AUDITING

AUDITING

JACK C. ROBERTSON, Ph.D., CPA
Associate Professor
The University of Texas at Austin

1979

Revised Edition

BUSINESS PUBLICATIONS, INC. Dallas, Texas 75243
Irwin-Dorsey Limited Georgetown, Ontario L7G 4B3

ISBN 0-256-02212-7
Library of Congress Catalog Card No. 78–61200

Printed in the United States of America

1 2 3 4 5 6 7 8 9 0 MP 6 5 4 3 2 1 0 9

Dedicated to
Jim Tom Barton
and
Albert L. Wade

PREFACE

This Revised Edition of *Auditing* reflects significant events and changes in the accounting and auditing profession since 1976 when the first edition was published. Incorporated throughout the text are references and explanations of the following:

- Congressional reports and hearings (Metcalf, Moss).
- Securities and Exchange Commission innovations concerning auditor involvement.
- Foreign Corrupt Practices Act of 1977 implications.
- Corporate Audit Committee developments.
- Commission on Auditors' Responsibilities recommendations.
- Auditing Standards Board organization.
- AICPA Division for Firms organization.
- Accounting and Review Services Committee.
- Quality Control Standards Committee.
- AICPA Code of Professional Ethics changes and disciplinary procedures changes.
- Standards for the Professional Practice of Internal Auditing.

All of these events and changes occurred in the short three-year span from 1976 to 1978. The pace of change is rapid, and students need the most current introduction to auditing possible. In order to stay current with developments in auditing standards and ethics interpretation pronouncements, a course in auditing should be supplemented with one or both of the following volumes of professional pronouncements:

- AICPA Professional Standards, *Auditing, Management Advisory Services, Tax Practice.*
- AICPA Professional Standards, *Ethics, Bylaws, Quality Control.*

While this revised edition remains quite comprehensive in its explanations of auditing standards, there is no sufficient substitute for the detail contained in the original professional pronouncements. Throughout the text the emphasis is on one's ability to make decisions within the framework of professional standards and acceptable professional behavior.

Decision-Making Orientation

An auditing course usually represents students' most concentrated introduction to the profession they are about to enter. One of the most important topics of the first course in auditing is an introduction to the practice of *professional* accounting and auditing. A central feature in such a professional practice is the art of making decisions in a variety of unstructured situations, which decisions demand a grasp of purpose, method, and judgment for their resolution.

A unifying thread that runs throughout this text is that of making decisions. An auditor is faced with decision problems daily: conceptual decisions, ethical decisions, accounting principles decisions, technical-procedural decisions, and reporting decisions. Whereas many accounting courses may have emphasized the "solution" of problems, this text emphasizes a structured scientific method for their "resolution."

Auditors and accountants work in a world of fast-paced change. As a result, the introductory auditing course and its accompanying textbook should provide a conceptual basis for coping with change as well as a basis in current auditing technology. This text is a blend of conceptual and technical material designed to serve both the long-range educational needs of auditors and the immediate demands for technical competence.

Organization

Each chapter of this text contains a conceptual introduction to technical standards and procedures. Through such an organization of the content a student may obtain not only an introductory familiarity with "how it is done" but also a thorough understanding of "why it is done." In the sequence of chapters the following content is developed:

Auditing is defined in terms of the objectives of independent auditors, internal auditors, and governmental auditors. A general scientific method for making audit decisions is introduced.

Auditing theory is given a full chapter with emphasis on the basic foundation of generally accepted auditing standards. Practice standards for management advisory services and tax practice, for governmental auditors, and in an EDP environment are integrated.

Professional ethics is given a full chapter, beginning with an introduction to general ethics and including a comprehensive discussion of the AICPA Rules of Conduct.

Some acquaintance with internal auditing is provided with Appendixes to each of Chapters 1, 2, and 3 dealing with internal auditors' responsibilities, ethics, and practice standards.

Legal liability also is given a full chapter including duties under both common law and statute. Coverage of the SEC and the Securities Acts is in this chapter. Significant court cases are briefed in two Appendixes.

The general theory of evidence, audit program planning, and documentation are introduced in a single chapter to provide an overview of the audit process.

Internal control is covered in three chapters. The material is organized systematically along these lines:

General characteristics, use of questionnaires, and flowchart techniques.

Compliance tests using attribute sampling, placing this statistical sampling method in the context of the internal control evaluation.

Internal control in an EDP environment, dealing with the special problems of EDP in connection with computer system reviews and compliance testing.

The use of generalized computer-audit software is covered immediately following the chapter on internal control in an EDP environment in order to place computer-related subjects in logical order.

Statistical decisions and statistical estimates receive thorough, up-to-date coverage with considerations of materiality, risk evaluation, and statistical estimation. Coverage includes the mean-per-unit (MPU) statistic, the difference statistic, stratified MPU estimates and dollar-unit sampling (DUS).

Technical audit program applications are condensed into six chapters by grouping together accounts related in a transaction cycle so that the interrelationships of audit procedures can be explained with a minimum of repetition. Each of these chapters contains the following features:

A business approach overview of audit objectives.

Flow charts of data processing systems.

Exhibits of audit programs—selected compliance testing and substantive testing procedures.

Application of general procedures explained in relation to the accounts and transactions.

A section on possibilities for fraud and misstatement of which an auditor should be aware.

Two chapters give thorough coverage to various report forms used by independent auditors. Many examples of real opinions are used as illustrations.

One chapter covers a new category of financial statement content—unaudited interim and replacement cost information in audited financial statements, and "non-opinion reports"—independent auditors' reports on internal control, and the reports of governmental and internal auditors and management advisory services consultants.

The final chapter contains forward-looking commentary on the Commission on Auditors' Responsibilities recommendations, the Accounting and Review Services Committee, forecasts, price level-adjusted statements, current value statements, and management auditing.

Throughout the text reliance has been placed on techniques and methods used by firms of certified public accountants. The material on statistics of attribute sampling is consistent with the style of coverage in professional development courses; the explanation of generalized audit software is based on a system developed and used by a major CPA firm; and the statistics of variables sampling is based on Section 320 of *Statement on Auditing Standards No. 1*. Problem materials have been revised and several discussion cases drawn from practice have been added to this revised edition.

Acknowledgments

The American Institute of Certified Public Accountants has generously given permission for liberal quotations from official pronouncements and other AICPA publications, all of which lend authoritative sources to the text. In addition, several publishing houses, professional associations, and accounting firms have granted permission to quote from their copyrighted material. Since a great amount of significant auditing thought exists in a wide variety of sources, I am especially grateful for the cooperation of all those interested in auditing education.

I gratefully acknowledge also the reviews and suggestions offered on the first edition by M. Tabibian and William C. Mair of Touche Ross & Co., Donald M. Roberts of the University of Illinois, Geraldine Dominiak of Texas Christian University, Norman C. Gillespie—professional philosopher, Michael Lovett of Peat, Marwick, Mitchell & Co., James Lahey of Northern Illinois University, and James Boatsman of Oklahoma State University. The revised edition especially benefited from reviews by Diane Allen of Price Waterhouse & Co., Frederick G. Davis and Michael T. Vanecek of North Texas State University, William C. Boynton of the University of Virginia, Michael Granof and Gary Grudnitski of The University of Texas at Austin, Gary L. Holstrum of the University of Florida, Hugh D. Grove of the University of Denver, and Harry Sieber of Franklin and Marshall College. Their suggestions greatly enhanced several portions of the text, but of course for all errors of commission and omission I remain responsible.

I owe a great debt of gratitude to two accountants who are truly professional in every meaning of the word. To Jim Tom Barton, himself an author of Texana literature, and Albert L. Wade, the book is dedicated in hope that it conveys to others the sense of professional values these two men have exhibited freely in their personal and professional lives. My wife Susan graduated from first-edition typist to editor and critic; daughter Sarah gave up criticism for her own studies; and daughter Elizabeth, who was born in the middle of the first edition, continues to offer her own creative diversions to authorship. To them all I express my appreciation for their joyful support and forbearance.

December 1978 JACK C. ROBERTSON

I [illegible] gratitude [illegible] professional [illegible]

[illegible]

[illegible] who was [illegible] in the middle of the [illegible] [illegible]

[illegible]

CONTENTS

PART ONE

Introduction to Professionalism

1

PROFESSIONAL PRACTICE

Since the early 1970s the auditing profession has experienced public attention, criticism, and change unequaled in all the previous years of its existence. Economic difficulties brought business failures, and the news media threw light on corporate briberies and payoffs. The question of "Where were the auditors?" brought pressure to bear on the organized profession. In 1974 the independent Commission on Auditors' Responsibilities was established to write a blueprint for change.

Events moved quickly in 1976 and 1977. A critical report entitled "Federal Regulation and Regulatory Reform" was issued in 1976 by the House Subcommittee on Oversight and Investigations under the leadership of Representative John E. Moss (D-California). Under the direction of the late Senator Lee Metcalf (D-Montana) the Senate Subcommittee on Reports, Accounting, and Management issued a staff report in 1977 entitled "The Accounting Establishment," which called for federal government takeover of many accounting and auditing functions performed by the independent Financial Accounting Standards Board and by the American Institute of Certified Public Accountants. At about the same time in 1977 the Commission on Auditors' Responsibilities issued its *Report of Tentative Conclusions,* which recommended several significant changes in auditors' approaches and attitudes.

The Senate Committee on Governmental Affairs' subcommittee on Reports, Accounting, and Management held hearings in 1977 and issued a final report late that year entitled "Improving the Accountability of Publicly-Owned Corporations and Their Auditors." Many of the Metcalf subcommittee staff report recommendations appeared in the final report, but the full subcommittee adopted a position of waiting to see whether the accounting profession could make the changes necessary to satisfy its critics. Just prior to the hearings the AICPA Council and Board of Directors had approved several changes in the organization and governing functions of the AICPA.

Soon thereafter, in January 1978, the Commission on Auditors' Responsibilities issued its final report entitled *Report, Recommendations, and Conclusions.* The Commission recommended a number of changes and innovations to be undertaken by the AICPA and by auditors. The AICPA Board of Directors endorsed a number of the recommendations and set to work to implement them.

As this implementation got underway, Representative Moss conducted congressional hearings to hear testimony about the efforts of the AICPA. The initial hearings closed in 1978 under a cloud of doubts expressed by Representative Moss. Potential federal regulatory legislation loomed on the horizon for the AICPA and the auditing profession.

The impact of these events is recognized throughout the chapters of this textbook. This attention is evidence of the important role auditors fill in American financial society, and it is an ever-changing role. Students and practitioners of auditing need to be careful to keep up to date with the tides of change.

We begin the study of auditing by considering definitions. *Auditing* may be defined in several ways depending upon what purpose is to be served. Four definitions are given below, beginning with a general one produced by a committee of the American Accounting Association. The next three definitions exhibit the purposes served by independent auditors, internal auditors, and governmental auditors.

AMERICAN ACCOUNTING ASSOCIATION DEFINITION

The AAA Committee on Basic Auditing Concepts (1971) has prepared the most comprehensive definition of auditing.

> Auditing is a systematic process of objectively obtaining and evaluating evidence regarding assertions about economic actions and events to ascertain the degree of correspondence between those assertions and established criteria and communicating the results to interested users.

This definition contains statements of concepts that permeate auditing theory and practice. Each of the concepts is explained below.

"Auditing is a systematic process . . ."

All definitions of auditing refer to auditing as a *process*. Process implies a dynamic activity. The important connotation in this phrase is that auditing is a *systematic* process. It is purposeful, logical, and based on the discipline of a structured, scientific approach to decision making. It is not haphazard, unplanned, or unstructured.

". . . of objectively obtaining and evaluating evidence . . ."

This second phrase contains one of the more important concepts in auditing—*evidence.* Evidence consists of all those influences upon the minds of auditors which ultimately guide their decision choices. The definition points out that auditing comprehends *objective* gathering and evaluation of evidence. There is no reference to nonsystematic methods of obtaining and evaluating evidence. The concept refers to the objectivity of methods of evidence gathering and evidence evaluation, but the evidence itself may be more or less objective, or even subjective in nature.

". . . regarding assertions about economic actions and events . . ."

This phrase identifies the general subject matter of the audit process—*assertions* about economic matters and the *information* (particularly accounting information) that is contained in the assertions. The word *assertions* is important to this phrase. When beginning an audit engagement, an independent auditor of financial statements is given financial statements and other disclosures by management and thus obtains management's explicit assertions about economic actions and events. These assertions may include statements about a company's system of internal accounting control.

Independent auditors generally begin work with explicit representations of management—the subject matter under audit. Other auditors, however, typically are not so well provided with definite and explicit assertions. An internal auditor may be assigned to "evaluate the economy of the company's policy to lease rather than purchase heavy equipment." A governmental auditor may be assigned to "determine whether goals of providing equal educational opportunity" have been achieved with federal grant funds. Oftentimes these latter two types of auditors must develop the explicit statements of performance for themselves.

However, no matter what the form of the assertions, all auditors should be open-minded enough to view accounting information broadly to include economic information needed by users for their informed judgments and decisions. A broad view of accounting information takes an auditor beyond the constraints of transaction information that can be captured in debit-credit entries. Accounting-economic information subject to audit may include many disclosures found only in footnotes and in annual report narratives outside the structure of the financial statement schedules.

". . . to ascertain the degree of correspondence between those assertions and established criteria . . ."

This phrase specifies why auditors are interested in assertions and related evidence. Auditors will ultimately communicate their findings to users, but in order to communicate in an efficient and understandable manner, some common ground of communication language must exist between the auditor and the user of the information. Such a common body of understanding constitutes the *established criteria* that are essential for effective communication.

Established criteria may be found in a variety of sources. For independent CPAs, governmental auditors, and Internal Revenue Service agents, the criteria largely consist of the generally accepted accounting principles. IRS agents also rely heavily on criteria specified in the Internal Revenue Code. Governmental auditors may rely on criteria established in legislation or regulatory agency rules. Bank examiners and state insurance board auditors look to definitions and rules of law. Internal auditors and governmental auditors rely a great deal on financial and managerial models of efficiency and economy as well as upon generally accepted accounting principles. All auditors rely to some extent on elusive criteria of general truth and fairness.

". . . and communicating the results to interested users."

The final activity, essential to the social usefulness of auditing, is the communication of findings and results to decision makers. With respect to the activities of independent auditors, this communication output is referred to as *attestation*. The essence of attestation is the act of *lending credibility* to information transmitted by management to users of financial statements.

The attestation communication is *one* possible output of an audit, and the independent CPA's opinions on financial statements are the most familiar examples. However, there are a variety of report forms and circumstances that are characteristic of internal audits, governmental audits, and other types of audits.

OTHER DEFINITIONS OF AUDITING

The American Accounting Association definition discussed above is broad and general enough to encompass independent, internal, and governmental auditing activity. However, other definitions also exist. Presented below are three definitions promulgated by organizations that have direct professional responsibility for the practice of auditing.

American Institute of Certified Public Accountants (AICPA)

In its first paragraph, *Statement on Auditing Standards No. 1* (1973) describes the principal objectives of a financial audit.

> The objective of the ordinary examination of financial statements by the independent auditor is the expression of an opinion on the fairness with which they present financial position, results of operations and changes in financial position in conformity with generally accepted accounting principles. The auditor's report is the medium through which he expresses his opinion or, if circumstances require, disclaims an opinion. In either case, he

> states whether his examination has been made in accordance with generally accepted auditing standards.[1]

The AICPA statement of objective restricts auditing interest to the independent CPA's examinations of the three traditional financial statements for the purpose of rendering a standard audit report. However, as the needs of users change, new audit objectives and reports are created to meet new needs. Thus the Statements on Auditing Standards also contain guides relating to reports on internal control, letters to underwriters, and special reports that are not prepared in conformity with generally accepted accounting principles. These other aspects of auditor's practice are discussed in Chapters 6, 18, and 19 of this text.

Comptroller General of the United States (GAO)

The U.S. Comptroller General is the chief executive officer of the U.S. General Accounting Office, which is an accounting, auditing, and investigative agency of the U.S. Congress. The first "basic premise" given in the 1972 statement entitled *Standards for Audit of Governmental Organizations, Programs, Activities, and Functions* expresses a broad description of governmental auditing:

> The term "audit" may be used to describe not only work done by accountants in examining financial reports but also work done in reviewing (*a*) compliance with applicable laws and regulations, (*b*) efficiency and economy of operations, and (*c*) effectiveness in achieving program results.

The GAO viewpoint does not restrict auditing to financial reports alone, as is implied by the AICPA statement, but extends audit interest to three elemental areas. The 1972 *Standards* statement defines each of these elements as follows:

1. *Financial and compliance*—determines (*a*) whether financial operations are properly conducted, (*b*) whether the financial reports of an audited entity are presented fairly, and (*c*) whether the entity has complied with applicable laws and regulations.
2. *Economy and efficiency*—determines whether the entity is managing or utilizing its resources (personnel, property, space, and so forth) in an economical and efficient manner and the causes of an inefficiencies or uneconomical practices including inadequacies in management information systems, administrative procedures, or organizational structure.
3. *Program results*—determines whether the desired results or benefits are being achieved, whether the objectives established by the legislative or other authorizing body are being met, and whether the agency has considered alternatives which might yield results at a lower cost.

---

[1] The Statements on Auditing Standards are authoritative AICPA pronouncements on auditing theory and practice. Statements on Auditing Procedures Numbers 1–54 were codified into *SAS No. 1* in 1973; and Statements on Auditing Standards numbered 2 through 22 had been issued by March 1978.

GAO auditing standards are presented in Chapter 2, and GAO reports are discussed more fully in Chapter 19 of this text.

The Institute of Internal Auditors (IIA)

The Institute of Internal Auditors adopted a statement of *Standards for the Professional Practice of Internal Auditing* in 1978. A summary of these standards is in the appendix to Chapter 2. The definition contained in the introduction to the 1978 standards views internal auditing as follows:

> Internal auditing is an independent appraisal function established within an organization to examine and evaluate its activities as a service to the organization. The objective of internal auditing is to assist members of the organization in the effective discharge of their responsibilities. To this end, internal auditing furnishes them with analyses, appraisals, recommendations, counsel, and information concerning the activities reviewed.

The Institute of Internal Auditors has also adopted a *Statement of Responsibilities of the Internal Auditor* (modified in 1947, 1957, and 1971). This statement is reproduced in the appendix to this chapter. The definition of internal auditing therein is slightly different from the one quoted above from the 1978 *Standards* statement and one can expect that the 1971 *Statement of Responsibilities* will be amended to reflect the change.

Internal auditors view auditing as extremely broad, as does the GAO, reaching not only to accounting data but also to compliance, control effectiveness, and performance quality. The internal auditors also add another dimension—reports recommending operating improvements. The full *Statement of Responsibilities of the Internal Auditor* contains a concise description of internal auditing. Reports of internal auditors are presented in Chapters 6 and 19 of this textbook.

Observation on Definitions

In comparison to the GAO and Internal Auditors, the AICPA's definition recognizes only a small portion of audit practice possibilities. However, the GAO and IIA statements of definition and objective serve to define *all* professional practice of governmental auditors and internal auditors. Likewise the AAA definition is stated broadly to include a wide variety of auditing practice.

The AICPA definition pertains to only one part of the professional practice of certified public accountants. Many CPA firms perform the same tasks as governmental auditors and internal auditors, but such engagements are either performed as management advisory services or are audits in every sense of the broadest definition except for the absence of the standard audit report. Independent CPAs generally are reluctant to call an engagement an "audit" unless its end product is an opinion on financial statements, regardless of the substantive nature of the work performed. The principal reasons for this reluctance have to do with legal liability questions and the absence of definitive standards.

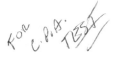

AUDITORS' REPORTS

The desire to obtain the services of an auditor reflects a natural human tendency of skepticism. Auditors' reports serve to reduce skepticism by adding credibility to information used for decisions. These decisions may involve a wide range of economic, political, and social considerations, and auditors can become involved in a variety of ways.

One of the prime concerns in the national and world economy is the efficient operation of orderly capital markets. Securities trading is facilitated by the existence of reliable information attested by *independent auditors.*

In a similar manner the managers of large organizations need to be informed of the efficiency and effectiveness of operations that are under their responsibility, yet not under their direct personal supervision. *Internal auditors* may serve the needs of such managers by facilitating the production of timely and accurate reports. Special studies conducted by internal auditors may also be used to control poor performances and highlight outstanding performances.

Governmental activities in the United States are pervasive, and their monetary impact is large. To help manage a federal budget in excess of $500 billion, Congress utilizes the auditors and experts in the *U.S. General Accounting Office.* This agency investigates programs and functions at the request of Congress and submits analytical reports, most of which are also available to the public.

Other agencies of government use auditing services in performing regulatory and compliance functions. *IRS auditors, bank examiners,* and *insurance department auditors* are indicative of a few of the kinds of audit work done by regulatory agencies. Their audit reports are usually transmitted directly to the responsible governmental agency.

The Standard Short-Form Report

Every audit engagement, whether performed by independent auditors, internal auditors, or by others, produces a report of the work performed and the conclusions reached. Reports may take a wide variety of form and content. This variety is considered in more detail in Chapters 17, 18, and 19. However, in order to obtain some orientation to the final output, some familiarity is required at the beginning of a study of auditing.

The most widely used standard report is the independent auditor's *unqualified short-form report.* The wording reproduced below is recommended by the AICPA and is widely used by auditors in the United States. The first paragraph is known as the *scope paragraph* and is a report of the character of the audit itself. The second paragraph is the *opinion paragraph* and contains the attestation communication by the auditor on the financial statements.

To the Board of Directors and Stockholders, Anycompany, Inc.:

We have examined the balance sheets of Anycompany, Inc., as of December 31, 19X2, and 19X1, and the related statements of income, retained earnings, and changes in financial position for the years then ended. Our examinations were made in accordance with generally accepted auditing standards and, accordingly, included such tests of the accounting records and such other auditing procedures as we considered necessary in the circumstances.

In our opinion, the financial statements referred to above present fairly the financial position of Anycompany, Inc., as of December 31, 19X2, and 19X1, and the results of its operations and the changes in its financial position for the years then ended, in conformity with generally accepted accounting principles applied on a consistent basis.

Nicholas A. Dixon Co.
Certified Public Accountants
February 28, 19___

Each elemental phrase in the short-form report has significant meaning for auditors, as explained below.

1. The report is addressed to the persons or organization that engage the auditor. Typically, these persons are the directors and stockholders of an organization, but in some cases an audit of one entity may be commissioned by another entity. For example, Corporation A engages and pays an auditor to audit Corporation B in connection with a proposed merger. The report on financial statements of Corporation B may then be addressed to the officers and directors of Corporation A.

2. The first sentence of the scope paragraph identifies the financial statements that were audited. Even though the standard wording names all three basic statements, it is important to realize (*a*) that a report mentions only the statements that the auditor has in fact audited and omits naming one(s) that have not been audited, and (*b*) that *financial statements* include related footnote disclosures as well as the structured formal financial schedules. This sentence also implies the fact that the statements and disclosures were produced by management and are the ultimate responsibility of management. (The auditor's responsibility is stated in the opinion paragraph.)

Notice that the financial statements are audited and not the books and records. Financial statements are drawn from management's books and records, but the audit is not strictly confined to the books and records. Evidence is sought from other sources as well.

3. The second sentence of the scope paragraph states in the first phrase that the examination was made in accordance with *generally accepted auditing standards.* These standards are the quality criteria for an audit, and this reference to them implies that a professionally competent level of audit performance has been attained. The standards are reviewed in more detail in Chapter 2.

4. The last phrase of the second scope sentence augments the reference to generally accepted auditing standards by stating, in effect, that the auditor has personally tailored the many available auditing procedures to the specific circumstances of the Anycompany, Inc., financial statements. It is not appropriate to list the procedures in the scope para-

graph for two reasons: (1) the procedures are too numerous to name specifically; and (2) a reader would have no way of knowing, even after reading a description of all procedures, whether they were appropriate in the circumstances and no way of knowing whether procedures not described were appropriately excluded. The reference to "tests of the accounting records" is notice that the auditors did not review 100 percent of the transactions executed during the period.

5. The opinion paragraph begins with the introductory words, "In our opinion. . . ." It is important to know that this paragraph should contain a clear, factual expression of the auditor's beliefs about the financial statements. The word "opinion" connotes belief or judgment stronger than impression, but less strong than positive knowledge. The auditor's professional opinion is an informed judgment based on evidence.

6. The financial statements are said to "present fairly the financial position . . . and the results of operations and the changes in financial position . . . in conformity with generally accepted accounting principles." The phrase "present fairly . . . in conformity with generally accepted accounting principles" is based on the auditor's judgment as to whether (*a*) the accounting principles selected and applied have general acceptance,[2] (*b*) the accounting principles are appropriate in the circumstances,[3] (*c*) the financial statements, including the related notes, are adequately informative for users, (*d*) the financial statement information is classified and summarized in a manner that is neither too detailed nor too condensed for users, and (*e*) the financial statements are accurate within practical materiality limits.

7. The last phrase of the opinion paragraph refers to the consistent use of accounting principles. It is important to realize that the standard wording refers to the consistent application of principles in all the years for which comparative financial statements are presented. If statements for only one year are presented, the consistency phrase refers to the latest year not presented.

8. The auditor's report is signed by the auditor and dated. The appropriate date is the day on which substantially all audit field work is completed. This date essentially defines the time limit of the auditor's responsibility for disclosing economic events that occur after the balance sheet date. The report date may be between one week to six weeks or more after the balance sheet date, depending upon the time it takes to complete the field work. ("Field work" is defined and explained in Chapter 2.)

Departures from the wording of the standard short-form report are the means of reporting fully on what the auditor has found when the situation

---

[2] According to *Statement on Auditing Standards No.* 5 (Sections 411.04–411.06) "general acceptance" is evidenced in the FASB pronouncements, APB opinions, AICPA accounting research bulletins, AICPA accounting interpretations, AICPA industry audit and accounting guides, AICPA statements of position issued by the Accounting Standards Executive Committee, pronouncements of other professional organizations and of regulatory agencies (such as the SEC), accounting textbooks and articles in professional journals.

[3] *SAS No.* 5 (Section 411.07) points out that this decision requires that the auditor consider the substance as well as the form of transactions.

is nonstandard. Alterations of the standard wording may take the following forms:

Scope Paragraph Qualification. When generally accepted auditing standards have not been observed (in whole or in part), the scope paragraph contains a description and explanation of the failure. Most cases involve a client-imposed restriction on the audit evidence-gathering work (e.g., a request to omit confirmation of receivables) or a restriction due to the circumstances (e.g., appointment as auditor after the physical inventory date).

Middle Paragraphs. Whenever something is nonstandard by reason of uncertainty, lack of evidence or by reason of failure to adhere to generally accepted accounting principles in the preparation of statements, a full explanation is given in a second paragraph designed to emphasize the matter.

Opinion Paragraph Other Than the Unqualified Opinion. An *adverse* opinion is the opposite of an unqualified opinion. In the adverse opinion, after an explanation of reasons, the auditor reports that the financial statements *do not* fairly present financial position, results of operations, and changes in financial position in conformity with generally accepted accounting principles.

A *qualified opinion* is one that expresses an overall opinion as to fair presentation in conformity with generally accepted accounting principles but also mentions the auditor's *exceptions* to such things as (1) information not audited because of a scope limitation, (2) information that is not presented in conformity with generally accepted accounting principles, and (3) information that is presented on a basis not consistent with that of the prior year. The recommended standard wording is "except for" language inserted in the opinion paragraph. The report may also be qualified with the words "subject to" with reference to an *uncertainty* affecting the company. Common uncertainties include such matters as pending litigation and questions about the realizable value of assets held for disposal.

A *disclaimer of opinion* is an expression of no opinion in which auditors give an explanation of their reasons and an explicit statement that no opinion is rendered. This disclaimer is generally used when there is a pervasive and important uncertainty or when there is not enough evidence upon which to base an opinion on the financial statements taken as a whole.

The foregoing description of the standard short-form report and the types of departures from the standard wording is a very brief introduction to the independent auditor's product. However, some preliminary knowledge of the reporting framework is useful for grasping the purpose and the context of auditing ethics, standards, and procedures that are explained in subsequent chapters. Matters of reporting variations are considered in more detail in the last four chapters of this book.

Other Reports

Communications without such structured wording as the standard short-form report include auditors' letters detailing internal accounting control weaknesses, internal auditors' reports on compliance with policy, and governmental auditors' reports on performance of specific programs and projects. Recommendation reports may be typified by management advisory service engagement findings about alternative solutions to a problem and by internal auditors' reports on specific analyses such as a lease-or-buy decision analysis. The nature and content of these communications is bounded only by the auditor's imagination. The goal is to produce a useful output. Several aspects of the reporting obligation involving nonopinion reports are covered in more detail in Chapter 19.

Commission on Auditors' Responsibilities (CAR)

The CAR report recommended significant changes for the form and content of independent auditors' reports on audited financial statements. The commission believes that management should write and publish a report on financial statements emphasizing their prime responsibility for preparing the statements. The commission further recommended an expanded standard report containing more than two paragraphs which would include the auditors' report of scope and opinion (as before) and additional comments on the nature of an audit, a report about internal accounting controls, a report about other financial information not within the formal financial statements and notes, a report about the company's system for producing quarterly financial statements, a report of a review of company policy statements on employee conduct (as related to illegal payments, for example) and a report of auditor contact with the audit committee of the board of directors. These recommendations were given to a special AICPA committee in 1978 for review and study with a goal of determining what should be done, if anything, about changing the form and content of reports.

SCIENTIFIC METHOD FOR AUDITING DECISIONS

Inherent in the definitions and objectives of auditing is a central emphasis on making decisions. The important aspect of audit decision making is the *method* of approaching and solving an audit problem. An inquiring "audit attitude" is very important, and a structured (scientific) approach to problems aids in the development of such an attitude.

The scientific method is both an attitude and an organized procedure for reaching logical and supportable conclusions. To be an auditor, one must possess the inquiring questioning mentality of a problem-solver. The ever-present question is "What economic action or event is being asserted?" Following closely is the next question: "Is it so?"

The use of the scientific method in auditing is a five-step process:

1. *Recognize* the assertion(s), problems, and preliminary data required to formulate a testable hypothesis statement.
2. *Formulate* the hypothesis in such a manner that either acceptance or rejection of it yields a useful auditing decision.
3. *Collect* competent evidence that contributes to the decision. Collec-

tion of evidence involves the following two aspects of audit program planning:
   a. *Selection* of applicable evidence-gathering techniques and procedures.
   b. *Performance* of techniques and procedures to obtain evidence.
4. *Evaluate* the evidence relative to the decision-problem hypothesis and assess its sufficiency for the decision choice.
5. *Make the decision* to accept or reject the problem-related hypothesis.

The most important step is the first one—to recognize the problem. Audit problems requiring decision are numerous, ranging from questions of the actual existence of things (e.g., assets, liabilities) and the actual occurrence of events (e.g., sales, cash receipts) to the proper accounting treatment for reporting purposes (e.g., classification, disclosure).

In the ordinary audit engagement the problem hypothesis is formulated first in the manner of a positive proposition. For example: "The recorded value of accounts receivable is a fair presentation," or "The contract terms are being met satisfactorily." However, the auditor must also be aware of alternative conditions—that the recorded value of accounts receivable is materially misstated, or that the contract terms have been violated. In general the auditor begins the decision process by explicitly stating a proposition (a hypothetical assertion) that expresses tentative belief in the truth of records and amounts. But if this initial belief is not supportable, the auditor is prepared to decide otherwise.

The third and fourth steps in the decision method are the technical-procedural aspects of audit testing of the problem statement. By collecting evidence, the auditor attempts to answer the ever-present question: "Is it so?"

The last step forces the auditor to choose one of the decision alternatives. As a practical matter, the auditor must decide whether, for example, the recorded value of the accounts receivable is materially correct or the contract terms are being met satisfactorily. The auditor must assess these assertions in light of the available evidence.

Consequently, the scientific method applied in auditing decisions is completed with this step: *Formulate a judgment on the conformity of the assertion with reality as the auditor perceives reality at the time of the evaluation of the evidence.* This final statement of the decision-making method incorporates the concept of the careful, prudent practitioner—one who is not omniscient but who is professionally competent, careful, and knowledgeable.

As an example of this method, consider the line item on a balance sheet entitled "Trade Accounts Receivable . . . $100,000." This single line contains several assertions, including the following:

All the accounts are due from trade customers.

None are due from officers, directors, or affiliates.

All are collectible within the next year (current assets).

None are due after one year.

The collectible amount is $100,000.

Allowance has been made for doubtful accounts.

Accounts are not pledged or otherwise restricted.

To keep this example brief, take the first two assertions for elaboration. With the assertions made explicit, the first two steps of the scientific method have been accomplished—the problem has been recognized and the hypotheses have been formulated. Now the auditor needs to identify customers, officers, and directors, and relate their identities to the names of the debtors. Evidence is gathered by comparing these names to the subsidiary accounts. The result of the comparison is evaluated to yield the facts about the actual identities and affiliations of the debtors. With the evidence and evaluation in hand, the auditor is now prepared to decide whether the first two assertions conform to reality as that reality is presently determinable.

This example is a preview of more complex assertions, procedures, and evidence-gathering techniques covered in more detail in the technical chapters of this textbook. Throughout these subsequent chapters, the scientific methodology for auditing decisions is relied upon as the essence of a practical, inquiring audit attitude.

ACCOUNTING AS A PROFESSION

Frequent references are made to professions, to professional men and women, and to professional activities. The activities of auditors and accountants are often characterized as "professional" without specific explanation of what is meant by the word. Five dimensions of a truly professional activity are reviewed and explained below with reference to accounting and auditing practice.

The five principal characteristics that help differentiate the professional fields of endeavor from other vocations are these:

1. A body of specialized knowledge acquired by formal education.
2. Admission to the profession governed by standards of professional qualifications.
3. A concomitant pair: recognition and acceptance by society of professional status, and concurrent recognition and acceptance of social responsibility by the professional.
4. Standards of conduct governing relationships of the professional with clients, colleagues, and the public.
5. A national organization devoted to the advancement of the social obligations of the professional group.

Specialized Knowledge and Formal Education

Higher education has not always been the means of acquiring preparation for careers in professional accounting. Collegiate schools of business were first created little more than 60 years ago. Since then, however, the world of accountancy has become much more complex. A college degree is truly prerequisite to becoming a professional accountant, and many people believe that a fifth year of study is necessary. Two or three states are considering a requirement of five years of study prior to taking the CPA examination.

In the last few years several colleges and universities have explored establishment of professional schools of accounting. A few have been started, and the accounting profession generally supports this development. The AICPA has published standards for programs and schools of professional accounting and is working actively with the American Accounting Association and the American Assembly of Collegiate Schools of Business (AACSB) on accounting program accreditation standards. Also, the Commission on Auditors' Responsibilities has recommended expanded formal schooling for accountants along the lines of a professional school program.

Professional Admission Standards

The most highly esteemed professions govern admission to the profession by standards of professional qualifications contained in state law. If legal recognition is considered a requisite of a profession, then the membership of the accounting profession is limited to holders of the CPA certificate and state licenses to practice. However, many other accountants consider themselves professionals by virtue of meeting other requirements. CPA admission standards involve examinations, experience requirements, and licensing by state accountancy boards.

Qualification by Examination. The Uniform CPA Examination which is administered in all U.S. states and territories consists of four parts: (1) accounting practice, (2) auditing, (3) accounting theory, and (4) commercial law. The examination is offered in May and November of each year. Further information on the CPA examination is available in the AICPA publication titled "Information for CPA Candidates" and from various state boards of accountancy.

The National Association of Accountants, operating through its Institute of Management Accounting, conducted the first examination leading to the Certificate in Management Accounting (CMA) in 1972. The CMA program was begun as an organized effort to formalize professionalism and to create a new goal for accountants who are not in public practice. The five parts of the CMA examination are (1) managerial economics and business finance, (2) organization and behavior, including ethical considerations, (3) public reporting standards, auditing, and taxes, (4) periodic reporting for internal and external purposes, and (5) decision analysis, including modeling and information systems.

In December 1972, the Institute of Internal Auditors gave final approval for its certified internal auditor program. Qualified candiates may take the CIA examination and upon passing all parts are entitled to use the designation Certified Internal Auditor. The written examination consists of four parts: (1) principles of internal auditing, (2) internal audit techniques, (3) principles of management, and (4) disciplines related to internal auditing. In order to take the CIA examination, a candidate must hold a baccalaureate degree from an accredited college-level institution.

Experience Requirements. In the past all states required a term of experience before granting the CPA certificate. Now a few states have no experience requirement, and most states have reduced their former requirements.

The CMA program requires experience of two years which may be obtained before or after passing the exam. Related professional experience in management accounting is defined as substantially full-time continuous experience at a level where judgments are regularly made that employ the principles of management accounting.

Internal auditors are required to have three years of experience in internal auditing before the CIA certificate will be granted.

License to Practice Accounting. Most states issue the CPA certificate and a license to practice at the same time. For a small fee this license is renewed periodically. State boards of accountancy have the power to license persons with the right to hold themselves out to the public as certified public accountants. This license is the manifestation of a legal aspect of qualification.

The Institute of Management Accounting and the Institute of Internal Auditors do not issue licenses to practice nor do they forbid practice to persons not holding their respective certificates. The CMA and CIA programs make it possible for an accountant to show evidence of accomplishment, but participation in the programs and attainment of certificates are not required as matters of law.

Continuing Professional Education. In 1971 the AICPA adopted a resolution favoring the continuing education and professional development of accountants. The recommendation was that accountants be expected to complete 120 hours of professional development courses every three years. More than 25 states have enacted required continuing professional education standards for renewal of the license to practice, and other states have encouraged voluntary programs. The SEC practice section and the private companies practice section of the AICPA division for firms, established late in 1977, require 40 hours of continuing professional education annually for all professionals (CPAs and non-CPAs) resident in the United States as a condition for continued membership of the firm in the section. The future holds promise of more, not less, education and training designed to upgrade and maintain the competence of accountants.

Social Recognition: A Reciprocal Relationship

No group of practitioners can become a "profession" merely by declaring itself to be one. There must exist a general recognition by society of the status of the group as a professional body. Today accountants and auditors are recognized by almost all elements of society as true professionals.

Such recognition, however, is not necessarily permanent. Society will not continue to honor as professional any activity that fails to serve a broad-based social and public interest. A profession must nurture and retain recognition of status in order to remain a widely respected profession. Thus there is another side to the coin of recognition: Accountants and auditors must reciprocate and accept the social responsibility inherent in professional activity endowed with the public interest. The problems of the profession mentioned at the beginning of this chapter and the work of the AICPA and of the Commission on Auditors' Responsibilities are evidence of the reciprocal social recognition relationship.

Standards of Conduct

In order to maintain social recognition, accountants and auditors must conduct themselves individually and collectively in a manner acceptable to clients, colleagues, and the public. CPAs may come under the jurisdiction of three codified statements of conduct rules. The AICPA *Code of Professional Ethics* applies to members of the AICPA. All state societies of CPAs have codes of ethics applicable to their members. All state boards of accountancy have codes applicable to license holders. All three agencies have trial boards and disciplinary committees that can try cases of alleged violation. All three agencies may reprimand and suspend; the CPA organizations may expel a member; and the state board may revoke a license to practice. Only the actions by state boards to suspend or revoke a license deny the right to practice. All the other actions are stamps of professional disapproval. The Institute of Internal Auditors has also promulgated a code of ethics for the guidance of certified internal auditors.

Professional Organizations

Since a profession continues to be recognized by virtue of its responsiveness to social change, there must exist an authoritative organization to initiate, stimulate, and direct dynamic activities of the profession as a whole. A central professional organization generally operates to refine the body of knowledge, to regulate admission, to effect social responsibility in new areas of concern, and to police the conduct of members. The organization exists to foster and maintain all of the first four elements that have been identified as the characteristics of a profession.

The Institute of Internal Auditors serves in this capacity as does the National Association of Accountants. However, broad-based social attention concerning auditors generally is focused on independent auditors represented by the American Institute of Certified Public Accountants.

The American Institute of Certified Public Accountants. The AICPA is the only national organization that limits its membership to certified public accountants. In all important respects, the AICPA is the central professional organization that initiates, stimulates, and directs professional change. As stated in its bylaws, the purposes of the AICPA are (1) to unite the accountancy profession in the United States, (2) to promote and maintain high professional and moral standards within the accountancy profession, (3) to assist in the maintenance of high standards for the certified public accountant certificate, (4) to develop and maintain standards for the examination of candidates for admission, (5) to safeguard the interests of certified public accountants, (6) to advance accounting research, (7) to develop and improve accountancy education, and (8) to encourage cordial relations among certified public accountants and accountants of similar status in other countries of the world.

In order to accomplish these objectives, the AICPA is organized into several divisions and committees. The auditing standards division has primary responsibility in the area of auditing practice. There are several senior committees (empowered to issue authoritative pronouncements governing practice) that operate in the area of accounting and auditing and practice management and oversight. The principal committees are these:

> *Auditing Standards Executive Committee (AudSEC)*—issues Statements on Auditing Standards and interpretations of the standards. These standards provide the basis for a large part of the theory and practice presented in this textbook.[4]
>
> *Accounting and Review Services Committee*—authorized in 1977 by Council of the AICPA to issue pronouncements concerning the conduct of nonaudit accounting work and small accounting firms/small business practice. This committee was formed in response to the criticism that the AICPA paid too little attention to this type of practice.
>
> *Quality Control Standards Committee*—authorized in 1977 by Council of the AICPA to issue pronouncements concerning quality-of-practice policies and procedures for auditing firms' activities. This committee was formed in response to continuing criticisms that the auditing profession has done little to promote and maintain high quality of performance in its practicing firms.

The AICPA ethics division also issues pronouncements (interpretations and rulings) concerning the rules of ethical conduct. These rulings directly affect auditors' practices.

In 1977 Council created a new division unique to the organizational structure of the AICPA—the Division for Firms. There are two *sections* in this division (1) SEC practice firms and (2) private companies practice firms. In all other respects, *individuals* are members of the AICPA, but *firms* are the membership unit in the new division. The goal is to establish rules and procedures to exercise "oversight" of the quality of performance in the audit practice units. This organizational structure was prompted by congressional critics' threats to legislate a governmental unit to do the same task and thus bring about greater control and monitoring of firms' practices. The new division was in its formative stages throughout 1978,

[4] At its meeting in May 1978, AICPA Council approved reorganization of the auditing standards division. Auditing activities will be headed by an AICPA Vice President—Auditing, and the Auditing Standards Executive Committee was renamed the Auditing Standards Board. While the board will serve the same authoritative function as its predecessor executive committee, it will have fewer members and will be supported by an advisory council and more AICPA staff resources. The impetus for this change came from the Commission on Auditors' Responsibilities' recommendation favoring a reorganization of the auditing standards-setting function within the AICPA.

and only time will tell whether it constitutes a sufficient response to outside pressures placed on the profession.

Other Professional Organizations. There are several other nationwide accountants' organizations that serve the interests of segments of the profession. Each of the ones listed below conducts research and makes various publications available upon request:

Organization	*Accountants*	*Journal Publication*
National Association of Accountants (NAA)	Accountants in industry, banking, insurance, not-for-profit, and other fields	*Management Accounting*
Institute of Internal Auditors (IIA)	Practicing internal auditors	*The Internal Auditor*
Financial Executives Institute (FEI)	Corporate accounting and financial officers	*The Financial Executive*
Association of Government Accountants (AGA)	Accountants in federal offices and agencies	*The Federal Accountant*
American Accounting Association (AAA)	Accounting educators	*The Accounting Review*
U.S. General Accounting Office (GAO)	Accountants and experts employed by GAO	*The GAO Review*

ORGANIZATION OF TEXTBOOK

This book is organized into four major sections:

Part One: Introduction to Professionalism, Chapters 1–4.
Part Two: General Technology of Auditing, Chapters 5–10.
Part Three: Audit Program Applications, Chapters 11–16.
Part Four: Reporting Obligations, Chapters 17–20.

Throughout the text, reference is made to "new" developments under way in 1977 and 1978. Since the auditing profession is experiencing rapid change, these developments may be "old" ones by 1979. Also, the 1978 final report of the Commission on Auditors' Responsibilities (CAR) is cited as the source for many recommendations for change. By 1979 or soon thereafter these recommendations may have become the subject of official pronouncements, and changes may already have been enacted. Thus this word of advice: Be alert to areas where change may have occurred and be aware that yesterday's rules and guides may have been superceded by new ones.

To assist with further study of auditing, each chapter in Parts One, Two, and Four is followed by a bibliography of sources and references.

SOURCES AND ADDITIONAL READING REFERENCES

Beamer, Elmer G. "Continuing Education—A Professional Requirement," *Journal of Accountancy,* January 1972, pp. 33–39.

Boyle, J. T., and Holton, T. L. "Peer Review in the Accounting Profession—Who Audits the Auditor?" *The CPA Journal,* January 1975, pp. 15–18.

Burns, D. C., and Haga, W. J. "Much Ado about Professionalism: A Second Look at Accounting," *Accounting Review,* July 1977, pp. 705–15.

Campfield, William L. "Approach to Formulation of Professional Standards for Internal Auditors," *Accounting Review,* July 1960.

______. "Professional Status for Internal Auditors," *Accounting Review,* October 1965, pp. 594–98.

Carey, John L. *The CPA Plans for the Future.* New York: American Institute of Certified Public Accountants, 1965.

"Certificate in Management Accounting Established by NAA," *Management Accounting,* March 1972, pp. 13–14 et seq.

Commission on Auditors' Responsibilities. *Report, Conclusions, and Recommendations.* New York: CAR, 1978.

Committee on Basic Auditing Concepts. "A Statement of Basic Auditing Concepts," *Accounting Review,* supplement to vol. 47, 1972.

Comptroller General of the United States. *Standard for Audit of Governmental Organizations, Programs, Activities, and Functions.* U.S. General Accounting Office, 1972.

"A Description of the Professional Practice of Certified Public Accountants," *Journal of Accountancy,* December 1966, p. 61.

Dowell, C. Dwayne, and Anderson, W. T. "CPA Requirements of the States," *Collegiate News and Views,* Fall 1977, pp. 5–10.

Gobeil, Robert E. "The Common Body of Knowledge for Internal Auditors," *The Internal Auditor,* November/December 1972, pp. 20–29.

Grady, Paul. "The Independent Auditing and Reporting Function of the CPA," *Journal of Accountancy,* November 1965, pp. 65–71.

The Institute of Internal Auditors. *Statement of Responsibilities of the Internal Auditor.* Altamonte Springs, Florida, 1971.

Layton, L., and Perry, W. E. "The Auditor's Responsibility: A Dialogue," *The Internal Auditor,* February 1977, pp. 12–21.

Mautz, R. K., and Sharaf, Hussein A. *The Philosophy of Auditing,* American Accounting Association Monograph no. 6. American Accounting Assn., 1961.

Roy, Robert H., and MacNeill, James H. *Horizons for a Profession.* American Institute of Certified Public Accountants, 1967.

Smith, William S. "Certification—A Giant Step," *The Internal Auditor,* November–December 1972, pp. 10–19.

Staats, Elmer B. "Governmental Auditing—Yesterday, Today, and Tomorrow," *The GAO Review,* Spring 1976, pp. 1–9.

"Standards for the Professional Practice of Internal Auditing," *The Internal Auditor,* October 1978, pp. 9–30.

REVIEW QUESTIONS

1.1. Define and explain auditing. What would be your answer if asked by an anthropology major, "What do auditors do?"

1.2. What is the meaning of the terms *attest* and *attest function*?

1.3. Why is the AICPA definition of auditing apparently so narrow in comparison to definitions given by other auditing organizations?

1.4. List and briefly explain the three elemental areas of interest in GAO audits.

1.5. What have been the sources of outside pressures on the auditing profession and how has the profession responded to them?

1.6. Why are users of financial statements likely to insist that the statements carry the opinion of an independent certified public accountant?

1.7. What three major representations are made by the independent auditor in the opinion paragraph of the standard short-form report?

1.8. Present a useful framework of a scientific, orderly approach to making an audit decision.

1.9. What *assertions* are made in the line entitled "Sales . . . $5,000,000" in an income statement?

1.10. What are the five principal characteristics of an organized profession?

1.11. Who is charged with primary responsibility for the form and content of published financial statements.

1.12. What is regulated by state accountancy laws?

1.13. What authoritative statements are the sources of (1) generally accepted auditing standards, and (2) generally accepted accounting principles?

EXERCISES AND PROBLEMS

1.14. The chairman of the board of directors of Hughes Corporation proposed that the board hire as comptroller a CPA who had been the manager on the corporation's audit performed by a firm of independent accountants. The chairman was of the opinion that the hiring of this person would make the annual audit unnecessary and would consequently result in a saving of the professional fees paid to the auditors. The chairman proposed to give this new comptroller a full staff to conduct such investigations of accounting and operating data as necessary. Evaluate this proposal.

1.15. Put yourself in the position of the person hired as comptroller in the situation above. Suppose that the chairman of the board makes a motion to discontinue the annual audit because Hughes Corporation now has your services on a full-time basis. You are invited to express your views to the board. Explain fully how you would discuss the nature of your job as comptroller and your views on the discontinuance of the annual audit.

1.16. A CPA in public practice and another person who is president of a large drug company are both engaged in providing services and goods that are important to society as a whole. May both persons claim membership in a profession—the CPA as a professional accountant and the president as a professional manager?

1.17. The independent auditor's standard unqualified report contains several important sentences and phrases. Give an explanation of why each of the following phrases is used instead of the alternative language indicated.

1. Address: "To the Board of Directors and Stockholders" instead of "To Whom It May Concern."
2. "We have examined the balance sheet of Anycompany, Inc., as of December 31, 19___, and the related statements of income and retained earnings and changes in financial position for the year then ended," instead of "We have audited the attached financial statements."
3. "Our examination was made in accordance with generally accepted auditing standards," instead of "Our audit was conducted with due audit care appropriate in the circumstances."
4. "In our opinion, the aforementioned financial statements present fairly . . . in conformity with generally accepted accounting principles," instead of "The financial statements are true and correct."

1.18. When an auditor conducts a professionally competent audit examination, why is the auditor's attest communication an expression of opinion rather than a statement of fact?

1.19. Attached to the two-year comparative financial statements of the Clark Corporation for 1977 and 1978 is a standard short-form opinion with no alteration in the recommended wording. Could you conclude that Clark Corporation is applying generally accepted accounting principles on the same basis as it did five years ago? Three years ago? Two years ago? One year ago? Explain.

1.20. Every independent auditor's attest opinion refers to the fair presentation of financial position in conformity with generally accepted accounting principles. Search the authoritative accounting and economics literature (or conduct interviews with practicing auditors) and find the official definition of *financial position*. Determine whether the definition(s) is adequate for you and defend your support or criticism of the definition.

1.21. You have 12 solid spherical objects, 11 of which have an identical weight and volume, but the other sphere has a *different* weight. All 12 spheres look exactly alike.

You have been given a balance scale (a weighing instrument), and you have 3 (and only 3) weighing trials in which to determine (*a*) which sphere has the weight different from the other 11, and (*b*) whether it is heavier or lighter than the other 11.

1.22. Call or write your state board of accountancy and learn the requirements for (*a*) sitting for all or part of the CPA examination, (*b*) grade scores required to pass and to retake exam parts if not passed the first time, (*c*) experience, (*d*) reciprocity, and (*e*) fees.

1.23. Upon completion of all field work on September 23, 1979, the following "short-form" report was rendered by Timothy Ross to the directors of the Rancho Corporation.

To the Directors of the Rancho Corporation:

We have examined the balance sheet and the related statement of income and retained earnings of the Rancho Corporation as of July 31, 1979. In accordance with your instructions, a complete audit was conducted.

In many respects, this was an unusual year for the Rancho Corporation. The weakening of the economy in the early part of the year and the strike of plant employees in the summer of 1979 led to a decline in sales and net income. After making several tests of sales records, nothing came to our attention that would indicate that sales have not been properly recorded.

In our opinion, with the explanation given above, and with the exception of some minor errors that are considered immaterial, the aforementioned financial statements present fairly the financial position of the Rancho Corporation at July 31, 1979, and the results of its operations for the year then ended, in conformity with pronouncements of the Accounting Principles Board and the Financial Accounting Standards Board applied consistently throughout the period.

Timothy Ross, CPA
September 23, 1979

Required:

List and explain deficiencies and omissions in the auditor's report.

Organize your answer by paragraph (scope, explanatory, and opinion) of the auditor's report. (AICPA adapted)

APPENDIX

Statement of Responsibilities of the Internal Auditor*

NATURE

Internal auditing is an independent appraisal activity within an organization for the review of operations as a service to management. It is a managerial control which functions by measuring and evaluating the effectiveness of other controls.[1]

OBJECTIVE AND SCOPE

The objective of internal auditing is to assist all members of management in the effective discharge of their responsibilities, by furnishing them with analyses, appraisals, recommendations and pertinent comments concerning the activities reviewed. The internal auditor is concerned with any phase of business activity where he can be of service to management. This involves going beyond the accounting and financial

* Source: From *Statement of Responsibilities of the Internal Auditor* by The Institute of Internal Auditors, Inc. Copyright 1971 by The Institute of Internal Auditors, Inc., 249 Maitland Avenue, Altamonte Springs, Florida 32701 U.S.A. Reprinted with permission.

[1] This definition was superceded in the 1978 statement of *Standards for the Professional Practice of Internal Auditing*.

records to obtain a full understanding of the operations under review. The attainment of this overall objective involves such activities as:

Reviewing and appraising the soundness, adequacy, and application of accounting, financial, and other operating controls, and promoting effective control at reasonable cost.

Ascertaining the extent of compliance with established policies, plans, and procedures.

Ascertaining the extent to which company assets are accounted for and safeguarded from losses of all kinds.

Ascertaining the reliability of management data developed within the organization.

Appraising the quality of performance in carrying out assigned responsibilities.

Recommending operating improvements.

RESPONSIBILITY AND AUTHORITY

The responsibilities of internal auditing in the organization should be clearly established by management policy. The related authority should provide the internal auditor full access to all of the organization's records, properties, and personnel relevant to the subject under review. The internal auditor should be free to review and appraise policies, plans, procedures, and records.

The internal auditor's responsibilities should be:

To inform and advise management and to discharge this responsibility in a manner that is consistent with the Code of Ethics of the Institute of Internal Auditors.

To coordinate his activities with others so as to best achieve his audit objectives and the objectives of the organization.

In performing his functions, an internal auditor has no direct responsibility for nor authority over any of the activities which he reviews: Therefore, the internal audit review and appraisal does not in any way relieve other persons in the organization of the responsibilities assigned to them.

INDEPENDENCE

Independence is essential to the effectiveness of internal auditing. This independence is obtained primarily through organizational status and objectivity:

The organizational status of the internal auditing function and the support accorded to it by management are major determinants of its range and value. The head of the internal auditing function, therefore, should be responsible to an officer whose authority is sufficient to assure both a broad range of audit coverage and the adequate consideration of and effective action on the audit findings and recommendations.

Objectivity is essential to the audit function. Therefore, an internal auditor should not develop and install procedures, prepare records, or engage in any other activity which he would normally review and appraise and which could reasonably be construed to compromise his independence. His objectivity need not be adversely affected, however, by his determination and recommendation of the standards of control to be applied in the development of systems and procedures under his review.

2

AUDITING THEORY AND PRACTICE STANDARDS

Statements of auditing theory and practice standards are useful for describing, explaining, and predicting various aspects of accounting and auditing practice. In some respects such theory statements are *normative* (describing what proper practice should be), and in other respects they are *positive* (describing what practices are really like).

As presently constituted, auditing theory is mostly a derivation from observed practices, and in this sense it is descriptively positive. However, the theory also contains ideal statements of what practice should be like, and in this sense it is normative. Theory and practice are complementary. The theory exists to guide practice, and practice developments provide the basis for refinements of the theory. At any given time, the practitioner who has a strong understanding of theoretical propositions is in a position to reach meaningful solutions to difficult decision problems. Lacking a thorough grounding in theory such solutions may be had only by chance, and chance is a poor basis for professional decisions.

THEORY STRUCTURE

The purpose of a study of theory and practice standards is to obtain a structure for organizing thoughts relevant to practical decision situations. Thus the most important element of theoretical thinking is to relate the theory to a scientific method for making decisions, as discussed in Chapter 1. As a practical matter, virtually all problems can be approached by relating the problem situation to one or more of the practice standards.

There are three main elements in auditing theory—*concepts*, *postulates*, and *standards*. The standards are sometimes called *precepts*, indicating that they are the most specific elements of the theory of auditing. A *postulate* is a belief fundamental to other beliefs which gives a basis for defining guides to actions. In the discussion below, the postulates of auditing are shown to contain ideas that help explain many of the auditing standards. A *concept* is a central organizing idea that helps a person categorize and classify elements of the theory. Postulates and concepts both lend explanatory power to auditing theory.

Auditing standards are criteria for the quality of audit performance. They are guides to action, which is a meaning of the word *precept.* It is important to realize that auditing standards are quite different from auditing *procedures,* which are the particular and specialized things auditors do on a specific audit engagement. Standards are the quality guides that remain the same through time and for all audits. Procedures, on the other hand, may vary depending upon the complexity of an accounting system, the type of company, and other factors unique to a particular job. This difference is the reason that the auditor's report refers to an audit "conducted in accordance with generally accepted auditing standards" rather than in accordance with auditing procedures.

Under the heading of precepts one may include the rules of ethics, which are also guides to action. Since the subject of professional ethics is extensive, discussion of these rules is deferred to Chapter 3. Practical applications and procedures also are extensive and complex, and these are covered in Chapters 5–16.

GENERAL STANDARDS

The AICPA and GAO statements of auditing standards are divided into three groups—general standards, field standards (AICPA) and examination and evaluation standards (GAO), and reporting standards.[1] The AICPA general standards relate to the personal integrity and professional qualifications of the auditor. The three standards in the general group are:

1. The examination is to be performed by a person or persons having adequate technical training and proficiency as an auditor.
2. In all matters relating to the assignment, an independence in mental attitude is to be maintained by the auditor or auditors.
3. Due professional care is to be exercised in the performance of the examination and the preparation of the report.

Conceptual Basis for General Standards

Three of the five central concepts of auditing theory provide the basis for the general standards. They are (1) ethical conduct, (2) independence, and (3) due audit care.

[1] The Standards for the Professional Practice of Internal Auditing are organized under somewhat different major categories. These standards are reprinted in the Appendix to this chapter.

Ethical Conduct. The concept of ethical conduct belongs equally to all professional accounting practice, not just to auditing practice. In addition to general notions of ethics that are applicable to all persons and in all places, accountants have a codified set of rules of conduct that guide their behavior. Two of the more important rules in this code deal with matters of general standards and with matters of independence. These rules are specifically applicable to all three of the general standards.

Independence. In auditing theory and practice, independence is generally considered a matter of ethics. However, independence is so important that it can stand alone as a central concept.

One important element of independence involves the characteristic of professionalism which was described in Chapter 1 as "the professional's acceptance of social responsibility accompanied by a concurrent recognition of professional status by society." Society, the public at large, expects independent auditors to *lend credibility* to financial communications. Only if the auditors are perceived as truly independent can the public continue to grant social recognition of professional status. Auditors have to adopt an attitude of impartiality as to their concerns with the client and their concerns over the needs of users of audited financial statements.

Some critics of the profession have pointed to the fact that auditors are paid by their clients as an undesirable arrangement, arguing that it is impossible to be independent from the party that pays the fee. Accountants generally have not taken such criticism very seriously because the alternative appears to be some form of public-government control of accounting fees. More significant, however, are the independence issues surrounding the concurrent performance of auditing services and management advisory services or tax advisory services. These issues are discussed in Chapter 3, and here are merely placed in perspective.

The notion of individual practitioner independence is more specific to the conduct of each audit engagement. The essence of this aspect of independence is that auditors must not subordinate their judgment to others and must keep themselves disassociated from influences that might warp their judgment. In more specific terms, auditors must preserve their independence in the following practical ways:

Programming independence. Auditors must remain free from interference by client managers intended to restrict, specify, or modify the procedures that they want to perform, including any attempts by others to assign personnel or otherwise control the audit work.

Investigative independence. Auditors must have free access to books, records, correspondence, and other evidential matter, and they must have the cooperation of management without any attempts to interpret or screen evidence that they need.

Reporting independence. Auditors must not let any feelings of loyalty to the client interfere with their obligation to report fully and fairly. Neither should management be allowed to exert pressure on or overrule auditors' judgment on the appropriate content of an audit report.

Due Audit Care. The concept of due audit care is of utmost importance to the performance of an audit. Indeed, the third general standard simply requires that due professional care is to be exercised. With regard to the first general standard, auditors must be competent and trained if they expect to be properly careful. Thus the general standards are all closely related to the concept of due audit care.

A useful notion for understanding due audit care is the *standard of the prudent auditor*. The idea of a prudent professional practitioner is present in other social science theories, for example, the "economic man" of economic theory and the "reasonable man" in law. In the law the prudent man is one who exercises judgment equal to that of the level of his community, who is not expected to be omniscient, who is presumed to have knowledge special to his profession, who is expected to be aware of his own ignorance. Additionally, the prudent man is expected to possess the skills of his profession whether he is a beginner or a veteran.

Adapting these dimensions from law, Mautz and Sharaf have summarized the qualities of the prudent auditor:

> A prudent practitioner is assumed to have a knowledge of the philosophy and practice of auditing, to have the degree of training, experience, and skill common to the average independent auditor, to have the ability to recognize indications of irregularities, and to keep abreast of developments in the perpetration and detection of irregularities. Due audit care requires the auditor to acquaint himself with the company under examination . . . to review the method of internal control operating in the company . . . to obtain any knowledge readily available which is pertinent to the accounting and financial problems of the company . . . to be responsive to unusual events and unfamiliar circumstances, to persist until he has eliminated from his own mind any reasonable doubts he may have about the existence of material irregularities, and to exercise caution in instructing his assistants and reviewing their work.[2]

Due audit care is a matter of what the auditor does and how well he does it. A determination of proper care must be reached on the basis of all the facts and circumstances in a particular case. When an auditor's work becomes the subject of a lawsuit, the question of due audit care is usually at issue as shall be seen in the law cases in Chapter 4.

Postulates Underlying the General Standards

As a practical matter, postulates in auditing theory are basic beliefs that may be accepted as a foundation for the auditing standards. However, the postulates should not be accepted blindly and without critical thought given to the circumstances of a particular audit engagement. In general, the postulates help explain many of the activities of auditors.

When considering the postulates, one should ask this question: "What would auditing practice be like if this assumption were not accepted?" At

[2] R. K. Mautz and H. A. Sharaf, *The Philosophy of Auditing* (American Accounting Association, 1961), p. 140.

the same time one should recognize that a postulated condition might be false in a particular audit engagement, and to act as if it were true (thus ignoring any evidence to the contrary) could result in negligent performance in the audit.

The postulates most closely related to the three general standards are considered next.

Potential Conflicts of Interest. The current social environment dictates this postulate: *There always exists a potential conflict of interest between the auditor and the management of the enterprise under audit.* Auditors have not always held this view. Until the mid-1970s, auditors preferred to believe that there was no necessary conflict of interest between themselves and management, but widespread disclosures of corporate bribes, kickbacks, and payoffs, and the resulting public clamor for auditors to "do something" have brought about changes.

Holding a belief that a potential conflict of interests always exists causes auditors to include procedures in their audit plans to search for errors or irregularities that would have a material effect on financial statements.[3] This tends to make audits more extensive for the auditor and more expensive for the client. The situation is not a desirable one in the vast majority of audits where no errors or irregularities exist. Nevertheless, auditors have responded in all audits to "do something" because of misdeeds perpetrated by a few managements.

Even though auditing theory contains a postulate about ever-existing potential conflict, auditors must be careful about this belief. Once an audit examination is under way and procedures designed to search for errors and irregularities have been performed, and none have been found, the auditor must be willing to accept the apparent fact that there is no evidence that the *potential* conflict is a *real* one. The overtones of suspicion can be dispelled by the evidence.

The exercise of due audit care requires a healthy skepticism on the part of the auditor—a disposition to question and test all material assertions made by management whether they be oral, written, or incorporated in the accounting records. However, this attitude of skepticism must be balanced with an open mind about the integrity of management. An auditor should not blindly assume that every management is dishonest nor should management be assumed perfectly honest without a thought. The key lies in the auditor's objectivity and in the audit attitude toward gathering the evidence necessary to reach reasonable, supportable audit decisions.

Exclusively an Auditor. The next postulate is: *When examining financial data for the purpose of expressing an independent opinion thereon, the auditor acts exclusively in the capacity of an auditor.* The essential concept implicit in this postulate is the auditor's independence. Although an auditor may act in other capacities to serve client management—as a consultant or tax adviser—these additional services

[3] *Statement on Auditing Standards No. 16* (Section 327.05), "The Independent Auditor's Responsibility for the Detection of Errors or Irregularities" (New York: AICPA, January 1977).

should be perceived as secondary to the principal duties and responsibilities expected in an audit engagement. If management advisory services or tax advice become of such importance that they interfere with the primary objective, then they can damage the professional standing of the auditor. These considerations imply an importance for professional obligations that is considered in the next postulate.

The notion of acting exclusively in the capacity of an auditor, while phrased in terms of independent audits by CPAs, is not necessarily limited to independent audits of financial statements. The basic assumption may also be applied to internal auditors' assignments to assess performance efficiency and especially to GAO auditors when assigned to evaluate programs that have sociopolitical implications.

Professional Obligations. A close relative of the preceding postulate is: *The professional status of the independent auditor imposes commensurate professional obligations.* One important facet of this idea is that auditors' primary responsibility is to the *users* of their work and the readers of their reports. The user audiences include both management and directors and outsiders who receive audit reports. This postulate is as much a basic assumption for all areas of accounting practice as it is for auditing practice. Chapters 3 and 4 on professional ethics and legal relationships draw their importance from this postulate. The point to be made for expressing professional obligations as a postulate is to make explicit the ethical foundation for several of the concepts and standards and to emphasize the role of professionalism in auditing practice.

General Standards in an EDP Environment

The AICPA auditing standards were first formulated in the early 1940s prior to the advent of computerized data processing systems. Nevertheless, the standards are as effective for guiding the audit of complex computer-based information systems as they are for guiding audits of simple hand-kept books and accounts.

An interpretive reexamination of the general standards is presented below. The authors, practicing CPAs, have ably placed these standards in their proper perspective in an EDP environment.[4]

Adequate Technical Training and Proficiency. In the EDP environment, the first general standard clearly requires that the auditor be trained in examining computer-based accounting systems. The use of such systems—not only through in-house computer facilities but also through EDP service bureaus—has become so prevalent that no auditor today can ignore the need for special training in the EDP area. Specifically, today's auditor must understand:

What computers can do and how data are processed in EDP systems.

How to test such systems and how to use the computer to achieve compliance with generally accepted auditing standards.

[4] E. M. Lamb and J. R. Nolan, "Computer Auditing in the Seventies." Reprinted, by permission, from *The Arthur Young Journal,* Winter/Spring 1970, special supplement, pp. 5–6. Copyright © 1970 by Arthur Young & Company.

The many peculiar auditing problems which result from a computer-based accounting system, whether it be a company's own system or that of a service bureau.

The language of the new environment, to permit effective communication with EDP personnel.

The types of system documentation employed in the EDP environment which are not generally found in other situations.

Training in each of these areas is an essential element in achieving compliance with the other general and field work standards.

An Independence in Mental Attitude. To be independent, the auditor must be capable of making his own judgments. If he lacks training in examining computer-based systems, he could well find himself relying on other specialists to make judgments for him—and sometimes he might even be unaware that such judgments are being made. It will not suffice, for example, to rely upon explanations of a computer-based accounting system received from a client's own EDP staff. Neither can the auditor rely upon a service bureau's system on the theory that it is "independent." An examination of the controls and workings of the system must be performed, and such an examination requires competence in computer auditing techniques.

Due Professional Care Is to Be Exercised. The exercise of due care requires a critical review at every level of audit supervision of the work done and the judgments made by those working on the examination. As certified public accountants, we hold ourselves out to clients and the public as possessing the necessary knowledge and skills to examine financial statements and the underlying records and systems. When these records are computerized, such necessary knowledge and skills must include the ability to use procedures specifically designed for the examination of computer-based systems.

General Standards of the GAO

The GAO standards for audit of governmental organizations, programs, activities, and functions are precepts for a wide variety of audit assignments. These standards are the generally accepted auditing standards insofar as governmental audits are concerned. Auditors, including independent CPAs, engaged on audits of governmental organizations, programs, activities, and functions are encouraged by the GAO to observe these auditing standards.

The AICPA general standards have been incorporated into the GAO general standards, but the GAO statement goes further to express standards related to the full scope of governmental audits, which may go beyond that contemplated by independent auditors of financial statements. The first three of the GAO standards below are essentially the same as the AICPA general standards, but the fourth one on the scope of an audit was added to cover the possible breadth of GAO assignments.

- The auditors assigned to perform the audit must collectively possess adequate professional proficiency for the tasks required.

- In all matters relating to the audit work, the audit organization and the individual auditors shall maintain an independent attitude.
- Due professional care is to be used in conducting the audit and in preparing related reports.
- The full scope of an audit of a governmental program, function, activity, or organization should encompass:
  - *a.* An examination of financial transactions, accounts, and reports, including an evaluation of compliance with applicable laws and regulations.
  - *b.* A review of efficiency and economy in the use of resources.
  - *c.* A review to determine whether desired results are effectively achieved.
- In determining the scope for a particular audit, responsible officials should give consideration to the needs of the potential users of the results of the audit.

FIELD WORK STANDARDS

The AICPA field work standards set forth quality criteria for the actual conduct of the audit, including the proper design and execution of auditing procedures. Some reflection on the field standards below will reveal that they cannot be followed effectively if the auditor has not also observed the general standards. The auditor's proficiency, independence, and due audit care are all necessary prerequisites for proper conformity with the field work standards.

1. The work is to be adequately planned and assistants, if any, are to be properly supervised.
2. There is to be a proper study and evaluation of the existing internal control as a basis for reliance thereon and for the determination of the resultant extent of the tests to which auditing procedures are to be restricted.
3. Sufficient competent evidential matter is to be obtained through inspection, observation, inquiries, and confirmations to afford a reasonable basis for an opinion regarding the financial statements under examination.

Conceptual Basis for Field Work Standards

The concept of due audit care is particularly evident in the first of the field standards. Adequate planning and proper supervision are indications of care, and their absence is an indication of careless work.

Timing Aspects of Due Audit Care. In order to plan an audit, auditors should accept an engagement before the client's fiscal year-end, and the more advance notice auditors can have, the better they are able to set aside time for planning. An early appointment of the auditor benefits both the auditor and the client. The auditor may be able to perform some work at an *interim date* (a time some weeks or months before the fiscal year-end).

At an interim date auditors may be able to perform a preliminary evaluation of internal control, audit some account balances, and possibly discover some problem areas of which they were unaware. This advance knowledge of problems can enable auditors to alter the audit program as necessary so that the year-end work (performed on and after the fiscal year-end date) can be performed efficiently. Advance planning for the observation of physical inventory counts and for the confirmation of accounts receivable is particularly important.

The Concept of Evidence. The fourth auditing concept to be mentioned thus far in this chapter is *evidence.* The concept of evidence provides the theoretical basis for technical auditing decisions, as witnessed by the important role of evidence in the scientific decision-making methodology. Evidence was defined earlier as consisting of "all those influences upon the mind of an auditor which ultimately guide his decision choices." The second and third field work standards are specifically concerned with the process of gathering evidence.

Relevant evidence may be quantified or it may be qualitative; it may be objective or it may have subjective qualities; it may be absolutely compelling to a decision or it may be only mildly persuasive. The auditor's task is to collect and evaluate sufficient competent evidence to afford a reasonable and logical basis for his or her decisions. Evidence has several important dimensions and features, and the process of gathering evidence is a principal feature of audit field work. Chapter 5 goes into the matter of evidence in more depth, along with an explanation of general procedures for gathering it.

Right now, however, turn to some other matters of basic assumptions that underlie the field standards.

Postulates Underlying the Field Standards

There are three postulates most closely related to the field standards which help explain the purposes for requiring a proper study and evaluation of internal control and the obtaining of sufficient competent evidential matter. As before, these basic assumptions should be received on their merits in a particular engagement, not merely accepted without a second thought.

Verifiability. The very first necessary assumption for an audit is: *Financial statements and financial data are verifiable.* To state an obviously necessary condition such as this one may seem trivial, but the explicit exposure of all underlying assumptions is the essence of a statement of postulates. If auditors had to assume that financial statements and financial data were not verifiable, then auditing would be presumed impossible at the outset.

The word "verifiable" is used in this postulate (and throughout auditing literature) with some qualification. "Verification" in auditing does not mean that fundamental truths are known as a result of evidence gathered and evaluated. The word generally refers merely to the ability to gather evidence about something.

Audit verification is the means by which auditors make the scientific approach to decisions operational, especially the steps involving collection and evaluation of evidence. Since absolute proof and absolute truth are unknown and unknowable, the audit decision maker must accept some risks of wrong decisions. These risks can be measured in some circumstances. This is why the third field work standard refers to "sufficient" rather than "absolute" evidence.

The verifiability postulate also sets some bounds on the scope of auditing practice, although different bounds may exist for independent auditors, internal auditors, IRS agents, GAO auditors, and others. Independent auditors accept tasks that possess a great potential for verifiability; internal auditors may accept assignments that require more subjective judgment than hard evidence; and GAO auditors may receive assignments to report on performance efficiency in situations where standards are not fully developed. Each type of auditor, in his own sphere of interest, nevertheless assumes some degree of verifiability that is consistent with his social role and congruent with the type of report expected. The verifiability proposition is of prime importance in consideration of the extension of auditors' responsibility to new kinds of information.

Internal Control and Reliability. The companion to the preceding postulate is: *The existence of a satisfactory system of internal control reduces the probability of irregularities.* The basic assumption provides the foundation for a major portion of present-day audit engagement conduct. Auditors always determine the state of control over the information processing system with the view to relying upon a satisfactory system to produce reasonably accurate financial and nonfinancial records.

Internal control may be defined simply as a system's capability to prevent and/or detect data processing errors and provide for their correction. In *Statement on Auditing Standards No. 1*, accounting controls are defined as methods and procedures that are concerned mainly with safeguarding assets from loss through errors and irregularities and with providing reliable financial records for external reporting purposes.[5] These definitions and other technical aspects of the proper study and evaluation of internal control are covered in more depth in Chapters 6, 7, and 8.

One should note, however, that the primary objective contemplated in the second field work standard is that auditors use the decision about an internal control system for planning subsequent audit procedures. Thus there is a direct connection between the reliance on a system and the criterion of *sufficient* evidence mentioned in the third field work standard.

The postulate provides the following necessary assumptions and results: (*a*) The better a system of controls over data processing accuracy, the more reliable is the output, and an auditor can thus feel free to minimize the extent of subsequent verification procedures; and conversely (*b*)

[5] *Statement on Auditing Standards No. 1* (Sections 320.10, 320.15, 320.17, 320.19, 320.28) (New York: AICPA, 1973).

the poorer a system of controls over data processing accuracy, the less reliable is the output, and an auditor must tend to maximize the extent of subsequent verification procedures. If auditors had to assume no relationship between the quality of accounting controls and the accuracy of output then proper study and evaluation of internal control would be pointless. Experience has shown that audit field work efficiencies can be realized if the auditor can rely on the existing system of internal control.

The Past Holds True for the Future. This controversial postulate holds a rather subtle meaning for auditing practice: *In the absence of clear evidence to the contrary, what has held true in the past for the enterprise under examination will hold true in the future.* The opening phrase of this assumption—"In the absence of clear evidence to the contrary . . ."—could be an appropriate preface to all the other postulates, but it is particularly relevant to the auditor's concern with future events.

Even in the audit of historical cost-basis financial statements, an auditor makes many inferences about the future. Examples of inferences about future events are most evident in (*a*) evaluating the collectibility of accounts receivable based upon collection experience; (*b*) evaluating inventory obsolescence on the basis of past usage patterns; (*c*) assessing the economic usefulness and useful lives of fixed assets based upon experience with similar assets; and (*d*) in a negative sense, expecting to encounter classification and valuation problems when management has been known to have made such accounting errors in the past.

With this postulate about the future, one can infer that the auditor's responsibility for predicting the future is limited. Auditors are responsible for decisions based upon knowledge available at the time the decisions were made. They are relatively protected from having their decisions judged on the basis of after-the-fact hindsight. The sufficiency and competency of evidence is judged in this perspective. If this assumption is released, the tendency would be to create a situation of massive uncertainty about current decisions vis-á-vis future developments, and audit decisions and reports would have to be phrased explicitly to recognize reservations based on undefined and undefinable uncertainties. In a utilitarian sense, the assumption that the past predicts the near future (lacking contrary evidence) has served reasonably well the needs of both auditors and society.

Field Work Standards in an EDP Environment

Turning again to the special environment of computer-based information systems, the field work standards may be reinterpreted with special emphasis on EDP. Since the technology of EDP is complex, the auditor should take into account special problems of planning and supervision, internal control features, and evidential matter. Lamb and Nolan have provided the additional considerations set forth below.

Adequate Planning and Supervision. The adequate plannning of an audit engagement includes a careful consideration of timing problems. In planning examinations of computerized records, the auditor should anticipate timing problems similar to those encountered in planning the observation of physical inventories. The nature and effectiveness of internal controls which are built into computer programs can have a major impact on the review and evaluation of controls outside the computer area. It is often desirable for this portion of the examination to be performed first, to permit an assessment of the impact of the computer system on the remainder of the examination. Occasionally situations will be encountered in which the only way the auditor can assure himself of the proper functioning of a computer-based accounting system is to make tests throughout the year—and these tests may have to be on a surprise basis. These are merely a few examples of the kinds of planning problems which arise in the computer environment.

Adequate supervision also implies that each supervisor is skilled in reviewing the procedures employed by his assistants in examining computerized records. Without such skill the supervisor cannot properly evaluate the judgments made by his assistants.

Study and Evaluation of Internal Control. The subject of internal control presents probably the most vivid illustration of the need for the auditor to develop new skills in order to perform examinations in the computer environment. It is insufficient in most instances for the auditor to limit his review to controls over transactions entering into the computer system and the resulting output therefrom. Attention must also be paid to the controls which exist (or which may not exist) within the computer system and in the EDP operating department. Controls that are written into computer programs must be evaluated and tested. Although in some cases such controls may be tested by obtaining detailed printouts of transactions processed, this procedure can be quite expensive. A company which has spent a substantial amount of money to incorporate adequate controls into its computer system will quite properly expect its auditors to use techniques of evaluation and testing similar to those which were used in developing the EDP system. Every computer system must be programmed and tested before it is used; the auditor can employ similar techniques.

Sufficient Competent Evidential Matter. The computer has brought with it new methods of accounting systems documentation. Flowcharts, logic diagrams, and decision tables, for example, are types of documentation not normally found in noncomputer systems; they will form part of the auditor's evidential matter. In obtaining such evidence when computer systems are present, the auditor should design his inquiries and tests to cover the peculiarities of the system. A typical internal control questionnaire, for example, oriented toward manual or tabulating machine systems, can be entirely inadequate as a guide for the review of an EDP system.

Examination and Evaluation Standards of the GAO

Like the AICPA field work standards, the GAO examination and evaluation standards are operational statements about the evidence-gathering phase of an audit. The major difference between the GAO and AICPA standards in this group is the GAO emphasis on compliance with legal and regulatory requirements. This seems natural because most if not all organizations, programs, activities, and functions examined by GAO auditors are created by law or regulation. Thus specific compliance is of particular interest to the recipients of GAO reports. The GAO standard on internal control evaluation also places more emphasis on the reliability of the system to provide for efficient and effective operations, something that is not necessarily required by independent auditors of financial statements.

- Work is to be adequately planned.
- Assistants are to be properly supervised.
- An evaluation is to be made of the system of internal control to assess the extent it can be relied upon to ensure accurate information, to ensure compliance with laws and regulations, and to provide for efficient and effective operations.
- Sufficient, competent, and relevant evidence is to be obtained to afford a reasonable basis for the auditor's opinions, judgments, conclusions, and recommendations.
- A review is to be made of compliance with legal and regulatory requirements.

The absence of an explicit AICPA field work standard specifying a review for compliance with rules, laws, and regulations does not mean that such work is not required. Independent auditors do in fact review for compliance with laws and regulations, especially those that may have an impact on the financial statements and related disclosures. Failure to do so would be a breach of due audit care, so this aspect of difference is not as major as it would seem from a comparison of the standards themselves.[6]

REPORTING STANDARDS

The ultimate objective of independent auditors—their report on the audit and their opinion on the financial statements—is guided by the four AICPA reporting standards. The importance of these standards cannot be overemphasized.

1. The report shall state whether the financial statements are presented in accordance with generally accepted accounting principles. ✓
2. The report shall state whether such principles have been consistently observed in the current period in relation to the preceding period. ✓
3. Informative disclosures in the financial statements are to be regarded as reasonably adequate unless otherwise stated in the report. ✓
4. The report shall either contain an expression of opinion regarding the financial statements, taken as a whole, or an assertion to the effect that an opinion cannot be expressed. When an overall opinion cannot be expressed, the reasons therefore should be stated. In all cases where an auditor's name is associated with financial statements, the report should contain a clear-cut indication of the character of the auditor's examination, if any, and the degree of responsibility he is taking. ✓

[6] Refer to *Statement on Auditing Standards No. 17* (Section 328), "Illegal Acts by Clients."

The first two reporting standards are straightforward directives about two features of the standard audit report. Recall from the illustration of standard short-form opinion wording given in Chapter 1 these phrases: "*In our opinion* the . . . financial statements present fairly the financial position . . . results of operations and the changes in financial position . . . *in conformity with generally accepted accounting principles* applied on a *basis consistent with that of the preceding year.*"

In this opinion paragraph auditors make a statement of fact about their belief (opinion). Since the auditor is the professional expert in attestation his or her belief is considered reliable and to be relied upon, the users of financial statements do in fact depend upon it. The standard wording carries the required references to conformity with generally accepted accounting principles and to consistency of their application.

Generally accepted accounting principles include not only financial reporting standards found in official pronouncements (e.g., Accounting Research Bulletins, Accounting Principles Board Opinions, Financial Accounting Standards Board Statements, SEC Regulations) but also the methods of applying the principles. In addition, there may exist practices having general acceptance but which are not covered in any official pronouncement. When auditors find such standards used, they must use their judgment and expertise to determine whether they have found general acceptance for reporting purposes.

The consistency phrase required by the second reporting standard has the objectives of (*a*) giving assurance that the comparability of financial statements has not been materially altered by accounting changes, and (*b*) requiring full disclosure if accounting changes have in fact occurred. Nevertheless, consistency does not absolutely assure *comparability* of comparative financial statements. There may have been changes in accounting estimates or substantially different transactions in one year that do not require consistency-related disclosure under the second reporting standard.[7]

The third reporting standard requires auditors to use professional judgment in deciding whether the financial statements and related disclosures contain all the important information that users might need for their decisions. Observance of this standard may mean disclosure of some information that is not covered by any written rules in official pronouncements of accounting principles. It may mean having to deal with a rare and unusual fact situation that nobody has encountered before. In this standard the auditor has great latitude for determining what is important and what is not. Likewise, users of financial statements also have the right to claim that certain information is necessary for adequate disclosure. In fact, many lawsuits are brought on this issue: Investors claim that certain information is (was) necessary that was not disclosed, and auditors must show reasons for lack of disclosure.

The fourth reporting standard is the most complex one. It contains three important elements. Each one is discussed in turn.

[7] Further details on consistency matters are found in *Statement on Auditing Standards No. 1* (Sections 420 and 546).

1. The report shall either contain an expression of opinion on the financial statements, taken as a whole, or an assertion to the effect that an opinion cannot be expressed.

This first sentence divides opinion statements into two classes: (*a*) opinions on statements *taken as a whole* (i.e., unqualified, adverse, and qualified opinions); and (*b*) the disclaimer of opinion. The second sentence adds to the idea of "statements taken as a whole" as follows:

2. When an overall opinion cannot be expressed, the reasons therefor should be stated.

An "overall opinion" here refers to the unqualified opinion. Thus when the adverse opinion, qualified opinions, or disclaimer of opinion is rendered all the substantive reasons for doing so must be explained. A middle paragraph is generally used for such an explanation.

The last sentence refers to both the scope paragraph and the opinion paragraph.

3. In all cases where an auditor's name is associated with financial statements, the report should contain a clear-cut indication of
   a. the character of the auditor's examination, if any, and
   b. the degree of responsibility he is taking.

This last sentence means precisely what it says when referring to "in all cases." Every time auditors (even when acting only as accountants) are associated by name or by action with financial statements they must report on their examination and their responsibility. The character of their examination is usually described by the standard short-form reference to an "examination conducted according to generally accepted auditing standards." But if the audit has been restricted in some way or if the statements are simply unaudited, the auditor must say so in the scope paragraph. This is especially important when an accountant prepares unaudited financial statements for a client.

The "degree of responsibility" is indicated by the form of the opinion. Auditors take full responsibility for their belief when they give the unqualified or the adverse opinion. They take no responsibility whatsoever when giving the disclaimer of opinion. They take responsibility when giving a qualified opinion for all matters except those mentioned as the reasons for the qualified opinion.

The Concept of Fair Presentation

The fifth and last concept in auditing theory is that of *fair presentation.* The critical test for the usefulness of auditing services rendered by independent auditors, internal auditors, governmental auditors, and others is the quality of the report. For independent auditors this report is the opinion on the fair presentation of financial statements and related disclosures. For internal auditors and governmental auditors the final communication output may involve a comprehensive, evaluative report on economy, efficiency, or program results.

Decisions about fair presentation may produce problems of conflict. In the first place, generally accepted accounting principles are usually presented as means of finding "answers" to disclosures and presentation problems, and they are usually presented as a fairly complete and unambiguous set of rules. Yet auditing theory, as a matter of postulate, accepts the accounting principles only with reservation on the grounds that there is nothing better available for a standard. With regard to reporting problems and fair presentation decisions, there are no quick and easy solutions because these issues are the most difficult ones facing the accounting profession today.

The first phrase in the standard opinion paragraph is: "In our opinion, the . . . financial statements *present fairly*. . . ." For auditors these two italicized words have the traditional meaning that the financial statements are free from material errors. These words are supposed to express the art of accounting—putting readers on notice that "exact" statements are not what are intended. Over the years, however, users of financial statements have forgotten (or never learned) this meaning and have become accustomed to reading these words literally in the context of general "fairness." Consequently, auditors sometimes find themselves embroiled in controversies over what is fair and what is misleading.

The Postulate of Fairness

The seventh and final postulate was first proposed with reservation in 1961, and it is subject to interpretation today: *Consistent application of generally accepted accounting principles (GAAP) results in the fair presentation of financial position and the results of operations.* This assumption makes explicit the merging of accounting and auditing for the process of financial communication. Nevertheless, the reliance on generally accepted accounting principles is expressed solely for the purpose of providing auditors with *some* standard. (The general argument is that if this postulate were not accepted then there would exist *no* statement of standards that auditors could use to judge fairness.)

Events since 1961 have revealed several views of GAAP. One survey showed that CPAs, in approximate equal proportions, believed (*a*) that financial statements are reported as fairly presented *and* in conformity with GAAP, (*b*) that financial statements are fair *because* of conformity with GAAP (this is the postulated condition), and (*c*) that financial statements are fair *despite* conformity with GAAP. The last view is typical of the critics of accountants and auditors.

The issue, however, has been resolved about as well as possible by *SAS No. 5.*[8] Financial accounting standards are constantly undergoing change and revision. What may have been an acceptable practice in one year may be prohibited the next. For example, deferral of research and develop-

---

[8] The most recent effort appeared in *Statement on Auditing Standards No. 5* (Section 411), "The Meaning of 'Present Fairly in Conformity with Generally Accepted Accounting Principles' in the Independent Auditor's Report" (July 1975).

ment costs was generally accepted until late 1974 when FASB *Statement No.* 2 required that most types of internal research and development costs be expensed.

The importance of the reporting standards cannot be overemphasized, and the problems of reporting cannot be swept away. Thus they will appear again and again throughout the remaining chapters in this textbook.

Reporting Standards of the GAO

The reporting standards exhibit the greatest difference between AICPA standards applicable in independent audits of financial statements and GAO standards applicable in audits of various programs, activities, and functions. In fact, the GAO statement contains a far more elaborate set of standards than the AICPA statement, but this detail is a function of the wider variety of GAO audit assignments. In other facets of the practice of public accounting, notably in management advisory services, many of the GAO reporting standards are relevant for communication of work done, results achieved, and recommendations offered.

GAO Financial Report Standards. The first two GAO reporting standards are essentially the same as the AICPA's four reporting standards. In this respect the GAO has incorporated audits of financial statements within its responsibility.

Each audit report containing financial reports shall:

> Contain an expression of the auditor's opinion as to whether the information in the financial reports is presented fairly in conformity with generally accepted accounting principles or with other specified accounting principles applicable to the organization, program, function or activity audited, applied on a basis consistent with that of the preceding reporting period. If the auditor cannot express such an opinion, the reasons should be stated in the audit report.

> Contain appropriate supplementary explanatory information about the contents of the financial reports as may be necessary for full and informative disclosure about the financial operations of the organization, program, function, or activity audited. Violations of legal or other regulatory requirements, including instances of noncompliance, shall be explained in the audit report. Material changes in accounting policies and procedures and their effect on the financial reports are to be explained in the audit report.

Distribution and Timing Standards. Since the GAO does not have "clients" in the same sense as public accountants and thus does not have a uniform delivery of reports, the following standards relate to distribution and timing.

> Written audit reports are to be submitted to the appropriate officials of the organizations requiring or arranging for the audits. Copies of the reports should be sent to other officials who may be responsible for taking action on audit findings and recommendations and to others responsible for taking action on audit findings and recommendations and to others responsible or

authorized to receive such reports. Copies should also be made available for public inspection.

- Reports are to be issued on or before the dates specified by law, regulation or other arrangements, and in any event, as promptly as possible so as to make the information available for timely use by management and by legislative officials.

Detail Report Content Standards. The last set of standards consists of a number of reporting guides that illustrate the diverse nature of GAO reports. Since GAO audit assignments may range from defense systems to food programs, there is no standard "form" for a report. The considerations listed below, however, serve as quality criteria for their reports.

Each report shall:

1. Be as concise as possible but at the same time clear and complete enough to be understood by the users.
2. Present factual matter accurately, completely, and fairly.
3. Present findings and conclusions objectively and in language as clear and simple as the subject matter permits.
4. Include only factual information, findings, and conclusions that are adequately supported by enough evidence in the auditor's working papers to demonstrate or prove, when called upon, the bases for the matters reported and their correctness and reasonableness. Detailed supporting information should be included in the report to the extent necessary to make a convincing presentation.
5. Include, when possible, the auditor's recommendations for actions to effect improvements in problem areas noted in his audit and otherwise to make improvements in operations. Information on underlying causes of problems reported should be included to assist in implementing or devising corrective actions.
6. Place primary emphasis on improvement rather than on criticism of the past; critical comments should be presented in balanced perspective, recognizing any unusual difficulties or circumstances faced by the operating officials concerned.
7. Identify and explain issues and questions needing further study and consideration by the auditor or others.
8. Include recognition of noteworthy accomplishments, particularly when management improvements in one program or activity may be applicable elsewhere.
9. Include recognition of the views of responsible officials of the organization, program, function, or activity audited on the auditor's findings, conclusions, and recommendations. Except where the possibility of fraud or other compelling reason may require different treatment, the auditor's tentative findings and conclusions should be reviewed with such officials. When possible, without delay, their views should be obtained in writing and objectively considered and presented in preparing the final report.
10. Clearly explain the scope and objectives of the audit.
11. State whether any significant pertinent information has been omitted because it is deemed privileged or confidential. The nature of such information should be described, and the law or other basis under which it is withheld should be stated.

Summary: Auditing Theory

The description of auditing theory has ranged over the AICPA standards, GAO standards, standards in an EDP environment, the conceptual basis for standards, and the postulates underlying the standards. Exhibit 2–1 organizes the main elements of auditing theory and summarizes their interrelationships. Abbreviated descriptions of the postulates and standards are used in the exhibit so that an overall picture may be obtained.

EXHIBIT 2–1
Auditing Theory Interrelationships

Concepts	*Postulates*	*Auditing Standards (AICPA, GAO)*
1. Ethical conduct 2. Independence 3. Due audit care	1. Potential conflicts of interest 2. Exclusively an auditor 3. Professional obligation	Proficiency as an auditor (AICPA, GAO) Independent attitude (AICPA, GAO) Due professional care (AICPA, GAO) Scope of audit (GAO) Needs of users (GAO)
4. Evidence	4. Verifiability 5. Internal control and reliability 6. Past holds true for the future	Planning and supervision (AICPA, GAO) Study and evaluation of internal control (AICPA, GAO) Sufficient, competent evidential matter (AICPA, GAO) Compliance review (GAO)
5. Fair presentation	7. Application of generally accepted accounting principles results in fair presentation	Generally accepted accounting principles (AICPA, GAO) Other specified accounting principles (GAO) Consistency (AICPA, GAO) Adequate informative disclosures (AICPA, GAO) Compliance violations (GAO) Expression of opinion or a disclaimer (AICPA, GAO) Distribution and timing (GAO) Detail report content (GAO)

MANAGEMENT ADVISORY SERVICES PRACTICE STANDARDS

Practice standards are as meaningful in management advisory services as they are in audit engagements. The AICPA management advisory services executive committee has codified eight MAS practice standards for the guidance of practitioners.[9] The term "practitioner" as used in these standards refers to all persons, whether CPAs or not, who perform management advisory services in CPA firms.

The first three standards are very much like the general group of the auditing standards. They are guides for assessing personal and professional qualities.

1. *Personal Characteristics.* In performing management advisory services, a practitioner must act with integrity and objectivity and be independent in mental attitude.
2. *Competence.* Engagements are to be performed by practitioners having competence in the analytical approach and process and in the technical subject matter under consideration.
3. *Due Care.* Due professional care is to be exercised in the performance of a management advisory services engagement.

The integrity, objectivity, and independence required of a management consultant are very similar to those same qualities required of an auditor. They mean that the consultant should ensure that his or her work and results are free of distortions and misstatements, and free of any bias unrelated to the engagement. A client generally expects the consultant to maintain an impartial attitude in the engagement.

Competence involves the consultant's ability to identify and define the client's problem, to determine and evaluate possible solutions, and to communicate recommendations effectively. This competence amounts to a facility with the scientific methodology described in Chapter 1 of this textbook. At the client's request, the consultant may participate in implementing management's choice of a solution alternative. But this type of participation tends to identify the consultant very closely with the management and is to be avoided if the consultant also performs the audit of the client's financial statements.

The standard of due professional care has the same meaning as the auditing standard of due care explained earlier in this chapter. To the extent that management advisory services are complex and require expertise beyond that normally held by accountants, the due professional care standard is extended to match the complexity of the task.

The next two standards relate directly to the client who engages the consultant.

4. *Client Benefit.* Before accepting an engagement, a practitioner is to notify the client of any reservations he has regarding anticipated benefits.
5. *Understanding with Client.* Before undertaking an engagement, a practitioner is to inform his client of all significant matters related to the engagement.

---

[9] American Institute of Certified Public Accountants, *Statements on Management Advisory Services* (New York, 1974). Also reprinted in the *Journal of Accountancy,* February 1975, pp. 78–81.

The generally accepted auditing standards have no guides parallel to these two, although auditors do try to inform clients of any problems and issues connected with an audit. But in management advisory services, because of the wide variety of management problem areas, the guides are useful to make the consultant aware that all management advisory services are expected to produce positive benefits. Sometimes these benefits are obvious, but in other cases a consultant may find the problem not serious enough to merit an expensive investigation.

The "significant matters" mentioned in the fifth standard are items that should go into an engagement letter or contract. Typically they include: (*a*) the scope and objective of the engagement, (*b*) the extent to which the consultant is expected to carry the study, (*c*) the roles and responsibilities of client personnel or other consultants involved in the study but not as members of the practitioner's staff, (*d*) the desired communication and report and the timetable for the study, and (*e*) the basis for the fee. All these matters should be agreed upon in advance, preferably in writing, so that later misunderstanding might be avoided.

The last three standards may be viewed as field work and reporting standards. Their similarity to the auditing standards is readily apparent.

6. *Planning, Supervision, and Control.* Engagements are to be adequately planned, supervised, and controlled.
7. *Sufficient Relevant Data.* Sufficient relevant data is to be obtained, documented, and evaluated in developing conclusions and recommendations.
8. *Communication of Results.* All significant matters relating to the results of the engagement are to be communicated to the client.

Planning, supervision, and control are elements of due professional care. Control is particularly important. Since management advisory services tend to be very diverse, more so than audit engagements, the practitioner should continually monitor the work in terms of accomplishment, time schedule, and quality of work.

The phrase "sufficient relevant data" in the seventh standard carries the same meaning as does "sufficient competent evidence" in the audit field work standards. The point is that consultants must gather and document support for their conclusions and recommendations.

The reporting standard, number eight, is simply an open-ended concise statement that a report is to be rendered without holding back any significant information from the client. Reports may be written or oral, and they may be made as the engagement progresses as well as when it is completed. The final report should include descriptions of significant alternatives considered by the practitioner, the rationale supporting his or her recommendations, and any assumptions made and the bases for them.

For more detail guides to report content, a practitioner might refer to the detail report content standards of the GAO presented earlier in this chapter. These standards contain something of a checklist of good ideas for informative reports.

RESPONSIBILITIES IN TAX PRACTICE STANDARDS

As of July 1, 1977, ten Statements on Responsibilities in Tax Practice had been issued by AICPA taxation committees. By early 1978 two other statements were in the exposure draft stage—one on *Communications between Successor and Predecessor Tax Advisers* and one on *Contingent Fees*. The U.S. Treasury Department also has published regulations on income tax preparers. The AICPA statements depend for their authority on the general acceptability of the standards expressed in them. The Treasury regulations have the force and effect of law. The AICPA statements are reviewed below.[10]

Signatures. A CPA should sign as preparer any federal tax return which requires such a signature if he prepares it for and transmits it to the taxpayer or another, whether or not the return was prepared for compensation. This requirement goes beyond Section 1.6065–1(*b*) (1) of the income tax regulations which requires the signature if the return is prepared for compensation.

A CPA may sign the preparer's declaration on a federal tax return if he reviews the return and thereby acquires knowledge with respect to it substantially equivalent to that which he would have acquired had he actually prepared the return.

When the preparer's declaration is signed, it should not be modified by the CPA (i.e., no penned changes to the wording to suit the CPA's taste).

Answers to Questions. A CPA should sign the preparer's declaration on a federal tax return only if he is satisfied that reasonable effort has been made to provide appropriate answers. Otherwise, the CPA should not sign an incomplete return that does not explain the reason for omitting answer(s) to question(s).

Administrative Proceedings of a Prior Year. A CPA may sign the preparer's declaration on a federal tax return when the client has selected a current tax treatment of an item that was the subject of an earlier administrative proceeding concluded by a waiver by the taxpayer. So long as the taxpayer is not bound to a particular treatment in closing an administrative proceeding, a similar tax treatment can be selected in subsequent tax returns.

Estimates and Errors in Tax Returns. A CPA may prepare federal tax returns involving the use of estimates, especially when it is impracticable to obtain exact data. However, the CPA should be satisfied that estimated amounts are not unreasonable.

When a CPA learns of an error in a client's previously filed federal tax return (or learns of the failure to file a required return), the client should be advised promptly with a recommendation to take appropriate corrective action. If the client requests the CPA to prepare subsequent returns, the CPA should consider the client's willingness (or lack of it) to correct previous errors before proceeding with preparation of current tax returns.

When a CPA is representing a client in an administrative proceeding

---

[10] U.S. Treasury Department regulations on income tax preparers differ in some respects from the AICPA Statements on Responsibilities in Tax Practice.

and knows of an error in a federal tax return, the CPA should request the client's agreement to disclose the error to IRS. The problem is a serious one because if IRS questions the item the CPA cannot lie about it, but to speak openly without the client's agreement might amount to a breach of the confidentiality relationship with the client. The best thing to do is obtain the client's agreement. Lacking that, the standards suggest that the CPA may be under a duty to withdraw from the engagement.

Advice to Clients. Keeping up with federal taxation changes is difficult at best. CPAs may carry on continuous communication with clients about changes. However, a CPA is not required to initiate such communication and keep a tax client informed unless there is a specific agreement with the client to do so.

Procedural Aspects of Return Preparation. When preparing a federal tax return, the CPA is not required to examine or review documents or other evidence supporting the tax information submitted by a client. However, a CPA should encourage clients to provide supporting data where appropriate. If the CPA recognizes information to be incorrect or incomplete, he is required to make inquiries, one of which would probably be for supporting data.

Contrary Positions. In a federal tax return a CPA may take positions contrary to Treasury Department or IRS interpretations of the code without disclosure, if there is reasonable support for the position. However, rare positions contrary to the Internal Revenue Code itself, even when there is reasonable support (e.g., a constitutional question or conflicts between two code sections), cannot be taken without disclosure. In light of possible penalties for negligence and fraud, it is probably a prudent idea to make disclosure of any type of contrary position.

SUMMARY

To aid students' comprehension of the contents of this chapter, the list below shows the variety of auditing theory and practice standards covered. One must be aware that standards exist in all areas of practice and some similarities exist across some of the statements. A little thought and organization will prevent confusion of one with another.

- AICPA Generally Accepted Auditing Standards (GAAS)
  - Conceptual basis for GAAS
  - Postulates underlying GAAS
- AICPA general and field work standards interpreted in an EDP environment.
- GAO Auditing Standards
- Management Advisory Services Practice Standards
- Responsibilities in Tax Practice Standards
- Standards for the Professional Practice of Internal Auditing (Appendix)

PUTTING THEORY TO WORK

The importance of having a thorough understanding of auditing theory and the practice standards can hardly be overemphasized. Throughout the remainder of this textbook, all topics have one or more roots in the concepts, postulates, and standards covered in this chapter. All practical problems can be approached by beginning with a consideration of the practice standard(s) in question. Auditing theory does not exist in a vacuum. It is put to work in numerous practical applications.

Particular practical applications of theoretical standards are evident in subsequent discussion of audit program planning, execution of auditing procedures, gathering evidence, and making auditing decisions. In effect these practical applications are the means of operationalizing the scientific method of decision making.

SOURCES AND ADDITIONAL READING REFERENCES

American Accounting Association Committee on Auditing Concepts. "A Statement of Basic Auditing Concepts," *Accounting Review,* supplement to vol. 47, 1972, pp. 15–76.

American Institute of Certified Public Accountants. *Statements on Management Advisory Services,* New York, 1974.

———. *Statements on Responsibilities in Tax Practice,* New York, 1973.

———. *Code of Professional Ethics,* New York, 1973.

Anderson, H. M.; Giese, J. W.; and Booker, Jon. "Some Propositions about Auditing," *Accounting Review,* July 1970, pp. 524–31.

Carey, J. L., and Doherty, W. O. "The Concept of Independence—Review and Restatement," *Journal of Accountancy,* January 1966.

Clarke, Robert W. "Extension of the CPA's Attest Function in Corporate Annual Reports," *Accounting Review,* October 1968, pp. 769–76.

Comptroller General of the United States, U.S. General Accounting Office. *Standards for Audit of Governmental Organizations, Programs, Activities, and Functions.* Washington, D.C.: U.S. Government Printing Office, 1972.

Dominiak, Geraldine F., and Louderback, Joseph G. "Present Fairly and Generally Accepted Accounting Principles," *CPA Journal,* January 1972, pp. 45–49.

Granof, Michael H. "Operational Audit Standards for Audits of Government Services," *CPA Journal,* December 1973, pp. 1079–85.

Hicks, E. L. "Standards for the Attest Function," *Journal of Accountancy,* August 1974, pp. 39–45.

The Institute of Internal Auditors, Inc. *Standards for the Professional Practice of Internal Auditing,* 1978.

Kramer, John L. "Disclosure of Positions Contrary to the IRC," *CPA Journal,* January 1978, pp. 41–45.

Lamb, E. M., and Nolan, J. R. "Computer Auditing in the Seventies," *The Arthur Young Journal,* Winter/Spring 1970, special supplement, pp. 5–6.

Lynn, B. B. "Auditing Contractor Compliance with Cost Accounting Standards," *Journal of Accountancy,* June 1975, pp. 60–70.

Mautz, R. K., and Sharaf, Hussein A. *The Philosophy of Auditing,* American Accounting Association Monograph No. 6, especially chap. 3, "The Postulates of Auditing" and chap. 10, "Auditing in Perspective." American Accounting Association, 1961.

Thorne, Jack F. "Tough Regulations for Tax Return Preparers," *CPA Journal,* May 1978, pp. 21–25.

Wood, Thomas D. "Auditors' Concern for Compliance with Laws," *CPA Journal*, January 1978, pp. 17–21.

REVIEW QUESTIONS

2.1 Of what usefulness is theory in auditing? Does "theory" exist only in college textbooks?

2.2 Explain the term "verification" as it is commonly used by auditors.

2.3. Why should auditors at first believe that there is always a potential conflict of interest between the auditor and the management of the enterprise under audit?

2.4. What are the three specific aspects of independence that an auditor should carefully guard in the course of an engagement?

2.5. For what reasons does an auditor conduct a proper study and evaluation of internal controls? Must such an evaluation *always* be made of every data processing subsystem?

2.6. By what standard would a judge determine the quality of *due audit care*? Explain.

2.7. Give some examples of how an auditor might assume that "what has held true in the past for the enterprise under examination will hold true in the future."

2.8. What are the seven underlying *postulates* of auditing theory?

2.9. What are the five major *concepts* in auditing theory?

2.10. Define audit evidence.

2.11. Distinguish between auditing *standards* and auditing *procedures*. (AICPA)

2.12. Are the GAO audit standards applicable for all audits and for all auditors? Explain.

EXERCISES AND PROBLEMS

2.13. The Lovett Corporation uses an IBM 360 system with peripheral card-to-tape and high-speed printer equipment. Transaction information is initially recorded on paper documents (e.g., sales invoices), then key-punched on cards before being inserted into a card-reader which produces a magnetic tape containing the data. These data file tapes are processed by a computer program; and printed listings, journals, and general ledger balances are produced on the high-speed printer equipment.

Required:

Explain how the audit standard requiring "adequate technical training and proficiency" is important for satisfying the other general and field work standards in the audit of Lovett Corporation's financial statements.

2.14. The MAL Transport Company operates a freight trucking line in seven southeastern states. Management has identified as one of its principal problems the regular scheduled maintenance of the fleet of trucks and trailers.

The maintenance supervisor once took a college course in operations management and realizes that the maintenance schedule creates a "waiting line" of freight contracted for shipment. This amount of freight not shipped fluctuates according to the availability of trucks and trailers, which may be unavailable because (1) they are undergoing maintenance in the shop or (2) they are broken down on the road. From the college course in operations management, the supervisor knows that maintenance scheduling is a "queuing problem" but does not know how to solve it. Therefore, the supervisor forwarded a request to the vice president in charge of operations that a consultant be engaged to study the problem and make recommendations.

Required:

Assume that the consulting engagement is accepted by an independent CPA firm.

a. What training and/or experience should a consultant have in order to undertake the assignment?

b. How is an independence in mental attitude relevant for the MAL maintenance problem?

c. Suppose that a consultant goes to the MAL company office and gathers data on (1) the capacity of trailers in the fleet and (2) shipping volume for the last year. The consultant divides the shipping volume by the trailer capacity and decides that 775 trailers are needed. (The company owns 800.) Believing that 75 extra trailers are needed to account for maintenance downtime, the consultant thus recommends the purchase of 50 additional trailers. Is this description of the work indicative of the exercise of due professional care on the engagement?

2.15. There are circumstances under which an auditor should qualify his opinion in reporting on financial statements, and other circumstances under which he should disclaim an opinion on the financial statements. Explain the general nature of the circumstances which would make each course of action necessary.

2.16. You have accepted the engagement of examining the financial statements of the Thorne Company, a small manufacturing firm that has been your client for several years. Because you were busy writing the report for another engagement, you sent an assistant accountant to begin the audit with the suggestion that she start with the accounts receivable. Using the prior year's working papers as a guide, the assistant prepared a trial balance of the accounts, aged them, prepared and mailed positive confirmation requests, examined underlying support for charges and credits, and performed such other work as she deemed necessary to obtain reasonable assurance about the validity and collectibility of the receivables. At the conclusion of her work you reviewed the working papers that she prepared and found that she had carefully followed the prior year working papers.

Required:

The opinion rendered by a CPA states "Our examination was made in accordance with generally accepted auditing standards. . . ."

List the three generally accepted standards of field work. Relate them to the above illustration by indicating how they were fulfilled or, if appropriate, how they were not fulfilled. (AICPA)

2.17. Your public accounting practice is located in a city of 15,000 population. Your work, which is conducted by you and two assistants, consists of the preparation for clients of monthly statements without audit, preparation of income tax returns for individuals from cash data, and partnership returns from books and records. You have a few corporate clients; however, service to them is limited to preparation of income tax returns and some assistance in year-end closings where bookkeeping is deficient.

One of your corporate clients is a retail hardware store. Your work for this client has been limited to the preparation of the corporation income tax return from a trial balance submitted by the bookkeeper.

On December 26 you receive from the president of the corporation a letter containing the following request:

> "We have made arrangements with the First National Bank to borrow $50,000 to finance the purchase of a complete line of appliances. The bank has asked us to furnish our auditor's certified statement as of December 31, which is the closing date of our accounting year. The trial balance of the general ledger should be ready by January 10, which should allow ample time to prepare your report for submission to the bank by January 20. In view of the importance of this certified report to our financing program, we trust you will arrange to comply with the foregoing schedule."

Required:

From a theoretical viewpoint, discuss the difficulties that are caused by such short notice of a request for an audit. (AICPA adapted)

2.18. Ray, the owner of a small company, asked Holmes, CPA, to conduct an audit of the company's records. Ray told Holmes that an audit is to be completed in time to submit audited financial statements to a bank as part of a loan application. Holmes immediately accepted the engagement and agreed to provide an auditor's report within three weeks. Ray agreed to pay Holmes a fixed fee plus a bonus if the loan was granted.

Holmes hired two accounting students to conduct the audit and spent several hours telling them exactly what to do. Holmes told the students not to spend time reviewing the controls but instead to concentrate on proving the mathematical accuracy of the ledger accounts and summarizing the data in the accounting records that support Ray's financial statements. The students followed Holmes's instructions and after two weeks gave Holmes the financial statements which did not include footnotes. Holmes reviewed the statements and prepared an unqualified auditor's report. The report, however, did not refer to generally accepted accounting principles nor to the year-to-year application of such principles.

Required:

Briefly describe each of the generally accepted auditing standards and indicate how the action(s) of Holmes resulted in a failure to comply with each standard. (AICPA adapted)

2.19. You are meeting with executives of Cooper Cosmetics Corporation to arrange your firm's engagement to examine the corporation's financial statements for the year ending December 31. One executive suggested that the audit work be divided among three audit staff members so one person would examine asset accounts, a second would examine liability accounts, and the third would examine income and expense accounts to minimize audit time, avoid duplication of staff effort, and curtail interference with company operations.

Advertising is the corporation's largest expense, and the advertising manager suggested that a staff member of your firm whose uncle owns the advertising agency which handles the corporation's advertising be assigned to examine the Advertising Expense account. The staff member has a thorough knowledge of the rather complex contract between Cooper Cosmetics and the advertising agency on which Cooper's advertising costs are based.

Required:

a. To what extent should a CPA follow his client's suggestions for the conduct of an audit? Discuss.

b. List and discuss the reasons why audit work should not be assigned solely according to asset, liability, and income and expense categories.

c. Should the staff member of your CPA firm whose uncle owns the advertising agency be assigned to examine advertising costs? Discuss. (AICPA)

2.20. The CPA firm of Gohlson and Jibset performed an audit of the financial statements of the Security Home Savings and Loan Association for the year ended December 31. An unqualified short form audit report was issued. Insofar as the conduct of the audit is concerned, what does the audit report say, directly or indirectly, about the quality of audit personnel and the depth and breadth of the audit work?

2.21. The Dilly Container Corporation has recently received an order from the Equal Employment Opportunity Commission (EEOC) requiring affirmative action in hiring and promotion practices respecting minority applicants and employees. The president of Dilly has approached you, as independent auditor, with a request that you examine the company's hiring and promotion practices. The president proposes to write a report addressed to the EEOC emphasizing the positive efforts embodied in the company's present practices. It is the president's belief that the company is a leader in nondiscriminatory hiring and promotion, and the president wants to give you full freedom to investigate every aspect so that you can give an opinion to be included in the president's report to EEOC.

Required:

Write a response to the president's request indicating whether you are willing to undertake such an engagement and render an opinion. Consider any limitations you might wish to impose, and indicate whether you would consider your report the result of an audit engagement or the result of a management services engagement.

2.22. The GAO audit standards state that each report should "include when possible the auditor's recommendations for actions to effect improvements in problem areas noted in his audit and otherwise to make improvements in operations." Suppose that a governmental unit accepts and implements such recommendations made by an auditor. Will this chain of events cause an impairment of the independence of the GAO auditor with respect to subsequent audits of this governmental unit? Explain.

2.23. The GAO General Standards state that "the auditors assigned to perform the audit must collectively possess adequate professional proficiency for the tasks required." What special skills or expertise, if any, must auditors possess if they are to undertake audits of governmental program effectiveness and efficiency (in addition or supplementary to the skills and expertise required for audits of financial statements only)? Must *each* auditor possess the required skills and expertise in a specific task?

2.24. In order for a governmental auditor to be able to determine whether the objectives of a program have been achieved, it must be determined what the objectives were in the first place. From what sources might an auditor obtain knowledge of the objectives of a governmental program?

2.25. Jones and Todd, a local CPA firm, received an invitation to bid for the audit of a local federally assisted program. The audit is to be conducted in accordance with the audit standards published by the General Accounting Office (GAO). Jones and Todd have become familiar with the GAO standards and recognize that the GAO standards are not inconsistent with generally accepted auditing standards (GAAS). The GAO standards, unlike GAAS, are concerned with more than the financial aspects of an entity's operations.

Jones and Todd have been engaged to perform the audit of the program, and the audit is to encompass all three elements that constitute the full scope of a GAO audit.

Required:

a. Jones and Todd should perform sufficient audit work to satisfy the financial and compliance element of the GAO standards. What should such audit work determine?

b. After making appropriate review and inquiries, what uneconomical practices or inefficiencies should Jones and Todd be alert to, in satisfying the efficiency and economy element encompassed by the GAO standards?

c. After making appropriate review and inquiries, what should Jones and Todd consider to satisfy the program results element encompassed by the GAO standards? (AICPA adapted)

2.26. In the short cases below, indicate whether the CPA's conduct was or was not in accordance with the AICPA Statements on Responsibilities in Tax Practice. Also, discuss whether the CPA's conduct is subject to criticism on any other grounds.

a. Rupert Rose, CPA, prepared, signed, and delivered his widowed mother's individual federal income tax return based on information she supplied. She claimed a $2,000 itemized deduction for charitable contributions, figuring her 200 hours of volunteer hospital work at $10 per hour. Rupert thought the item was a cash contribution but did not ask to see her receipt or canceled checks.

b. Susan Bugg, CPA, was engaged by an audit client to review the client's federal business income tax return. In the course of the review she acquired knowledge with respect to the return substantially equivalent to that which would have been acquired had she prepared the return. The client asked her to sign the return. Being somewhat uncertain, since she did not actually prepare it, Bugg changed the declaration to read as follows:

reviewer
Declaration of ~~preparer~~ (other than taxpayer) is based on all information
reviewer
of which ~~preparer~~ has any knowledge.

c. Lois Hughes, CPA, obtained a new tax client, Gordon Printing Company, and while preparing the current year federal tax return discovered an error in the previous year's return. The previous year's depreciation deduction had been calculated in error, resulting in a $10,000 overstatement of the deduction. But the year had been a good business period and taxable income was $47,000 anyway, about the same as in earlier years. Hughes pointed out the error to Gordon's controller and suggested that the company file an amended return. The controller stated that he would be happy to pay any additional tax due if a revenue agent found the error but would not file an amended return. He said "Just reduce this year's depreciation by $10,000. This year is not too good anyway. Taxable income will then be about $25,000." Hughes thought this position was reasonable, prepared the return, and signed it.

d. Daniel Carrol, CPA, prepared, signed, and delivered A. Capone's individual federal income tax return after discussing Mr. Capone's reluctance to supply information on the question about taxpayer's having authority over a bank account in Bermuda. Mr. Capone believed that his inactive accounts were of no concern to IRS, and anyway, something in the Constitution of the United States probably made it unlawful for IRS to ask taxpayers the question. Carrol transmitted the return without attaching any explanations to it.

APPENDIX

Summary of General and Specific Standards for the Professional Practice of Internal Auditing*

100 *INDEPENDENCE*—INTERNAL AUDITORS SHOULD BE INDEPENDENT OF THE ACTIVITIES THEY AUDIT.

110 *Organizational Status*—The organizational status of the internal auditing department should be sufficient to permit the accomplishment of its audit responsibilities.

120 *Objectivity*—Internal auditors should be objective in performing audits.

200 *PROFESSIONAL PROFICIENCY*—INTERNAL AUDITS SHOULD BE PERFORMED WITH PROFICIENCY AND DUE PROFESSIONAL CARE.

---

* Source: *Summary of Standards for the Professional Practice of Internal Auditing,* by The Institute of Internal Auditors, Inc. Copyright 1978 by The Institute of Internal Auditors, Inc., 249 Maitland Avenue, Altamonte Springs, Florida, 32701. Reprinted with permission.

The Internal Auditing Department

210 *Staffing*—The internal auditing department should provide assurance that the technical proficiency and educational background of internal auditors are appropriate for the audits to be performed.

220 *Knowledge, Skills, and Disciplines*—The internal auditing department should possess or should obtain the knowledge, skills, and disciplines needed to carry out its audit responsibilities.

230 *Supervision*—The internal auditing department should provide assurance that internal audits are properly supervised.

The Internal Auditor

240 *Compliance with Standards of Conduct*—Internal auditors should comply with professional standards of conduct.

250 *Knowledge, Skills, and Disciplines*—Internal auditors should possess the knowledge, skills, and disciplines essential to the performance of internal audits.

260 *Human Relations and Communications*—Internal auditors should be skilled in dealing with people and in communicating effectively.

270 *Continuing Education*—Internal auditors should maintain their technical competence through continuing education.

280 *Due Professional Care*—Internal auditors should exercise due professional care in performing internal audits.

300 *SCOPE OF WORK*—THE SCOPE OF THE INTERNAL AUDIT SHOULD ENCOMPASS THE EXAMINATION AND EVALUATION OF THE ADEQUACY AND EFFECTIVENESS OF THE ORGANIZATIONS SYSTEM OF INTERNAL CONTROL AND THE QUALITY OF PERFORMANCE IN CARRYING OUT ASSIGNED RESPONSIBILITIES.

310 *Reliability and Integrity of Information*—Internal auditors should review the reliability and integrity of financial and operating information and the means used to identify, measure, classify, and report such information.

320 *Compliance with Policies, Plans, Procedures, Laws, and Regulations*—Internal auditors should review the systems established to ensure compliance with those policies, plans, procedures, laws, and regulations which could have a significant impact on operations and reports and should determine whether the organization is in compliance.

330 *Safeguarding of Assets*—Internal auditors should review the means of safeguarding assets and, as appropriate, verify the existence of such assets.

340 *Economical and Efficient Use of Resources*—Internal auditors should appraise the economy and efficiency with which resources are employed.

350 *Accomplishment of Established Objectives and Goals for Operations or Programs*—Internal auditors should review operations or programs to ascertain whether results are consistent with established objectives and goals and whether the operations or programs are being carried out as planned.

400 ***PERFORMANCE OF AUDIT WORK***—AUDIT WORK SHOULD INCLUDE PLANNING THE AUDIT, EXAMINING AND EVALUATING INFORMATION COMMUNICATING RESULTS, AND FOLLOWING UP.

410 *Planning the Audit*—Internal auditors should plan each audit.

420 *Examining and Evaluating Information*—Internal auditors should collect, analyze, interpret, and document information to support audit results.

430 *Communicating Results*—Internal auditors should report the results of their audit work.

440 *Following Up*—Internal auditors should follow up to ascertain that appropriate action is taken on reported audit findings.

500 ***MANAGEMENT OF THE INTERNAL AUDITING DEPARTMENT***—THE DIRECTOR OF INTERNAL AUDITING SHOULD PROPERLY MANAGE THE INTERNAL AUDITING DEPARTMENT.

510 *Purpose, Authority, and Responsibility*—The director of internal auditing should have a statement of purpose, authority, and responsibility for the internal auditing department.

520 *Planning*—The director of internal auditing should establish plans to carry out the responsibilities of the internal auditing department.

530 *Policies and Procedures*—The director of internal auditing should provide written policies and procedures to guide the audit staff.

540 *Personnel Management and Development*—The director of internal auditing should establish a program for selecting and developing the human resources of the internal auditing department.

550 *External Auditors*—The director of internal auditing should coordinate internal and external audit efforts.

560 *Quality Assurance*—The director of internal auditing should establish and maintain a quality assurance program to evaluate the operations of the internal auditing department.

3

PROFESSIONAL ETHICS

This chapter is divided into two main parts. The first sections contain an introduction to general principles of ethics that help guide persons in making ethical decisions. The latter sections are explanations of specific rules of conduct that guide the professional behavior of accountants and auditors. Some brief coverage of controversial independence issues is given in the final sections.

A sense of proper ethical conduct must underlie all human activity, and a pervasive sense of ethics is particularly important to professional persons. In addition to a general concept of ethics, accountants and auditors—like physicians and attorneys—have found it necessary to promulgate specific rules of ethics in order to demonstrate to the public that the profession as a whole is prepared to govern its own members' professional conduct. Thus there are two aspects of ethics that operate in the professional environment—general ethics (the spirit) and professional ethics (the rules). Mautz and Sharaf have contributed the following thoughts to the association of general ethics and professional ethics:

> The theory of ethics has been a subject of interest to philosophers since the beginnings of recorded thought. Because philosophers are concerned with the good of all mankind, their discussions have been concerned with what we may call general ethics rather than the ethics of small groups such as the members of a given profession. We cannot look, therefore, to their philosophical theories for direct solutions to our special problems. Nevertheless, their work with general ethics is of primary importance to the development of an appropriate concept in any special field. *Ethical behavior in auditing or in any other activity is no more than a special application of the general notion of ethical conduct devised by philosophers for men generally. Ethi-*

cal conduct in auditing draws its justification and basic nature from the general theory of ethics. Thus we are well advised to give some attention to the ideas and reasoning of some of the great philosophers on this subject. [Emphasis added.]

Overview

What is ethics? Wheelwright defines ethics as follows: "Ethics (is) that branch of philosophy which is the systematic study of reflective choice, of the standards of right and wrong by which it is to be guided, and of the goods toward which it may ultimately be directed."[1] In this definition one can detect three key elements: (1) that ethics involves questions requiring reflective choice (i.e., decision problems), (2) that ethics involves guides of right and wrong (i.e., moral principles), and (3) that ethics is concerned with the consequences (i.e., *goods*) of decisions.

What is an ethical problem? *A problem situation* exists when one has to make a choice among alternatives, and the right choice is not absolutely clear. An *ethical problem situation* may be described as one in which the choice of alternative actions affects the well-being of other persons.

What is ethical behavior? There are two standard philosophical answers to this question: (1) ethical behavior is that which produces the greatest good, and (2) ethical behavior is that which conforms to moral rules and moral principles. The most difficult problem situations arise when there is a conflict of two or more rules or when there is a conflict between a rule and the criterion of "greatest good." Some cases are given later in this chapter to illustrate these difficulties.

Why does an individual or group need a code of ethical conduct? While it has been said that a person should *be* upright and not be *kept* upright, a code serves a useful purpose as a reference and a benchmark for individuals. A code makes explicit some of the criteria for conduct that are peculiar to the profession, and in this way codes of professional ethics are able to provide some direct solutions that may not be available in general theories of ethics. Furthermore, the individual is better able to know what the profession expects. From the viewpoint of the organized profession, a code is a public declaration of principled conduct, and it is a means of facilitating *enforcement* of standards of conduct. Practical enforcement and professionwide internal discipline would be impossible if members were not first put on notice of the standards.

A Variety of Roles

While one of the main purposes of ethics is to guide the actions of decision makers, the role of decision maker does not fully describe the professional person's entire obligation. Each person acts not only as an individual but also as a member of a profession and as a member of society. Hence, accountants and auditors are also *spectators* (observing the

[1] Philip Wheelwright, *A Critical Introduction to Ethics*, 3d ed. (New York: The Odyssey Press, Inc., 1959), p. 4.

decisions of colleagues), *advisors* (counseling with coworkers), *instructors* (teaching accounting students or new employees on the job), *judges* (serving on disciplinary committees of a state society, a state board of accountancy, or the AICPA), and *critics* (commenting on the ethical decisions of others). All of these roles are relevant to the practice of professional ethics.

AN ETHICAL DECISION PROCESS

In considering general ethics the primary goal of accountants and auditors is to arrive at a set of acceptable methods for making ethical decisions. Consequently an understanding of some of the general principles of ethics can contribute background for a detailed consideration of the behavior directed by the AICPA *Code of Professional Ethics* and other similar statements of ethical rules. (Each state society of CPAs and state regulatory board has a code of ethics, but all of them are more or less modeled after the AICPA Code of Ethics.)

In the earlier definition of ethics, one of the key elements was *reflective choice*. This element bears a great similarity to the process described in Chapter 1 as scientific decision-making methodology. Both of these methodologies involve an important sequence of events beginning with the recognition of a decision problem, the identification of alternative actions, the assessment of evidence, and ending with a decision and appropriate action. The process of moral deliberation, or reflective choice, is characterized by these beginning steps:

First. Examine and clarify the alternative actions. Ask what are the relevant possibilities for action in the circumstances. Search for all the action alternatives available.

Second. Think through the consequences of each possible action. Try to predict a hypothetical future state of affairs that would follow action on each alternative.

Third. Use imagination to project yourself into these hypothetical future states of affairs. Think about what it will be like to live with your decision.

Fourth. Identify yourself with the points of view of other people who will be affected by your decision. Put yourself in *their* shoes in these hypothetical futures.

These steps of method bring a decision maker to the point of choice. A review of some of the principles of ethics that may help guide one's choice is given next.

PRINCIPLES IN ETHICS

Theory, whether it be ethical theory or technical theory, has primary value in its ability to serve as a guide to decisions and actions. We could dispense with the following discussion of ethical theories if we were willing to accept a simple rule: "Let conscience be your guide." Such a rule is appealing because it is a call on the individual's own judgment which may be based on wisdom, insight, adherence to custom, or an authoritative code. But it might also be based on caprice, immaturity, ignorance, stubborness, or misunderstanding. Consciences, individually and collectively, sometimes fail to show the consistency, clarity, practicability, impartiality, and adequacy that are essential for maintaining ethical standards and behavior.

In a similar manner, it is not always enough to rely on the opinions of others or on the weight of opinion of a particular social group. Another person or a group of persons may perpetuate a custom or habit that is wrong. To adhere blindly to custom or to group habits is to abdicate individual responsibility. Titus and Keeton summarized this point succinctly: "Each person capable of making moral decisions is responsible for making his own decisions. The ultimate locus of moral responsibility is in the individual."[2] Thus the function of ethical *principles* is not to provide a simple and sure rule but rather to provide some insight into alternative guides for decisions and actions.

Two illustrations are given below to show some problem situations that for most persons would present difficult choices. Consider them in light of the method of reflective choice and in terms of the *imperative*, the *utilitarian*, and the *generalization* theories explained afterward.

> ***Illustration.*** As a result of your fine reputation as a public accountant, you were invited to become a director of a local bank, and you were pleased to accept the position. While serving on the board for a year, you have learned that a bank director is under a duty to use care and prudence in administering the affairs of a bank, and failure to do so in such a way that the bank suffers a financial loss means that the director(s) may be held liable for damages. This month, in the course of an audit, you discover a seriously weakened financial position in a client who has a large loan from your bank. Prompt disclosure to the other bank directors would minimize the bank's loss, but since the audit report cannot be completed for another three weeks such disclosure would amount to divulging confidential information gained in the course of an audit engagement (prohibited by AICPA Rule 301). You can remain silent and honor Rule 301 (and fail to honor your duty as a bank director), or you can speak up to the other directors (thus violating Rule 301). Which shall it be?

> ***Illustration.*** In your work as an auditor you discover that the cashier, who has custody over the petty cash fund, has forged several vouchers in order to cover innocent mistakes and to make the fund balance each month when it is replenished. Your investigation reveals that the amount involved during the year is $240. The cashier is a woman, age 55, and the president of the company is a man who can tolerate no mistakes, intentional or otherwise, in the accounting records. In fact, he is unyielding in this respect. He asks you about the results of your audit. Not doubting that the cashier would be fired if the forgeries were known, should you remain silent and thus not tell the truth?

---

[2] Harold H. Titus and Morris Keeton, *Ethics for Today*, 4th ed. (New York: American Book Co., 1966), p. 131.

The Imperative Principle

An imperative theory directs a decision maker to act according to the requirements of an ethical rule. Strict versions of imperative theories maintain that the decision should be made without looking to see which alternatives will probably create the greatest balance of good over evil. Ethics in this sense is a function of moral rules and principles and not a situation-specific calculation of the consequences.[3]

The philosopher Immanuel Kant (1724–1804) is perhaps the foremost advocate of the imperative school. Kant was unwilling to rely solely upon decision makers' inclinations and value preferences for choice in various circumstances. He strongly preferred rules without exceptions to the varied and frequently inconsistent choices of individuals. He maintained that *reason* and the strict *duty to be consistent* governed the formulation of his first law of conduct: "Act only on that maxim whereby you can at the same time will that it should become a universal law." This law of conduct is Kant's first formulation of his *categorical imperative*, meaning that it specifies an *unconditional obligation.* One such maxim (rule), for example, is "Lying is wrong."

Suppose someone were to believe it proper to lie by remaining silent about the cashier's attempts to cover mistakes (or any other specific kind of lie). The Kantian test of the morality of such a lie is: Can this maxim be a moral rule which should be followed without exception by all persons when asked about the results of audit work? In order for all persons to follow a rule, all persons must know of it, and when everyone knows that the rule is to lie about the results of some audit work, then no one is fooled by the auditor's silence (or false response).

A lie succeeds only when the hearer of it does not know that it is a lie. The nature of a universal rule is universal knowledge of it; therefore, any manner of lying is bound to fail the test because no one would believe the speaker of the lie. Thus lying is wrong because, when made universal, no one could be believed and virtually all common communication would become impossible.

A decision maker who followed the imperative principle would be on the horns of a dilemma in the case of conflicting duties as bank director and auditor. To remain silent to the other directors could be construed as a lie since a director's duty is to speak up, but to speak up would mean that the auditor's implicit promise to the client not to divulge confidential information would be a lie. However, following the imperative, the auditor in the other illustration would tell the employer about the forged vouchers. By this principle it does not matter that the circumstances might be different (for example, the cashier was a 22-year-old man, the amount was $24,000). Kant maintained that motive and duty alone define a moral act, not the consequences of the act. Thus an ethical person is not responsible for the consequences of his or her acts.

The general objection to the imperative principle is the belief that no universal rule can be made that does not admit exceptions. The general

---

[3] I. Kant, *Foundations of the Metaphysics of Morals* (originally published in 1785), trans. Lewis W. Beck (Indianapolis: Bobbs-Merrill Co., Inc., 1959).

response to this objection is that if the rule is properly stated to include the exceptional cases, then the principle is still valid. The problem with this response, however, is that human experience is sufficiently complicated that extremely complex universal rules would have to be constructed in order to encompass all possible cases.[4]

One value of the Kantian categorical imperative with its emphasis on universal, unconditional obligations is that it lets you know when you are faced with ethical decision problems. When only one rule derived from the categorical imperative is applicable, a person may have no trouble following it. But when two rules or two duties are in conflict a serious problem exists. Assume for the sake of illustration that there is another rule which is "Live up to all your professional duties." In the illustrative case, these two rules ("Lying is wrong," and "Live up to all your professional duties") may be in conflict. Such conflicts of rules and duties create difficult problems of ethical choice because adherence to one of the rules means the breaking of the other.

The Kantian imperative theory, however, does not provide an easy way to make the decision. Someone who is rule-bound may find himself or herself in an insoluble dilemma. Just this kind of dilemma is what prompts persons to look for ways to weigh the consequences of actions, and one way is described by the theory of utilitarianism discussed in the next section below.

Most professional codes of ethics have characteristics of the imperative type of theory. As a general matter, professionals are expected to act in a manner in conformity with the rules. However, the current mood of society is to question not only conduct itself but the rules on which conduct is based. Thus a dogmatic imperative approach to ethical decisions may not necessarily be completely sufficient for the maintenance of professional standards. Society may question the rules, and conflicts among them are always possible. Thus a means of estimating the consequences of alternative actions may be useful.

The Principle of Utilitarianism

The principle of utilitarianism maintains that the ultimate criterion of an ethical decision is the balance of good over evil consequences produced by the action.[5] The emphasis in utilitarianism is on the consequences of action rather than on the following of rules, and the criterion of producing the greater good is made an explicit part of the decision process.

In *act-utilitarianism* the center of attention is the individual act as it is affected by the specific circumstances of a situation. An act-utilitarian's ethical decision problem may be framed in this way: "What effect will my

[4] Several rules in the AICPA Rules of Conduct are explicitly phrased in such a way as to provide for exceptions to the general rules, notably Rules 203 and 301. Imperative rules also seem to generate borderline cases, so the AICPA ethics division issues *interpretations* and *rulings* to explain the applicability of the rules.

[5] J. S. Mill, *Utilitarianism* (originally published in 1861), Oskar Piest, ed. (Indianapolis: Bobbs-Merrill Co., Inc., 1957).

doing this act in this situation have on the general balance of good over evil?" This theory admits general guides like "telling the truth is probably always for the greatest good." However, the emphasis is always on the specific situation, and decision makers must determine whether they have independent grounds for thinking that it would be for the greatest general good not to tell the truth (for example) in a particular case.

The general difficulty with act-utilitariansim is that it seems to sanction too many exceptions to well-established rules. By focusing attention on individual acts, the long-run effect of setting examples for other people appears to be ignored. If an act-utilitarian decision is to break a moral rule, then the success of the decision usually depends on everyone else's adherence to the rule. For example, to benefit from tax evasion for a good reason depends on everyone else not having an equally good reason not to pay their taxes.

Rule-utilitarianism, on the other hand, emphasizes the centrality of rules for ethical behavior while still maintaining the criterion of the greatest universal good. This kind of utilitarianism means that decision makers must first determine the rules which will promote the greatest general good for everyone. The initial question is not which *action* has the greatest utility, but which *rule*. Thus the rule-utilitarian's ethical decision problem can be framed as follows: "What effect will everyone's doing this kind of act in this kind of situation have on the general balance of good over evil?" The principle of utility becomes operative not only in determining what particular action to take in a specific decision situation in which rules conflict but also in determining what the rules should be in the first place.

The statement of the rule-utilitarian's problem may be given a very commonsense expression: "What would happen if everybody acted this way?" In this form the question is known as *generalization*.

The Generalization Argument

For all practical purposes the generalization argument may be considered a judicious combination of the imperative and utilitarian principles. Stated succinctly, the argument is: "If everyone were to act in a certain way and the consequences would be undesirable, then no one ought to act in that way without a reason.[6] The argument should be interpreted to apply to similar persons acting under similar circumstances.

A more everyday-language expression of the argument is the question: "What would happen if everyone acted in that certain way?" If the answer to the question is that the consequences would be undesirable, then one's conclusion according to the generalization test is that the way of acting is not ethical and ought not be done.

The key ideas in the generalization test are "similar persons" and "similar circumstances." These features provide the needed flexibility for

[6] Marcus G. Singer, *Generalization in Ethics* (New York: Atheneum, 1961, 1971), especially pp. 5, 10–11, 61, 63, 73, 81, 105–22.

persons to consider the many variations that may arise in real decision problem situations. They also demand that the decision maker exercise considerable judgment in determining whether persons and circumstances are genuinely different or are just arbitrarily rationalized as different so that a preconceived preference can be "explained" as right.

The problem over conflict of duties as a bank director and public accountant arises only when accounting clients are customers of the bank. The circumstances are those of the situation described in the illustration. As long as these circumstances do not exist, the question of "What if every CPA served as a bank director of a bank with whom no accounting clients did business?" is easily answerable. There is no problem because no conflict can arise. But when the *potential* for conflict exists, the question becomes "What if every CPA were exposed to conflict-of-duty situations like this one?" In this case the results would be undesirable, and the conclusion would be that no CPAs should serve as bank directors unless none of their accounting clients did business with the bank.

Assume in the other illustration that the custodian of the petty cash fund had forged vouchers involving $24,000 instead of $240. Now one feature of the circumstances is decidedly different. When posing the generalization question, the auditor must judge whether the money amount tips the balance. Would it make a difference if it were $1, $241 or $23,999? The money amount characteristic helps determine whether the case is insignificant or important, and accountants and auditors are constantly called upon to make judgments about the importance of money amounts in a variety of decisions.

This brief review of principles in ethics hopefully provides some guide to the ways that many persons may think about and approach difficult decision problems. The greatest task is to take a general notion of ethics—the imperative, utilitarianism, generalization—and apply it to a real decision. Their application through codes of professional ethics is a challenge.

CODES OF ETHICS

Various codes of professional ethics can usually be distinguished from each other in one important respect—they tend to be either general statements of ideals and purposes or they tend to be specific and definite about prohibited acts. General codes are subject to wide interpretation and consequently are very difficult to enforce. Specific codes are more amenable to enforcement, but the professional group must take care to review the rules for periodic revision lest they become outdated and inappropriate to the changing social environment. The code of ethics for certified internal auditors, reprinted in the Appendix to this chapter, is an example of a code that is quite general.

The AICPA *Code of Professional Ethics* consists of four parts. (1) The "Concepts of Professional Ethics" contains five essays that are statements of general ideals and purposes. These essays are found in the AICPA booklet entitled *Restatement of the Code of Professional Ethics* and in the annual *AICPA Professional Standards Volume* 2 published for the AICPA by

Commerce Clearing House, Inc. The Concepts section does not contain enforceable rules of ethics. (2) The "Rules of Conduct" section contains definitions and rules that are the enforceable ethical standards applicable to members of the AICPA. (3) The "Interpretations of Rules of Conduct" are explanatory rulings issued by the AICPA Division of Professional Ethics that serve as guidelines as to the scope and applicability of the Rules of Conduct. The interpretations are not themselves enforceable, but anyone who departs from their guidelines has the burden of justifying the departure in any disciplinary hearing. (4) The ethics division also publishes "rulings" on the applicability of rules in specific situations. Like the interpretations, members must be able to justify departures from the rulings.

AICPA Rules of Conduct

The AICPA *Code of Professional Ethics* derives its authority from the bylaws of the AICPA. The penalties for violating the rules are admonishment, suspension of membership, and expulsion from membership. The rules apply to all auditing practice, and some rules are applicable in tax and management advisory services.

Members of the AICPA are held responsible for compliance with the rules by all persons associated with them in their practice, including employees, partners, and shareholders. In addition, members may not permit other people to carry out on their behalf acts which are prohibited by the rules. Most of the rules relate specifically to the practice of public accounting. However, members of the AICPA who are not in public practice must observe Rules 102 and 501.

The rules of conduct are discussed next under the five major articles. The rules are quoted verbatim. The analysis that follows each article is not a part of the enforceable *Code of Professional Ethics*.

Independence, Integrity, and Objectivity:

A certified public accountant should maintain his integrity and objectivity and, when engaged in the practice of public accounting, be independent of those he serves.

Rule 101—Independence. A member or a firm of which he is a partner or shareholder shall not express an opinion on financial statements of an enterprise unless he and his firm are independent with respect to such enterprise. Independence will be considered to be impaired if, for example:

A. During the period of his professional engagement, or at the time of expressing his opinion, he or his firm
   1. *a.* Had or was committed to acquire any direct or material indirect financial interest in the enterprise; or
      b. Was a trustee of any trust or executor or administrator of any estate if such trust or estate had or was committed to acquire any direct or material indirect financial interest in the enterprise; or

2. Had any joint closely held business investment with the enterprise or any officer, director, or principal stockholder thereof which was material in relation to his or his firm's net worth, or
3. Had any loan to or from the enterprise or any officer, director, or principal stockholder thereof. This latter proscription does not apply to the following loans from a financial institution when made under normal lending procedures, terms, and requirements:
   a. Loans obtained by a member of his firm which are not material in relation to the net worth of such borrower.
   b. Home mortgages.
   c. Other secured loans, except loans guaranteed by a member's firm which are otherwise unsecured.

B. During the period covered by the financial statements, during the period of the professional engagement or at the time of expressing an opinion, he or his firm
   1. Was connected with the enterprise as a promoter, underwriter or voting trustee, a director or officer or in any capacity equivalent to that of a member of management or of an employee, or
   2. Was a trustee for any pension or profit-sharing trust of the enterprise.

The above examples are not intended to be all-inclusive.

Rule 102—Integrity and Objectivity. A member shall not knowingly misrepresent facts, and when engaged in the practice of public accounting, including the rendering of tax and management advisory services, shall not subordinate his judgment to others. In tax practice, a member may resolve doubt in favor of his client as long as there is reasonable support for his position.

As of late 1977 the ethics division had issued six interpretations related to Rule 101 on the subjects of directorships, retired partners and firm independence, accounting services, effect of family relationships on independence, meaning of the term "normal lending procedures, terms and requirements," and the effect of actual or threatened litigation on independence. No interpretations of Rule 102 have been issued. A total of 59 rulings on Rules 101 and 102 have been issued, of which 56 have not been superceded by later rulings.

Analysis:

The concept of independence is the cornerstone of the accounting profession. Since the principal purpose of independent financial auditing is to lend credibility to financial assertions and representations made by management, auditors must in fact be impartial and unbiased with respect to both the client management and the client entity itself.

Not only must auditors be independent *in fact,* but they must also *appear* independent to outside decision makers who rely on their attestation. Independence *in fact* is truly a mental condition of intellectual honesty—a quality difficult to demonstrate by physical or visual means. Thus some appearances of lacking independence are the unethical actions prohibited specifically in parts A and B of Rule 101.

Section 101(A) deals with financial interests in an audit client. Note that the "period covered by the financial statements" is not relevant to this section as it is in Section B. An auditor may divest of any prohibited financial interest before the first audit of a new client begins, after which it is improper to reinvest when the engagement will continue for future years' audits. *Any direct* financial interest (e.g., common stock, perferred stock, convertible debt) is prohibited, even the beneficial ownership of a single share, no matter how acquired. This rule is the strictest one in the code. There are no exceptions in the wording of the rule. *Indirect* financial interests, on the other hand, are allowed up to the point of materiality (with reference to the auditor's wealth). This provision permits auditors to hold mutual fund shares and have some limited business transactions with audit clients so long as they do not reach material proportions. Items 2 and 3 of 101(A) define certain specific types of prohibited and allowed indirect financial interests.

Section 101(B) prohibits activities that amount to the abilities to make decisions for the audit client—to act as management, broadly defined. The appearance of independence is impaired if such a connection existed at any time during the period covered by the financial statements, regardless of whether the association was terminated prior to the beginning of the audit work. The presumption is that auditors cannot be independent and objective when auditing decisions in which they took part or with which they appeared to be connected.

Rule 102 essentially reaffirms the general concept of independence and extends the requirement of maintaining integrity and objectivity to tax and management advisory services. This rule specifically allows the CPA to act in a client's best interests—to act as an advocate—in tax practice. Neither Rule 101 nor Rule 102 prohibits direct or material indirect financial interests or other business relationships with nonaudit clients (tax and/or management advisory services engagements) but such relations are not recommended, and some public accounting firms extend the rule to these other areas of practice.

In terms of the principles of ethics, these rules may be justified on a *rule-utilitarian* basis as far as direct financial interests are concerned. The logic is something like this: The greatest good is created by making a situation free of any suspicious circumstances, no matter how innocent they may be in truth, because the goodwill of public reliance and respect is greater than the CPA's sacrifice of the opportunity to invest in securities of audit clients.

Competence and Technical Standards:

A certified public accountant should observe the profession's technical standards and strive continually to improve his competence and the quality of his services.

Rule 201—General Standards. A member shall comply with the following general standards as interpreted by bodies designated by Council and must justify any departures therefrom.

a. *Professional competence.* A member shall undertake only those engagements which he or his firm can reasonably expect to complete with professional competence.
b. *Due professional care.* A member shall exercise due professional care in the performance of an engagement.
c. *Planning and supervision.* A member shall adequately plan and supervise an engagement.
d. *Sufficient relevant data.* A member shall obtain sufficient relevant data to afford a reasonable basis for conclusions or recommendations in relation to an engagement.
e. *Forecasts.* A member shall not permit his name to be used in conjunction with any forecast of future transactions in a manner which may lead to the belief that the member vouches for the achievability of the forecast.

Rule 202—Auditing Standards. A member shall not permit his name to be associated with financial statements in such a manner as to imply that he is acting as an independent public accountant unless he has complied with the applicable generally accepted auditing standards promulgated by the Institute. Statements on Auditing Standards issued by the Institute's Auditing Standards Executive Committee [Board] are, for purposes of this rule, considered to be interpretations of the generally accepted auditing standards, and departures from such statements must be justified by those who do not follow them.

Rule 203—Accounting Principles. A member shall not express an opinion that financial statements are presented in conformity with generally accepted accounting principles if such statements contain any departure from an accounting principle promulgated by the body designated by Council to establish such principles which has a material effect on the statements taken as a whole, unless the member can demonstrate that due to unusual circumstances the financial statements would otherwise have been misleading. In such cases his report must describe the departure, the approximate effects thereof, if practicable, and the reasons why compliance with the principle would result in a misleading statement.

Rule 204—Other Technical Standards. A member shall comply with other technical standards promulgated by bodies designated by Council to establish such standards, and departures therefrom must be justified by those who do not follow them.

As of late 1977 the ethics division had issued one interpretation related to Rule 201 on the subject of competence, one related to Rule 202 on unaudited financial statements, two related to Rule 203 on departures from established accounting principles and the status of FASB interpretations, and one related to Rule 201(*e*) on forecasts. In addition the ethics division has issued nine rulings related to the four competence and technical standards rules.

Analysis:

Rule 201 quoted above was approved by the AICPA membership on March 31, 1978. This new rule seeks to satisfy the need for a comprehensive statement of general standards which accountants would be expected to observe in all areas of practice. Upon analysis, one can see in Rule 201 elements of the generally accepted auditing standards and MAS practice standards discussed in Chapter 2 of this textbook. The new rule embodies the *general standards* previously published by the AICPA for auditing and MAS practice, and it represents the first official expression of such standards for CPAs' tax practice.

Rule 201 effectively prohibits the acceptance of any engagement that the CPA knows that he or she cannot handle. Such engagements may involve audits that require extensive capability with computers—knowledge that the auditor may lack—or tax consultation on obscure provisions that are not understood, or management advisory services in areas unknown to the practitioner. This rule includes all areas of public accounting practice. Of course, a CPA may have to do some research to learn more about a unique problem or technique and may engage a colleague as a consultant.

Section 201(*e*) of Rule 201 is not new. (The rule relation to forecasts was previously designated as Rule 204.) Rule 201(*e*) reflects auditors' reluctance to be associated with the uncertainties of the future. However, the rule limits association only to the extent of the accountant's predictions about achievability. Several other varieties of association short of asserting achievability are possible, and some CPA firms are moving into work related to published forecasts. Accountants in Great Britain currently offer reports on certain types of forecasts, and some aspects of this service will probably emerge in the United States.

Rule 202, requiring that an auditor comply with generally accepted auditing standards, has more meaning if viewed in relation to the former Rule 2.02 that was in effect until 1973. The earlier rule defined "acts discreditable to the profession" (prohibited by current Rule 501) as the following conduct of an auditor:

1. He fails to disclose a material fact known to him which is not disclosed in the financial statements but disclosure of which is necessary to make the financial statements not misleading.
2. He fails to report any material misstatement known to him to appear in the financial statement.
3. He fails to direct attention to any material departure from generally accepted accounting principles or to disclose any material omission of generally accepted auditing procedure applicable in the circumstances.
4. He is materially negligent in the conduct of his examination or in making his report thereon.
5. He fails to acquire sufficient information to warrant an expression of an opinion, or his exceptions are sufficiently material to negative the expression of an opinion.

The first three of these discreditable acts essentially enforced the reporting standards, and the last two essentially enforced the field work standards of the generally accepted auditing standards. The current Rule 202 lacks the forceful language of "discreditable acts," but one may be reasonably certain that enforcement of the rule will follow the spirit of the one that it replaced.

Rule 203 clearly requires adherence to Accounting Research Bulletins of the Committee on Accounting Procedure (to 1959), Opinions of the Accounting Principles Board (1959–1973), and statements and interpretations issued by the Financial Accounting Standards Board (1973 to present) with the important exception in unusual circumstances where adherence would create misleading statements. Thus the rule itself admits that unusual circumstances may exist, permits auditors to decide for themselves the applicability of official pronouncements, and places on them the burden of an ethical decision. The rule is not strictly imperative because it allows the auditor to exercise a utilitarian calculation for special circumstances.

Note that Rule 203 requires adherence to official pronouncements *unless* such adherence would be misleading. The consequence of misleading statements to outside decision makers would be financial harm, so presumably the greater good would be realized by explaining a departure and thereby "breaking the rule of generally accepted accounting principles." During 1978 a special committee was at work developing an interpretation which will set forth criteria for determining when the result of applying FASB pronouncements may be misleading due to unusual circumstances.

Rule 204 quoted above is also a new rule approved by the AICPA membership on March 31, 1978. It is a future-oriented rule. Council of the AICPA may sometime decide to designate the Management Advisory Services Committee, the Federal Taxation Executive Committee, or other senior committees as bodies having authority to promulgate standards enforceable under the Code of Ethics.

Responsibilities to Clients:

A certified public accountant should be fair and candid with his clients and serve them to the best of his ability with professional concern for their best interests, consistent with his responsibilities to the public.

Rule 301—Confidential Client Information. A member shall not disclose any confidential information obtained in the course of a professional engagement except with the consent of the client.

This rule shall not be construed (*a*) to relieve a member of his obligation under Rules 202 and 203, (*b*) to affect in any way his compliance with a validly issued subpoena or summons enforceable by order of a court, (*c*) to prohibit review of a member's professional practices as a part of voluntary quality review under Institute authorization, or (*d*) to preclude a member from responding to any inquiry made by the ethics division or Trial Board of the Institute, by a duly constituted investigative or disciplinary body of a state CPA society, or under state statutes.

Members of the ethics division and Trial Board of the Institute and professional practice reviewers under Institute authorization shall not disclose any confidential client information which comes to their attention from members in disciplinary proceedings or otherwise in carrying out their official responsibilities. However, this prohibition shall not restrict the exchange of information with an aforementioned duly constituted investigative or disciplinary body.

Rule 302—Contingent Fees. Professional services shall not be offered or rendered under an arrangement whereby no fee will be charged unless a specified finding or result is attained, or where the fee is otherwise contingent upon the findings or results of such services. However, a member's fees may vary depending, for example, on the complexity of the service rendered.

Fees are not regarded as being contingent if fixed by courts or other public authorities or, in tax matters, if determined based on the results of judicial proceedings or the findings of governmental agencies.

As of late 1977 the ethics division had issued one interpretation related to Rule 301 on confidential information and technical standards. No interpretations on Rule 302 have been issued, but 6 of the 15 rulings on Rules 301 and 302 deal with matters of contingent fees.

Analysis:

Confidential information, according to Rule 301, is information that should not be disclosed to outside parties unless demanded by a court or an administrative body having subpoena power. Privileged information, on the other hand, is information that cannot even be demanded by a court. Common-law privilege exists as to husband-wife and attorney-client relationships, and physician-patient and priest-penitent relationships have obtained the privilege through state statutes. No federal statute provides for privilege, and only the Fifth Amendment to the U.S. Constitution is available in federal proceedings to withhold testimony. In all these relationships the professional person is obligated to observe the privilege, which can be waived only by the client, patient, or penitent. (These persons are said to be the holders of the privilege.)

Rule 301 does not assume accountant-client relations to be privileged, although several states have statutes granting modified privilege. Few states extend the privilege to information gained during an audit engagement, and the AICPA *Code of Professional Ethics* specifically provides that the confidential relationship must not infringe upon the auditor's independence and obligation to report fully and fairly on audited financial statements.

The rules of privileged and confidential communication are both based on the premise that they facilitate a free flow of information between parties to the relationship. The nature of accounting services makes it necessary for the accountant to have access to information about salaries, products, contracts, merger or divestment plans, and other data that are required for the best possible professional work. Managers would be less likely to reveal such information if they could not trust the accountant to keep it confidential.

Of course, it is possible for conflicts to arise. Information about past or near-future adverse financial events might be considered confidential by management. For example, management might not want to disclose the failure of a major research and development project which, if written off, would give signals to industry competitors. Auditors have no choice but to insist upon proper accounting or appropriate disclosure in their reports in keeping with the requirements of the reporting standards of generally accepted auditing standards.

Different problems arise when the information gained by the auditor reveals a shady or illegal practice. Consider the following illustrative example.

Illustration. The independent auditor decided that she needed to substantiate the amount of an account payable, shown in the records as $500,000, which had not been paid since its original entry 20 months ago. She wanted to write a letter of confirmation to the creditor, but the controller refused and explained that the charge was the estimated cost of the complete overhaul of a catalytic cracking tower which had been performed two years ago by a large engineering firm. The cost, classified as a fixed asset, had never been billed by the engineering firm; and the controller wanted to let the statute of limitations run out, then "write off" the account payable.

What should an auditor do in a situation like this one? The Rules of Conduct do not give a direct answer to the specific situation. What is required is an exercise in reflective choice guided by a sense of general ethics. What are the alternative actions? What are the consequences of each? What would users of financial statements want to know? What would you do? These questions of reflective choice are the essence of ethical decision making.

Rule 302 prohibits fees that are contingent upon findings that are the product of an audit engagement. For example, a fee of $10,000 for each 1 cent per share income increase over last year's per share income, or a fee dependent upon approval of a bank loan based on audited financial statements, or a fee that cannot be paid unless an unqualified opinion is rendered are all considered contingent fees. The pressures on independence and the probable erosion of public confidence in such arrangements are reasons for this prohibition. However, a contingent fee based upon the setting of an amount of tax refund or renegotiation claim is permitted because the basis for the contingency is not within the accountant's power, and because in such cases the accountant is acting in the role of advocate. Fees that depend upon number of hours or days worked or on technical qualifications of accountants are not considered contingent on the findings or results of auditing services.

Responsibilities to Colleagues:

A certified public accountant should conduct himself in a manner which will promote cooperation and good relations among members of the profession.

Rule 401—Encroachment. A member shall not endeavor to provide a person or entity with a professional service which is currently provided by another public accountant except:

1. He may respond to a request for a proposal to render services, and may furnish service to those who request it. However, if an audit client of another independent public accountant requests a member to provide professional advice on accounting or auditing matters in connection with an expression of opinion on financial statements, the member must first consult with the other accountant to ascertain that the member is aware of all the available relevant facts.
2. Where a member is required to express an opinion on combined or consolidated financial statements which include a subsidiary, branch, or other component audited by another independent public accountant, he may insist on auditing any such component which in his judgment is necessary to warrant the expression of his opinion.

A member who receives an engagement for services by referral from another public accountant shall not accept the client's request to extend his service beyond the specific engagement without first notifying the referring accountant, nor shall he seek to obtain any additional engagement from the client.

As of late 1977 the ethics division had issued two interpretations related to Rule 401 on the subjects of relations with clients also served by other public accountants and reliance in the work of others. Seven rulings had also been issued on questions arising from Rule 401.

Analysis:

Rule 401 is really a rule of etiquette that puts accountants on notice that pirating the clients of other accountants is subject to discipline. Part 2 of the rule contains a provision that effectively encourages referrals and complements the competence requirements of Rule 201. Accountants should not have to fear loss of all work for a client if there is a need to refer some work beyond his or her competence to another accountant. Section 1 of the rule is aimed at the undesirable practice of client managers searching around for an auditor who will agree with their accounting and thus give an unqualified opinion. If an auditor is approached for a new engagement, he or she must first consult with the auditor being replaced.[7] Presumably the new auditor might thus learn about disagreements over accounting principles, but of course, the outgoing auditor must be careful with regard to confidential information. Recognizing the problem, the SEC in 1972 ruled that companies changing auditors must submit a statement of reasons to the SEC, *and* the outgoing auditor must submit a letter stating whether or not management's reasons are the real ones. In this way, the SEC hopes to have knowledge of auditor changes involving a conflict over accounting principles and auditing standards. The letters are public documents. This SEC rule can be explained as an exercise in utilitarian ethical theory.

Other Responsibilities and Practices:

A certified public accountant should conduct himself in a manner which will enhance the stature of the profession and its ability to serve the public.

Rule 501—Acts Discreditable. A member shall not commit an act discreditable to the profession.

Rule 502—Advertising and Other Forms of Solicitation. A member shall not seek to obtain clients by advertising or other forms of solicitation in a manner that is false, misleading, or deceptive. A direct uninvited solicitation of a specific potential client is prohibited.

---

[7] *Statement on Auditing Standards No.* 7 (Section 315), "Communications between Predecessor and Successor Auditors" points out matters that a successor should ask the predecessor about. However, it also emphasizes that the client must give permission to the predecesso auditor to talk about the engagement. Rule 301, as it is written, does not contain an except that allows a predecessor auditor to speak freely to a successor auditor without the fo client's permission.

Rule 503—Commissions. A member shall not pay a commission to obtain a client, nor shall he accept a commission for a referral to a client of products or services of others. This rule shall not prohibit payments for the purchase of an accounting practice or retirement payments to individuals engaged in the practice of public accounting or payments to their heirs or estates.

Rule 504—Incompatible Occupations. A member who is engaged in the practice of public accounting shall not concurrently engage in any business or occupation which would create a conflict of interest in rendering professional services.

Rule 505—Form of Practice and Name. A member may practice public accounting, whether as an owner or employee, only in the form of a proprietorship, a partnership, or a professional corporation whose characteristics conform to resolutions of Council. (See Exhibit 3–1.)

A member shall not practice under a firm name which includes any fictitious name, indicates specialization, or is misleading as to the type of organization (proprietorship, partnership, or corporation). However, names of one or more past partners or shareholders may be included in the firm name of a successor partnership or corporation. Also, a partner surviving the death or withdrawal of all other partners may continue practice under the partnership for up to two years after becoming a sole practitioner.

A firm may not designate itself as "Member of the American Institute of Certified Public Accountants" unless all of its partners or shareholders are members of the Institute.

As of late 1977 the ethics division had issued one interpretation related to Rule 501 on the subject of retaining a client's records and the accountant's work papers. One interpretation had been issued on Rule 503 concerning fees in payment for services, one on Rule 504 concerning incompatible occupations, and one on Rule 505 concerning investment in a commercial accounting corporation.

Rule 502 is a new rule approved by the AICPA membership on March 31, 1978. Prior to that date the AICPA Code of Ethics prohibited advertising. A great deal of enforcement effort was generated by the old rule, and 15 interpretations and over 150 rulings on various questions had been issued. However, pressures from critics in the Federal Trade Commission and the U.S. Department of Justice, not to mention Representative Moss and Senator Metcalf, forced change. The rule change was brought to a vote, and the new Rule 502 permits advertising with only a few limitations.

Analysis:

Rule 501 may be called the "morals clause" of the code. It is seldom the basis for disciplinary action, instead penalties are normally invoked under Article V of the AICPA Bylaws, which provides penalties for members found by a court to have committed any fraud, or convicted of any criminal offense, or found by the Trial Board (AICPA) to have been guilty of an act discreditable to the profession.

Practicing accountants have had to become accustomed to a new environment with regard to permitted advertising. Customary advertising practices will no doubt develop as time passes. To help make the transition from prohibition of advertising to the permissive rule, the ethics division prepared four interpretations that were also effective March 31, 1978. These interpretations are reproduced below as a means of explaining the new rule.

Interpretation 502-1—Informational Advertising. Advertising that is informative and objective is permitted. Such advertising should be in good taste and be professionally dignified. There are no other restrictions, such as on the type of advertising media, frequency of placement, size, art work, or type style. Some examples of informative and objective content are—

1. Information about the member and the member's firm, such as—
   a. Names, addresses, telephone numbers, number of partners, shareholders or employees, office hours, foreign language competence, and date the firm was established.
   b. Services offered and fees for such services, including hourly rates and fixed fees.
   c. Educational and professional attainments, including date and place of certifications, schools attended, dates of graduation, degrees received, and memberships in professional associations.
2. Statements of policy or position made by a member or a member's firm related to the practice of public accounting or addressed to a subject of public interest.

Interpretation 502–2—False, Misleading, or Deceptive Acts. Advertising or other forms of solicitation that are false, misleading, or deceptive are not in the public interest and are prohibited. Such activities include those that—

1. Create false or unjustified expectations of favorable results.
2. Imply the ability to influence any court, tribunal, regulatory agency, or similar body or official.
3. Consist of self-laudatory statements that are not based on verifiable facts.
4. Make comparisons with other CPAs.
5. Contain testimonials or endorsements.
6. Contain any other representations that would be likely to cause a reasonable person to misunderstand or be deceived.

Interpretation 502–3—Other Forms of Solicitation. CPAs may engage in a variety of activities to enhance their reputations and professional stature with the objective of expanding their clientele. Such indirect forms of solicitation, which include giving speeches, conducting seminars, distributing professional literature, and writing articles and books, are considered to be in the public interest and are permitted. A direct uninvited solicitation of a specific potential client in person or in a communication tailored in content to that specific recipient by a member relating to his professional services is prohibited. However, invitations that are not tailored in content to the specific recipient can be issued to potential clients to invite them to attend seminars conducted by the member.

Interpretation 502–4—Self-Designation as Expert or Specialist. Claiming to be an expert or specialist is prohibited because an AICPA program with methods for recognizing competence in specialized fields has not been developed and self-designations would be likely to cause misunderstanding or deception. A member or a member's firm may indicate the services offered but may not state that the practice is limited to one or more types of service.

One word of warning is in order, however. Even though the AICPA Code of Ethics no longer prohibits advertising, state societies of CPAs and state licensing boards may or may not be quick to enact similar rules. Since CPAs are subject to discipline in state jurisdictions, knowledge of local rules is essential. A similar situation exists with respect to competitive bidding by CPAs.

Prior to July 6, 1972, the AICPA *Code of Professional Ethics* prohibited competitive bidding for engagements under the theory that bidding-based price competition could lead to cheap and substandard professional service. The consequences of such substandard service would be to cause accountants to be overly concerned with break-even and to cause a general deterioration of service quality. The U.S. Department of Justice, however, was of the opinion that the rule violated antitrust laws, and so the code prohibition was repealed by the AICPA. Nevertheless, accountants must still be careful on at least two counts: (1) submission of an unrealistically low bid in order to "buy" an engagement may be construed as prohibited solicitation under state ethics rules, and (2) some state boards of accountancy have not dropped the antibidding rules in their licensing jurisdictions.

Rule 503 prohibits the giving or receiving of commissions or referral fees for recommendation of products or services (e.g., business forms, consulting services) or solely for obtaining a client by referral. The intent of this rule is to eliminate payments that would not produce professional accounting services of direct benefit to clients.

Rule 504, in its first phrase, complements the rules on independence, integrity, and objectivity by prohibiting concurrent work in another occupation that might adversely influence the auditor's objectivity. This rule was also changed in the March 31, 1978, vote by the AICPA membership. The old rule prohibited CPA's involvement in incompatible occupations that could serve as a "feeder to his practice." Such incompatible occupations included such financial-oriented professions as loan broker, insurance agent, and mutual fund salesman. At present, it is not entirely clear exactly what kinds of occupations could create a "conflict of interest" in rendering professional services. Each CPA will have to decide about situations on a case-by-case basis.

Rule 505 allows members to practice in any form of organization but with severe limitations on the characteristics of the corporate form. Incorporation of accounting practices was prohibited by ethics rules until 1969 when the membership voted to change the rule and allow corporations that conform to the resolution reprinted in Exhibit 3–1.

The main arguments against the corporate form were that such an organization would depersonalize practice (i.e., such fictitious names as Pen & Ink, Inc.), would generate "conglomeration" of many incompatible occupations under a corporate shell, would allow control of accounting practices to fall into the hands of nonaccountants, and would limit the liability and thus the public perception of responsibility of the professional accountants. The resolution of Council in its seven provisions voids each

EXHIBIT 3–1

RESOLUTION OF COUNCIL APPROVED AT THE SPRING MEETING OF COUNCIL ON MAY 6, 1969 (AS AMENDED)

RESOLVED, that members may be officers, directors, stockholders, representatives or agents of a corporation offering services of a type performed by public accountants only when the professional corporation or association has the following characteristics:

1. *Name.* The name under which the professional corporation or association renders professional services shall contain only the names of one or more of the present or former shareholders or of partners who were associated with a predecessor accounting firm. Impersonal or fictitious names, as well as names which indicate a speciality, are prohibited.

2. *Purpose.* The professional corporation or association shall not provide services that are incompatible with the practice of public accounting.

3. *Ownership.* All shareholders of the corporation or association shall be persons engaged in the practice of public accountancy as defined by the Code of Professional Ethics. Shareholders shall at all times own their shares in their own right and shall be the beneficial owners of the equity capital ascribed to them.

4. *Transfer of Shares.* Provision shall be made requiring any shareholder who ceases to be eligible to be a shareholder to dispose of all of his shares within a reasonable period to a person qualified to be a shareholder or to the corporation or association.

5. *Directors and Officers.* The principal executive officer shall be a shareholder and a director, and to the extent possible, all other directors and officers shall be certified public accountants. Lay directors and officers shall not exercise any authority whatsoever over professional matters.

6. *Conduct.* The right to practice as a corporation or association shall not change the obligation of its shareholders, directors, officers, and other employees to comply with the standards of professional conduct established by the American Institute of Certified Public Accountants.

7. *Liability.* The stockholders of professional corporations or associations shall be jointly and severally liable for the acts of a corporation or association, or its employees—except where professional liability insurance is carried, or capitalization is maintained, in amounts deemed sufficient to offer adequate protection to the public. Liability shall not be limited by the formation of subsidiary or affiliated corporations or associations each with its own limited and unrelated liability.

In a report approved by Council at the fall 1969 meeting, the board of directors recommended that professional liability insurance or capitalization in the amount of $50,000 per shareholder/officer and professional employee to a maximum of $2,000,000 would offer adequate protection to the public. Members contemplating the formation of a corporation under this rule should ascertain that no further modifications in the characteristics have been made.

of these negative arguments, and what remains for the incorporated practice is the *form* of a corporation and the *substance* of a partnership.

The last paragraph of Rule 505 effectively blocks formal partner designation of persons who are not CPAs. (A person cannot be a member of the AICPA unless he or she is a CPA.) This rule section creates problems for tax and management advisory services personnel who are not CPAs. They cannot be admitted to full partnership or become shareholders without causing the other partners who are CPAs to be in violation of the rule. Thus a firm may employ non-CPAs who are high on the organization chart, but these persons may not be unrestricted partners under current rules.

Summary: AICPA Rules and Ethical Principles:

Specific rules in the AICPA Rules of Conduct may not necessarily be classified under one of the ethics principles. Decisions based on a rule may involve imperative, or utilitarian, or generalization considerations, or elements of all three. The rules have the form of imperatives (because that is the nature of a code); however, elements of utilitarianism and generalization seem to be apparent in the underlying rationale for most of the rules. If this perception is accurate, then these two principles may be utilized by the auditor in difficult decision problems where adherence to a rule would produce an undesirable result.

Recent Developments: Ethics Enforcement:

Critics of the profession have been particularly harsh on what they perceive as a lenient AICPA ethics division. They have complained that unethical behavior often goes unpunished, that Trial Board proceedings are often delayed (especially when the behavior in question relates to a case in the process of court litigation), and guilty members are often protected by the division's discretion not to publish their names. The AICPA responded to such criticisms by announcing some policy changes in September 1977. There will no longer be an automatic delay in proceedings until related litigation is completed, and the names of all persons disciplined under the code will be published.

THE SEC ON INDEPENDENCE

The Securities and Exchange Commission was established in 1935 to administer the Securities Act of 1933, the Securities Exchange Act of 1934, and several other regulatory acts pertaining to holding companies and regulated investment companies. In addition to administrative powers, the SEC also has rule-making and judicial powers. The SEC relies heavily on the accounting profession and has a great interest in auditing standards and standards of professional conduct.

The SEC position on independence is contained in Rule 2.01(*b*) of *Regulation S–X*, as follows:

> *b.* The commission will not recognize any certified public accountant or public accountant as independent who is not in fact independent. For exam-

ple, an accountant will be considered not independent with respect to any person or any of its parents, its subsidiaries, or other affiliates (1) in which, during the period of his professional engagement to examine the financial statements being reported on or at the date of his report, he or his firm or a member thereof had, or was committed to acquire, any direct financial interest or any material indirect financial interest or (2) with which, during the period of his professional engagement to examine the financial statements being reported on, at the date of his report or during the period covered by the financial statements, he or his firm or a member thereof was connected as a promoter, underwriter, voting trustee, director, officer, or employee, except that a firm will not be deemed not independent in regard to a particular person if a former officer or employee of such person is employed by the firm and such individual has completely dissociated himself from the person and its affiliates and does not participate in auditing financial statements of the person or its affiliates covering any period of his employment by the person.

For the purposes of Rule 2–01 the term "member" means all partners in the firm and all professional employees participating in the audit or located in an office of the firm participating in a significant portion of the audit.

The AICPA and SEC positions on independence are quite similar in the letter of the rules, but there is a major difference in their views on two aspects of the appearance of independence. First, the SEC tends to define any business transaction between auditor and client to be a prohibited "direct financial interest." Second, the SEC believes that almost all forms of recordkeeping for a client are impairments of independence. Accountants are not prohibited from having these two relationships with a client, but when they exist, the accountant cannot then also serve as independent auditors with respect to financial statements filed with the SEC.

Accounting Series Release No. 126 (July 1972)[8] gives numerous examples of situations in which independence is considered impaired. The following are some cases involving keeping of records:

NOT INDEPENDENT

1. Accounting firm provided services to client which included writing up books, making adjusting entries, and preparing financial statements.
2. In order to keep certain information confidential, the client asked the accounting firm to prepare the executive payroll and maintain selected accounts in a private ledger.
3. Accounting firm proposed to use its computer to correct errors in the stockholders' ledger and to provide for subsequent maintenance and updating to reflect future transactions.

The next cases involve financial interests that would impair independence:

1. Accounting Firm A is considering a merger with Firm B, one of whose partners owns stock in a client of Firm A. The partner proposed to put the stock in a irrevocable trust for the benefit of his children and controlled by two unassociated trustees.

---

[8] *ASR No. 234* was issued in December 1977 in order to deal with cases and questions on independence that had arisen since the issuance of *ASR No. 126* in 1972. *ASR No. 126* was not superceded. *ASR No. 234* expresses the SEC views on accountants' independence in cases relating to foreign accountants, family relationships, retired partners, business with clients, accounting services to clients, unpaid fees, and litigation involving accountants and clients.

2. A partner in an accounting firm, whose proposed client was a wholly owned subsidiary of the registrant, owned 1 percent of the stock of the parent company.

3. Accounting firm plans to rent block time on its computer to a client on a regular basis.

ASR No. 126 gives other brief fact situations involving conflicting occupations and family relationships that impair independence, of which the following two are examples:

1. A partner in an accounting firm also acted as legal counsel for an audit client, receiving fees for such legal services and, through the accounting partnership, for accounting services rendered concurrently.

2. An accountant has a sister-in-law whose husband is a 40-percent stockholder of a client company.

The distinction between keeping books and processing data and the design of information systems is a fine one. *ASR No. 126* states: "Systems design is a proper function for a qualified certified public accountant. Computer programming is an aspect of systems design and does not constitute a bookkeeping service." However, the SEC is equally as definite about the impairment of independence when an accounting firm in any way audits the records that it has helped prepare. So far, the SEC has not ruled that systems *design* is equivalent to systems *operation*. This distinction brings us to the subject of two particularly sensitive areas of practice—tax and management advisory services—and their relationships to independence.

INDEPENDENCE ISSUES

Independence and Management Advisory Services (MAS)

MAS in accounting practice defies definition because the field is so dynamic. MAS includes information systems design, actuarial consulting on pension plans, industrial engineering, and cost-budget-forecast analyses to name a few. Many of the largest CPA firms offer as varied a range of services as the financial and personnel departments of large corporations and the non-CPA management consulting firms themselves. Accountants are justifiably proud of being able to serve business on such a wide scale.

However, some critics have suggested that accounting firms may get so involved in the managerial advice business that they lose their independent perspective in the audit function. Oftentimes, this criticism is raised as a question of the "compatibility of MAS and independence." Of course, independence in the audit sense is not required for straight MAS engagements, although integrity and objectivity are required. All accountants and all critics would agree, though, that when an accounting firm becomes too closely identified with managerial decisions and interests, the appearance of independence for audit purposes is impaired.

To analyze the independence issues involved when MAS work is performed by the same firm that does the audit, one needs to understand the process of managerial decision making. This method is much the same as the scientific method described in Chapter 1.

1. First a manager must recognize a problem situation or a potential problem that demands a solution.
2. A manager must define the problem and seek out alternative courses of action.
3. A manager must assess the costs and benefits of each of the alternative solutions.
4. A manager must determine subjective probabilities of success of each alternative, thus allowing calculation of expected costs and benefits.
5. A manager must then choose one alternative solution.
6. Finally, a manager must implement, supervise, and control the operation of the alternative.

All management consulting activities involve some of the above functions of a manager. The important question relative to audit independence is one of how far the auditor can go and still not be too closely identified with management. No accountant who wants to maintain independence would perform steps 5 and 6. Choice and implementation are clearly the responsibility of management. On the other hand, a large number of accountants (and critics) would go as far as step 3—allowing problem identification, definition of alternatives, and assessment of costs and benefits. Steps 3 and 4 are the gray areas. Once the probabilities of success are estimated, the cost-benefit data then generally point to the most profitable alternative. Exercise of step 4 effectively makes the choice according to some, and according to others there are still too many "nonquantifiables" to say that the determination of probabilities amounts to the same thing as choice.

In response to public and congressional pressure, however, the AICPA has taken steps to prohibit certain management advisory services. A firm that is a member of the SEC practice section commits itself not to perform advisory services that:

Would create a loss of the firm's independence for the purpose of expressing opinions on financial statements of such clients.

Are predominantly commercial in character and inconsistent with the firm's professional status as CPAs.

Consist of the following types of services:
- Psychological testing.
- Public opinion polls.
- Merger and acquisition assistance for a finder's fee.

The executive committee of the SEC practice section may prohibit other advisory services as time passes. As of 1978, this executive committee had tentative plans to prohibit a variety of marketing consulting activities which are essentially nonfinancial in nature and unrelated to accounting control systems (e.g., market testing, product and package design, advertising development) and plant layout services that consist of product design, plant site selection, and design and construction of productive facilities. The committee has taken executive search and actuarial services under study as possible candidates for prohibition. However, the executive committee of the private companies practice section has not proposed prohibition of any management advisory services performed by member firms of that section.

Independence and Tax Advisory Services

Rule 102 effectively defines the role of an accountant tax advisor as an *advocate* of reasonably supportable positions taken by the taxpayer-client. All other ethics rules that do not refer specifically to the audit function, however, are equally applicable to the accountant in the role of tax practitioner. In addition, the AICPA series entitled "Statements on Responsibilities in Tax Practice" defines specific quality criteria for tax practice. Generally, these statements set forth the dimensions of accountants' responsibilities for fair dealing in the complex area of tax practice.

Perhaps the most relevant observation for an auditing textbook is that the preparer's signature at the bottom of a tax return does not represent an audit opinion on financial statements in the return. The declaration on a tax return reads as follows:

> Under penalties of perjury, I declare that I have examined this return, including accompanying schedules and statements, and to the best of my knowledge and belief it is true, correct, and complete. Declaration of preparer (other than taxpayer) is based on all information of which he has any knowledge.

Accountants are not obligated to perform an audit in order to sign a tax return as preparer. However, they cannot close their eyes to unreasonable or contradictory data that place taxpayer-provided information in doubt. Sufficient inquiries to resolve reasonable doubts are expected of the careful tax accountant.

Audits of tax returns are performed by Internal Revenue Service auditors. IRS may select returns with certain signal characteristics (e.g., large charitable deductions relative to income) and ask the taxpayer to show evidence to support the deduction. IRS agents epitomize independence from their "clients." Their methods of gathering evidence in the normal investigation do not differ from the methods of other auditors, but IRS auditors may be armed with special investigative powers to pursue cases of suspected fraud and concealment. In this respect they are quite different from other auditors.

For accountants who perform both tax and audit services for the same client, there exists a dual role of advocate and independent auditor. In some engagements, auditors prepare the client's tax return, thus establishing amounts for tax expenses and tax liability in the financial statements under audit. Clearly this dual service can result in auditors auditing their own tax work. If accountants are acting as advocate for allowance of a controversial deduction (thus a lower tax liability), they must somehow take into account as an auditor the probability that some part of the deduction may be disallowed by IRS. It is not easy (some would say impossible) to serve two masters in this manner—the taxpayer-client and the users of published financial statements. Some writers have suggested that auditors should exercise considerable care to reflect the possibility of a deficiency assessment in the tax liability account while at the same time advocating the validity of the tax item in question in the tax return.

PROFESSIONALISM REVISITED

Of the five characteristics of professionalism defined in Chapter 1, two are of utmost importance to the individual accountant: recognition by society with a reciprocal recognition of responsibility by the accountant, and a stated and observed code of conduct. The individual accountant by good deeds or by misdeeds can have a direct influence on society's view of the accounting profession, and one's observance or nonobservance of the letter and the spirit of the rules of conduct determines whether actions are favorably or unfavorably received.

Accountants must not lose sight of the layman's perspective in making ethical and technical decisions. For no matter how complex or technical a decision may be, there is always a simplified lay view of it that tends to cut away details of specialized technical issues to get directly to the heart of the matter. A sense of professionalism coupled with a sensitivity to the impact of decisions on other persons are invaluable in the practice of accounting.

SOURCES AND ADDITIONAL READING REFERENCES

American Institute of Certified Public Accountants. *Restatement of the Code of Professional Ethics.* New York.

Brenner, S. N., and Molander, E. A. "Is the Ethics of Business Changing?" *Harvard Business Review,* January/February 1977, pp. 57–71.

Burton, John C., ed. *Corporate Financial Reporting: Ethical and Other Problems.* New York: American Institute of Certified Public Accountants, 1972.

Carmichael, D. R., and Sweiringa, R. J. "Compatibility of Auditing Independence and Management Services—An Identification of Issues," *Accounting Review,* October 1968, pp. 697–706.

"Conflict of Interest: The Moral Climate Changes," special report, *Business Week,* April 14, 1973, pp. 56–62.

Darling, John R. "Attitudes toward Advertising by Accountants," *Journal of Accountancy,* February 1977, pp. 48–53.

Editorial. "The SEC and the Auditor's Independence," *Journal of Accountancy,* September 1972, p. 37.

"Final Report of the Ad Hoc Committee on Independence," *Journal of Accountancy,* December 1969, pp. 51–56.

Fletcher, Joseph. *Situation Ethics.* Philadelphia, Pa.: The Westminster Press, 1966.

Frankena, William K. *Ethics*. Englewood Cliffs, N.J.: Prentice-Hall, Inc., 1963.

Goldman, Arieh, and Barlev, Benzion. "The Auditor-Firm Conflict of Interests: Its Implications for Independence," *Accounting Review*, October 1974, pp. 707–18.

Grenside, J. P. "Accountants' Reports on Profit Forecasts in the U.K.," *Journal of Accountancy*, May 1970, pp. 47–53.

Hartley, R. V., and Ross, T. L. "MAS and Audit Independence: An Image Problem," *Journal of Accountancy*, November 1972, pp. 42–52.

Higgins, Thomas G. "Professional Ethics: A Time for Reappraisal," *Journal of Accoutancy*, March 1962, pp. 29–35.

Lavin, David. "Perceptions of the Independence of the Auditor," *The Accounting Review*, January 1976, pp. 41–50.

Loeb, Stephen E. "A Code of Ethics for CPAs in Industry; A Survey," *Journal of Accountancy*, December 1971, pp. 52–60.

Mautz, R. K., and Sharaf, Hussein A. *The Philosophy of Auditing*, American Accounting Association monograph no. 6, especially chap. 8, "Independence" and chap. 9, "Ethical Conduct," American Accounting Assn., 1961.

Mead, George. "Auditing, Management Advisory Services, Social Service, and the Profit Motive," *Accounting Review*, October 1960, pp. 659–66.

Raby, William L. "Ethics in Tax Practice," *Accounting Review*, October 1966, pp. 714–20.

______. "Advocacy versus Independence in Tax Liability Accrual," *Journal of Accountancy*, March 1972, pp. 40–47.

SEC Accounting Series Release No. 126, "Independence of Accountants: Guidelines and Examples of Situations Involving the Independence of Accountants," reprinted in *Journal of Accountancy*, September 1972, pp. 83–89.

Singer, Marcus G. *Generalization in Ethics*. New York: Atheneum, 1961, 1971.

Sprague, W. D. "The Advertising Dilemma," *The CPA Journal*, January 1977, pp. 27–30.

Titard, Pierre. "Independence and Management Advisory Services—Opinions of Financial Statement Users," *Journal of Accountancy*, July 1971, pp. 47–52.

Ways, Max. "Business Faces Growing Pressures to Behave Better," *Fortune*, May 1974, pp. 193 et seq.

Weygandt, Jerry J. "The CPA and His Duty to Silence," *Accounting Review*, January 1970, pp. 60–75.

Wheelwright, Philip. *A Critical Introduction to Ethics*. New York: The Odyssey Press, Inc., 1959.

Wilcox, Edward B. "Ethics: The Profession on Trial," *Journal of Accountancy*, November 1955, pp. 72–79.

REVIEW QUESTIONS

3.1 What *roles* must a professional accountant be prepared to occupy in regard to ethical decision problems?

3.2 What are the steps of the decision process called *reflective choice*?

3.3 Why might the rule "Let conscience be your guide" not be sufficient basis for your personal ethics decision? For your professional ethics decisions?

3.4. Assume that you accept the following ethical rule: "Failure to tell the whole truth is wrong." In the text illustrations about (*a*) your position as a bank director and (*b*) your knowledge of the cashier's forgeries, what would this rule require you to do? Why is an unalterable rule like this classed as an element of *imperative* ethical theory?

3.5. How does *utilitarian* ethics differ from *imperative* ethics theory?

3.6. Which of the AICPA Rules of Conduct apply to a member (*a*) in tax practice, (*b*) in management advisory services practice, (*c*) in practice exclusively outside the United States, and (*d*) who is not engaged in the practice of public accounting (for example, an internal auditor, GAO auditor, IRS agent)?

3.7. What ethical responsibilities do members of the AICPA have for acts of nonmembers who are under their supervision (for example, recent college graduates who are not yet CPAs)?

3.8. Why is competitive bidding for professional engagements no longer prohibited by the AICPA Rules of Conduct?

3.9. Is an incorporated accounting practice substantially different from an accounting practice organized in the form of a partnership?

3.10. Draw a line down the center of a sheet of paper. In the left-hand column, write each of the articles of the Code of Ethics for Certified Internal Auditors. Opposite each of these articles, in the right-hand column, write the AICPA Rules of Conduct that are related.

3.11. The Institute of Internal Auditors expresses a position on independence in the *Statement of Responsibilities of the Internal Auditor.* Compare this position with the AICPA ethical concept of independence.

3.12. Compare the AICPA and SEC views on independence. How are they similar? How do they differ?

3.13. What are the six phases of the managerial decision process? Why should accountants in public practice be concerned with this kind of decision process?

EXERCISES AND PROBLEMS

3.14. Is there any moral difference between a disapproved action in which you are caught and the same action that never becomes known to anyone else? Do many persons in business and professional society make a distinction between these two circumstances? If you respond that *you* do (or do not) perceive a difference while *persons in business and professional society* do not (or do), then how do you explain the difference in attitudes?

3.15. You are treasurer of a church. A member approaches you with the following proposition: "I will donate stock to the church on October 15 if, on October 16, you will sell it back to me. All you will have to do is convey the certificate with your signature to me in return for my check, which will be for the "asking" price of the stock quoted that day without reduction for commissions."

The member's objective, of course, is to obtain the income tax deduction for the value of the stock on October 15, but he wants to maintain his ownership interest. The policy of the church board is not to hold any stock but to sell shares within a reasonably short time.

Consider:

1. Should the treasurer accommodate the member? Would you if you were treasurer?
2. Would your considerations and conclusion be any different if:
   a. The church were financially secure and the gift was small in amount?
   b. The church were financially secure and the gift was large?
   c. The church would be in a deficit position for the year were it not for this gift?

3.16. Is the AICPA prohibition (Rule 201(*e*)) of vouching for the achievability of a forecast a complete prohibition of an accountant's association with forecasts of financial results? What are the ethical theory reasons underlying the existence of Rule 201(*e*)? (Hint: Try the steps of reflective choice using a utilitarian theory as a guide.)

3.17. Would a CPA be considered independent for an examination of the financial statements of a—
a. Church for which he or she is serving as treasurer without compensation? Explain.
b. A club for which a spouse is serving as treasurer-bookkeeper if the CPA is not to receive a fee for the examination? Explain.

3.18. Your client, Newsell Corporation, requested that you conduct a feasibility study to advise management of the best way the corporation can utilize electronic data processing equipment and which computer, if any, best meets the corporation's requirements. You are technically competent in this area and accept the engagement. Upon completion of your study the corporation accepts your suggestions and installs the computer and related equipment that you recommended.

Required:
a. Discuss the effect acceptance of this management advisory services engagement would have upon your independence in expressing an opinion on the financial statements of Newsell Corporation.
b. Instead of accepting the engagement, assume that you recommended Iva Mackey, of the CPA firm of Brown and Mackey, who is qualified in specialized services. Upon completion of the engagement your client requests that Ms. Mackey's partner, John Brown, perform services in other areas. Should Brown accept the engagement? Discuss.
c. A local printer of data processing forms customarily offers a commission for recommendation as a supplier. The client is aware of the commission offer and suggests that Mackey accept it. Would it be proper for Mackey to accept the commission with the client's approval? Discuss. (AICPA adapted)

3.19. Gilbert and Bradley formed a corporation called Financial Services, Inc., each man taking 50 percent of the authorized common stock. Gilbert is a CPA and a member of the American Institute of CPAs. Bradley is a CPCU (Chartered Property Casualty Underwriter). The corporation performs auditing and tax services under Gilbert's direction and insurance services under Bradley's supervision. The opening of the corporation's office was announced by a three-inch, two-column "card" in the local newspaper.

One of the corporation's first audit clients was the Grandtime Company. Grandtime had total assets of $600,000 and total liabilities of $270,000. In the course of his examination, Gilbert found that Grandtime's building with a book value of $240,000 was pledged as security for a ten-year-term note in the amount of $200,000. The client's statements did not mention that the building was pledged as security for the ten-year-term note. However, as the failure to disclose the lien did not affect either the value of the assets or the amount of the liabilities and his examination was satisfactory in all other respects, Gilbert rendered an unqualified opinion on Grandtime's financial statements. About two months after the date of his opinion, Gilbert learned that an insurance company was planning to loan Grandtime $150,000 in the form of a first-mortgage note on the building. Realizing that the insurance company was unaware of the existing lien on the building, Gilbert had Bradley notify the insurance company of the fact that Grandtime's building was pledged as security for the term note.

Shortly after the events described above, Gilbert was charged with a violation of professional ethics.

Required:

Identify and explain the rules of the AICPA Code of Professional Ethics violated by Gilbert and the nature of the violations. (AICPA adapted)

3.20. Alex Pratt, a retired partner of your CPA firm, has just been appointed to the board of directors of Palmer Corporation, your firm's client. Pratt is also an ex officio member of your firm's income tax advisory committee which meets monthly to discuss income tax problems of the partnership's clients, some of which are competitors of Palmer Corporation. The partnership pays Pratt $100 for each committee meeting attended and a monthly retirement benefit, fixed by a retirement plan policy, of $1,000. Discuss the effect of Pratt's appointment to the board of directors of Palmer Corporation on your partnership's independence in expressing an opinion on the Palmer Corporation's financial statements, and discuss other matters of ethics involved in this situation. (AICPA adapted)

3.21. An auditor's report was appended to the financial statements of Worthmore, Inc. The statements consisted of a balance sheet as of November 30, 1978, and statements of income, retained earnings, and changes in financial position for the year then ended. The first two paragraphs of the report contained the wording of the standard unqualified short form report, and a third paragraph read as follows:

> The wives of two partners of our CPA firm owned a material investment in the outstanding common stock of Worthmore, Inc., during the fiscal year ended November 30, 1978. These individuals disposed of their holdings on December 3, 1978 in a transaction that did not result in a profit or a loss. This information is included in our audit report in order to comply with disclosure requirements of the *Rules of Conduct* of the American Institute of Certified Public Accountants.
>
> Bell and Davis
> *Certified Public Accountants*

Required:

a. Was the CPA firm of Bell and Davis independent with respect to the fiscal 1978 audit of Worthmore, Inc.'s financial statements? Explain.

b. Do you find Bell and Davis' audit report satisfactory? Explain.

c. Change the fact situation of this problem such that the financial interest consisted not of common stock held by members of partners' families but instead that the financial interest consisted of an unsecured loan of $10,000 from Worthmore to the Bell and Davis partnership for the purpose of financing the purchase of computer hardware. The net worth of the CPA partnership was $150,000. Is independence impaired?

d. Change the facts once again such that Worthmore is a lending institution which holds the mortgage on partner Davis's home. Is independence impaired? (AICPA adapted)

3.22. Ready and Able, CPAs, regularly perform the audit of the First National Bank, and the firm is preparing for the audit of the financial statements for the year ended December 31, 1978. For each of the following fact situations explain why independence would or would not be impaired.

a. Two directors of the First National Bank became partners in Ready and Able, CPAs, on July 1, 1978, resigning their directorships on that date.

b. During 1978 the former controller of the First National Bank, now a partner of Ready and Able, was frequently called upon for assistance regarding loan approvals and the bank's minimum checking account policy. In addition, he conducted a computer feasibility study for First National. (AICPA adapted)

3.23. The Moore Corporation is indebted to a CPA for unpaid fees and has offered to give the CPA unsecured interest-bearing notes. Would the CPA's acceptance of these notes have any bearing upon the CPA's independence in the audit engagement with the Moore Corporation? Would your conclusion be the same if Moore Corporation had offered to give two shares of its common stock, after which 10,002 shares would be outstanding? Discuss all facets of these two separate fact situations. (AICPA adapted)

3.24. A CPA has discovered a way to eliminate most of the boring work of processing routine accounts receivable confirmations by contracting with the Jiffy Mail Service. After the auditor has prepared the confirmations, Jiffy will stuff them in envelopes, mail them, receive the return replies, open the replies, and return them to the auditor. Is this arrangement acceptable under the AICPA Rules of Conduct? Explain why or why not.

3.25. A client, without consulting its CPA, has changed its accounting so that it is not in accordance with generally accepted accounting principles. During the regular audit engagement the CPA discovers that the statements based on the accounts are so grossly misleading that they might be considered fraudulent.

Required:

a. Discuss the specific action to be taken by the CPA.

b. In this situation what obligation does the CPA have to outsiders if he is replaced? Discuss briefly.

c. In this situation what obligation does the CPA have to a new auditor if he is replaced? Discuss briefly. (AICPA)

3.26. A CPA who had reached retirement age arranged for the sale of his practice to another certified public accountant. Their agreement called for the transfer of all working papers and business correspondence to the accountant purchasing the practice. Is this arrangement suitable and in accordance with the AICPA Rules of Conduct?

3.27. Martha Jacoby, CPA, withdrew from the audit of Harvard Company after discovering irregularities in Harvard's income tax returns. One week later, Ms. Jacoby was telephoned by Jake Henry, CPA, who explained that he had just been retained by Harvard Company to replace Ms. Jacoby, Mr. Henry asked Ms. Jacoby why she withdrew from the Harvard engagement. What should she reply? Explain.

3.28. Caroline Daniel, CPA, is approached by a prospective tax client who promises to pay a fee of "4 percent of whatever amount you save me in taxes." Can the CPA accept the tax engagement under this fee arrangement? Explain.

3.29. David Moore, CPA, offers a consulting service to clients in which he reviews their needs for computer-related supplies (magnetic tapes, disks, cards, paper, and so on) and places their orders with Computographics, Inc. This supplier offers a special discount price because of the volume of business generated by Moore. Would Moore be in violation of the AICPA Code of Professional Ethics if he:

a. Charged the clients no fee, instead accepted a 3 percent commission from Computographics, Inc.? Explain.

b. Charged his regular hourly consulting rate of $60 per hour? Explain.

c. Charged a consulting fee figured at 3 percent of the amount of supplies ordered by the client? Explain.

3.30. Justify the provision in Rule 302 of the AICPA Rules of Conduct that permits the accountant to accept an engagement on a contingent fee basis when it is based on the results of judicial proceedings or the findings of governmental agencies.

3.31. Sarah Ehlan and Elizabeth Hughes, both CPAs, have engaged in the practice of public accounting in Big City since 1974. Their practice consisted of 50 percent audit work, 10 percent tax work and 40 percent consulting, mainly in the area of pension and employee benefit plans. Their staff has grown to a complement of 40 professionals.

The consulting business is quite profitable, and in a move to expand, Sarah and Elizabeth plan to buy the computer programs, library, and other assets and assume the employment contracts of 15 persons all of which constitute the actuarial and compensation services of an insurance brokerage firm. They plan to merge these services into their existing consulting practice. None of the new employees will be partners of the firm.

Before this investment is completed, they wish to have an authoritative opinion on whether their plan would put them in the position of engaging in an occupation incompatible with the practice of public accounting. What is your opinion?

3.32. Which, if any, of the following might constitute incompatible occupations prohibited under Rule 504? Explain your opinion.

a. Operating an employment agency.

b. Operating a finance company.

c. Being an insurance broker affiliated with an agency.

d. Selling insurance.

e. Serving as a loan broker for industrial and commercial loans.
f. Serving as a collection agent under state license to perform collection services for clients only.

3.33. With the approval of its board of directors, the Thames Corporation made a sizable payment of advertising during the year being audited. The corporation deducted the full amount in its federal income tax return. The controller acknowledges that this deduction probably will be disallowed because it relates to political matters. He has not provided for this disallowance in his federal income tax provision and refuses to do so because he fears that this will cause the revenue agent to believe that the deduction is not valid. What is the CPA's responsibility in this situation? Explain with regard to ethical responsibilities, audit responsibilities, and tax practice responsibilities. (AICPA)

DISCUSSION CASES

3.34. **Disclosure Dilemma**

The Roberts-On Ringer Corporation, a conglomerate, acquired the Granof Grain Storage Company in 1978. Unbeknownst to Roberts's management, Granof Grain executives had engaged in illegal price-fixing activities during the period 1961–1977. This year, 1979, one of those executives died and curiously included in his last will and testament a full account of the illegal activities. The president of Roberts in a moment of indiscretion allowed the auditor (you) to see a copy of this document; thus, you have full knowledge of the situation.

With regard to matters of timing, you are auditing the financial statement for the year ended December 31, 1979, and you plan to complete the field work and write the report on February 15, 1980. It is now January 28, 1980. The will and testament will be read in open probate court on February 28. Assume that the statute of limitations which will bar lawsuit action runs out on February 20. In other words, after February 20 no prosecution can take place.

As you begin to complete the field work and write your report, you realize that only you and the president know the facts. Fourteen other Granof executives know, but they have remained silent. The customers of Granof are apparently unaware of the price-fixing situation in 1961–1977. Roberts's total assets amount to $1 billion, stockholders' equity is $300 million, and net current assets amount to $100 million. Treble damages that could arise from this kind of violation are conservatively estimable at $150 million. The president of Roberts-On has implored you to forget having seen the documents.

Required:

a. Discuss the ethical and technical decision problems the auditor faces in this situation.
b. What should the auditor do? Why?
c. What may be the consequence of the auditor's decision(s)? Explain.

3.35. **Peter Hampden, CPA***

Peter Hampden, a third-year member of his firm's audit staff, was debating whether he should continue working as a public accountant. During his

* By David F. Hawkins, professor of business administration, Harvard University, as published in John C. Burton, ed., *Corporate Financial Reporting: Ethical and Other Problems* (New York: AICPA, 1972).

college years, he had considered himself to be somewhat of an idealist with a strong sense of public responsibility. Over the last few years, he had increasingly found himself questioning some of the decisions of his superiors on matters which he considered involved ethical issues—the responsibility of the profession to the client and statement users, and "fair" reporting. Hampden realized these issues were difficult to resolve—especially those involving concepts of right and wrong as applied to auditor behavior. He also recognized that his ethical standards were changing as he grew older and that he "did not have all the answers." Therefore, before he reached his career decision, he sought the opinion of a second person.

Hampden spoke to the firm's senior partner about his problem. The partner said that Hampden's seniors had rated him "excellent and definite partner material if he continued to develop in the future as he had in the past." The senior partner was also sympathetic to Hampden's concern and suggested they spend some time together during the following week discussing it.

To facilitate their planned discussion, the senior partner suggested Hampden prepare for him thumbnail descriptions of some of the situations involving financial reporting that had troubled him over the last few years. The senior partner also suggested that Hampden outline the "ethically correct" action he would have taken if he had been the partner in charge. The following is a copy of the material Hampden submitted to his senior partner.

(a) Disclosure of Anticipated Accounting Change

A client company had invited the partner in charge of their audit to discuss with their president some decisions made at a board of directors meeting at which the preliminary third quarter results and the accounting principles policies to be followed in the annual report were discussed. The publication of the third quarter results was to follow this meeting with the president. The audit partner had brought me to this meeting to expand my knowledge of how to maintain effective top management-auditor relations.

At its meeting the board had decided "if it is feasible" to change the depreciation accounting policy followed in their annual report to stockholders. It was anticipated that this change, if made, would permit the company to show improved earnings per share over the previous year's results. If the old depreciation policy were followed, the company would most likely show a decline in earnings.

The board had asked the president to request their auditor to review the company's accounting department's proposed adjustments to the asset accounts. Also, the president indicated that before the annual report was submitted to stockholders other accounting principle changes might be necessary "in order to put the company's accounting on a more realistic basis." If these changes were made, the president planned to discuss them with the company's auditors.

In my opinion, the auditor should have insisted that the company indicate in its third quarter report to stockholders that they were contemplating a change in accounting practices. None of the directors apparently thought this was necessary, and neither did the audit partner.

(b) Disclosure of Tax Status of Lease Transaction

Our company had been requested to help a client draw up some sale and leaseback agreements that would qualify for tax and financial reporting purposes as leases and not as conditional sales. Subsequently, at the insistence of the Internal Revenue Service, the agreements were treated for tax purposes as conditional sales. The client was very disturbed by this ruling, but on the advice of the company counsel decided not to challenge it. This lawyer, who had replaced the company counsel involved in the original transaction, described the sale and lease agreement as "a classic example of the type of lease agreement involving nominal purchase options used to teach law students how not to try and fool the tax authorities."

After making his tax decision, the client discussed the financial reporting implications of the decision with the partner in charge of the audit. In the process of this discussion, the client indicated that he was very upset at the "poor advice" given by his auditors and that he preferred to continue treating the sale and leaseback as a lease for financial reporting purposes. If the lease were capitalized, the company's long-term liabilities would have increased about 17 percent.

The partner in charge of the audit later agreed with the client's treatment of the transaction as a lease. In his opinion, since the agreement had been drawn up prior to the most recent accounting pronouncement on leases, the provisions of the pronouncement did not apply. No mention of the agreement's tax status was indicated in the footnotes to the annual statements.

Comment. In my opinion, at least the lease's tax status should have been disclosed; preferably, the lease should have been capitalized. Not taking either of these actions leaves the auditor open to the criticism of (1) trying to cover up his earlier poor advice and (2) being biased in his opinion of what constitutes a full and fair presentation of financial data.

The economic substance of the lease transaction was equivalent to a sale under accounting principles. The legal and tax authorities used the same criteria as stated in accounting principles to make their decision. These criteria are similar to those presented in tax guides to distinguish between genuine leases and conditional sales disguised as leases.

(c) Responsibility for Disclosing Control and Reporting Deficiencies

The founder-president of a client company raised $20 million through a public stock sale for his new company to develop, manufacture, market, and lease on a cancelable basis at an unusually low monthly rental price a revolutionary photo-copying system. To date, no major company had been able to develop the technology and production capability needed to make this kind of equipment at the low rental levels proposed by the client company. At the time of the public offering, the client company also had not developed the needed technology or production capability.

Soon after the public issue the stock's price soared to four times its offering price of $12.50. This upward movement was accompanied by optimistic articles in the financial and trade press on the company's prospects for success.

Shortly after these funds were raised, I attended a public seminar during which the client company's president discussed his technique for raising venture capital. He said:

> Raising money is very much like running for office. You have to put a campaign together. . . . The business plan you prepare must be a lie

> . . . but it must be a detailed and precise lie rather than a vague and general lie. . . . If you promise enough risk, loss, and catastrophe, the financier will begin to wonder whether you're hiding something from him. . . . Go public as fast as you can.

Subsequently, the company went into bankruptcy, losing some $18 million on sales of $700,000. The principal causes for failure were poor control over production costs and a decision to sell rather than lease its equipment. This decision led to the cancellation of a number of letters of intent to purchase.

Comment. In cases such as these, is it acceptable by the public's standards for the auditor simply to comment on the fairness of the financial statements and their adherence to generally accepted accounting principles? Whose standards of conduct should prevail? Those of the AICPA or some other? Who is responsible for telling the public about the poor control over production costs and the cancellation of the letters of intent? Indeed, should the public be told at all?

I have no answer to this kind of problem beyond saying that it is management's responsibility to disclose unfavorable information. If they will not, the auditor should use all of his power to see that they do. Yet, is this his function?

(d) Responsibility of the Financial Press

In order to reflect better a change in their business, a client company changed from accelerated to straight-line depreciation and started capitalizing certain product development expenses. We agreed with the client that these changes were desirable.

Subsequently, a prominent financial writer used this accounting change as a perfect example of how companies change their accounting methods to boost earnings. The writer failed to mention any of the reasons presented by management in their annual report for the change in accounting.

Comment. As an individual auditor, I suspect that I cannot do much to impose more responsible standards on the press; yet, this kind of reporting disturbs me. What can be done about it? Can I as an individual auditor do anything?

(e) Responsibilities of Financial Analysts

Incidentally, while I am raising questions about the way financial reporters discuss our client's financial report, I would like to discuss the implications for me as an auditor of this kind of reporting of our client's situation:

> The 10 percent stock dividend recently announced by ________ makes ________ an attractive investment at current prices.
>
> If you have not got ________ in your portfolio, now would be an appropriate time to make a purchase at the current depressed levels.
>
> At present, the company is making huge capital investments, and one can expect a return within the next two or three years. Investors should not worry about the auditors qualifying ________'s recent record profits by $1.4 million. It is only an accountant's wrangle.

In any case, look at provisions in the income statment for depreciation which is up from $10.0 million to $12.5 million this year. Such a provision is no more than a way of creating reserves out of profits.

This company's earnings for the current year were about the same as the prior year. We disagreed with the company's deferred tax accounting practices. They refused to apply comprehensive tax allocation to some mining expenditures that they capitalized for book purposes but wrote off on their tax return as incurred. The stock is traded over-the-counter.

Comment. Why should auditors struggle to determine what are "fair" reporting practices while this kind of reporting persists?

Questions for Discussion

1. If you were the senior partner, how would you respond to the cases presented to you by Hampden? Do these involve ethical issues? Accounting principle issues? Audit judgment issues?
2. Is it desirable that the auditor behave in the manner suggested by Hampden?

3.36. **Effect of Actual or Threatened Litigation on Independence (AICPA Ethics Interpretation 101–6)**

For each of the following situations (1) discuss whether independence of the auditor should be considered impaired, (2) explain why or why not, and (3) indicate what action the auditor should take.

(*a*–1) Your client, Contrary Corporation, is very upset over the fact that your audit last year failed to detect an $800,000 inventory overstatement caused by employee theft and falsification of the records. The board has discussed the matter and authorized its attorneys to explore the possibility of a lawsuit for damages.

(*a*–2) Contrary Corporation filed a lawsuit alleging negligent audit work and seeking $1 million in damages.

(*a*–3) In response to the lawsuit by Contrary, you have decided to start litigation against certain officers of the company alleging management fraud and deceit. You are asking for a damage judgment of $500,000.

(*a*–4) The Allright Insurance Company paid Contrary Corporation $700,000 under fidelity bonds covering the employees involved in the inventory theft. Both you and Contrary Corporation have dropped your lawsuits. However, under subrogation rights, Allright has sued your audit firm for damages on the grounds of negligent performance of the audit.

(*b*) Your audit client, Science Tech, Inc., installed a cost accounting system devised by the management advisory services department of your firm. The system failed to account properly for certain product costs (according to management), and the system had to be discontinued. Science Tech management was very dissatisfied and has filed a lawsuit demanding return of the $10,000 MAS fee. The audit fee is normally about $50,000, and $10,000 is not an especially large amount for your firm. However, you believe that Science Tech management operated the system improperly. While you are willing to do further MAS work at a reduced rate to make the system operate, you are unwilling to return the entire $10,000 fee.

(*c*) A group of dissident shareholders filed a class action lawsuit against both you and your client, Amalgamated, Inc., for $30 million. They allege there was a conspiracy to present misleading financial statements in connection with a recent merger.

APPENDIX

Certified Internal Auditor Code of Ethics

The full text of the CIA code is reprinted below. The code itself is neither long nor complex. Notice in the preamble the sentence: "A Certified Internal Auditor shall realize that individual judgment is required in the application of these principles." This is a clear call for each person to exercise fully his or her powers of ethical decision making.

The CIA code does not express a preference for one guiding theory of ethics. However, in the context of the preamble, there are implications for both a universal utilitarianism (in the phrase "conduct himself so that his good faith and integrity should not be open to question") and for a narrowly defined utilitarianism (in the objective "to the end of advancing the interest of his company or organization"). One could hope that the advancement of broad, social-economic ends would not conflict with advancement of the interest of a single employer organization, but in consideration of real-world pressures, the CIA must recognize that a conflict situation may be faced when a difficult choice must be made.

In general the CIA ethics rules correspond to the spirit of similar AICPA Rules of Conduct. However, throughout the CIA rules there is an underlying thread of strong commitment to the employer, whereas in the AICPA rules there is a spirit of commitment to a broad public interest. The similarities point up a commonality of technical professionalism among accountants. The differences reflect the employee-employer-client structural characteristics of the two branches of auditing practice.

In considering the CIA Code of Ethics, one must not overlook the criteria for independence expressed in the *Statement of Responsibilities of the Internal Auditor* (reproduced in the Appendix to Chapter 1). The references therein to independence with regard to procedures, records, and review of systems may be usefully compared to related views of the SEC and AICPA.

Certified Internal Auditor Code of Ethics*

The Certified Internal Auditor has an obligation to his profession, management, stockholders, and the general public to maintain high standards of professional conduct in the performance of his profession. In recognition of these obligations the board of regents has adopted the following Code of Ethics.

Adherence to this code, which is based on the Code of Ethics of The Institute of Internal Auditors, Inc., is a prerequisite to maintaining the designation Certified Internal Auditor. A Certified Internal Auditor who is judged in violation of the provisions of the code by the ethics committee of the board of regents shall forfeit the CIA designation.

Preamble

The provisions of this Code of Ethics cover basic principles in the various disciplines of internal auditing practice. A Certified Internal Auditor shall realize that individual judgment is required in the application of these principles. He has a responsibility to conduct himself so that his good faith and integrity should not be open to question. While having due regard for the limit of his technical skills, he will promote the highest possible internal auditing standards to the end of advancing the interest of his company or organization.

Articles

I. A Certified Internal Auditor shall have an obligation to exercise honesty, objectivity, and diligence in the performance of his duties and responsibilities.

II. A Certified Internal Auditor, in holding the trust of his employer, shall exhibit loyalty in all matters pertaining to the affairs of the employer or to whomever he may be rendering a service. However, a Certified Internal Auditor shall not knowingly be a party to any illegal or improper activity.

III. A Certified Internal Auditor shall refrain from entering into any activity which may be in conflict with the interest of his employer or which would prejudice his ability to carry out objectively his duties and responsibilities.

IV. A Certified Internal Auditor shall not accept a fee or a gift from an employee, a client, a customer, or a business associate of his employer without the knowledge and consent of his senior management.

V. A Certified Internal Auditor shall be prudent in the use of information acquired in the course of his duties. He shall not use confidential information for any personal gain or in a manner which would be detrimental to the welfare of his employer.

VI. A Certified Internal Auditor, in expressing an opinion, shall use all reasonable care to obtain sufficient factual evidence to warrant such expression. In his reporting, a Certified Internal Auditor shall reveal such material facts known to him which, if not revealed, could either distort the report of the results of operations under review or conceal unlawful practice.

VII. A Certified Internal Auditor shall continually strive for improvement in the proficiency and effectiveness of his service.

* Source: From *Certified Internal Auditor Code of Ethics* by The Institute of Internal Auditors, Inc. Copyright by The Institute of Internal Auditors, Inc., 249 Maitland Avenue, Altamonte Springs, Florida 32701. Reprinted with permission.

4

LEGAL RELATIONSHIPS AND FRAUD DETECTION

The making of law, both common law and statutory law, is a society's means of formalizing the ethics rules that members of the society must observe. Thus, the law may be perceived as an extension of the self-imposed general and professional ethics considered in Chapter 3. This chapter reviews auditors' liability exposure under common law and statutory law, and the auditors' responsibilities for fraud detection.

Accountants are potentially liable for monetary damages and even subject to criminal penalties (fines, jail terms) for failure to perform professional services properly. They can be sued by clients, clients' creditors, investors, and by the government.

Litigation has resulted from accountants' unvarnished lawbreaking (e.g., conviction for bribing IRS agents, embezzlement), from failure to discover material misstatements in financial statements, from failure to disclose information considered essential, and from misunderstandings over the nature and requirements of an engagement. Lawsuits have multiplied since the early 1960s, and the threat of them has prompted some major changes in the way accountants go about doing their work in audits, in management advisory services, and in tax practice.

RESPONSIBILITIES FOR FRAUD DETECTION

Fraud is a term accountants prefer to avoid because it covers a wide variety of sources for material misstatements in financial statements. Thus auditing standards deal with auditors' responsibilities regarding related party transactions (*SAS No. 6*, Section 335), errors and irregularities (*SAS No. 16*, Section 327), and illegal acts (*SAS No. 17*, Section 328).

Before reviewing dimensions of common law and statutory liability, an explanation of the current environment of auditors' responsibilities for fraud detection will set the stage.

In 1976, under a program of voluntary disclosure, some 250 American companies notified the Securities and Exchange Commission that they had made illegal or questionable payments in the United States and abroad. Millions of dollars were involved in some cases, as were high officials in this country, Europe, and Japan. These disclosures were begun with discovery of some corporate political contributions involved in the Watergate investigations and with a dramatic story of political payoffs in a Central American country. The pattern of payments involved contributions to U.S. and foreign politicians, bribes to win overseas contracts, and under-the-table payments to expedite performance of services. Some payments were made with the apparent consent of chief executive officers, while others were authorized at lower management levels without the knowledge of top executives. Some disbursements came from general corporate funds and others from secret "slush funds" maintained off the books.

A rising tide of public indignation and impatience with wrongdoing prompted several agencies into action. The principal results are set out in the sections below.

Foreign Corrupt Practices Act of 1977

This law—an amendment of the Securities Exchange Act of 1934—makes it a criminal offense for U.S. companies to give anything of value (i.e., give a bribe) to a foreign official, foreign political party, or candidate for foreign political office for the purpose of influencing acts or decisions in favor of the business interests of the company. The law also prohibits such bribes on the part of every U.S. domiciled company and individual. Companies may be fined up to $1 million and individuals up to $10,000 and imprisoned up to five years for violations.

The law also amends the Securities Exchange Act of 1934 to include some accounting and internal control standards which require companies registered with the SEC to (1) keep books, records, and accounts which, in reasonable detail, accurately and fairly reflect the transactions and dispositions of the assets of the company, and (2) devise and maintain a system of internal accounting controls sufficient to provide reasonable assurance that the following four objectives are met:

Transactions are executed in accordance with management's general or specific authorization;

Transactions are recorded as necessary (*a*) to permit preparation of financial statements in conformity with generally accepted accounting principles or any other criteria applicable to such statements, and (*b*) to maintain accountability for assets;

Access to assets is permitted only in accordance with management's general or specific authorization; and

The recorded accountability for assets is compared with the existing assets at reasonable intervals and appropriate action is taken with respect to any differences.

These four objectives are quoted directly from *Statement on Auditing Standards No. 1* (Section 320.28). The effect of the Foreign Corrupt Practices Act of 1977 was to make a company's failure to satisfy them a violation of federal law in addition to being merely a matter of nonconformity with auditing standards. (However, the monetary fines and the prison term penalties that apply to bribes do not apply to violations of the accounting and internal control requirements.)

The law gives the Securities and Exchange Commission another avenue for bringing action against companies. Only three months after the law was passed, the SEC brought action against a company, charging the officers with making false entries in the books and records and failing to devise an adequate accounting control system. No allegations of foreign bribery were made, so the case was apparently based entirely on the accounting and internal control requirements of the Foreign Corrupt Practices Act.

Audit Committees

Audit committees of boards of directors have been encouraged since 1939. The objective is to constitute a committee of the board which would bear the first responsibility for overseeing the independent audit engagement, internal auditors' activities, and other related exploratory and investigative matters related to financial accounting and internal controls. This committee would stand as auditors' direct pipeline to the board, opening up communications channels to the top of the corporate organization.

The SEC, in a number of investigations and disciplinary hearings, has forced corporations to form audit committees made up of outside (nonmanagement) directors. Court decisions have also required formation of audit committees and judges have specified their duties and responsibilities.

After many years of encouraging voluntary formation, the New York Stock Exchange required all listed domestic companies to establish audit committees no later than June 30, 1978. The committee members are to be outside directors free from relationships (other than board membership) which might interfere with their exercise of independent judgment. The emphasis on outside directors is meant to ensure that the interests of shareholders are not subordinated to any conflicting responsibilities that an officer-director might have.

AICPA: Statements on Auditing Standards (SAS's)

Several Statements on Auditing Standards (SASs) issued by the Auditing Standards Executive Committee (AudSEC) were designed to establish standards of auditor responsibility for various sources of material misstatement in financial statements. Collectively, the SASs explained below form the basis of professional responsibility in this sensitive area. Only the bare essentials of the standards are explained below, so study of the complete statements is recommended.

SAS No. 6 (Section 335)—Related Party Transactions. Several cases involving materially misleading financial statements resulted from corporate officers dealings among themselves, with affiliated companies, with family members, and with shell companies. Transactions included borrowing or lending funds at interest rates below the current market, selling real estate at prices significantly different from its appraised value, exchanging property and making loans with no repayment schedule. *SAS No. 6* specifies procedures for determining the existence of related parties, identifying transactions with related parties, examining the identified transactions, and making appropriate disclosure in the financial statements.

SAS No. 16 (Section 327)—The Independent Auditor's Responsibility for the Detection of Errors or Irregularities. *Errors* are basically defined as unintentional mistakes and *irregularities* refer to intentional distortions of financial statements. Auditors' concerns with these arise from the fact that persons who rely on financial statements look to entities' controls and independent audits to provide reasonable assurance that financial statements are not materially misstated as a result of errors or irregularities.

Under generally accepted auditing standards the independent auditor has the responsibility, within the inherent limitations of the auditing process, to (1) plan the examination to search for errors or irregularities that would have a material effect on the financial statements, and (2) exercise due skill and care in the conduct of that examination. In addition to the procedures the auditor judges appropriate in order to form an opinion on financial statements, extended procedures are required if evidence indicates that material errors or irregularities might exist. *SAS No. 16* goes on to say that an independent auditor's standard report implicitly indicates a belief that the financial statements taken as a whole are not materially misstated as a result of errors or irregularities.

Two terms used above deserve some closer scrutiny and definition. *Reasonable assurance* is a concept that recognizes relative costs and benefits. In terms of internal control (*SAS No. 1*, Section 320.32) the concept of reasonable assurance recognizes that the cost of internal control should not exceed the benefits expected to be derived. The concept, however, is hard to work with because it is hard to measure the costs and benefits involved. In the context of *SAS No. 16*, the injunction to obtain reasonable assurance that financial statements are not materially misstated as a result of errors or irregularities means that diligent effort should be made to obtain evidence, but the auditor is not expected to disregard *all* costs and *all* time constraints and make audits so minutely detailed that they are completed only at great cost after a long delay.

The second term is *inherent limitations of the auditing process*. Like *reasonable assurance* the concept of inherent limitation is based on time and cost considerations. Audits incorporate many tests of samples of transactions. When the audit is anything less than a census examination, there is a risk that material errors or irregularities, if they exist, will not be detected. Another source of inherent limitation is the fact that other persons might lie to the auditor and actively conceal evidence that the auditor can obtain only through their cooperation.

The subsequent discovery that errors or irregularities existed during the period of an audit does not necessarily indicate inadequate performance on the part of the auditor. If the matter goes before outside reviewers (e.g., judge, jury), the determination will be one of deciding whether the substance of *SAS No. 16* standards was observed. Much depends on the reviewers' attitude toward what constitutes due skill and care in the circumstances. Hopefully, reviewers will realize that the auditor should not be expected to serve as an absolute insurer or guarantor.

SAS No. 17* (*Section 328*)—*Illegal Acts by Clients. Many of the corporate disclosures of the mid-1970s involved illegal and "questionable" payments. *SAS No. 17* explains auditors' responsibilities for paying attention to the possibility that illegal acts may have occurred and for reporting them.

An auditor is neither a legal expert nor an administrative enforcement agent. However, auditors should have enough acquaintance with law in general to recognize a questionable act or transaction and seek expert legal advice. This is especially true of financially-related transactions that enter into the accounting system (e.g., income tax transactions, selling prices controlled by legislation or administrative rules). Actions that exist outside the accounting system, such as violation of health and safety laws and pollution control laws, are much less likely to come to the auditor's attention.

SAS No. 17 explains some procedures that may help identify illegal acts by clients. If one is discovered, the auditor is directed to assess its materiality with due regard to possible ramifications. For example, outside knowledge of a relatively small bribe (say $100,000 in a $1 billion-size company) may endanger a large contract, a business license, or the right to operate in a foreign country. Findings should be reported to a high level in the client organization, up to and including the audit committee, for appropriate action and decision about financial statement disclosure.

Depending upon management's decisions on disclosure in the financial statements, the auditor may have to qualify his opinion or give an adverse opinion if an unqualified opinion is not warranted. In some cases where management and directors fail to give the matter proper consideration, the auditor may consider withdrawing from the engagement, because it may be better to withdraw than to continue association with such a client. Auditing standards do not require an auditor to report unresolved questions of illegal acts to persons outside the company (e.g., law enforcement agencies), but an auditor must be careful to be sure that silence does not make him or her a co-conspirator or accessory to a criminal act.

SAS No. 19* (*Section 333*)—*Client Representations. One of the most useful auditing procedures for obtaining evidence is to ask client personnel about a matter under investigation. For example, subjects of inquiries may include questions about related party transactions, collectibility of receivables, obsolescence of inventory, possible litigation and loss contingencies, plans to discontinue a line of business, and a host of others. Ordinarily an auditor can corroborate clients' responses by obtaining evidence from other sources, but in some cases there is no other source (e.g., plans to discontinue a line of business), and in others the corroborating evidence may be very difficult to find (e.g., some kinds of related party transactions). Thus auditors may have to rely on client cooperation in important areas. *SAS No. 19* contains an illustrative list of 20 items about which representations should be obtained.

Important client representations have to be in writing. If management refuses to furnish a written representation that the auditor believes is essential, the scope of the audit is considered limited and a qualified opinion may be appropriate.

SAS No. 20 (Section 323)—Required Communications of Material Weaknesses in Internal Accounting Control. Prior to 1977 most auditors followed a practice of reporting internal control weaknesses to management in a "management letter." This letter was a private communication between auditor and management and was viewed as an additional service to management as a result of the audit. *SAS No. 20* established a *requirement* that auditors report material weaknesses in internal control to senior management and the board of directors or its audit committee.

A "material weakness in internal accounting control" is defined in *SAS No. 1*, Section 320.68 as follows:

> . . . a condition in which the auditor believes the prescribed procedures or the degree of compliance with them does not provide reasonable assurance that errors or irregularities in amounts that would be material in the financial statements being audited would be prevented or detected within a timely period by employees in the normal course of performing their assigned functions.

A report of a material weakness may indicate a violation of the accounting and internal control standards section of the Foreign Corrupt Practices Act of 1977.

The Commission on Auditors' Responsibilities recommended development of public reports on internal control. This recommendation is under study, but *SAS No. 20* does not require public reports. Standards for voluntary public-type internal control reports, however, exist in *SAS No. 1*, Sections 640 and 641. Generally accepted auditing standards as set forth in *SAS No. 20* do not require the auditor to evaluate each and every control feature for the purpose of rendering a report to management. The auditor can evaluate those controls on which reliance is to be placed (in accordance with the second AICPA standard of field work) and is not required to go further.

The purpose of this required communication is to assist management in discharging its primary responsibility for establishing and maintaining a system of internal accounting control. Since internal control is the first line of defense against errors and irregularities, this kind of information is very important to managers and directors. If the auditor does not become aware of any material weaknesses during the audit, this fact may be reported to management but the auditor is not required to do so.

Corporate Policy and Internal Audit

The internal audit department can perform an important role in detecting and preventing fraud, especially when it is functionally independent. Internal auditors can be assigned to tasks such as the following: Review the company's policies regarding questionable payments; investigate compliance with the policies; audit large, abnormal, or unexplained expenditures, especially where higher than normal levels of authority are involved in overriding regular approval controls; audit sensitive expenses like legal fees, consultants' fees, advertising and foreign sales commissions; and audit company contributions that appear to be nonnormal.

Many corporate managements and boards of directors are busy formulating company policy statements on proper business behavior and ethics. They are becoming aware of sensitive areas and trying to institute controls in order to prevent the occurrence of errors, irregularities, and illegal acts. This task is not easy because sometimes it is hard to imagine just what kinds of problems might arise. The checklist shown in Exhibit 4–1 was designed to alert managers to potential problems. The list can also serve as a guide to auditors of conditions that may alert them to be especially careful and alert during an audit.

EXHIBIT 4–1
Danger Signals: A Checklist for Executives and Directors

Some conditions within a company may create an environment in which fraudulent or irregular practices are more likely to occur. The presence of any combination of the following conditions should alert directors and executives to the need for corrective action:

Tight credit, high interest rates, and reduced ability to acquire credit.

Pressure to finance expansion via current earnings rather than through equity or debt.

A profit squeeze as a result of sales and revenues not having kept pace with increasing costs and expenses.

The need for additional collateral to support existing obligations.

Significant reduction in sales order backlog, heralding a future sales decline.

A cash shortage, negative cash flow, or lack of sufficient working capital and/or credit to continue the business.

Difficulties in collection of accounts receivable from classes of customers who may be experiencing severe economic pressures, e.g., energy-dependent businesses and real estate investment trusts.

Massive demands for new capital in a developing industry and/or unusually heavy competition.

EXHIBIT 4–1 (*continued*)

Dependence for success on a single product or a small number of products, customers, or transactions.

A declining industry or one characterized by a large number of business failures.

Competition from low-priced imports.

Excess capacity due to economic or other conditions such as energy shortages.

Existing loan agreements, with little flexibility in their working-capital ratios, limits on additional debt, and the terms of the payment schedule.

Existence of revocable (and possibly imperiled) licenses necessary for continuation of the business.

Management tendency to exert extreme pressure on executives to meet budgets.

Urgent desire to maintain a continued favorable earnings record in the hope of supporting the price of the company's stock.

Reluctance by management to provide additional information to improve the clarity and comprehensiveness of the company's financial statements.

Numerous acquisitions of speculative ventures in pursuit of diversification.

Significant inventories and other assets that require special expertise for valuation.

A long manufacturing cycle, which may have an adverse impact when costs are rising and products have to be sold at fixed prices or in competitive markets.

Unusually rapid expansion of product lines.

Significant danger of product obsolescence in a high-technology industry.

Sizable inventory increases without comparable sales increases.

Progressive deterioration in the "quality" of earnings, e.g., adoption of straight-line depreciation to replace sum-of-the-years'-digits depreciation without good reason.

Existence of significant litigation, especially between shareholders and management.

Suspension or delisting from a stock exchange.

Significant tax adjustments by the IRS, especially when they occur with some regularity.

Unmarketable collateral.

Executives with records of malfeasance.

Source: Reprinted from the *Coopers & Lybrand Newsletter*, published by Coopers & Lybrand, April 1977, p. 4.

LIABILITY UNDER COMMON LAW

Legal liabilities of professional accountants may arise from lawsuits brought on the basis of the law of contracts or as a tort action for negligence. Breach of contract is a claim that the contract was not performed in the manner agreed upon, and this basis is most characteristic of lawsuits involving the accountant and the client. Tort actions cover civil complaints other than breach of contract, including fraud, deceit, and injury.

Suits for civil damages under common law usually result when someone suffers a financial loss after relying upon audited financial statements that are later found to be materially misleading. However, legal liability may also arise between accountants and their clients for breach of contract and tort in connection with tax practice and management advisory services practice. As the legal liability exposure of accountants and auditors is considered, bear in mind that clients also have duties and responsibilities in the accountant-client relationship, and thus the dimensions of liability do not run entirely in the accountant's direction.

Characteristics of Common Law Actions

When an injured party considers himself damaged by an accountant and brings a lawsuit, he generally asserts all possible causes of action, including breach of contract, tort, deceit, fraud, and whatever else may be relevant to his claim. Actions brought under common law place most of the burdens of affirmative proof on the plaintiff, who must prove (1) that he was damaged or suffered a loss, (2) that the financial statements were materially misleading or the accountant's advice was faulty, (3) that he relied upon the statements or advice and that they were the proximate cause of his loss, and (4) that the accountant was negligent, grossly negligent, deceitful, or otherwise responsible for unlawful behavior. The defendant accountant, on the other hand, must offer evidence to mitigate or refute the plaintiff's claims and evidence. In a subsequent section dealing with the securities acts, one sees how the statutes shift some of these burdens of affirmative proof to the professional accountant.

Clients may bring a lawsuit for breach of contract. The relationship of direct involvement between parties to a contract is known as *privity*. When privity exists, it is usually sufficient for a plaintiff to show that the defendant accountant was negligent. (*Ordinary negligence*—a lack of reasonable care in the performance of professional accounting tasks—is usually meant when the word *negligent* stands alone.) If negligence is proved, the accountant may be liable, provided that the client has not been involved in some sort of contributory negligence in the dispute.

Fifty years ago it was very difficult for parties other than contracting clients to succeed in lawsuits against auditors. Other parties are not in privity, so they had no cause of action for breach of contract. However, the court opinion in the case known as *Ultramares* (Appendix 4–A) expressed the view that if negligence were so great as to constitute *gross negligence*—lack of even minimum care in performing professional duties, indicating reckless disregard for duty and responsibility—there might be grounds for concluding that the accountant had engaged in *constructive fraud.* Actual fraud is characterized as positive and intentional acts entered into with intent to deprive someone else of a right or to do an injury. Constructive fraud, however, may not have the elements of being positive and intentional, but the result is the same—to deprive or injure another unsuspecting party. Fraud is a basis for liability in tort, so parties not in privity with the accountant may have causes of action. These other parties—primary beneficiaries, actual foreseen and limited classes of persons, and all other injured parties—are discussed next.

Primary beneficiaries are third parties for whose primary benefit the audit or other accounting service is performed. Such a beneficiary will be identified to or reasonably foreseeable by the accountant prior to or during the engagement, and the accountant will know that his work will influence the primary beneficiary's decisions. For example, an auditor may be informed that his report is needed for a bank loan application at the First National Bank. Recent cases indicate that proof of ordinary negligence may be sufficient to make accountants liable for damages to primary beneficiaries.

Accountants may also be liable to parties other than known primary beneficiaries such as creditors, investors, or potential investors who rely on accountants' work. If the accountant is reasonably able to *foresee* a limited class of potential users of his work (for example, local banks, regular suppliers), liability may be imposed for ordinary negligence. This, however, is an uncertain area, and liability in a particular case depends entirely on the unique facts and circumstances.

However, beneficiaries of the types mentioned above and all other injured parties may recover damages if they are able to show that the accountant was grossly negligent and perpetrated a constructive fraud. Several significant American common law cases are briefed in Appendix 4–A. Each of these cases carries some weight of precedent that is relevant to modern auditing practice.

Typical Lawsuits

While lawsuits can be enumerated and identified for study, one must recognize that thousands of accounting engagements are performed without any kind of legal conflict. The exposure to examples of court cases and lawsuits is useful as a learning device, but these cases represent a small segment of activity among the daily activities of accountants.

In a study conducted in the mid-1960s, Bakay surveyed the claims files of two U.S. companies that write professional liability insurance for small practice accountants. (Large firms carry insurance with Lloyd's of London and were not included in the survey.) Approximately half the claims for the period surveyed were on accounting, auditing, and general practice actions. The other half were over tax practice issues such as late filings that resulted in penalties and interest and tax advice that proved to be costly.

Of the 96 accounting-auditing claims reviewed 32 concerned undiscovered defalcations, 17 were countersuits against suits brought by accountants for fees, 9 were in connection with buy-sell engagements, 8 concerned alleged defamation, 9 concerned alleged overstatement of owners' equity, 6 were over accountants' bad investment advice, and 15 others involved bookkeeping errors, divorce settlement disagreements, improper legal advice, and loss of the client's books. In many cases the controversy arose out of a misunderstanding of the terms, nature, and scope of the engagement, and in several cases it was apparent that claimants were just trying to find a scapegoat for their own bad business judgment.

Some general and specific lessons can be gleaned from this survey: Have a clear understanding with the client about the accountant's responsibility with regard to discovery of defalcations. Don't sue for an unpaid fee until all the facts and circumstances are reviewed, and the work is believed to have been acceptable. Obtain a written engagement letter specifying the terms, nature, and scope of the work. Don't venture into areas of investment advice or legal advice when competence is lacking.

Bakay's report of the survey also yielded the following examples which illustrate the role of ethical decision problems that may precede legal difficulties.

> ***Illustration.*** The president of the claimant company used company funds for personal expenditures without the knowledge of other board members. The auditor was convinced by the president that the funds would be repaid, and he was persuaded not to mention the "borrowing" in his report.

> ***Illustration.*** The accountant knew that $26,000 of receivables reflected in an unaudited report had been assigned to a factor because he had helped to arrange the assignment. The report did not disclose the assignment.

> ***Illustration.*** The auditor accepted the statement of management regarding valuation of its receivables and the underlying security without independent confirmation. The receivables were the most important asset to be examined.

> ***Illustration.*** The accountant who prepared financial statements for a business which later became bankrupt was a member of the board of directors, treasurer, minority stockholder, and a creditor of the business.

RELATIONSHIPS UNDER STATUTORY LAW

Several federal statutes provide sources of potential liability for accountants, among them the following: Federal False Statements Statute, Federal Mail Fraud Statute, Federal Conspiracy Statute, Securities Act of 1933, and Securities and Exchange Act of 1934. The securities acts contain provisions defining certain civil and criminal liabilities of accountants. Because a significant segment of accounting practice is under the jurisdiction of the securities acts, the following discussion will concentrate on duties and liabilities under these laws. First, however, some familiarity with the scope and function of the securities acts and the Securities and Exchange Commission (SEC) is necessary.

Federal securities regulation in the United States was enacted in 1933 not only as a reaction to the events of the early years of the Great Depression and in the spirit of the New Deal era but also as a culmination of attempts at regulation by the states over many years. The Securities Act of 1933 and the Securities and Exchange Act of 1934 are statutes that require disclosure of all information required for an informed investment decision. No government agency, including the SEC, rules on the quality of the underlying investment. The law has been characterized as "truth in securities" law, and the spirit of the law favors the otherwise uninformed investing public, while *caveat vendor* applies to the issuer (i.e., let the *seller* beware of violations).

The 1933 act was first administered by the Federal Trade Commission until the SEC was created in 1934. Presently the SEC administers the 1933 and 1934 acts, the Public Utility Holding Company Act of 1935, the Trust Indenture Act of 1939, the Investment Company Act of 1940, and the Investment Advisers Act of 1940. The latter four laws are fairly specialized in their applicability and so are not considered further in this text. The SEC also has important functions under the Securities Investor Protection Act of 1970 (amending the Securities Exchange Act of 1934), serves as advisor to federal courts in proceedings under Chapter X of the National Bankruptcy Act, and has duties under section 851 of the Internal Revenue Code (relating to investment companies).

Regulation of Accountants and Accounting

Like other government agencies, the SEC has promulgated rules governing the conduct of persons practicing before it. (Rule 2.01 relative to auditor independence appeared in Chapter 3.) Rules are found in Article 2 of *Regulation S–X,* which is the compendium of accounting rules and regulations. In addition the SEC has released a body of Rules of Practice of which Rule 2 relates to appearance and practice before the commission. Thus one of the first ways an accountant may suffer penalty is under administrative-rule stemming from securities law.

Rule of Practice 2(*e*) provides that the commission may deny, temporarily or permanently, the privilege of practice before the commission (i.e., signing any documents filed) to any person found (1) not to possess the requisite qualifications to represent others, or (2) to be lacking in character or integrity or to have engaged in unethical or improper professional conduct, or (3) to have violated willfully any provision of the federal securities laws or their rules and regulations. Amendments in 1971 strengthened the commission's powers of regulation by providing for censure or disqualification of accountants and other experts who have been permanently enjoined from violating the laws or rules, regardless of whether the accountant consented to the injunction with or without admitting the facts. A full trial and judgment is not required because the commission is authorized to act in a quasi-judicial manner, but its decisions are tempered by hearing the facts and by whether a violation was willfully committed. Numerous cases of discipline of accountants are, however, in evidence.

Section 19 of the 1933 act and Section 13 of the 1934 act give the commission power to set accounting principles and rules. For the most part, however, the SEC has deferred this power to the organized accounting profession, except for a few cases. The fact that the SEC does not frequently promulgate principles should not be misinterpreted to mean that the SEC is inactive. There is, in fact, great cooperation between the AICPA, FASB, and SEC during the process of formulating principles and standards. When an official body (e.g., FASB, Auditing Standards Board) is considering an official pronouncement, a meeting is generally held with SEC staff to obtain indications of agreement or disapproval. If disapproval is the result, the professional body generally incorporates changes, but there have been cases of pronouncements being contrary to SEC views.

Accounting Series Release No. 4 (1938) expresses the profession-SEC environment of the force and effect of accounting principles. Apparently, it is still a good guide today. The major points are these:

> 1. When financial statements filed with the commission are prepared according to principles that have no authoritative support, they will be *presumed to be misleading. Other disclosures or footnotes will not cure this presumption.*
> 2. When financial statements involve a principle on which the commission disagrees, but has promulgated no explicit rules or regulations, and the principle has substantial authoritative support, *then supplementary disclosures will be accepted in lieu of correction of the statements.*
> 3. When financial statements involve a principle that (1) has authoritative support in general, but (2) the commission has ruled against its use, then the statements will be *presumed misleading. Supplementary disclosures will not cure this presumption.*[1]

An auditor therefore must be thoroughly familiar not only with generally accepted accounting principles but also with the principles that have been formally disapproved by the commission. The SEC issues Staff Accounting Bulletins (SABs) to inform practitioners about how the staff treats various detailed accounting matters. The SABs are like "interpretations" of *Regulation S-X.*

In comparison to the matters of accounting principles, the SEC's involvement in auditing standards and procedural matters has been minimal since the developments of the McKesson and Robbins affair (see Appendix 4-A). In brief, following an investigation of the McKesson case, the SEC ruled that auditors' reports must state that an examination must be in accordance with "generally accepted auditing standards." At that time (1938) the ten standards had not been officially promulgated by the AICPA. They were written and adopted soon afterwards.

Regulation of Securities Sales and Trading

For the most part the 1933 act regulates the issue of securities, and the 1934 act regulates trading in securities. Section 5 of the 1933 act provides that no person may lawfully buy, sell, offer to buy, or offer to sell any security by the means of interstate commerce unless a registration statement meeting the requirements of Sections 7 and 10 is in effect. This

---

[1] *Accounting Series Release No. 150* (1973) affirmed that pronouncements of the FASB will be considered to constitute substantial authoritative support of accounting principles standards and practices. Other sources of authoritative support are enumerated in *SAS No. 5*. (See discussion in Chapter 1 of this textbook.)

EXHIBIT 4–2

FORM S–1: GENERAL REGISTRATION STATEMENT

This is the form most commonly used to register securities under the 1933 act. A brief indication of the scope and content of a registration statement on Form S–1 is indicated by the following listing of the items of information required to be included in the form.

Part I. Information Required in the Prospectus:

Item 1. Offering price information and distribution spread.
Item 2. Plan of distribution, names of underwriters and their participations, and nature of the underwriters' obligation.
Item 3. Use of proceeds to registrant.
Item 4. Sales of securities otherwise than for cash.
Item 5. Capital structure.
Item 6. Summary of earnings.
Item 7. State and date of incorporation and type of organization of the registrant.
Item 8. Parents of the registrant and basis of control.
Item 9. Description of the business and its development during the past five years. This is the item which requires disclosure in certain cases of information with respect to principal lines of business, ...
Item 10. Description and location of principal plants, mines, and other physical properties.
Item 11. If organized within five years, names of and transactions with promoters.
Item 12. Pending legal proceedings other than routine litigation.
Items 13. 14, and 15. Information as to capital stock, funded debt, or other securities being registered.
Item 16. Names of directors and executive officers and the principal occupations of the latter during the past five years.
Item 17. Remuneration paid by the affiliated group during latest fiscal year to (1) each director, and each of the three highest paid officers, of the registrant who received more than $30,000, and (2) all directors and officers as a group.
Item 18. Outstanding options to purchase securities from the registrant or subsidiaries.
Item 19. Principal holders of registrant's securities.
Item 20. Interest of directors, officers, and certain other persons in certain material transactions during last three years or in any proposed transactions.
Item 21. Financial statements.

Part II. Information Not Required in the Prospectus:

Item 22. Arrangements limiting, restricting, or stabilizing the market for securities being offered.
Item 23. Expenses of the issue.
Item 24. Relationship with registrant of experts named in the registration statement (including accountants).
Item 25. Sales of securities to special parties.

EXHIBIT 4–2 (*continued*)

Item 26.	Recent sales of unregistered securities.
Item 27.	List of subsidiaries of the registrant.
Item 28.	Franchises or concessions held by the registrant and subsidiaries.
Item 29.	Indemnification arrangements for officers and directors.
Item 30.	Accounting for proceeds from sale of capital stock being registered.
Item 31.	List of financial statements and exhibits.

Source: Louis H. Rappaport. *SEC Accounting Practice and Procedure*, Third Edition, copyright © 1972, The Ronald Press Company. Reprinted by permission of John Wiley & Sons, Inc.

prohibition should be interpreted literally: *No person* can *buy or sell any security* by the means of *interstate commerce* (i.e., telephone, highway, national bank), unless a registration statement is in effect.

Section 5 is all-encompassing, but Sections 3 and 4 offer exemptions. In general Section 3 exempts government securities, charitable and eleemosynary institutions, securities of business subject to regulation by the ICC, a number of other relatively uncommon securities, and wholly intrastate issues of any security. Section 3 also exempts issues of $1.5 million[2] or less (referring to a cumulative total, generally over two years). Section 4 exempts certain specified *transactions*, principally any transaction *not* involving a "public offering," and transactions by any person who is *not* an issuer, underwriter, or dealer (e.g., the small investor).

The general point relevant to most auditors about applicability of the 1933 act is that *all* sales must be registered, except those exempted by Sections 3 and 4. One fine point of the law is that *offerings* are registered, but specific securities are not. This means that a corporation that holds treasury stock or a large shareholder (10 percent or more) must consult the law before selling. Even if the shares held were acquired pursuant to an earlier registration, subsequent sales may have to be registered anew.

A registration statement must be filed and must be *effective* before a sale is lawful. On the basis of Sections 7 and 10 of the 1933 act, the SEC adopted a series of forms for use in registrations. There are several forms in the "S" series, most of them applicable to special situations, but the most commonly used form is S–1, the general form. The form is not a set of blank pages to fill in, but a list of items of disclosure to include. The scope and content of an S–1 form is shown in Exhibit 4–2. Part I, the prospectus, is the section that must be distributed to the public in order to make an offer lawful. Parts I and II taken together constitute the complete registration statement.

The sequence of events preceding closing of a sale is shown in Exhibit 4–3. The relative duties and time periods hold great significance for auditors.

The 1934 act primarily regulates daily trading in securities and re-

[2] This limit is subject to legislative change. The $1.5 million limit was enacted in 1978.

EXHIBIT 4–3
Sequence of Events in Registration Process

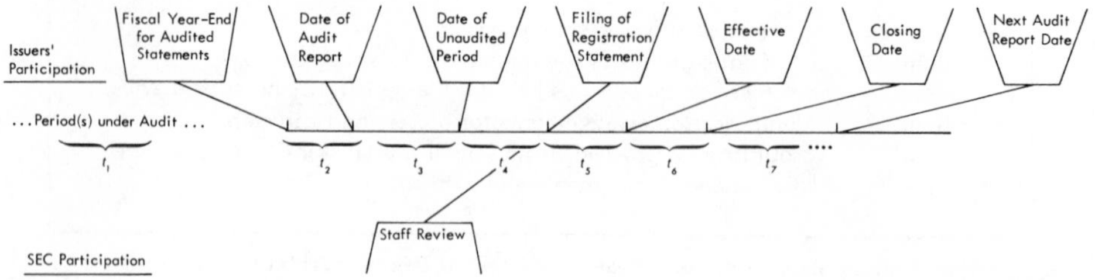

The time periods indicated by t are:

t_1 The periods under audit and covered by the auditor's opinion.

t_2 The period subsequent to the balance sheet date for which the auditor has responsibility for discovery and disclosure of significant subsequent information in all audits whether involving a registration or not.

t_3 plus period t_2 is the period exhibited by *unaudited* financial statements with which the auditor is "associated."

t_4 The brief time period required for printing of the registration statement.

t_5 The period of review. Generally the effective date is 30 days or less after the filing date unless amendments are required. The auditors' responsibility for disclosure of significant events subsequent to the balance sheet date extends over $t_2 + t_3 + t_4 + t_5$ to the effective date.

t_6 The actual sale date follows the effective date by only a few days.

t_7 plus periods t_6, t_5, t_4, and t_3 is the time after issuance of an audit opinion during which the auditor is responsible for disclosing information that *may come to his attention.* The degree of care and requirements for examination are significantly lesser in t_7 than in prior time periods t_3, t_4, and t_5.

quires registration of most securities traded in interstate commerce. All issuers having total assets of $1 million or more and a class of securities holders of 500 or more persons are required to register under the 1934 act. The purpose of these size and number criteria is to define securities in which there is a significant public interest.

For auditors and accountants the most significant aspect of the 1934 act is the requirement for annual reports, quarterly reports, and periodic special reports. Respectively these reports are referred to by the form numbers 10–K, 10–Q, and 8–K. A company's regular annual report to shareholders may be filed as a part of the 10–K to provide part or all of the information required by law. This ability to use the regular annual report coupled with the fact that 10–K filings are public documents has greatly influenced the content of corporate reports disseminated directly to the public. The 10–Q quarterly report is filed after each of the first three fiscal year quarters, and its contents are largely financial statement information. Form 8–K, the "current events report," is required whenever certain significant events occur, such as changes in control, legal proceedings, and changes in accounting principles.

One of the events considered significant for an 8–K report is a change of auditors. When there is a change of auditors, the registrant must report the fact and state whether in the past 18 months there had been any disagreement with the auditors concerning matters of accounting principles, financial statement disclosure, or auditing procedure. At the same time, the former auditor must submit a letter stating whether he agrees with the explanation as offered by the registrant, and if he disagrees, give particulars. These documents are available to the public on request and their purpose is to make available information about client-auditor conflicts that might have a bearing on financial presentations and consequent investment decisions. This information item was first required in 1971. Through April 1976, 1,667 companies had reported changing auditors, and 165 companies reported disagreements. These disagreements included disputes over recoverability of asset cost, revenue recognition timing, expense recognition timing, amounts to be reported as liabilities, and necessity for certain auditing procedures.

Other sections of the 1934 act regulate trading by requiring distribution of proxy material and reports of trading by insiders.

Liability Provisions: Securities Act of 1933

Section 11 of the 1933 act is of great interest to auditors because it alters significantly the duties and responsibilities otherwise required by common law. This section contains the principal criteria defining civil liabilities under the statute. Portions of Section 11 pertinent to auditors' liability are extracted below:

> Sec. 11(a) . . . any person acquiring such security [in a registered offering] . . . may sue
>
> Every person who signed the registration statement.
> Every person who was a director of . . . or partner in, the issuer.
> Every accountant, engineer, or appraiser.
> Every underwriter with respect to such security.
>
> If such person acquired the security after the issuer has made generally available to its security holders an earning statement covering a period of at least 12 months beginning after the effective date of the registration statement, then the right of recovery . . . shall be conditioned on proof that such person acquired the security relying upon . . . the registration statement. . . .
>
> Sec. 11(b) Notwithstanding the provisions of subsection (a) no person, other than the issuer, shall be liable as provided therein who shall sustain the burden of proof . . .
>
> that (A) as regards any part of the registration statement *not purporting to be made on the authority of an expert,* . . . he had, after reasonable investigation, reasonable ground to believe . . . that the statements therein were true and that there was no omission to state a material fact . . .
>
> and (B) as regards any part of the registration statement *purporting to be made upon his authority as an expert* . . . he had, after reasonable in-

vestigation, reasonable ground to believe . . . that the statements therein were true and that there was no omission to state a material fact . . .

and (C) as regards any part of the registration statement *purporting to be made on the authority of an expert (other than himself)* . . . he had no reasonable ground to believe . . . that the statements therein were untrue or that there was an omission to state a material fact. . . .

Sec. 11(c) In determining, for the purpose of . . . subsection (b) of this section, what constitutes reasonable investigation and reasonable ground for belief, the standard of reasonableness shall be that required of a prudent man in the management of his own property. . . .

Sec. 11(e) . . . if the defendant proves that any portion or all of such damages [claimed in a lawsuit] represents other than the depreciation in value of such security resulting from such part of the registration statement, with respect to which his liability is asserted, not being true or omitting to state a material fact required to be stated therein . . . such portion of or all such damages shall not be recoverable.

The effect of Section 11 of the statute is to shift the major burdens of affirmative proof from the injured plaintiff to the expert accountant. Recall that under the common law, the *plaintiff* had to allege and prove misleading statements, reliance, proximate cause, damages, negligence, and close relationship (e.g., privity, third-party beneficiary). Under Section 11 the plaintiff still has to show that he or she was damaged and has to allege and show proof that financial statements in the registration statement were materially misleading, but here the plaintiff's duties are essentially ended. Exhibit 4–4 summarizes these common law and statutory duties.

The plaintiff does not have to be in privity with the auditor. Section 11 provides that *any purchaser* may sue the accountant. The purchaser-plaintiff does not have to prove that he or she relied on the financial statements in the registration statement. In fact, the purchaser may not have even read them.[3] Neither does the purchaser have to show that the misleading statements caused him or her to make an unwise decision and thus suffer a consequent loss.

Section 11 was written with the protection of the investing public in mind, not the protection of the expert auditor. The first significant court case under Section 11 was *Escott et al.* v. *BarChris Construction Corp. et al.* (Refer to Appendix 4–B.) The ruling in this case was that the auditors did not conduct a reasonable investigation and thus did not satisfy Section 11(b)(B).

Section 13 of the 1933 act defines the statute of limitations in such a way that suit is barred if not brought within one year after discovery of the misleading statement or omission, or in any event if not brought within three years after the public offering. These limitations and the reliance

[3] This matter of reliance is modified by Section 11(a) to the extent that when enough time has elapsed *and* the registrant has filed an income statement covering a 12-month period beginning after the effective date, then the plaintiff must prove that he or she purchased after that time in reliance on the registration statement. However, the plaintiff may prove reliance without proof of actually having read the registration statement.

EXHIBIT 4–4
Comparison of Common Law and Statutory Litigation

Under Common Law	*Under 1933 Act Section 11*	*Under 1934 Act Section 18*
Plaintiff proves damages or loss and necessary privity or beneficiary relationship.	Plaintiff proves damages or loss, but any purchaser may sue the accountant.	Plaintiff proves damages or loss, but any purchaser or seller may sue the accountant.
Plaintiff alleges, shows evidence, and the court decides whether financial statements were misleading.	Same	Same
Plaintiff proves he relied on the misleading statements, and they were the proximate cause of his loss.	Proof of purchaser's reliance not required unless a 12-month earnings statement had been issued.	Same as common law.
Plaintiff proves the requisite degree of negligence by the accountant.	Accountant must prove he performed a reasonable investigation (due diligence).*	Accountant must prove he acted in good faith and did not know the statements were misleading.

* Upon failing to prove due diligence, the accountant may try to prove that plaintiff's loss was caused by something other than the misleading financial statements (the *causation* defense).

limitation mentioned in footnote 3 restrict auditors' liability exposure to a determinable time span.

Section 11 also states the means by which the auditor can prove himself or herself not liable. Section 11(b) enunciates what is known as the "due diligence" defense. If the auditor can prove that a *reasonable* examination was performed, then the auditor is not liable for damages. Section 11(c) states the standard of reasonableness to be that degree of care required of a prudent person in the management of his own property. In a context more specific to the auditor, a reasonable investigation would be shown by the conduct of an audit in accordance with generally accepted auditing standards in both form and substance.

Section 11(b) also gives a diligence defense standard for portions of a registration statement made on the authority of an expert. Any person who relies upon an "expert" is not required to conduct a reasonable investigation of his own, but only to have no reasonable grounds for disbelief. Thus the auditor who relies on the opinion of an actuary or engineer need not make a personal independent investigation of that expert's area. Similarly, any officer, director, attorney, or underwriter connected with a registration has a far lesser diligence duty respecting any information that is covered by the auditor's expert opinion. In the *BarChris* judgment officers, directors, attorneys, and underwriters were found lacking in diligence *except* with respect to audited financial statements.

Section 11(e) defines the last line of defense available to an auditor when lack of diligence has been proved. This defense is known as the "causation defense." Essentially, if the auditor can prove that the plaintiff's damages (all or part) resulted from something other than the misleading and negligently prepared registration statement, then all or part of the damages will not have to be paid. This defense may create some imaginative "other reasons." In the *BarChris* case at least one plaintiff had purchased securities *after* the company had gone bankrupt. The presumption that the loss in this instance resulted from events other than the misleading registration statement is fair, but this claim was settled out of court, so there is no judicial determination for reference.

Section 17 of the 1933 act is the antifraud section. The wording and intent of this section is practically identical to Section 10(b) and Rule 10(b)(5) under the 1934 act which give accountants and others liability exposure. The difference between the two acts is the 1933 act reference to "offer or sale" and the 1934 act reference to "use of securities exchanges." The pertinent portion of Section 17 is as follows:

> Section 17. (a) It shall be unlawful for any person in the offer or sale of any securities by the use of any means or instruments of transportation in interstate commerce or by the use of the mails, directly or indirectly—(1) to employ any device, scheme, or artifice to defraud, or (2) to obtain money or property by means of any untrue statement of a material fact or any omission to state a material fact . . . (3) to engage in any transaction, practice, or course of business which operates or would operate as a fraud or deceit upon the purchaser.

Section 24 sets forth the criminal penalties imposed by the 1933 act. Criminal penalties are characterized by monetary fines and/or prison terms. The key words in Section 24 are *willful* violation and *willfully* causing misleading statements to be filed.

> Section 24. Any person who willfully violates any of the provisions of this title, or the rules and regulations promulgated by the commission under authority thereof, or any person who willfully, in a registration statement filed under this title, makes any untrue statement of a material fact or omits to state any material fact required to be stated therein or necessary to make the statements therein not misleading, shall upon conviction be fined not more than $5,000 or imprisoned not more than five years, or both.

Liability Provisions: Securities and Exchange Act of 1934

Section 10 of the 1934 act is being used against accountants with increasing frequency. Like Section 17 of the 1933 act, Section 10 is a general antifraud section. The law itself reveals Section 10(b) as follows:

> Section 10. It shall be unlawful for any person, directly or indirectly, by use of any means or instrumentality of interstate commerce or of the mails,

> or of any facility of any national securities exchange—. . . (b) to use or employ, in connection with the purchase or sale of any security registered on a national securities exchange or any security not so registered, any manipulative or deceptive device or contrivance in contravention of such rules and regulations as the commission may prescribe as necessary or appropriate in the public interest or for the protection of investors.

Rule 10b–5, which is equally as actionable as the statute itself, is more explicit. The rule is quoted below:

> *Rule 10b–5. Employment of Manipulative and Deceptive Devices.* It shall be unlawful for any person, directly or indirectly, by the use of any means of instrumentality of interstate commerce, or of the mails, or of any facility of any national securities exchange,
>
> (1) To employ any device, scheme, or artifice to defraud,
>
> (2) To make any untrue statement of a material fact or to omit to state a material fact necessary in order to make the statements made, in the light of the circumstances under which they were made, not misleading, or
>
> (3) To engage in any act, practice, or course of business which operates or would operate as a fraud or deceit upon any person in connection with the purchase or sale of any security.

The *Hochfelder* decision (Appendix 4–B) explains this section more fully.

Section 18 sets forth the pertinent civil liability definition under the 1934 act as follows:

> Section 18. (a) Any person who shall make or cause to be made any statement . . . which . . . was at the time and in the light of the circumstances under which it was made false or misleading with respect to any material fact shall be liable to any person (not knowing that such statement was false or misleading) who, in reliance upon such statement, shall have purchased or sold a security at a price which was affected by such statement, for damages caused by such reliance, unless the person sued shall prove that he acted in good faith and had no knowledge that such statement was false or misleading.

Under Section 18 an auditor may be liable to both purchasers and sellers of securities. (Recall that under Section 11 of the 1933 act liability was only to purchasers.) Consequently, an overly conservative bias to the extent of misinformation may harm a seller and give him or her a cause of action. No such suit to challenge the accountants' traditional conservatism has ever been brought, so the bastion of conservatism remains intact to date.

Interestingly, under Section 18, a plaintiff has to prove reliance on misleading statements and damages caused thereby—the same requirement as under common law. As a defense the auditor must then prove action in good faith and no knowledge of the misleading statement. This requirement appears to be the *Ultramares* rule written into statute, to the extent that proving good faith is equivalent to showing that any negligence was no greater than ordinary negligence. (The *Ultramares* decision is reviewed in Appendix 4–A.)

Section 32 states the criminal penalties for violation of the 1934 act. Like Section 24 of the 1933 act, the critical test is whether the violator acted "willfully and knowingly." The defendant accountants in the *Continental Vending* case (*U.S.* v. *Simon*) and in *U.S.* v. *Natelli* discussed in Appendix 4–B were charged with violation of Section 32.

> Section 32. (a) Any person who willfully violates any provision of this title, or any rule or regulation thereunder . . . or any person who willfully and knowingly makes, or causes to be made, any statement . . . which . . . was false or misleading with respect to any material fact, shall upon conviction be fined not more than $10,000, or imprisoned not more than two years, or both . . . but no person shall be subject to imprisonment under this section for the violation of any rule or regulation if he proves that he had no knowledge of such rule or regulation.

To the credit of the accounting profession, litigation under the securities acts has not been widespread when considered in the light of many thousands of documents filed with the SEC. Nevertheless, the suits that have gone to trial have resulted in judgments rich with many implications for practice and laden with portents of the judicial atmosphere of the future. Several of these cases are briefed in Appendix 4–B. Exhibit 4–5 below summarizes the liability sections of the 1933 and 1934 acts.

EXHIBIT 4–5
Summary of Securities Acts Liability Sections

	1933 Act	*1934 Act*
Financial statement liability	Section 11	Section 18
Fraud liability	Section 17	Section 10, Rule 10b–5
Criminal liability	Section 24	Section 32

EXTENT OF LIABILITY

Auditing students may be interested in knowing about *who* suffers exposure and penalties in lawsuits—the accounting firm, partners, managers, senior accountants, staff assistants, or all of these? Most lawsuits center attention on the accounting firm and on the partners and managers involved in the audit or other accounting work. However, court opinions have cited the work of senior accountants, and there is no reason that the work of new staff assistant accountants should not come under review. All persons involved in professional accounting work are exposed to potential liability.

Statement on Auditing Standards No. 22. (Section 311.12) entitled "Planning and Supervision," however, offers some important thoughts for accountants who question the validity of some of the work. Accountants can express their own positions and let the working paper records show the nature of the disagreement and the resolution of the question. *SAS No.* 22 expresses the appropriate action as follows:

The auditor with final responsibility for the examination and assistants should be aware of the procedures to be followed when differences of opinion concerning accounting and auditing issues exist among firm personnel involved in the examination. Such procedures should enable an assistant to document his disagreement with the conclusions reached if, after appropriate consultation, he believes it necessary to disassociate himself from the resolution of the matter. In this situation, the basis for the final resolution should also be documented.

SOURCES AND ADDITIONAL READING REFERENCES

"AICPA Brief in Natelli-Scansaroli," *Journal of Accountancy*, May 1975, pp. 69–76.

"AICPA-NYSSCPA Brief in 1136 Tenants' Corporation Case," *Journal of Accountancy*, March 1971, pp. 57–73.

Bakay, Virginia H. "A Review of Selected Claims against Public Accountants," *Journal of Accountancy*, May 1970, pp. 54–58.

Causey, Denzil Y. *Duties and Liabilities of the CPA*, rev. ed. Austin: Bureau of Business Research, The University of Texas at Austin, 1976.

_____. "Foreseeability as a Determinant of Audit Responsibility," *Accounting Review*, April 1973, pp. 258–67.

_____. "Newly Emerging Standards of Auditor Responsibility," *The Accounting Review*, January 1976, pp. 19–30.

Chazen, C., and Solomon, K. I. "The Art of Defensive Auditing," *Journal of Accountancy*, October 1975, pp. 66–71.

"The Continental Vending Case," *Journal of Accountancy*, November 1968, pp. 54–62.

"Continental Vending Decision Affirmed," *Journal of Accountancy*, February 1970, pp. 61–69.

Dunfee, T. W., and Gleim, I. N. "Criminal Liability of Accountants: Sources and Policies," *American Business Law Journal*, Spring 1971, pp. 1–20.

Isbell, David B. "The Continental Vending Case: Lessons for the Profession," *Journal of Accountancy*, August 1970, pp. 33–40.

_____, and Carmichael, D. R. "Disclaimers and Liability—The Rhode Island Trust Case," *Journal of Accountancy*, April 1973, pp. 37–42.

"McKesson & Robbins, Inc.: Summary of Findings and Conclusions of the SEC," *Journal of Accountancy*, January 1941, pp. 90–95. Also SEC *Accounting Series Release No. 19*, December 1940.

Mautz, R. K., and Neumann, F. L. *Corporate Audit Committees: Policies and Practices*. Cleveland: Ernst & Ernst, 1977.

Olson, Norman O. "The Auditor in Legal Difficulty—What's the Answer?" *Journal of Accountancy*, April 1970, pp. 39–44.

"1136 Tenants' Corporation—Decision of the Appellate Division of the Supreme Court of the State of New York," *Journal of Accountancy*, November 1971, pp. 67–73.

"Rappaport, Louis H. *SEC Accounting Practice and Procedures*, 3d ed. New York: Ronald Press, 1972.

"Report of the Special Committee on Equity Funding." New York: AICPA, 1975.

Saxe, Emanuel. "Unaudited Financial Statements: Rules, Risks, and Recommendations," *CPA Journal*, June 1972, pp. 457–64.

Securities and Exchange Commission. "In the Matter of Peat, Marwick, Mitchell & Co." *Accounting Series Release No. 173.* July 2, 1975.

Slavin, Nathan S. "The Elimination of 'Scienter' in Determining Auditors' Statutory Liability," *The Accounting Review*, April 1977, pp. 360–68.

Solomon, K. I., and Muller, H. "Illegal Payments: Where the Auditor Stands," *Journal of Accountancy*, January 1977, pp. 51–58.

Stoppleman, John S. "Accountants and Rule 10b-5: After Hochfelder," *Journal of Accountancy*, August 1977, pp. 49–54.

Wade, Allison. "Launching a Stock Registration—A Joint Accountant-Attorney Effort to Lead the Client through the Maze," *CPA Journal*, April 1972, pp. 279–87, and May 1972, pp. 399–402.

Whalen, Richard J. "The Big Skid at Yale Express," *Fortune*, November 1965, pp. 144–49.

Williams, Harold M. "Audit Committees—The Public Sector's View," *Journal of Accountancy*, September 1977, pp. 71–75.

REVIEW QUESTIONS

4.1. What similarities and differences are there between rules of ethics and rules of law? Consider scope, enforcement, and penalty in your answer.

4.2. In what form of the law will one find provision for criminal penalties? Civil remedies?

4.3. Give four general ways that public accountants can get themselves into legal difficulty.

4.4. What must be proved by the plaintiff in a common law action seeking recovery of damages from an independent auditor of financial statements? What must the defendant accountant do in such a court action?

4.5. What legal theory is derived from the *Ultramares* decision? Can auditors rely on this *Ultramares* rule today?

4.6. On what grounds were the auditors judged liable for damages in the *Rhode Island Hospital Trust* case? Explain.

4.7. Do any pronouncements of the AICPA, other than the rules of ethics, define duties and responsibilities of accountants in nonaudit engagements?

4.8. What are the auditor's responsibilities for reporting on events subsequent to the balance sheet date (*a*) up to the date of the auditor's report, (*b*) up to the date of the filing of a registration statement, (*c*) up to the effective date of a registration statement, and (*d*) after the audit report has been issued?

4.9. Assume that in the course of an audit you find that the client has sold treasury stock without having registered under the Securities Act of 1933. How might you determine whether the sale was legal?

4.10. What must be proved by the plaintiff in a suit under Section 11 of the Securities Act of 1933 seeking recovery of damages from an independent auditor of financial statements? What must the defendant auditor do in such a court action?

4.11. How does Section 11 of the Securities Act of 1933 change the legal environment that previously existed under common law?

4.12. What are the 10–K, 10–Q, and 8–K reports? To which securities act do they relate? How has the 8–K report been used to strengthen the independent auditor's position?

4.13. Why should officers, directors, and underwriters want auditors to include under the audit opinion such information as the plan for use of the proceeds of an offering, the description of the organization and business, the description of physical properties, and other quasi-financial information such as plant floor space and sales order backlog?

4.14. What liability exposure for accountants is found in Section 17 of the Securities Act of 1933? In Section 10(b) of the Securities Exchange Act of 1934? In Section 18 of the Securities Exchange Act of 1934?

4.15. What liability exposure for accountants is found in Section 24 of the Securities Act of 1933? In Section 32 of the Securities Exchange Act of 1934?

4.16. With reference to the *BarChris* and *Continental Vending* decisions, what lessons might be learned about the force and effect of generally accepted accounting principles?

4.17. With reference to the *BarChris* decision, what lessons might be learned about the force and effect of generally accepted auditing standards?

EXERCISES AND PROBLEMS

4.18. In conducting the examination of the financial statements of the Farber Corporation for the year ended September 30, Harper, a CPA, discovered that Nance, the president, who was also one of the principal stockholders, had borrowed substantial amounts of money from the corporation. He indicated that he owned 51 percent of the corporation, that the money would be promptly repaid, and that the financial statements were being prepared for internal use only. He requested that these loans not be accounted for separately in the financial statements, but be included in the other current accounts receivable. Harper acquiesced in this request. Nance was correct as to his stock ownership and the fact that the financial statements were for internal use only. However, he subsequently became insolvent and was unable to repay the loans.

Required:

What is Harper's liability to the other stockholders under common law? Explain. (AICPA)

4.19. Risk Capital Limited, a Delaware corporation, was considering the purchase of a substantial amount of the treasury stock held by Florida Sunshine Corporation, a closely held corporation. Initial discussions with the Florida Sunshine Corporation began late in 1977.

Wilson and Wyatt, Florida Sunshine's accountants, regularly prepared quarterly and annual unaudited financial statements. The most recently prepared financial statements were for the year ended September 30, 1978.

On November 15, 1978, after protracted negotiations, Risk Capital agreed to purchase 100,000 shares of no par, Class A capital stock of Florida Sunshine at $12.50 per share. However, Risk Capital insisted upon audited statements for calendar year 1978. The contract which was made available to Wilson & Wyatt specifically provided:

Risk Capital shall have the right to rescind the purchase of said stock if the audited financial statements of Florida Sunshine for calendar year 1978 show a material adverse change in the financial condition of the corporation.

The audited financial statements furnished to Florida Sunshine by Wilson and Wyatt showed no such material adverse change. Risk Capital relied upon the audited statements and purchased the treasury stock of Florida Sunshine. It was subsequently discovered that as of the balance sheet date, the audited statements were incorrect and that in fact there had been a material adverse change in the financial condition of the corporation. Florida Sunshine is insolvent and Risk Capital will lose virtually its entire investment.

Risk Capital seeks recovery against Wilson and Wyatt.

Required:

Assuming that only ordinary negligence is proven, will Risk Capital prevail:

a. Under the *Ultramares* decision?

b. Under the *Rusch Factors* decision?

Explain. (AICPA adapted)

4.20. Walter Young, doing business as Walter Young Fashions, engaged the CPA partnership of Small & Brown to examine his financial statements. During the examination, Small & Brown discovered certain irregularities which would have indicated to a reasonably prudent accountant that James Smith, the head bookkeeper, might be engaged in a fraud. More specifically, it appeared to Small & Brown that serious defalcations were taking place. However, Small & Brown, not having been engaged to discover defalcations, submitted an unqualified opinion in their report and did not mention the potential defalcation problem.

Required:

What are the legal implications of the above facts as they relate to the relationship between Small & Brown and Walter Young? Explain. (AICPA)

4.21. Cragsmore & Company, a medium-sized partnership of CPAs, was engaged by Marlowe Manufacturing, Inc., a closely held corporation, to examine its financial statements for the year ended December 31, 1978.

Prior to preparing the auditor's report, William Cragsmore, a partner, and Fred Willmore, a staff senior, reviewed the disclosures necessary in the footnotes to the financial statements. One footnote involved the terms, costs, and obligations of a lease between Marlowe and Acme Leasing Company.

Fred Willmore suggested that the footnote disclose the following: "The Acme Leasing Company is owned by persons who have a 35-percent interest in the capital stock and who are officers of Marlowe Manufacturing, Inc."

On Cragsmore's recommendation, this was revised by substituting "minority shareholders" for "persons who have a 35-percent interest in the capital stock and who are officers."

The auditor's report and financial statements were forwarded to Marlowe Manufacturing for review. The officer-shareholders of Marlowe who also owned Acme Leasing objected to the revised wording and insisted that the footnote be changed to describe the relationship between Acme and Marlowe as merely one of affiliation. Cragsmore acceded to this request.

The auditor's report was issued on this basis with an unqualified opinion. But the working papers included the drafts that showed the changes in the wording of the footnote.

Subsequent to delivery of the auditor's report, Marlowe suffered a substantial uninsured fire loss and has been forced into bankruptcy. The failure of Marlowe to carry any fire insurance coverage was not noted in the financial statements.

Required:

What legal problems under common law are suggested by these facts for Cragsmore & Company? Discuss. (AICPA adapted)

4.22. The Chriswell Corporation decided to raise additional long-term capital by issuing $3 million of 8-percent subordinated debentures to the public. May, Clark & Company, CPAs, the company's auditors, were engaged to examine the June 30, 1978, financial statements which were included in the bond registration statement.

May, Clark & Company completed its examination and submitted an unqualified auditor's report dated July 15, 1978. The registration statement was filed and became effective on September 1, 1978. On August 15 one of the partners of May, Clark & Company called on Chriswell Corporation and had lunch with the financial vice president and the controller. He questioned both officials on the company's operations since June 30 and inquired whether there had been any material changes in the company's financial position since that date. Both officers assured him that everything had proceeded normally and that the financial condition of the company had not changed materially.

Unfortunately the officers' representation was not true. On July 30, a substantial debtor of the company failed to pay the $400,000 due on its account receivable and indicated to Chriswell that it would probably be forced into bankruptcy. This receivable was shown as a collateralized loan on the June 30 financial statements. It was secured by stock of the debtor corporation which had a value in excess of the loan at the time the financial statements were prepared but was virtually worthless at the effective date of the registration statement. This $400,000 account receivable was material to the financial condition of Chriswell Corporation, and the market price of the subordinated debentures decreased by nearly 50 percent after the foregoing facts were disclosed.

The debenture holders of Chriswell are seeking recovery of their loss against all parties connected with the debenture registration.

Required:

Is May, Clark & Company liable to the Chriswell debenture holders under Section 11 of the Securities Act of 1933? Explain. (AICPA adapted.)

4.23. Meglow Corporation manufactured ladies' dresses and blouses. Because its cash position was deteriorating, Meglow sought a loan from Busch Factors. Busch had previously extended $25,000 credit to Meglow but refused to lend any additional money without obtaining copies of Meglow's audited financial statements.

Meglow contacted the CPA firm of Watkins, Winslow & Watkins to perform the audit. In arranging for the examination, Meglow clearly indicated that its purpose was to satisfy Busch Factors as to the corporation's sound financial condition and thus to obtain an additional loan of $50,000. Watkins, Winslow & Watkins accepted the engagement, performed the examination in a negligent manner, and rendered an unqualified auditor's opinion. If an adequate examination had been performed, the financial statements would have been found to be misleading.

Meglow submitted the audited financial statements to Busch Factors and obtained an additional loan of $35,000. Busch refused to lend more than that amount. After several other factors also refused, Meglow finally was able to persuade Maxwell Department Stores, one of its customers, to lend the additional $15,000. Maxwell relied upon the financial statements examined by Watkins, Winslow & Watkins.

Meglow is now in bankruptcy, and Busch seeks to collect from Watkins, Winslow & Watkins the $60,000 it loaned Meglow. Maxwell seeks to recover from Watkins, Winslow & Watkins the $15,000 it loaned Meglow.

Required:

Under common law:

a. Will Busch recover? Explain.

b. Will Maxwell recover? Explain. (AICPA adapted)

4.24. The CPA firm of Bigelow, Barton, and Brown was expanding very rapidly. Consequently it hired several new accountants, including a man named Small. Subsequently, the partners of the firm became dissatisfied with Small's production and warned him that they would be forced to discharge him unless his output increased significantly.

At that time Small was engaged in audits of several clients. He decided that to avoid being fired, he would reduce or omit entirely some of the standard auditing procedures listed in audit programs prepared by the partners. One of the CPA firm's clients, Newell Corporation, was in serious financial difficulty and had adjusted several of its accounts being examined by Small to appear financially sound. Small prepared fictitious working papers in his home at night to support purported completion of auditing procedures assigned to him although he in fact did not examine the adjusting entries. The CPA firm rendered an unqualified opinion on Newell's financial statements which were grossly misstated. Several creditors subsequently extended large sums of money to Newell Corporation relying upon the audited financial statements.

Required:

Would the CPA firm be liable to the creditors who extended the money in reliance on the erroneous financial statements if Newell Corporation should fail to pay them? Explain. (AICPA)

4.25. 1. The partnership of Zelsch & Co., CPAs, has been engaged to audit the financial statements of Snake Oil, Inc., in connection with filing an S–1 registration statement under the Securities Act of 1933. Discuss the following two statements made by the senior partner of Zelsch & Co.

a. "The partnership is assuming a much greater liability exposure in this engagement than exists under common law."

b. "If our examination is not fraudulent, we can avoid any liability claims that might arise."

2. State whether the following are true or false. Explain each.

   Xavier, Francis & Paul are a growing medium-sized partnership of CPAs located in the midwest. One of the firm's major clients is considering offering its stock to the public. This will be the firm's first client to go public.

   a. The firm should thoroughly familiarize itself with the Securities Act of 1933, the Securities Exchange Act of 1934 and *Regulation S–X*.
   b. If the client is unincorporated, the Securities Act of 1933 will not apply.
   c. If the client is going to be listed on an organized exchange, the Securities Act of 1934 will not apply.
   d. The Securities Act of 1933 imposes an additional potential liability on firms such as Xavier, Francis & Paul.
   e. So long as the company engages in exclusively intrastate business, the federal securities laws will not apply.

4.26. Your client, Lux Corporation, is a small food manufacturing company with a single plant located in its state of incorporation and has outstanding 200,000 shares of $10 par value common stock which is selling at about that price in infrequent sales. Lux desires to raise $3 million of additional working capital and is considering the following alternatives:

1. Sale of $3 million of a new issue of convertible debentures to Kelly, a sophisticated investor who formerly had been an executive of the company. Kelly retired and now lives in a neighboring state.
2. Sale of $3 million of additional common stock to local business executives and other local investors.

Required:

Discuss the impact of the registration requirements of the Securities Act of 1933 as it applies to each alternative.

4.27. Huffman & Whitman, a large regional CPA firm, was engaged by the Ritter Tire Wholesale Company to audit its financial statements for the year ended January 31, 1979. Huffman & Whitman had a busy audit engagement schedule from December 31 through April 1, and they decided to audit Ritter's purchase vouchers and related cash disbursements on a test sample basis. They instructed staff accountants to select a random sample of 300 purchase transactions and gave directions about what to look for. Boyd, the assistant in charge, completed the working papers, properly documenting the fact that 30 of the purchases sampled had been recorded and paid without the receiving report (required by stated internal control procedures) being included in the file of supporting documents. Whitman, the partner in direct charge of the audit, showed the findings to Lock, Ritter's chief accountant. Lock appeared surprised but promised that the missing receiving reports would be inserted into the files before the audit was over. Whitman was satisfied, noted in the work papers that the problem was solved, and did not say anything to Huffman about it.

Unfortunately Lock was involved in a fraudulent scheme in which he diverted shipments to a warehouse leased in his name and sent the invoices to Ritter for payment. He then sold the tires for his own profit. Internal auditors discovered the scheme during a study of slow-moving inventory items. Ritter's inventory was overstated by about $200,000—the amount Lock had diverted.

Required:

a. Did Lock's activity amount to an error or an irregularity?

b. Were any related party transactions involved?

c. Assume that no one had been assigned the job of determining whether receiving reports were obtained before invoices were paid. Does a material weakness in internal control exist? If so, does Huffman & Whitman have any reporting responsibility? Explain.

d. Was the audit conducted in a negligent manner?

APPENDIX 4–A

Cases in Common Law

Smith* v. *London Assur. Corp. (Appellate Division, New York, 1905, 109 App. Div. 882, 96 N.Y.S. 820). This was the first American case involving an auditor. The auditor sued for an unpaid fee, and the company counterclaimed for a large sum that had been embezzled by one of its employees which they claimed would not have occurred except for the auditor's breach of contract. The evidence indicated that the auditors indeed failed to check cash accounts at one branch office as stipulated in an engagement contract. The court recognized the auditors as skilled professionals and held them liable for embezzlement losses which could have been prevented by nonnegligent performance under the contract.

Landell* v. *Lybrand (Supreme Court of Pennsylvania, 1919, 264 PA. 406, 107 ALT. 783). This was the earliest American case where the CPA's liability to a third party was at issue. Plaintiff sued the auditor claiming loss as a result of having relied upon a false report negligently prepared. The court held that since there was no intent to deceive and because there was no contract the defendants were not liable for negligent conduct. This case is no longer considered good law. In modern courts auditors may be liable for negligent conduct to specific third parties whom they can foresee as recipients and users of a report.

Ultramares Corp.* v. *Touche (Court of Appeals of New York, 1931, 255 N.Y. 170, 174 N.E. 441). *Ultramares* is considered an important landmark case for accountants because it dealt specifically with issues of contract, privity, tort, deceit, degrees of negligence, and third-party beneficiaries. Nevertheless, the gross negligence test for liability to third parties applied in *Ultramares* is beginning to be modified in more current decisions.

Ultramares Corp. relied upon financial statements audited by Touche and made loans to the Fred Stern & Co., Inc., an importer of rubber. Stern went bankrupt and the evidence presented in court indicated that Touche had failed to investigate the significance of penciled sales–accounts receivable entries at the bottom of the last month's sales journal which turned out to be fictitious.

Ultramares suffered damages in the amount of the loans that could not be collected.

The *Ultramares* decision stated criteria for an auditor's liability to third parties for *deceit* (a tort action). In order to prove deceit: (1) a false representation must be shown, (2) the tort-feasor must possess *scienter*—either knowledge of falsity or insufficient basis of information, (3) an intent to induce action in reliance must be shown, (4) the damaged party must show justifiable reliance, and (5) there must have been a resulting damage. The court held that an accountant could be liable when he did not have sufficient information (audit evidence) to lead to a sincere or genuine belief. In other words, an audit report is deceitful when the auditor purports to speak from knowledge when knowledge there is none.

However, the court also held that the auditor was not liable to unidentified third parties for negligence. The plaintiff was not known to Touche at the time the report was issued, although the auditor knew that it would be shown to and used by third parties. Only this lack of identification caused the court to say:

> If liability for negligence exists, a thoughtless slip or blunder, the failure to detect a theft or forgery beneath the cover of deceptive entries, may expose accountants to a liability in an indeterminate amount for an indeterminate time to an indeterminate class.

The court also wrote that the degree of negligence might be so gross, however, as to amount to a constructive fraud. Then the auditor could be liable in tort to a third party beneficiary. Some modern court decisions are currently modifying the *Ultramares* rule by holding the auditor liable for negligence to third parties who can be foreseen by the auditor. (Refer to the discussion of *Rusch Factors* v. *Levin* below.)

The McKesson & Robbins, Inc., case. In 1938 a receiver was appointed to oversee the affairs of McKesson & Robbins, Inc., and an introductory chapter in American auditing was begun. The company had, out of a total of $87 million in assets, an approximate $10 million inventory overstatement and $9 million in fictitious accounts receivable. The trustee's claim against the auditor was settled without litigation by refund of over $500,000 previously paid in audit fees since 1933.

At the time this audit was conducted, acceptable audit procedure did not include independent confirmation of accounts receivable or observation of inventories. Certain company officials had simply taken advantage of their knowledge of auditing to create false entries for purchases and sales, thereby creating a paper empire.

In a subsequent investigation by the SEC (*Accounting Series Release No. 19,* 1940), the following findings were made:

1. The auditors failed to employ that degree of vigilance, inquisitiveness, and analysis of the evidence available that is necessary in a professional undertaking and is recommended in all well-known and authoritative works on auditing. Meticulous verification of the inventory was not needed to discover the fraud.
2. Even though the auditors are not guarantors and should not be responsible for detecting all fraud, the discovery of gross overstatements in the accounts is a major purpose in an audit even though every minor defalcation might not be disclosed.

The response of accountants and auditors was the development of auditing standards and the beginning in 1939 of the series of Statements on Auditing Procedure.

State Street Trust Co.* v. *Ernst (278 N.Y. 104, 15 N.E. 2d 416, 1938). This case is very similar to *Ultramares* except that here the auditors *did examine* receivables but failed to detect an overstatement due to the uncollectibility of many accounts. The court found that auditors could be liable to third parties and expressed the criteria forthrightly as follows:

> Accountants, however, may be liable to third parties, even where there is lacking deliberate or active fraud. A representation certified as true to the knowledge of the accountants when knowledge there is none, a reckless misstatement, or an opinion based on grounds so flimsy as to lead to the conclusion that there was no genuine belief in its truth, are all sufficient upon which to base liability. A refusal to see the obvious, a failure to investigate the doubtful, if sufficiently gross, may furnish evidence leading to an inference of fraud so as to impose liability for losses suffered by those who rely on the balance sheet. In other words, heedlessness and reckless disregard of consequence may take the place of deliberate intention.
>
> In *Ultramares Corp.* v. *Touche* (255 N.Y. 170) we said with no uncertainty that negligence, if gross, or blindness, even though not equivalent to fraud, was sufficient to sustain an inference of fraud. Our exact words were: "In this connection we are to bear in mind the principle already stated in the course of this opinion that negligence or blindness, even when not equivalent to fraud, is none the less evidence to sustain an inference of fraud. At least this is so if the negligence is gross."

CIT Financial Corp.* v. *Glover (U.S. Court of Appeals for the Second Circuit, 1955, 224 F. 2d 44). In this case plaintiff had suffered losses on loans and claimed that audited financial statements were materially misleading. The suit alleged negligence and gross negligence. The court interpreted *Ultramares* to mean that auditors are liable to third parties for ordinary negligence if their reports are for the primary benefit of the third party. Thus the privity criterion may not serve as a defense when third party beneficiaries are known. However, the jury evaluated evidence presented in court and determined (1) that there was no negligence because the report adequately communicated the auditor's opinion and knowledge, and (2) that the auditor's report was not for the primary benefit of the third party.

Rusch Factors, Inc.* v. *Levin (U.S. District Court for the District of Rhode Island, 1968, 248F. Supp. 85). The plaintiff had relied upon audited financial statements to make loans to a company that soon after went bankrupt. These circumstances are not different from earlier cases, but the court in *Rusch Factors* did three things of note: (1) liberalized the liability exposure rule respecting the privity defense, (2) modified the *Ultramares* rule to shift more responsibility to the accountant, and (3) quoted and applied the Restatement (Second) of Torts (1966). These parts of the court opinion are of sufficient importance to quote them below in their entirety.

> Privity of contract is clearly no defense in a fraud action. An intentionally misrepresenting accountant is liable to all those persons whom he should reasonably have foreseen would be injured by his misrepresentation. (*Ultramares* v. *Touche & Co.*) . . . Neither actual knowledge by the accountant of the third person's reliance nor quantitative limitation of the class of reliant persons is requisite to recovery for fraud. . . . The same broad perimeter prevails if the misrepresenter's conduct is heedless enough to permit an inference of fraud. (*State St. Trust Co.* v. *Ernst*). . . . There are several reasons which support the broad rule of liability for fraudulent misrepresentation. First, liability should extend at least as far in fraud, an intentional tort, as it does in negligence cases resulting in personal injury or property damage. Second, the risk of loss for intentional wrongdoing should invariably be placed on the wrongdoer who caused the harm, rather than on the innocent victim of the harm. Finally, a broad rule of liability may deter future misconduct. . . . The court determines, for the above stated reasons, that the plaintiff's complaint is sufficient in so far as it alleges fraud.
>
> The wisdom of the decision in *Ultramares* had been doubted, . . . and this court shares the doubt. Why should an innocent reliant party be forced to carry the weighty burden of an accountant's professional malpractice? Isn't the risk of loss more easily distributed and fairly spread by imposing it on the accounting profession, which can pass the cost of insuring against the risk onto its customers, who can in turn pass the cost onto the entire consuming public? Finally, wouldn't a rule of foreseeability elevate the cautionary techniques of the accounting profession? For these reasons it appears to this court that the decision in *Ultramares* constitutes an unwarranted inroad upon the principle that "the risk reasonably to be perceived defines the duty to be obeyed." . . .
>
> This court need not, however, hold that the Rhode Island Supreme Court would overrule the *Ultramares* decision, if presented the opportunity, for the case at bar is qualitatively distinguishable from *Ultramares*. There, the plaintiff was a member of an undefined, unlimited class of remote lenders and potential equity holders not actually foreseen but only foreseeable. Here the plaintiff is a single party whose reliance was actually foreseen by the defendant. . . .
>
> With respect, then to the plaintiff's negligence theory, this court holds that an accountant should be liable in negligence for careless financial misrepresentations relied upon by actually foreseen and limited classes of persons. According to the plaintiff's complaint in the instant case, the defendant knew that his certification was to be used for, and had as its very aim and purpose, the reliance of potential financiers of the Rhode Island corporation. The defendant's motion is, therefore, denied. The court does not rule upon, but leaves open for reconsideration in the light of trial development, the question of whether an accountant's liability for negligent misrepresentation ought to extend to the full limits of foreseeability.

Rhode Island Hospital Trust National Bank* v. *Swartz (455 F.2d 847 4th Cir., 1972). This case is similar to *Rusch Factors* in the court's citation and reliance on the Restatement of Torts. The client company in its financial statements represented that certain additions to fixed assets in the form of self-construction of warehouse improvements had been made at several locations. The auditors *disclaimed* an opinion and stated in their report, in part: "Additions to fixed assets in 1963 were found to include principally warehouse improvements and installation of machinery and equipment in (several locations named). . . . Unfortunately, fully complete detailed cost records were not kept of these improvements and no exact determination could be made as to the actual cost of said improvements."

In fact *no* cost records were kept, and the asset additions did not exist at all. The court held that the auditor was negligent in failing to give a clear explanation of the reasons for the qualification (the disclaimer of opinion) and of the effect on financial position and results of operations as required by AICPA *Statement on Auditing Procedures No. 33,* Chapter 10, paragraphs 1 and 9. Being ruled negligent, under the Restatement of Torts, the auditors were held liable for plaintiff's damage.

1136 Tenants' Corp.* v. *Max Rothenberg & Co. (Appellate Division, New York, 1967, 27 A.D. 2d 830, 277 N.Y.S. 2d 996). This is one of the leading cases involving unaudited financial statements and the accountant's responsibilities to stockholder-users of the statements.

The accountant Rothenberg had been engaged to perform "write-up" work for a fee of $600 per year for Riker & Company—a managing agent that handled maintenance payments of several cooperative apartment houses including the plaintiffs'. The accountant prepared statements of receipts and disbursements, and Riker sent these to the tenants. The statements showed that various taxes and expenses had been paid, but in fact these were not paid and Riker had embezzled the money. The statements carried the legend "unaudited," and a cover letter stated that "the statements were prepared from the books and records of the corporation and no independent verifications were undertaken thereon."

Despite claims to the contrary the court found that defendant was engaged to audit and not merely "write-up" plaintiffs' books and records. The accountant had in fact performed some limited auditing procedures including preparation of a worksheet entitled "Missing Invoices 1/1/63–12/31/63." These were items Riker claimed to have paid but did not. The court held that even if accountants were hired only for "write-up" work they had a duty to inform plaintiffs of any circumstances that gave reason to believe that a fraud had occurred (e.g., the record of "missing invoices").

The plaintiffs recovered damages of about $237,000. This decision prompted the AICPA to issue a booklet entitled *Guide for Engagements to Prepare Unaudited Financial Statements* which sets forth professional standards applicable to "write-up" work.

APPENDIX 4–B

Cases under the Securities Acts

Escott et al.* v. *BarChris Construction Corporation et al. (U.S. District Court for the Southern District of New York, 1968, 283 F. Supp. 643). Suit was brought on October 25, 1962, under Section 11 of the Securities Act of 1933 by purchasers of the company's 5½ percent convertible subordinated debentures. The company had filed a registration statement on March 30, 1961, which became effective May 16, 1961; and 17 months later, on October 29, 1962, it filed under Chapter XI of the Bankruptcy Act. The auditors had given an unqualified opinion on the balance sheet as of December 31, 1960, in a report dated February 23, 1961.

BarChris was in the business of constructing bowling alleys. Usually the completed structures were sold to an operator who made a down payment and gave an installment note for the balance. BarChris would then discount the note with a factor and receive proceeds reduced by an amount withheld by the factor as a loss reserve. As the purchaser paid the note, a proportionate part of this loss reserve would be remitted to BarChris. On at least one occasion a customer could not take possession, so BarChris sold the bowling alley at a gain to the factor, who then leased it to a wholly owned BarChris subsidiary for operation. BarChris accounted for construction operations on the percentage-of-completion method.

The important points of the court opinion were these:

1. Plaintiffs charged in general that the 1960 financial statements were materially misleading, that the percentage-of-completion method was erroneous and misleading, and that even if the method were appropriate, it was applied in error to cause the statements to be materially misleading.
    a. The court ruled that the percentage-of-completion method was a widely used generally accepted accounting method and was thus appropriate and did not of itself cause financial statements to be misleading.
    b. The court ruled that errors had been made in applying the method but that the errors were not material. The auditor had treated two contracts as 100 percent complete, relying on management's oral representations, when they were in fact only partially completed.
    c. The court ruled that the sale and subsequent leaseback of a bowling alley was not in fact a sale because the property did not leave the company's control, thus sales and gross profits were overstated. (This sale occurred in 1960, prior to issuance of APB *Opinion No.* 5 in 1964. Before 1964, profits on sale and leaseback could be recognized currently with full disclosure, but only after APB 5 was this prohibited.)
    d. The court ruled that the income statement data was not materially misstated. Sales were overstated by 8 percent, net operating

income by 16 percent, and earnings per share by 15 percent. The apparent reasoning for ruling these overstatements not material was that sales and earnings were significantly greater in 1960 than in 1959 even with the overstatements removed. Sales were up 256 percent instead of the reported 276 percent, net operating income up $1,055,093 instead of $1,301,698, and earnings per share up 97 percent (to 65 cents) instead of up 128 percent (to 75 cents).

e. The court ruled that the balance sheet data, especially the current assets and liabilities, were materially misstated. Noncurrent assets (a temporary cash advance from a nonconsolidated subsidiary, and the factor's loss reserve retentions) were improperly classified as current, an allowance for uncollectibility was judged erroneous, and some current liabilities were omitted. Altogether these errors caused the current ratio to be shown as 1.9 : 1 and the court decided that it was properly 1.6 : 1.

In brief outline then, the *BarChris* court made judgments that both upheld and disregarded then-current generally accepted accounting principles and judgments that distinguish both material and immaterial error.

2. Defendant accountants, officers, directors, attorneys, and underwriters all asserted the defense of due diligence.

   The court ruled that the auditors were the only *experts* under Section 11 and specifically ruled that the attorneys were not considered experts.

   In individual findings against all defendants (except the auditors) the court generally ruled that they had not conducted reasonable investigations to form a basis for belief and that they had not satisfied the diligence requirement, *except to the extent that they had relied upon the portions of the prospectus expertised by the auditors*. (A lesser diligence requirement.) The court ruled that the auditors had also failed to perform a diligent and reasonable investigation. Particularly the court specified the misclassification of the factor's loss reserve retentions, the exercise of bad judgment in evaluating collectibility of a receivable, and a "useless" S–1 review. This last point is of particular relevance to the responsibility for subsequent events running to the effective date. The S–1 review is a common term for the audit program for review of subsequent events, and the auditors had prepared a program in full accord with the then-current Chapter 11 of *SAP 33*. However, the court found that the auditor had spent "only" 20½ hours in this review, had read no important documents, and, "He asked questions, he got answers that he considered satisfactory, and he did nothing to verify them . . . He was too easily satisfied with glib answers to his inquiries."

This final finding of the court caused the judge to write the following, the first sentence of which has become famous (or infamous) enough to be quoted many times. The phrases following it, however, have not been quoted nearly as often.

> Accountants should not be held to a standard higher than that recognized in their profession. *I do not do so here.* [Accountant's name] *review did not come up to that standard. He did not take some of the steps which* (the) *written program prescribed. He did not spend an adequate amount of time on a task of this magnitude.* [Emphasis added.]

3. The defendant accountants asserted the causation defense, citing general economic conditions and particularly the decline in the bowling industry. The court did not rule on this defense because of the diverse circumstances of the plaintiffs and because some cross-claims among the defendants had to be settled first. One plaintiff had purchased his debentures after the bankruptcy, so one may assume that the causation defense was complete as to his claim.

United States* v. *White (124 F. 2d 181, 2d Cir., 1941). In this 1941 case an accountant was convicted of using the mails to defraud in violation of Section 17 of the 1933 act. The auditor's defense was that he had extracted facts from the books and from what management had told him in apparent disregard of other factual circumstances and events. The prosecution maintained that anyone with the auditor's experience and intelligence would have been aware of the irregularity. The jury apparently decided guilt on the basis of the auditor's being "so credulous or so ill acquainted with his calling" that a finding of innocence was not undeniably demanded by the evidence.

Fischer* v. *Kletz., popularly styled the "*Yale Express* case" (U.S. District Court for the Southern District of New York, 266 F. Supp. 180, 1967). This decision is actually only the court's ruling to deny defendant's motion to dismiss the suit. No other public record exists because the suit was later settled without trial. Plaintiff's allegations were based on common law deceit, Section 18 of the 1934 act and Section 10(b) and Rule 10(b)–5 under the 1934 act. The case was complicated by the accounting firm's involvement in a management services engagement *following* the financial statement audit. Thus there are many instructive dimensions to this ruling: Reading of the complete decision is recommended.

Stockholders and debenture holders of Yale Express System, Inc., sued the auditor, alleging their false certification of false financial statements and failure to disclose subsequently acquired information. The 1963 financial statements, with auditor's opinion, were released around April 9, 1964, showing net income of $1,140,000. Sometime around June 29, 1964, the company filed a 10–K report with the SEC reporting essentially the same information. Early in 1964 (the exact date was disputed) the accounting firm that did the 1963 audit was engaged to perform special studies of the company's past and current income and expenses. In the course of this nonaudit engagement the accountants discovered that the 1963 financial statements were materially in error. The plaintiffs contended that the misstatement was known before the 10–K report was filed, and the defendants maintained that discovery was later. In any event, the misstatement was disclosed around February or May 1965, when the 1964 audit was completed. At that time (which was also in dispute) the financial statements and auditor's report revealed that 1963 net income had been revised downward to a *loss* of $1,254,000 (not considering $629,000 in special charges to retained earnings).

In brief, the court's findings dealt with the following subjects: (1) The accounting firm's role of consultant and not that of statutory independent auditor on the management services engagement. (2) The aspect of silence and inaction rather than affirmative misrepresentations as criteria for deceit. (3) The dimensions of "aiding and abetting" in connection with Section 10(b) and Rule 10(b)–5 liability. (4) The responsibilities of an auditor in connection with unaudited interim financial statements.

The *Yale Express* case stimulated promulgation of *SAP No. 41*, "Subsequent Discovery of Facts Existing at the Date of the Auditor's Report" (1969). This SAP requires positive action by the CPA who later becomes aware of facts existing at the date of his report which might have affected his audit opinion had he then known those facts. The CPA is required to disclose his knowledge to client management and seek wider disclosure and, failing that, notify the SEC and stock exchanges as appropriate representatives of the public interest. (See *Statement on Auditing Standards,* Section 561.)

United States* v. *Benjamin (328 F. 2d 854, 2d Cir., 1964). The judgment in this case resulted in conviction of an accountant for willingly conspiring by use of interstate commerce to sell unregistered securities and to defraud in the sale of securities, in violation of Section 24 of the 1933 act. The accountant had prepared "pro forma" balance sheets and claimed that use of the words "pro forma" absolved him of responsibility. He also claimed that he did not know that his reports would be used in connection with securities sales. The court found otherwise, showing that he did in fact know about the use of his reports and that certain statements about asset values and acquisitions were patently false and the accountant knew that they were false. The court made two significant findings: (1) that the willfulness requirements of Section 24 may be proved by showing that due diligence would have revealed the false statements, and (2) that use of limiting words such as "pro forma" do not justify showing false ownership of assets in any kind of financial statements.

United States* v. *Simon (United States Court of Appeals for the Second Circuit, 425 F. 2d, 796, 1969). Defendants (two partners and an audit manager) were prosecuted for filing false statements with a government agency, mail fraud, and violation of Section 32 of the 1934 Act. The first trial resulted in a jury hung in favor of acquittal and a mistrial was declared. The second jury trial in 1968 resulted in conviction, which was confirmed by the appeals court in 1969. The U.S. Supreme Court denied certiorari in 1970. In 1973, the defendants received a full presidential pardon. In related civil suits, the accounting firm settled out of court for slightly less than $2 million. Coupled with the sensational nature of the case, there are many practical lessons to be learned from the various briefs and judgments. (Refer to the reading list at the end of Chapter 4.)

The auditors were engaged in the audit of Continental Vending Machine Corporation. Roth was president and owner of about 22 percent of the stock of Continental, and he also owned about 25 percent of the stock of Valley Commercial Corporation and supervised that company's operations. Continental would issue notes to Valley who would discount them with banks and remit the proceeds to Continental. These transactions created the account known as the "Valley payable." In an unrelated series of transactions, Roth would have Continental "lend" cash to Valley, who would then lend to Roth for his personal use, thus creating the account known as the "Valley receivable." For the fiscal years 1960–1962 the relative account balances were as follows:

September 30	*Receivable from Valley*	*Payable to Valley*
1960	$ 397,996	$ 949,852
1961	848,006	780,472
1962	3,543,335	1,029,475

In the financial statements, the receivable was classified among the assets and the payable among the liabilities, but in the footnote disclosure (the alleged false statement at issue in the trials), the two accounts were *netted together*. When asked why the offset of liability against an asset, clearly contrary to accounting principles, the auditors admitted error and explained that sometime in the past someone had netted the two amounts, and it just was not questioned. So lesson one is: Never rely only on the fact that "this is the way we did it last year."

Continental's auditors learned that Valley was probably not in any position to repay the receivable, so Roth and others put up collateral *to Valley*. (Knowledge was not certain because other auditors were engaged to audit Valley's statements, and their report was not delivered to Continental's auditors.) This collateral largely consisted of stock in Continental which the court characterized as singularly unsuitable to secure the receivable. The footnote disclosure revealed only (1) Roth's relation to Valley as "officer, director, and stockholder," (2) that the collateral, assigned by Valley to Continental, exceeded the *net* receivable, (3) that the collateral consisted of "equity in certain marketable securities."

The government contended that the disclosure should have included the following information: (1) that the Valley receivable was uncollectible since Valley had loaned approximately the same amount to Roth who was unable to pay; (2) that the Valley receivable and payable could not be offset; (3) that the Valley receivable was $3,900,000 (It had increased since the fiscal year-end to the February 15, 1963, date of the audit report.); (4) that the value of the collateral was $2,978,000; and (5) that approximately 80 percent of the collateral was in securities of Continental. In fact the unencumbered value of the collateral was only $1,978,000 because of prior liens that the auditors had not discovered.

The audited financial statements were dismal anyway. When they were released, Continental stock plunged, the value of the collateral evaporated, and the accounting firm then withdrew its opinion on the financial statements.

The case, as it progressed, became a *cause celebre* over the role of generally accepted accounting principles as standards of the profession fixing the responsibility of professional accountants. The defense brought an array of well-versed accountants to testify that standards did not require an auditor to inquire deeply into the affairs of an affiliated company that was not an audit client (Valley) to the extent of learning what practices it conducted (the loans to Roth), and that GAAP did not require disclosure of the *nature* of any collateral. Their problem was that no authoritative written source for GAAP spells out these positions, so the strength of their testimony rested entirely on "general acceptability" as it was perceived by the common sense of practicing accountants.

The jury was not convinced, and the trial judge instructed them that knowledge of generally accepted accounting principles could be highly persuasive, *but not necessarily conclusive.* Later the appeals judge in affirming the conviction stated that it should be the auditor's responsibility to report factually whenever corporate activities are carried out for the benefit of the president and when "looting" has occurred.

Thus two other lessons may be inferred: (1) that generally accepted accounting principles to be forceful in a court of law will have to be written, and (2) that auditors should be careful to be knowledgeable of the financial affairs of affiliated companies, even to the extent of insisting upon auditing them directly. The events connected with this case led in part to the issuance of *SAS No.* 6 (Section 335) entitled "Related Party Transactions" and to the addition of Part 2 to ethics Rule 401, which allows auditors to insist on auditing a subsidiary, branch, or other component which in their judgment is necessary to warrant the expression of an opinion.

United States* v. *Natelli (U.S. Ct. Appeals, 2d Circuit, 1975, F. 2d). This case is better known as the *National Student Marketing Corporation* (*NSMC*) case. Two auditors were charged with violation of Section 32(a) of the Securities Exchange Act of 1934 which provides criminal penalties for any person who willfully and knowingly makes, or causes to be made, any statement filed under the act which was false or misleading with respect to any material fact.

Natelli was in charge of the audit of NSMC, a company whose first issue of stock had risen from $6 to $80 per share in five months. The company sold marketing programs to companies for promotions on college campuses. Many of the programs had heavy front-end development costs before they were ready, and accounting decisions had been made to apply percentage-of-completion accounting for revenue recognition. This accounting resulted in recording of certain "unbilled receivables" representing commitments from customers. Some commitments totaling $1.7 million in fiscal 1968 were not in writing, but these were nonetheless included in the financial statements for that year.

As fiscal year 1969 proceeded about $1 million of these commitments were written off, and indications were that they were not valid in the first place. Some decisions were made to adjust the 1968 figures. This is where the accountants got into trouble.

NSMC had acquired several companies in pooling transactions. A footnote in financial statements included in a proxy statement filed in 1969 showed 1968 sales and income figures exhibited below:

	1968
Net sales	
Originally reported	$ 4,989,446
Pooled companies reflected retroactively	6,552,449
Per statement of earnings	11,541,895
Net earnings	
Originally reported	388,031
Pooled companies reflected retroactively	385,121
Per statement of earnings	773,152

The footnote also explained that certain retroactive adjustments had a net affect of reducing net earnings for the year 1968 by $21,000.

The trouble arose out of the fact that about $350,000 of the write-offs were recorded in the year 1969 and about $678,000 was subtracted from the 1968 sales figures of the pooled companies and not from the "originally reported" net sales. Also, the net income effect was really a $210,000 *reduction*, but the firm's tax department had reported that a deferred tax item in the amount of $189,000 should be reversed. The accountant improperly netted these two items together to report in the footnote a rather minor $21,000 income reduction.

The appeals court stated: "It is hard to probe the intent of a defendant. . . . When we deal with a defendant who is a professional accountant, it is even harder at times to distinguish between simple errors of judgment and errors made with sufficient criminal intent to support a conviction, especially when there is no financial gain to the accountant other than his legitimate fee." Nevertheless, the court affirmed one accountant's conviction by the lower trial court because of his apparent motive and action to conceal the effect of the accounting adjustments. The footnote in particular, as it was written, failed to reveal what it should have revealed—the write-off of $1 million of "sales" (about 20 percent of the amount previously reported) and the large operating income adjustment ($210,000 compared to $388,031 originally reported). The court concluded that the concealment of the retroactive adjustments to NSMC's 1968 revenues and earnings were properly found to have been intentional for the very purpose of hiding earlier errors.

Ernst & Ernst* v. *Hochfelder (U.S. Supreme Court, 1976). This decision is considered a landmark for accountants because it relieved them of liability for negligence under Section 10(b) of the Securities Exchange Act of 1934 and its companion SEC Rule 10b–5. The point of law at issue in the case was whether scienter is a necessary element for a cause of action under 10(b) or whether negligent conduct alone is sufficient. *Scienter* refers to a mental state embracing intent to deceive, manipulate, or defraud. Section 10(b) makes unlawful the use or employment of any manipulative or deceptive device or contrivance in contravention of Securities and Exchange Commission rules. The respondents (Hochfelder) specifically disclaimed any allegations of fraud or intentional misconduct on the part of Ernst & Ernst, but they wanted to see liability under 10(b) imposed for negligence. The court reasoned that Section 10(b) in its reference to "employment of any manipulative and deceptive device" meant that intention to deceive, manipulate, or defraud is necessary to support a private cause of action under Section 10(b), and negligent conduct is not sufficient.

Ernst & Ernst was retained by First Securities Company of Chicago, a small brokerage firm, to perform periodic audits and did so from 1946 until 1967. Respondents (Hochfelder) were customers of First Securities who invested in a fraudulent securities scheme perpetrated by Leston B. Nay, president of First Securities and owner of 92 percent of its stock. Nay induced some clients to invest funds in "escrow" accounts to earn high rates of return (12 percent at first and later 9 percent). They did so from 1942 through 1966. There were no such accounts because Nay converted the funds to his own use. Hence, there were never any accounts of this type available for Ernst & Ernst to audit.

Investors were instructed to make checks payable to Nay, and he instituted a "mail rule" at First Securities to ensure that he alone received them. The "mail rule" was that only he could open mail addressed to him at First Securities or addressed to First Securities to his attention, even if it arrived in his absence.

Ernst & Ernst was charged with having aided and abetted Nay's scheme by negligent failure to conduct a proper audit, specifically the failure to discover the "mail rule." The premise was that, upon discovery, disclosure would have been made to the SEC of an irregular procedure that prevented an effective audit, and the whole scheme would have been exposed by a subsequent investigation. Ernst & Ernst did have a duty to perform an audit in accordance with generally accepted auditing standards, which under SEC rules includes a review of the accounting system, the internal accounting control, and procedures for safeguarding securities (held by a brokerage firm).

Ernst & Ernst advanced the view that Nay's mail rule was not relevant to the system of internal control and that First Securities did in fact maintain adequate internal accounting controls. The Hochfelder group countered with three expert witnesses who testified that the mail rule represented a material inadequacy in internal control. A "material inadequacy" in internal accounting control is defined in the AICPA audit guide *Audits of Brokers and Dealers in Securities* (1963) as:

> . . . a condition that would permit a person acting individually in the brokerage concern's organization to perpetrate errors or irregularities involving the accounting records, assets of brokerage concern, and/or assets of customers that could not be detected through the internal control procedures in time to prevent material loss or misstatement of the concern's financial statements, or serious violation of rules of the regulatory agencies.

The trial court granted Ernst & Ernst's motion for summary judgment and dismissal on the grounds that there was no genuine issue of material fact with respect to whether Ernst & Ernst had conducted proper audits. In effect the trial court decided that there was no negligence on the part of Ernst & Ernst. The appeals court later reversed the trial court and remanded the case for trial saying there were genuine issues of material fact to be decided, namely (1) whether Nay's "mail rule" constituted a material inadequacy in First Securities' system of internal accounting control, and (2) whether Ernst & Ernst failed to exercise due care in that it did not discover a material inadequacy. Before a new trial could decide these issues, Ernst & Ernst appealed to the Supreme Court, which rendered the decision explained at the beginning of this brief. So the substantive issues of material inadequacy and auditor's due care were never taken before a trial jury.

The Supreme Court did not, however, address the issue of whether reckless behavior and disregard for duty can be considered a form of intentional conduct (scienter) for purposes of imposing liability under Section 10(b) and Rule 10b–5. Thus one might expect future cases of this type, lacking an allegation of scienter to allege that accountants acted in such a reckless way as to constitute intent. Nevertheless, this standard is more forgiving than a standard of mere negligence.

PART TWO

General Technology of Auditing

5

AUDIT OVERVIEW: EVIDENCE, PROGRAM PLANNING, DOCUMENTATION

This chapter deals with four major topics:

- An overview of an audit engagement sequence of events,
- Evidence—defined in specific terms and related directly to auditing problems,
- Procedures—activities performed by auditors to gather evidential matter, and
- Program planning and documentation—the process of specifying procedures to meet audit objectives and the techniques of recording the evidence in audit working papers.

AUDIT ENGAGEMENT OVERVIEW

An audit engagement consists of several sequential elements or phases, beginning with decisions about client acceptance and continuance and ending with reviews of the quality of the completed audit work. In between lie steps that constitute the technical audit tasks of gathering sufficient competent evidence upon which an audit report may be based.

The phases illustrated in the chart and explained in the following pages pertain to an independent audit of financial statements. Internal audits and governmental audits may be conceptually similar in many cases, but they may also differ from independent audits in some of the details.

A first-time audit usually requires more audit work than a repeat engagement. If the company has never been audited, this additional work includes audit of the beginning of the year account balances because these amounts affect the current year income and funds flow statements. This work may involve going back to audit several years' transactions that make up permanent accounts—those accounts whose balances are car-

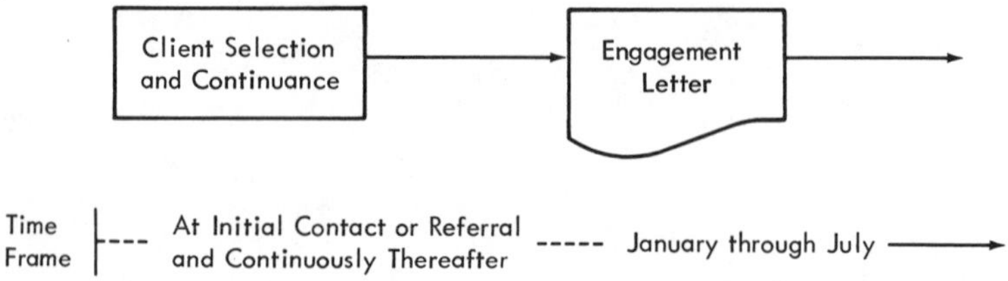

ried forward for a long time (e.g., fixed assets, patents, bonds payable). If the company has been audited by other auditors, the new first-time auditor may facilitate the audit by asking for information from the previous auditor and by reviewing the previous auditor's working papers concerning the permanent accounts and other matters. In any event a first-time auditor will have to obtain an understanding of the new client's business and the company's methods of operation.[1]

Client Selection, Continuance. The first element of an audit firm's quality control policies and procedures is a system for initially deciding to accept a new client and, on a continuing basis, deciding whether to resign from audit engagements. Auditing firms are not obligated to accept undesirable clients nor are they obligated to continue to audit clients when relationships deteriorate or client management comes under a cloud of suspicion.

All audit firms have procedures related to client acceptance and continuance. Some may be more formal and systematic than others. Policies and procedures may include (1) obtaining and reviewing financial information about the prospective client—annual reports, interim statements, registration statements, Forms 10–K and reports to regulatory agencies, (2) inquiring of the prospect's banker, legal counsel, underwriter, or other persons who do business with the company for information about the company and its management, (3) communicating with the predecessor auditor, if any (see *SAS No. 7*, Section 315), for information on the integrity of management, on disagreements with management about accounting principles, auditing procedures or similar matters, and on the reasons for a change of auditors, (4) considering whether the engagement would require special attention or involve unusual risks, and (5) evaluating the audit firm's independence with regard to the prospect and considering the need for special skills (e.g., computer auditing, specialized industry knowledge).

Decisions to continue auditing a client are similar to acceptance decisions, except that the audit firm will have had more first-hand experience with the company. Continuance review may be done periodically (e.g., annually) or upon occurrence of some major events such as changes in management, directors, ownership, legal counsel, financial condition, litigation status, nature of the client's business, or scope of the audit engagement. In general, conditions which would have caused the audit firm to reject a prospective client may develop and lead to a decision to discon-

[1] *Statement on Auditing Standards No.* 22, (Section 311), "Planning and Supervision," specifies numerous considerations involved in planning and conducting an audit.

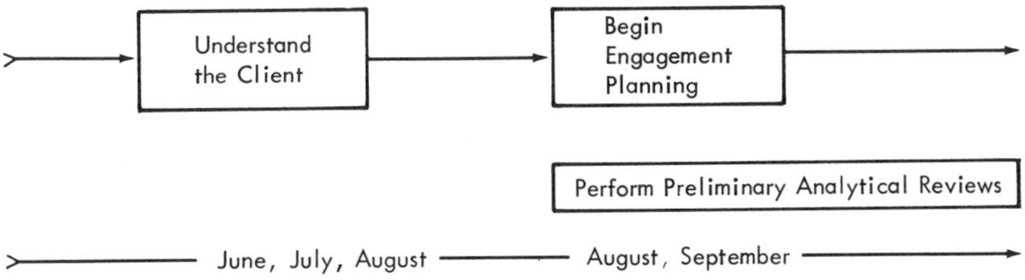

tinue the engagement. As examples: A client company may expand and diversify on an international scale to the extent that a small audit firm may not have the competence to continue the audit; in an actual event, an audit firm discontinued the audit of seven companies under the managerial influence of one person who had admitted falsifying some financial statements and using corporate funds for his personal benefit.

Engagement Letters. Upon acceptance, and preferably on a continuing basis, the audit firm should prepare an *engagement letter.* This letter sets forth the terms of the engagement and the auditor-client understandings. In effect it is the audit contract. It may contain special requests and assignments undertaken by the auditor, or it may be a rather standard letter stating that an audit of financial statements will be performed in accordance with generally accepted auditing standards. An engagement letter is highly recommended as a means of avoiding misunderstandings with the client and as a means of avoiding legal liability for claims that the auditor did not perform the work promised. A standard type of letter is illustrated in Exhibit 5–1.

Obtain an Understanding of the Client. It is imperative to obtain a working knowledge of the client. An auditor must understand the broad economic environment in which the client operates, including such things as the effects of national economic policies (e.g., price regulation, import restriction), the geographic location and its economy (e.g., northeastern states or "sunbelt" states), and developments in the taxation and regulatory areas (e.g., the encouragement of more price competition in air transport and trucking). Next, the industry characteristics are important. Banking, insurance, and savings and loan companies operate in an industry environment altogether different from auto manufacture and chemicals processors. At the client level the personnel, products, production methods, and financing methods utilized in the business are important for efficient, effective audit work. Sources of this information include general business and economics magazines, industry and trade journals, Moody's and Standard and Poor's records, and company histories contained in registration statements and in the auditor's permanent file working papers. An auditor must be well read. In addition a walking tour of the client's plant and offices can contribute a great deal toward first-hand acquaintance with the layout, physical facilities, and accounting personnel and information systems.

Begin Engagement Planning. The first steps of planning the audit work have the goals of: (1) developing time budgets, (2) assigning audit staff personnel, and (3) scheduling dates for interim and year-end audit

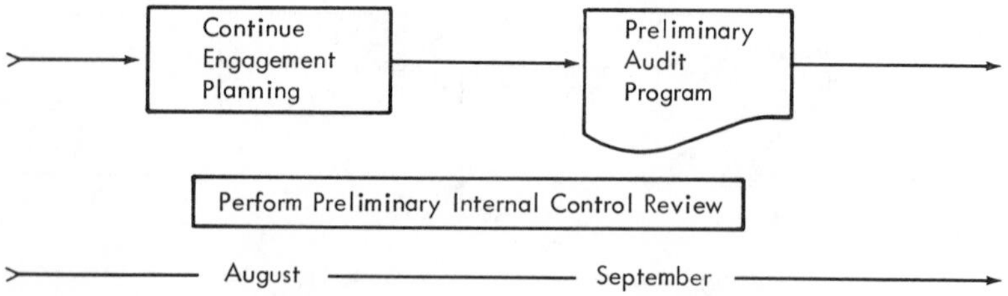

procedures. A time budget sets forth the number of hours expected to complete the audit, broken down by categories; for example, 40 hours for work on cash, 80 for work on inventories, 20 for report preparation, 25 for partner review and so forth. Audit staff personnel should be assigned to clients according to (1) capability, (2) availability, (3) rotation among clients, and (4) opportunity for on-the-job training and advancement. *Interim audit work* refers to a time period prior to the client's fiscal year-end when the audit team does work on testing compliance with the system of internal accounting control and substantive testing work on account balances available at that time. *Year-end procedures* refer to the kind of cutoff procedures, substantive tests of balances procedures and subsequent event review that are usually done on and after the client's fiscal year-end. (Other sections of this chapter and other chapters explain these elements in more detail.)

Preliminary analytical reviews play a large role in the initial engagement planning phase. A very useful type of review involves obtaining industry statistics from services such as Dun and Bradstreet and Robert Morris Associates. These statistics include industry averages for important financial yardsticks like the gross profit margin, return on sales, current ratio, debt/net worth, and many others. A comparison with client data may reveal out-of-line statistics indicating a relatively strong feature of the client, a weak financial position, or possibly an error or misstatement in the client's financial information. On an exception basis, ratio comparisons may aid in the audit program planning and time budgeting process. The client's own internal and interim financial statements should also be reviewed at this stage.

Other reviewing procedures helpful in planning may be carried out at this stage. The corporate charter and bylaws, articles of partnership, terms of a government grant (for grant-holding agencies), minutes of the meetings of directors, executive committee, audit committee, finance committee, and important new contracts and leases all should be reviewed with an eye to authorization of important accounting and auditing matters which should be followed up by subsequent evidence-gathering procedures. Pertinent minutes should be extracted or copied for inclusion in the working papers.

Preliminary Internal Control Review. This phase of continued engagement planning moves the audit team into some of the actual audit field work. The *review phase* of a proper study and evaluation of existing internal accounting control (described in detail in Chapter 6) involves the auditor in obtaining specific information about the client's major account-

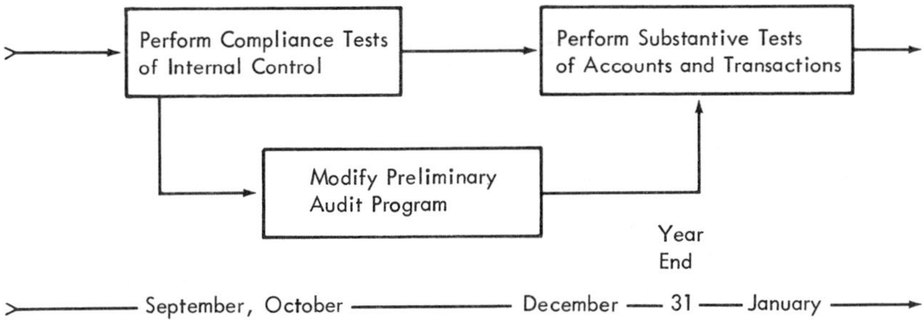

ing systems, the books and records of the client, internal accounting reports, major classes of transactions, and the procedures used to control for errors and irregularities in the accounting process. Auditors use the tools and techniques of interviews with client personnel, completion of internal control questionnaires (control checklists), and preparation of systems flowcharts to obtain an understanding of the existing internal accounting control system. At this stage enough detailed work should be done to determine whether management's design of internal control systems is satisfactory. This is not the systems compliance testing phase, however. It comes next in the sequence of events. This preliminary work on internal control is intended to provide the audit manager with better information for the task of preparing the preliminary audit program. At this point the auditor is primarily interested in knowing enough about the accounting systems to avoid adverse and unanticipated difficulties later on in the audit field work.

Preliminary Audit Program. An audit *program* is a listing of evidence-gathering *procedures* considered necessary to satisfy specific *practical audit objectives*. The program planning stage thus begins with recognition of specific objectives (for example: Determine whether inventories actually exist.), followed by a specification of procedures designed to produce sufficient competent evidential matter relevant to the objective (for example: On November 30, observe the client's count of inventory and personally test-count 350 randomly chosen inventory items selected from the perpetual inventory records.). Program planning is covered in more detail in this chapter and in Chapters 11–16. It involves segmentation of the audit work into manageable categories (e.g., cash, inventories), identification of material transactions and balances and attention to possible sources of errors and irregularities. Preliminary programs are prepared for both compliance testing of the internal accounting control system and substantive testing of account balances.

Compliance Testing Phase. Compliance tests of the existing system of internal accounting control upon which the auditor intends to rely are required by the second standard of field work. A proper study and evaluation of internal control includes two types of compliance tests—observation tests (auditor observance of control procedures that leave no audit trail of documentation) and detail tests of transactions (examination of documents that indicate performance of control procedures). Controls and testing procedures are explained in more detail in Chapters 6, 7, and 8.

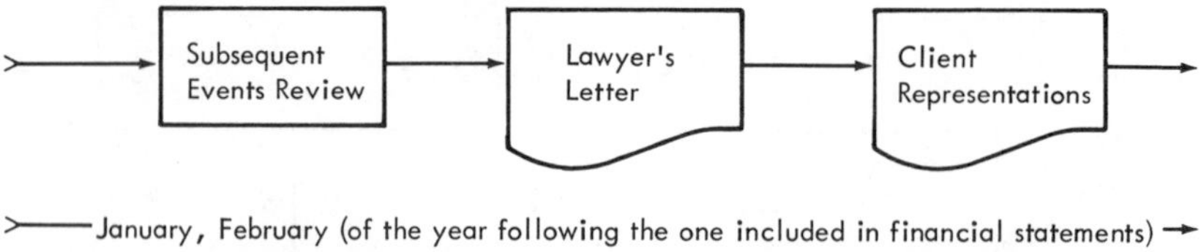

SAS No. 1, Section 320.65 explains a four-step logical approach to the evaluation of internal control, which focuses directly on the control purpose of preventing or detecting material errors and irregularities in financial statements. For each major class of transactions and related assets:

Consider the types of errors and irregularities that could occur.

Determine the accounting control procedures that should prevent or detect such errors and irregularities.

Determine whether (*a*) the necessary procedures are prescribed—review phase, and (*b*) they are being followed satisfactorily—compliance testing phase.

Evaluate weakness, if any. Decide what effect the absence or nonobservance of control procedures have on (*a*) the nature, timing, or extent of other auditing procedures, and (*b*) suggestions to be made to the client.

Modifying the Audit Program. The results of compliance tests may reveal new information about material weaknesses in internal accounting control. If so, the auditor should compensate by changing the preliminary audit program. For example, the plan may have included observation of inventory-taking on November 30 and reliance on a satisfactory perpetual record-keeping system thereafter to December 31 for the inventory numbers in financial statements. However, the auditor may move the inventory-taking date to December 31 if compliance tests show many errors in perpetual inventory transaction processing (e.g., failure to post purchases, many errors in figuring issues). This is an example of a *timing* change. Other changes involve the *nature* and *extent* of substantive tests and are discussed in more detail later.

Substantive Tests. The audit field work sequence is progressing to the requirement of the third AICPA field work standard—obtaining sufficient competent evidence to afford a reasonable basis for an opinion. Two classes of auditing procedures are involved: (1) tests of details of the money amounts of transactions and balances, and (2) analytical review of significant ratios and trends and resulting investigation of unusual fluctuations and questionable items. There are many specific substantive tests that can be applied, and these are covered in Chapters 11–16. Their specification (nature), timing, and extent (sample size) are fundamental audit programming decisions. One objective right around December 31 is to determine proper *cutoff*—whether transactions were recorded in the proper accounting period.

Subsequent Events Review. Independent auditors perform substantive procedures *after* the client's balance sheet date. There is a responsi-

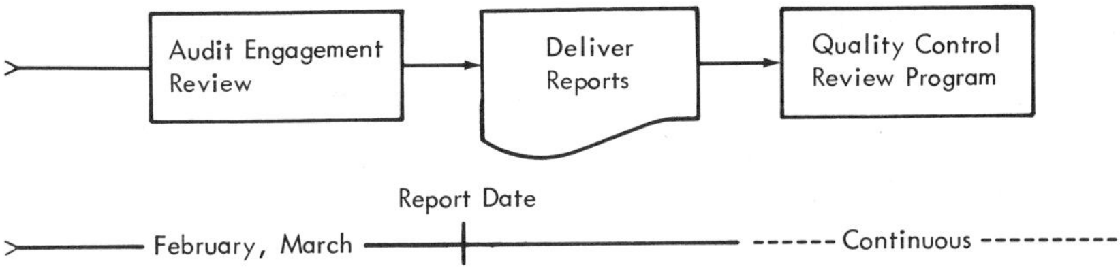

bility to report on significant events that occur between the balance sheet date and the date of the auditor's report. Sometimes these procedures are called the "post-balance-sheet review" or, in an SEC registration engagement, a "S–1 review."

Two types of subsequent events are important. The first is actually subsequent *knowledge* of conditions that existed at the balance sheet date which affect the measurement of financial statement amounts. For example, news of the bankruptcy of a major debtor on February 1 is new knowledge indicating that the customer's account receivable may not have been collectible as of December 31 (when the conditions of financial difficulty leading to bankruptcy probably existed). This type of event usually calls for adjustment of the financial statements. The second type involves events that arise after the balance sheet date but are significant enough to require disclosure in the financial statements (but no adjustment to accounts in the December 31 financial schedules). Examples include sale of new stock, acquisition of a business, and catastrophes such as fire or flood. Subsequent events review is covered in more detail in Chapter 16 under the topic of "Completion of Field Work."

Lawyers' Letters. *SAS No. 12* (Section 337) describes standards for "Inquiry of a Client's Lawyer concerning Litigation, Claims, and Assessments." These standards are closely aligned with FASB *Statement No. 5*, "Accounting for Contingencies." One standard procedure performed near the end of the field work is to obtain representations from the client's lawyers about litigation in process and unasserted claims that may represent risks and uncertainties in the client's business. Reporting on risks and uncertainties has always been troublesome, and since legal analyses are beyond the competence of auditors, help must be sought from attorneys. The client's lawyers are asked to give information about pending or threatened litigation, claims, and assessments and to comment on the completeness of a list prepared by management of unasserted claims and assessments that may eventually arise and have an unfavorable outcome. More details and an illustrative inquiry letter are in *SAS No. 12*.

Client Representations. *SAS No. 19* (Section 333, discussed in Chapter 4) requires that important client representations be reduced to writing. This step is considered necessary for completion of the audit so there can be as little room as possible for misunderstandings about where primary responsibility for financial statements lies and about important information transmitted by client personnel to the auditor.

Engagement Review. Auditing executives (partners, managers, and senior accountants in CPA firms, and their counterparts in internal and governmental audit organizations) participate in the review of work done

EXHIBIT 5–1
Engagement Letter

Anderson, Olds and Watershed
Certified Public Accountants
Chicago, Illinois
July 15, 1978

Mr. Larry Lancaster, Chairman
Apple Blossom Cologne Company
Chicago, Illinois

Dear Mr. Lancaster:

This will confirm our understanding of the arrangements made with you covering the examination which you wish us to make of the financial statements of Apple Blossom Cologne Company for the year ending December 31, 1978.

It is contemplated that, as in previous years, our work will consist of an examination of the balance sheet at December 31, 1978, and the related statements of income, retained earnings, and changes in financial position for the year ending that date. Our examination will be made in accordance with generally accepted auditing standards and, accordingly, will include such tests of the accounting records and such other auditing procedures as we consider necessary to enable us to express an opinion regarding your financial statements.

Our examination will be based on selective tests of recorded transactions. We will plan these tests and other procedures to search for material errors and irregularities that may affect your financial statements. Within the inherent limitations of our test-based audit we expect to obtain reasonable but not absolute assurance that major misstatements do not exist. Our findings regarding your system of internal accounting control, including information about material weaknesses, will be reported to you in a separate letter at the close of the audit.

At your request we will perform the following other services: (1) timely preparation of all required federal tax returns, and (2) a review and report on the company's methods for estimating unaudited replacement cost information in accordance with SEC *Accounting Series Release No. 190*.

Mr. Dalton Wardlaw will be the partner in charge of all work performed for you. He will inform you immediately if we encounter any circumstances which could significantly affect our fee estimate of $46,000 discussed with you on July 1, 1978. He is aware of the due date for the audit report, May 10, 1979. You should feel free to call on him at any time.

If the specifications above are in accordances with your understanding of the terms of our engagement, please sign below and return the duplicate copy to us. We look forward again to serving you as independent public accountants.

Sincerely yours,

Arnold Anderson

Arnold Anderson, CPA

Accepted by ______________________________ Date __________________________ on an audit engagement. The senior accountant reviews the work of the assistant accountants; the manager reviews the work of the seniors; and the partner in charge of the engagement reviews all the work. At each review stage, memoranda of additional work "to do" or questions to answer are prepared by the reviewer. These notes and questions must be cleared up before the audit is completed. The review and quality control process is an essential element of the exercise of due audit care. In particular, attention is given to adjusting entries and reclassification entries proposed by the audit team. Clients' cooperation in considering these changes to financial statements is very important.

Many audit firms practice what is known as a "cold review." In such a review a partner who is not otherwise associated with an engagement will take the report (in draft copy) and all the working papers and review the entire engagement with a fresh start. The purpose of a "cold" review is to obtain the unbiased view of a professional expert who has not become involved in client or audit personnel affairs and who is in no way committed to the particular engagement or its problems. A review of this nature is believed to be in keeping with the highest standards of professional practice.

Reports. The reports are finally ready to be delivered. The auditors prepare the appropriate audit report and opinion—unqualified, qualified, disclaimed, or adverse. The required communication on material weaknesses in internal accounting control is prepared and delivered (*SAS No. 20*, Section 323). This communication may be oral, and it may be delivered at an earlier date. Tax returns may be completed at this time if a part of the engagement, and ancillary services such as management services advice may be completed and reported.

Quality Control Review Programs. Monitoring the quality of a firm's practices is continuous and not confined strictly to the period of an engagement. The AICPA approved a Voluntary Quality Control Review Program for CPA Firms in 1976, after several years of developmental work and after the 1974 issuance of *SAS No. 4* (Section 160), "Quality Control Considerations for a Firm of Independent Auditors." In 1977 the AICPA formed the Quality Control Standards Committee which will issue pronouncements, and the AICPA section of SEC practice firms plans to make formal quality control reviews mandatory. Further details about quality control review programs are given in Chapter 16.

EVIDENCE IN AUDITING

The art of auditing has no codified rules governing the admissibility of evidence, and there are no universally applicable standards for the required quantity of evidence. However, the following four characteristics of audit evidence are useful for a general understanding of the quality and quantity of evidence: (1) relevance, (2) objectivity, (3) freedom from bias, and (4) persuasiveness. The first three characteristics define *competency* of evidence, and the last one has to do with the *sufficiency* of evidential matter as a basis for an audit decision.

Relevance. In the theory of legal evidence, and similarly for auditing, relevance is not an inherent characteristic of any item of evidence. Relevance is (1) a *quality* by which evidence is perceived as logically related to some matter required to be proved, and (2) a *relationship* between an item of evidence and a proposition sought to be proved.

The important point for auditors is that the gathering of irrelevant evidence is, at best, an inefficiency that can be costly both in unbillable time and in poor client relations. At worst irrelevant evidence can lead to entirely erroneous conclusions.

> ***Illustration.*** Auditor Larry Kermson prepared and mailed confirmations on all the clients' accounts payable with balances greater than zero as reflected in the subsidiary ledger. Upon receiving responses indicating no exceptions, he concluded that accounts payable were fairly stated. Actually Kermson's conclusion is spurious because he confirmed only those accounts that *were recorded.* His evidence (confirmation responses) was not relevant for proving the proposition that "No material accounts payable were *unrecorded,*" which is an important consideration for deciding whether the total of accounts payable is fairly stated. However, the evidence would support the proposition that all *recorded* accounts payable are proper obligations of the company.

Objectivity. Objectivity can be interpreted in auditing as it is in accounting: Evidence is objective if two or more different auditors can reach essentially the same decision based upon the same evidence. If widely different interpretations can be derived by prudent professional practitioners, then objectivity is lacking. Independent auditors have more stringent objectivity requirements than internal and governmental auditors because the latter two are able to report and evaluate in extended discussions and lengthy reports unlike those typically issued by CPAs.

> ***Illustration.*** Auditors sometimes have to determine whether a company is a "going concern" in order to apply accounting principles properly in financial statements. This decision involves at least an informal forecast of uncertain future events, and reasonable auditors may justifiably reach different conclusions. The "evidence" in the form of guesses, hopes, and promises may be so lacking in objectivity as to be unreliable for going-concern decision problems.

Freedom from Bias. This characteristic is also similar to an analogous concept in financial accounting. The essence is that evidence must be free from any biasing influence that may tend to support unfairly one decision alternative to the exclusion of evidence that would support a contrary alternative.

Bias in evidential matter is generally a function of the source of the evidence, but bias can also be a result of the auditor's choice of items for audit attention. The possibility that bias may exist should cause the auditor to retain some healthy skepticism throughout the evidence-gathering process. As examples, positive responses taken from executives concerning internal control procedures, recoverability of costs, and subjective judgments on income tax disputes should be dutifully sought, but the auditor should subsequently test for compliance with control procedures, evaluate the possibilities for cost recovery, and identify the settlement probabilities in income tax controversies.

The more difficult task is to guard against bias in the auditor's own selection of procedures and selection of items for audit. Auditors sometimes concentrate time and effort on high-dollar-value items and on documents that tend to have many errors. There is nothing inherently wrong about allocating audit time and effort to cover the most dollars and discover the most errors. However, when the concentration forces auditors to give only passing attention to small-dollar items and apparent low-error documents, then they have created bias in their evidence.

Illustration. Independent auditors typically begin an evaluation of internal accounting control by obtaining questionnaire responses from a ranking accounting officer. These responses mostly refer to things supposedly done by other personnel and not by the officer. This information is in the nature of hearsay, and the auditor must later obtain better direct evidence that duties and procedures are actually performed by subordinate personnel. However, a negative declaration (for example, "The bank statement has not been reconciled for ten months.") may be taken as relatively convincing; but the statement "Sure, Smith reconciles the bank statement every month" is definitely a matter not to be taken on the officer's word standing alone.

Illustration. Auditor Elizabeth Bugg was assigned the task of testing the client's calculations of inventory extensions (quantity multiplied by unit price). She selected a small random sample and found a few errors, including misplaced decimals and price-per-gross applied to quantities counted in dozens. Having found these errors, she decided to extend her testing by recalculating all the inventory items extended to an amount of $10,000 or more. On this basis she found several more errors, and she summarized the total dollar amount of error for a recommended adjusting journal entry. Ms. Bugg has injected bias by selecting for recalculation those items that were most likely to have errors of *overstatement.* An amount erroneously calculated too low (as $9,000 instead of $90,000) would not be detected. By correcting for the amount of detected error, Ms. Bugg may be responsible for causing a material inventory understatement as a result of her systematic exclusion of calculations likely to contain errors of understatement.

The three characteristics of relevance, objectivity, and freedom from bias define *competency of evidence*, a criterion required by the AICPA and GAO standards of field work. The next characteristic defines sufficiency of evidence which is also an integral element of the field work standards.

Persuasiveness. In the context of a scientific decision process the evidence must provide an adequate basis for a conclusion. Audit decisions must be based on enough evidential matter of a competent nature that they can stand the test of review by other auditors and by outsiders. The auditing profession has no officially expressed and universally applicable standards for how much evidence is enough. Like the theoretical matter of relevance, the determination is left to the logic, expertise, and ability of the individual auditor.

Sources and Relative Strengths of Evidence

In the process of describing the four characteristics above, some indications of the sources and relative persuasive strengths of evidence have emerged. In general, evidence may be categorized as follows (in descending order of relative strength):

1. Mathematical evidence.
2. Physical observation (eyewitness) evidence.
3. External evidence.
4. External-internal evidence.
5. Internal evidence.

Mathematical evidence may be strictly compelling on the auditor's decision process, but in this sense mathematical evidence is limited. Calculations such as column footings, sales commission calculations, depreciation calculations, medicare reimbursement formula calculations, and pension cost actuarial computations can be recalculated by the auditor, and he or she can determine absolutely whether they are mathematically correct. The limitations are (1) the underlying bases must be audited (a correct calculation with erroneous inputs is still erroneous), and (2) some mathematical calculations such as ratio analyses depend both on audited data and on comparisons with independent data (e.g., externally prepared industry statistics) which must be obtained from a reliable source.

Eyewitness, physical observation evidence is also highly persuasive, but this evidence is limited to tangible assets. An auditor can count inventory and petty cash, observe and tally fixed assets, but here the use of observation ends. (The count-observation of notes receivable and investment security certificates is actually the physical observation of the paper form of an intangible, but observation of this type may also be considered eyewitness evidence.)

External evidence is evidential matter that is obtained from the other party to an arm's-length transaction or from outside independent agencies. Purely external evidence reaches the auditor directly and does not pass through the hands of client management or the client's data processing system. Examples are confirmations of accounts receivable, cutoff bank statements, and industry statistics from a trade association or government agency.

External-internal evidence, on the other hand, is documentary material that originates outside the bounds of client management but which has passed through the client's information processing system. The regular monthly bank statement, invoices from vendors, and cash remittance advices from customers are examples of documents that originate outside but are viewed by the auditor after internal information processing. Canceled checks are documents that originate in the company, are sent out to third parties, and later returned to the information system. In a sense, such evidential matter is slightly "tainted," not considered as reliable as purely external evidence but more reliable than purely internal evidence.

Internal evidence consists of verbal and documentary material that is produced, circulates, and finally resides within the client's information processing system. Such evidence either is not touched by outside parties at all or is several steps removed from third-party attention. This is the least convincing evidence of all, consisting largely of such things as bank reconciliations, insurance policy files, customer or patient history records, credit records, internal reports, cost distribution work sheets, and many other forms of paperwork characteristic of a bureaucratic organization. Internal evidence may be relied upon only to the extent that it is produced under conditions of satisfactory internal control. Not to be overlooked are oral and written representations by client management. These too are internal evidence.

When planning and executing an audit program for gathering and evaluating evidence, an auditor must always consider the competency and sufficiency of the evidence, as well as the relative strengths and sources of it. Of course, evidence of different types may be combined to form a persuasive evidential base (e.g., internal evidence of adequate sales invoice processing with external evidence from confirmations of accounts receivable). With these considerations in mind, the procedures and methods for gathering appropriate audit evidence are considered next.

AUDIT OBJECTIVES AND PROCEDURES

The most important technical aspects of auditing are to know *why* something is being done (i.e., objectives) and *how* it is to be done (i.e., procedures). Other important aspects are concerned with *when* procedures are performed and *by whom*. All of these facets may come under the heading of planning and programming an audit.

Practical Audit Objectives

The ultimate objective for the independent auditor is to render the attestation on financial statements. Internal auditors and GAO auditors have the objective of producing effective information reports of findings. Subordinate to these ultimate output objectives, however, are several more specific goals that may be termed *practical audit objectives*. They provide nuclei around which procedures may be grouped to form an audit program. The most important practical objectives are *existence-occurrence*, *valuation*, *cutoff*, *accounting principles and disclosure*, *compliance*, and *effectiveness*.

The first objective is to establish with evidence that assets, liabilities, and equities actually exist and that sales and expense transactions actually occurred. Thus an auditor will count cash and inventory, confirm receivables and insurance policies, and search for unrecorded liabilities to discover whether the actual tangible things or economic claims are real. One must be careful at this point because the finding of existence alone generally proves little about the other objectives.

The next objective is to determine whether proper values have been assigned to assets, liabilities, equities, revenue, and expense. Thus auditors will reconcile bank accounts, look up inventory costs and obtain lower-of-cost-or-market data, evaluate collectibility of receivables, trace insurance policy terms to actuarial computations of liabilities, and search for payment of unrecorded liabilities. In many cases preliminary dollar valuation evidence may be obtained concurrently with existence evidence but only when the counting unit is dollars. (The counting unit for accounts receivable is dollars, whereas inventory physical quantities are counted first, then unit prices are multiplied to yield an extension and a dollar total.)

The cutoff objective is a special case of accounting period propriety. The auditor must determine that transactions recorded in the period under audit do not belong in the periods preceding or following, and that transactions recorded in the periods preceding or following do not belong in the period under audit. Auditors' terminology includes the term "cutoff date" which refers to the fiscal year-end. Transactions recorded in two- or three-week periods before and after the cutoff date receive special attention in keeping with the cutoff objective.

Financial audits for which there is to be an attestation also have the objective of determining whether accounting principles are properly selected and applied and whether disclosures are adequate. The facets of this objective include proper current and long-term balance sheet classification, mathematical accuracy of figures, and footnote disclosure of accounting policies. The accounting principles objective is the meeting place for accounting principles and audit reporting standards.

Many auditors would include as an objective the determination of *ownership* of assets. This is highly important and should not be overlooked in terms of proper accounting principles application. However, some capitalized assets are not "owned" in the legal sense (e.g., leased assets), and some balances on the liability side are not "owed" in a legal sense (e.g., deferred tax credits and estimates of warranty liability). Determination of ownership is usually an audit objective, but other economic relationships are reflected in financial statements under generally accepted accounting principles.

Compliance with laws and regulations is very important for the business, and disclosure of known noncompliance is usually necessary for the fair presentation of financial statements in conformity with generally accepted accounting principles. (See *SAS No. 17*, Section 328, "Illegal Acts by Clients.") Independent auditors should be familiar with financially-related laws and regulations such as federal and state securities acts, labor laws (e.g., payroll tax withholding, minimum wages, 1974 pension reform act), wage and price controls, income tax laws, and specialized industry regulations. Compliance with legal terms of the company's private contracts (e.g., merger agreements, bond indentures) is also important for financial statement presentations.

Compliance with laws and regulations is also a special objective that is always characteristic of governmental audits (GAO, IRS, bank examiners) and is generally an objective for an internal auditor with respect to managerial policies.

Effectiveness is an objective typical of GAO audits and internal audits whose purpose is to evaluate the results of a program and/or the performance of managers. Such evaluation involves the requirement to know of performance goals and related performance management. Independent audits include this objective only as a subsidiary matter of added service to the client, although in management advisory services engagements it may be the only objective.

The major point to express about practical audit objectives is that they serve as focal points for organizing procedures. If auditors can discern each objective for each audit problem, then they can more easily identify the sources of competent evidence and the procedural means of obtaining the evidence.

General Evidence-Gathering Procedures

There are seven basic types and sources of evidence and eight general procedures that auditors use to gather evidence. One or more of these eight procedures may be used no matter what account balance, transaction flow, or program event is under audit. Arrangements and combinations of the procedures constitute an audit program. Exhibit 5–2 shows the seven types of evidence and the procedures most closely related to each.

EXHIBIT 5–2
Types of Evidence and Related Audit Procedures

Types of Evidence	*Evidence-Gathering Procedures*
1. Auditor's calculations	1. Recalculation by the auditor
2. Physical observation	2. Observation and examination by the auditor
3. Statements by independent parties	3. Confirmation by letter
4. Statements by client personnel	4. Verbal inquiry and written representations
5. Authoritative documents prepared by independent parties	5. Vouching (examination of documents)
6. Authoritative documents prepared by the client	6. Retracing • Vouching
7. Data interrelationships	7. Scanning 8. Analysis of interrelationships

1. Recalculation by the auditor of calculations previously performed by client personnel produces mathematical evidence that can be compelling. A prior calculation is either right or wrong. Such mathematical evidence can serve the objectives of both existence and valuation for financial statement amounts that exist principally as calculations; for example, depreciation, pension liabilities, actuarial reserves, statutory bad debt reserves, and product guarantee liabilities. Recalculation, in combination with other procedures, is also used to provide evidence of valuation for all other financial data.

2. *Physical observation* and examination of tangible assets provides compelling evidence of existence and may provide tentative evidence of condition and quality. In a strict sense, physical observation is limited to tangible assets and formal documents such as securities certificates. In a broader sense, the procedure of physical observation is utilized whenever the auditor views the activity of a client's personnel and the physical facilities on the inspection tour, when watching personnel carry out data processing activities, when participating in a surprise payroll distribution, and by a general awareness of events in the client's offices.

3. *Confirmation* by direct correspondence with independent parties is a widely used procedure in auditing. Most transactions involve outside parties, and theoretically, written correspondence could be conducted even on such items as individual paychecks. However, auditors limit their use of confirmation to major transactions and balances about which outside parties could be expected to provide information. A selection of confirmation applications is shown below:

Banks—account balances
Customers—receivables balances
Borrowers—note terms and balances
Agents—inventory on consignment or in warehouses
Lenders—note terms and balances
Policyholders—life insurance contracts
Vendors—accounts payable balances
Registrar—number of shares of stock outstanding
Attorneys—litigation in progress
Trustees—securities held, terms of agreements
Lessors—lease terms

Confirmations of receivables and payables may take two forms—positive confirmation or negative confirmation. An example of a positive confirmation is shown in Exhibit 5–3. The negative confirmation form is

EXHIBIT 5–3
Positive Confirmation Form

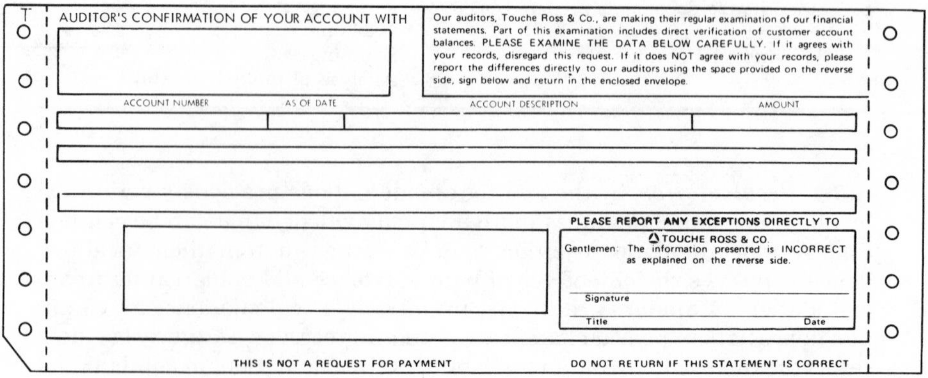
AUDITOR'S CONFIRMATION OF YOUR ACCOUNT WITH

Our auditors, Touche Ross & Co., are making their regular examination of our financial statements. Part of this examination includes direct verification of customer account balances. PLEASE EXAMINE THE DATA BELOW CAREFULLY. If it agrees with your records, disregard this request. If it does NOT agree with your records, please report the differences directly to our auditors using the space provided on the reverse side, sign below and return in the enclosed envelope.

ACCOUNT NUMBER	AS OF DATE	ACCOUNT DESCRIPTION	AMOUNT

PLEASE REPORT ANY EXCEPTIONS DIRECTLY TO

TOUCHE ROSS & CO.
Gentlemen: The information presented is INCORRECT as explained on the reverse side.

Signature

Title Date

THIS IS NOT A REQUEST FOR PAYMENT

DO NOT RETURN IF THIS STATEMENT IS CORRECT

simply a request for a response only if something is wrong with the balance, thus nonresponses are considered evidence of propriety. Generally a positive confirmation includes a recitation that an audit is being performed with a request to provide specified information directly to the auditor. Confirmations should be signed by client's officers, although they are controlled in preparation, in mailing, and in return by the auditor.

4. ***Verbal inquiry*** is a procedure that generally involves the collection of oral evidence from independent parties and client officials. Written statements must be obtained in response to an important inquiry. An auditor begins to use this procedure with the early office and plant tour and continues to use it to the end of the audit when a representation letter is obtained and when conferences in connection with post-balance-sheet events are conducted. Evidence gathered by formal and informal inquiry generally cannot stand alone as convincing, and the auditor usually has to corroborate this evidence with independent findings based on other procedures. An exception to this general rule is a negative statement where someone volunteers adverse information such as an admission of defalcation or use of an accounting policy that is misleading.

Formal inquiries may be distinguished from the informal in two ways. First, the responses to formal inquiries are generally written. Second, formal inquiries deal with important substantive matters. One of the most visible forms is the internal control questionnaire which is illustrated in Chapter 6. Another form is the client representation letter. Other verbal inquiries may request a wide variety of responses, and the auditor may tailor them to the requirements of each audit engagement. In internal audits, representations may refer to a wide variety of manager's assertions, and as evident in the GAO reporting standards some of these representations may appear in the audit report.

5. ***Vouching*** means the *examination of documents*. The important aspect of the vouching procedure is the *direction* of the search for audit evidence. Generally an item of financial information is selected from an account (e.g., the posting of a sales invoice in a customer's account), then the auditor goes *backward* through the bookkeeping-filing system to find the source documentation that supports the item selected (e.g., looking for the journal entry, the sales summary, the sales invoice copy, and the shipping documents). With vouching of documents an auditor can decide whether all *recorded data* are adequately supported, but he does not yet have relevant evidence to decide whether all events were recorded. (This latter problem is covered by the next procedure—*retracing*.)

Vouching is useful for gathering evidence contained in authoritative documents prepared by independent parties and in authoritative documents prepared by the client.

Authoritative documents prepared by independent outside parties. A great deal of documentary evidence is external-internal in nature. The most convincing of this documentation is that which has been prepared by other parties and sent to the client. The signatures, seals, engraving, or other distinctive artistic attributes of formal authoritative documents make such sources more reliable (less susceptible to alteration) than ordinary authoritative documents prepared by outsiders. Some examples of both types of documents are shown below:

Formal Authoritative Documents	*Ordinary Authoritative Documents*
Bank statements	Vendors' invoices
Canceled checks	Customers' purchase orders
Insurance policies	Loan applications
Notes receivable (on unique forms)	Insurance policy applications
Securities certificates	Notes receivable (on standard bank forms)
Indenture agreements	Simple contracts
Elaborate contracts	Correspondence
Title papers (e.g., autos)	

Authoritative documents prepared and processed within the entity under audit. Documentation of this type has the characteristics of internal evidence. Some such documents may be quite informal and not very authoritative or reliable at all. As a general proposition the reliability of these documents depends upon the quality of internal control under which they were produced and processed. Some of the more usual kinds of these documents are listed below:

Sales invoice copies	Shipping documents
Sales summary reports	Receiving reports
Cost distribution reports	Requisition slips
Loan approval memos	Purchase orders
Budgets and performance reports	Credit memoranda
Documentation of transactions with subsidiary or affiliated companies	

6. ***Retracing*** is a procedure that is essentially the opposite of vouching. When an auditor performs retracing, he or she selects sample items of basic source documents and *proceeds forward* through the bookkeeping process (whether manual or electronic) to find the final recording of the accounting transactions. Thus samples of payroll payments are traced to cost and expense accounts, sales invoices to the sales accounts, cash receipts to the accounts receivable subsidiary, and cash disbursements to the accounts payable, to name a few examples.

Using the retracing procedure, an auditor can contribute evidence to decisions about whether all events were recorded, thus complementing the evidence obtained from the vouching procedure. However, care must be taken to be alert to events that may not have been captured in the source documents and thus not even entered in the system. For example, the search for unrecorded liabilities for materials must include examination of invoices received in the period following the fiscal year-end and examination of receiving reports dated near the year-end. In nonmanufacturing businesses the retracing search for a relevant basic population may include loan-approval files, correspondence with attorneys, life insurance file search, and many other unique sources of evidence.

7. ***Scanning*** is oftentimes termed "scrutinizing" in auditing literature and practice. Scanning is the procedural means by which auditors exercise their general alertness to unusual items and events in documentation. A typical scanning directive in an audit program is: "Scrutinize the expense accounts for credit entries, vouch any to source documents."

In general, scanning is an "eyes-open" approach of looking for anything unusual in order to identify such items for vouching or retracing. The scanning procedure usually does not produce direct evidence itself, but it does produce questions for which evidence must be obtained by the careful auditor. Thus such things as debits in revenue accounts, credits in expense accounts, unusually large accounts receivable write-offs, unusually large paychecks, unusually small sales volume in the month following the year-end, and large cash deposits just prior to year-end are typical questions turned up by the scanning effort.

Scanning is a valuable procedure to use when random sampling and statistical methods are applied in audit decisions. When a random sample is the basis for selection of items for audit, there always exists the risk of choosing a sample that does not actually reflect the entire population of items. Such an event may cause a decision error. Auditors can subjectively mitigate this risk by scanning items not selected in the random sample in order to guard against decision error.

8. ***Analyses of interrelationships with other data*** constitute a major aspect of the analytical reviews and tests used by auditors. There are several major types of analyses used regularly: (1) ratio and trend analysis, (2) comparison analysis, (3) correlation with audit of related accounts, and (4) references to statistical data produced by independent agencies.

Ratio and trend analysis performed as a part of the preliminary review involves the computation and study of financial ratios and amounts based on a client's *unaudited* financial statements for comparison to ratios and amounts based on prior years' audited data. The fact that current-year calculations are based on unaudited data enables the auditor to notice out-of-line conditions that may be caused by accounting errors; for example, when the gross profit margin shows a decline, the auditor will want to investigate closely the recording of sales, inventory pricing, and the valuation of ending inventory. An auditor must also be alert to situations in which changes *should have occurred* but are not evident in the unaudited numbers; for example, if the auditor knows that credit sales have increased, then he or she may also expect to find an increase in the ratio of doubtful accounts to total accounts receivable. However, generalizations about ratio relationships that *could* materialize are tentative because each company and each audit situation is unique. Ratio and trend analysis performed near the end of the field work may also involve comparison of the company's audited operating statistics with comparable industry data and audited data from prior years.

Comparison analysis generally involves the construction of an array of minor accounts (e.g., small-balance expense accounts) of the current year in parallel with the same accounts of the prior year. The auditor may study these for significant changes in amounts from year to year (a rough variety of trend analysis) and may detect a clue for further investigation. Again, the auditor must be alert for the situation in which a balance has not changed much from one year to the next when other facts indicate that it should have changed; for example, if the client's accountant records a property tax accrual based on the prior year's rate and valuation when those assessments have in fact changed, then the comparison will show no significant change when one should have been recorded. The auditor must know about such general economic conditions as price changes, local tax rates, and a variety of other matters that aid the procedure of comparison analysis. Comparisons of actual performance data with budget expectations are also useful, especially when followed up with management's explanation of why actual results differed from the budget.

Many financial accounts are *paired* in that the data in one is a function of the data in another. Thus by an audit of both accounts the findings related to one can support findings related to the other. Some of these account relationships are item-by-item direct, and others are related in general. For example, each item of interest expense should relate to a specifically identifiable interest-bearing liability. Failure to match an interest payment with a liability may indicate an unrecorded liability and a misstatement in another account as well, and failure to find an interest payment or accrual in accordance with borrowing terms may indicate an understatement of expense, perhaps a default on a debt, and possibly a need for some adjustments or explanatory disclosure. General relationships involve the auditor in analyses of related account balances. When sales increase, cost of sales should also increase; when inventories and purchases increase, accounts payable should also increase. A list of some of the major related accounts is given below:

Sales—Cost of sales	Interest expense—Interest-bearing liabilities
Sales—Sales returns	Purchases—Accounts payable
Sales—Accounts receivable	Net income—Income taxes
Accounts receivable—Bad debts	Capital stock—Professional fees
Fixed assets—Depreciation	Legal fees—Contingent liabilities
Investment income—Investments	Insurance expense—Fixed assets
Demand deposits—Loans	

PREPARATION AND MODIFICATION OF AUDIT PROGRAMS

The process of actually putting together an audit program is an exercise of the scientific decision methodology that is emphasized throughout this text. Financial audits are organized along the lines of typical balance sheet and income statement account titles—cash, securities, receivables, accounts payable, capital stock, sales, and so forth. For each of these segments the auditor faces the basic problem of deciding whether the assertions of economic things and events represented by each category are fair representations of real things and events. In brief, for each segment auditors must design the program along the following lines:

1. Recognize the explicit and implicit assertions presented in financial classifications, amounts, and supplementary disclosures.

2. Identify clearly the pertinent features of the practical audit objectives and select appropriate procedures that will produce sufficient competent evidence related to existence, valuation, cutoff, accounting principles and disclosure, compliance, and effectiveness (to the extent that each is within the scope of the engagement).
3. Write the selected procedures in an instructional form so that senior and assistant accountants will know what to do in order to gather the evidence.

Programs for Independent Audits

As an illustration, consider the problem of constructing an audit program for the audit of the expense account entitled Officers' Salaries. The assertions offered by this account title and the amount are not too complex. Basically the assertions are:

- All officers are properly employed by the company.
- Officers' salary amounts are approved by the board of directors.
- Salaries were all paid and recorded in the expense account.
- Salaries were not improperly classified in other accounts.
- Other forms of compensation, if any, were properly paid or accrued and properly classified (e.g., stock option and bonus plans).
- Disclosures concerning officers' compensation are complete (some details are required in SEC filings).
- Individual officers and the company complied with their respective duties under employment contracts.

Inherent in the assertions are features of existence, valuation, accounting principles and disclosure, cutoff, and compliance. The list of procedures, arranged under headings for these practical objectives is shown in Exhibit 5–4. Notice that each of these procedures defines the evidence to be gathered by the auditor.

Programs for Internal Audits

Internal audit staffs are well advised to develop long-range planning programs as well as individual assignment audit programs. The internal auditing function, unlike the independent audit engagement, is characterized by an ongoing, everyday association with company affairs and management. A long-range planning program is necessary for scheduling assignments, assigning staff personnel, supporting the funding allocation for the internal audit function, involving top management in requests for audit assignments and coordinating with management's operating plans. Also the long-range plan enables internal audit executives to evaluate the performance of their own staffs and facilitates coordination of internal audit activities with the independent auditor's engagement.

Modern internal auditors pay particular attention to their audit objectives as a means of carefully aligning the audit with the needs of management. An example of the contrast between independent auditors' ob-

EXHIBIT 5–4

AUDIT PROGRAM: OFFICERS' SALARY EXPENSE

A. *Existence*

1. Obtain a current organization chart and make a list of officers.
2. Vouch this list to salary authorizations in directors' minutes.
3. Observe the individuals and their office locations.

B. *Valuation*

1. From step A–2 above, list authorized salaries.
2. Select a sample of entries in the expense account and vouch to—
   - *a.* Payroll journal.
   - *b.* Employee earnings record.
   - *c.* Canceled checks.
3. Add up the authorized salaries and compare to the expense account balance.
4. Retrace payroll journal entries to posting in the expense account.

C. *Accounting Principles and Disclosure*

1. Inquire about the existence of any stock option or bonus plans.
2. Scan stock issue records for issue of shares to officers.
3. Confirm with stock registrar any reservation of shares for such plans.
4. If there is a bonus plan, recalculate the bonus amount and determine that it has been paid or accrued.
5. Review detail disclosures about salaries, compensation, stock options, bonuses for correspondence with basic evidence.

D. *Cutoff*

This objective is essentially satisfied with procedures B–3, B–4, and C–4 above.

E. *Compliance*

1. Obtain and read employment contracts, if any, and determine whether their terms have been satisfied.
2. Determine whether there are any unrecorded expense and liability amounts based on the contracts.

F. *General*

Working papers should fully document all evidence obtained by the above procedures, including evidence of errors and deficient disclosure. Curative adjustments and disclosures should be recommended and documented.

jectives and internal auditors' objectives respecting audit of payroll is exhibited below.

Independent auditors' approach

1. Review internal checks designed to:
   - *a.* Prevent improper additions of names to the payroll and the prompt deletion of the names of those separated from the rolls.

   b. Assure the accuracy of the hours worked.
   c. Control the mechanics of calculating net and gross pay.
   d. Protect against misuse of check stock and signature plates.
2. Review legislation concerning various deductions.
3. Analyze distribution of labor costs to operating or overhead areas.
4. Examine wage rates and related matters defined in the union agreement.[2]

Internal auditors' approach

1. An examination of the payroll department's assignment of duties, organization, staffing, and work flow. Payroll work is subject to peak loads followed by sharp dips in activity. There is generally a tendency to staff for the peaks. The valleys will see overstaffing, lowered efficiency, and loss of morale. Lowered efficiency will affect the peaks, calling for still further staffing. The cycle could be vicious.
2. An analysis of overtime payments—the incidence and the factors behind them. Why, for example, should a man work 35 hours in one week and 45 hours in the next? Does this happen often? Does this happen in a number of departments? Are there indications of poor planning and manloading?
3. An evaluation of labor turnover—whether it is high, low, or average for the industry and what reasons are advanced or determined for high turnover.
4. A check of night premium payments. Why, for instance, are only 20 percent of the maintenance people on night premium when 70 percent of routine maintenance can be dealt with more effectively after the operating departments are shut down?[3]

In addition to audits of payroll functions, internal auditors may be involved in a wide variety of analyses that require equally imaginative viewpoints. Some examples of assignments are listed below:

1. Acquisition of new EDP equipment.
2. Acquisitions of other companies.
3. Budgets for research and development projects.
4. Marketing cost analysis.
5. Marketing research evaluation.
6. Marketing strategy analysis.
7. Evaluation of management objectives.
8. Evaluation of management plans.
9. Evaluation of organization structure.

The major difference between programs for independent audits and programs for internal audits is the ultimate objective. For the former, the ultimate objective is the opinion on financial statements, but for the latter it is an evaluation designed to report on and enhance managerial efficiency. Consequently, the objectives of efficiency takes dominance in an internal audit, and the other practical objectives dominate the independent auditor's program of procedures.

---

[2] Lawrence B. Sawyer, *The Practice of Modern Internal Auditing* (Altamonte Springs, Florida: The Institute of Internal Auditors, Inc., 1973), p. 156.

[3] Sawyer, *The Practice of Modern Internal Auditing*, pp. 156–57.

Modification of Audit Programs

Essentially, the discussion thus far has reviewed the evidence produced by, and the relevance of, procedures. Also quite important in program planning and execution are the following:

1. *Nature.* *Which* audit procedures are to be performed.
2. *Timing.* *When* the audit work is performed.
3. *Extent.* *How much* audit evidence is obtained.

Nature of Auditing Procedures. During the planning phase of the audit, when auditors construct a preliminary audit program, they select procedures that they would like to perform. For a particular audit problem, alternative procedures may be available. For example, if the company has inventories stored in outside warehouses, the auditor might (1) if related internal controls are strong, obtain evidence of existence with a confirmation from the warehouseman; otherwise the auditor might (2) visit the warehouse and conduct a physical inspection. The *nature* of these procedures is different.

Generally an auditor will choose first the procedure that will produce the strongest evidence. But if that procedure is too costly (visiting a distant warehouse, for example), the auditor might settle for alternative procedures such as (*a*) confirmation from the warehouseman and (*b*) vouching of shipping reports related to the inventory. Such a combination of several sources of evidence of lesser strength than physical observation may produce sufficient evidence for a decision.

Timing of Procedure Applications. A significant portion of an audit can be done during an interim work period prior to the fiscal year-end. In many important respects, an audit of a nine- or ten-month period can be completed. At interim the auditor can evaluate internal accounting control and arrive at conclusions that are definite as to the period reviewed and at least tentative as to the after-interim period. If internal control is strong, confirmation of receivables and observation of inventory may be planned for a date prior to the fiscal year-end. Likewise all recalculations, document examinations, analyses of accounts and vouching of major transactions, analyses of interrelationships, inquiries, and scanning relevant to the period covered by interim work can be completed. The results are thus three-fold: (1) a major portion of the audit will have been accomplished in otherwise slack time; (2) year-end audit work may be minimized and limited to an updating of all work that could not be completed at interim; or (3) the auditor may gain information leading to modification of the nature and extent of auditing procedures that were in the preliminary program for year-end work.

At worst the auditor could learn that internal accounting control over data processing accuracy operated so poorly that little reliance could be placed on the client's records. This finding might mean that important procedures such as confirmation of receivables and observation of inventories would have to be performed on the year-end date. Some account analyses and some vouching could be performed, but most work would have to be done later when the full year's data were available. Learning of serious record deficiencies early can also make it possible for the auditor to do more vouching work at interim rather than crowding overtime into a tight December audit schedule.

Other aspects of timing include the planning of surprise appearances. Unannounced audits of banks and savings and loan associations are common. Surprise observation of payroll distributions, surprise petty cash counts, and unscheduled tests of computer programs are typical means of finding operations in their "natural" state. Such appearances prevent any preparatory good-behavior activities on the part of a client's personnel.

Extent of Procedure Applications. Perhaps the most crucial question for the execution of audit procedures is "How much evidence?" This question relates technical performance directly to the general and field standards of due care, evaluation of internal control, and sufficiency of evidence. For instance: How many accounts receivable to confirm? How many inventory items to test count and to vouch for prices? How many receipts and disbursement items to retrace and vouch? How many sales invoices to examine? How many fixed asset additions to vouch? How many depreciation calculations to recalculate? How many demand deposits to confirm? When does the auditor have *enough* evidence?

At risk of oversimplifying, one can observe that judgment, expertise, and experience can serve the veteran auditor well in deciding how much. The veteran has a "sixth sense" about how much evidence is enough, acquired through encountering many and varied audit situations. All this is of small comfort to the beginning auditor, and little of it is amenable to textbook presentation in a scientific approach to auditing decision problems.

The inputs of judgment that help decide questions of extent of procedural applications are these:

1. *Information about characteristics of the data population.* This preliminary information includes the potential number of data items, whether they are of widely varied dollar amounts, and whether they are from the same information system as all other similar items. In statistical applications this information is condensed into the parameters of population size, population strata, and estimated population standard deviation.
2. *The relative risk factor.* This factor generally refers to the relatively greater likelihood that assets may be overstated rather than understated and that liabilities are more likely to be understated than overstated. Other considerations such as financial instability of the company or knowledge of nonarm's-length transactions with affiliates are elements of relative risk.
3. *Materiality of balances and error amounts.* Large dollar amounts, the unique character of a basic event (e.g., litigation for damages), and the financial impact of possible measurement errors define materiality for the auditor. In statistical applications a material amount of

allowable error must be specified in order to perform a mathematical evaluation of audit findings.

4. *Internal control strength or weakness.* The amount of subsequent audit work depends largely on the reliability of the records, which is inferred from a proper study and evaluation of information system control. Essentially, the internal accounting control evaluation gives the auditor some indication of the likelihood that material error has gone undetected.
5. *Other situation-specific factors.* Other miscellaneous factors cannot be ignored. Oftentimes these overlap with the four criteria described above, and they are often unique to a particular audit engagement. Other situations include:

   - Audits in which management's and auditor's interests appear to be in definite conflict.
   - When estimates of future events foretell that historical trends cannot be relied upon.
   - When collusion and unusual irregularities have been detected.
   - When amounts and events lack evidential qualities to make them verifiable and thus auditable.

The auditor's preliminary decisions relative to these judgment inputs can cause modification of a preliminary audit program in accordance with the circumstances. Each modification designed to collect more or less evidential matter will bear upon the question of "how much evidence." Mathematical-statistical applications can assist in decisions about sample size and the extent of audit, and these methods are discussed in Chapters 7 and 10.

WORKING PAPER DOCUMENTATION

The planning and execution of an audit program is not complete without the preparation of proper working paper documentation. Working papers are the auditor's own evidence of compliance with generally accepted auditing standards and of the decisions respecting all procedures necessary in the circumstances unique to the audit engagement. The working papers are a record of the solution of numerous decision problems that in the aggregate constitute the audit engagement. Even though the auditor is the legal owner of the working papers, professional ethics require that they not be transferred without consent of the client because of the confidential information that is necessarily recorded in them. Detail auditing standards concerning working papers are in *SAS No. 1,* Section 338.

Working papers can be classified in three categories for explanation purposes: (1) permanent file papers, (2) audit administrative papers, and (3) audit evidence papers.

Permanent File Papers

The permanent file contains papers of continuing interest over many years' audits of the same client. This file can be used year after year, while each year's current audit evidence papers are filed away once they have served their purpose. Documents of permanent interest and applicability include copies or excerpts of the corporate or association charter, bylaws, or partnership agreement; copies or excerpts of continuing contracts such as leases, bond indentures, and royalty agreements; a history of the company, its products, markets, and background; copies or excerpts of stockholders, directors, and committee minutes on matters of lasting interest; and continuing schedules of accounts whose balances are carried forward for several years, such as owners' equity, retained earnings, partnership capital, and the like. Copies of prior years' financial statements and audit reports may also be included.

The permanent file is a ready source of information for first-time familiarization with the client by new personnel on the engagement.

Audit Administrative Papers

Administrative records contain the fruit of the early planning phases of the audit. Usually these papers are bound together with the current year's audit evidence papers. All the work that goes on in the course of audit planning, the assignment of personnel, the preparation of a time budget, the study and evaluation of internal control, and the audit program preparation is a part of audit administration and is documented in the working papers.

In general, the following items may appear in the front of each year's current file:

1. Engagement letter.
2. Memoranda of conferences with management.
3. Memoranda of conferences with the directors' audit committee.
4. Memoranda of review notes and unfinished procedures (all cleared by the end of the field work).
5. Audit engagement time budget.
6. Internal control questionnaire.
7. Management controls questionnaire.
8. EDP control questionnaire.
9. Internal control system and program flowcharts.
10. Audit program.
11. A working trial balance of general ledger accounts.
12. Working paper record of preliminary adjusting and reclassifying entries.

Audit Evidence Papers

The current year audit evidence working papers contain the record of the procedures followed, the tests performed, the evidence obtained, and the decisions made in the course of the audit. These papers are themselves communications of the quality of the audit, thus they must be clear, concise, complete, neat, well-indexed, and informative. Each separate working paper (or multiple pages that go together) must be complete in the sense that it can be removed from the working paper file and considered on its own, with proper cross-reference available to show how the paper coordinates with other working papers. (Quality review committees and plaintiffs' attorneys are known for taking specific working papers out of a file for review and study or for presentation to a jury.)

The most important facet of the current audit evidence papers is the requirement that they show the auditor's decision problems and their conclusions. Thus the papers must record the propositions to be tested (book values or qualitative disclosures), the evidence gathered to test the proposition, and the final decision. These records can take many forms—numerical, narrative, pictorial—depending on the decision problem, the

EXHIBIT 5–5
Current Working Paper File

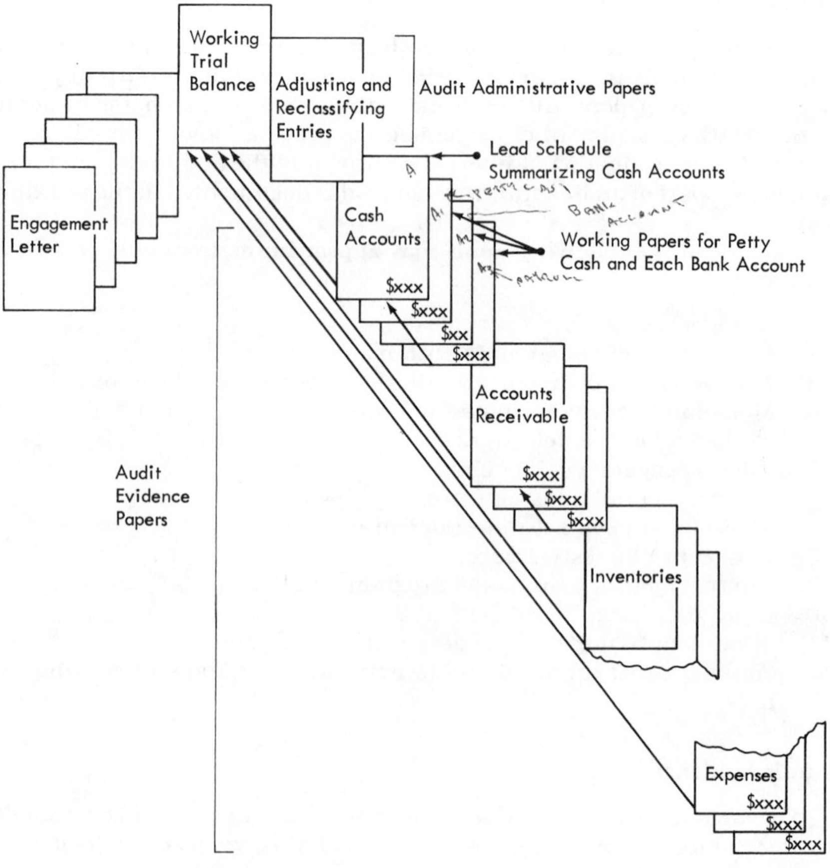

unique circumstances of the engagement, and the type of report to be rendered.

Working Paper Arrangement and Indexing

Each auditing organization has a different method of arranging and indexing working papers. In general, however, the papers are grouped in order behind the adjusting and reclassifying entry papers according to balance sheet and income statement captions. Usually the current assets appear first, followed by fixed assets, other assets, liabilities, equities, income and expense accounts. The typical arrangement is shown in Exhibit 5–5.

There are several working paper preparation techniques that are quite important for the quality of the finished product. The points explained below are illustrated in Exhibit 5–6.

EXHIBIT 5–6
Illustrative Working Paper

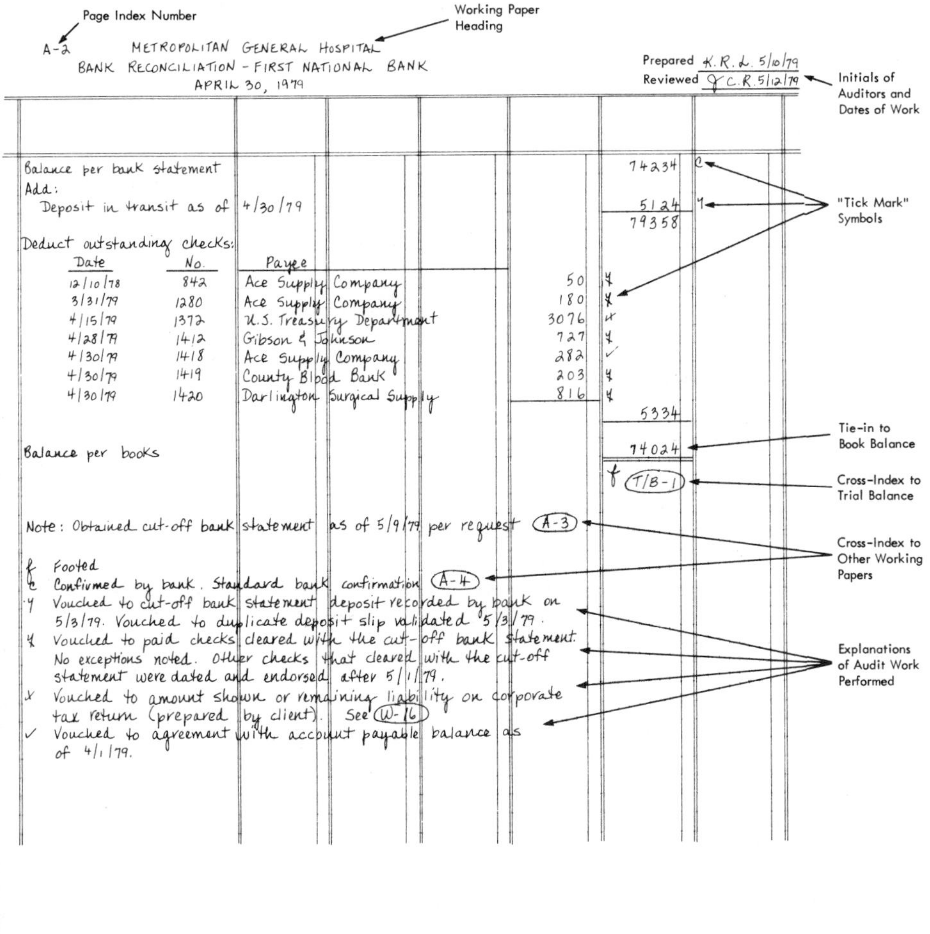

Indexing. Each paper is given an index number, like a book page number, so that it can be found, removed, and replaced without loss.

Cross-indexing. Numbers or memoranda that are carried forward to other papers carry the index of the other paper(s) so that the flow of events can be followed.

Heading. Each paper is titled at a minimum with the name of the company, the period under audit date, and a descriptive title of the contents of the working paper. (When an audit manager is reviewing audits of several companies, he cannot afford to file an untitled paper in the wrong company's folder.)

Signatures and initials. The auditor who performs the work and the supervisor who reviews it must sign the papers so that personnel can be identified at a later date.

Dates of audit work. The dates of performance and review are recorded on the working papers so that reviewers of the papers can tell when the work was performed.

Tick marks and explanations. "Tick marks" are the auditor's shorthand for abbreviating comments on work performed, but always with reference to a full explanation.

SOURCES AND ADDITIONAL READING REFERENCES

Andrews, Wesley T. "Obtaining the Representations of Legal Counsel," *CPA Journal,* August 1977, pp. 37–40.

Bencivenga, Joseph V. "Improving Reviews of Audit Examinations," *CPA Journal,* April 1978, pp. 33–38.

Benis, Martin. "The Small Client and Representation Letters," *Journal of Accountancy,* September 1978, pp. 78–85.

Bettauer, Arthur. "Extending Audit Procedures—When and How," *Journal of Accountancy,* November 1975, pp. 69–72.

Davis, G. B.; Neter, J.; and Palmer, R. R. "An Experimental Study of Audit Confirmations," *Journal of Accountancy,* June 1967, pp. 36–44.

Doege, Richard L. "Photogrammetrics in Auditing," *Journal of Accountancy,* April 1972, pp. 60–63.

Hull, James, C. "A Guide to Better Workpapers," *Journal of Accountancy,* February 1969, pp. 44–52.

Kissinger, John N. "A General Theory of Evidence as the Conceptual Foundation in Auditing Theory: Some Comments and Extensions," *The Accounting Review,* April 1977, pp. 322–39.

Koontz, Robert P. "An Approach to Auditing Scientific Projects," *The GAO Review,* Winter 1975, pp. 55–60.

Krogstad, J. L.; Grudnitski, G.; and Bryant, D. W. "PERT and PERT/Cost for Audit Planning and Control," *Journal of Accountancy,* November 1977, pp. 82–91.

McGraw, R. J., and Walter, E. F. "Auditing the FBI," *The GAO Review,* Fall 1976, pp. 43–46.

Mautz, R. K. "The Nature and Reliability of Audit Evidence," *Journal of Accountancy*, May 1958, pp. 40–47.

______, and Sharaf, Hussein A. *The Philosophy of Auditing*, American Accounting Association Monograph No. 6, especially chap. 5, "Evidence," and chap. 6, "Due Audit Care," American Accounting Assn., 1961.

Neumann, Frederick L. "The Auditor's Analytical Review—Some Sources of Information," *Journal of Accountancy*, October 1974, pp. 88–92.

Sawyer, Lawrence B. *The Practice of Modern Internal Auditing*. Altamonte Springs, Florida: The Institute of Internal Auditors, Inc., 1973.

Tipgos, Manual A. "Prior Year's Working Papers: Uses and Dangers," *CPA Journal*, September 1978, pp. 19–25.

Toba, Yoshihide. "A General Theory of Evidence as the Conceptual Foundation in Auditing Theory," *Accounting Review*, January 1975, pp. 7–24.

REVIEW QUESTIONS

5.1. Briefly explain the concept of "relevance" as a characteristic of evidence.

5.2. Briefly explain the concept of "objectivity" as a characteristic of evidence.

5.3. How might an auditor introduce bias into the evidential matter he or she considers in making a decision?

5.4. Explain how the four characteristics of audit evidence define the concepts of competency and sufficiency.

5.5. Define external, external-internal, and internal evidence.

5.6. Describe each phase of an audit engagement, and give for each one an example of a procedure involved in it, a letter delivered or received, or a report produced.

5.7. List and briefly explain the six practical audit objectives.

5.8. Explain what is meant by "vouching," "retracing," and "scanning."

5.9. Generally, what three steps are taken in designing each segment of an audit program?

5.10. What are the general considerations in determining the *necessary extent* of audit procedures in a given circumstance?

5.11. What information would you expect to find in a permanent audit file? In the front of a current working paper file?

5.12. What is considered the most important content of the auditor's current audit working papers?

EXERCISES AND PROBLEMS

5.13. The first generally accepted auditing standard of field work requires, in part, that "the work is to be planned adequately." An effective tool that aids the auditor in adequately planning the work is an audit program.

Required:

What is an audit program, and what purposes does it serve? (AICPA)

5.14. Auditors frequently refer to the terms "Standards" and "Procedures." Standards deal with measures of the quality of the auditor's performance. Standards specifically refer to the generally accepted auditing standards expressed in the Statements on Auditing Standards. Procedures relate to those acts that are performed by the auditor while trying to gather evidence. Procedures specifically refer to the methods or techniques used by the auditor in the conduct of the examination. Procedures are also expressed in the Statements on Auditing Standards.

Required:

List at least eight different types of procedures that an auditor would use during an examination of financial statements. For example, a type of procedure that an auditor would frequently use is the observation of activities and conditions. Do not discuss specific accounts. (AICPA adapted)

5.15. In late spring of 1977 you are advised of a new assignment as in-charge accountant of your CPA firm's recurring annual audit of a major client, the Lancer Company. You are given the engagement letter for the audit covering the calendar year December 31, 1977, and a list of personnel assigned to this engagement. It is your responsibility to plan and supervise the field work for the engagement.

Required:

Discuss the necessary preparation and planning for the Lancer Company annual audit prior to beginning field work at the client's office. In your discussion include the sources you should consult, the type of information you should seek, the preliminary plans and preparation you should make for the field work, and any actions you should take relative to the staff assigned to the engagement. *Do not write an audit program.* (AICPA)

5.16. What are the general objectives or purposes of the CPA's observation of the taking of the physical inventory? (Do not discuss the procedures or techniques involved in making the observation.) (AICPA adapted)

5.17. When a CPA has accepted an engagement from a new client who is a manufacturer, it is customary for the CPA to tour the client's plant facilities.

Required:

Discuss the ways in which the CPA's observations made during the course of the plant tour would be of help to him as he plans and conducts his audit. (AICPA)

5.18. A CPA accumulates various kinds of evidence upon which he will base his auditor's opinion on the fairness of financial statements he examines. Among this evidence are confirmations from third parties and written representations from his client.

Required:

a. (1) What is an audit confirmation?
   (2) What characteristics should an audit confirmation possess if a CPA is to consider it as valid evidence?

b. (1) What is a written representation?
   (2) What information should a written representation contain?
   (3) What effect does a written representation have on a CPA's examination of a client's financial statements?

c. (1) Distinguish between a positive confirmation and a negative confirmation in the auditor's examination of accounts receivable.
(2) In confirming an audit client's accounts receivable, what characteristics should be present in the accounts if the CPA is to use negative confirmations?

5.19. Overall tests and ratios are used during preliminary audit reviews to determine whether there are any areas that need special audit attention in the preliminary audit program. When an auditor notices a significant change in a ratio compared with a prior year, the reasons for the change must be considered. Explain possible reasons for (*a*) an increase in the rate of inventory turnover—ratio of cost of sales and average inventory—when Lifo is used, and (*b*) an increase in the number of days' sales in receivables—ratio of credit sales and average daily accounts receivable.

5.20. Staff accountants of E. Z. Campbell & Company, CPAs, are planning the preliminary audit program for the examination of Model Manufacturing Company accounts for the year ended February 28, 1979. You have obtained the company's third quarter financial statements dated November 30, 1978, and your task is to analyze significant ratios and trends in order to understand Model's business and determine whether audit efforts should be concentrated in any particular areas. The financial statements as of November 30, 1978 and 1977, and for the nine months ending on each of these dates are condensed below.

Balance Sheets

Assets	*1978*	*1977*
Cash	$ 12,000	$ 15,000
Accounts receivable, net	93,000	50,000
Inventory	72,000	67,000
Other current assets	5,000	6,000
Plant and equipment, net of depreciation	60,000	80,000
	$ 242,000	$ 218,000
Equities		
Accounts payable	$ 38,000	$ 41,000
Federal income tax payable	30,000	14,400
Long-term liabilities	20,000	40,000
Common stock	70,000	70,000
Retained earnings	84,000	52,600
	$ 242,000	$ 218,000

Income Statements

Net sales	$1,684,000	$1,250,000
Cost of goods sold	927,000	710,000
Gross margin on sales	$ 757,000	$ 540,000
Selling and administrative expenses	682,000	504,000
Income before federal income taxes	$ 75,000	$ 36,000
Income tax expense	30,000	14,400
Net income	$ 45,000	$ 21,600

Model's sales are all on credit—no cash sales. A review of the monthly financial statements has shown that the November 30 balances are comparable to the monthly averages for each year.

The controller figures the allowance for uncollectible accounts receivable each month and has provided the following information.

	1978	*1977*
Current accounts	40,000	30,000
Accounts 30–60 days past due	47,653	12,000
Accounts 60–90 days past due	4,000	5,000
Accounts over 90 days past due	2,000	4,105
Allowance for uncollectible accounts	(653)	(1,105)
	93,000	50,000

The controller ordinarily figures the allowance for uncollectible accounts as 2 percent, 5 percent, and 15 percent of each of the past due categories, and she has been fairly accurate for the last three years. As of November 30, 1978, she explains that a new discount chain customer let a $40,000 account go past due, but the amount is considered fully collectible. This customer has purchased and paid for $685,000 of goods since December 1977.

Required:

a. Compute the accounts receivable turnover ratio. Identify and explain procedures that might be used to audit the accounts receivable.

b. Compute the current ratio. Review its composition and discuss whether any additional audit attention appears necessary.

c. Compute ratios of costs, margin, expenses, and taxes, and discuss whether any additional audit attention appears necessary.

5.21. Kermit Griffin, an audit manager, had begun a preliminary analytical review of selected statistics related to the Majestic Hotel. His objective was to obtain an understanding of this hotel's business in order to draft a preliminary audit program. He wanted to see whether he could detect any troublesome areas or questionable accounts that might require special audit attention. Unfortunately Mr. Griffin caught the flu and was hospitalized. From his sickbed he sent you the following schedule he had prepared and asked you to write a memorandum identifying areas of potential errors and irregularities or other matters that the preliminary audit program should cover.

Required:

a. Write a brief description of Majestic's operating characteristics compared to the "industry average" insofar as you can tell from the statistics.

b. Write the memorandum using good working paper style.

c. Specify the auditing procedures you would recommend regarding the areas noted in your memorandum.

EXHIBIT 5.21–1

AP-6

Majestic Hotel
Preliminary Analytical Review
FYE 3/31/79

Prepared by KG
Reviewed by ____

The Majestic Hotel, East Apple, New Jersey, compiles operating statistics on a calendar year basis. Hotel statistics below were provided by the controller, A. J. Marcelli, for 1978. The parallel column contains industry average statistics obtained from Welsh's Hotel Industry Guide.

	Majestic	Industry
Sales: Rooms	60.4%	63.9%
Food and beverages	35.7	32.2
Other	3.9	3.9
Costs: Rooms department	15.2%	17.3%
Food and beverages	34.0	27.2
Administrative and general	8.0	8.9
Management fee	3.3	1.1
Advertising	2.7	3.2
Real estate taxes	3.5	3.2
Utilities, repairs, maintenance	15.9	13.7
Profit per sales dollar	17.4%	25.4%
Rooms dept. ratios to rooms sales $		
Salaries and wages	18.9%	15.7%
Laundry	1.0	3.7
Other	5.3	7.6
Profit per rooms sales $	74.8%	73.0%
Food/Beverage ratios to F/B Sales $		
Cost of food sold	42.1%	37.0%
Food gross profit	57.9%	63.0%
Cost of beverages sold	43.6%	29.5%
Beverages gross profit	56.4%	70.5%
Combined Gross profit	57.7%	64.6%
Salaries and wages	39.6%	32.8%
Music and entertainment	—	2.7%
Other	13.4	13.8
Profit per F/B Sales $	4.7%	15.3%
Average annual % room occupancy	62.6%	68.1%
Average room rate per day	$16.16	$15.94
Number of rooms available per day	200	148

5.22. The third generally accepted auditing standard of field work requires that the auditor obtain sufficient competent evidential matter to afford a reasonable basis for an opinion regarding the financial statements under examination. In considering what constitutes sufficient competent evidential matter, a distinction should be made between underlying accounting data and all corroborating information available to the auditor.

Required:

a. Discuss the nature of evidential matter to be considered by the auditor in terms of the underlying accounting data, all corroborating information available to the auditor, and the methods by which the auditor tests or gathers competent evidential matter.

b. State the three general presumptions that can be made about the validity of evidential matter with respect to comparative assurance, persuasiveness, and reliability. (AICPA)

5.23. The preparation of working papers is an integral part of a CPA's examination of financial statements. On a recurring engagement a CPA reviews his audit programs and working papers from his prior examination while planning his current examination to determine their usefulness for the current engagement.

Required:

a. (1) What are the purposes or functions of audit working papers?
(2) What records may be included in audit working papers?

b. What factors affect the CPA's judgment of the type and content of the working papers for a particular engagement?

c. To comply with generally accepted auditing standards a CPA includes certain evidence in his working papers, for example, "evidence that the engagement was planned and work of assistants was supervised and reviewed." What other evidence should a CPA include in audit working papers to comply with generally accepted auditing standards?

d. How can a CPA make the most effective use of the preceding year's audit programs in a recurring examination? (AICPA)

5.24. You were engaged to examine the financial statements of Ronlyn Corporation for the year ended June 30.

On May 1, two months before the fiscal year-end, the corporation borrowed $500,000 from Second National Bank to finance plant expansion. The long-term note agreement provided for the annual payment of principal and interest over five years. The existing plant was pledged as security for the loan.

Due to unexpected difficulties in acquiring the building site, the plant expansion did not begin on time. To make use of the borrowed funds, management decided to invest in stocks and bonds, and on May 16, the $500,000 was invested in securities.

Required:

a. What are the audit objectives in the examination of long-term debt?

b. How could you audit the security position of Ronlyn at June 30? (AICPA adapted)

5.25. The inspection of the minutes of meetings is an integral part of a CPA's examination of a corporation's financial statements.

Required:

a. A CPA should determine if there is any disagreement between transactions recorded in the corporate records and actions approved by the corporation's board of directors. Why is this so and how is it accomplished?

b. Discuss the effect each of the following situations would have on specific audit steps in a CPA's examination and on his auditor's opinion:

(1) The minute book does not show approval for the sale which was consummated during the year of an important manufacturing division.

(2) Some details of a contract negotiated during the year with the labor union are different from the outline of the contract included in the minutes of the board of directors.

(3) The minutes of a meeting of directors held after the balance sheet date have not yet been written, but the corporation's secretary shows the CPA notes from which the minutes are to be prepared when the secretary has time.

c. What corporate actions should be approved by stockholders and recorded in the minutes of the stockholders' meetings? (AICPA)

5.26. Identify the types of procedure(s) employed in each situation described below (e.g., vouching, retracing, recalculation, observation, and so on):

1. The auditor selects accounts payable with debit balances and checks amounts and computations to purchase orders and receiving documents.
2. The auditor examines property insurance policies and checks insurance expense for the year. The auditor then reviews the expense in light of changes and ending balances in fixed asset accounts.
3. The auditor examines perpetual inventory records and discovers several slow-moving items. The client states that the items are obsolete and have already been written down; the auditor checks journal entries to support the client's statements.
4. The auditor reviews cash remittance advices to see that allowances and discounts are appropriate and that receipts are posted to the correct customer accounts in the right amounts, and reviews the documents supporting unusual discounts and allowances.
5. The auditor observes the client's taking a physical inventory. A letter is also received from a public warehouseman stating the amounts of the client's inventory stored in the warehouse. The company's cost-flow assumption, Fifo, is then tested by the auditor.

5.27. 1. Classify the following evidential items by *type* (e.g., mathematical, external, and so on), and rank them in order of reliability.

a. Amounts shown on monthly statements from creditors.

b. Amounts shown "paid on account" in the voucher register.

c. Amount of "discounts lost expense" computed from unaudited supporting documents.

d. Amounts shown in letter received directly from creditor.

2. Classify the following evidential items by *type* (e.g., mathematical, external, and so on) and rank them in order of reliability.

a. Amounts shown on letter received directly from independent bond trustee.

b. Amounts obtained from minutes of board of directors' meetings.

c. Computation of bond interest and amortization expense when remaining terms and status of bond are audited.

d. Amounts shown on canceled checks.

5.28. The propositions which the independent auditor seeks to prove include the following:

1. Propriety of leased property transactions and asset balances with respect to existence-occurrence, valuation, and accounting principles.
2. Propriety of capital stock transactions and asset balances (except inventories and fixed assets) with respect to existence-occurrence and valuation (independent transfer agent and registrar not used).
3. Propriety of bond indebtedness transactions and balances with respect to existence-occurrence, valuation, and accounting principles.
4. Propriety of inventory balances (retail enterprise) with respect to existence-occurrence and valuation.
5. Propriety of fixed asset transactions and balances with respect to existence-occurrence and valuation.

The following are sources of evidence which the auditor may use to assist him or her in resolving the five propositions:

1. Bank deposit slips.
2. Cash disbursements journal.
3. Purchase orders.
4. Vendors' invoices.
5. Equipment work orders.
6. Minutes of board of directors' and officers' meetings.
7. Confirmation letter from third parties to auditors.
8. Voucher register.
9. Bank statements.
10. General ledger.
11. Materials receiving reports.
12. Insurance policies covering client properties.
13. Property tax bills.
14. Equipment subsidiary ledger.
15. Formal agreements and contracts.
16. Stockholder ledger.
17. Stock certificate book.
18. Client's regular internal reports.
19. Copy of client's completed inventory worksheet.
20. Deeds.
21. Repair and maintenance expense vouchers.
22. Verbal representations of clients' management and other employees.
23. Cash receipts journal.
24. Assets themselves (as observed by the auditor).
25. Materials subsidiary records.
26. Plant and equipment budget.
27. Purchase requisitions.

Required:

For each proposition, list the sources of evidence which the auditor might use to facilitate the reaching of reasonable conclusions.

5.29. Assigned to audit plant asset balances, an assistant auditor began by footing the equipment subsidiary ledgers and reconciling the total to the general ledger account. He checked the mathematical accuracy for the depreciation expense calculation (fixed percent on declining base), giving due consideration to additions and retirements of equipment noted in the subsidiary ledgers. Depreciation expense was traced to the trial balance and the income statement. All amounts were mathematically accurate, and the auditor concluded no adjustments were necessary.

Required:

a. What evidence-gathering techniques did the auditor rely upon in determining the propriety of plant asset balances? Explain.

b. Does the evidence gathered by the auditor afford a reasonable basis for his conclusion? Explain.

c. How might the auditor obtain *firsthand* evidence of the existence of plant assets?

d. What are the auditor's objectives with specific reference to plant equipment? (Refer to the *practical audit objectives* presented in the chapter).

5.30. In the examination of financial statements, an auditor must judge the validity of the audit evidence he or she obtains.

Required:

Assume that you have evaluated internal accounting control and found it satisfactory.

a. In the course of the examination, the auditor asks many questions of client officers and employees.
  (1) Describe the factors that the auditor should consider in evaluating oral evidence provided by client officers and employees.
  (2) Discuss the validity and limitations of oral evidence.

b. An auditor's examination may include computation of various balance sheet and operating ratios for comparison to prior years and industry averages. Discuss the validity and limitations of ratio analysis.

c. In connection with the examination of the financial statements of a manufacturing company, an auditor is observing the physical inventory of finished goods, which consists of expensive, highly complex electronic equipment. Discuss the validity and limitations of the audit evidence provided by this procedure. (AICPA)

5.31. Z. Summers was assigned to the audit of a new client that had never been audited before. The engagement letter specified that the audit report would cover the statement of financial position, the statement of results of operations and retained earnings, and the statement of changes in financial position of the current year. No comparative financial statements will be issued. Consequently, Z decided to do no audit work on the beginning balances of cash, accounts receivable, inventory, fixed assets, accounts payable, and long-term debt.

Required:

a. What is wrong with Z's reasoning?

b. What would he do about beginning balances if they had been audited in prior years by (1) his firm, (2) another CPA firm?

5.32. Johnson, Inc., a closely held company, wishes to engage Norr, CPA, to examine its annual financial statements. Johnson was generally pleased with the services provided by its prior CPA, Diggs, but thought the audit work performed was too detailed and interfered excessively with Johnson's normal office routines. Norr asked Johnson to inform Diggs of the decision to change auditors, but Johnson did not wish to do so.

Required:

a. List and discuss the steps Norr should follow before accepting the engagement.

b. What additional procedures should Norr perform on this first-time engagement over and beyond those Norr would perform on the Johnson engagement of the following year?

5.33. A CPA has been asked to audit the financial statements of a publicly held company for the first time. All preliminary verbal discussions and inquiries have been completed between the CPA, the company, the predecessor auditor, and all other necessary parties. The CPA is now preparing an engagement letter.

Required:

a. List the items that should be included in the typical engagement letter in these circumstances and

b. Describe the benefits derived from preparing an engagement letter. (AICPA)

6

INTERNAL CONTROL THEORY AND REVIEW TECHNIQUES

One of the first technical audit program planning tasks is to design a proper study and evaluation of the existing internal control system.[1] The results of the study become inputs to the planning of procedures to be performed in making further substantive tests of amounts and balances shown in financial statements and other reports. The internal control investigation is most relevant in independent financial audits, in special systems study engagements by internal auditors and consultants, and in special engagements designed to produce only a report on internal control. It is less relevant to special decision-oriented analyses such as a lease-or-buy analysis by an internal auditor.

The four major topics covered in this chapter are (1) definition of internal accounting control and explanation of the theoretical characteristics of a satisfactory system, (2) explanation of two major phases of the study and evaluation—the initial *review phase* and the subsequent *compliance testing phase*, (3) explanation and illustration of the tools and techniques used in the review phase, and (4) reporting on internal control.

Exhibit 6–1 contains a diagrammatic explanation of the audit program planning process. This exhibit contains more detail than the overview presented in Chapter 5. It begins after the engagement letter is obtained. Evaluation and consideration of internal accounting control is shown to be important at several decision points, indicated by the letters A, B, C, D, and E.

[1] A careful distinction should be made between the ideas of "designing a proper study and evaluation of a system" and "designing an effective internal control system." The former idea expresses the auditor's task—to evaluate the system that exists. The latter idea expresses the consultant's task—to *create* a new system or *change* an existing system.

EXHIBIT 6–1
Overview of the Audit Program Planning Process

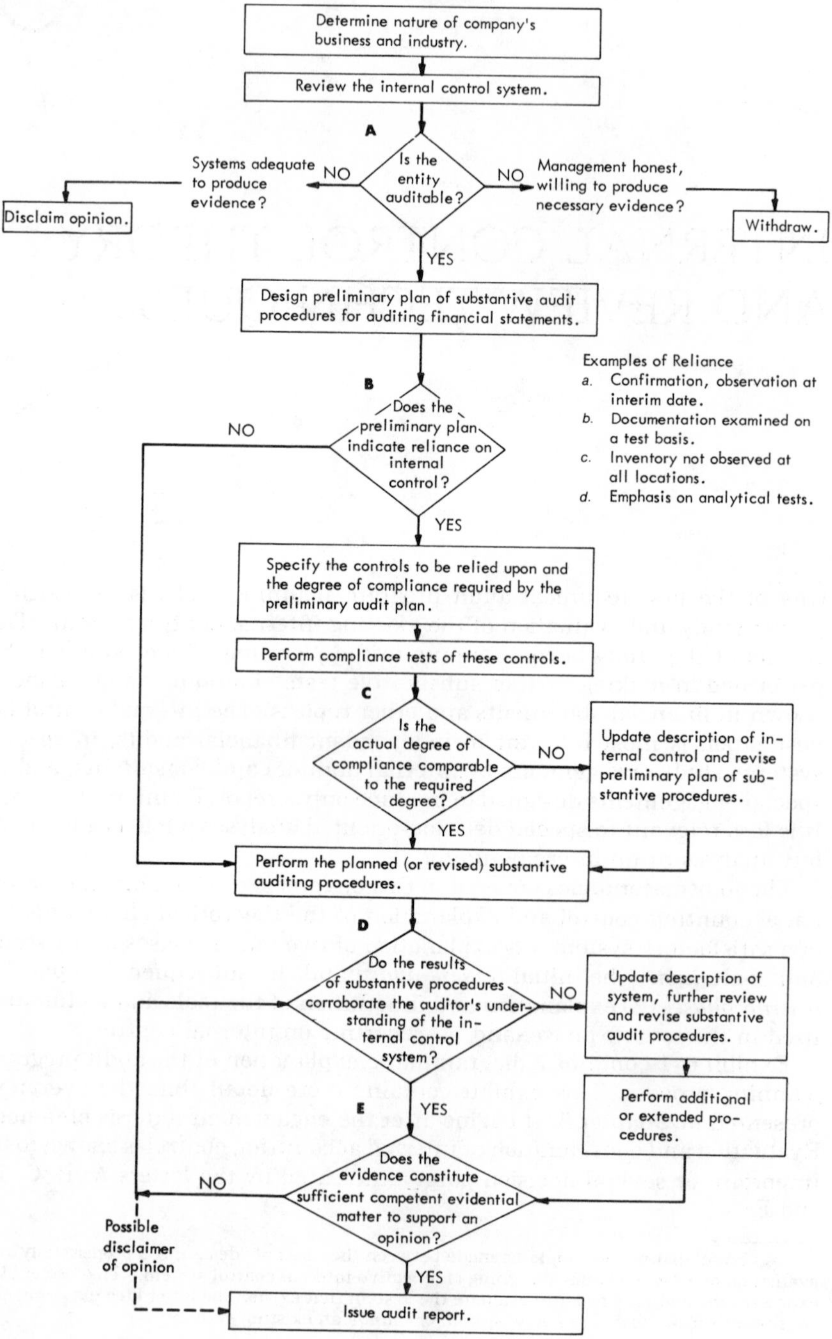

A. After reviewing internal accounting control (review phase) decide whether the entity is auditable; that is, whether controls may exist at a level of minimum acceptability.
B. Decide what particular controls will be relied upon. These will be tested for compliance.
C. Evaluate compliance with controls in comparison to the auditor's requirements for reliance.
D. When performing substantive tests, determine whether additional evidence about internal control is consistent with earlier conclusions. (This is the *dual-purpose* characteristic of some substantive tests.)
E. Evaluate the substantive evidence and decide what form of audit report to render.

CONTROL DEFINITIONS

The following is a concise definition of internal control as it relates to the second standard of field work: *Internal accounting control is the means by which errors in accounting data are detected and corrected.*

By definition, a perfect system of accounting data processing control is one that detects and provides for the correction of all errors. A reliable system, however, may be short of perfection. The auditor's problem, according to the theory in the standards of field work, is to find out how much reliance, if any, can be placed on the system. The primary purpose of the independent auditor's study and evaluation of internal accounting control is to assist in determining the nature, extent, and timing of other auditing tests to be performed subsequently. The second purpose, added by *SAS 20* (Section 323) in 1977, is to render a required report to the client.

Managers and internal auditors are also interested in the reliability of information system control. However, their interest is much broader than that of the independent auditor. Management bears the responsibility to establish and maintain a system of internal control. The internal auditor enters the picture when he or she evaluates information system control as a service to management.

Internal control is defined comprehensively in auditing theory as follows:

> Internal control comprises the plan of organization and all of the coordinate methods and measures adopted within a business to safeguard its assets, check the accuracy and reliability of its accounting data, promote operational efficiency, and encourage adherence to prescribed managerial policies. This definition possibly is broader than the meaning sometimes attributed to the term. It recognizes that a "system" of internal control extends beyond those matters which relate directly to the functions of the accounting and financial departments.[2]

---

[2] *Statement on Auditing Standards No. 1* (Section 320.09).

Two dimensions of internal control are the administrative controls and the accounting controls. Internal auditors are constantly interested in both dimensions. Independent auditors are most interested in the accounting controls, but not to the complete exclusion of the administrative controls.

Administrative control includes, but is not limited to, the plan of organization and the procedures and records that are concerned with the decision processes leading to management's authorization of transactions. Such authorization is a management function directly associated with the responsibility for achieving the objectives of the organization and is the starting point for establishing accounting control of transactions.

Accounting control comprises the plan of organization and the procedures and records that are concerned with the safeguarding of assets and the reliability of financial records and consequently are designed to provide reasonable assurance that

a. Transactions are executed in accordance with management's general or specific authorization.
b. Transactions are recorded as necessary (1) to permit preparation of financial statements in conformity with generally accepted accounting principles or any other criteria applicable to such statements and (2) to maintain accountability for assets.
c. Access to assets is permitted only in accordance with management's authorization.
d. The recorded accountability for assets is compared with the existing assets at reasonable intervals and appropriate action is taken with respect to any differences.[3]

In an audit engagement the distinction between administrative controls and accounting controls may be difficult to make. The distinction should not be made artificially in order to avoid dealing with some controls that may be labeled "administrative." Accounting controls in which the independent auditor is primarily interested are those methods and procedures that bear directly and importantly on the reliability of financial records. Administrative controls, in contrast, generally relate only indirectly to the accounts.

For example, a company may have a system for planning, approving, and controlling expenditures on major advertising projects. The part of the system concerning approval and payment of these expenses are accounting controls that impact directly on the amount shown in the expense account. At the same time the company may maintain marketing analysis records of the sales generated by the advertising projects. These records and analyses serve as administrative controls for the purpose of evaluating the effectiveness of the marketing effort and for planning future promotions. An independent auditor would normally not be primarily concerned with these marketing analyses. However, such records might

[3] *Statement on Auditing Standards No. 1* (Section 320.27–320.28). Companies registered under the Securities Exchange Act of 1934 are required by law to maintain internal control systems having these characteristics. Refer to the discussion of the Foreign Corrupt Practices Act of 1977 in Chapter 4.

prove useful if the auditor needs to explain unusual sales fluctuations as a part of his or her audit of the sales revenue accounts.

Other administrative controls effected through such devices as budgets, statistical production analyses, quality control data, investments analysis, and maintenance schedules are in a class of controls with the marketing analyses mentioned above. These data are usually not a part of the transaction-processing accounting system itself. Yet they may turn out to be useful in resolving some questions that arise during an audit. A thorough understanding of the client and its business includes an understanding of the administrative controls.

Internal auditors, on the other hand, may be concerned equally as much with administrative controls as with internal accounting controls. Exhibit 6–2 compares the context of the work of internal and independent auditors respecting a study and evaluation of information system control.

EXHIBIT 6–2
Differentiated Audit Objectives

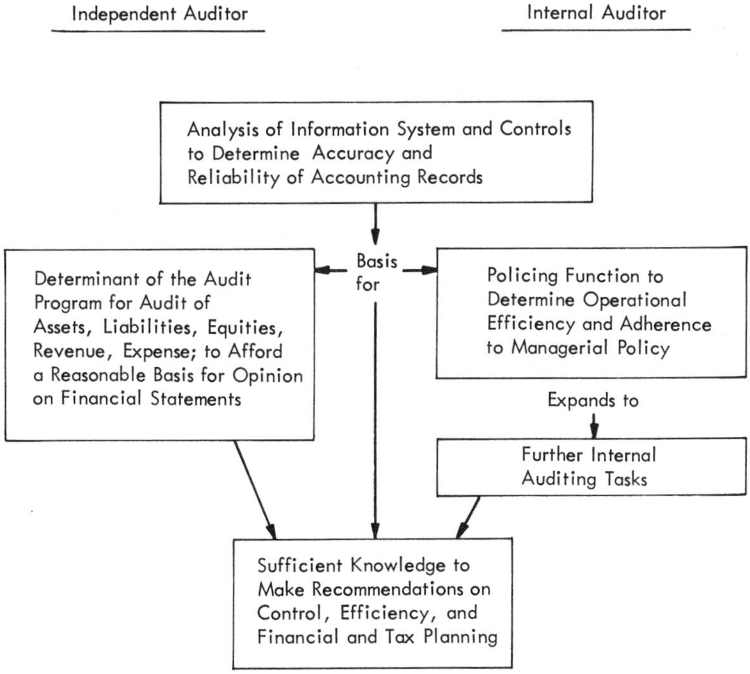

Source: Adapted from R. I. Anderson, "Analytical Auditing: Does It Work?" *The Internal Auditor,* July/August 1972. Copyright 1972 by The Institute of Internal Auditors, Inc., 249 Maitland Ave., Altamonte Springs, Florida. Reprinted with permission.

PHASES OF STUDY AND EVALUATION

The work of independent auditors and internal auditors (and others that may be concerned with information system control) may be differentiated by the various purposes of their studies and by the extent or depth of study. All auditors, however, follow common approaches and use common methods for evaluating the reliability of a system. Exhibit 6–3 is a diagram of an auditor's approach showing two phases—the review phase and the compliance testing phase—that are coordinated elements.

EXHIBIT 6–3
Phases of Study and Evaluation of Information System Control

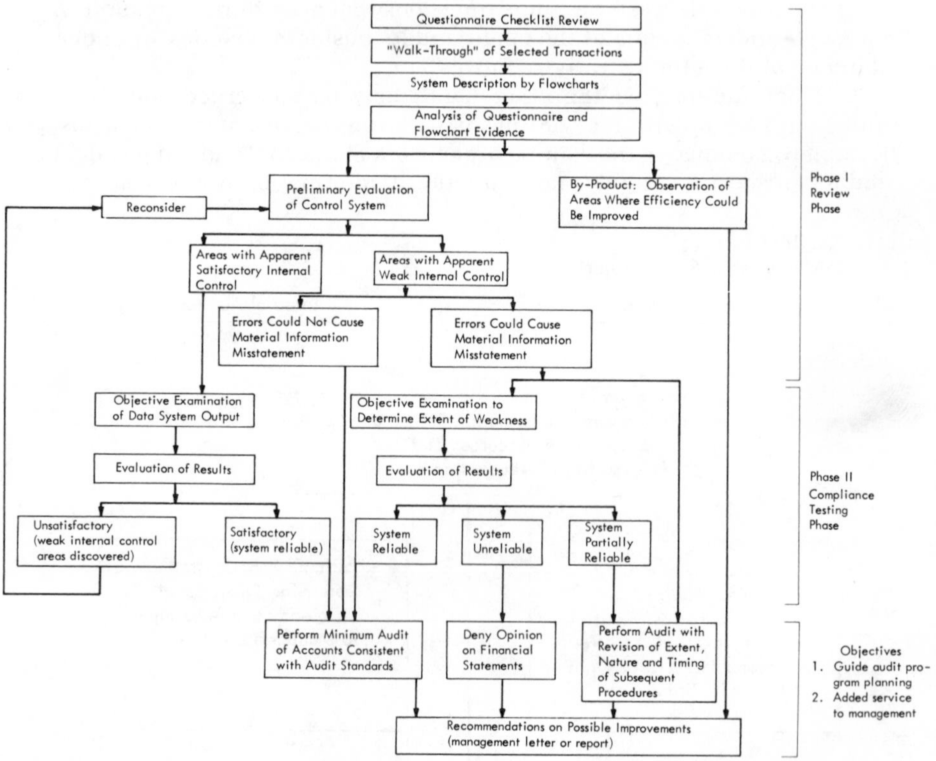

Source: Adapted from R. I. Anderson, "Analytical Auditing: Does It Work?" *The Internal Auditor*, July/August 1972. Copyright 1972 by The Institute of Internal Auditors, Inc., 249 Maitland Ave., Altamonte Springs, Florida. Reprinted with permission.

As the methods of study and evaluation are explained in subsequent sections, the discussion is divided into methods of review and methods of compliance testing.

CHARACTERISTICS OF RELIABLE INTERNAL CONTROL SYSTEMS

A satisfactory system of internal control is one that exhibits the following qualitative characteristics:

1. A plan of organization which provides appropriate segregation of functional responsibilities.
2. A system of authorization and record procedures adequate to provide reasonable accounting control over assets, liabilities, revenues, and expenses.
3. Sound practices to be followed in performance of duties and functions of each of the organizational departments.
4. Personnel of a quality commensurate with responsibilities.[4]
5. A reliable system of internal control actually operates effectively to detect and correct data processing errors.

The first four elements of this statement of internal control characteristics were first written in 1949, making the statement one of the most long-lived theory statements in auditing literature and practice. The reason it has lasted so long in a rapidly changing world is that it gives an auditor a broad, yet firm basis for conducting a study of internal accounting control. Starting with the first characteristic, an auditor may proceed systematically to sound conclusions about the subjective quality and reliability of the accounting information control system. Before reaching a final evaluation, however, the auditor must gather further evidence that is best described by the fifth characteristic—evidence that the system actually functions effectively.

This fifth characteristic emphasizes that a control system may be *designed* to be effective, but the auditor is really interested in whether it *actually operates* effectively. Such a conclusion is reached only by performing the objective compliance testing phase of examination while, on the other hand, the first four characteristics may be tentatively judged on the basis of the review phase.

Segregation of Responsibilities

The first qualitative characteristic calls for an "appropriate segregation of functional responsibilities." Sometimes this requirement is referred to as "division of duties." There are three general duties that should be performed by different departments or at least by different persons on the client's accounting staff.

1. Authorization to execute a transaction. This authorization refers to the person who has authority and responsibility to initiate recordkeeping of a transaction. Authorization may be general, referring to a class of transactions (e.g., all purchases), or it may be specific (e.g., sale of an important asset).
2. Recording of the transaction. This duty refers to the accounting and recordkeeping function (bookkeeping) which in some organizations may be partially delegated to an electronic data processing system. If

[4] Committee on Auditing Procedure, special report. *Internal Control* (New York: AICPA, 1949), p. 6. Also in *Statements on Auditing Procedure No. 33* (New York: AICPA, 1963), pp. 28–29.

EDP is used, an additional level of control over the machine system is required.

3. Custody of assets involved in the transaction. This duty refers to the actual physical possession or effective physical control of property.

The idea underlying separation of these duties is that no one person should have control of two or three of the functional responsibilities. The first duty is a management function, the second is an accounting function, and the third is a custodial function. If different departments or persons are forced to deal with these different elements of transactions, then two benefits accrue: (1) deliberate introduction of error is made more difficult because it would require collusion of two or more persons, and most persons hesitate to seek aid of another to perpetrate a wrongful act; and (2) by acting in a coordinated manner (handling different aspects of the same transaction), it is more likely that innocent error will be found and flagged for correction. The latter point is a variation on the cross-check or "two heads are better than one" idea of error detection.

Authorization and Record Procedures

The second qualitative characteristic refers to "a system of authorization and record procedures." In general, such a system means that approved procedures and methods should be employed by the client's accounting staff. The system consists of the chart of accounts, procedures manuals, computer program and system documentation manuals, flowcharts of transaction processing, and the variety of paperwork forms and approval signature provisions that characterize large-volume transaction data files.

Sound Practices

The quality characteristic of "sound practices in the performance of duties and functions" adds another dimension to the first two characteristics. There is overlap among this characteristic and the first two because "sound practices" also include appropriate division of duties and appropriate authorization and record procedures. The sound practices dimension refers to the many and varied error-checking routines that may be performed in connection with recordkeeping, including periodic comparison of recorded amounts with existing assets and liabilities. A few examples of sound practices are:

In payroll processing the checking of job time tickets to clock cards to determine that cost accounting and payroll departments will account for the same number of labor hours.

In cash receipts recordkeeping, the comparison of total cash deposited (deposit slip) to total credits to accounts receivable.

In accounts receivable recordkeeping, the periodic check to determine that the subsidiary ledger total agrees with the control account balance.

In sales invoice processing, the prenumbering of all blank sales invoice documents so that a missing one can be detected easily.

A computer-programmed limit check designed to cause a printout of unusually large or unusually small transactions for human review.

These are only a few of the many error-checking routines available. One very important factor in the area of sound practices is the existence of a well-organized internal auditing function. An internal audit assignment is often the means of "comparing existing assets and liabilities to the accounting records." (Refer to part *d* of the definition of *accounting control.*)

Quality of Personnel

The fourth characteristic is both the most important and the most difficult to evaluate. In fact, auditors have very limited means for discovering whether a client's personnel possess "a degree of quality commensurate with responsibilities." Oftentimes, this quality is referred to as the "competence of personnel." Auditors do not administer intelligence tests, dexterity tests, or knowledge exams to determine directly whether personnel are competent. Perhaps the best that can be said is that auditors can generally identify the very capable people and the very incapable people. But these two extremes occur with too little frequency to be of much practical help in audits. The next best means of assessing competence is to observe and audit the output generated by the people which is direct evidence of their work and indirect evidence of their abilities. This task leads to evidence gathering in the objective compliance testing phase and relates the study and evaluation of internal control to the fifth system characteristic.

Actual System Performance

Any system may be beautifully designed with complex organization charts, voluminous manuals, and detailed statements of operating procedures, but if the people do not operate the system as it is designed, then the elaborate system exists only on paper. Only tentative conclusions may be based on the evaluation of the first four characteristics. An auditor *must* perform objective tests on important controls which he intends to rely upon to determine whether the system actually operates effectively as it is designed. In the absence of objective tests, the auditor proceeds with only paper knowledge and hearsay evidence—a potentially dangerous combination. In essence the objective compliance testing phase consists of vouching and retracing source documents to account records and from account records to source documents, with attention paid to all the intermediate processing steps, including those that may be performed by EDP programs and equipment.

INTERNAL CONTROL AND BUREAUCRACY

The foregoing explanation of internal control contains an underlying thread of organization behavior theory that is not explicitly stated. A theory of internal control which relies on the first four quality characteristics is implicitly based on the organization form known as *bureaucracy*. This word is not used in a derogatory manner to imply a cumbersome, inefficient form, but only as a name tag to identify an organization built on certain basic assumptions. The opposite organization type may be called an *open organization*. The behavioral dimensions discussed next are important for relating internal control theory to large organizations (characterized by bureaucratic norms) and to small organizations (characterized by open norms). The first dimension is specialization of duties.

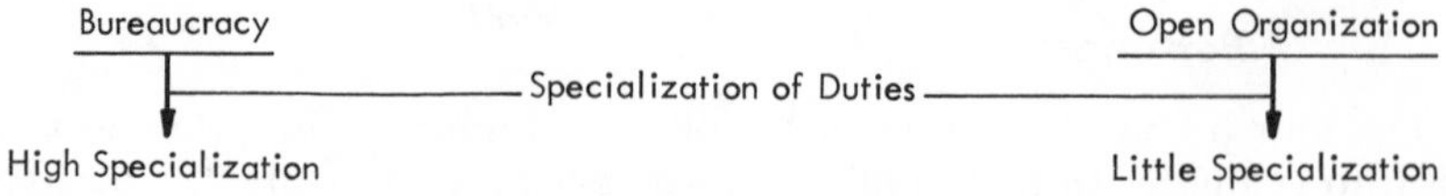

High specialization of duties and a detailed division of labor are characteristic of bureaucratic organizations. The classical theory of management suggests that greater efficiency and effectiveness is obtained when persons are assigned only a few limited tasks in which they can become expert. Hence, one finds in internal control theory the notions of division of duties to enhance data processing accuracy and to facilitate error detection. In open organizations persons may be assigned or reassigned periodically to a variety of tasks, and they will tend to experience little specialization. In small businesses there may be too few employees to accomplish all proper segregations of duties.

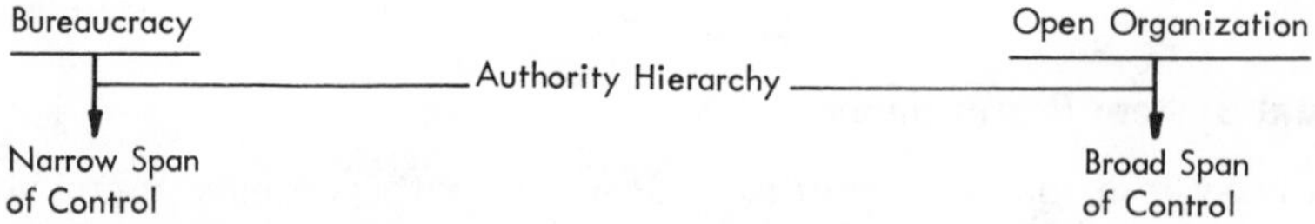

The dimension of authority hierarchy describes the shape of the organization chart. A bureaucracy would appear as a triangle with steep sides, each manager having only a few subordinates reporting to him or her; while an open organization would appear as a triangle with a flat top—in the extreme with all employees reporting to one manager. The point relevant to internal control theory is that the bureaucratic form gives more opportunity for closer counsel and supervision of personnel, more approval of their work, and greater specialization in managerial functions. An open organization or a small business, on the other hand, cannot be expected to have a different supervisory manager for every functional operation, and employees may operate very much on their own without close supervision.

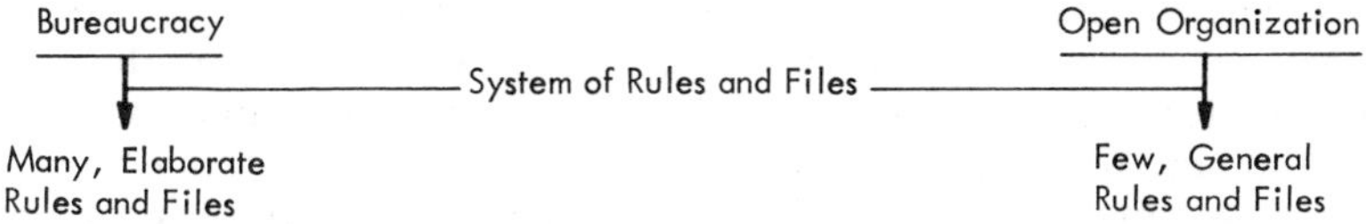

Bureaucracy thrives on having a procedure, rule, or approved method for almost all activities. In addition, the wheels of bureaucracy are greased with paper. Every action should be written, catalogued, and filed for future reference. The halls of government, business, and education virtually bulge with files. One can observe reliance on this dimension in the internal control characteristic of a system of authorization and record procedures. Auditors rely heavily on written records for evidence that a system exists and has operated as it was designed. Hence, auditors look for account charts, procedures manuals, vouchers, journals, ledgers, and all the other documents that testify to the existence and operation of a system. An open organization, however, is one that does not demand extensive paperwork and does not require that a written rule or procedure exist for every activity. Such informality is generally characteristic of small businesses.

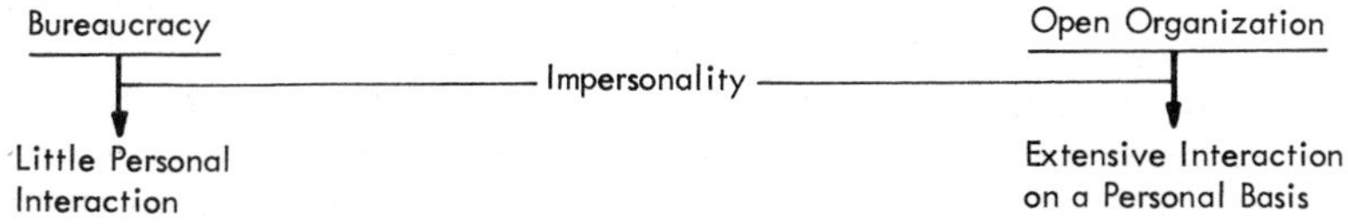

Bureaucracy assumes that on the job persons act not as unique individuals doing "their own thing" but as *role-occupants* performing the tasks defined by their specialized duties. In its strictest form, bureaucratic theory would also suggest that persons do not discuss work problems or other matters with persons other than their supervisors or immediate colleagues and then only in accordance with approved procedures. Thus if a person transfers from the sales order department to the data processing department, he or she becomes a data processor and leaves the sales orderer role behind and forgotten. The extreme form of impersonality is relatively rare in business, but an auditor must be aware that the theory literature of internal control depends greatly on the concept of role performance. (This aspect is particularly relevant to the theory that division of duties reduces the probability of collusion and complicated fraud.) Open organizations and small businesses do not compartmentalize people in roles but provide for operation and interaction extensively across departmental lines whenever to do so would be efficient and effective.

This brief digression into organization theory is not intended to make the auditor into an organizational behavior analyst. However, it is very important that auditors be aware of why the four quality characteristics are supposed to mark a satisfactory system of internal control. When an auditor is able to discern that the organization under audit is more like an open organization and less like a bureaucracy, then he or she must be very careful about relying on the professed existence of division of duties and elaborate rule-file systems when these characteristics may not be observed in actual operation.

Open organizations are not easy to describe by examples, but most often they appear in not-for-profit institutions and research-oriented institutions. Small businesses might be bureaucratic if size permitted. Limited operations and few employees, however, make most small businesses look like open organizations.

INTERNAL CONTROL IN SMALL BUSINESSES

One can have specialization, steep hierarchy, and impersonality only if there are enough people to fill all the roles. A business organization is considered small if it cannot build a bureaucracy, and this may mean anywhere from one to ten persons involved in the business.

The key person in internal control in a small business is the owner-manager. Because the business is small, it does not yet exhibit the complexity that creates demand for elaborate internal control. A diligent owner-manager may be able to oversee and supervise all the important authorization, recordkeeping, and custodial functions, and to assure data processing accuracy to his own and the auditor's satisfaction. Thus the auditor, in evaluating internal accounting control, may find himself studying the extent of the owner-manager's involvement in the operation of the information system and may find himself evaluating the competence and integrity of the owner-manager. This latter task emphasizes the importance of the "competent personnel" quality characteristic of internal control theory.

As a small business begins to grow from, say, 4 people to 10 or 15, the transition to more formalized internal control tends to lag behind. The owner-manager may become overburdened with control duties and may tacitly delegate these to others. The intermediate size stage represents a turning point where both owner-manager and auditor need to be very careful. At this point some measures such as limited specialization and surety bonding of employees may help traverse the transition, and an auditor may offer many suggestions to the owner-manager as an added service.

In the next section, methods of the review phase are considered in some detail, including a look at the use of internal control questionnaires. Exhibit 6–4 contains a portion of a questionnaire designed specifically for use in small businesses. While this exhibit is only a sample of the kind of questions relevant to the small business, it does enable one to see the great reliance placed on the role of the owner. This questionnaire may be compared with others designed for large organizations presented in the next section.

EXHIBIT 6–4

THE SMALLTIME COMPANY
Internal Control Questionnaire

	Yes	*No*
1. General		
a. Are accounting records kept up to date and balanced monthly?	______	______
b. Is a chart of accounts used?	______	______
c. Does the owner use a budget system for watching income and expenses?	______	______
d. Are cash projections made?	______	______
e. Are adequate monthly financial reports available to owner?	______	______
f. Does the owner appear to take a direct and active interest in the financial affairs and reports which should be or are available?	______	______
g. Are the personal funds of the owner and his personal income and expenses completely segregated from the business?	______	______
h. Is the owner satisfied that all employees are honest?	______	______
i. Is the bookkeeper required to take annual vacations?	______	______
2. Cash Receipts		
a. Does the owner open the mail?	______	______
b. Does the owner list mail receipts before turning them over to the bookkeeper?	______	______
c. Is the listing of the receipts subsequently traced to the cash receipts journal?	______	______
d. Are over-the-counter receipts controlled by cash register tapes, counter receipts, etc?	______	______
e. Are receipts deposited intact, daily?	______	______
f. Are employees who handle funds bonded?	______	______
3. Cash Disbursements		
a. Are all disbursements made by check?	______	______
b. Are prenumbered checks used?	______	______
c. Is a controlled, mechanical check protector used?	______	______
d. Is the owner's signature required on checks?	______	______
e. Does the owner sign checks only after they are properly completed? (Checks should not be signed in blank.)	______	______
f. Does the owner approve and cancel the documentation in support of all disbursements?	______	______
g. Are all voided checks retained and accounted for?	______	______
h. Does the owner review the bank reconciliation?	______	______
i. Is an imprest petty cash fund used?	______	______
4. Accounts Receivable and Sales		
a. Are work order and or sales invoices prenumbered and controlled?	______	______
b. Are customers' ledgers balanced regularly?	______	______

EXHIBIT 6–4 (*continued*)

	Yes	*No*
c. Are monthly statements sent to all customers?	____	____
d. Does the owner review statements before mailing them himself?	____	____
e. Are account write-offs and discounts approved only by the owner?	____	____
f. Is credit granted only by the owner?	____	____
5. Notes Receivable and Investments		
a. Does the owner have sole access to notes and investment certificates?	____	____
6. Inventories		
a. Is the person responsible for inventory someone other than the bookkeeper?	____	____
b. Are periodic physical inventories taken?	____	____
c. Is there physical control over inventory stock?	____	____
d. Are perpetual inventory records maintained?	____	____
7. Property Assets		
a. Are there detailed records available of property assets and allowances for depreciation?	____	____
b. Is the owner acquainted with property assets owned by the company?	____	____
c. Are retirements approved by the owner?	____	____
8. Accounts Payable and Purchases		
a. Are purchase orders used?	____	____
b. Does someone other than the bookkeeper always do the purchasing?	____	____
c. Are suppliers' monthly statements compared with recorded liabilities regularly?	____	____
d. Are suppliers' monthly statements checked by the owner periodically if disbursements are made from invoice only?	____	____
9. Payroll		
a. Are the employees hired by the owner?	____	____
b. Would the owner be aware of the absence of any employee?	____	____
c. Does the owner approve, sign, and distribute payroll checks?	____	____

10. Brief Narrative of Auditor's Conclusions as to Adequacy of Internal Control

____

____

____

____

Source: Herbert J. Stelzer, "Evaluation of Internal Control in Small Audits," *Journal of Accountancy*, November 1964, pp. 58–59.

TECHNIQUES OF THE REVIEW PHASE

The proper study and evaluation of internal accounting control is essentially an evidence-gathering and decision-making process that can be approached in the light of the scientific method outlined in Chapter 1. The internal control review and examination may be generalized in parallel with the first three methodological steps.

1. Recognize the assertion(s), problems, and preliminary data required to formulate a testable hypothesis statement.	1. Most managements represent that an adequate system of data processing control is in operation, although in some audits it may be admitted to be deficient at the outset of the audit. In either case the auditor knows the importance of control for program planning, and he or she must determine the *degree* of reliability no matter what management says in conversations. Thus the hypothesis to be tested is really a question of degree: "How reliable is the system of internal accounting control?"
2. Formulate the hypothesis in such a manner that either acceptance or rejection of it yields a useful auditing decision.	2. An auditor cannot simply reject a hypothesis that internal accounting control is reliable (upon finding contrary evidence) but must go on to further audit work (except when the situation is hopeless). Thus a useful form of the question-type hypothesis is: "Internal control over accounting data processing is (0) excellent, (1) good, (2) fair, (3) poor, or (4) unreliable." The major hypothesis is that internal accounting control is excellent, but there are four alternative hypotheses available in descending order of reliability, and a choice of any of the five yields useful information for planning the nature, extent, and timing of subsequent auditing tests.*
3. Collect competent evidence that contributes to the decision (i.e., a choice of the degree of reliability), by first selecting the applicable auditing evidence-gathering techniques and procedures. Then perform the tasks called for by the procedures.	3. Evidence that contributes to the decision includes evidentiary material about the five quality characteristics of operative effectiveness. The applicable techniques are questionnaire inquiry, flowchart description, and transaction-testing (vouching and retracing procedures).

* The degree of reliability decision generally depends upon some *specific* and *important* control point strength or weakness. The idea of an overall rating (excellent, good, fair, and so on) should be interpreted as a way of evaluating some specific type of control.

Internal Control Questionnaire and Narrative

The most efficient means of gathering initial evidence and knowledge about internal accounting control is to conduct a formal interview with a knowledgeable manager, using the checklist type of internal control questionnaire. Exhibit 6–4 contains a sample of such questions relevant for small businesses, and Exhibit 6–5 illustrates the type of questions appropriate for a larger enterprise. Questionnaires are also tailored for use in computer-based information systems, and the questions are designed to produce information about the operation of the EDP installation and the individual data processing subsystems.

These questionnaires are designed to help the auditor gather evidence about the division of duties, the system of authorization and record procedures, and many practices that are considered good error-checking routines. Answers to the questions, however, are *not competent and sufficient enough* for final conclusions about the reliability of internal accounting control. Questionnaire evidence is like hearsay evidence because its source is generally a single person who, while knowledgeable, is still not the person who actually does the work that the questionnaire asks about. This person may give answers that reflect what he or she believes the system should be, rather than what it really is; or he or she may be unaware of informal ways in which duties have been changed, or may be innocently ignorant of the details of the system.

Nevertheless, questionnaires are useful when the manager tells of a weak feature. An admission adverse to the criterion of effectiveness is fairly convincing to an auditor. Another strong point is that questionnaires are complete—usually containing hundreds of questions dealing with most conceivable points of internal control interest. With such a checklist an auditor is less likely to forget to cover some important point. Also, questions are generally worded such that a "No" answer points out some weakness or control deficiency, thus making analysis of the evidence easier.

However, there are pitfalls in questionnaire use. Sometimes it is tempting to complete the questionnaire for the current year audit while using the prior year's questionnaire as a crutch. Such a shortcut might cause the auditor to miss a change in the system. A mechanical checking off of "Yes" and "No" answers with cursory comments in the "Remarks" column—a manifestation of viewing the questionnaire as just another form to fill out—does not contribute much to a careful decision about the reliability of internal accounting control, and the quality of subsequent audit work may suffer. Also, since questionnaires may be standardized and thus contain every conceivable question, it is inevitable that many of them might not be applicable to a particular audit client.

One way to tailor this inquiry evidence-gathering operation to a unique system is to write a narrative description of each important control subsystem. Such a narrative would appear very much like the text portion of the problems at the end of the chapter which describe data processing and control procedures. The narrative description may be efficient in audits of very small businesses, although concurrent use of specialized questionnaires is also recommended. The greatest drawbacks to the narrative description is that its writing takes time and skill; the evaluation of what is described requires experience and insight; and as the years pass, its revision becomes physically cumbersome because with any major change the entire narrative must be rewritten.

In summary, the formal inquiry to gather preliminary evidence about internal accounting control may be documented with a complete questionnaire, with a narrative description, or with both. In any event, the auditor should make sufficient note of admitted weak points and design the audit program accordingly. For all other points of importance that appear to be reliable, objective tests must still be performed, but they may be limited to those controls that will be relied upon when substantive tests are performed.

The questionnaire section shown in Exhibit 6–5 covers accounts receivable and sales transaction control matters. This part of the questionnaire relates to the fact situation described in Exercise 6.11 at the end of this chapter. The system flowcharts presented next and the objective tests of transactions illustrated in Chapter 7 and Chapter 8 are all coordinated with Exercise 6.11 in order to give continuity to the proper study and evaluation of internal accounting control for this specific subsystem. At this point a reading of Exercise 6.11 is recommended. Along with the exercise are illustrative working papers documenting some of the internal accounting control decisions.

Internal Control System Flowcharts

Another method for gathering preliminary evidence is to construct a flowchart or diagram of the data processing system. Flowcharting is in wide use by auditors. The advantages of flowchart diagrams can be summarized by an old cliche: "A picture is worth a thousand words." Flowcharts can enhance the auditor's evaluation, and annual updating of the chart is relatively easy (compared to narrative descriptions) with additions or deletions to the symbols and lines.

The disadvantages of flowcharting are said to be its greater time requirement and greater expertise in a rather unique art form. In response to the disadvantages one might say that the greater time requirement contributes to a much better internal accounting control evaluation and hence possibly to a better and more efficient overall audit. As for the required expertise, the "disadvantage" is largely illusory and may be overcome by study and practice.

Construction of a flowchart takes more time because the auditor does not finish drawing it until he or she has consulted firsthand all the operating personnel involved in the system, seen all the machines, and gathered exhibits of all the documents. Thus the information for the flowchart, like the narrative description, involves a lot of legwork and observation. When the flowchart is complete, the result is an easily evaluated, informative description of the system.

EXHIBIT 6–5
Internal Control Questionnaire for Sales and Accounts Receivable

Client: Kingston Company Audit Date: December 31, 1978

Names and Positions of Client Personnel Interviewed: Mr. Samuel Carboy (Controller), Mr. Julian Grace (Chief Accountant)

Auditor: Harold Groody (Senior Account.) Date Completed: September 17, 1978

Reviewed by: Titus Balstrade (Manager) Date Reviewed: September 20, 1978

Question	Answer: NA	Yes	No	Remarks*
SALES:				
1. Briefly describe method of recording sales.				Billing clerk matches invoice with sales order, enters prices, extends and foots. Sends daily batches to keypunch for EDP preparation.
2. Are customers' orders subjected to review and approval before invoice is prepared:				
a. By sales or order department?		✓		
b. By credit department?		✓		
3. Are blank invoices prenumbered?		✓		
4. Are blank invoices available only to authorized personnel?		✓		
5. Are sales and order department personnel denied custodial access to assets?		✓		
6. Are bill of lading forms prenumbered?			✓	Potential loss of data control.
7. Are back orders or pending files reviewed periodically? How often?		✓		Weekly.
8. Are invoices checked for accuracy of:				
a. Quantities billed?		✓		
b. Prices used?		✓		
c. Mathematical calculations?		✓		
d. Credit terms?		✓		
9. Are completed invoices compared with customer orders?		✓		By billing clerk.
10. Are returned items cleared through the receiving department?		✓		
11. Does the system provide control over:				
a. Sales to officers and employees?		✓		
b. Sales to subsidiaries and affiliates?		✓		
c. Scrap and waste sales?		✓		
d. Sales of equipment?		✓		
e. C.O.D. sales?	✓			
f. Cash sales?		✓		
12. Are there accuracy checks on data prepared for EDP departments:				Control totals are prepared but not used for control.
a. Control totals?		✓		
b. Key verification?		✓		
13. List and describe programmed EDP controls. Self-checking customer code; Limit check on sales amount				Unique code for each customer for sales over $5,000.

* In the case of a "No" answer, the "Remarks" column should (1) cross-reference to the audit program steps designed to recognize the weakness or to a supporting memorandum which explains related adequate controls or lack of importance of the item, and (2) indicate whether the item is to be included in the draft of the letter to management on internal accounting control.

EXHIBIT 6–5 (*continued*)

Question	NA	Yes	No	Remarks*
	Answer			
ACCOUNTS RECEIVABLE:				
1. Are cash postings made simultaneously with the posting of the cash receipts records by means of a machine bookkeeping device? (If not, give brief description of method used.)		✓		EDP of daily document batches.
2. Are the duties of the accounts receivable bookkeeper separate from any cash functions?		✓		
3. If there is more than one accounts receivable bookkeeper, are the account sections for which they are responsible changed from time to time?		✓		
4. Are monthly statements sent to all customers?		✓		
5. Are statements independently checked to accounts and kept under control to insure their being mailed by someone other than the accounts receivable bookkeeper?			✓	monthly statements are maintained, prepared, and mailed by the AR department.
6. Are customer accounts regularly balanced with control?		✓		
7. Are the accounts aged periodically for review?		✓		
8. Are accounts independently confirmed by client's personnel with customers?			✓	No internal auditors.
9. Are credit memoranda approved by proper authority and are they under numerical control?		✓		
10. Is approval of credit department a prerequisite to payment of customer credit balances?		✓		
11. Are delinquent accounts periodically reviewed by an officer?		✓		Only every six months
12. Are write-offs of bad debts and adjustment credits approved by an officer?		✓		
13. Is proper control exercised over bad debts after they have been written off?		✓		
14. Are allowances for discounts in violation of regular terms of sale specifically authorized by a responsible official?		✓		
15. Is the collection department independent of and does it constitute a check on accounts receivable bookkeepers?		✓		
16. Is the management of the credit department completely divorced from the sales department?		✓		
17. Are there accuracy checks on data prepared for EDP departments?		✓		Control totals are prepared but Not used for control.
18. Are there post-processing accuracy checks on EDP output?				
a. Comparison of sales and accounts receivable control account entries.		✓		
b. Comparison of control account entry to subsidiary detail.		✓		
19. List and describe programmed EDP controls. Self-checking customer code; Limit check on sales amount; Count, hash, and batch totals				Unique code for each customer for sales over $5,000. Control totals are generated by computer processing.

EXHIBIT 6–6
Abbreviated Set of Standard Flowcharting Symbols

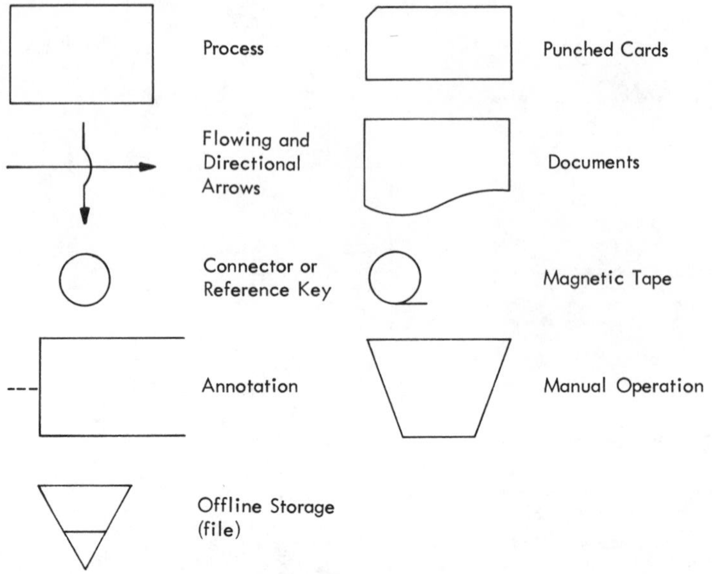

Source: American National Standards Institute, Inc. (1971).

Exhibit 6–6 contains a few simple symbols that will be used in further illustrations and in problem solutions. For any flowcharting application, it is important that the chart be understandable to a reasonably knowledgeable audit supervisor, without his or her having to consult a lengthy index of symbols for interpretation of the chart.

Before proceeding to drawing techniques, one should be aware of some elementary cautions. First, a flowchart should be drawn with a template and ruler: A messy chart is hard to read. Second, the starting point in the system should, if possible, be placed at the upper left-hand corner: It's frustrating to pick up a chart and have to hunt around for the place to start. The flow of procedures and documents should be from left to right and from top to bottom as much as is possible: A chart that has lines going back and forth is hard to decipher. Narrative explanations should be written on the face of the chart as annotations or written in a readily available reference key.

All these cautions emphasize one main point: The flowchart should communicate all relevant information and evidence about division of duties, authorization and procedures, and sound practices in a visually understandable form. Exhibit 6–7 contains a flowchart representation of the data processing system for the illustrative sales–accounts receivable system.

With reference to Exhibit 6–7 one can note some characteristics of flowchart construction and some characteristics of this data processing

Sales Transaction Processing System Flowchart

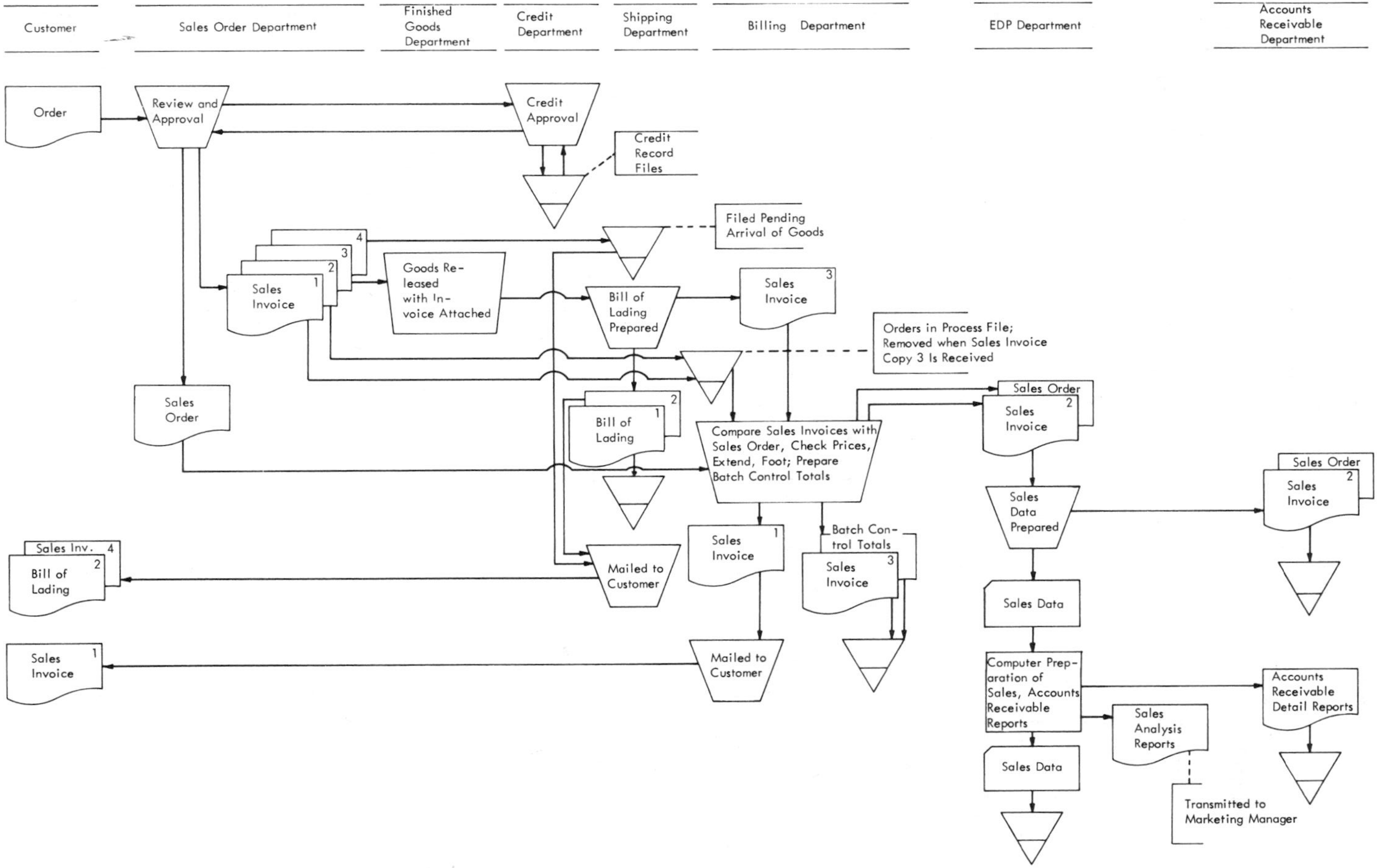

system. By reading *down* the columns headed for each department, notice that transaction initiation authority (both credit approval and sales invoice preparation), custody of assets, and transaction recordkeeping are appropriately separated. Notice also that all the invoice-completion procedures, including preparation of a batch control total, are performed in the billing department. There is no apparent double-check on data accuracy, although both the batched invoice copy 2 and the EDP report on accounts receivable are eventually filed in the accounts receivable department. Also, the chart shows that the *batch control total is not used*, which indicates that the auditor may have to test more carefully to determine whether the keypunch data-transformation process is performed accurately (e.g., select a sample of daily batches and compare machine totals run on the cards to adding machine batch totals). Note that all documents have an intermediate or final resting place in a file. This feature of a flowchart gives the auditor information about where to find audit evidence later.

The review phase of the study and evaluation of internal control is not complete until the auditor *analyzes* the flowchart and other evidence for signs of control strengths, deficiencies, or weaknesses. Reliable control system elements, which will be subject to compliance testing, and control weaknesses may be found by analyzing the flowchart. The auditor's findings and preliminary conclusions should be written up for the working paper files.

Program Flowcharts

Another type of flowcharting, generally called *program flowcharting*, is utilized to describe the features of a computer program. A program flowchart is an important element in the documentation of an EDP system. The system flowchart in Exhibit 6–7 contains a process box labeled "Computer Preparation of Sales and Accounts Receivable Reports" which is the place where the program flowchart is important for describing precisely the nature of computer programs and processing. While detailed study of techniques is better left to more lengthy books and courses of study, a brief review of program flowcharts is in order to place them in an auditing context.

The flowchart of a program is a step-by-step explanation of all the operations that are supposed to be performed by the computer. Auditors need to know how to read and review simple flowcharts that document a client's EDP programs. A portion of a program that could be used to process sales and accounts receivable transactions illustrated in this chapter is presented in Exhibit 6–8. This program flowchart is part of the documentation needed to complete the system flowchart shown in Exhibit 6–7.

The auditor can review the computer program in connection with his or her review of internal accounting control in two ways: (1) check the coded program instructions for proper controls and logic, and (2) review the flowchart for proper controls and logic. The first method requires consid-

EXHIBIT 6–8
Portion of Computer Program Flowchart: Sales and Accounts Receivable Transaction Processing

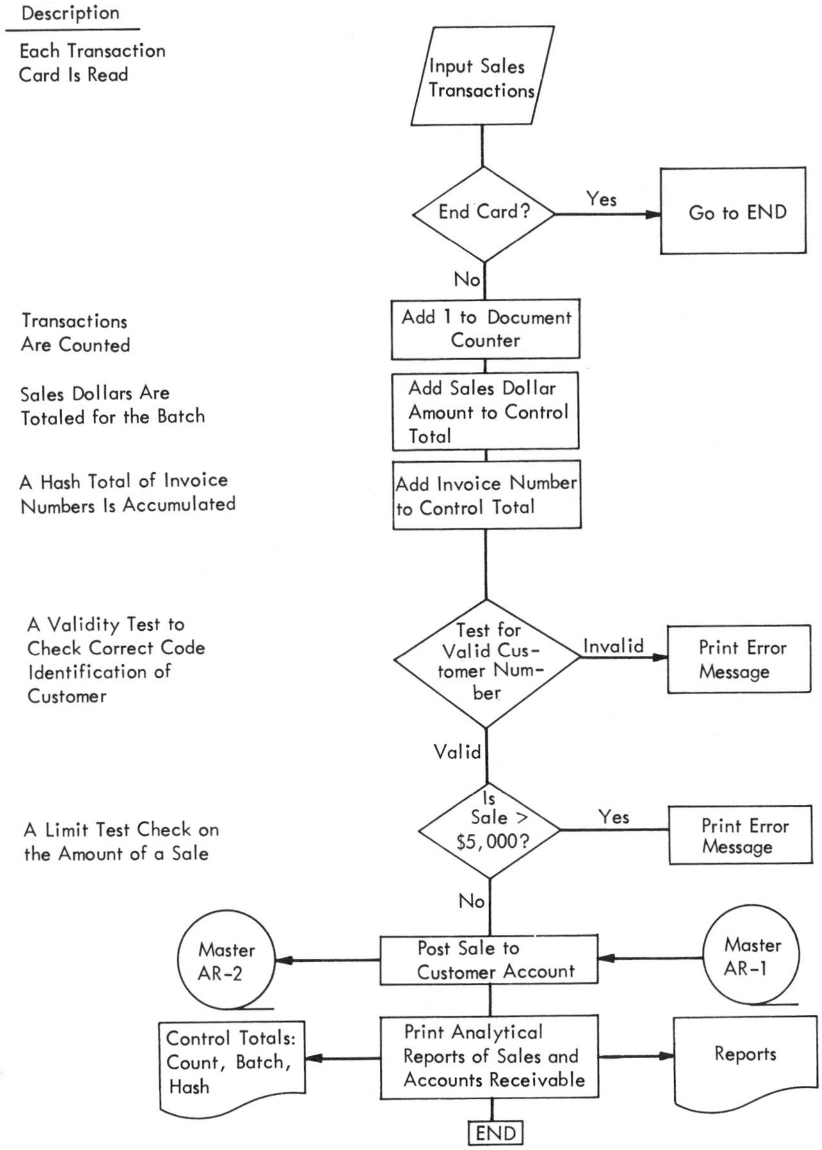

erable expertise in computer languages and much diligence in poring over a printout of the program. The second method avoids the need to know the programming language, but it still requires careful study to perform a critical analysis of the program. Both methods are subjective because the auditor is reading and reviewing documents that purport to be the real system, but the auditor is not testing the real system. These two methods of review have the same tentative evidential weight as an internal control questionnaire. In Exhibit 6–8 one can notice that the computer generates control totals that can be checked for agreement to totals prepared prior to EDP processing, and one can notice two kinds of validity tests—customer number and large-sale limit tests—that are typical of programmed controls. These and other matters of review and objective examination are covered in more detail in Chapter 8.

OBJECTIVE EXAMINATION

In this chapter the theoretical groundwork has been laid, and the tools and techniques for obtaining preliminary evidence about an internal accounting control system have been explained and illustrated. There yet remains the auditor's task of determining whether a system actually operates in an effective manner. A general term for finding such objective evidence is the class of procedures involved in compliance tests (or "tests of transactions"), which include use of the vouching, retracing, scanning, and recalculation procedures explained in Chapter 5.

In the next chapter the tools and techniques of compliance testing are explored in the context of the application of statistical methods to audit work. The methods of *sampling for attributes* is a scientific framework that provides a ready vehicle for explaining tests of transactions and subsequent evaluation decisions about internal accounting control reliability. Also, the framework provides a means of introducing and integrating mathematical-statistical concepts in the study of auditing.

REPORTING ON INTERNAL CONTROL

The Commission on Auditors' Responsibilities studied the need for reports on internal control and concluded that some form of public report is needed, especially by financial analysts. The commission recommended that management should write a report commenting upon its accounting system and its control over it and describe the company's response to material weaknesses identified by the independent auditor. The auditor's report, according to the commission, could take exception to management's comments about internal accounting control, if exceptions were warranted. These recommendations are being studied by the AICPA.

Existing auditing standards regarding reporting on internal control exist in *SAS No. 1*, Section 640 ("Reports on Internal Control"), *SAS No. 1*, Section 641 ("Reports on Internal Control Based on Criteria Established by Governmental Agencies"), and *SAS No. 20*, Section 323 ("Required Communication of Material Weaknesses in Internal Accounting

Control"). *SAS No. 20* was reviewed in Chapter 4 in connection with standards concerning auditors' responsibilities for fraud detection.

SAS No. 1, Sections 640 and 641 express the view that reports on internal control can serve a useful purpose when submitted to management, regulatory agencies, and other independent auditors—in other words, to persons who have training and experience enough to understand the nature of internal control and the auditor's evaluation of it. The standards also conclude that the "general public" has varying abilities to understand and evaluate a report on internal control, thus it is the responsibility of management and/or any regulatory agency having jurisdiction to decide whether to require dissemination of the report.[5]

Recommended language for a report to the public on internal accounting control is given in *SAS No. 1*, Section 640.12. The form (oral or written) of the report required[6] under *SAS No. 20* is optional, but language for written reports identical to Section 640.12 is suggested. Exhibit 6–9 is an illustration of a required report to management, the first two paragraphs of which contain the wording suggested in *SAS No. 20*.

Following Exhibit 6–9 is an illustration of an internal auditor's report to management on results of an evaluation of controls (Exhibit 6–10).

EXHIBIT 6–9
Independent Auditor's Communication of Material Weaknesses in Internal Accounting Control

Mr. Albert B. Conroe, President
Electro Manufacturing Company

We have examined the financial statements of Electro Manufacturing Company for the year ended December 31, 1978, and have issued our report thereon dated February 23, 1979. As a part of our examination, we made a study and evaluation of the company's system of internal accounting control to the extent we considered necessary to evaluate the system as required by generally accepted auditing standards. Under these standards, the purposes of such evaluation are to establish a basis for reliance on the system of internal accounting control in determining the nature, timing, and extent of other auditing procedures that are necessary for expressing an opinion on the financial statements and to assist us in planning and performing our examination of the financial statements.

---

[5] Internal control reports by independent auditors have appeared in some bank financial statements and are required by certain government agencies and by the SEC (with regard to controls of brokers over securities held for customers). See: D. R. Carmichael. "Opinions on Internal Control," *Journal of Accountancy*, December 1970, pp. 47–53.

[6] *SAS No. 20*, which is an element of auditing standards, *requires* auditors to render the communication (oral or written) on material weaknesses in internal accounting control to senior management and the board of directors or its audit committee. However, even though this required communication may not have been made, the auditor can still state in the standard scope paragraph that his examination (audit of financial statements) was made in accordance with generally accepted auditing standards. The required communication on material weakness is considered incidental to the performance of an audit in accordance with generally accepted auditing standards. (*SAS No. 20*, Section 323).

EXHIBIT 6–9 (*continued*)

Our examination of the financial statements made in accordance with generally accepted auditing standards, including the study and evaluation of the company's system of internal accounting control for the year ended December 31, 1978, that was made for the purposes set forth in the first paragraph of this report, would not necessarily disclose all weaknesses in the system because it was based on selective tests of accounting records and related data. However, such study and evaluation disclosed the following conditions that we believe to be material weaknesses.

Receivables. Indications are that credit and collection procedures are not formalized and are not in writing. Receivables of doubtful collection have increased from 17 percent in 1977 to 24 percent in 1978, and accounts in the hands of collection agents have increased to $16,000. Credit sales continue to be made to customers with existing balances overdue by 150 days or more.

We recommend that credit granting and collection policies be reduced to writing in order to define responsibilities for granting credit on new accounts and for continuing credit on old accounts. Credit limits for customers would be useful, and salesmen should receive information on past-due accounts so that they can assist in the collection effort.

Inventories. The perpetual inventory records have not been used for planning and controlling inventory. Item records were not adjusted according to the semiannual inventory count in March, and several item records reflect a negative quantity on hand. The computer-printed inventory reports are not reliable for determining production and purchasing requirements. In addition, these same reports are being used to prepare interim financial statements which have been inaccurate.

We recommend that the reports be reviewed monthly for obvious errors (such as negative quantities). Major dollar items and important materials should be counted and inspected at least every three months. All adjustments and error corrections should be made to the records and to the computer input. Interim financial statements should incorporate these adjustments.

Data Processing Department. We found that the operator or EDP manager acts as the EDP librarian on an informal basis. The librarian has the responsibility of accounting for card and tape files and programs. We suggest that this function be assigned to a person who will physically control tapes and punched cards and will make them available to the operators on an as-needed basis. This type of arrangement provides several benefits—maintenance of a formal record of program and tape usage, prevention of unauthorized or unscheduled program runs, and assurance that all important master files and programs are being physically safeguarded.

In reviewing specific data processing applications, we noted that end of file labels with record counts, control totals, and other control information are not being incorporated in the internal control system for the EDP department. This type of control is uniquely and easily adaptable to magnetic media files. Each program should develop comparative control totals to be compared to those end of file labels. The results of the end of file comparison should be printed out and given to the control clerk. All run-to-run balancing should be reported on a standard form and periodically reviewed and approved by the data processing manager.

The foregoing conditions were considered in determining the nature, timing, and extent of audit tests to be applied in our examination of the financial statements, and this report of such conditions does not modify our report dated February 23, 1979, on such financial statements. We will be pleased to discuss these matters further, at your request.

Very truly yours,
Anderson, Olds & Watershed
Certified Public Accountants

EXHIBIT 6–10
Excerpt from an Internal Audit Report (audit of the knit division of a large mill)

This report covers the audit of a knitting division of the mill. The auditing department addresses its report to the president of the division being audited. Copies of the report are sent to the corporate president, the treasurer, and the corporate controller. The report is sent by a brief memorandum of transmittal.

The report begins with the scope of the examination and indicates a broad audit coverage. Immediately thereafter, the findings are briefly summarized and are divided between items on which action has been taken and those on which action is still required.

The summary is followed by brief discussions of the findings, grouped according to functional activity. The report is signed by the head of the audit department.

The excerpts that follow are from the summary of findings and the related detailed findings and recommendations.

INTERNAL AUDIT REPORT
AUDIT OF THE KNIT DIVISION

Scope of Examination

Our review covered the analysis of operations at the E.F.G. plant, the customer service center and the sales office. We examined the policies and procedures followed in order-booking, invoicing, shipping, receiving, claims, purchasing, payroll, waste control, quality audit, and production scheduling and control.

Summary of Findings

A. *Items on Which Action Has Been Taken*
1. Revised procedures covering packing, shipping, and billing of retail sales items expected to result in additional income of $129,000 a year.
2. Elimination of overtime amounting to $14,000 annually.
3. Collection of $3,000 excessive freight paid due to failure to deduct proper allowances on yarn invoices.
4. Revised handling of unclaimed wages to conform to company policy.
5. Discontinuation of allowing sales personnel to charge personal telephone calls to the company.

B. *Items on Which Action Is to Be Taken*
1. Improve control over cash received for retail sales.
2. Improve control in accounting for and safeguarding purchase orders.
3. Establish procedures to insure that quantities of materials and supplies received agree with quantities paid for.
4. Improve control over bills of lading to insure that all goods shipped are billed.
5. Establish control routines governing use of company truck and gasoline purchases.
6. Require medical examinations for new employees.
7. Have proper authorization for employee insurance deductions.
8. Compare number of dependents claimed for tax withholding with those used in computing net pay.
9. Process leaves of absence and terminations in accordance with company policy.

EXHIBIT 6–10 (*continued*)

10. Follow company policy on:
    a. Approval of time orders.
    b. Travel expenses paid from petty cash.
    c. Preparation of exit interview forms.
    d. Wage and work notices.
    e. Bulletin board notices.
11. Eliminate unnecessary copies of reports and use multilith instead of more expensive copier service; savings of approximately $4,750 annually.
12. Improve control over and accounting for movement of inventories, and eliminate duplicate grey goods inventory maintained in sales office.
13. Consolidate mail between plants; estimated savings of about $1,300 annually.
14. Establish preventive maintenance program and control over spare parts to provide accurate maintenance and supply costs for each machine.
15. Install program for accurately determining and reporting waste generated by each production operation.
16. Have department managers approve time sheets in accordance with company policy.
17. Have plant employees charge reimbursable mileage from plant base for better control.
18. Develop written operating procedures for training employees, defining problems, and coordinating activities.
19. Exclude nonbusiness visitors from enclosed parking lot to prevent possible company liability for personal injury and to provide better plant security.
20. Have proper and timely follow-up of late purchase orders.

Detailed Findings and Recommendations

1. *Retail Sales*
   A. Tests revealed that approximately 10 percent of goods shipped were not being billed because of quantity differences between shipping documents and invoices and because of errors in measuring the quantities packed. The adoption of procedures to make sure that all quantities are billed will result in additional income of about $129,000 annually based on current sales volume projections. Procedures to insure accurate packing, shipping, and billing have been adopted.
   B. Internal control of cash receipts for retail sales is weakened by the fact that the person receiving cash also prepares original sales documents and by the further fact that the sales documents are not accounted for numerically.

Source: From Lawrence B. Sawyer, *The Practice of Modern Internal Auditing,* pp. 414–15. Copyright 1973 by The Institute of Internal Auditors, Inc., 249 Maitland Ave., Altamonte Springs, Florida. Reprinted with permission.

SOURCES AND ADDITIONAL READING REFERENCES

Anderson, R. I. "Analytical Auditing: Does It Work?" *The Internal Auditor,* July/August 1972, pp. 36–54.

Bower, J. B., and Schlosser, R. E. "Internal Control—Its True Nature," *Accounting Review,* April 1965, pp. 338–44.

Carmichael, D. R. "Behavioral Hypotheses of Internal Control," *Accounting Review*, April 1970, pp. 235–45.

Cushing, Barry E. "A Mathematical Approach to the Analysis and Design of Internal Control Systems," *Accounting Review*, January 1974, pp. 24–41.

"Flowchart Symbols and Their Usage in Information Processing," American National Standards Institute, Inc., 1971.

A Guide for Studying and Evaluating Internal Accounting Controls. Chicago: Arthur Andersen & Co., 1978.

Konrath, Larry F. "The CPA's Risk in Evaluating Internal Control," *Journal of Accountancy*, October 1971, pp. 53–56.

Mautz, R. K., and Mini, Donald L. "Internal Control Evaluation and Audit Program Modification," *Accounting Review*, April 1966, pp. 283–91.

Morris, W., and Anderson, H. "Audit Scope Adjustment for Internal Control," *CPA Journal*, July 1976, pp. 15–20.

Rennie, Robert. "Flow Charts for Audit Purposes," *The Quarterly* (Touche Ross & Co., March 1965), pp. 13–22.

Sawyer, Lawrence B. *The Practice of Modern Internal Auditing*. Altamonte Springs, Florida: The Institute of Internal Auditors, Inc., 1973.

Stelzer, Herbert J. "Evaluation of Internal Control in Small Audits," *Journal of Accountancy*, November 1964, pp. 55–61.

Zannetos, Zenon S. "Some Thoughts on Internal Control Systems of the Firm," *Accounting Review*, October 1964, pp. 860–68.

REVIEW QUESTIONS

6.1. Distinguish between accounting controls and administrative controls in a properly coordinated system of internal control. (AICPA)

6.2. Define and explain *compliance tests*, *substantive tests* and *dual-purpose tests*.

6.3. How do the goals of internal auditors differ from those of independent auditors with respect to the conduct of a routine audit of an information control system?

6.4. List and discuss the general elements or basic characteristics of a satisfactory system of internal accounting control. (AICPA)

6.5. Is it necessary that the review phase of internal control study always be followed by performance of procedures to obtain objective evidence of system performance? (AICPA)

6.6. Is the general theory of internal control embodied in the basic characteristics equally applicable to large and small enterprises? Discuss.

6.7 What are the advantages to a CPA of reviewing internal accounting control by using (1) an internal control questionnaire, (2) a narrative memorandum, and (3) a flowchart? (AICPA)

6.8. List and discuss the scientific methodological steps which the auditor takes in a review of internal accounting control.

6.9. List and discuss the general guides for preparing system flowcharts.

6.10. Distinguish between a system flowchart and a program flowchart.

EXERCISES AND PROBLEMS

Exercise 6.11 is a comprehensive internal control study and evaluation problem which is incorporated in Chapters 6, 7, and 8. Portions of the problem relate review methods (Chapter 6), statistical applications (Chapter 7), and EDP variants (Chapter 8) to the explanation in these three chapters. Solutions are reproduced as exhibits in the chapters and as working papers at the end of the chapters. The full statement of the problem situation is given in 6.11. Problem requirements relating to Chapters 7 and 8 are given in Exercises 7.11 and 8.11, respectively.

6.11. The Kingston Company operates as a regional wholesale distributor of small home appliances, shipping electric toothbrushes, carving knives, can openers, and many other such items to large and small retail outlets in a six-state area. The sales order and billing and shipping procedures are standardized for efficient operation and have been described by the controller and observed by the senior accountant on the audit as follows:

1. *Sales order department and credit department:* Customer orders are received in the mail and over the telephone by sales order clerks who review the order request. The clerks show the order to the credit department supervisor, giving an estimate of the amount of the order, and approval for credit is written on the order. If credit is not approved, the customer is requested to forward a 75-percent advance payment before shipment. After credit approval is obtained, or a payment received, a four-copy sales invoice is prepared. Copy 1 (customer copy) and Copy 2 (billing copy) are sent to the billing department. Copy 4 (packing list copy) is sent directly to the shipping department where it is held pending movement of goods out of inventory. Copy 3 (shipping copy) is sent to the finished goods warehouse location.
2. *Finished goods warehouse:* Products are removed from shelves and bins only upon receipt of Invoice Copy 3 which is authorization for personnel to gather the order and move it to the shipping department where it will be packed properly. Copy 3 is attached to the goods as they are sent to shipping.
3. *Shipping department:* When the products are received for packing, Invoice Copy 4 is taken from the pending file and quantities actually shipped are entered on both Copies 3 and 4. A bill of lading is made out in two copies for shipments by common carrier truckers. Copy 2 of the bill of lading and Invoice Copy 4 are packed with the shipment. Invoice Copy 3 is transmitted to the billing department.
4. *Billing department:* When Invoice Copy 3 is received, Copies 1 and 2 are taken from an orders in process file, and unit prices, according to a current price list, are entered. The invoice is compared to the original customer order, to Invoice Copy 3, and all the arithmetic is completed. Invoice Copy 1 is immediately mailed to the customer. Invoice Copy 3 is filed in a shipped order file. The sales order and Invoice Copy 2 are stapled together, and a daily batch is accumulated for which the billing clerks obtain control totals for number of invoices, a hash total of invoice numbers, and a batch total of sales dollar amounts. The prenumbered numerical sequence of invoices is not checked because invoices seldom come from shipping in the sequence they were prepared by the sales order department. The daily batches are forwarded to the keypunch department for card and input preparation.

5. *Keypunch and data processing:* Keypunch operators prepare data cards with relevant dates, customer code numbers, shipping document data, quantities, and prices. Equipment operator personnel then take the cards and perform the daily sales analysis and accounts receivable updating runs. The sales order and Invoice Copy 2 are sent to the accounts receivable department and filed. Sales analysis and accounts receivable detail reports are transmitted to marketing managers and accounts receivable accounting clerks, respectively. (The general accounting office also receives summary reports for general ledger bookkeeping purposes. The accounts receivable department periodically performs functions of analyzing the accounts for an aged trial balance and mailing of monthly statements.)

Required:

In performing a proper study and evaluation of internal accounting controls, an auditor must first review the system, then perform compliance tests in order to determine whether the system actually operates effectively.

a. Design an internal control questionnaire for the sales and accounts receivable information processing subsystem. (See Exhibit 6–5 in the text.)

b. Construct a flowchart to describe the internal accounting control over sales and accounts receivable transactions. (See Exhibit 6–7 in the text.)

6.12. Sally's Craft Corner was opened in 1972 by Sally Moore, a fashion designer employed by Bundy's Department Store. Sally is employed full-time at Bundy's and travels frequently to shows and marts in New York and San Francisco. She enjoys crafts, wanted a business of her own, and saw an opportunity in the city—Billmore, Colorado, population about 100,000. The Corner sells regularly to about 300 customers now, but business only began to pick up in 1976. The staff presently includes two sales people and four office personnel, and Sally herself helps out on weekends.

Sales have grown as has the Corner's reputation for quality crafts. The history is as follows:

	1972	*1973*	*1974*	*1975*	*1976*	*1977*	*1978*
Sales	$16,495	$18,575	$17,610	$18,380	$23,950	$29,470	$37,230
Discounts, allowances	500	550	520	570	950	1,480	2,230
Net sales	$15,995	$18,025	$17,090	$17,810	$23,000	$27,990	$35,000

With an expanding business and a need for inventory, the Corner is now cash poor. Prices are getting higher every month and Sally is a little worried. The net cash flow is only about $400 per month after allowance of a 3-percent discount for timely payments on account. So she has engaged you as auditor and asks for any recommendations you might have about the cash flow situation. The Corner has never been audited before.

During your preliminary review of internal accounting control, you have learned the following about the four office personnel.

Janet Bundy is the receptionist and also helps customers. She is the daughter of the Bundy Department Store owner and a long-time friend of Sally's and helped her start the Corner in 1972. They run around together when Sally is in town. She opens all the mail, answers most of it herself, but turns over payments on account to Sue Kenmore.

Sue Kenmore recently graduated from high school and started working as a bookkeeper-secretary at the Corner in 1976. She wants to go to college but cannot afford it right now. She is very quiet at the office, but you noticed that she has some fun with her friends in her new Porsche. In the office she gets the mailed-in payments on account from Janet, takes payments over the counter in the store, checks the calculation of discounts allowed, enters the cash collections in the cash receipts journal, prepares a weekly bank deposit (and mails it), and prepares a list (remittance list) of the payments on account. The list shows amounts received from each customer, discount allowed and amount to be credited to customer's account. She is also responsible for approving the discounts and credits for merchandise returned.

Ken Murphy has been the bookkeeper-clerk since 1972. He also handles other duties, among them: He receives the remittance list from Sue, posts the customers' accounts in the subsidiary ledger, and gives the remittance list to David Roberts. Ken also prepares and mails customers' monthly statements. Ken is rather dull, interested mostly in hunting on weekends, but he is a steady worker. He always comes to work in a beat-up pickup truck—an eyesore in the parking lot.

David Roberts is the bookkeeping supervisor. He started work in 1973 after giving up his small practice as a CPA. He posts the general ledger (using the remittance list as a basis for the cash received on account entries) and prepares monthly financial statements. He also approves and makes all other general ledger entries and reconciles the monthly bank statement. David is very happy not to have to contend with the pressures he experienced in his practice as a CPA.

Required:

a. Draw a simple flowchart of the cash collection and bookkeeping procedures.

b. Identify any material weakness in internal accounting control. Explain any reasons you might have to suspect that errors or irregularities may have occurred.

c. Recommend corrective measures you believe necessary and efficient in this business.

6.13. Discuss briefly what you regard as the more important deficiencies in the system of internal control in the following situation, and in addition include what you consider to be a proper remedy for each deficiency:

> The cashier of the Easy Company intercepted customer A's check payable to the company in the amount of $500 and deposited it in a bank account which was part of the company petty cash fund, of which he was custodian. He then drew a $500 check on the petty cash fund bank account payable to himself, signed it and cashed it. At the end of the month while processing the monthly statements to customers, he was able to change the statement to customer A so as to show that A had received credit for the $500 check that had been intercepted. Ten days later he made an entry in the cash received book which purported to record receipt of a remittance of $500 from customer A, thus restoring A's account to its proper balance, but overstating cash in bank. He covered the overstatement by omitting from the list of outstanding

checks in the bank reconcilement, two checks, the aggregate amount of which was $500. (AICPA)

6.14. You are auditing the Alaska Branch of Far Distributing Company. This branch has substantial annual sales which are billed and collected locally. As a part of your audit you find that the procedures for handling cash receipts are as follows:

Cash collections on over-the-counter sales and C.O.D. sales are received from the customer or delivery service by the cashier. Upon receipt of cash the cashier stamps the sales ticket "paid" and files a copy for future reference. The only record of C.O.D. sales is a copy of the sales ticket which is given to the cashier to hold until the cash is received from the delivery service.

Mail is opened by the secretary to the credit manager, and remittances are given to the credit manager for his review. The credit manager then places the remittances in a tray on the cashier's desk. At the daily deposit cutoff time the cashier delivers the checks and cash on hand to the assistant credit manager who prepares remittance lists and makes up the bank deposit which he also takes to the bank. The assistant credit manager also posts remittances to the accounts receivable ledger cards and verifies the cash discount allowable.

You also ascertain that the credit manager obtains approval from the executive office of Far Distributing Company, located in Chicago, to write off uncollectible accounts, and that he has retained in his custody as of the end of the fiscal year some remittances that were received on various days during last month.

Required:

a. Construct a flowchart to describe the procedures now in effect for handling cash collections and remittances. What irregularities might occur undetected under this system?

b. Give procedures that you would recommend to strengthen internal accounting control over cash collections and remittances. (AICPA adapted)

6.15. The 12 partners of a regional-sized CPA firm met in special session to discuss audit engagement efficiency. Jones spoke up, saying: "We all certainly appreciate the firmwide policies set up by Martin and Smith, especially in connection with the audits of the large clients that have come our way recently. Their experience with a large national firm has helped build up our practice. But I think the standard policy of conducting reviews and compliance tests of internal accounting control on all audits is raising our costs too much. We can't charge our smaller clients fees for all the time the staff spends on this work. I would like to propose that we give engagement partners discretion to decide whether to do a lot of work on internal control. I may be an old mossback, but I think I can finish a competent audit without it." Discussion on the subject continued but ended when Martin said, with some emotion: "But we can't disregard generally accepted auditing standards like Jones proposes!"

What do you think of Jones's proposal and Martin's view of the issue? Discuss.

6.16. The following four short cases represent separate fact situations bearing on internal controls under specific conditions.

a. Suppose you find during a review of internal accounting control procedures that the client's clerks responsible for accounting for construction contract costs were (1) all hired within the last six weeks, (2) not trained in accounting methods used by the company, and (3) had no previous accounting employment. What effect would this knowledge have on your evaluation of the existing system of internal control and your substantive auditing procedures related to construction costs?

b. The warehouse inventory of your client consists of CB radios, audio accessories, batteries, cables, and antennae. The warehouse is located three blocks from the company's retail store outlet. It is a wood frame building in which the items are stored on open shelves. There is no permanent staff at the warehouse, but employees go there almost every two hours to remove items upon customers' requests. Each night the main door is carefully locked by the watchman who patrols the retail store area. Do the physical safeguards over this inventory appear to be adequate?

c. Marketable securities owned by the client are kept locked in the treasurer's desk drawer. The treasurer instituted this practice seven years ago. He has been with the company for ten years and works so diligently that he has never had time for a vacation. Do these circumstances suggest any possibility that errors or irregularities may have occurred?

d. The client has experienced several instances of having paid a vendor's invoice twice. This becomes known when vendor's monthly statements show both payments for one charge. What may have happened, and what control procedure appears to be absent?

6.17. The town of Commuter Park operates a private parking lot near the railroad station for the benefit of town residents. The guard on duty issues annual prenumbered parking stickers to residents who submit an application form and show evidence of residency. The sticker is affixed to the auto and allows the resident to park anywhere in the lot for twelve (12) hours if four quarters are placed in the parking meter. Applications are maintained in the guard office at the lot. The guard checks to see that only residents are using the lot and that no resident has parked without paying the required meter fee.

Once a week the guard on duty, who has a master key for all meters, takes the coins from the meters and places them in a locked steel box. The guard delivers the box to the town storage building where it is opened, and the coins are manually counted by a storage department clerk who records the total cash counted on a "Weekly Cash Report." This report is sent to the town accounting department. The storage department clerk puts the cash in a safe, and on the following day the cash is picked up by the town's treasurer who manually recounts the cash, prepares the bank deposit slip, and delivers the deposit to the bank. The deposit slip, authenticated by the bank teller, is sent to the accounting department where it is filed with the "Weekly Cash Report."

Required:

a. Describe weaknesses in the existing system and

b. Recommend one or more improvements for each of the weaknesses to strengthen the internal accounting control over the parking lot cash receipts. Organize your answers as follows: (AICPA adapted)

Weakness	*Recommended Improvement(s)*

6.18. Anthony, CPA, prepared the flowchart on the following page which portrays the raw materials purchasing function of one of his clients (a medium-sized manufacturing company) from the preparation of initial documents through the vouching of invoices for payment in accounts payable. The flowchart was a portion of the work performed on the audit engagement to evaluate internal accounting control.

Required:

Identify and explain the systems and control weaknesses evident from the flowchart. Include the internal accounting control weaknesses resulting from activities performed or not performed. All documents are prenumbered. (AICPA)

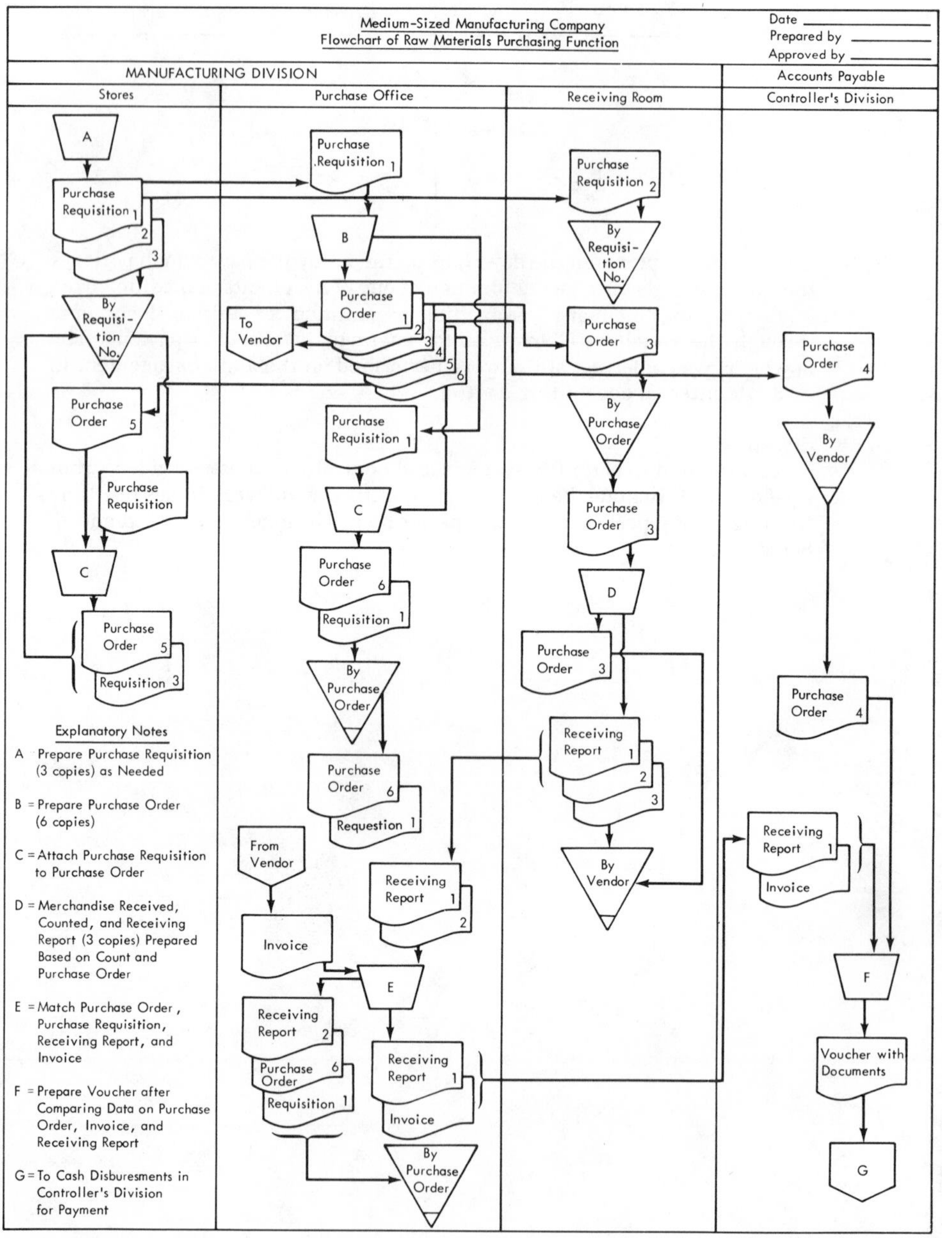
Medium-Sized Manufacturing Company
Flowchart of Raw Materials Purchasing Function
Date
Prepared by
Approved by
MANUFACTURING DIVISION
Accounts Payable
Stores
Purchase Office
Receiving Room
Controller's Division
A
Purchase Requisition 1
2
3
By Requisition No.
Purchase Order 5
Purchase Requisition
C
Purchase Order 5
Requisition 3
Purchase Requisition 1
B
Purchase Order 1
2
3
4
5
6
To Vendor
Purchase Requisition 1
C
Purchase Order 6
Requisition 1
By Purchase Order
Purchase Order 6
Requestion 1
From Vendor
Invoice
Receiving Report 1
2
E
Receiving Report 2
Purchase Order 6
Requisition 1
Receiving Report 1
Invoice
By Purchase Order
Purchase Requisition 2
By Requisition No.
Purchase Order 3
By Purchase Order
Purchase Order 3
D
Purchase Order 3
Receiving Report 1
2
3
By Vendor
Purchase Order 4
By Vendor
Purchase Order 4
Receiving Report 1
Invoice
F
Voucher with Documents
G
Explanatory Notes
A Prepare Purchase Requisition (3 copies) as Needed
B = Prepare Purchase Order (6 copies)
C = Attach Purchase Requisition to Purchase Order
D = Merchandise Received, Counted, and Receiving Report (3 copies) Prepared Based on Count and Purchase Order
E = Match Purchase Order, Purchase Requisition, Receiving Report, and Invoice
F = Prepare Voucher after Comparing Data on Purchase Order, Invoice, and Receiving Report
G = To Cash Disburesments in Controller's Division for Payment

7

COMPLIANCE TESTS OF INTERNAL CONTROL AND ATTRIBUTE SAMPLING

The study and evaluation of internal accounting control includes *compliance tests*—observation tests and tests of transaction details. The first purpose of this chapter is to explain and illustrate the procedures involved in performing tests of transaction details. The second purpose is to explain the use of statistical sampling for attributes when testing transaction details.

Combining the two purposes, the overall objective of the chapter is to explain the process of making decisions about the reliability of internal accounting control procedures. Such decisions are shown to be a blend of professional judgment and statistical measurement. As in Chapter 6 the illustrations in this chapter are based on the fact situation described in Exercise 6.11.

COMPLIANCE TESTS OF TRANSACTION DETAILS

The practice of testing transaction details on a sample basis for evidence of compliance with internal accounting control procedures is well established in auditing. Whether applied through statistical or nonstatistical methods, the common purpose is to form a conclusion about a whole population by auditing only a part of it (the sample). The goal of sampling is to achieve audit efficiency in terms of time and cost.

Compliance tests of transaction details should be applied to transactions executed throughout the period under audit because the auditor's conclusions are going to encompass the entire period. However, it is a common practice to perform a major portion of compliance tests during the *interim* audit work period—some weeks or months prior to the client's fiscal year-end. When this has been done, the auditor must determine what to do about the period remaining (for example, the period October–December after compliance tests were performed in late September). Factors influencing the decision of whether to continue testing include (*a*) the results of interim tests, (*b*) responses to inquiries made during the period, (*c*) the length of the remaining period, (*d*) the nature and dollar amount of transactions involved, and (*e*) evidence of compliance obtained from the results of substantive tests performed near the year-end and results of work done by the client's internal auditors.[1] Depending on the circumstances indicated by these considerations, the auditor may decide either to perform more compliance tests of transaction details or to rely on evidence already on hand.

The key consideration involved in designing compliance tests of transaction details is that the audit sample must be *representative* of the population of transactions (and their accompanying controls) about which decisions will be made. These decisions, of course, are the ones dictated by the second AICPA standard of field work—the decisions about reliance on the system of internal accounting control and about the nature, timing, and extent of subsequent auditing procedures. The primary product of a proper study and evaluation of existing internal accounting control is the information it provides for modifying (or not modifying) the preliminary audit program, and the secondary product is the information on material weaknesses communicated to the client.

In Chapter 6, internal accounting control was concisely defined as—"the means by which errors in accounting data are detected and corrected." Specific control procedures are designed in a system to detect and correct errors, and an auditor is obligated to determine whether the specific controls on which he or she intends to rely are operating effectively. To make this determination the auditor can select a sample of transactions that are *supposed* to show documentary evidence of effective control and examine them to see if the controls seem to have worked. For a carefully defined, specific control, the control feature will have worked or it will not have worked. The auditor will find either a "yes" or "no" answer to the question of effectiveness.

The characteristics of specific controls are called *attributes* of control, hence the name given to *attribute sampling*. For example, a billing system should provide procedures for matching a customer's order with an invoice and with a shipping document before a sale is recorded in order to control the possibility of recording a sale improperly (a wholly fictitious "sale", or merely recording one too early—before the goods are shipped). The specific control attribute in this example may be called "Assure that recorded sales transactions are valid by comparing sales invoices to shipping documents."

Other specific attributes and exceptions to them are explained in this and subsequent chapters. Below are listed categories that describe attributes of interest to auditors and an example of how each might fail its control purpose.

---

[1] *SAS No. 1* (Section 320.61).

Control Attribute Categories	*Exceptions to Control Attributes*
1. Assure that recorded transactions are valid by comparing supporting documentation.	Fictitious sales are recorded without supporting shipping documents.
2. Assure that all valid transactions are recorded, and none are omitted	Clerks fail to invoice shipments to customers.
3. Assure that transactions are authorized according to company policy.	Sales invoices are prepared without proper credit approval.
4. Assure that transaction dollar amounts are properly calculated.	Customers are billed for greater or lesser quantities than shipped, and incorrect unit prices are used.
5. Assure that transactions are properly classified in the accounts.	Sales transactions are classified in the wrong business segment account.
6. Assure that transactions are accounted for completely.	Billings fail to be posted to customer accounts even though properly posted to the control account.
7. Assure that transactions are accounted for in the proper period.	Sales invoices are dated and recorded prior to the actual shipment date.

Elements of Professional Judgment

The quantitative statistical evaluation involved in compliance tests of transaction details includes elements of professional judgment and statistical calculations.

Internal accounting controls are not expected to operate perfectly all the time to detect and correct all errors and irregularities. Thus an auditor should be willing to tolerate some degree of imperfection, but just how much depends upon the individual auditor's preferences, the nature and importance of the control, the transactions involved and their total dollar amounts, and the particular circumstances of the audit engagement. However, the auditor should not insist upon being certain about the decision reached. *Certainty* means to have no doubt about making a decision error, but it is obtained at the cost of auditing all the transactions subject to the control under audit. A risk of being wrong coexists with any sample-based audit test. This risk can be *measured* using statistical calculations.

Acceptable Upper Precision Limit (AUPL). The AUPL is the auditor's quantification of a professional judgment. It is the proportion of exceptions that might exist in the operation of a specific control but still permit the control to be considered effective and allow the auditor to place reliance on it. In general, auditors are willing to rely on systems that might produce a relatively high proportion of exceptions so long as they might be expected to have a minor effect on financial statements and financial data and so long as subsequent audit procedures are likely to detect any material misstatement. Conversely, auditors demand a relatively low exception proportion when the exceptions could have a direct and possibly material effect on financial statements and operating reports. One major public accounting firm has expressed the policy shown below on acceptable exception proportions. Each proportion refers to specific controls identified by the auditor, not to all control features in general.

Auditor's Judgment of Required Degree of Compliance with a Specific Control	*Recommended Range for the Acceptable Upper Limit of Exception Proportion**
High	2 to 4 percent
Intermediate	5 to 8 percent
Low	9 to 12 percent

* Another public accounting firm expresses "compliance" literally by viewing not the exception rate but the rate of compliance. Thus for "High" the recommended lower limit for compliance would be 98 percent to 96 percent. The principle is the same.

***Required Reliability* (*R*%).** The required reliability is often called the *required confidence level.* Reliability is explained in AICPA auditing standards (*SAS No. 1,* Section 320B. 23) as follows: "The reliability level is related to the probability that the auditor's conclusion . . . will be correct." It is further explained as the "complement of the level of sampling risk he is willing to assume that his conclusion will be incorrect." Thus, in the special context of attribute sampling: (1) Reliability = 1 − Risk, and (2) Risk = 1 − Reliability.

This risk is an auditor's quantitative expression of "how important is the decision about this particular internal accounting control feature." If a great deal of reliance is to be placed on the control and follow-up substantive auditing procedures are not especially effective, the auditor may wish to take very little risk, say 1 percent. On the other hand, if the control procedure is not particularly crucial and/or follow-up substantive procedures are effective and extensive, the auditor may be willing to tolerate greater risk, say 20 percent. These two examples point to reliabilities (R%) of 99 percent and 80 percent, respectively.

Risk is an auditor's assessment of the situation and of how important it is in a particular engagement to avoid making an initial wrong decision about internal control effectiveness. Further examples in this chapter use only R% = 99 percent for convenience only, not because auditors use 99 percent uniformly.

Combining these two elements of professional judgment, the quantitative aspect of an auditor's decision criteria may be stated like this: "I will decide that an internal accounting control is operating effectively if I can estimate the population exception proportion of applying this control to be less than or equal to AUPL, with R% reliability."

Statistical Measurements

The primary statistical measurements involved in compliance tests of details are (1) the computed upper precision limit (CUPL) and (2) the computed reliability (CR%) of the CUPL measurement. Underlying these measurements is the auditor's interest in obtaining evidence about the proportion of control exceptions that might exist in a population of transactions subject to the control.

Unbiased Estimate of a Population Proportion (π). An auditor is most interested in obtaining an unbiased estimate of the proportion of exceptions in the population of transactions subject to the controls. The population exception proportion is usually symbolized in statistics by the Greek letter π (pi). The higher this proportion, the less effective the controls have been, and vice versa.

Auditors use the proportion of exceptions found in a sample as an estimate of π. The proportion is:

$$p = \frac{x}{n}$$

where

p is the sample proportion—an unbiased point estimate (single value number) of π,
x is the number of exceptions discovered, and
n is the number of items (transactions) in the sample.

For example, if 420 recorded sales are vouched to supporting documents, and in 2 cases no shipping document can be located (defined as a control exception), the sample proportion is $p = 2/420 = 0.0048$.

Computed Upper Precision Limit (CUPL). Even though the sample proportion ($p = 0.0048$) can be calculated easily, an auditor cannot simply conclude that it is equal to the population proportion (π). The random sample of 420 recorded sales may not in fact be representative of the population as a whole, because even *random* samples may include or omit more of the exceptions than is characteristic of all transactions. This is called *sampling error* and is handled by computing an interval or range of proportions around the sample proportion. (Recall from your earlier statistics courses the concept of *confidence interval* or *precision interval* measurement.)

A confidence interval has a lower limit and an upper limit. The upper limit is called the computed upper precision limit (CUPL), and it is more important with regard to internal control evaluation than the lower limit.[2] The CUPL may be defined as: "The worst likely exception proportion, computed at CR% reliability."

The important point here is that the auditor must calculate and interpret the CUPL. A CUPL greater than zero should be considered acceptable because (1) control systems are generally not expected to operate per-

[2] Refer to *SAS No. 1* (Sections 320B.17, .22, and .23).

fectly all the time, and (2) sample-based evidence will never produce a zero CUPL.

However, for any set of audit findings (for example, $n = 420, x = 2, p = 0.0048$), more than one CUPL can be calculated. Each one is based on a different reliability, in this case a statistically computed reliability, which may be called CR% to distinguish it from the judgmental reliability (R%) discussed earlier.

***Computed Reliability* (CR%).** The CR% is a product of a *cumulative binomial probability function*:

$$CR\% = 1 - \sum_{k=o}^{x} \binom{n}{k} \text{CUPL}^k (1\text{–CUPL})^{n-k}$$

where

n is the sample size—the number of transactions audited,
x is the number of exceptions found—the number of times a specific control procedure was not effectively applied, and
$\binom{n}{k}$ is the number of combinations of n events taken k at a time.[3]

By definition, *computed risk* is:

$$\text{Computed risk} = \sum_{k=o}^{x} \binom{n}{k} \text{CUPL}^k (1\text{–CUPL})^{n-k}$$

The computed reliability, computed risk, and CUPL are definitely not the same concepts as the reliability, risk, and AUPL discussed earlier. The statistics described in this section (CR%, CUPL) are *calculated* on the basis of objective audit findings. The decision criteria (R%, AUPL) described earlier are products of the auditor's professional judgment.

The equations given above may be used to calculate attribute sampling statistical results.

1. Given sample results (for example, $n = 420$, $x = 2$) and a hypothetical CUPL, the CR% can be calculated directly. This CR% is the "probability that more than 2 exceptions would have been found in a random sample of 420 *if* the population error rate (π) were exactly equal to CUPL."
2. Given the same circumstances above, the computed risk is the "probability that 2 or fewer exceptions would have been found in a random sample of 420 *if* the population error rate (π) were exactly equal to CUPL."
3. Given the same sample results and a CR% (say, 99 percent), the CUPL can be calculated by an iterative method (trying CUPLs in the equation until CR% = .99 is the result). This CUPL may be described

[3] *Combination* is a counting calculation.

$$\binom{n}{k} = \frac{n!}{(n-k)!\,k!}$$

The exclamation mark indicates "factorial," which is a multiplication, for example, $5! = 5 \cdot 4 \cdot 3 \cdot 2 \cdot 1$. Zero factorial is one. ($0! = 1$).

as the "worst likely value of the population exception proportion with 99 percent computed reliability." A different (lower) CUPL would be computed as the "worst likely population exception proportion with 80 percent reliability."

Strictly speaking the CR% is an expression of the results of many repetitive random samples of the same size (for example, $n = 420$) taken from the same population. CR% says "If the actual but unknown population exception proportion (π) exceeds CUPL (say, 2 percent), then CR% (say, 99 percent) of all possible samples of the same size that could be selected from the same population would produce CUPLs greater than 2 percent." In other words CR% = 99 percent means that the auditor can have some comfort (confidence) that he could be right about CUPL $\leq$ 2 percent 99 times out of 100.

Auditors seldom use the equations to calculate CR% and CUPL. Calculations are packaged in tables such as the ones in Appendix 7–C. The CUPLs for CR%'s of 99 percent, 95 percent, and 90 percent have been rounded off, but they are accurate enough for most auditing purposes. Tables can be found elsewhere,[4] or calculations can be based on the Poisson and Normal approximations of the binomial probability function. The statistics involved in these approximations are beyond the scope of this textbook.

Quantitative Evaluation

An auditor can use statistical measurements of the exception proportion to *help* make a decision about internal control reliability. However, the quantitative measurements are by no means the only evidence that can or should be used. The statistical information is employed in a quantitative evaluation by comparing the CUPL obtained from objective compliance test evidence to the AUPL set up as a judgmental criterion (both expressed at the same reliability or confidence level). Basically the auditor is testing an hypothesis: "The population exception proportion (π) is equal to or less than AUPL." The alternative hypothesis is: "The population exception proportion (π) is greater than AUPL."

When CUPL is less than or equal to AUPL (CUPL $\leq$ AUPL) the auditor has a basis for believing that the controls are reliable. This is the first decision alternative shown in Exhibit 7–1. The "true state" of the controls may be one of reliability (i.e., $\pi \leq$ AUPL), and the decision would be correct. This is outcome O_{11} in Exhibit 7–1. However, CUPL can turn out to be less than or equal to AUPL when the controls are actually *not* reliable (i.e., $\pi >$ AUPL). The auditor runs a sampling risk of making this erroneous decision. This is a "Type II error," whose probability is β (beta), of failing to reject a false hypothesis. This erroneous decision is shown as outcome O_{12} in Exhibit 7–1.

---

[4] See Herbert Arkin, *Handbook of Sampling for Auditing and Accounting*, 2d ed. (New York: McGraw-Hill Book Co., 1974).

EXHIBIT 7–1
A Generalized Internal Control Decision Matrix

Decision Alternatives	*Unknown Condition ("true state") of Internal Accounting Controls*	
	Reliable	*Not Reliable*
The controls are reliable	Correct decision O_{11}	Erroneous decision O_{12}
The controls are not reliable	Erroneous decision O_{21}	Correct decision O_{22}

When CUPL is greater than AUPL (CUPL > AUPL), the auditor has a basis for believing that the controls are *not* reliable. This is the second decision alternative shown in Exhibit 7–1. The "true state" of the controls may be one of *not reliable* (i.e., $\pi >$ AUPL), and the decision would be correct. This is outcome O_{22} in Exhibit 7–1. However, CUPL can turn out to be greater than AUPL when the controls actually are reliable (i.e., $\pi \leq$ AUPL). The auditor runs a sampling risk of making this erroneous decision too. This is a "Type I error," whose probability is α (alpha), of rejecting a true hypothesis. This erroneous decision is shown as outcome O_{21} in Exhibit 7–1.

An example of quantitative evaluation is shown in Exhibit 7–7. However, several steps are involved in applying statistical sampling methods before an auditor gets to the quantitative evaluation stage. These steps are summarized in the next section below and explained in more detail in the one following.

SUMMARY OF SAMPLING METHODOLOGY

1. Define the objective(s) of the audit tests.
   a. Define the specific control attribute(s) to be tested.
   b. Define the "exception" conditions.
2. Define the relevant data population(s) (transactions) from which to sample.
   a. Write the audit program for compliance test procedures.
3. Determine sample size (number of transactions to audit).
   a. Judgmental determination.
   b. Mathematically aided (statistical) determination.
      (1) Specify AUPL.
      (2) Specify R%.
      (3) Estimate the exception occurrence proportion in the population.
      (4) Calculate *n* (Appendix 7–B).
4. Select the sample.

5. Audit the sample items (transactions).
6. Evaluate evidence from the sample.
   a. Qualitative.
      (1) Perform error analysis.
      (2) Apply professional judgment.
   b. Quantitative.
      (1) Calculate CUPL at CR% = R%.
      (2) Compare CUPL to AUPL.
      (3) Generalize the results to the population of transactions.
7. Make final decisions.
   a. Reliability of internal accounting controls.
   b. Modification of nature, timing, or extent of substantive audit procedures in the preliminary audit program.
   c. Material weaknesses to be communicated to the client.

SAMPLING FOR ATTRIBUTES

Sampling for attributes consists of the seven major steps shown above. *Statistical sampling* and *judgmental sampling* methods can be distinguished from one another on three points: (1) Statistical sampling typically involves using a mathematical basis for figuring *sample size* (although arbitrary sizes are sometimes used), whereas judgmental sampling uses no mathematical assistance, (2) statistical sampling requires the use of *randomly* chosen sample items, whereas judgmental sampling does not, and (3) statistical sampling employs *mathematical measurement of audit findings,* whereas judgmental sampling cannot do so. The sample must be random in order to use the statistical mathematics. Lacking randomness, any calculations are meaningless.

Exhibit 7–2 displays these seven steps and compares judgmental and statistical sampling methods. Both methods are acceptable according to generally accepted auditing standards, but many auditors are employing statistical methods in whole or in part these days.

Judgmental sampling effectiveness depends entirely on the ability, experience, and expertise of the auditor. These qualities may or may not be highly developed in an individual. In general, judgmental sampling has been usefully applied in countless audit engagements, but the method is believed to have the following disadvantages:

Arbitrary sample sizes may represent too little or too much audit effort. There is no standard (such as mathematical calculations of CUPL at CR%) to guide the decision of how much auditing is enough. A judgmental size might be: "Select two days' sales transactions for test."

Sample item selection may be biased in an unknown way, causing the sample to produce proportionately fewer or proportionately more exceptions than is characteristic of the population as a whole. To select two days, an auditor might pick his or her birthday and anniversary, or two slow-sale days because the audit is running behind time, or two days that both preceded a turnover of client employees involved in the control procedures. Unknown bias is treacherous simply because the effect of it is unknown.

EXHIBIT 7–2
Transaction Test Methodology: Judgmental and Statistical

Judgmental Sampling	*Statistical Sampling*
1. *Define the objective(s) of the audit tests;* for example, to determine that all sales were recorded.	1. Same.
2. *Define the relevant population(s) from which to sample;* for example, the shipping document file.	2. Same.
3. *Determine sample size;* for example, an arbitrary number of all shipments on two days.	3. *Determine sample size* according to the mathematical relationship of acceptable exception proportion and reliability suitable for reaching a useful audit conclusion.
4. *Select the sample;* for example, by picking two days arbitrarily.	4. *Select the sample* by choosing the required number of shipping documents *at random* for the entire period under audit.
5. *Audit the sample* by reviewing the shipping documents for propriety and arithmetic accuracy and retracing the bookkeeping through to the sales account. (This may involve assessment of accurate transformation to EDP input and machine processing.)	5. Same.
6. *Evaluate evidence from the sample;* for example, determine how many errors and their importance. *Decide* how reliable the system is with reference to experience and ability.	6. *Evaluate the evidence from the sample* by counting number of exceptions. *Decide* how reliable the system is with reference to predetermined acceptable exception proportion and reliability criteria.*
7. *Final decision.* The internal control over omission of sales recordings is either (*a*) adequate or (*b*) unreliable.	7. *Final decision.* The internal control over omission of sales is one of (0) excellent, (1) good, (2) fair, (3) poor, or (4) unreliable—depending upon the proportion of exceptions the system fails to detect.

* These criteria are matters of auditor judgment, but they are quantified and made explicit in statistical sampling methods.

Results cannot be measured. Evaluation is limited strictly to the auditor's judgment. No mathematical assistance is available.

Generalizations about the population from which the sample was drawn cannot be made, strictly speaking. Auditors make such generalizations all the time, however. But the user of statistical sampling has the science of statistics behind him to justify the generalizations.

Statistical sampling is said to have the following advantages:

Measurements of audit findings are objective and defensible because widely accepted statistical principles underlie the calculations. Generalizations about the population can be made.

A judgmentally sufficient sample size can be figured before the sample is selected.

The requirement for randomness tends to force samples to meet the *representativeness* criterion expressed in generally accepted auditing standards.

The need to define attributes and exceptions clearly induces care and attention on the part of the auditor. This discipline of the method tends to produce better working paper documentation of the work performed, results obtained, and the decisions reached.

Samples taken by auditors working at different locations (e.g., branch offices) on the same client can be brought together for an overall evaluation. Year-to-year variations on the same client may be avoided. Large firms can guide the quality of audit work by setting statistical standards.

The following explanations of the seven steps use illustrations drawn from the fact situation in Exercise 6.11. Further requirements are given in Exercise 7.11 at the end of this chapter. A review of Exercise 6.11 at this time will facilitate understanding of the remainder of this chapter.

Define the Objectives of the Audit Tests

Generally accepted auditing standards suggests the following conceptually logical approach to the evaluation of controls, focusing directly on their purpose of preventing or detecting material errors and irregularities in financial statements (*SAS No. 1*, Section 320.65):

Consider the types of errors and irregularities (exceptions) that could occur.

Determine the accounting control procedures that should prevent or detect them.

Determine whether the necessary procedures are (a) prescribed, and (b) being followed satisfactorily.

Evaluate any weaknesses. . . .

In the sales-accounts receivable illustration (Exercises 6.11, 7.11) the types of exceptions that could occur include:

a. Inadequate credit files available for credit checking.
b. Accounting data entered erroneously into the computer.
c. Shipments failed to be invoiced to customers.
d. Recorded invoices do not represent goods actually shipped.
e. Sales were recorded erroneously (classification, posting).
f. Invoices were mathematically inaccurate.
g. Credit approval was not obtained.
h. Recorded sales were not invoiced to customers.

This kind of specification of exception possibilities accomplishes two things. It helps the auditor define the objectives of the compliance test procedures—in general, to determine whether appropriate controls over each kind of exception are operating effectively—and it helps the auditor define the specific exception conditions. Ultimately the auditor will evaluate evidence regarding the estimated population proportion of exceptions for each type of error or irregularity that might occur.

Define the Relevant Data Populations

Upon defining specific exception conditions, the relevant data populations from which samples should be drawn are relatively apparent. In general, a relevant population is the file or source of basic documents that constitutes the records of the transaction(s) being tested. For example, if the test were for errors of failing to bill for goods shipped, the relevant population is the file of shipping documents. If the test is for errors of overbilled quantities or for the irregularity of fictitious sales, the relevant population is the file of recorded sales (i.e., the sales journal list of invoices).

For most accounting transactions there are dual objectives that require the definition of two populations. First, there is the objective of determining extent of error related to all *recorded* data—and the relevant population is the individual *recorded* items or amounts. Second, there is the objective of determining the extent of errors of *omission* (items *not recorded*)—and the relevant data population is the set of physical things or source transaction records that *should* have been recorded. The first type calls for use of a vouching procedure, and the second calls for use of a retracing audit procedure for gathering evidence.

A convenient method for describing relevant populations is to lay out a form like a flowchart, this time with columns headed by data files (which should be identified in a systems flowchart). Such a layout is shown in Exhibit 7–3. This layout identifies populations that are represented by credit files, daily batch total files, invoice with sales order attached file, customer accounts (a file of subsidiary accounts), and the shipping department file of bills of lading. For appropriate objectives, each of these files must be sampled and audited for control attributes.

EXHIBIT 7–3
Illustration: Data Population Locations, Samples, and Procedures

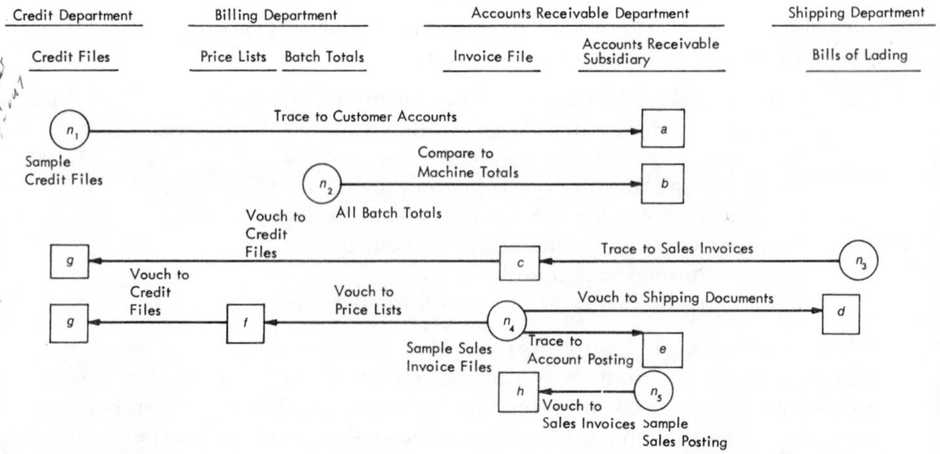

Key: Alphabetical index letters *a* through *h* refer to program steps shown in Exhibit 7–4. Sample designations n_1 through n_5 are also explained in the program steps shown in Exhibit 7–4. Sample sizes are computed in Exhibit 7–5.

In order to plan audit procedures properly, each of the attributes in each population must be identified and the auditor must judge their importance. This detailed specification of attributes amounts to an operational definition of the objectives of the tests. The specification also lends itself to the organization of an audit program. The program is shown in Exhibit 7–4.

EXHIBIT 7–4
Compliance Test Audit Program

Kingston Company December 31, 1978	Prepared by AG Date 9–20–78

a. Select a sample of credit files (n_1 = 300).* Determine whether each is up to date with reference to customers' ledger accounts.
b. Compare all daily batch totals (n_2 = all 260) of invoices to EDP-produced totals to determine whether EDP input was accurate.
c. Select a sample of bills of lading (n_3 = 340). Trace to sales invoices to determine whether shipments were invoiced, recorded, and charged to the right customer. (See also step *g* below.)
d. Select a sample of recorded sales invoices (n_4 = 420). Scan numerical sequence for missing invoice numbers. Vouch invoice data to supporting shipping documents, contracts, or correspondence files. Compare quantities billed to quantities shipped. Determine whether invoices are adequately supported.
e. Trace invoice information (220 from n_4) to EDP input media to determine accuracy of data transformation. Trace data to posting in customers' accounts and control accounts. Determine whether posting and classification was accurate.
f. Vouch invoice prices (650 prices used in sample n_4 invoices) to approved price lists to determine pricing accuracy. Recalculate amounts to prove mathematical accuracy.
g. Vouch invoiced sales (280 from sample n_4) to credit files to determine whether credit sales were properly approved.
h. Select a sample of accounts receivable sales debits (n_5 = 900) or sales account credits. Vouch to sales invoices to determine whether recorded items are properly supported.

* See Exhibit 7–5 for sample sizes.

Taken together, Exhibit 7–3 and the compliance test audit program (Exhibit 7–4) show (1) that each file is audited in two directions, one for validity of data in the file, and the other to test the file for completeness of correspondence with a related file and (2) that audit program procedures are organized around specific objectives. Notice that at this stage the methods of judgmental sampling and statistical sampling are exactly alike. The differences arise in the methods of sample size determination, the method of sample item selection, and in the evaluation of audit findings.

Sample Size Determination

Judgmental sample size is simply the number of transactions the auditor believes will provide adequate evidence. There is no science or mathematics involved in determining the number. Sometimes this is called the "magic number" theory. Some auditors like 50, others like 80, and still others prefer 163.

Statistical sampling can also work with "magic number" sample sizes. The difference is that when chosen randomly and evaluated mathematically the adequacy of the sample size can be assessed. In the final analysis, sample sizes prove themselves "adequate" or "inadequate" at the evaluation stage, not before.

Nevertheless, statistical methods provide a means of estimating a sample size in advance. The ability to do so may help the auditor avoid choosing too large a sample. The calculation (using the graphs in Appendix 7–B) is based upon two elements of judgment and one estimate (which may be a guess). To predetermine sample size the auditor must:

Specify AUPL—the professional judgment of the proportion of exceptions that might exist but the control would still be considered reliable.

Specify R%—the professional judgment of required reliability (confidence level) that expresses the auditor's preference about the risk of making an erroneous decision.

Estimate the expected rate (proportion) of occurrence of control exceptions in the population—a judgmental rather than statistical estimate (guesstimate, guess, or last year's sample exception proportion). This expresses the variance of the binomial probability function and is a factor used only to estimate a sample size in advance. It is not used later in any calculations. (Incidentally, the estimate must be less than AUPL, otherwise the sample size would equal the population size.)

The sample size is "calculated" using graphs. In Appendix 7–B locate the graph for R%, the bar for the estimated rate of occurrence, and find the intersection of the bar with the AUPL at the bottom of the graph, then read the sample size at the left or right margin. The graph is a little crude, so exact calculation of a sample size such as 423 is not possible, but such exactness is not required for audit purposes. For example, the sample size for attribute *a* in Exhibit 7–5 is:

AUPL = 10 percent

R% = 99 percent

Estimated rate of occurrence = 6 percent

n = 300 (n could be as small as 280 or as large as 320.)

This explanation of sample size determination does not mention the population size as a factor. Population size has very little influence on sample size. While this phenomenon may not be intuitively obvious, it is a mathematical fact. The graphs in Appendix 7–B are good for all populations of 1,000 or more transactions and show sample sizes a little larger than necessary for populations smaller than 1,000. Theoretically, however, larger populations require slightly larger sample sizes, all other factors constant.

EXHIBIT 7–5
Attribute Sample Size Determination

Attribute of Interest*	Reliability	Expected Exception Proportion†	Acceptable Upper Precision Limit	Precision‡	Population Size (assumed)	Sample Size	Sample
a. Credit files up to date	.99	6%	10%	4%	5,000 files	300	n_1
b. Batch totals agree	.99	0	0	0	260 totals	all 260	n_2
c. Shipments invoiced	.99	1%	3%	2%	10,000 bills	340	n_3
d. Recorded sales represent actual shipments	.99	0	1%	1%	10,000 invoices	420	n_4
e. Sales properly recorded	.99	1%	4%	3%	10,000 sales	220	n_4
f. Invoices priced correctly, arithmetically accurate	.99	3%	5%	2%	100,000 invoice items	650	n_4
g. Credit approvals adequate	.99	2%	5%	3%	10,000 invoices	280	n_4
h. Recorded sales were properly invoiced	.99	1%	2%	1%	10,000 postings	900	n_5

* Refer to the audit program in Exhibit 7–4.
† Auditors must *expect less error* than they are willing to tolerate, otherwise sampling is not appropriate.
‡ Zero precision is equivalent to specifying that exact knowledge is required. Thus, all items in the population must be audited.

Auditors often speak of the *precision* of a statistical specification or of a statistical measurement. Precision is merely the difference between the point estimate (p) of a population proportion and the lower and upper limits of an interval around it. Auditors usually pay attention only to the upper limit—a "one-tail" measurement. For example, if an auditor said: "I expect a 6-percent exception rate but can live with ± 4 percent precision," he or she is saying that an exception proportion of 10 percent is still satisfactory (AUPL = 6 percent + 4 percent = 10 percent). In the sampling plan described above, this specification yields the same sample size (provided R% = 99 percent). Likewise if a sample yields $p = 23/300 = 0.0767$ and CUPL = 0.12 at CR% = 99 percent, the *achieved precision* is 0.0433—the difference between p and CUPL (0.0433 = CUPL − p).

With some study and comparison of the graphs in Appendix 7–B, one can see the following relationships, with all factors but the one mentioned held constant.

One Factor Changed at a Time	*Change in Predetermined Sample Size*
Higher required reliability (R%)	Larger
Higher AUPL	Smaller
Higher estimated rate of occurrence	Larger
Larger difference between AUPL and estimated rate of occurrence	Smaller
Larger population size (not shown in Appendix 7–B graphs)	Larger, but not very much

Sample Item Selection

The criterion that defines randomness in sample item (transaction) selection is that *each item in the population has an equally likely chance of being included in the sample.* The auditor must be careful to define an *item.* In the sales-accounts receivable system *items* are customer credit files, daily batch totals, individual bills of lading, sales invoices, arithmetic calculations on invoices, and accounts receivable debits. Notice that a daily batch of invoices is not an item; thus a random selection of two days' invoices would not necessarily satisfy the criterion of equal likelihood for each sales invoice.

Equal likelihood of selection is of paramount importance because without it no generalizations about the population are possible. The mathematical evaluation of sample results is premised upon random selection.

Random Number Table. The simplest, although most time-consuming, selection device is a random number table. (See Appendix 7–A). This table contains rows and columns of numbers from 0 to 9 in random order. When items in the population are associated with numbers in a random number table, choice of random numbers amounts to choice of sample items, and the resulting sample is random. Such a sample is called an *unrestricted random sample.* For example, in the population of 10,000 sales invoices, assume that the first invoice in the year was 32059 and that the last one was 42058. By obtaining a random start in the table and proceeding systematically through it, 420 invoices may be selected for testing.[5] Assume that a random start is obtained at the number in the second row, fifth column—number 29094—and that the reading path in the table is down to the bottom of the column then to the top of the next column, and so on. The first usable number and first invoice is 40807, the second is 32146, and so forth. Note that several of the random numbers were skipped because they do not correspond with the invoice number sequence.[6]

Systematic Random Sampling. Another selection method that is commonly used in auditing because of its simplicity and relative ease of application is *systematic selection*. This method of choice is used when direct association of the population with random numbers is cumbersome. Systematic selection consists of (*a*) dividing the population size by the sample size, obtaining a quotient k; (*b*) obtaining a random start in the population file; and (*c*) selecting every kth item for the sample. The file of credit records provides a good example. These may be filed alphabetically with no numbering system. Therefore, to select 300, first find $k = 5{,}000/300 = 16.7$, then obtain a random start in the set of files and pull out every 17th one, progressing systematically to the end of the file and returning to the beginning of the file to complete the selection. This method only approximates randomness, but the approximation can be improved by taking more than one random start in the process of selection. But when more than one start is used, the interval k is changed. For example, if 2 starts are used, then every 34th item would be selected. Auditors usually require five or more random starts.

Computerized Selection. Most audit organizations have computerized random number generators available to cut short the drudgery of poring over printed random number tables. Such routines can print a tailored series of numbers with relatively brief turnaround time. Even so, some advance planning is required, and knowledge of how a random number table works is useful.

Stratified Random Sampling. *Stratification* merely means dividing up a single population into two or more populations from which sample items will be drawn. Populations can be subdivided any way the auditor desires in order to satisfy his or her compliance test objectives. The following are some examples of stratification dimensions:

Large dollar value sales transactions and small dollar value sales transactions if control procedures are different (for example, credit approval on sales over $1,000).

Transactions processed by different persons supposedly performing the same control procedures (e.g., each of several billing clerks).

---

[5] A random start in a table may be obtained by poking a pencil at the table, or by checking the last four digits on a $50 bill to give row and column coordinates for a random start.

[6] Most auditors will not allow the same sample item to appear twice in a selection—duplicate selections are counted only once. Strictly speaking this amounts to *sampling without replacement* and the hypergeometric probability distribution is appropriate instead of the binomial distribution. The binomial probabilities are exact only when each sample item is *replaced* after selection, thus giving it an equally likely chance of appearing in the sample more than once. For audit purposes the practice of ignoring the distribution is acceptable because the difference is mathematically insignificant.

Transactions processed before changeover to an EDP system and transactions processed afterward.

Intercompany transactions and all other transactions.

Transactions processed during the two weeks before and two weeks after the balance sheet date (relevant to proper cutoff information).

Population stratification does not change any other elements of the kind of sampling plan described in this chapter. In effect, stratification creates two or more populations where before there was one. It is a way of giving special attention to areas an auditor believes important, thereby enhancing the exercise of due audit care.

However, stratification in attribute sampling tends to increase total sample size. For example, if 300 is an appropriate sample size for a population of 5,000 transactions and that population is stratified into one containing 2,000 and the other 3,000, the sample will be 300 for *each stratum* (provided AUPL, R%, and the estimated exception proportion are the same in both cases)—a total sample of 600.

Block and Haphazard Sampling. Block sampling refers to the method of selecting several days' sales, or selections of transactions in number sequence, or several weeks' cash receipts. The block is convenient because many clients' recordkeeping systems provide files by blocks. Block sampling on a judgmental basis is not contrary to generally accepted auditing standards so long as the selection of blocks produces a sample that is *representative* of the transactions processed during the period under audit. In statistical methodology, *cluster sampling* is a scientific adaptation of block selection that can be evaluated mathematically. However, cluster sampling mathematics is beyond the scope of this textbook.

Haphazard sampling is hard to explain. Picture an auditor standing before a messy file—papers sticking out at odd angles. He is dipping his hand in, eyes closed, "randomly" picking out items to audit. Haphazard sampling is simply any unsystematic way of choosing sample items, but there is no way to tell whether such a sample is random. The trouble with haphazard sampling is that the sample selection method actually used cannot be performed by someone else trying to find the same sample items. Applying mathematical evaluation to a haphazard selection would be a mistake because the sample may not be random.

Audit the Sample Items

The actual audit procedures—the "how-to-do-it" steps—are given in the audit program in Exhibit 7–4. One may observe that the compliance testing phase of a proper study and evaluation of internal accounting control has synthesized the practical aspects of the theory of evidence. Compliance testing incorporates audit objectives, program planning, and procedures specification, elements of internal control theory, and audit practice related thereto. The tasks remaining now are the evaluation of evidence gained from the sample-based audit, the making of decisions respecting reliability of output, and the documentation of the audit decisions. (An illustration of documentation for the sales-accounts receivable system is presented following Exercises 7.11 and 8.11.)

Evaluation of Evidence

Evaluation of the evidence produced by audit procedures involves both *quantitative* and *qualitative* levels of analysis. The qualitative evaluation is as important as the statistical-quantitative evaluation because awareness of the *nature* of control deficiencies is the only way to know how to modify or extend subsequent audit work. A detailed presentation of qualitative evaluation is presented in the working paper documentation illustration accompanying Exercise 7.11.

The qualitative evaluation is sometimes called *error analysis*, because each error or exception to a prescribed control procedure is audited to determine its nature, cause, and probable effect on financial statements. The analysis is essentially judgmental and involves the auditor's determination of whether the exception is (1) a pervasive error in principle made systematically on all like transactions or just a mistake on a particular transaction, (2) a deliberate or intentional control breakdown rather than unintentional, (3) due to misunderstanding of instructions or careless inattention to control duties, or (4) directly or remotely related to a money amount measurement in the financial statements. One can see that different qualitative perceptions of the seriousness of an exception would result from error analysis findings.

In order to illustrate the quantitative analysis, some hypothetical audit results are assumed and presented in Exhibit 7–6. They relate to the sales-accounts receivable illustration utilized in this chapter.

The quantitative evidential matter consists of the number of observed exceptions (Exhibit 7–6, column 3) and the sample exception proportion (Exhibit 7–6, column 4). For the required reliability (column 5) the computed upper precision limit (CUPL in column 6, Exhibit 7–6) is obtained from the tables in Appendix 7–C. These tables essentially express the cumulative binomial probability, CR% (equal in this example to .99), that the actual population exception proportion is less than or equal to CUPL *given* the sample size (n) and the observed number of exceptions (x). For example, whatever may be the true exception proportion for failure to invoice shipments (attribute c), the quantitative evidence indicates with .99 reliability that the proportion is less than or equal to 2 percent (i.e., approximately 200 or fewer shipments failed to be invoiced, thus understating actual sales, with perhaps a related overstatement existing in the inventory records). Since the AUPL for attribute c is 3 percent, this control meets the auditor's quantitative criterion. All the CUPL-AUPL comparisons are shown in Exhibit 7–7.

Final Decision

The final step shown in Exhibit 7–2 suggests that internal control may be evaluated as excellent, good, fair, poor, or unreliable. The quantitative evidence (calculated upper precision limit, CUPL) may serve as a guide to this evaluation—the higher the exception proportion, the less reliable the system. However, the five grades of internal control shown in Exhibit 7–2 may be too many for some control procedures and too few for others. How fine the distinctions should be depends upon the auditor's ability to mod-

EXHIBIT 7–6
Hypothetical Audit Results

(1) Attribute of Interest	(2)* Number in Sample = n	(3) Number of Exceptions = x	(4) Sample Exception Proportion = (3) ÷ (2)	(5) Statistical Evaluation: Probability Is . . .	(6) . . . That $\pi \leq$ CUPL
a. Credit files up to date	300	23	7.67%	.99	$\pi \leq 12\%$
b. Batch totals agree	all 260	0	0	1.00	$\pi = 0$
c. Shipments invoiced	340	1	.29	.99	$\pi \leq 2$
d. Recorded sales represent actual shipments	420	2	.48	.99	$\pi \leq 2$
e. Sales properly recorded	220	0	0	.99	$\pi \leq 3$
f. Invoices priced correctly, arithmetically accurate	650	19	2.92	.99	$\pi \leq 5$
g. Credit approvals adequate	280	16	5.71	.99	$\pi \leq 10$
h. Recorded sales were properly invoiced	900	2	.22	.99	$\pi \leq 1$

where:

π symbolizes the actual, but unknown, exception proportion.
CUPL is the computed upper precision limit found by reading tables in Appendix 7–C.1.

* Refer to Exhibit 7–5 for sample sizes.

EXHIBIT 7–7
Quantitative Evaluation

	Attribute of Interest	*CUPL** *CR% = 99%*	*AUPL†* *R% = 99%*	*Quantitative Result*
a.	Credit files up to date	12%	10%	Control deficient.
b.	Batch totals agree	NA	NA	Control reliable.
c.	Shipments invoiced	2	3	Control reliable.
d.	Recorded sales represent actual shipments	2	1	Control deficient.
e.	Sales properly recorded	3	4	Control reliable.
f.	Invoices priced correctly, arithmetically accurate	5	5	Control reliable.
g.	Credit approvals adequate ..	10	5	Control deficient.
h.	Recorded sales were properly invoiced	1	2	Control reliable.

* See Exhibit 7–6.
† See Exhibit 7–5.

ify subsequent auditing procedures. If subsequent procedures can be fine-tuned in terms of various sample sizes for audit (for example, the number of accounts receivable confirmations to be mailed), then a fine distinction among grades of control in data processing may be useful. However, if for reason of nature or timing only a satisfactory-unreliable dichotomy is needed (for example, in determining whether to accept a client's physical inventory count or to request a complete recount), then the finer distinctions may be superfluous.

As an example assume that an auditor is able to quantify the judgment on attribute *h* ("Recorded sales were properly invoiced.") as shown below.

CUPL	*Internal Control*	*Substantive Procedures*
2 percent or less	Excellent	Analyze sales totals for trend and comparison with prior years and for internal consistency (e.g., gross margin test)
3 percent	Good	Audit some additional (say, 50) recorded sales and perform analyses as specified above.
4 percent	Fair	Audit additional recorded sales (say, 200) at the year-end date; perform analyses; and correlate sales quantities with production and shipping records.
5 percent	Poor	Audit recorded sales extensively, using methods of sampling for dollar amounts in order to audit the sales balance through a thorough audit of transactions.
6 percent or more	Unreliable	Inform client that sales data should be analyzed extensively. Possibility that sufficient evidence will not be obtainable at a reasonable fee.

For different computed upper precision limits, the results could be distinguished, and decisions could be made respecting (1) the reliability of the system for detecting invoices recorded in error and (2) the nature, timing, and extent of further audit work necessary to audit the sales revenue account.

The definition of grades of control by relation to CUPLs is one aspect of the qualitative professional judgment input to evaluation. After the evidence has been evaluated both in qualitative and quantitative terms, the decisions about internal accounting control system reliability are almost self-evident. However, one must be careful to distinguish between a *statistical expression* and an *auditing expression* of the decision. The statistical expression flows from the relationships of acceptable upper precision limits used as predetermined decision criteria and the computed upper precision limits calculated on the basis of audit sample evidence. The statistical expressions are like these: "The exception proportion regarding adequacy of credit files (attribute *a*) appears to be at most 12 percent, which exceeds the criterion of 10 percent," and "the discovery of one failure to invoice a shipment (attribute *c*) indicates maximum likely error of 2 percent, which is less than the decision criterion of 3 percent." These statistical expressions indicate the nature of the auditing decision, but they are rather neutral about what audit work must follow.

Therefore, an auditor must give the decision an auditing expression and an audit meaning. The specification of effect on subsequent audit work is the essence of the internal control *evaluation*. The following examples relate to the sales–accounts receivable illustration:

Auditing Decision Expression	*Effect on Subsequent Work*
1. Credit policy and procedure. Credit files are not adequately up to date and approvals of customer credit do not meet minimum requirements of performance.	1. In confirmation of accounts receivable, pay particular attention to large and to overdue accounts and confirm more than the minimum. Perform additional work on collectibility question at year-end date, including possible second confirmation on questionable accounts.
2. Possible understatement of sales. Examination of bills of lading files and accounting accuracy indicate that understatement is unlikely.	2. Perform the usual ratio and comparison overall tests relative to volume and dollars of sales. No need to audit for omission of sales recordings or to search for unrecorded receivables.
3. Possible overstatement of sales. Missing bills of lading and arithmetic errors appear to indicate that some sales items may not have been shipped. (Refer to the qualitative nature of the exceptions in the analysis presented with Exercise 7.11.)	3. Confirm accounts receivable extensively at interim date and consider second confirmation at year-end. Perform additional vouching of any unusual transactions, particularly noncash credit allowances. The minimum audit program will not be sufficient.
4. EDP data input accuracy. Data transformation to machine-readable form is accurate.	4. Perform usual error report and test deck or parallel simulation analysis of processing programs.

One can observe that the use of statistics and statistical evaluation aids and guides audit decisions, but it is still up to the auditor to provide a proper interpretation of the evidence. The statistics are quite helpful in deciding whether evidence is *sufficient* when no exceptions are detected, but when some errors are found qualitative judgment and a complete follow-up of the errors are required in order to give the decision audit meaning.

DISCOVERY SAMPLING

Discovery sampling is essentially another kind of sampling design directed toward a specific objective. However, discovery sampling statistics also offer an additional means of evaluating the *sufficiency* of audit evidence in the event that no exceptions are found in a sample of transactions.

A discovery sampling table is shown in Appendix 7–D. A discovery sampling plan deals with this kind of question: "If I believe some important kind of error or irregularity might exist in the records, what sample size will I have to audit to have assurance of finding at least one example of the exception?" Ordinarily, discovery sampling is used for designing tests to search for such things as examples of forged checks or intercompany sales improperly classified as sales to outside parties. The auditor must quantify "assurance" with an R%, as discussed earlier, and must specify an upper precision limit (AUPL) that is called a "critical rate of occurrence." Generally, the "critical" rate is very low because the exception is something very sensitive and important.

The R% in this case represents the desired probability of including at least one occurrence (example of the exception) in a sample. In Appendix 7–D, one can read down a specified critical rate column to the specified R%, then read the required sample size at the left margin. This discovery sampling table expresses a type of cumulative binomial probability (CR%) of finding one or more exceptions ($x > O$) in a sample of a particular size (n), if the actual exception proportion is equal to a given critical occurrence rate (AUPL).[7]

Suppose that in the compliance tests of attribute h ("Recorded sales are properly supported by invoices") the auditor was especially concerned about finding an example of an exception if as few as 100 exceptions existed in the population of 10,000 recorded invoices (a "critical rate" of 1 percent). Furthermore, suppose the auditor wanted to achieve at least 99 percent reliability for the test. Appendix 7–D indicates a required sample of 460 recorded sales. If a sample of this size were audited and no exceptions were found, the auditor could conclude with computed reliability (CR%) of 99 percent that the actual rate of occurrence in the population was *less than* 0.01.

This feature of discovery sampling evaluation provides the additional means of evaluating the *sufficiency* of audit evidence whenever the sample

[7] The equation is: CR% = Probability ($x > O$) = $1 - (1 - \text{AUPL})^n$. Appendix 7–D, however, is based on the more complicated *hypergeometric function* which corrects the binomial function for population size effects. The equation in this footnote therefore is an approximation of Appendix 7–D.

turns up zero exceptions. Regardless of whether the discovery sampling table was consulted, the auditor can read across from the sample size audited (say 200) to a probability (CR%) that in his or her judgment represents reasonable assurance. Then reading up the column, the "critical rate" is found. This is very nearly the case for the attribute *e* ("Sales are properly recorded") results shown in Exhibit 7–6. In that result, 220 items were audited and no errors were found. The discovery sampling table tells the auditor that if the exception occurrence rate were 2 percent, the probability of including at least one in a sample of 200 is about 0.985. None were found, so with about 98.5 percent reliability the auditor can believe that the occurrence rate is 2 percent or less.

LIMITATIONS AND NONSAMPLING ERROR

Limitations on Conclusions. One brief warning must accompany the discussion of attribute sampling for transaction tests of internal control effectiveness: *Conclusions about internal control do not yield sufficient information to support conclusions that dollar balances are or are not fairly stated.* As long as the statistic is the "error" or "no-error" measurement, *the magnitude* of the effect of a CUPL is not determinable. Only by measuring in terms of dollars may conclusions about dollar amounts be reached. The AICPA's second field standard implies that internal control is *evaluated for the determination of the resultant extent of the tests to which subsequent auditing procedures are to be restricted.* The term "restricted" does not mean "eliminated," and the third field standard is not satisfied as to material financial data by virtue of reliance only on internal accounting control.[8]

Nonsampling Error. The measurement expressed statistically as a computed upper precision limit is a way of expressing the probable amount of *sampling error*—the error that may occur because the randomly selected sample does not exactly mirror the true population characteristic. However, other sources of error exist, and unfortunately there is no applicable measurement. Such sources are the kinds of *nonsampling error,* or human error, that may occur in any sampling application whether judgmental or statistical. An auditor must be aware of these several pitfalls and be wary of them:

Failure to recognize an error when one exists in the sample. This failure is particularly important in a small random sample because one error can make the difference between an acceptable and an unacceptable computed upper precision limit.

Failure to obtain a random start for selection of a sample, or otherwise inadvertently choosing a biased sample when a random selection is desired.

Inclusion of transactions selected by judgment in a random sample. The mix of random and nonrandom items damages the validity of

[8] *Statement on Auditing Standards No. 1* (Section 320.71).

mathematical evaluation and inference about the population as a whole.

Lack of logic and care in the final evaluation of findings. If too much reliability is assigned to a high exception proportion transaction set, even if the high proportion is the acceptable upper precision limit, subsequent audit tests may not produce sufficient evidential matter.

PERVASIVENESS OF INTERNAL CONTROL

This chapter has been very detailed in explaining objective tests with relation to the illustrative sales–accounts receivable system described in Exercises 6.11 and 7.11. However, the important points are those related to the compliance tests of transactions in general and application of statistical methods in particular. Internal control considerations pervade all aspects of auditing procedure and decision making, as is illustrated further in Chapters 11 through 16 with regard to other data processing subsystems. Since the decisions about internal accounting control reliability provide the primary basis for judging the nature, timing, and extent of subsequent audit work, the theory and practice of a proper study and evaluation are very important.

In the next chapters the concepts of internal control evaluation in an EDP environment, in computer applications, and in statistical-based decisions are explained in more detail.

SOURCES AND ADDITIONAL READING REFERENCES

Arkin, Herbert. *Handbook of Sampling for Auditing and Accounting*, 2d. ed. New York: McGraw-Hill Book Co., 1974.

———. "Discovery Sampling in Auditing," *Journal of Accountancy*, February 1961.

Cyert, R. M., and Davidson, H. J. *Statistical Sampling for Accounting Information*. Englewood Cliffs, N.J.: Prentice-Hall, Inc., 1962.

Elliott, R. K., and Rogers, J. R. "Relating Statistical Sampling to Audit Objectives," *Journal of Accountancy*, July 1972, pp. 46–55.

Hill, H. P.; Roth, J. L.; and Arkin H. *Sampling in Auditing*. New York: Ronald Press, 1962.

Ijiri, Yuji, and Kaplan, R. S. "A Model for Integrating Sampling Objectives in Auditing," *Journal of Accounting Research*, Spring 1971, pp. 73–87.

Roberts, Donald M. "A Statistical Interpretation of SAP No. 54." *Journal of Accountancy*, March 1974, pp. 47–53.

Smith, Kenneth. "Internal Control and Audit Sample Size," *Accounting Review*, April 1972, pp. 260–69.

Stringer, Kenneth. "Some Basic Concepts of Statistical Sampling in Auditing," *Journal of Accountancy*, November 1961.

Tracy, John A. "Bayesian Statistical Methods in Auditing," *Accounting Review*, January 1969, pp. 90–98.

Trentin, H. G. "Sampling in Auditing—A Case Study," *Journal of Accountancy*, March 1968, pp. 39–43.

Trueblood, R. M., and Cyert, R. M. *Sampling Techniques in Accounting.* Englewood Cliffs, N.J.: Prentice-Hall, Inc., 1957.

REVIEW QUESTIONS

7.1. Why does an auditor sample?

7.2. What are the advantages in applying statistical sampling and evaluation techniques in audit tests of transactions instead of judgmental sampling and evaluation methods? (AICPA adapted)

7.3. *a.* What decisions involving professional judgment must be made by an auditor in applying statistical techniques to compliance tests of transactions audit procedures?

b. What courses of action are available to auditors when they find that the computed upper precision limit is greater than the predetermined acceptable upper precision limit?

7.4. If an audit test of transactions reveals an exception proportion of 0.02 for a selected attribute of interest, what is the computed upper precision limit (at .99 reliability) if the sample size was 50? 100? 200? 300? 500? 800? 1,000? What is the computed upper precision limit in the above cases for reliability of .95? .90?

7.5. What is the relationship of sample size with regard to various population sizes, expected exception proportions, reliability levels, and acceptable upper precision limits?

7.6. What criterion must be met in order that a sample from a well-defined population be truly random? Explain the importance of a *representative* sample for compliance tests of transactions.

7.7. List the steps involved in systematic random sampling.

7.8. Distinguish between the statistical quantitative evaluation and the qualitative evaluation of sample results in regard to internal control.

7.9. What is "sampling error" and what is "nonsampling error?" Explain how each may occur in a sample of transactions.

7.10. Why does the second AICPA standard of field work imply that internal control is evaluated for the determination of the resultant extent of the tests to which subsequent auditing procedures are to be *restricted* instead of *eliminated*?

EXERCISES AND PROBLEMS

7.11. This problem is a continuation of the fact situation presented in 6.11 at the end of Chapter 6. Additional requirements related to statistical applications are given below. Exhibit solutions are shown in Exhibits 7.11–1, 7.11–2 and 7.11–3.

Required:

For the compliance test of transactions, apply methods of statistical sampling and evaluation. The following are guides.

1. Define the objectives of the audit tests. Refer to the worksheets, Exhibit 7.11–1 and 7.11–2 following.

2. Identify the relevant attributes of interest, make an estimate of the expected exception proportion, and specify an acceptable upper precision limit. See the discussion in the text, and refer to Exhibits 7.11–1 and 7.11–2 for a documentation illustration.
3. Prepare a file layout and identify the data populations, the samples to be

EXHIBIT 7.11–1
Attributes Sampling Data Sheet

ATTRIBUTES SAMPLING DATA SHEET

Client Kingston Company By H. Groody

Period covered January, 1978-Sept. 17, 1978 Date 9-17-78

Define the objective(s) Obtain assurance that (1) Credit files are adequate, (2) EDP batch totals agree with reports, (3) Goods shipped were invoiced (billed to customers)

Population: description (1) Credit department files -- 5000 files (2) Billing dept. EDP batch totals - 260 totals (3) Bills of lading numbered 00001-10,000.

Sampling unit (1) Credit file (2) Batch total (3) Bill of Lading

Random selection procedures (1) Systematic sample of credit department files, (2) all batch totals (3) Random numbers associated to bill of lading numbers

Attributes tested (Error definition)	Required Conf. Lev.	Required Accept. UPL	Expected Exception Proportion	Planned Sample Size	Actual Results Sample Size	Occurrence No.	Occurrence Rate	CUPL*
1. Credit files up to date	99%	10%	6%	300	300	23	7.67%	12%
2. Batch totals agree with EDP reports	99%	-0-	-0-	all 260	all 260	-0-	-0-	-0-
3. Bill of lading agrees with								
4. related sales invoice	99%	3%	1%	340	340	1	.29%	2%
5.								
6.								
7.								
8.								
9.								
10.								

Intended use of sampling results:

1. Effect on audit plan: Credit approval procedure may be deficient, causing problems with collectibility of accounts receivable -- extend procedures related to allowance for uncollectible accounts.
2. Recommendation to management: (1) Credit approval files should be brought up to date (2) Use the EDP batch totals to control for EDP input-processing-output errors.
3. Other action:

*Whenever CUPL > AUPL there must be some action.

EXHIBIT 7.11–2
Attributes Sampling Data Sheet

ATTRIBUTES SAMPLING DATA SHEET

Client Kingston Company By H. Groody

Period covered January, 1978 - Sept. 17, 1978 Date 9-17-78

Define the objective(s) Obtain assurance that sales invoices are (1) in agreement with related bills of lading, (2) posted properly to control and sub accounts (3) arithmetically correct, properly priced, (4) on approved credit (5) supported by shipping documents.

Population: description Sales invoices -- 10,000 numbered from #32059 - #42058.

Sampling unit Sales invoice

Random selection procedures Random number associated with sales invoice number

Attributes tested (Error definition)	Required Conf. Lev.	Required Accept. UPL	Expected Exception Proportion	Planned Sample Size	Actual Results Sample Size	Occurrence No.	Occurrence Rate	CUPL
1. Invoice agrees with bill of lading	99%	1%	-0-	420	420	2	.48%	2%
2. Invoice recorded properly	99%	4%	1%	220	220	-0-	-0-	3%
3. Invoices arithmetically correct, properly priced	99%	5%	3%	650	650	19	2.92%	5%
4. Credit approval or sales	99%	5%	2%	280	280	16	5.71%	10%
5. Recorded sales supported by								
6. shipping documents	99%	2.9%	1%	900	900	2	.22%	1%
7.								
8.								
9.								
10.								

Intended use of sampling results:

1. Effect on audit plan: (1) May have a problem with unsupported (fictitious?) sales -- at year end vouch carefully a sample of the largest sales invoices and confirm a larger sample of receivables than planned (2) Poor credit approval procedure -- vouch receipts on account after Dec 31, 1978, extend procedure on doubtful acct. analasis
2. Recommendation to management: Need better clerical review of invoices, File bill of lading copy with sales invoice copy 2.
3. Other action:

*Whenever CUPL > AUPL there must be some action.

EXHIBIT 7.11–3

By: *H. Broody*
Date: 9-17-78

KINGSTON COMPANY

ERRORS IN TEST OF TRANSACTIONS: SALES INVOICE DOCUMENTS

DECEMBER 31, 1978

ERROR / EXCEPTION	DISPOSITION
Invoice #36421 – No credit approval	New customer. Credit mgr. states that approval was obtained after shipment. Approval memo examined.
Invoice #32146 – Arithmetic error of $18.00 too much	Clerical error not caught in review.
Invoice #38000 – Priced incorrectly; price corresponds to following item on price list	Clerical error. Caught by customer and corrected with credit memo (examined, O.K.).
Invoice #37619 – No bill of lading or other evidence of shipment could be located	Shipping clerk explained that it must have been lost or misfiled. Could not locate.
Invoice #33021 – Arithmetic error of $72 in favor of customer	Never corrected.
Invoice #35211 – No credit approval	New customer. Approval was formalized in a memo after shipment.
Invoice #34999 – Invoice quantities do not agree with bill of lading quantities	Invoice copy 3 was not completed to show that some items ordered were not shipped. Customer caught error and was issued a credit memo.
Invoice #36555 – No bill of lading or other evidence of shipment could be located	Shipping clerk explained that it must have been lost, misfiled or possibly sent in error to the customer.

ALL NOW ERRORS DISCOUNTED BEFORE CALCULATIONS OF CUPL

Ex THE FIRST ONE

selected, and the procedures to be performed. See Exhibit 7–3 and Exhibit 7–4 in the text.

4. Audit the transaction samples and make a working paper record of all findings of error with notes describing subsequent follow-up. See Exhibit 7.11–3 for an abbreviated working paper containing some of the findings in the audit of the sales invoices shown on Exhibit 7.11–2.

7.12. Coil steel comprises one half of the inventory of the Watermore Manufacturing Company. At the beginning of the year the company installed a system to control coil steel inventory.

The coil steel is stored within the plant in a special storage area. When coils are received, a two-part tag is prepared. The tag is prenumbered and each part provides for entry of supplier's name, receiving report number, date received, and coil weight and description. Both parts of the tag are prepared at the time the material is received and weighed and the receiving report prepared. The "A" part of the tag is attached to the coil, and the "B" part of the tag is sent to the stock records department with the receiving report. The stock records department files the tags numerically by coil width and gauge. Using the receiving report, the stock records department also maintains perpetual stock cards on each width and gauge by total weight. In a sense, the cards are a control record for the tags. No material requisitions are used by the plant, but as coils are placed into production, the "A" part of the tag is removed from the coil and sent to stock records as support for the production report, which is the basis of entries on the perpetual inventory cards.

When the "A" part of the tag is received by the stock records department, it is matched with the "B" part of the tag and the "A" part is destroyed. The "B" part is stamped with the date of use, processed, and retained in a "Consumed" file by width and gauge.

The coils are neatly stacked and arranged, and all tags are visible.

Physical inventories are taken on a cycle basis throughout the year. About one twelfth of the coil steel inventories are counted each month. The coil steel control account and the perpetual stock cards are adjusted as counts are made. Internal control over inventories is considered good.

In previous years the client had taken a complete physical inventory of coil steel at the end of the year (the client's fiscal year ends December 31), but none is to be taken this year. You are engaged for the current audit in September. You audited the financial statements last year.

Required:

a. Construct a flowchart to describe the system of control for coil steel inventory. Identify at least six files or locations of data subject to tests of transactions.

b. Prepare a file layout and show thereon the samples of data to be examined, the audit comparisons to be made, and the procedures to be performed.

c. Write an audit program for the audit of the coil steel portion of the inventory with respect to (1) study and evaluation of internal control effectiveness, (2) existence of the inventory, and (3) valuation, at cost, of the inventory. (AICPA adapted)

7.13. The Cowslip Milk Company's principal activity is buying milk from dairy farmers, processing the milk, and delivering it to retail customers. You are engaged in auditing the retail accounts receivable of the company and determine the following:

1. The company has 50 retail routes; each route consists of 100 to 200 accounts, the number that can be serviced by a driver in a day.
2. The driver enters cash collections from the day's deliveries to each customer directly on a statement form in record books maintained for each route. Mail remittances are posted in the route record books by office personnel. At the end of the month the statements are priced, extended,

and footed. Photocopies of the statements are prepared and left in the customers' milk boxes with the next milk delivery.

3. The statements are reviewed by the office manager, who prepares a list for each route of accounts with 90-day balances or older. The list is used for intensive collection action.
4. The audit program used in prior audits for the selection of retail accounts receivable for confirmation stated: "Select two accounts from each route, one to be chosen by opening the route book at random and the other as the third item on each list of 90-day or older accounts."

Your review of the accounts receivable leads you to conclude that statistical sampling techniques may be applied to their examination.

Required:

a. Since statistical sampling techniques do not relieve CPAs of their responsibilities in the exercise of their professional judgment, of what benefit are they to the CPA? Discuss.

b. Give the reasons why the audit procedure previously used for selection of accounts receivable for confirmation (as given in (4) above) would not produce a valid statistical sample.

c. What are the audit objectives or purposes in selecting 90-day accounts for confirmation? Can the application of statistical sampling techniques help in attaining these objectives or purposes? Discuss.

d. Assume that the company has 10,000 accounts receivable and that your statistical sampling disclosed 6 exceptions of the same kind in 6 different customers' accounts out of a sample of 200 accounts. Is it reasonable to assume that 300 accounts in the entire population are in error? Explain. (AICPA adapted)

7.14. 1. Discovery sampling is concerned with the occurrence proportion of a characteristic and therefore may be considered a special case of—

a. Random sampling.
b. Sampling for attributes.
c. Sampling for variables.
d. Stratified sampling.

2. CPAs using discovery sampling are looking for characteristics which, if discovered in the sample, might be indicative of more widespread irregularities or serious errors in the financial statements examined. If a CPA discovers one such error while using a discovery sampling plan, the CPA—

a. Is satisfied.
b. Must test more extensively.
c. Must expand the testing to 100 percent.
d. May not use any sampling plan.

3. A CPA who believes the occurrence proportion of a certain characteristic in a population being examined is 3 percent and who has established a maximum acceptable occurrence proportion at 5 percent should use (a) (an)—

a. Attribute sampling plan.
b. Discovery sampling plan.
c. Stratified sampling plan.
d. Variable sampling plan.

4. The statement, "A CPA tests disbursement vouchers to determine whether or not compliance deviations exceed .2 percent," omits which of the following necessary elements of a discovery sampling plan?

a. Characteristic being evaluated.
b. Definition of the population.
c. Maximum tolerable occurrence rate.
d. Specified reliability.

5. To determine the proper sample size in a discovery sampling plan, a CPA need not know the—
   a. Estimated occurrence proportion in the population.
   b. Maximum tolerable occurrence proportion.
   c. Population size.
   d. Specified reliability of the sample.
6. As the specified reliability is increased in a discovery sampling plan for any given population and critical occurrence proportion, the required sample size—
   a. Remains the same.
   b. Decreases.
   c. Increases.
   d. Cannot be determined.

7.15. Using the *discovery sampling* table in Appendix 7–D, fill in the missing data in each case below.

	(a)	(b)	(c)	(d)	(e)	(f)	(g)	(h)	(i)
Critical rate of occurrence	.4%	.5%	1.0%	2.0%	1.0%	.5%	—	—	—
Required reliability	99	99	99	—	—	—	70	85	95
Sample Size (minimum)	—	—	—	240	240	240	300	460	700

7.16. In determining your answers to items 1 to 5, consider the information given in the following statement of facts.

A CPA's client is considering the adoption of statistical sampling techniques. Accordingly, the client has asked the CPA to discuss these techniques at a meeting of client employees. In connecting with this presentation, the CPA prepared the following table which shows the comparative characteristics of two populations and the samples to be drawn from each. (For example, in case 1 the expected exception proportion of population 1 is smaller than that of population 2, whereas the populations are of equal size and the samples to be drawn from them have equal acceptable upper precision limits and equal required reliabilities [confidence levels]).

	Population 1 Relative to Population 2		*Sample from Population 1 Relative to Sample from Population 2*	
	Size	*Expected Exception Proportion*	*Acceptable Upper Precision Limit*	*Required Reliability*
Case 1	Equal	Smaller	Equal	Equal
Case 2	Smaller	Equal	Equal	Higher
Case 3	Equal	Equal	Higher	Equal
Case 4	Larger	Equal	Lower	Equal
Case 5	Equal	Greater	Equal	Higher

Using the table and the technique of unrestricted random sampling with replacement, meeting participants are to be asked to determine the relative required sample sizes to be drawn from the two populations. Each of the five cases is independent of the other four and is to be considered separately. Select one of the following answer choices.

a. Larger than the required sample size from population 2.
b. Equal to the required sample size from population 2.
c. Smaller than the required sample size from population 2.
d. Indeterminate relative to the required sample size from population 2.

(1) The required sample size from population 1 in case 1 is ________.
(2) The required sample size from population 1 in case 2 is ________.
(3) The required sample size from population 1 in case 3 is ________.
(4) The required sample size from population 1 in case 4 is ________.
(5) The required sample size from population 1 in case 5 is ________.

7.17. *Exercises in Sample Selection:*

a. Sales invoices beginning with number 0001 and ending with number 5000 are entered in a sales journal. You want to choose 50 invoices for audit. Start at row 5, column 3 of the random number table in Appendix 7–B and select the first 5 usable numbers, using the first four digits in the column.

b. There are 9,100 numbered checks in a cash disbursements journal, beginning with number 2,220 and ending with number 11,319. You want to choose 100 disbursements for audit. Start at row 11, column 1 of the random number table in Appendix 7–B and select the first 5 usable numbers.

c. During the year the client wrote 45,200 vouchers. Each month the numbering series started over with number 00001, prefixed with a number for the month (January = 01, February = 02, and so on) so that the voucher numbers had 7 digits, the last 5 of which were in overlapping series. You want to choose 120 vouchers for audit. Evaluate each of the following suggested selection methods:

(1) Choose a month at random and select 120 at random in that month by association with a 5-digit random number.
(2) Choose 120 usable 7-digit random numbers.
(3) Select ten vouchers at random from each month.

d. Explain how you could use systematic sampling to select the first five items in each case above. For case (*c*) assume that the random start is at voucher 03–01102.

7.18. Using the tables in Appendix 7–D, find the computed upper precision limit for each case below:

	(*a*)	(*b*)	(*c*)	(*d*)	(*e*)	(*f*)	(*g*)	(*h*)	(*i*)
Required reliability	99	95	90	95	95	95	95	95	95
Sample size	300	300	300	100	200	400	100	100	100
Exception occurrences	6	6	6	2	4	8	10	6	0
Actual sample exception proportion	—	—	—	—	—	—	—	—	—
Computed upper precision limit	—	—	—	—	—	—	—	—	—

7.19. Tom Barton, an assistant accountant with a local CPA firm, has recently graduated from The Other University. He studied statistical sampling in tests of transactions in his auditing course and wants to impress his employers with his knowledge of modern auditing methods.

He decided to select a random sample of payroll checks for audit, using an acceptable upper precision limit of 5 percent and a required confidence level of 95 percent. The senior accountant told Tom that 2 percent of the checks audited last year had one or more errors in the calculation of net pay.

Tom decided to audit 100 random checks. Since supervisory personnel had larger paychecks than production workers, he selected 60 of the larger checks and 40 of the others. He was very careful to see that the selection of 60 from the April payroll register and 40 from the August payroll register was random.

The audit of this sample yielded two exceptions, exactly the 2 percent rate experienced last year. The first exception was the deduction of federal income taxes based on two exemptions for a supervisory employee, when his W–4 form showed four exemptions. The other was payment to a production employee at a rate for a job classification one grade lower than his actual job. The worker had been promoted the week before, and Tom found that in the next payroll he was paid at the higher correct rate.

When he evaluated this evidence, Tom decided that these two findings were really not control exceptions at all. The withholding of too much tax did not affect the expense accounts, and the proper rate was paid the production worker as soon as the clerk caught up with his change orders. Tom decided that having thus found zero exceptions in a sample of 100, the computed upper precision limit at 95 percent confidence was 3 percent, which easily satisfied his predetermined criterion.

The senior accountant was impressed. Last year he had audited 15 checks from each month, and Tom's work represented a significant time savings. The reviewing partner on the audit was also impressed because he had never thought that statistical sampling could be so efficient and that was the reason that he had never studied the method.

Required:

Identify and explain the mistakes made by Tom and the others.

To gain a better understanding of the application of statistical sampling techniques, the next two problems involve a comprehensive simulation of sampling for attributes in auditing. These problems are adapted from Robert W. Vanasse, *Statistical Sampling for Auditing and Accounting Decisions: A Simulation*, 2d ed. (New York: McGraw-Hill Book Co., 1976). The Vanasse simulation is necessary for completion of exercises 7.20 and 7.21.

7.20. Internal Control—Test of compliance with company payroll procedures: Based on Problem 6–1, Vanasse Simulation.

Required:

With the information given below, prepare a Vanasse Worksheet showing your application of statistical sampling techniques to estimate the foreman's compliance with the requirement to initial payroll clock cards.

Population definition: Payroll clock cards.

Population items: Table A, pp. A–1 to A–10.

Field size: 1,000.

Column number: (1).

Error: C (=Absence of foreman's initials).

Nonerrors: A, B, D, E, G.

Error rate in prior tests: 5 percent.

Acceptable upper precision limit: 9 percent.

Required reliability: 90 percent.

7.21. Internal Control—Test of erroneous quantities in perpetual inventory records. Based on Problem 6–3, Vanasse Simulation.

Required:

With the information given below, prepare a Vanasse Worksheet showing your application of statistical sampling techniques to estimate the proportion of inventory errors defined as the event when a physical count does not agree with the quantity in the perpetual records.

Population definition: Inventory records.

Population items: Table A, pp. A–1 to A–10.

Field size: 1,000.

Column number: (2).

Errors: J, L (= Lack of correspondence between physical count and perpetual record quantity)

Nonerrors: K, M, O, P.

Error rate in prior tests: 9 percent.

Acceptable upper precision limit: 14 percent.

Confidence level: 95 percent.

7.22. **Application Case—Compliance Testing**

Abbot Mills, Inc., produces mixed chemical fertilizers in a plant in southern Iowa. Dry chemical compounds are stored in a warehouse and removed for production mixing when a workman presents prenumbered issuance slips (in duplicate) filled out and initialed by the production foreman. The dated issuance slips specify the production order number and the type, quantity, and grade of dry chemicals to be used. The warehouseman writes the actual quantity removed on an issuance slip, initials it, and sends both copies to the accounting department.

In the accounting department, inventory control clerks insert unit costs on both copies and use one copy to update the perpetual inventory records. This copy is then filed in numerical order. The other copy is sent to the cost clerks who figure the materials costs, enter them on a copy of the production order, staple the issuance slips to the production order, enter the total production cost in the Finished Mix Inventory records, and ultimately in Cost of Goods Sold when the mix is shipped to a customer. It is normal for the cost clerks to have to hold a production order until all the issuance slips come in because chemicals are not all issued at the beginning of production. Thus, when more than one issuance slip is attached to a finished production order, they may not all be in numerical order. The production order is filed in its numerical order with the issuance slips attached.

In connection with the annual audit these internal accounting control procedures are considered important because:

a. Proper use of issuance slips enables inventory clerks to keep accurate perpetual inventory records of raw materials quantities and cost prices.

b. Accurate recording of quantities and prices on issuance slips enable cost clerks to enter proper amounts in the Finished Mix Inventory and Cost of Goods Sold accounts.

Required:

a. Identify and define the types of errors or irregularities that could occur. Specify the attributes to be tested. (Hint: It helps to organize the analysis around the seven general categories that describe types of attributes as discussed in Chapter 7. An example is given below.)

Example	*Attribute to Test*
1. Invalid recorded transactions. Raw materials records reduced (credited) improperly.	Issuance slips exist to support credits to raw materials inventory.

b. Using the problem description and the flowchart in Exhibit 7.22–1:

(1) Identify the control procedures in use to prevent or detect the errors or irregularities identified in requirement *a.* above, and

(2) Identify control procedures that apparently are *not* in use.

EXHIBIT 7.22–1
Abbot Mills, Inc., Inventory Procedures

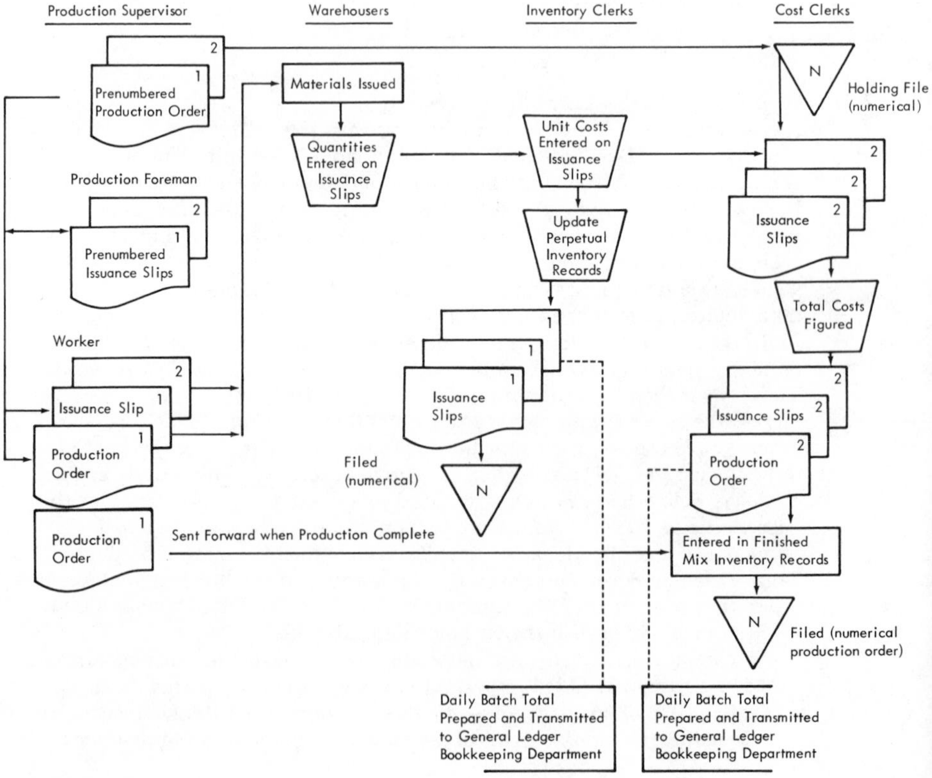

EXHIBIT 7.22–2
Attributes Sampling Data Sheet

ATTRIBUTES SAMPLING DATA SHEET

Client Abbot Mills, Inc. By DMA

Period covered January 1978 - November 1, 1978 Date 11-4-78

Define the objective(s) Determine whether raw materials and finished mix perpetual records are maintained reliably enough to justify counting physical inventory on November 30, 1978

Population: description Production orders -- 2,000 numbered from #75294 - #77,293

Sampling unit Production order (PO)

Random selection procedures Unrestricted random number association with document number sequence.

Attributes tested (Error definition)	Required Conf. Lev.	Required Accept. UPL	Expected Exception Proportion	Planned Sample Size	Actual Results Sample Size	Actual Results Occurrence No.	Actual Results Occurrence Rate	CUPL*
1. Production order exists	95%							
2. PO'S signed by supervisor	95%							
3.								
4.								
5.								
6.								
7.								
8.								
9.								
10.								

Intended use of sampling results:

1. Effect on audit plan:

2. Recommendation to management:

3. Other action:

*Whenever CUPL > AUPL there must be some action.

c. Prepare a working paper in the form outlined in Exhibits 7.22–2 and 7.22–3. The important exercise is to define the attributes that will be tested (Examples are given in Exhibits 7.22–2 and 7.22–3). Also, try your judgment at specifying criteria and determining sample size for the tests.

EXHIBIT 7.22–3
Attributes Sampling Data Sheet

ATTRIBUTES SAMPLING DATA SHEET

Client Abbot Mills, Inc. By DMA

Period covered January 1978-November 1, 1978 Date 11-4-78

Define the objective(s) Determine whether raw materials and finished mix perpetual inventory records are maintained reliably enough to justify counting physical inventory on November 30, 1978

Population: description Issuance slips -- 6,500 numbered from #1123-#7622

Sampling unit Issuance slip (IS)

Random selection procedures Unrestricted random number association with document numbering sequence

Attributes tested (Error definition)	Required Conf. Lev.	Required Accept. UPL	Expected Exception Proportion	Planned Sample Size	Actual Results Sample Size	Actual Results Occurrence No.	Actual Results Occurrence Rate	CUPL
1. Issuance slip exists	95%							
2. Is properly initialed	95%							
3.								
4.								
5.								
6.								
7.								
8.								
9.								
10.								

Intended use of sampling results:

1. Effect on audit plan:

2. Recommendation to management:

3. Other action:

*Whenever CUPL > AUPL there must be some action.

APPENDIX 7–A: Table of Random Digits

32942	95416	42339	59045	26693	49057	87496	20624	14819
07410	99859	83828	21409	29094	65114	36701	25762	12827
59981	68155	45673	76210	58219	45738	29550	24736	09574
46251	25437	69654	99716	11563	08803	86027	51867	12116
65558	51904	93123	27887	53138	21488	09095	78777	71240
99187	19258	86421	16401	19397	83297	40111	49326	81686
35641	00301	16096	34775	21562	97983	45040	19200	16383
14031	00936	81518	48440	02218	04756	19506	60695	88494
60677	15076	92554	26042	23472	69869	62877	19584	39576
66314	05212	67859	89356	20056	30648	87349	20389	53805
20416	87410	75646	64176	82752	63606	37011	57346	69512
28701	56992	70423	62415	40807	98086	58850	28968	45297
74579	33844	33426	07570	00728	07079	19322	56325	84819
62615	52342	82968	75540	80045	53069	20665	21282	07768
93945	06293	22879	08161	01442	75071	21427	94842	26210
75689	76131	96837	67450	44511	50424	82848	41975	71663
02921	16919	35424	93209	52133	87327	95897	65171	20376
14295	34969	14216	03191	61647	30296	66667	10101	63203
05303	91109	82403	40312	62191	67023	90073	83205	71344
57071	90357	12901	08899	91039	67251	28701	03846	94589
78471	57741	13599	84390	32146	00871	09354	22745	65806
89242	79337	59293	47481	07740	43345	25716	70020	54005
14955	59592	97035	80430	87220	06392	79028	57123	52872
42446	41880	37415	47472	04513	49494	08860	08038	43624
18534	22346	54556	17558	73689	14894	05030	19561	56517
39284	33737	42512	86411	23753	29690	26096	81361	93099
33922	37329	89911	55876	28379	81031	22058	21487	54613
78355	54013	50774	30666	61205	42574	47773	36027	27174
08845	99145	94316	88974	29828	97069	90327	61842	29604
01769	71825	55957	98271	02784	66731	40311	88495	18821
17639	38284	59478	90409	21997	56199	30068	82800	69692
05851	58653	99949	63505	40409	85551	90729	64938	52403
42396	40112	11469	03476	03328	84238	26570	51790	42122
13318	14192	98167	75631	74141	22369	36757	89117	54998
60571	54786	26281	01855	30706	66578	32019	65884	58485
09531	81853	59334	70929	03544	18510	89541	13555	21168
72865	16829	86542	00396	20363	13010	69645	49608	54738
56324	31093	77924	28622	83543	28912	15059	80192	83964
78192	21626	91399	07235	07104	73652	64425	85149	75409
64666	34767	97298	92708	01994	53188	78476	07804	62404
82201	75694	02808	65983	74373	66693	13094	74183	73020
15360	73776	40914	85190	54278	99054	62944	47351	89098
68142	67957	70896	37983	20487	95350	16371	03426	13895
19138	31200	30616	14639	44406	44236	57360	81644	94761
28155	03521	36415	78452	92359	81091	56513	88321	97910
87971	29031	51780	27376	81056	86155	55488	50590	74514
58147	68841	53625	02059	75223	16783	19272	61994	71090
18875	52809	70594	41649	32935	26430	82096	01605	65846
75109	56474	74111	31966	29969	70093	98901	84550	25769
35983	03742	76822	12073	59463	84420	15868	99505	11426

Source: The Rand Corporation. *A Million Random Digits with 100,000 Normal Deviates* (Glencoe: The Free Press, 1955), p. 102.

APPENDIX 7–B.1

Graph for Selecting Sample Size—Confidence Level 99 Percent

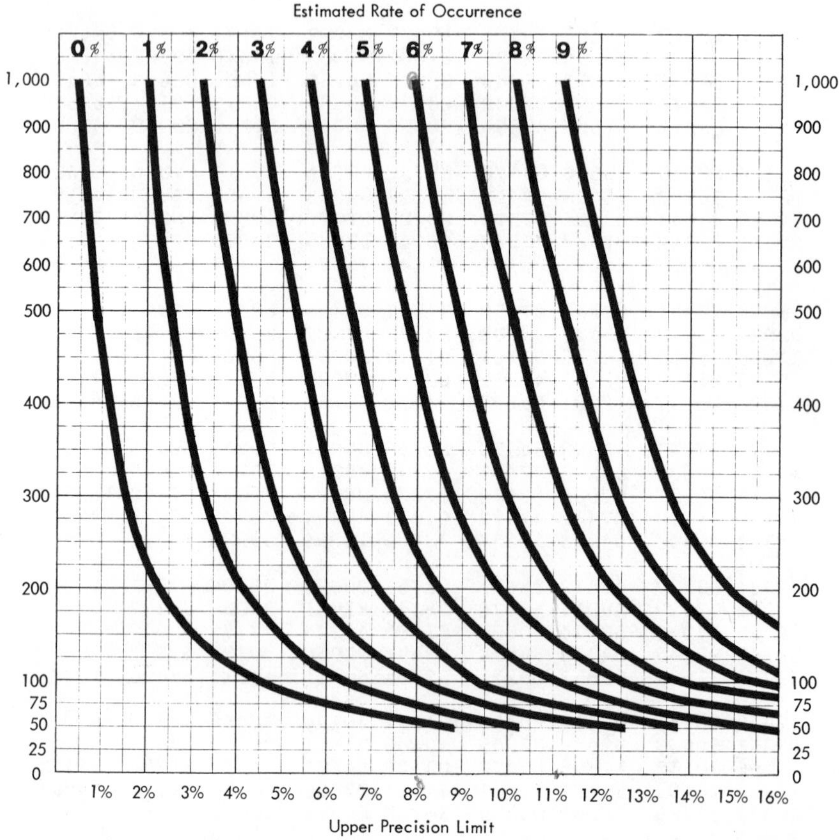

This graph is based upon an infinite field size. If the field is small (1,000 or less), slightly smaller samples sizes than those indicated by the graph are adequate.

Source: Used with permission of the American Group of CPA firms.

APPENDIX 7–B.2

Graph for Selecting Sample Size—Confidence Level 95 Percent

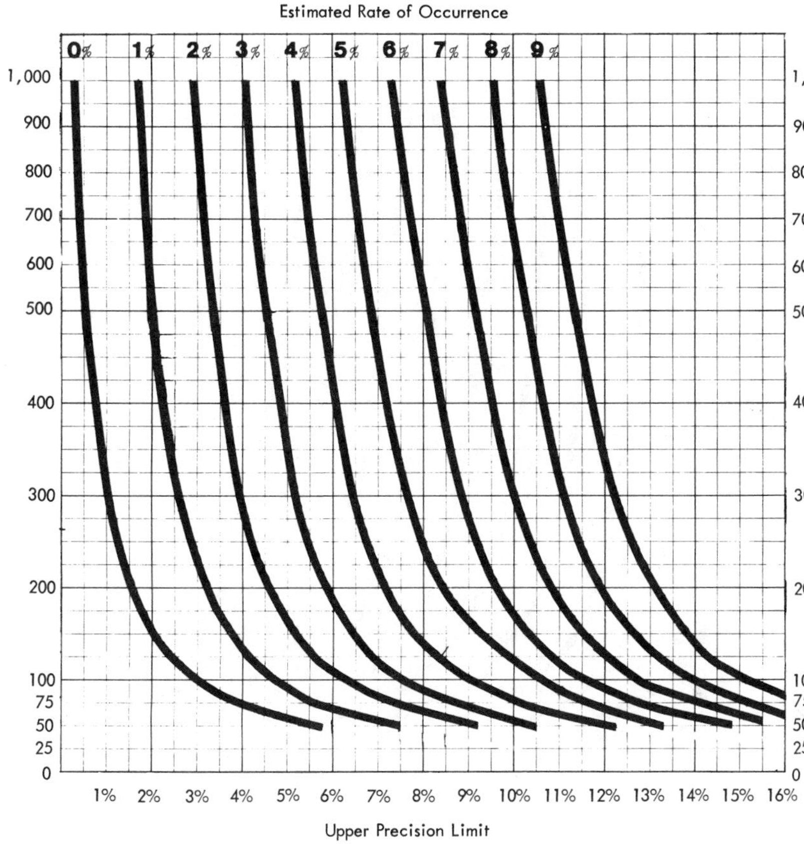

This graph is based upon an infinite field size. If the field is small (1,000 or less), slightly smaller samples sizes than those indicated by the graph are adequate.

Source: Used with permission of the American Group of CPA firms.

APPENDIX 7–B.3

Graph for Selecting Sample Size—Confidence Level 90 Percent

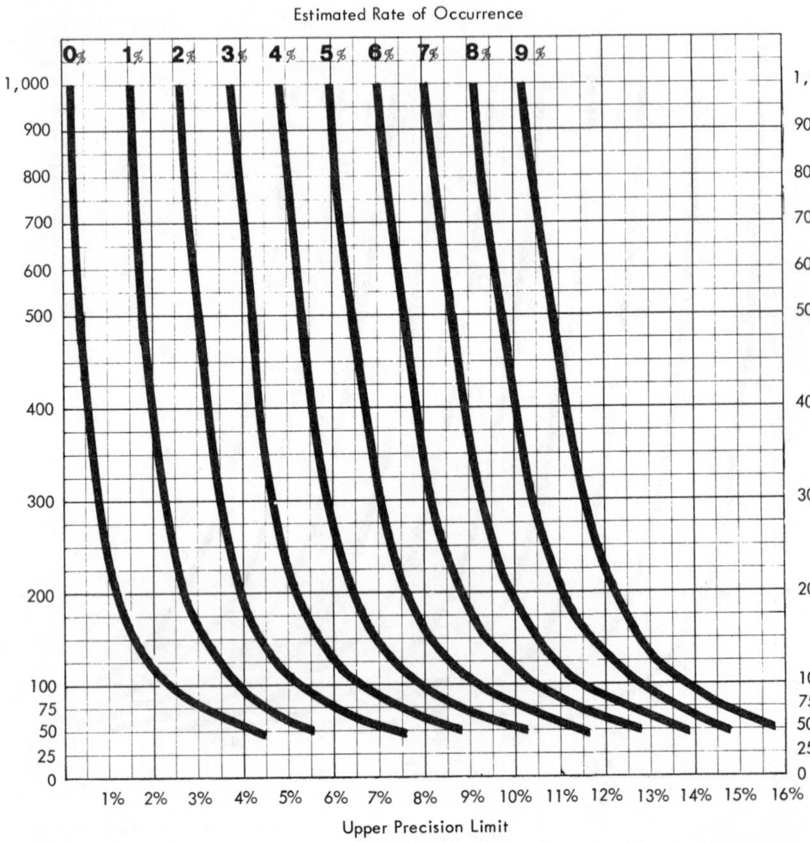

This graph is based upon an infinite field size. If the field is small (1,000 or less), slightly smaller samples sizes than those indicated by the graph are adequate.

Source: Used with permission of the American Group of CPA firms.

APPENDIX 7–C.1

Attribute Evaluation Table

EVALUATION OF RESULTS, RELIABILITY = 99 percent (number of observed occurrences)

Sample Size	Computed Upper Precision Limit: Percent Rate of Occurrences																				
	1	*2*	*3*	*4*	*5*	*6*	*7*	*8*	*9*	*10*	*12*	*14*	*16*	*18*	*20*	*25*	*30*	*35*	*40*	*45*	*50*
10																			0		
20																0	1		2	3	4
30													0			1	3	4	5	6	8
40											0		1		2	3	5	7	8	10	12
50									0			1	2		3	5	7	9	11	13	16
60								0			1	2	3		4	7	9	12	14	17	20
70							0			1	2	3	4	5	6	9	11	14	18	21	24
80						0			1		2	4	5	6	7	10	14	17	21	25	29
90					0			1		2	3	5	6	7	9	12	16	20	24	29	33
100					0		1		2	3	4	6	7	9	10	14	19	23	28	33	37
120				0		1	2		3	4	6	8	9	11	13	18	24	29	35	40	46
140				0	1	2	3		4	5	7	10	12	14	16	22	29	35	42	48	55
160			0		1	2	3	5	6	7	9	12	14	17	20	27	34	41	49	56	64
180			0	1	2	3	4	6	7	8	11	14	17	20	23	31	39	47	56	65	73
200			0	1	3	4	5	7	8	10	13	16	19	23	26	35	44	54	63	73	83
220			0	2	3	5	6	8	10	11	15	18	22	26	30	39	50	60	70	81	92
240		0	1	2	4	6	7	9	11	13	17	21	25	29	33	44	55	66	78	89	101
260		0	1	3	5	6	8	10	12	14	19	23	27	32	36	48	60	72	85	97	110
280		0	2	3	4	7	9	12	14	16	21	25	30	35	40	53	65	79	92	106	120
300		0	2	4	6	8	10	13	15	18	23	28	33	38	43	57	71	85	99	114	129
320		0	2	4	7	9	11	14	17	19	24	30	35	41	47	61	76	91	107	122	138
340		1	3	5	7	10	13	15	18	21	26	32	38	44	50	66	82	98	114	131	148
360		1	3	6	8	11	14	16	19	22	28	35	41	47	54	70	87	104	122	139	157
380		1	3	6	9	12	15	18	21	24	30	37	44	50	57	75	93	111	129	148	166
400		1	4	7	10	13	16	19	22	26	32	39	46	54	61	79	98	117	136	156	176
420		2	4	7	10	14	17	20	24	27	35	42	49	57	64	84	103	124	144	164	185
460	0	2	5	8	12	15	19	23	27	31	39	47	55	63	72	93	114	136	159	181	204
500	0	3	6	10	13	17	21	26	30	34	43	52	60	70	79	102	125	149	174	198	223
550	0	3	7	11	15	20	24	29	34	38	48	58	68	78	88	113	139	166	192	219	247
600	0	4	8	13	17	22	27	32	37	43	53	64	78	86	97	125	153	182	211	241	271
650	0	4	9	14	19	25	30	36	41	47	58	70	82	94	106	136	167	198	230	262	294
700	1	5	10	16	21	27	33	39	45	51	64	76	89	102	115	148	181	215	249	283	318
800	1	7	13	19	25	32	39	46	53	60	74	89	103	118	133	171	209	248	287	326	366
900	2	8	15	22	29	37	45	53	61	69	85	101	118	135	152	194	237	281	325	369	414
1,000	2	9	17	25	34	42	51	60	69	78	96	114	133	151	170	218	266	314	363	412	462

Source: Adapted from "Tables of the Cumulative Binomial Probability Distribution," from *The Annals of the Computation Laboratory of Harvard University*, volume 35.

APPENDIX 7–C.2

Attribute Evaluation Table

EVALUATION OF RESULTS, RELIABILITY = 95 percent (number of observed occurrences)

Sample Size	*Computed Upper Precision Limit: Percent Rate of Occurrence*																				
	1	*2*	*3*	*4*	*5*	*6*	*7*	*8*	*9*	*10*	*12*	*14*	*16*	*18*	*20*	*25*	*30*	*35*	*40*	*45*	*50*
10																	0		1		
20												0				1	2	3		4	5
30										0			1		2	3	4	5	7	8	10
40								0			1		2		3	5	6	8	10	12	14
50						0				1		2	3	4	5	7	9	11	13	16	18
60					0			1			2	3	4	5	6	9	11	14	17	20	23
70					0		1		2		3	4	5	7	8	11	14	17	20	24	27
80				0		1		2		3	4	5	7	8	9	13	16	20	24	28	32
90				0		1	2		3	4	5	6	8	9	11	15	19	23	27	32	36
100			0		1		2	3	4		6	8	9	11	13	17	22	26	31	36	41
120			0	1		2	3	4	5	6	8	10	12	14	16	21	27	33	38	44	50
140			0	1	2	3	4	5	6	7	10	12	14	17	19	26	32	39	46	52	59
160		0	1	2	3	4	5	6	8	9	12	14	17	20	23	30	38	45	53	61	69
180		0	1	2	3	5	6	8	9	11	14	17	20	23	26	35	43	52	60	69	78
200		0	1	3	4	6	7	9	11	12	16	19	23	26	30	39	48	58	68	77	87
220		0	2	3	5	7	8	10	12	14	18	22	25	29	33	44	54	64	75	86	97
240		1	2	4	6	8	10	12	14	16	20	24	28	33	37	48	59	71	83	94	106
260		1	3	4	7	9	11	13	15	17	22	26	31	36	41	53	65	77	90	103	116
280		1	3	5	7	10	12	14	17	19	24	29	34	39	44	57	71	84	98	111	125
300	0	1	3	6	8	11	13	16	18	21	26	31	37	42	48	62	76	91	105	120	135
320	0	2	4	6	9	11	14	17	20	22	28	34	40	45	51	66	82	97	113	128	144
340	0	2	4	7	10	12	15	18	21	24	30	36	42	49	55	71	87	104	120	137	154
360	0	2	5	8	10	13	17	20	23	26	32	39	45	52	59	76	93	110	128	146	163
380	0	2	5	8	11	14	18	21	24	28	34	41	48	55	62	80	98	117	135	154	173
400	0	3	6	9	12	15	19	22	26	29	37	44	51	59	66	85	104	123	143	163	183
420	0	3	6	9	13	16	20	24	27	31	39	46	54	62	70	90	110	130	151	171	192
460	0	4	7	11	15	18	22	26	31	35	43	51	60	68	77	99	121	143	166	188	211
500	1	4	8	12	16	21	25	29	34	38	47	56	66	75	84	108	132	157	181	197	221
550	1	5	9	14	18	23	28	33	38	43	53	63	73	83	94	120	146	173	200	227	255
600	1	6	10	15	20	26	31	36	42	47	58	69	80	92	103	132	161	190	219	249	279
650	2	6	12	17	23	28	34	40	46	52	64	76	88	100	112	143	175	207	239	271	303
700	2	7	13	19	25	31	37	43	50	56	69	82	95	108	122	155	189	223	258	292	327
800	3	9	15	22	29	36	43	51	58	65	80	95	110	125	141	179	218	257	296	336	376
900	4	10	18	26	34	42	50	58	66	74	91	108	125	142	159	203	247	291	335	379	424
1,000	4	12	20	29	38	47	56	65	74	84	102	121	140	159	178	227	275	324	374	423	473

Source: Adapted from "Tables of the Cumulative Binomial Probability Distribution" from *The Annals of the Computation Laboratory of Harvard University*, volume 35.

APPENDIX 7–C.3

Attribute Evaluation Table

EVALUATION OF RESULTS, RELIABILITY = 90 percent (number of observed occurrences)

Sample Size	Computed Upper Precision Limit: Percent Rate of Occurrence																				
	1	2	3	4	5	6	7	8	9	10	12	14	16	18	20	25	30	35	40	45	50
10																0		1		2	
20											0				1	2		3	4	5	6
30								0				1		2		4	5	6	8	9	10
40						0				1		2	3		4	6	7	9	11	13	15
50					0			1			2	3	4	5		8	10	12	15	17	19
60				0			1		2		3	4	5	6	7	10	13	15	18	21	24
70				0		1		2		3	4	5	6	8	9	12	15	18	22	25	29
80			0		1		2		3	4	5	6	8	9	10	14	18	22	25	29	33
90			0		1	2		3	4		6	7	9	11	12	16	20	25	29	33	38
100			0	1		2	3	4		5	7	9	10	12	14	19	23	28	33	38	43
120		0		1	2	3	4	5	6	7	9	11	13	15	17	23	29	34	40	46	52
140		0	1	2	3	4	5	6	7	9	11	13	16	18	21	27	34	41	48	54	61
160		0	1	2	4	5	6	8	9	10	13	16	19	22	25	32	40	47	55	63	71
180		0	2	3	4	6	7	9	10	12	15	18	22	25	28	37	45	54	63	71	80
200		1	2	4	5	7	8	10	12	14	17	21	24	28	32	41	51	60	70	80	90
220		1	2	4	6	8	10	12	13	15	19	23	27	31	35	46	56	67	78	89	99
240	0	1	3	5	7	9	11	13	15	17	21	26	30	35	39	50	62	74	85	97	109
260	0	1	3	5	8	10	12	14	17	19	24	28	33	38	43	55	68	80	93	106	119
280	0	2	4	6	8	11	13	16	18	21	26	31	36	41	46	60	73	87	101	114	128
300	0	2	4	7	9	12	14	17	20	22	28	33	39	45	50	64	79	93	108	123	138
320	0	2	5	7	10	13	16	18	21	24	30	36	42	48	54	69	85	100	116	132	148
340	0	3	5	8	11	14	17	20	23	26	32	38	45	51	58	74	90	107	123	140	157
360	0	3	6	9	12	15	18	21	25	28	34	41	48	55	61	79	96	113	131	149	167
380	0	3	6	9	13	16	19	23	26	30	37	44	51	58	65	83	102	120	139	158	177
400	1	4	7	10	14	17	21	24	28	31	39	46	54	61	69	88	107	127	146	166	186
420	1	4	7	11	14	18	22	26	29	33	41	49	57	65	73	93	113	134	154	175	196
460	1	4	8	12	16	20	24	28	33	37	45	54	63	71	80	102	124	147	170	192	215
500	1	5	9	13	18	22	27	31	36	40	50	59	69	78	88	112	136	160	185	210	235
550	2	6	10	15	20	25	30	35	40	45	55	66	76	87	97	124	150	177	204	232	259
600	2	7	12	17	22	28	33	39	44	50	61	72	84	95	107	135	165	194	224	253	283
650	2	8	13	19	24	30	36	42	48	54	66	79	91	104	116	147	179	211	243	275	308
700	3	8	14	20	27	33	39	46	52	59	72	85	99	112	126	159	194	228	262	297	332
800	4	10	17	24	31	38	46	53	61	68	83	99	114	129	145	183	222	262	301	341	381
900	4	12	20	28	36	44	52	61	69	78	95	112	129	146	164	207	251	296	340	385	430
1,000	5	13	22	31	40	49	59	68	77	87	106	125	144	164	183	232	280	330	379	429	479

Source: Adapted from "Tables of the Cumulative Binomial Probability Distribution" from *The Annals of the Computation Laboratory of Harvard University*, volume 35.

APPENDIX 7–D

Discovery Sampling Table*

Sample Size	*Upper Precision Limit: Critical Rate of Occurrence*							
	.1%	*.2%*	*.3%*	*.4%*	*.5%*	*.75%*	*1%*	*2%*
50	5%	10%	14%	18%	22%	31%	40%	64%
60	6	11	17	21	26	36	45	70
70	7	13	19	25	30	41	51	76
80	8	15	21	28	33	45	55	80
90	9	17	24	30	36	49	60	84
100	10	18	26	33	40	53	64	87
120	11	21	30	38	45	60	70	91
140	13	25	35	43	51	65	76	94
160	15	28	38	48	55	70	80	96
200	18	33	45	56	64	78	87	98
240	22	39	52	62	70	84	91	99
300	26	46	60	70	78	90	95	99+
340	29	50	65	75	82	93	97	99+
400	34	56	71	81	87	95	98	99+
460	38	61	76	85	91	97	99	99+
500	40	64	79	87	92	98	99	99+
600	46	71	84	92	96	99	99+	99+
700	52	77	89	95	97	99+	99+	99+
800	57	81	92	96	98	99+	99+	99+
900	61	85	94	98	99	99+	99+	99+
1,000	65	88	96	99	99	99+	99+	99+
1,500	80	96	99	99+	99+	99+	99+	99+
2,000	89	99	99+	99+	99+	99+	99+	99+

* Reliability, in percent, of including at least one occurrence in a sample for populations between 5,000 and 10,000.

Source: Used with permission of Ernest & Ernst.

8

AUDITING INTERNAL CONTROL IN AN EDP ENVIRONMENT

The field of auditing technology known as "EDP auditing" has two facets for an auditor: (1) the proper study and evaluation of internal control and (2) the utilization of the computer to *perform* some audit work that would otherwise be performed by the auditor's own hand. The first of these two facets is the subject of this chapter. Methods of using the computer to perform substantive audit work are described more fully in Chapter 9.

The distinction between evaluating internal accounting control and using the computer to perform audit work is somewhat artificial because the computer itself and computer programs may be involved in both cases. Perhaps the most useful way to distinguish the two facets is to recognize two different purposes: (1) The purpose of the internal control study and evaluation is to determine whether *general* controls in a computer facility are satisfactory and whether *application* controls are properly designed and operate effectively and (2) the purpose of using the computer to perform audit tasks, operating on machine-readable records, is to obtain sufficient competent evidential matter pertaining to the fair presentation or usefulness of *output* information.

EVALUATION APPROACHES FOR EDP SYSTEMS

An auditor's special concern with EDP systems arises because personnel duties and control procedures that would ordinarily be separated in manual systems tend to be *concentrated* and *combined* within the hardware and software of a computerized system. Controls take on a special technological form in man-machine systems, and organizational charts differ from manual systems. When businesses started using computers, two terms were used to describe the nature of auditing work on EDP systems. *Auditing around the computer* meant that the auditor attempted to isolate and ignore the computer—treating it like a "black box"—and find audit assurance by tracing and vouching data from output to source documents and from source documents to output. As long as the computer was used as a speedy calculator, this method was generally adequate. In fact it may be satisfactory today if the computer system simply replaces the hands of numerous clerks, when source documents take familiar hard-copy form, and when journals and ledgers are all printed out as they would be under a manual system.

The second term was *auditing through the computer*, and it referred to the auditor's actual use of the hardware and software to determine the reliability of operations that could not be viewed by the human eye. *Auditing through* has become more common in practice because more and more EDP systems do not operate as "many clerks" but have significant control procedures built into the system. Thus to ignore the computer system and the controls built into it would amount to ignoring important characteristics of internal accounting control.

Two new terms have more recently been coined to describe the auditor's approach to EDP systems: (1) auditing *without* using the computer and (2) auditing *with* the computer. The first of these terms essentially describes an "around" approach. One prerequisite for auditing without using the computer is the existence of printed records that may be used like handwritten records. The auditor under this approach may audit the input data, the machine-produced error listings, the visible control points (e.g., use of batch totals), and the detailed printed output.

On the other hand, to audit *with* the computer refers to two aspects: (1) to use the computer hardware, the data processing programs, and real or simulated data to operate the system as it would operate under normal conditions and (2) to use specialized programs to perform other audit tasks. Thus one may see that "auditing around" and "auditing without" have essentially the same meaning, but "auditing through" is not as extensive as "auditing with."

EDP System Review

A study and evaluation of EDP-based internal accounting control begins with a *preliminary review*. This review has the primary purpose of enabling the auditor to understand the flow of transactions in the client's business, specifically (1) how the books are kept when a computer is used, (2) the extent to which EDP is used in each significant accounting application, and (3) the basic structure and interrelationships of manual and EDP controls. The preliminary review should identify:

Significant computer applications in the accounting system.

The extent EDP is used in each significant application.

The basic structure of controls.

The preliminary review phase starts with inquiries directed to knowledgeable EDP managers. Auditors use extensive questionnaires to guide this effort. Several questionnaire items are illustrated later in this chapter. Manual controls and procedures related to the EDP applications are also reviewed at the same time. In effect, the review of EDP applications and controls is an extension of the review phase discussed in Chapter 6 to cover the more technologically complex EDP function. However, manual *and* EDP controls must be understood by the auditor as a complete, integrated accounting control system.

The preliminary review gives the auditor initial evidence about the apparent reliability of the general controls and application controls. If the decision is to rely upon elements of the computer system, the auditor must then perform some *compliance tests* of the particular controls upon which reliance is planned. This logic scheme is the same as for the review, compliance testing, and reliance on manual systems.

GENERAL EDP INTERNAL CONTROL CHARACTERISTICS

All of the desired internal control characteristics discussed in Chapter 6 apply equally to EDP systems. However, when EDP is used in an accounting system, an additional dimension of control is present because of the removal of data processing from the traditional accounting function and because of the complex technology involved. An auditor needs to understand a client's EDP system, whether simple or complex, sufficiently to enable him or her to identify and evaluate its essential accounting control features.

According to *SAS No. 3* (Section 321.06–.08)—"The Effects of EDP on the Auditor's Study and Evaluation of Internal Control"—EDP controls are classified in two categories:

1. *General controls* relate to all EDP activities, and include:
   Plan of organization and operation of the EDP activity,
   Procedures for documenting, reviewing, testing and approving systems or computer programs (and changes made to them),
   Hardware controls built in by computer manufacturers,
   Controls over access to computer equipment, data files, and programs.
2. *Application controls* relate to specific tasks performed by an EDP system (applications such as payroll processing, for example) and consist of:
   Input controls,
   Processing controls, and
   Output controls.

Taken together, general and application controls should operate to provide reasonable prevention and detection assurance concerning the following types of errors or irregularities that might occur:

1. Errors in converting transaction data to machine-readable form (e.g., punched cards, magnetic tape),

2. Errors in correcting and resubmitting data initially rejected by the system,
3. Destruction or damage of machine-readable files,
4. Processing invalid transactions,
5. Failing to process valid transactions,
6. Processing unauthorized transactions,
7. Improper valuation of transaction data,
8. Erroneous classification of transaction data,
9. Failing to post control and subsidiary accounts properly,
10. Erroneous dating and recording of transactions.

The first three items in the list above are unique to EDP systems. The last seven are the same as the exceptions to control attributes shown and discussed in Chapter 7. This similarity is not accidental because EDP systems should accomplish the same control purposes as any other kind of system. Only some aspects of the organization and technology are different.

Organization and Access Control within the EDP Activity

The proper segregation of functional responsibilities among authority to authorize transactions, custody of assets, and recordkeeping is as important in EDP systems as in manual systems. However, EDP systems involve systems analysis, programming, data conversion, library functions, and machine operations that are unique. Therefore, a further separation of duties is recommended as illustrated in Exhibit 8–1.

Because of the exacting accuracy and logic required in EDP system design, programming, and operation, the capability of personnel is a highly significant characteristic. Nevertheless, direct evaluation by the auditor is difficult, so reliance must be placed on the condition of documentation and on the operative effectiveness of error-checking routines.

The essential division of duties are among the functions of analyst, programmer, and operators. The duties of these and other roles are defined as follows:

Systems analyst. Analyzes requirements for information. Evaluates the existing system and designs new or improved data processing procedures. Outlines the system and prepares specifications which guide the data communication specialists and programmers.

Programmer. Flowcharts the logic of the computer programs required by the overall system designed by the systems analyst. Codes the logic in the computer program. Prepares documentation.

Computer operator. Operates the computer according to the operating procedures for the installation and the detailed procedures for each program found in the computer operator instructions.

Data conversion operators. Prepare data for machine processing. Traditionally, these individuals operated keypunch machines and produced punched cards. In more recent times these operators may also con-

EXHIBIT 8–1
Structure of a Large EDP Organization

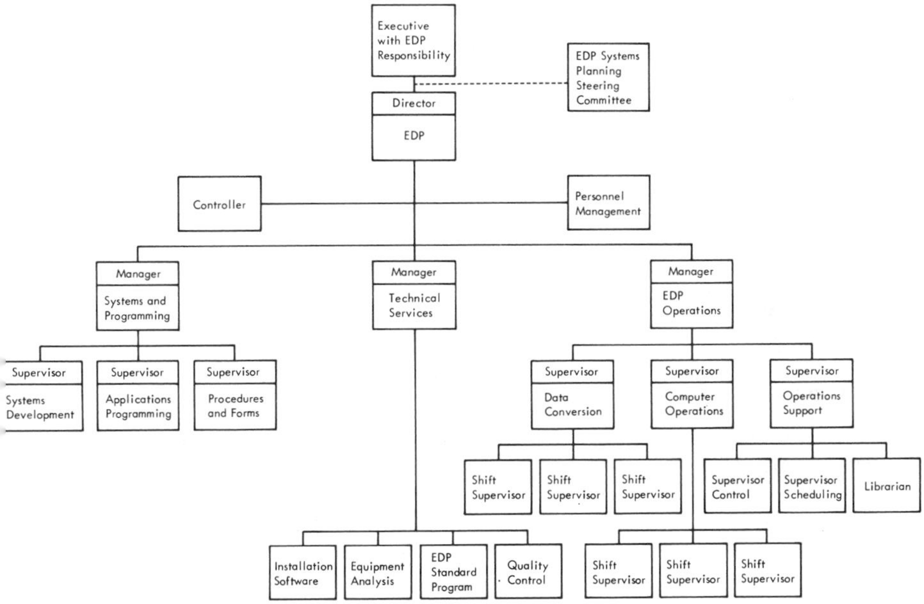

Source: From *Computer Control and Audit* by W. C. Mair, D. R. Wood, and K. W. Davis by permission of The Institute of Internal Auditors, Inc., 249 Maitland Avenue, Altamonte Springs, Florida 32701. Reprinted with permission.

vert data to magnetic tape, operate optical character reading equipment and cathode ray tube equipment, and data transmission terminals.

Librarian. There may be two librarian functions in an EDP facility—one for system and program documentation and the other for the actual program and data files. The purpose of the system/program documentation library is to maintain control over documentation of the design and redesign stages of EDP information systems. The purpose of the program input/output library is to maintain control over the files and programs actually used from day to day.

Quality control group. The quality control group operates with a specialized internal audit mission that includes periodic tests of the hardware and software. On a more regular basis, the control group compares control totals to EDP output, reviews document sequence numbers, reviews and processes error messages, monitors actual processing, and distributes output.

It is important to separate the duties performed by analysts, programmers, and operators. The general idea is that anyone who designs a processing system should not also do the technical programming work, and anyone who performs either of these tasks should not also be the computer operator when "live" data is being processed. Persons performing each function should not have *access* to the other's work, and only the computer operators should have access to the equipment. EDP systems are too susceptible to manipulative handling to consider lack of separation as anything other than a serious weakness in general controls.

> ***Illustration.*** A programmer employed by a large savings and loan association wrote a special subroutine that could be activated by throwing a switch on the computer console. The computation of interest on deposits and certificates was programmed to truncate calculations at the third decimal place. The special subroutine instructed the program to accumulate the truncated mills, and when processing was complete, to credit the amount to the programmer-operator's savings account. Whenever this person was on duty for the interest calculation run, she could "make" several hundred dollars! She had to be on duty in order to manipulate the control figures "properly" so that the error of overpaying interest on her account would not be detected by the control group. She was a programmer with computer operation duties.

Physical security and limited access to files and EDP equipment are important. Access controls help prevent improper use or manipulation of data files, unauthorized or incorrect use of computer programs, and improper use of the computer itself. The librarian functions should control access to systems documentation and to program and data files by using a check-out log to record use by authorized persons. Someone in possession of both documentation and data files could have enough information to alter data and programs for his or her own purposes.

Locked doors, security passes, and check-in logs (including logs produced by the computer) can be used to limit access to the computer hardware. These logs are often called "console logs" because they are produced at the computer "console"—a keyboard with printer used by the computer operator. Having definite schedules for running computer applications is a way to detect unauthorized access because the computer software can produce reports in the form of console logs that can be compared to the preset schedule. Variations can then be investigated.

Weakness or absence of organizational and access controls decrease the overall integrity of the EDP system. The auditor should feel uncomfortable when weaknesses exist and should weigh their impact in the overall evaluation of internal accounting controls.

Some typical questions asked by auditors are shown in the box below. A full set of questions, of which these are a part, is one method of reviewing the organization and access control of an EDP facility.

Documentation

The general internal control characteristic that requires a "system of authorization and record procedures" establishes the relevance of extensive documentation of EDP systems. The following purposes may be served by EDP system documentation, the elements of which are shown in Exhibit 8–2.

SELECTED QUESTIONNAIRE ITEMS*

Organization

Prepare or obtain an organization chart of the EDP organization. Determine position titles, job descriptions, and names of persons in these positions.

Is there a segregation of duties such that:

a. The functions and duties of system design and programming are separate from computer operation?

b. Programmers do not operate the computer for regular processing?

c. Computer operators are restricted from access to data and program information not necessary for performing their assigned task?

d. The employees in data processing are separated from all duties relating to the initiation of transactions and initiation of requests for changes to the master files?

Are the operators assigned to individual applications rotated periodically?

Are the computer operators required to take vacations?

The Control Function

Is there a person or group charged with responsibility for the control function in the data processing department? Obtain description of duties.

If there is an internal auditing group, does it perform EDP control activities related to:

a. Review or audit?

b. Day-to-day control activities?

Control over the Console

Are provisions adequate to prevent unauthorized entry of program changes and/or data through the console?

Are adequate machine operations logs being maintained?

Is there an independent examination of computer logs to check the operator performance and machine efficiency?

* Source: Excerpts from Gordon B. Davis, *Auditing and EDP* (New York: AICPA, 1968), pp. 325–40.

1. Provide explanatory material necessary for a supervisory review of proposed systems and computer programs.
2. Simplify program revisions by providing full detail in support of each program.
3. Provide the data necessary for answering inquiries regarding the operation of a computer program.
4. Aid in instructing new personnel by providing background on previous programs and serving as a guideline for new programs.
5. Provide operator with current operating instructions.
6. Serve as one basis for evaluation of internal control.[1]

The problem definition section is a record of the problem that required an EDP solution. A definition, description, feasibility, and approval of the

[1] Gordon B. Davis, *Auditing and EDP* (New York: AICPA, 1968), p. 23.

EXHIBIT 8–2
EDP Application Documentation

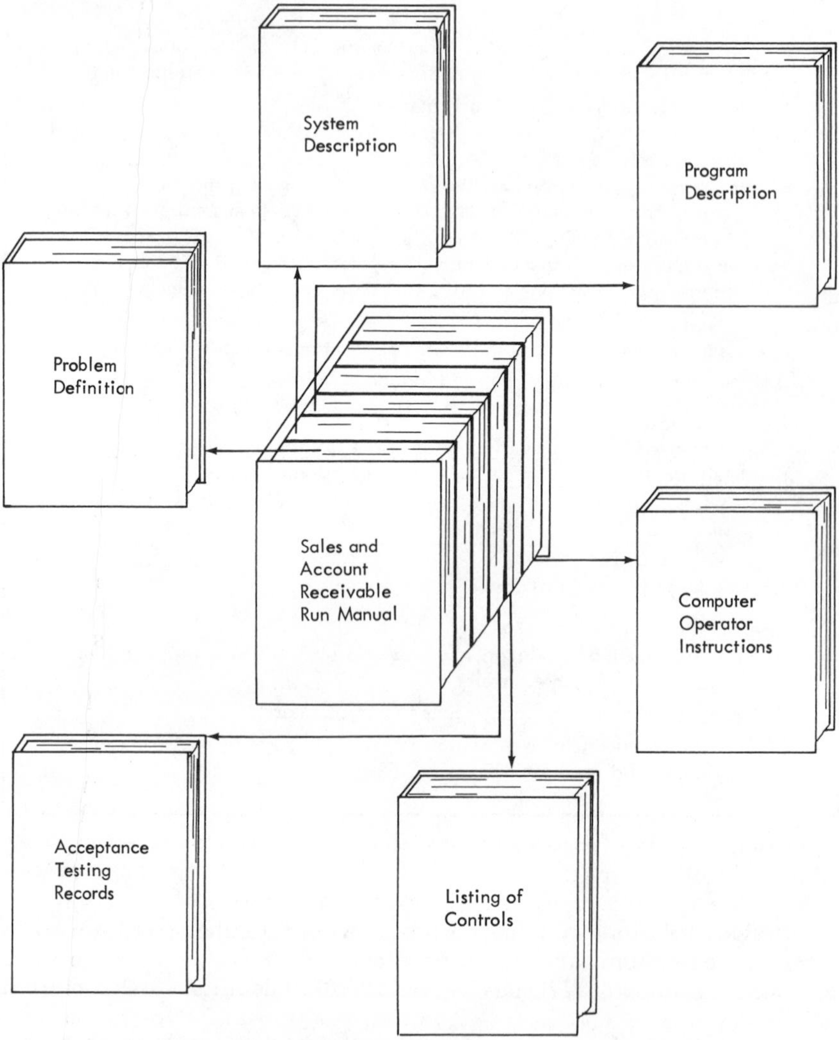

Source: Gordon B. Davis, *Auditing and EDP* (New York: AICPA, 1968), p. 25.

problem and its proposed solution may be found in this section. Also there is a description of how this solution system fits into the overall data processing plan.

The system description section follows behind the problem definition and expands the solution system with a statement of how the system was actually designed. This section includes the system flowcharts, decision tables, data record formats, lists of computer codes, and control features. The data record format, or "layout," is of particular interest to the auditor because this system element is important with regard to testing the system input and processing. An example of a multiple-card layout form is shown in Exhibit 8–3.

EXHIBIT 8–3

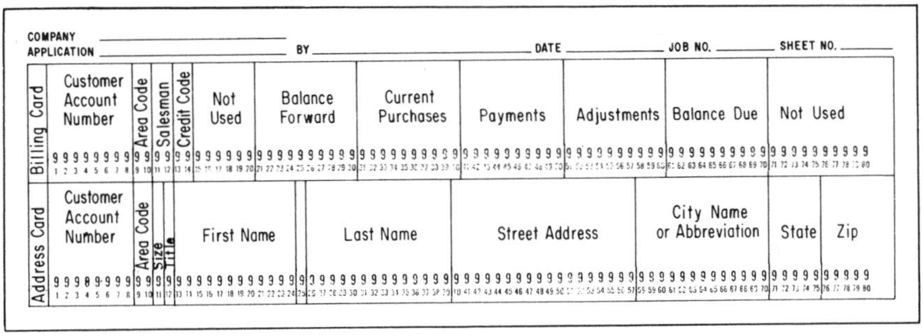
COMPANY
APPLICATION
BY
DATE
JOB NO.
SHEET NO.
Billing Card
Customer Account Number
Area Code
Salesman
Credit Code
Not Used
Balance Forward
Current Purchases
Payments
Adjustments
Balance Due
Not Used
Address Card
Customer Account Number
Area Code
Size
Title
First Name
Last Name
Street Address
City Name or Abbreviation
State
Zip

Source: Gordon B. Davis, *Auditing and EDP* (New York: AICPA, 1968), p. 28.

The program description section explains every detail of the processing software program itself. This description may take the form of a program flowchart, program decision tables, storage and memory locations, console switch settings, minor program modifications not included in the programmed language, and a printed program listing. This section provides the auditor with a source of evidence for the review phase study of how the system is supposed to function.

The operator's instruction section repeats the instructions from the program description section for use of hardware, console switches, file header and trailer labels, and other operating details. Some instructions such as the particular tape and disk drives to be used and the daily time schedule may appear only in the operator instructions.

The controls section contains a description and listing of the control features over input accuracy, programmed controls, error listing formats, and output control checks. An auditor will find this section very informative for beginning his or her tests of the system. However, the most crucial point to be alert to is the *omission* of needed controls because they generally are not mentioned in the controls section unless omission was planned and noted.

The acceptance section is the documentation of debugging and testing procedures performed before the system was brought into production. Input and output test data, error messages, and other validity checks should be fully documented. Any recommendations for alteration of the system should also be in the written record. An auditor may wish to review the tests performed by the EDP group before beginning to design audit tests.

Some typical questionnaire items asked about documentation are shown in the box below.

SELECTED QUESTIONNAIRE ITEMS*

Documentation

Is a run manual prepared for each computer run?

Are operator instructions prepared for each run?

Are documentation practices adequate? Does the normal documentation for an application include the following?

Problem statement.
System flowchart.
Record layouts.
Program flowcharts.
Program listing.
Test data.
Operator instructions.
Summary of controls.
Approval and change record.

Is documentation kept up to date?

Program Revisions

Is each program revision authorized by a request for change properly approved by management or supervisory personnel?

Are program changes together with their effective dates, documented in a manner which preserves an accurate chronological record of the system?

Are program revisions tested in the same manner as the new programs?

* Source: G. B. Davis, *Auditing and EDP* (New York: AICPA, 1968).

The run manual documentation described above is an indispensable record of the EDP system. As a last resort, it might have to be used to reconstruct an entire system or subsystem if everything else is destroyed. The documentation library function thus is quite important. Measures should be in effect to avoid loss or destruction of the run manual by providing check-out requirements and additional copies in separate off-site storage.

Even more important and sensitive, however, are the input, program, and output files that are maintained on cards, magnetic tapes, disks, or other magnetic media. These media are particularly subject to damage or destruction by such elements as bending-folding-mutilating, dust, magnetic fields, temperature extremes and other conditions that can cause loss of data stored in the form of magnetic impulses. The auditor is interested in controls to prevent such losses because file destruction, either massive or minor, can cause great audit reliance problems concerning the valid reconstruction of records.

Some of the more important security and retention devices and methods are discussed below.

External labels are paper labels on the outside of a file (punched cards or magnetic tape reels). The label merely identifies the contents, such as "Accounts Receivable Master File," so that the probability of using the file inappropriately, for example in a payroll run, is minimized.

File protection rings are used to prevent writing over data on a magnetic tape. The ring has the appearance of a circular plastic gasket inserted in the center of a tape reel where the reel would be mounted on a tape drive. The ring must be attached to a tape reel before the computer can write on the tape. Of course, an operator could simply insert the ring, mount the tape, and write on it; but the purpose of the file protection ring is to prevent inadvertent, not intentional, data destruction.

Header and trailer labels are special parts of magnetic tapes and disks. They are magnetic impressions on the tape or disk, but instead of containing data, they hold label information similar to the external file label. Sometimes the header and trailer labels are called *internal labels*. Essentially their function is to serve as controls to prevent use of the wrong file during processing, so the header label will contain the name of the file and relevant identification codes. The trailer label gives a signal that the end of the tape has been reached, and sometimes these trailer labels are designed to contain accumulated control totals to serve as a check on loss of data during operation.

File security is enhanced by many physical devices such as storage in fireproof vaults, in remote locations, and in printed or microfilmed form. In the majority of cases the exposure to risk of loss warrants insurance on program and data files.

File retention practices are closely related to *file security*, but in general retention may provide the first line of defense against relatively minor loss

EXHIBIT 8–4
Grandfather, Father, and Son in Magnetic Tape Files

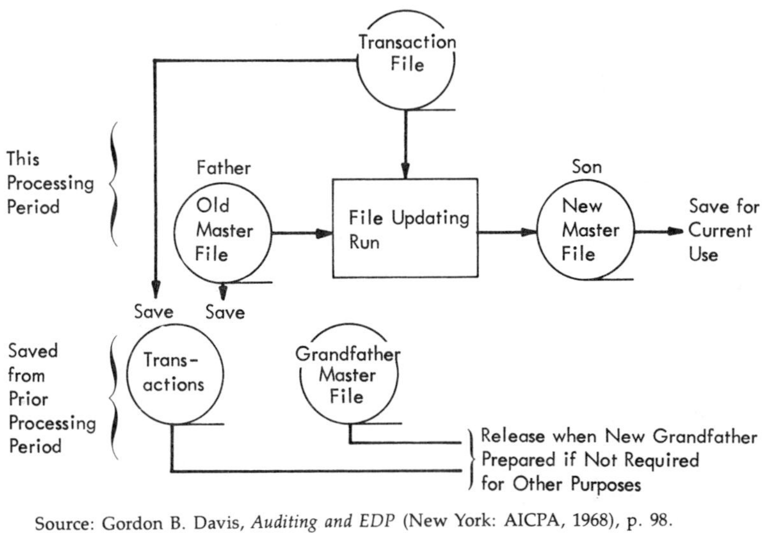

Source: Gordon B. Davis, *Auditing and EDP* (New York: AICPA, 1968), p. 98.

while security generally conceives of all measures taken to safeguard files against total loss. In essence the problem is one of how to reconstruct records and files once they have been damaged. One of the most popular methods is the "grandfather-father-son" concept. This concept involves the retention of backup files such as the current transaction file and the prior master file with which the current master file can be reconstructed. Exhibit 8–4 illustrates the file retention plan. Particularly important files may be retained to the great-grandfather generation if considered necessary.

Disk files are more difficult to reconstruct than tape files because the process of updating old records with new ones is "destructive." The old or superceded data on a record is removed ("destroyed") when new data is entered in the same place on a disk. One expensive means of reconstruction is to have a disk file "dumped" onto tape periodically (each day or each week). This file copy along with the related transaction file also retained can serve as the grandfather-father to the current disk file (son).

Some typical questionnaire items asked about file security and retention are shown in the box below.

SELECTED QUESTIONNAIRE ITEMS*

Physical Safeguards over Files

Are important computer programs, essential documentation, records, and files kept in fireproof storage?

Are copies of important programs, essential documentation, records, and files stored in off-premises locations?

Procedural Controls for Safeguarding Files

Are external labels used on all files?

Are internal labels used on all magnetic tape files?

Are file header labels checked by programs using the files?

Are file protection rings used on all magnetic tape files to be preserved?

Is the responsibility for issuing and storing magnetic tape or portable disk packs assigned to a tape librarian, either as a full-time or part-time duty?

Capability for File Reconstruction

Are there provisions for the use of alternative facilities in the event of fire or other lengthy interruption?

Is there data processing insurance (other than fire coverage)?

* Source: G. B. Davis, *Auditing and EDP* (New York: AICPA, 1968).

Hardware Controls

Modern computer equipment is highly reliable. Machine malfunctions that can go undetected are relatively rare. The auditor is not expected to be a computer systems engineer, but he or she should be familiar with some of the hardware controls so that they will not completely escape attention and so that the auditor can converse knowledgeably with EDP personnel.

The first such control that auditors should look for is the maintenance contract with the computer vendor. Then they should look for the record of regular maintenance work. If little or none is in evidence, they should have doubts about the complete reliability of the hardware and should consider consultation with a technical expert. Other general evidence may be obtained with a review of operating reports and computer downtime logs.

APPLICATION CONTROLS

Application control features are categorized as (1) input controls; (2) processing controls; and (3) output controls. Input control refers to the weakest link in EDP information systems—the point at which transaction data is transformed from hard-copy source documents into machine-readable cards or tape, or when direct entry is made with a communication device such as a teletype or remote terminal. When undetected errors are entered originally, they may not be detected during processing, and if detected, they are troublesome to correct. Processing control refers to error-condition check routines written into the computer program. These take a variety of forms. Output control refers primarily to control over the distribution of reports, but feedback on errors is also a part of this "last chance" control point.

Input Controls

According to *SAS No. 3* (Section 321.08), input controls are designed to provide reasonable assurance that data received for processing by EDP have been properly (1) authorized, (2) converted into machine-sensible form, and that (3) data have not been (*a*) lost, (*b*) suppressed, (*c*) added, (*d*) duplicated, or (*e*) otherwise improperly changed. These controls also apply to correction and resubmission of data initially rejected as erroneous. The following control areas are particularly important.

Only properly authorized and approved input should be accepted for processing by EDP. Authorization is usually a clerical (non-EDP) procedure involving a person's signature or stamp on a transaction document. However, some authorizations can be general (for example, a management policy of automatic approval for sales under $50), and some authorizations can be machine-controlled (for example, automatic production of a purchase order when an inventory item reaches a predetermined reorder point).

Code verification procedures should be used. Code numbers are often used in computer systems in lieu of customer names, vendor names, and so forth. One common type of code verification procedure is the calculation of a *check digit*. A check digit is an extra number, precisely calculated, that is tagged onto the end of a basic number, such as a customer number. The basic code with its check digit is sometimes called a self-checking number. An electronic device can be installed on a keypunch or the calculation can be programmed in an edit routine. The device or the program calculates the correct check digit and compares it to the one on the data input. When the digits do not match an error message should be printed out.[2]

Conversion of data into machine-sensible form is a source of many errors. Control procedures include the following:

- Key verification involves repunching the data on a verifying keypunch. When a datum is keyed differently the second time, the verifier machine locks (or cuts a notch in the card) and the operator can investigate the reason. Similar devices can be used on magnetic tape encoders. However, optical scanning equipment that "reads" hard copy does not have a rereading verification capability.
- Record counts are tallies of the number of transaction documents submitted for data conversion. The known number submitted can be compared to the count of records produced by the data conversion device (e.g., number of punched cards or count of magnetic tape entries coded). A count mismatch indicates a lost item or possibly one converted twice. Record counts are also used as *control totals* during processing and at the output stage—wherever the comparison of a known count can be made with a machine-generated count.
- Batch totals are used in the same way as record counts, except the batch total is the sum of some important amount (for example, the total sales dollars in a batch of invoices or the total payroll hours on time cards sent to the keypunch operator). Batch totals are also useful during processing and at the output stage.
- Hash totals are similar to batch totals, except the hash total is a sum not meaningful for accounting records (for example, the sum of all the invoice numbers on invoices submitted to the keypunch operator).

Various computer-programmed *editing routines* can be used to detect data conversion errors. Some of these are:

- Valid code tests to check codes against a control file of acceptable codes.

---

[2] One check digit algorithm is the "Modulus 11 Prime Number" method.

a. Begin with a basic code number: 814973.

b. Multiply consecutive prime number weights of 19, 17, 13, 7, 5, 3 to each digit in the basic code number

8	1	4	9	7	3
× 19	17	13	7	5	3

= 152 + 17 + 52 + 63 + 35 + 9 = 328

Note: the sequence of weights is the same for all codes in a given code system.

c. Add the result of the multiplication = 328.

d. Determine the next higher multiple of 11, which is 330.

e. Subtract the sum of the multiplication (330 − 328 = 2). This is the check digit.

f. New account number: 8149732.

Now if this number is entered incorrectly, say it is keypunched as 8419732, the check digit will not equal 2 and an error will be indicated. (Source: J. G. Burch, Jr., and F. R. Strater, Jr. *Information Systems: Theory and Practice*. Santa Barbara: Hamilton Publishing Co., 1974, p. 165.)

- Valid character tests to check data fields to see if they contain numbers where they are supposed to have numbers, and alphabetic letters where they are supposed to have letters.
- Valid sign tests check data fields for appropriate plus or minus signs.
- Missing data tests to check data fields to see if any are blank when they are not supposed to be blank.
- Sequence tests to check for numerical sequence of documents when sequence is important for processing. This edit procedure can also check for missing documents in a prenumbered series.
- Limit or reasonableness tests are very important. This is a computerized check to see whether data values exceed some predetermined limit. For example, a payroll application may have a limit test to flag for review any weekly time record of 50 hours or more or of 30 hours or less; or all sales over $5,000 may be flagged for a double-check of credit approval. The limit tests are a computerized version of *scanning*—the general audit procedure of reviewing data for indication of anything unusual which might turn out to be a data error.

Movement of data from one department to another or one processing program to another should be controlled. One useful control is *run-to-run* totals. "Run-to-run" refers to sequential processing operations—*runs*—on the same data. These totals are record counts, batch totals, and/or hash totals obtained at the end of one processing step that are compared to corresponding totals produced at the end of the next step.

Error correction and resubmission should be subject to review. Usually the EDP department itself is responsible only for correcting its own errors (keypunch errors, for example). Other kinds of errors should be referred to and handled by other persons. It is a good idea to have a control group or internal auditors review the contents of error reports and error logs in order to monitor the nature, disposition, and proper correction of rejected data. Unless properly supervised and monitored the error-correction process itself can become a source of data input error.

Some typical questionnaire items that may be asked during a review of input controls are shown in the box below. These questions should be asked about each kind of EDP application (e.g., payroll processing, sales invoice processing).

Processing Controls

According to *SAS No. 3* (Section 321.08), processing controls are designed to provide reasonable assurance that data processing has been performed as intended without any omission or double-counting of transactions. Many of the specific processing controls are the same as the input controls, but they are used in the actual processing phases rather than at the time input is prepared.

SELECTED QUESTIONNAIRE ITEMS*

Control over Input for an Application

Are there adequate controls over the creation of data and its conversion to machine-readable form?

a. Procedural controls.
b. Mechanical or visual verification.
c. Check digit.

Is there adequate control over transmittal and input of data to detect loss or nonprocessing? Note data field controlled.

Field

a. Financial control totals ______
b. Hash control totals ______
c. Document counts ______
d. Sequential numbering of input documents ______

Are the input control totals and run-to-run control totals for each application checked by someone other than the equipment operator? By whom? ______

Is input data adequately tested for validity, correctness, and sequence?

Fields Tested

a. Validity tests.
  (1) Valid code ______
  (2) Valid character ______
  (3) Valid sign ______
  (4) Missing data ______
b. Sequence.
c. Limit.
d. Reasonableness.
e. Other.

Control over Handling of Errors

Are all error corrections reviewed and approved by persons who are independent of the data processing department?

Does the program provide an adequate console printout of control information (console settings, control violations, operator intervention, and so on)?

Are there adequate controls over the process of identifying, correcting, and reprocessing data rejected by the program?

Inquire into handling of unmatched transactions (no master record corresponding to transaction record). Is it adequate?

* Source: G. B. Davis, *Auditing and EDP* (New York: AICPA, 1968).

Control totals—record counts, batch totals, hash totals, and run-to-run totals—should be produced during processing operations. These totals should be printed out, and someone should have responsibility for comparing and/or reconciling them to input totals or to totals from earlier processing runs. Loss or duplication of data may thus be detected.

File controls and operator controls should be used. External and internal labels are means of assuring that the proper files are used in applications. The systems software should produce a console log to identify operating personnel and instructions entered by the operator and to make a record of time and use statistics for application runs. These logs should be reviewed by supervisory personnel.

Limit and reasonableness tests should be programmed to assure that illogical conditions do not occur; for example, depreciating an asset below its cost, or calculating an inventory quantity less than zero. These conditions, and others considered important, should generate error reports for supervisory review. Other logic and edit checks such as the ones described earlier under the heading of input edit checks can also be used during processing.

Some typical questionnaire items that might be asked about processing controls are shown in the box below.

SELECTED QUESTIONNAIRE ITEMS*

Programmed Control over Processing

Are control totals used to check for completeness of processing? These may include trailer file labels, run-to-run totals, and so on.

Are programmed controls used to test processing of significant items? (e.g., limit and reasonableness test).

Control over Program and Data Files

Is there adequate up-to-date documentation for the application?

a. Application summary.
b. Run manuals.
c. Operator instructions.

Is test data documented and kept up to date?

Are controls over master file changes adequate?

a. Written request for change from outside data processing.
b. Register of all changes reviewed by initiating department.
c. Supervisory or other review of changes.

Are there adequate provisions for periodically checking master file contents?

a. Periodic printout and review.
b. Periodic test against physical count.

* Source: G. B. Davis, *Auditing and EDP* (New York: AICPA, 1968).

Output Controls

Output controls are the final check on the accuracy of the results of EDP processing. These controls should also be designed to assure that only authorized persons receive reports or have access to files produced by the system.

Control totals produced as output should be compared and/or reconciled to input control totals or totals produced during processing. An independent control group or the internal auditors should be responsible for the review of output control totals and investigation of differences.

Master file changes should be investigated in detail because an error can be pervasive; for example, changing product selling prices incorrectly can cause all sales to be priced wrong. Someone should test changes to original source documents for assurance that the data is correct.

Systems output should be distributed only to persons authorized to receive it. A distribution list should be maintained and used to deliver report copies. The number of copies produced should be restricted to the number needed.

Some typical questionnaire items that might be asked about output controls are shown below.

SELECTED QUESTIONNAIRE ITEMS*

Management or Audit Trail

Do the records or references adequately provide the means to:

a. Trace any transaction forward to a final total?
b. Trace any transaction back to the original source document or input?
c. Trace any final total back to the component transactions?

When ledgers (general or subsidiary) are maintained on computer media, does the system of processing provide:

a. An historical record of activity in the accounts?
b. A periodic trial balance of the accounts?

Are source documents retained for an adequate period of time in a manner which allows identification with related output records and documents?

* Source: G. B. Davis, *Auditing and EDP* (New York: AICPA, 1968).

Summary

Apparent weaknesses in any of the input, processing, and output controls are matters of concern for the auditor. However, absence of a control at the input stage may be offset by another control at later stages. For example, if check digits are not calculated when the input is prepared but are calculated and used during processing, the control is likely to be satisfactory and effective. Of course, it is usually more efficient to catch any errors early rather than late, but the control can still be considered reliable insofar as the accounting records and financial statements are concerned. Internal auditors, however, may be very interested in *when* controls are applied since they are concerned about the efficiency of EDP operations.

Material weaknesses in manual and EDP controls, however, become a part of the independent auditor's evaluation of internal accounting control. Input controls (or lack of them) may permit data to be lost or double-counted; poor processing control can permit accounting calculation, allocation, and classification errors to occur; poor output controls over distribution of reports and other output (e.g., negotiable checks) can be the source of errors and irregularities that could make financial statements materially misleading.

The auditor may use expertise and judgment, based on the findings from a review, including responses to questionnaire items like the ones shown in this chapter. Sample-based tests, using attribute sampling statistical methods, can also be used to gather evidence about how well (or how poorly) some of the controls actually operate. Some aspects of objective examination of EDP controls, however, must be performed with the computer.

COMPLIANCE TESTING OF EDP CONTROLS

With compliance tests auditors are interested in determining (1) whether necessary control procedures were performed, (2) how they were performed, and (3) by whom they were performed. Manual procedures are useful to a limited extent in examining records produced by the quality control group—error reports and documentation of error-correction procedures; in observing access security measures and library operations; and in vouching documentation of program changes and approvals. However, auditors quickly reach the point in the compliance testing of computer-based control where they have to utilize the computer to perform operations on data that cannot be viewed unaided. Thus a consideration of using the computer as an auditor's assistant is the next topic for study.

General Objective Approaches

A business processes real transaction data with a real system. In addition to these two realities an auditor may create simulated transaction data and a simulated system. In conjunction, the real and the simulated generate combinations that identify three general objective approaches as shown in Exhibit 8–5.

EXHIBIT 8–5
General Objective Approaches

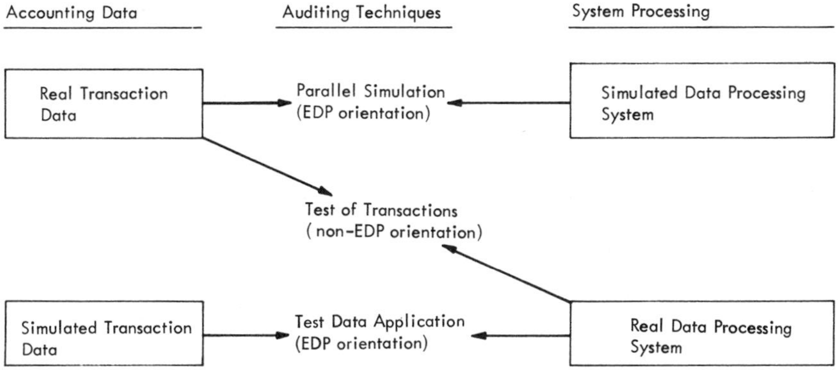

Attribute sampling can be applied to tests of the accuracy of keypunching operations or other methods of transforming data into machine-readable punched cards and magnetic tape. The application of *test data* and *parallel simulation* methodology are considered next as means of using the computer in the compliance tests of EDP controls.

Test Data

A *test deck* is a sample of one of each possible combination of data fields that may be processed through the real system. "Test deck" is a term that refers to the earliest days of computer system operation when all input was prepared on punched card media. The purpose of utilizing a test deck is to determine whether controls operate as indicated by questionnaire responses and/or program and program flowchart reviews. Today, of course, simulated test data can be on tape or disk as well as on punched cards, and they may be entered into an on-line system through computer terminals as well as through a card reader. Test transactions may consist of abstractions from real transactions and of simulated transactions generated by the auditor's imagination.

The greatest problem with utilization of test data is the auditor's imagination. Auditors must be very familiar with the nature of the business and the logic of the program in order to anticipate all data combinations that might exist as transaction input or which might be generated by processing, and they must be able to assign degrees of audit importance to each kind of error-checking control method. One pitfall in designing test data is the tendency to learn and to follow the real program logic too closely, thus losing perspective on some omitted error condition tests that are literally taken for granted not to occur. The following illustration is to the point:

Illustration. A test deck was designed to audit the exception-reporting provisions of an installment loan system of a commercial bank. The test deck verified that all edit features of the computer program were functioning as specified. However, a separate analysis uncovered the existence of a number of negative balances for accounts in the installment loan file—one in the amount of $30,000. In this case, since negative balances are improbable for installment loans, no tests had been built into the program (or into the test data) to report such situations. The auditor's utilization of the test data approach lacked the broad perspective necessary for an effective audit examination.[3]

Consider an example of the processing of sales transactions using the illustration that was begun earlier in Chapter 6. Assume that the punched card record layout for a sales invoice appears as in Exhibit 8–6.

Assume also that the objective of the test is to check the controls over accuracy of input data and controls over the same data as processing takes place. The problem is to assemble a set of transactions that includes all

[3] Adapted from W. C. Mair, "New Techniques in Computer Program Verification," *Tempo* (Touche Ross & Co., Winter 1971–72), p. 13.

EXHIBIT 8–6
Illustrative Punched Card Layout

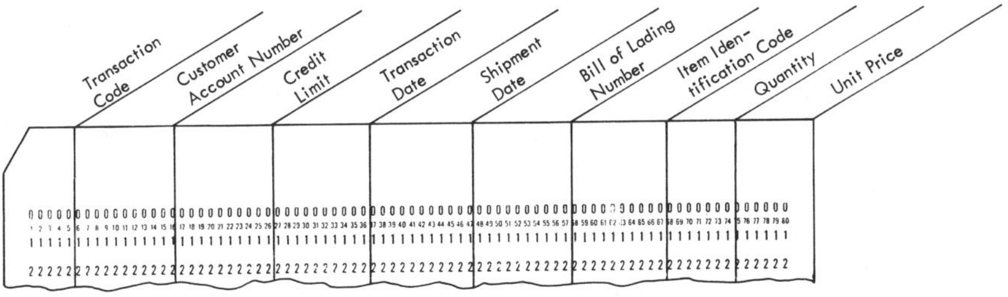

important error conditions in order to determine whether the input and processing controls can detect them.

For example, the auditor can create hypothetical transactions with the following conditions:

No customer code number.

Invalid customer code number.

Bill of lading document number not in field.

Sale amount greater than $5,000.

Sale amount equal to $5,000. (The system bases a limit test on $5,000.)

Sale amount equal to zero.

Sale amount less than zero.

These seven conditions generate many possible combinations of transactions. An exhibit of 15 of them is shown in a decision table presented with Exercise 8.11 (Exhibit 8.11–1) at the end of this chapter. Computerized "test data generators" are also available to help the auditor develop the simulated transactions. The auditor knows that transactions having no customer code number or bill of lading document number (missing data test), invalid customer code number (self-checking number test), sale amount greater than $5,000 (limit test), sale amount equal zero (missing data test) and sale amount less than zero (sign test) should produce error messages, and transactions with valid conditions should not. The auditor arranges to run these simulated transactions on the client's system and find out whether the controls operate.

Test data are used at one point in time on a client program that is supposed to have been used during the period under audit. Following the analysis of test output the auditor still has to make an inference about processing during the entire period. In order to do so the auditor must be satisfied by a review of documentation that any program changes have been revealed and that they are, or are not, significant. If changes are significant, the auditor may decide to duplicate the test for the data processed before the change. Some auditors occasionally perform test data procedures on a surprise basis at irregular intervals during the year.

Parallel Simulation

In parallel simulation, the auditor constructs a computer program which is designed to process real data in an accounting-adequate manner. This technique is actually a computer-utilizing method of auditing around the EDP system. With this method auditors have come full circle from ignoring the EDP system, to "auditing through the computer" with test data, to constructing a parallel simulated system to avoid direct testing of the actual system. The results of a parallel simulation can be compared to the real data processed by the real system. The concept of this method is illustrated in Exhibit 8–7.

EXHIBIT 8–7
System Concept of Parallel Simulation

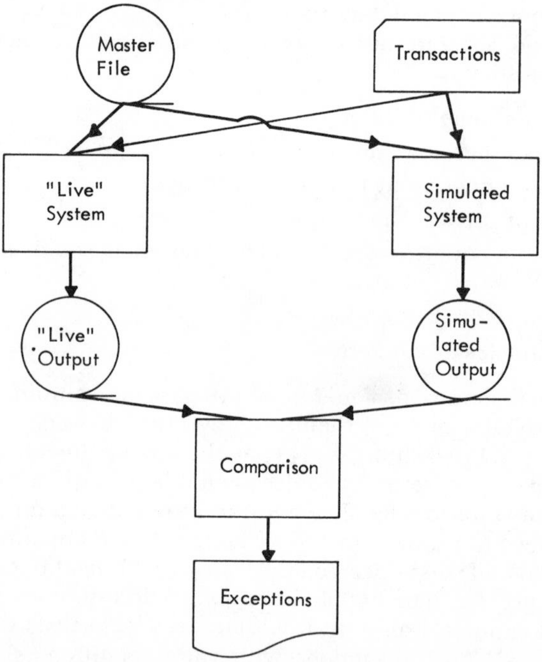

Source: W. C. Mair, "New Techniques in Computer Program Verification," *Tempo* (Touche Ross & Co., Winter 1971–72), p. 14.

Auditors have always had the options of (1) using the client's real program for tests, (2) having client personnel write special audit programs to perform tests, or (3) writing their own special audit programs. The first option requires test data utilization. The second option requires close supervision and testing. The third option requires significant programming expertise on the audit staff or close liaison with expert independent programmers.

With the advent in the mid-1960s of generalized audit software, however, the third option has become much more attractive. The generalized audit software programs developed by several organizations consist of numerous prepackaged subroutines that can perform most tasks needed in auditing and business applications. The user's programming task consists of writing simple instructions on preprinted specification forms that call up one or more of the subroutines. Thus there is no need to write complete complex programs, and the expertise to use the generalized software can be acquired in one week of training. (A closer examination of these programs and their capabilities is in Chapter 9.)

Using the generalized audit program capabilities an auditor can construct a system of data processing that will accept the same input as the real program, use the same files, and attempt to produce the same results. This simulated system will contain all the controls that the auditor believes appropriate, and in this respect the thought process is quite similar to the logic that goes into compilation of test data. The simulated-system outputs are then compared to the real system output for correspondence or difference, and at this point the audit evidence is similar to the evidence obtained by using test data with the real program. Conclusions can be reached about the error-detection capability of the real system.

The first audit application of parallel simulation may be very costly, although it will probably be more efficient than auditing without the computer or utilizing test data. Real economies are revealed, however, in subsequent audits of the same client, and a "model" simulated system may be used in other audit engagements.

The auditor must take care to determine that the real transactions selected for processing are "representative." Thus some exercise in random selection and identification of important transactions may be required in conjunction with parallel processing. The following illustration is based on the illustrative sales-accounts receivable system described in Exercise 6.11.

> ***Illustration.*** A simulation of a manufacturer's sales invoice and accounts receivable processing system revealed that invoices which showed no bill of lading or shipment reference were processed and charged to customers with a corresponding credit to sales. Further audit of the exceptions in the test sample showed that the real data processing program did not contain a missing data test and did not provide error messages for lack of shipping references. This finding led to (1) a more extensive test of attributes based on the sales invoice population with comparison to shipping documents and (2) a more extensive audit of accounts receivable for customers who were charged with such sales.

The ultimate goal of the methods of compliance testing is to reach a conclusion about the actual operation of controls in an EDP system. This conclusion allows the auditor to determine the reliability of the data processing system and provides the auditor with logical grounds for restricting or extending the scope of subsequent auditing procedures. This internal control decision is particularly crucial in EDP systems because subsequent audit work may be performed using magnetic files that are produced by the computerized information system. The data processing control over such files is important because their content is utilized in subsequent computer-assisted work.

Other Objective Testing Methods

Controlled reprocessing may be viewed as a type of parallel simulation. Once a client data processing program has been thoroughly tested and found adequate (using test data or by other methods), the auditor may obtain a copy of the program and retain it in his or her own files. With this controlled copy the auditor can run selected batches of the client's transactions and compare the output to the client's regular output. The procedure now is the same as parallel processing except that the program is a faithful copy of the client's production program.

Integrated test facility (ITF), the "minicompany" approach, is a technique used by the client's program maintenance personnel, but it can be used by auditors. It involves creating a dummy department or branch, complete with employees, customers, products, receivables, payables, and other accounts. The ITF has master file records, carefully coded (e.g., "99"), included among the real master file records. Simulated transactions (i.e., test data) are inserted along with real transactions and the same operating program(s) operate on both the test data and the real transactions. Since the auditor knows what the ITF output should be, he can review the actual results of processing (output reports, error reports) to determine whether the processing program is functioning properly. A great deal of care is required to use ITF because fictitious master file records, transactions, and account outputs are placed in the system and in the business records. The account amounts and other output data must be carefully reversed or adjusted out of the financial statements. Also, care must be taken not to damage or misstate any of the real master file records and account balances.

Systems control audit review file (SCARF) is a method in which the auditor has special limit, reasonableness or other edit tests built into the data processing programs. These tests produce reports of transactions selected according to the auditor's criteria, and the reports are delivered directly to the auditor for review and follow-up. The SCARF procedure is especially attractive to internal auditors, particularly when EDP systems developers do not want to incorporate the tests for the purpose of regular control review.

A sample audit review file (SARF) technique is similar to SCARF, except that instead of programming an auditor's test criteria a random sampling selection scheme is programmed. This produces a report of transactions which the auditor can review after each production run. The SARF method is efficient for producing representative samples of transactions processed over a period by EDP.

Snapshot is a special programmed technique that provides a report of the complete "audit trail" of selected transactions tagged with a special code. When the program is activated by the special code, each processing step within the production program for that transaction is printed out in a hard-copy report for audit review. The analogy to photography is very good because the auditor can "see" what happens to the transaction within the program. Snapshot can be very useful to systems development and programming personnel and may be used to advantage by internal and independent auditors.

The last four techniques—ITF, SCARF, SARF, and Snapshot—are not widely used by external auditors but have considerable potential for internal quality control personnel and internal auditors who have to monitor systems on a continuous basis. On the independent auditor's side, some persons have suggested audit involvement on a continuous basis. The SEC seems to lean toward heavier independent auditor involvement in a concept it calls the "auditor of record" and the Commission on Auditor's Responsibilities has suggested that a financial audit should be perceived as a process that is carried out throughout a time period rather than an engagement that is begun and ended in a few months each year. If these ideas gain headway, computer auditing techniques that lend themselves to "continuous auditing" may become more widely used by external auditors.

COMPUTER ABUSE

Computer fraud is a matter of concern for managers and investors as well as auditors. A more general term which includes computer fraud is *computer abuse*, which has been defined as follows:

> Any incident associated with computer technology in which a victim suffered or could have suffered loss and a perpetrator by intention made or could have made gain.[4]

This definition of computer abuse is broad enough to include such acts as intentional damage or destruction of a computer, use of the computer as a tool to assist in a fraud, and using the mystique of a computer to promote business. Computers have indeed been damaged by vandals, an abuse which is best prevented by physical security measures. The computer was used by perpetrators of the Equity Funding fraud to print thousands of fictious records and documents that would otherwise have occupied the time of hundreds of clerks. Some services (e.g., "computerized" dating services) have promoted business on the promise of using computers when none are actually used.

However, in a business environment, auditors are particularly concerned with acts of computer abuse that could result in theft or embezzlement of assets or material misstatements in published financial statements. In order to perpetrate abuses of these types, persons must have access to one or more of the following:

The computer itself,
Data files,

[4] Donn B. Parker, *Crime by Computer* (New York: Charles Scribner's Sons, 1976), p. 12.

Computer programs,
System information, and/or
Time and opportunity to convert assets to personal use.[5]

The most important preventive controls are those that limit access to computers, data files, programs and system documentation to the minimum number of persons needed to operate the EDP system for legitimate business purposes. Definition of duties, segregation of functional responsibilities, dual-person access, enforced vacations for computer personnel, physical security, and electronic security (e.g., access-code "passwords") are all methods of limiting access to computer resources.

Computer experts generally agree that an ingenious programmer can commit theft or misappropriation of assets which is difficult, if not impossible, to detect. Notwithstanding this situation, such abuses generally produce an unsupported debit balance in some account, although this is not always the case. For example, someone might manipulate the computer to cause purchased goods to be routed to his own warehouse. In this case the business inventory balances would probably be overstated. One bank employee caused checking account service charges to be credited to his own account instead of to the appropriate revenue account. In this case the service charge revenue account would be less than the sum of charges to the checking account customers. Thorough auditing of the accounting output records might result in detection of computer-assisted frauds such as these.

Non-EDP auditing methods, as well as some computer-assisted methods, may be employed to try to detect computer abuse. Direct confirmations with independent outside parties, analytical review of the output of the system for typical relationships, and comparison of output with independently maintained files may reveal errors and irregularities in EDP-produced accounting records. All too often auditors and managers, however, are surprised by computer abuses reported to them by consciousstriken participants, anonymous telephone messages, tragic suicides, or other random means. Nevertheless, auditors working in an EDP environment are expected to possess the expertise required to identify serious computer control weaknesses. When any such weaknesses are believed to exist, the best strategy is to use the services of a computer specialist to help plan and execute technical procedures for further study and evaluation of the computer control system.

BEYOND INTERNAL CONTROL

A proper study and evaluation of internal control may consume a significant portion of audit time and cost. However, after the internal control decisions are made, there remain the all-important tasks of gathering sufficient, competent evidential matter concerning events, important transactions, balances, amounts, and activities. To this point in the text very

---

[5] W. C. Mair, D. R. Wood, and K. W. Davis. *Computer Control and Audit* (Altamonte Springs, Fla.: The Institute of Internal Auditors, 1976, 1978) pp. 412–20.

little has been said about making final decisions on the fair presentation of financial statement numbers or about decisions on amounts and totals that reflect characteristics of operations. The next two chapters take up two pervasive tools for making such decisions. Chapter 9 covers the use of the computer to perform audit work and is placed in this sequence in order to maintain some continuity in the EDP topic begun in this chapter. Chapter 10 covers the use of statistical sampling applications for testing hypotheses and making decisions about dollar values.

SOURCES AND ADDITIONAL READING REFERENCES

Allen, Brandt. "The Biggest Computer Frauds: Lessons for CPAs," *Journal of Accountancy,* May 1977, pp. 52–63.

Auditing Standards Division. *Audits of Service-Center Produced Records,* especially chapter 2, "Evaluating Controls at Service Centers." New York: AICPA, 1974.

Burns, D. C., and Loebbecke, J. K. "Internal Control Evaluation: How the Computer Can Help," *Journal of Accountancy,* August 1975, pp. 60–70.

Cash, J. I., Jr.; Bailey, A. D., Jr.; and Whinston, A. B. "A Survey of Techniques for Auditing EDP-Based Accounting Information Systems," *Accounting Review,* October 1977, pp. 813–32.

Computer Services Executive Committee. *The Auditor's Study and Evaluation of Internal Control in EDP Systems.* New York: AICPA, 1977.

Davis, Gordon B. *Auditing and EDP*. New York: AICPA, 1968.

Equity Funding, Report of the Special Committee. New York: AICPA, 1975.

Jancura, E. G., and Drefs, J. A. "EDP Auditing Tips for Neophytes," *Internal Auditor,* April 1976, pp. 67–73.

Jancura, E. G., and Lilly, F. L. "SAS No. 3 and the Evaluation of Internal Control," *Journal of Accountancy,* March 1977, pp. 69–74.

Mair, W. C. "New Techniques in Computer Program Verification," *Tempo.* Touche Ross & Co., Winter 1971–72, pp. 10–19.

Mair, W. C.; Wood, D. R.; and Davis, K. W. *Computer Audit & Control.* Altamonte Springs, Fla.: The Institute of Internal Auditors, Inc., 1976, 1978.

Mason, J. O., and Connelly, W. E. "The Application and Reliability of the Self-Checking Digit Technique," *Management Advisor,* September/October 1971, pp. 27–34.

Mason, J. O., and Davies, J. J. "Legal Implications of EDP Deficiencies," *CPA Journal,* May 1977, pp. 21–24.

Newgarden, Albert, ed. *Computer Auditing in the Seventies,* special supplement *Arthur Young Journal,* Winter/Spring 1970.

Parker, Donn B. *Crime by Computer.* New York: Charles Scribner's Sons, 1976.

Porter, W. T., and Perry, W. E. *EDP: Controls and Auditing,* 2d ed. Belmont, Calif: Wadsworth Publishing Co., Inc., 1977.

Reneau, J. Hal. "Auditing in a Data Base Environment," *Journal of Accountancy,* December 1977, pp. 59–65.

Rittenberg, L. E., and Davis, G. B. "The Roles of Internal and External Auditors in Auditing EDP Systems," *Journal of Accountancy,* December 1977, pp. 51–58.

Romney, Marshall. "Fraud and EDP," *CPA Journal,* November 1976, pp. 23–28.

Schlegel, F. A. "A Test Data Generator," *Internal Auditor*, January–February 1976, pp. 80–86.

Stanford Research Institute. *Systems Control and Auditability: Control Practices Report and Audit Practices Report.* Altamonte Springs, Fla.: The Institute of Internal Auditors, Inc., 1977.

REVIEW QUESTIONS

8.1. Distinguish between auditing "through the computer" and auditing "with the computer."

8.2. What duties should be segregated within the EDP activity?

8.3. What is the difference between an external label and an internal label in magnetic file media?

8.4. What aspects of documentation, file security, and retention and control procedures are unique to EDP systems?

8.5. What does an auditor need to know about computer hardware controls?

8.6. What is a self-checking number? Can you give an example of one of your own?

8.7. What must an auditor know about application controls and their capability? Why?

8.8. What kind of work is involved in testing a system by *parallel simulation*?

8.9. Define an "audit trail." How might an EDP system audit trail differ from one in a manual system?

8.10. List five things to which a person must have access in order to commit a computer fraud.

EXERCISES AND PROBLEMS

8.11. This problem is a continuation of the fact situation presented in Exercise 6.11 at the end of Chapter 6. Additional requirements related to internal control tests in an EDP environment are given below. The conditions tested are illustrated in the form of a decision table. Requirement 6 below asks for a return to Exhibits 7.11–1 and 7.11–2 (in problems section at the end of Chapter 7) for final conclusions about internal control.

Required:

5. Prepare test data for testing EDP applications controls identified in the text. See Exhibit 8.11–1 for an illustrative set of simulated transactions. (For this illustrative exercise assume that the applications controls were believed to be reliable except that there was no missing data test on the bill of lading document data field.)
6. Complete the working papers, Exhibits 7.11–1 and 7.11–2, and make audit decisions about the reliability of the system; the nature, timing, and extent of subsequent audit procedures; and management letter recommendations for improving the system.

EXHIBIT 8.11–1

Kingston Company, Test Data Transactions: EDP Controls Tests (December 31, 1978)

	Test Data Transactions														
Conditions	(1)	(2)	(3)	(4)	(5)	(6)	(7)	(8)	(9)	(10)	(11)	(12)	(13)	(14)	(15)
Customer code number in field	*y*	*y*	*y*	*y*	*y*	*n*	*n*	*n*	*n*	*n*	*y*	*y*	*y*	*y*	*y*
Customer number is valid	*y*	*y*	*y*	*y*	*y*	*n*	*n*	*n*	*n*	*n*	*n*	*n*	*n*	*n*	*n*
Bill of lading document number in field	*y*	*n*	*n*	*n*	*n*	*y*	*n*	*n*	*n*	*n*	*y*	*n*	*n*	*n*	*n*
Sale amount 5,000	*n* 11,000	*n* 5,500	*n*	*y*	*y*	*n* 20,000	*n* 5,720	*n*	*y*	*y*	*n* 10,001	*n* 9,999	*n*	*y*	*y*
Sale amount = 5,000	*n*	*n*	*y*	*n*	*n*	*n*	*n*	*y*	*n*	*n*	*n*	*n*	*y*	*n*	*n*
Sale amount = 0	*n*	*n*	*n*	*y*	*n*	*n*	*n*	*n*	*y*	*n*	*n*	*n*	*n*	*y*	*n*
Sale amount < 0	*n*	*n*	*n*	*n*	*y* −100	*n*	*n*	*n*	*n*	*y* −5,000	*n*	*n*	*n*	*n*	*y* −1
Actions															
Error message ..	X	X		X	X	X	X	X	X	X	X	X	X	X	X
No error message			X												

Document count control total = 15.

Sale dollar batch control for test = $77,220 positive amounts
5,101 negative amounts
$72,119

y = valid condition.
n = invalid condition.

8.12. You have been engaged by Central Savings and Loan Association to audit its financial statements for the year ended December 31, 1978. The CPA who audited the financial statements at December 31, 1977 rendered an unqualified opinion.

In January 1978 the association installed an on-line real-time computer system. Each teller in the association's main office and seven branch offices has an on-line input-output terminal. Customers' mortgage payments and savings account deposits and withdrawals are recorded in a centralized computer data base from data input by the teller at the time of the transaction. The teller keys the proper account by account number and enters the information in the terminal keyboard to record the transaction. The accounting department at the main office has both batch processing and typewriter input-output devices. The computer is located at the main office.

Required:

You would expect the association to have certain internal controls in effect because an on-line real-time computer system is employed. List the internal controls which should be in effect solely because this system is employed, classifying them as:

a. Those controls pertaining to input of information.

b. All other types of computer controls. (AICPA adapted)

8.13. CPAs may audit "around" or "through" computers in the examination of the financial statements of clients who utilize computers to process accounting data.

Required:

a. Describe the auditing approach referred to as auditing "around" the computer.

b. Under what conditions does the CPA decide to audit "through" the computer instead of "around" the computer?

c. In auditing "through" the computer, the CPA may use a "test deck."

(1) What is a "test deck"?

(2) Why does the CPA use a "test deck"?

d. How can the CPA be satisfied that the computer program tapes presented to him or her are actually being used by the client to process its accounting data? (AICPA)

8.14. You are the senior accountant in charge of the annual audit of the Onward Manufacturing Corporation for the year ending December 31. The company is of medium size, having only 300 employees, but the payroll system work is performed by electronic data processing. The 300 employees are all union members paid by the hour at rates set forth in a union contract, a copy of which is furnished to you. Job and pay rate classifications are determined by joint union-management conference and a formal memorandum is placed in each employee's personnel file.

Every week, clock cards prepared and approved in the shop area are collected and transmitted to the payroll department. The total of labor hours is obtained on an adding machine and entered on each card. Batch and hash totals are obtained for the following: (1) last four digits of social security numbers and (2) labor hours. These data are keypunched onto cards and sent to the EDP department. The clock cards (with cost classification data) are sent to the cost-accounting department.

Payroll checks are written by the computer as follows: As each person's card is processed, the social security number is matched to a table (in internal memory) to obtain job classification and pay rate data, then the pay rate is multiplied by the number of hours and the check is printed. (Ignore payroll deductions for the following requirements.)

Required:

a. What audit procedures would you recommend to obtain evidence that payroll data are accurately totaled and transformed into machine-readable cards? What exception proportion might you expect? What upper limit of exception proportion might you tolerate? What "items" would you sample? What would be the size of your sample?

b. What audit procedures would you recommend to obtain evidence that persons' pay rates are appropriately assigned and used in figuring gross pay? In what way, if any, would these procedures be different if the gross pay were calculated by hand instead of on a computer?

8.15. *Part A:* The eight following items contain examples of internal control deficiencies observed by a CPA in his client's computer data processing system. For each of these conditions or situations, select from the list of control features or procedures given the one which, if properly utilized, would have been *most* useful in either preventing the error or in ensuring its immediate and prompt correction.

1. The night operator understood more about programming than anyone realized. Working through the console, the night operator made a change in a payroll program to alter the rate of pay for an accomplice in an operating department. The fraud was discovered accidentally after it had been going on for several months. The best control procedure would be—
   a. Review of console log for unauthorized intervention.
   b. Payroll review and distribution controls outside of data processing.
   c. Audit trail use of payroll journal output.
   d. Control total review.
2. A customer payment recorded legibly on the remittance advice as $13.01 was entered into the computer from punched cards as $1,301. The best control procedure would be—
   a. A limit test.
   b. A valid field test.
   c. Keypunch verification.
   d. A check digit.
3. A program for the analysis of sales provided questionable results, and data processing personnel were unable to explain how the program operated. The programmer who wrote the program no longer worked for the company. The best control procedure would be—
   a. A run manual.
   b. Operator instructions.
   c. Layouts.
   d. Assembly run checking.
4. Due to an unusual program error which had never happened before, the accounts receivable updating run did not process three transactions. The error was not noted by the operator because the operator was busy working on a card punch malfunction. There were control totals for the

file which were printed out. An examination of the console printout would have disclosed the error. The best control procedure would be—

a. An error message requiring operator response before processing continues.
b. Reconciliation of control totals by control clerk.
c. Internal audit review of console log.
d. Label checking by next computer program.

5. A new computer program to process accounts payable was unreliable and would not handle the most common exceptions. The best control procedure would be—
a. Test data.
b. Documentation.
c. An error report.
d. Assembly run error printouts.

6. A batch of cards was next to the computer waiting for processing. The personnel manager, showing some visitors through the installation, pulled a card from the batch to show the visitors what it looked like. Absentmindedly the card was put into the personnel manager's pocket rather than back into the batch. The missing card was not detected when the batch was processed. The best control procedure would be a—
a. Trailer label.
b. Transmittal control log.
c. Control total.
d. Missing data check.

7. An apparent error in input describing an inventory item received was referred to the originating department for correction. A week later the department complained that the inventory in question was incorrect. Data processing could not easily determine whether or not the item had been processed by the computer. The best control procedure would be—
a. Input edit checks.
b. Missing data validity check.
c. Transmittal control.
d. An error log.

8. The master inventory file, contained on a removable magnetic disk, was destroyed by a small fire next to the area where it was stored. The company had to take a special complete inventory in order to reestablish the file. The best control procedure would be—
a. Fire insurance.
b. Data processing insurance.
c. A copy of the disk.
d. Remote storage of a copy of the disk and the transactions since the disk was copied.

Part B: The eight following items contain examples of internal control deficiencies observed by a CPA in his client's computer data processing system. For each of these conditions or situations, select from a list of control features or procedures given the one which, if properly utilized, would have been most useful in either preventing the error or in ensuring its immediate detection and prompt correction.

1. The master file for inventory did not seem right. The file was printed out and many errors were found. The best control procedure would be—
a. Trailer label control totals.
b. A periodic test against physical count.

c. A parity check.
d. Limit tests.

2. The master payroll file on magnetic tape was inadvertently written on by another processing run. The best control procedure would be a—
   a. File protection ring.
   b. File destruction date on header label.
   c. Control figure.
   d. Trailer label check.
3. A weekly payroll check was issued to an hourly employee based on 98 hours worked instead of 38 hours. The timecard was slightly illegible and the number looked somewhat like 98. The best control procedure would be—
   a. A hash total.
   b. A code check.
   c. Desk checking.
   d. A limit test.
4. In preparing payroll checks, the computer omitted 24 of a total of 2,408 checks which should have been processed. The error was not detected until the foremen distributed the checks. The best control procedure would be—
   a. A parity check.
   b. A module N check.
   c. Control totals.
   d. Desk checking.
5. The magnetic tape containing accounts receivable transactions could not be located. A data processing supervisor said that it could have been put among the scratch tapes available for use in processing. The best control procedure would be a—
   a. Header label.
   b. Trailer label.
   c. External label.
   d. File protection ring.
6. A sales transaction document was coded with an invalid customer account code (7 digits rather than 8). The error was not detected until the updating run when it was found that there was no such account to which the transaction could be posted. The best control procedure would be—
   a. Parity checks.
   b. Keypunch verification.
   c. A hash total check.
   d. A check digit.
7. The operator, in mounting the magnetic tape containing the cash receipts for the processing run to update accounts receivable, mounted the receipts tape from the preceding rather than the current day. The error was not detected until after the processing run was completed. The best control procedure would be a—
   a. Header label check.
   b. Trailer label check.
   c. Parity check.
   d. Hash total check.
8. An expense report was prepared by the cost center. One executive questioned one of the amounts and asked for the source documents which

support the total. Data processing was not able to routinely do so. The best control procedure would be—

a. An error listing.
b. An audit trail.
c. Transmittal control.
d. Documentation. (AICPA)

8.16. At a meeting of the corporate audit committee, attended by the general manager of the products division and yourself, representing the internal audit department, the following dialogue took place:

Jones (committee chairman): Mr. Marks has suggested that the internal audit department conduct an audit of the products division computer activities.

Smith (general manager): I don't know much about the technicalities of computers, but the division has some of the best computer people in the company.

Jones: Do you know whether the internal controls protecting the system are satisfactory?

Smith: I suppose they are. No one has complained. What's so important about controls anyway, so long as the system works?

Jones turns to you and asks you to explain about EDP internal controls. Address your response to the following points:

a. State a principal objective of achieving control over
 (1) Input.
 (2) Processing.
 (3) Output.

b. Give at least three methods of achieving control over the following:
 (1) Source data.
 (2) Processing.
 (3) Output.

8.17. The audit of the financial statements of a client that utilizes the services of a computer for accounting functions compels the CPA to understand the operation of his client's electronic data processing (EDP) system.

Required:

a. The first requirement of an effective system of internal control is a satisfactory plan of organization. List the characteristics of a satisfactory plan of organization for an EDP department, including the relationship between the department and the rest of the organization.

b. An effective system of internal control also requires a sound system of records control of operations and transactions (source data and its flow) and of classification of data within the accounts. For an EDP system, these controls include input controls, processing controls, and output controls. List the characteristics of a satisfactory system of input controls. (Confine your comments to a batch-controlled system employing punched cards and to the steps that occur prior to the processing of the input cards in the computer.) (AICPA)

8.18. George Beemster, CPA, is examining the financial statements of the Louisville Sales Corporation, which recently installed an off-line electronic computer. The following comments have been extracted from Mr. Beemster's notes on computer operations and the processing and control of shipping notices and customer invoices:

To minimize inconvenience, Louisville converted without change its existing data processing system, which utilized tabulating equipment. The computer company supervised the conversion and has provided training to all computer department employees (except keypunch operators) in systems design, operations, and programming.

Each computer run is assigned to a specific employee, who is responsible for making program changes, running the program and answering questions. This procedure has the advantage of eliminating the need for records of computer operations because each employee is responsible for his or her own computer runs.

At least one computer department employee remains in the computer room during office hours, and only computer department employees have keys to the computer room.

System documentation consists of those materials furnished by the computer company—a set of record formats and program listings. These and the tape library are kept in a corner of the computer department.

The company considered the desirability of programmed controls but decided to retain the manual controls from its existing system.

Company products are shipped directly from public warehouses which forward shipping notices to general accounting. There a billing clerk enters the price of the item and accounts for the numerical sequence of shipping notices from each warehouse. The billing clerk also prepares daily adding machine tapes ("control tapes") of the units shipped and the unit prices.

Shipping notices and control tapes are forwarded to the computer department for keypunching and processing. Extensions are made on the computer. Output consists of invoices (in six copies) and a daily sales register. The daily sales register shows the aggregate totals of units shipped and unit prices which the computer operator compares to the control tapes.

All copies of the invoice are returned to the billing clerk. The clerk mails three copies to the customer, forwards one copy to the warehouse, maintains one copy in a numerical file, and retains one copy in an open invoice file that serves as a detail accounts receivable record.

Required:

Describe weaknesses in internal control over information and data flows and the procedures for processing shipping notices and customer invoices, and recommend improvements in these controls and processing procedures. Organize your answer sheets as follows:

Weakness	*Recommended Improvement*

(AICPA)

8.19. Roger Peters, CPA, has audited the financial statements of the Solt Manufacturing Company for several years and is making preliminary plans for the audit for the year ended June 30. This year, however, the company has installed and used an EDP system for processing a portion of its accounting data.

The following processing runs are made monthly:

1. Cash disbursements listed by check number.
2. Outstanding payables balances (alphabetized).
3. Purchase journals arranged by (*a*) account charged and (*b*) vendor.

Vouchers and supporting invoices, receiving reports and purchase order copies are filed by vendor code. Purchase orders and checks are filed numerically.

Company records as described above are maintained on magnetic tapes. All tapes are stored in a restricted area within the computer room. A grandfather-father-son policy is followed by retaining and safeguarding tape files.

Required:

a. Explain the grandfather-father-son policy. Describe how files could be reconstructed when this policy is used.

b. Discuss whether company policies for retaining and safeguarding the tape files provide adequate protection against losses of data. (AICPA adapted)

8.20. One way in which small enterprises can obtain the advantages of an EDP system without incurring large hardware, personnel, and programming costs is by use of a computer service center. Some typical characteristics of service centers are (1) data conversion is performed by either the user or the center, (2) the user delivers the input data to the center, (3) permanent (master) files are retained by the center, (4) record retention responsibility rests with the user, and (5) the service center usually retains only the records necessary for reconstruction of files in the event of loss, destruction, or significant error.

Required:

For each of the following six control categories shown below, list *two* applicable EDP controls which the auditor will look for in connection with a client who uses a computer service center for data processing. (Assume that data is converted by the service center.)

a. Control over data transmitted for processing.

b. Control over master file changes.

c. Control over error correction and resubmissions.

d. Control over output.

e. Adequate management inquiry trail.

f. Adequate protection and security.

8.21. The flowchart in Exhibit 8.21–1 depicts one part of an EDP system for *recording* of labor in a job order cost accounting system. The basic timekeeping tools are (1) the plastic employee badge, prepunched with identifying information; and (2) the job card, prepunched with the job number and other information about a particular job. A badge is assigned permanently to each employee, and the job cards follow the jobs. Additionally, there are *indirect* labor cards and other special cards located in racks adjacent to recording devices.

EXHIBIT 8.21–1

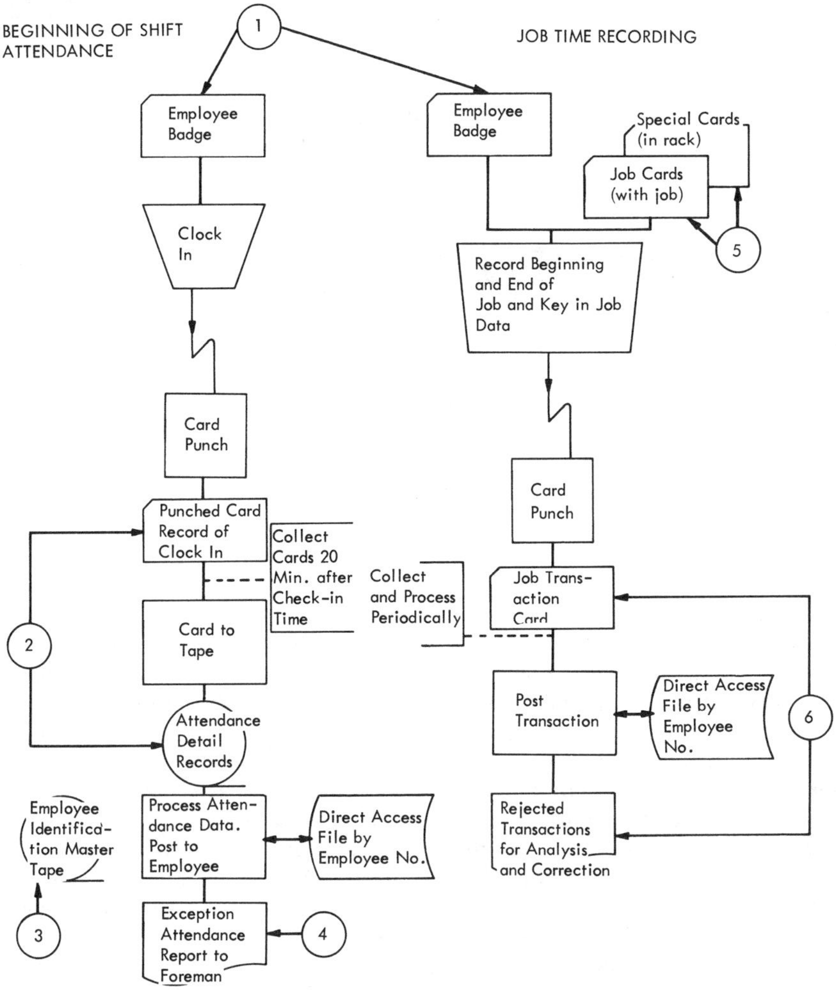

Required:

Each number on the flowchart locates a control point in the labor processing system. Make a list of the control points and for each point describe the corresponding internal control feature which is *most* appropriate.

8.22. Suppose that a credit sale was made to John Q. Smyth, customer account number 8149732. The last digit is a check digit calculated by the "Modulus 11 Prime Number" method. The keypunch operator made an error and punched the customer number as 8419732.

Required:

a. Calculate the check digit for the number that was keypunched.

b. How would the self-checking number control detect this data input error?

9

GENERALIZED AUDIT SOFTWARE

This chapter builds upon the computer-related concepts and terminology introduced in Chapter 8, but the emphasis is shifted from evaluation of internal control to techniques of using the computer to assist with gathering substantive evidential matter about transaction flows and account balances. In this chapter the technology of generalized audit software programs is explained in terms of a set of functions that may be utilized to read, compute, and operate on machine-readable records.

Auditors who deal with many different clients are in a peculiar position. They must be able to audit the output of a wide variety of data processing systems which may have a variety of technical characteristics. When clients' systems have common basic characteristics, the problem of differing systems is not a great one. These common basic characteristics would include the use of detailed general and special journals, files of paper hard-copy documents, and human-readable data in records and files. However, when EDP is utilized, the differing structure of files among clients and the fact that data cannot be read with the naked eye combine to create technical problems that require technical EDP-using solutions.

Two circumstances—voluminous data and machine-readable records—create the auditor's initial problems and the need to use computer capabilities to perform some audit procedures. Of course, an auditor could avoid these problems by requiring that the client print out in hard copy form all the required records and data files but to do so would be inadvisable because (1) the resultant manual-oriented audit would be inefficient in dealing with masses of printed records, probably to the point of lacking due audit care and (2) client goodwill would wither with the auditor's inability to work with a system designed for efficiency and effectiveness.

AUDITING WITH THE COMPUTER

It is important to realize that the techniques and methods previously introduced in Chapter 8 do not completely describe the range of computer-assisted auditing. In the previous chapter attention was focused on the general internal control features of EDP systems, concentrating on terminology, on the importance of input, processing and output controls, and on the use of test data, parallel simulation and other auditing tools (controlled reprocessing, ITF, SCARF, SARF, and Snapshot). All these topics were presented as having special relevance to decisions about internal control reliability as inputs to the planning of subsequent auditing work.

The audit problems following evaluation of internal accounting control in an EDP environment are to read the machine-readable detail records, to select samples of items for manual audit testing, to perform calculations and analyses of entire data files, and to produce hard-copy reports of the work performed. Auditors have utilized computer capabilities in three ways to solve these problems—with programs written by client personnel, with programs written by the auditor personally, and with the generalized audit software applied by the auditor.

Programs Written by the Client

Internal audit staffs or other client personnel may have created programs for special analytical or internal audit studies.[1] These programs may be for aging of accounts receivable, analysis of slow-moving inventory, variance analysis of labor costs, selection and printing of confirmations, and other similar applications.

If a client's computer audit programs are used, the independant auditor will have to study the program documentation and test the program in a manner similar to the study and evaluation of an original transaction-data processing program. Upon obtaining satisfaction that the program actually performs the operations as it is supposed to do, the auditor may proceed to use it to perform his or her own audit procedures.

Using client-prepared programs thus involves auditors in many procedures of evaluation and testing that are complex and time-consuming. Additionally, the auditor must possess EDP expertise in programming as well as in methods and techniques of testing computer programs.

Programs Written by the Auditor

One way to avoid the necessity of testing a client-prepared program is for auditors to write the program personally. Obviously this method

[1] In some circumstances an independent auditor may utilize the work and reports of the internal auditors. Refer to *SAS No. 9* (Section 322) "The Effect of an Internal Audit Function on the Scope of the Independent Auditor's Examination."

eliminates the need to audit the program, but it does not eliminate the processes of debugging and testing incidental to all programming tasks. Writing such a program enables auditors to tailor it to their specific needs, but it also requires full programming expertise.

Many large CPA firms and other audit organizations have special in-house EDP-audit task forces that can provide this expertise. Oftentimes a CPA firm will borrow management advisory services personnel to assist the audit staff. This approach has the advantages of superior control and specific tailoring capability, but it also has the disadvantages of being time-consuming and limited to a specific client. The third approach has both of these advantages and neither of the disadvantages.

Generalized Audit Software

Generalized audit software packages were developed by CPA firms in the mid-1960s for specific application to audit engagements. The essential advantages of a generalized audit software package are these:

Original programming is not required. The generalized software package consists of a set of preprogrammed editing, operating, and output subroutines.

The required programming is easy to do. A simple, limited set of programming instructions using preprinted specification forms are used to call up the subroutines in the package.

Training time is short. About one week of intensive training is sufficient to learn how to program using the specification forms.

For special-purpose analyses of data files, the generalized software is more efficient than special programs written from scratch because of the little time required for writing the instructions to call up the appropriate functions of the generalized software package. Also, the same software can be used on various clients' data bases. Control and specific tailoring are achieved through the auditor's own ability to program and operate the system.

A large number of generalized programs are currently available through CPA firms and consulting firms.[2] The explanations and illustrations given in this chapter are based on the system known as STRATA (System by Touche Ross for Audit Technical Assistance). Technical details about STRATA are presented in the Appendix at the end of the chapter.

GENERALIZED AUDIT SOFTWARE CAPABILITIES

In terms of the general audit procedures described in Chapter 5, the computer can perform the following tasks with application of generalized audit software subroutines:

1. *Recalculations* of numbers (e.g., depreciation) can be performed with the computer with more speed and accuracy than by hand. The com-

[2] For a list of these and their capabilities, see D. L. Adams, and J. F. Mullarkey, "A Survey of Audit Software," *Journal of Accountancy*, September 1972, pp. 39–66.

puter can recalculate all items, thus eliminating any need for a sample-based test.

2. *Confirmations* can be printed on forms ready for mailing. The process is one of using a high-speed printer and special paper forms to transcribe machine-readable records onto a confirmation letter. One such confirmation is shown in Exhibit 5–3.
3. *Analyses* of various ratio, trend, data population characteristics, and comparative amounts can be performed by the computer. Specific analyses may include:
   a. Stratification of populations for sample selection.
   b. Random selection of items for vouching, counting, or confirmation.
   c. Comparisons of budgeted, standard, and prior year data with current year data.
   d. Computation of operating ratios.
   e. Comparisons of audited data supplied by the auditor with unaudited data on file (e.g., inventory test counts of quantity may be merged with perpetual inventory records to produce an exception report.)
4. *Retracing* of transactions through calculation and classification operations can be done by the computer, although these tasks are generally associated with the evaluation of internal accounting controls.
5. *Scanning* with the computer is particularly powerful because the machine will not misinterpret or overlook items of interest. Relevant aspects of scanning include selection of unusual items for manual vouching (as specified by the auditor), identification of slow-moving inventory, overdue accounts, and other such items.

GENERALIZED AUDIT SOFTWARE LIMITATIONS

Notwithstanding the powers of the computer, several general auditing procedures are outside its reach. The computer cannot observe and count physical things (e.g., inventory), but it can compare numerous manmade counts to the records.

The computer cannot examine external and internal documentation, thus it cannot vouch accounting output to sources of basic evidence. (An exception would exist in an advanced EDP system that stored the basic source documents only on magnetic media. The auditor would have to test the controls over creation of the file but then would have no choice but to treat the file as a basic "document" source.)

In connection with vouching, however, computer-assisted selection of sample items is a great efficiency. Finally, the computer cannot conduct an inquiry in the limited sense that the inquiry procedure refers to questionnaires and conversations.

USING GENERALIZED AUDIT SOFTWARE

For the most part the widely used generalized audit software packages are very similar. Five primary steps carried out by auditors when using generalized software are explained below.

Define Audit Objectives

The first step in applying a generalized audit software package is to review the computer system and its applications to be audited. Based on this review, a plan is prepared which specifies audit test procedures most appropriate. Formulation of a plan depends upon the auditor acquiring a thorough understanding of the overall purpose and function of the application, especially noting the roles played by its various files. This may be accomplished by examining available documentation related to the application, such as systems flowcharts, systems narratives, file descriptions retention schedules, record layouts, and so forth. After the review is complete, the auditor should identify data elements to be tested, tests to be applied, and specific criteria to be used in evaluating the results.

As an example of an application, suppose the client keeps fixed asset records on a magnetic tape. This tape is called the *master* file. Each month a *transaction* file tape is created from cards punched with the information about the month's fixed asset transactions. The transaction file is then processed against the master file to *update* the master file, causing it to contain individual records of each fixed asset. The master file is the *data* file with which the auditor will work when applying generalized audit software. One fixed asset record on such a data file is illustrated in Exhibit 9A–5 in the Appendix to this chapter.

Specify Data Characteristics

The auditor's specification on preprinted forms of the client's data files, records and detail machine-readable fields on magnetic media describes the structure of the client's data base. This step is needed in order to set up the generalized software package to work on the particular client's data files. File organization, storage media, mode of access, and other technical characteristics are listed. Each data element is named, its size is specified, and its form (e.g., alphabetic, numeric, alphanumeric, binary) is defined.

In the fixed assets illustration shown in the Appendix at the end of this chapter, the auditor will identify the fixed asset data file by name and/or number. He or she will also specify the technical characteristics of the storage media (e.g., nine-track magnetic tape); give the access information (e.g., tape drive sequential access); and specify the data fields, their lengths, and technical forms. These specifications are made only for the data fields on the client's magnetic tape which the auditor will use. (An illustration form is shown in Exhibit 9A–4 of the Appendix.)

Specify Processing Steps

Most generalized audit software packages have an extensive repertoire of powerful instructions to facilitate processing of data files and preparing audit output. Using a processing specification form, the auditor defines the operations to be performed by the generalized audit software in terms of file access, file format representation, arithmetic and logical steps to be followed, statistical routines to be used and data file manipulations that may entail sequencing, consolidation, updating, or comparison operations.

Prepare Output Specification

Output is the end product of the application of generalized audit software. It can take three forms: printed tabulations, listings, or reports; confirmation statements; and machine-readable files (cards, tapes, or disks). The generalized audit software packages have a flexible capability to show spaces (e.g., single-space, double-space) and subtotals in the report specified by the auditor. An illustrative specification is shown in Exhibit 9A–9 in the Appendix.

Process the Data Base Using Generalized Audit Software and Evaluate the Results

The selected fields from the client's data file are processed in the computer according to the instructions prepared by the auditor. The auditor then reviews and evaluates the results. These instructions may involve scanning a file for unusual items, selecting a random sample for vouching, or calculating numbers that are meaningful in terms of audit evidence.

For example, with a fixed asset file the auditor may write instructions and obtain a report of (1) unusual items—all asset acquisitions of over $1,000 each in the year under audit, (2) a random sample of recorded assets so that someone can inspect them, and (3) depreciation recalculations of the depreciation previously calculated by the client.

GENERALIZED AUDIT SOFTWARE APPLICATION

When generalized audit software is applied in practice, the application typically constitutes a relatively small part of the total auditing effort. The computer cannot perform all the necessary evidence-gathering procedures, although its capabilities in dealing with voluminous machine-readable records are of great importance. Chapter 14 (Audit of Fixed Assets with EDP Applications) has been written to correspond with the examples given in Chapter 9 and the Appendix in order to illustrate further the role of the computer in auditing a specific account group. In the audit of fixed assets, the generalized audit software application is placed in the context of all the other procedures relevant for proper auditing.

SOURCES AND ADDITIONAL READING REFERENCES

Adams, D. L., and Mullarkey, J. F. "A Survey of Audit Software," *Journal of Accountancy*, September 1972, pp. 39–66.

Cash, J. I., Jr.; Bailey, A. D., Jr.; and Whinston, A. B. "A Survey of Techniques for Auditing EDP-Based Accounting Information Systems," *Accounting Review*, October 1977, pp. 813–32.

Computer Services Executive Committee. *Management, Control and Audit of Advanced EDP Systems.* New York: AICPA, 1977.

Dale, C. "The Systems Life-Cycle Approach to EDP Auditing," *The Internal Auditor,* April 1977, pp. 59–63.

Leishman, R. O. "The Computer as an Audit Tool," *The Internal Auditor,* January/February 1971.

McGuire, P. T. "EDP Auditing—Why? How? What?" *The Internal Auditor,* June 1977, pp. 27–34.

Mair, W. C.; Wood, D. R.; and Davis, K. W. *Computer Control & Audit.* Altamonte Springs, Fla.: The Institute of Internal Auditors, Inc., 1976, 1978.

Porter, W. T. "Generalized Computer-Audit Programs," *Journal of Accountancy,* January 1969, pp. 54–62.

Porter, W. T., and Perry, W. E. *EDP: Controls and Auditing,* 2d ed. Belmont, Calif.: Wadsworth Publishing Co., Inc., 1977.

Reid, G. F., and Demiak, J. A. "EDP Implementation with General Purpose Software," *Journal of Accountancy,* July 1971, pp. 35–46.

Samson, T. F. "Computer Auditing," *The Arthur Young Journal,* Autumn/Winter 1972–73 special edition, pp. 26–34.

Wagner, J. W. "EDP and the Auditor of the 1970s," *Accounting Review,* July 1969, pp. 600–604.

Weber, R. "The Demise of Generalized Audit Software Packages," *Journal of Accountancy,* November 1974, pp. 46–48.

REVIEW QUESTIONS

9.1. What is a generalized audit software package?

9.2. What advantages are derived from using generalized software to perform recalculations and confirmations?

9.3. Give examples of analyses which might be performed by generalized audit software.

9.4. Explain the *create* function. (Refer to the Appendix.)

9.5. Explain what is meant by (*a*) work record layout, (*b*) data file definition, and (*c*) data field selection. (Refer to the Appendix.)

9.6. Explain what is meant by each of the following functions: (*a*) update, (*b*) summarize, (*c*) sort, and (*d*) calculate. (Refer to the Appendix.)

EXERCISES AND PROBLEMS

9.7. You have been assigned to create a *work file* for inventory observation work and to find obsolete and slow-moving inventory items. Information in the *work file* should be sufficient to allow you to verify quantities observed and review stock movement for the year *in relation to quantity on hand.*
The manager on the engagement has suggested the following criteria for including data on the *work file:*

1. All items with current inventory value of $1,000 or more should be selected for *observation.*
2. All items with total cost balance over $500 *and* turnover for the year of two times or less should be selected for *obsolescence review.*

Description of the data file:

Control field (part number and location).
Description of inventory item.
Quantity—prior month-end.
Current month purchases.
Current month issues.
Current month adjustment (purchases minus issues).
Unit price.
Date of last purchase.
Vendor code.
Date of last issue.
Quantity issued year to date.
Quantity issued last year.

Required: (Refer to the Appendix at the end of this chapter.)

a. Copy the description of the data file shown above. After each field which is necessary for your *observation* of inventory, place an O. After each field which is necessary for your *obsolescence review,* place a T.

b. Describe how data fields and functions (e.g., merge, sort, calculate) are used to insure that each item over $1,000 is selected for *observation*. Identify which generalized computer audit *procedure* is being used for each operation you perform.

c. Describe how data fields and functions are used to insure that each item with a value over $500 *and* a turnover for the year of two times or less is selected for obsolescence review. Identify which generalized computer audit *procedure* is being used for each operation you perform.

9.8. Your audit assignment is the testing of depreciation expense in connection with the annual audit of Weaver Wool Company. Your plan to use generalized audit software to prepare a *work file* which contains information enabling you to identify each asset for which your recalculated depreciation expense differs from the client's depreciation expense by over $100. Additionally, you wish to determine whether total depreciation expense calculated by you does not differ by more than 2 percent from the total amount calculated by Weaver.

You have obtained the additional information shown below:

1. Depreciation is all *straight line* with 10 percent salvage value.
2. Management's policy is that a full year's depreciation is taken in the year of acquisition, and no depreciation is taken in the year of disposition.
3. Description of data file for all depreciable assets:

   Control field (serial number and location code).
   Cost.
   Use code.*
   Description.

---

* Note: Use codes are:
A—Weaving equipment.
B—Maintenance equipment.
C—Buildings.
F—Asset no longer in use (disposed or held for sale).

Vendor code.
Date of last repair.
Salvage value.
Repair expense for year.
Useful life.
Accumulated depreciation to date.
Date of last inventory.
Cumulative repair expense.
Date acquired.
Depreciation expense—current year.

Required: (Refer to the Appendix.)

a. List the data fields which contain information you would probably include in your *work file*.

b. Using your *work file*, state the operations you would perform to test the calculation of depreciation expense (and select items for further investigation).

9.9. Roger Peters, CPA, has examined the financial statements of the Munro Manufacturing Company for several years and is making preliminary plans for the audit for the year ended June 30. During this examination Mr. Peters plans to use a set of generalized computer audit programs. Munro's EDP manager has agreed to prepare special tapes of data from company records for the CPA's use with the generalized programs.

The following information is applicable to Mr. Peters's examination of Munro's accounts payable and related procedures:

1. The formats of pertinent tapes are shown in Exhibit 9.9–1.
2. The following monthly runs are prepared:
   a. Cash disbursements by check number.
   b. Outstanding payables.
   c. Purchase journals arranged (1) by account charged and (2) by vendor.
3. Vouchers and supporting invoices, receiving reports and purchase order copies are filed by vendor code. Purchase orders and checks are filed numerically.
4. Company records are maintained on magnetic tapes. All tapes are stored in a restricted area within the computer room. A grandfather-father-son policy is followed for retaining and safeguarding tape files.

Required:

a. Describe the controls that the CPA should maintain over:
   (1) Preparing the special tape.
   (2) Processing the special tape with the generalized computer audit programs.

b. Prepare a schedule for the EDP manager outlining the data that should be included on the special tape for the CPA's examination of accounts payable and related procedures. This schedule should show the:
   (1) Client tape from which the item should be extracted.
   (2) Name of the item of data. (AICPA adapted)

EXHIBIT 9.9–1

Master File—Vendor Name

Vendor Code	Recd Type	Space	Blank	Vendor Name	Blank	Card Code 10

Master File-Vendor Address

Vendor Code	Recd Type	Space	Blank	Address—Line 1	Address—Line 2	Address—Line 3	Blank	Card Code 120

Transaction File—Expense Detail

Vendor Code	Recd Type	Voucher Number	Blank	Batch	Voucher Number	Voucher Date	Vendor Code	Invoice Date	Due Date	Invoice Number	Purchase Order Number	Debit Account	Prd Type	Product Code	Blank	Amount	Quantity	Card Code 160

Transaction File—Payment Detail

Vendor Code	Recd Type	Voucher Number	Blank	Batch	Voucher Number	Voucher Date	Vendor Code	Invoice Date	Due Date	Invoice Number	Purchase Order Number	Check Number	Check Date	Blank	Amount	Blank	Card Code 170

9.10. You are using generalized audit software to prepare accounts receivable confirmations during the annual audit of the Eastern Sunrise Services Club. The company has the following data files:

Master file—debtor credit record.

Master file—debtor name and address.

Master file—account detail.

Ledger number.

Sales code.

Customer account number.

Date of last billing.

Balance (gross).

Discount available to customer (memo account only).*

Date of last purchase.

Required:

List the information from the *data files* shown above that you would include on the confirmation requests. Identify the file from which the information can be obtained.

9.11. You are supervising the audit field work of Sparta Springs Company and need certain information from Sparta's fixed asset records which are maintained on magnetic tape. The particular information is: (1) Net book value of assets, so that your assistant can reconcile the subsidiary ledger to the general ledger control accounts. The general ledger contains an account for each asset *type* at each plant *location*, and (2) sufficient data to enable your assistant to find and inspect selected assets.

Description of data file:

Asset number.

Description.

Asset type.

Location code.

Year acquired.

Cost.

Accumulated depreciation, end of year (includes accumulated depreciation at the beginning of the year plus depreciation year to date).

Depreciation for year to date.

Useful life.

Required:

a. List the information from the data file described above needed to verify correspondence of the subsidiary detail records with the general ledger accounts. Does this work complete the audit of fixed assets?

b. What additional data is needed to enable your assistant to inspect the assets?

9.12. A CPA's client, Boos & Backer, Inc., is a medium-sized manufacturer of products for the leisure time activities market (camping equipment, scuba

* The discount field represents the amount of discount available to the customer if the customer pays within 30 days of the invoicing date. The discount field is cleared for expired amounts during the daily updating, and you have determined that this is properly executed.

gear, bows and arrows, and the like). During the past year a computer system was installed, and inventory records of finished goods and parts were converted to computer processing. The inventory master file is maintained on a disk. Each record of the file contains the following information:

Item or part number.
Description.
Size.
Unit of measure code.
Quantity on hand.
Cost per unit.
Total value of inventory on hand at cost.
Date of last sale or usage.
Quantity used or sold this year.
Economic order quantity.
Code number of major vendor.
Code number of secondary vendor.

In preparation for year-end inventory the client has two identical sets of preprinted inventory count cards. One set is for the client's inventory counts, and the other is for the CPA's use to make audit test counts. The following information has been keypunched into the cards and interpreted (printed out) on their face:

Item or part number.
Description.
Size.
Unit of measure code.

In taking the year-end inventory, the client's personnel will write the actual counted quantity on the face of each card. When all counts are complete, the counted quantity will be keypunched into the cards. The cards will be processed against the disk file, and quantity-on-hand figures will be adjusted to reflect the actual count. A computer listing will be prepared to show any missing inventory count cards and all quantity adjustments of more than $100 in value. These items will be investigated by client personnel, and all required adjustments will be made. When adjustments have been completed, the final year-end balances will be computed and posted to the general ledger.

The CPA has available a general-purpose computer audit software package that will run on the client's computer and can process both card and disk files.

Required:

a. In general and without regard to the facts above, discuss the nature of general-purpose computer audit software packages and list the various types and uses of such packages.

b. List and describe at least five ways a general-purpose computer audit software package can be used to assist in all aspects of the audit of the inventory of Boos & Backer, Inc. (For example, the package can be used to read the disk inventory master file and list items and parts with a high unit cost or total value. Such items can be included in the test counts to increase the dollar coverage of the audit verification.) (AICPA adapted)

APPENDIX 9–A

The STRATA Generalized Audit Software System

An introductory explanation of the STRATA system is given in Exhibit 9A–1. Exhibit 9A–2 shows the STRATA processing cycle.

EXHIBIT 9A–1

INTRODUCTION TO STRATA

Touche Ross has developed a group of computer programs which allow a large number of data processing requirements to be satisfied without additional programming. These programs make up the system called STRATA, designed to run on an IBM 360 or 370. STRATA allows a nonprogrammer to work with information from any number of existing computer files. This information can be sorted, summarized, and manipulated as desired, and printed reports can be produced on an exception basis.

STRATA was originally developed to provide a means of examining and testing a company's computer files in conjunction with an audit of the company. In order to meet the wide variety of audit applications, it was necessary that the STRATA programs be generalized, much like the software provided by computer equipment manufacturers to support their hardware. An additional design requirement was that STRATA be fully usable by auditors without the assistance of programmers or other computer technicians. As a result of these design constraints, STRATA is extremely easy to use; yet it satisfies a wide variety of needs, not only of a company's auditors, but also of its management.

The user of STRATA need only complete a few specification forms defining the functions he requires and submit these forms for keypunching. (Note: Due to differences between IBM's DOS and O/S operating systems, there are a few STRATA forms which have separate DOS and O/S versions.) The punched cards are then processed on the computer by the STRATA diagnostic routine. As the cards are read, a diagnostic report is produced which is a printed interpretation of the operations to be performed. The diagnostic report also identifies any errors in the specifications which would prevent successful execution of the required functions. When the cards are error-free, the STRATA diagnostic routine automatically calls upon other STRATA routines to execute the specified functions.

The heart of the STRATA system is the WORK record concept. STRATA does not operate directly upon the user's input files (known as DATA files to STRATA). Instead STRATA creates new records in computer core storage from records on the DATA file. These new records contain only the information from the DATA fields which are necessary for the STRATA application. These new records are known as WORK records. The user does not have to be concerned with the handling of these WORK files, but he does have to describe the format of the WORK record.

The executive phase performs all of the user-specified STRATA functions except sorts which utilize standard IBM sort routines. All processing routines utilize a WORK record: the create and update functions move data from input records into the WORK record; the summarize routine produces a single WORK record with accumulations from several WORK records; calculation and selection steps act on fields of the WORK record; and detail lines of reports come only from WORK records.

Source: Touche Ross & Co., "An Introduction for Users of STRATA," rev. ed. (November 15, 1973), pp. 3–4.

EXHIBIT 9A–2
The STRATA Processing Cycle

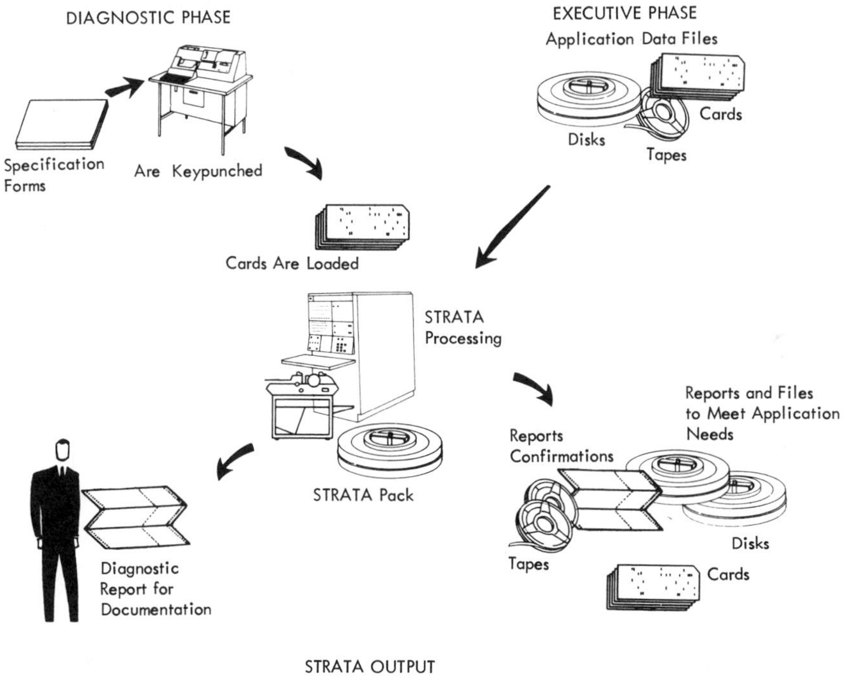

Source: Touche Ross & Co., "An Introduction for Users of STRATA," rev. ed. (November 15, 1973), p. 12.

STRATA FUNCTIONS

Each of the functions of STRATA is described and explained below. Examples relating to the audit of fixed assets are also given in order to provide some illustrative context to the rather abstract functions.

Diagnostic Phase

The first phase of a STRATA application is the auditor's analysis and debugging operations of his or her own programmed instructions. Preprogrammed diagnostic routines review the auditor's instructions for proper format and logic errors. Errors are identified and printed in a report. When errors have been corrected and the application is ready, the diagnostic routines will produce flowcharts and reports of instructions, fields, and files for working paper documentation.

Create Function

The major problem that stimulated production of *generalized* audit software packages was the fact that no two clients used exactly the same equipment configurations or designed identical data-storage formats for their files. The *create* function is a reading operation with which STRATA reads the basic *data file* (having been programmed as to the description, location, and format of data) and stores relevant data for a *work file* (having been programmed as to the field location and format). Auditors can select from the data file those fields that will be used (e.g., acquisition cost) and can omit from the work file data fields that will not be used (e.g., the GNP implicit deflator index at the date of acquisition). After the work file is created, the client's data file may be returned and all other operations may be performed using the work file contents. Thus it is very important to be able to identify audit-relevant data at the beginning.

The creation of a work file is accomplished by instructions written on four specification forms:

The *general systems specification* form contains the location of the input data file, the location of the output work file, and the media (e.g., magnetic tape, disk) on which the work file is to be written.

The *work record layout* form (Exhibit 9A–3) specifies the name, location, and technical description of the fields that the auditor will use.

The *data file definition* form specifies the data file name and its technical characteristics.

The *data field selection* form (Exhibit 9A–4) specifies the technical characteristics of the client's data fields and which work field they will fill.

The specification forms in Exhibit 9A–3 and Exhibit 9A–4 are filled out properly to build the work file shown in Exhibit 9A–5.*

Update (Merge) Function

The update function refers to the process of adding to a work file data that are contained in a second data file (other than the one used to create the work file). This operation makes it possible to assemble more information on one work file than is found in a single data file. The example illustrated in Exhibit 9A–6 is based on the assumption that a separate insurance data file contains a field for asset identification number that corresponds to the asset identification number on the property data file. After the update run, the updated property work file contains all asset identification numbers for insured property that is on the work file, but uninsured property will have a blank field in work field W15 (see Exhibit 9A–5).

Summarize Function

The summarizing operation enables the auditor to condense some multiple-transaction and multiple-record data into a single summary rec-

* Explanations of some technical data shown on the forms are not given in this text because they are not necessary for an understanding of the general capabilities of the system.

EXHIBIT 9A–3
Work Record Layout Specification Illustration

TOUCHE ROSS
STRATA 360

WORK RECORD LAYOUT

DOS OR O/S – SEE REVERSE FOR CONTINUATION

Sequence Number: W F 0 2 (1–4); 1 (5)

1. *WORK* TOTAL FIELD — W 0 5 (6–8)
   Enter numeric non-indicative *WORK* field for pass control totals – for DOS or O/S
2. EXTANT *WORK* FILE IDENTIFICATION (1)
   A. RECORD SIZE – ENTER FOR DOS or O/S (9–11)
   B. If DOS, ENTER DOS FILE LABEL — Version No. (12), Run No. (16), Application Heading (20–28)
   – – or – –
   IF O/S, ENTER O/S DATA SET NAME — T R Ø S (12) Version No. (16) . R Run No. (20) . W WF# (28)
   C. O/S Only — STRATA File Code (6) (29–30); Unit JCL Parameter (31–38); Work File Vol. Ser. No. (39–44); Tape Den. Parameter (45); 7 Track TRTCH (46–47)
3. O/S Only–Enter maximum number of work records (48–54)
4. *WORK* FIELD CHARACTERISTICS

5	*WORK* FIELD NUMBER (6–8)	*WORK* FIELD NAME (2) (9–22)	STORAGE FORMAT (3) ALPHA-NUMERIC LENGTH (23–25)	NUMERIC (4) Decimal Places (26)	NUMERIC (4) Indicative Y - Yes (27)	REDEFINITION (5) STARTING WORK FIELD (28–30)	REDEFINITION (5) STARTING LOCATION (31–33)	DO NOT PUNCH	Do Not Punch LEFT MOST BYTE LOCATION Memo Only
2	W 0 1	ASSET NUMBER	10						
2	W 0 2	DESCRIPTION	15						
2	W 0 3	CLASS CODE	2						
2	W 0 4	DATE ACQUIRED	5						
2	W 0 5	COST		2					
2	W 0 6	ACCUM DEPRC		2					
2	W 0 7	CURR DEPRC EXP		2					
2	W 0 8	DEPRC METHOD	3						
2	W 0 9	USEFUL LIFE	3						
2	W 1 0	SALVAGE VALUE		2					
2	W 1 1	STATUS CODE	1						
2	W 1 2	VENDOR IDENT	2						
2	W 1 3	BUDGET		0					
2	W 1 4	DEPRC AUDIT		2					
2	W 1 5	INSURANCE NO	15						
2	W 1 6	OBSERV ASSET #	10						
2	W 1 7	OBSERV CLASS	2						
2	W 1 8	OBSERV STATUS							
2	W 9								
2	W 0								
2	W 1								
2	W 2								
2	W 3								
2	W 4								
2	W 5								
2	W 6								
2	W 7								
2	W 8								
2	W 9								
2	W 0								

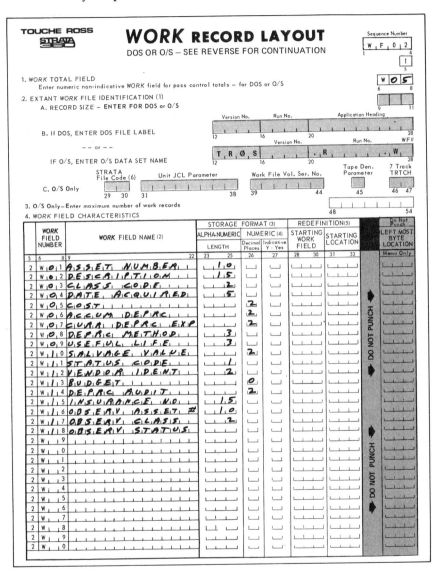

EXHIBIT 9A–4
Data Field Selection Specification Illustration

TOUCHE ROSS STRATA

DATA FIELD SELECTION

FIXED SECTION OR REPEATING SECTION
(See Reverse for Continuation)

F or R — Sequence Number: F S 0 5 (1–4)

1 (5)

1. RECORD ID's TO BE SELECTED.
Enter right justified 1 to 3 Record-ID specifications.
All criteria must be met for a record to be selected.

	RECORD-ID Location (1)	Length	Format	Criteria	SELECTION Value
ID 1	6–9	10	11	12–13	14–18
ID 2	19–22	23	24	25–26	27–31
ID 3	32–35	36	37	38–39	40–44

2. DESCRIPTION OF REPEATING SECTION – **ENTER ONLY WHEN USING FORM FOR REPEATING SECTIONS**

Location (Number of Bytes preceeding left most byte) of first repeating section of record.	Length of the record section that is repeated.	Maximum number of repeating sections.
45–48	49–52	53–55

3. ***DATA*** **FIELD DEFINITION**

5	LOCATION (1) OF *DATA* FIELD (6–9)	SIZE OF *DATA* FIELD (10–12)	FORMAT (2) (13)	DECIMAL PLACES IN NUMERIC FIELDS (14)	*DATA* FIELD NAME (3) ALPHA-NUMERIC CONSTANT (15) / NUMERIC CONSTANT (21–28)	RECEIVING *WORK* FIELD (4) (29–31)
2	0	10	C		ASSET NUMBER	W01
2	10	15	C		DESCRIPTION	W02
2	25	2	C		CLASS CODE	W03
2	27	5	C		DATE ACQUIRED	W04
2	35	5	P	2	COST	W05
2	40	5	P	2	ACCUM DEPRC	W06
2	45	5	P	2	CURR DEPRC EXP	W07
2	50	3	C		DEPRC METHOD	W08
2	53	3	C		USEFUL LIFE	W09
2	56	4	P	2	SALVAGE VALUE	W10
2	60	1	C		STATUS CODE	W11
2	61	2	C		VENDOR IDENT	W12
2	63	4	P		BUDGET	W13
2						W
2						W
2						W
2						W
2						W
2						W
2						W
2						W
2						W
2						W
2						W
2						W
2						W

(1) Number of bytes preceeding the left-most byte of the ***DATA*** field.

(2) C for character
B for binary
P for packed (signed)
L for constant
U for unsigned packed
R for unsigned packed right
X for unsigned packed left
A for unsigned packed all
H for addressing bits
V for variable length fields preceded by 1 byte
D for variable length fields preceded by 2 bytes
*Do not use on RS

(3) Constants can be entered into a ***WORK*** field, by entering constant value here. Alpha Numeric Constant will be moved to work field from left, and Numeric Constant from right.

(4) Do not specify a numeric indicative *WORK* field as the receiving WORK field for more than one DATA field. Indicative fields are not summarized.

(5) If using more than one FSnn sheet to describe one *DATA* record the FSnn sequence numbers on each sheet are to be the same.

EXHIBIT 9A–5
Creation of Work File from Data File

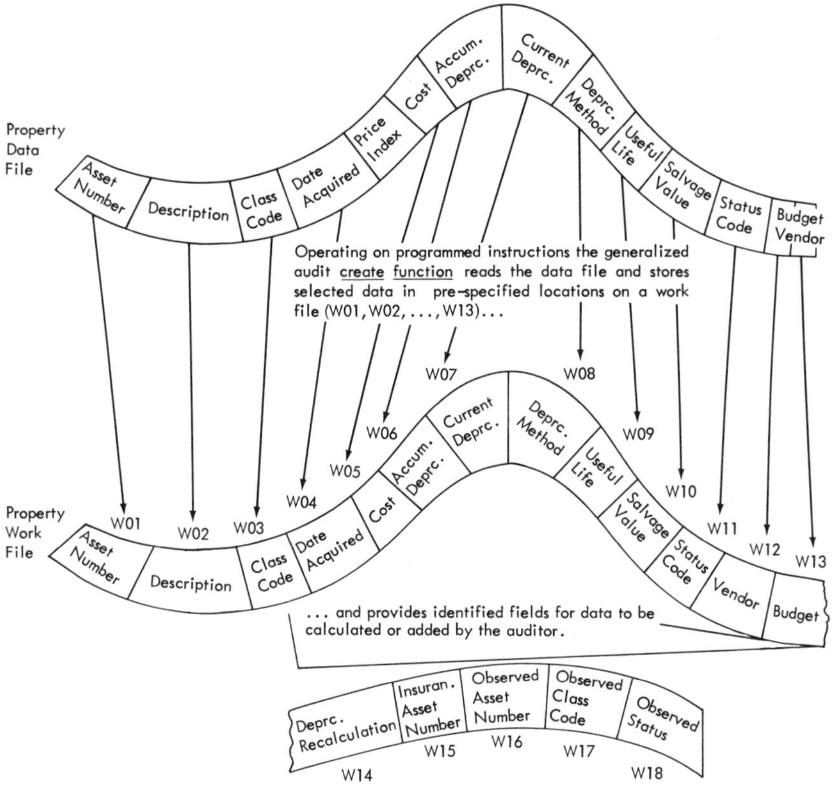

EXHIBIT 9A–6
Update of Existing Work File

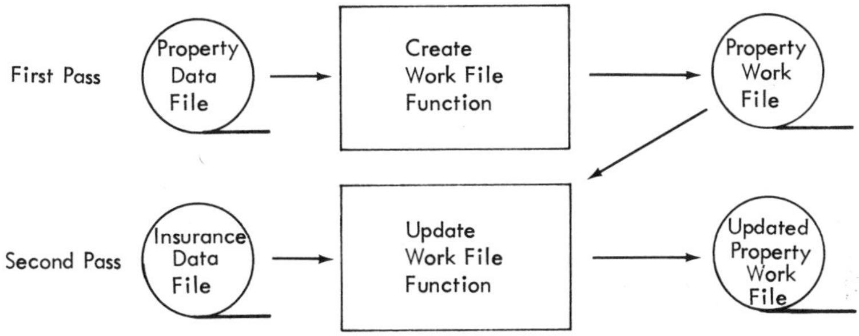

ord. (A *record* is a specified group of data fields such as the record shown in Exhibit 9A–5. A file may consist of thousands of records.) For example, the fixed asset file may contain many records holding transactions recording the purchase and refurbishing of a single asset (e.g., a building). With the summarize function the auditor can add all costs and other data on the same asset into a single number for each field. Of course, if the detailed transactions are to be audited, they must be identified before summarization. After the summarize operation, only the summary record is retained on the work file. The summarize function is illustrated in Exhibit 9A–7.

EXHIBIT 9A–7
Illustration of Summarize Function

Input Work File

Asset Number	Description	Cost	Accumulated Depreciation	Current Deprc.	Deprc. Method
701	Auto	3000	1000	200	SL
602	Typewriter	500	100	50	SL
603	Adder	300	175	35	SL
701	Auto	5000	500	750	SL

Output Work File (summarized)

Asset Number	Description	Cost	Accumulated Depreciation	Current Deprc.	Deprc. Method
701	Auto	8000	1500	950	SL
603	Adder	300	175	35	SL
602	Typewriter	500	100	50	SL

Sort Function

At any point in the application the work file can be sorted into a desired order to enhance the efficiency of subsequent auditing procedures. Suppose that the auditor intends to inspect a random sample of equipment items. After the computer selects the sample, the items may be sorted in order of location prior to obtaining a printed report. With the items grouped by location, the auditor can inspect them without having to group items by hand and without having to dash back and forth between buildings to look at one that was missed when reading an unsorted report. Sorting also facilitates the production of orderly printed reports with meaningful subtotals for items sorted into categories (e.g., autos, buildings, land).

Calculate Functions

Several arithmetical functions are available. In addition to the ordinary add, subtract, multiply, and divide operations, STRATA has comparison functions such as the ones below ("A" and "B" refer to contents of data fields in the work file).

Symbols	*Function*
L	A less than B
E	A equal B
G	A greater than B
LE	A less than or equal to B
NE	A not equal B
GE	A greater than or equal to B

Take the "A greater than B" for an example. For this operation, the symbol G is used to program the instructions. Let field W05 be asset cost, field W06 accumulated depreciation, and field W10 salvage value (refer to Exhibit 9A–5).

Programmed instruction: W06 *ADD* W10 *G* W05

This instruction is all that is needed to add field W06 (accumulated depreciation) to field W10 (salvage value) and compare for "greater than" field W05 (asset cost), and thereby detect assets that have been depreciated below salvage value. A report of exceptions can be printed out for further analysis. The instruction given above is illustrated in the specification form shown in Exhibit 9A–8.

The arithmetic functions hold a wide range of usefulness for recalculation, scanning (based on a limit test), stratification of a population, comparisons, and computations of trends. Any audit test whose criteria can be quantified can be performed by the computer using the calculate functions.

A random selection algorithm is also available in many software systems. Programmed input of sample parameters and population descriptions is required to activate a random number generator that selects numbers, associates them with data, and prints the sample selection for further audit work. STRATA has the capability to compute a population standard deviation.

Output Options

STRATA users may have as many as five output modes. (See Exhibit 9A–2.) These include output in the forms of tapes, disks, punched cards, printed reports, and printed confirmations. The most frequently used forms are the latter three—cards, hard-copy reports, and confirmations ready for mailing. Punched cards are convenient when they can be used to

EXHIBIT 9A–8
STRATA Calculate—Stratify Specification

TOUCHE ROSS
STRATA 360

CALCULATE-STRATIFY

SEE REVERSE FOR CONTINUATION PAGE

Sequence Number: C S 5 7 (1–4)

LINE NO. (5–7)	FIELD A (8–10)	OPERATION (1) (11–13)	FIELD B (14–16)	CONSTANT VALUE (3) (4) NUMERIC / ALPHA-NUMERIC (17–24)	DEC. PL. (25)	FIELD C RESULT (26–28)	GO TO (1) (29–32)
1 0 5	W06	ADD	W10			T01	
1 1 0	T01	G	W05				END
1 1 5							
1 2 0							
1 2 5							
1 3 0							
1 3 5							
1 4 0							
1 4 5							
1 5 0							
1 5 5							
1 6 0							
1 6 5							
1 7 0							
1 7 5							
1 8 0							
1 8 5							
1 9 0							
1 9 5							

CONDITIONAL OPERATIONS (1)	MATHEMATICAL AND OTHER OPERATIONS (2)	GO TO OPTIONS (1)
L - A less than B **E** - A equal to B **G** - A greater than B **RS** Random Selection of nn%. nn is a numeric constant from 01 to 99. For nn% of the records chosen at random, the condition is met.(3) **LE** - A less than or Equal to B **NE** - A not equal to B **GE** - A greater than or equal to B **SC** Tests *STRATA* Code field of the **WORK** record. If equal to the two-digit Alpha-Numeric constant, the condition is met.(4) EXIT ROUTINE – AVAILABLE IN O/S ONLY XIT – EXTPROG3 – Allows exiting from STRATA to a user coded subroutine to act upon STRATA Work record. Enter "XIT" in Operation column and user exit member name in the constant value field.	**ADD** A + B → C **MUL** A × B → C **SUB** A − B → C **DIV** A ÷ B → C **ANL** Analyze Field B Optional – To obtain "Variance" of Field B with Analyze results, enter ANL in "Operation" column and "V" in column 17. ***Available in 65K STRATA only.*** **MOV** B → A, Moves Alpha-Numeric field B or Constant to field A. **COD** Enters any two digit Alpha-Numeric Constant in the ***STRATA*** code field of the **WORK** record.(4) **EOP** Enter EOP to stop all processing in that STRATA Pass.	**END** pass current **WORK** record to next ***STRATA*** function. (After Calculate/Stratify.) **READ** reject current **WORK** record from any further ***STRATA*** function by getting the next record. **CSnn** branch to page number nn. **EX** CSnn Perform steps on page nn and return. Put EX in "Operation Field" and **CSnn** in "Go To" field. **blank** if any conditional operation fails, a blank "Go To" will cause a branch to the next page.

(1) In Conditional Operations:
- if the tested condition is met the next sequential operation is performed.
- if the tested condition fails, *STRATA* takes "Go To" option.

(2) After performing a mathematical or other operation (except for EOP) STRATA performs the next sequential operation unless the "Go To" field is non blank.

(3) Enter Numeric Constants and Random Selection percent right justified in Constant Value field.

(4) Enter Alpha-Numeric Constants and two digit *STRATA* Codes left justified in Constant Value field.

collect other audit data, for example, the physical test count for a selected inventory item or the observed status code of an asset. The auditor can take the card along for the inspection, note data on it, have it keypunched, and then merged back into the work file for further processing.

Printed confirmations are perhaps the most ingenious output application. With appropriate programming the auditor can have account data printed at high speed on special forms. The printing on the special forms produces a file copy, a spare copy, and a sealed envelope containing the confirmation and a reply envelope. Only postage is needed to complete the confirmation mailing. (The short form of such a confirmation is shown in Exhibit 5–3.)

Printed reports may take whatever form and content the auditor needs. The basic STRATA specifications for a printed report may include the following:

1. *Quantified selection criteria.* The criteria for selecting items of information for inclusion in the report are programmed by the auditor.
2. *Report title.* The contents of the report are identified with a heading.
3. *Sort control field selection.* The data field(s) (on the work file) that defines the order of items printed is specified.
4. *Totals and spacing.* The frequency of subtotals (major groupings, intermediate, and minor), page totals, and grand totals are specified.
5. *Report content and format.* The fields to be printed are specified and the horizontal position of columns on the page may be specified.

Exhibit 9A–9 is a reproduction of a select and print specification form that is used to produce a report on the STRATA system. This report contains a listing of assets that have been depreciated below salvage value. This "select and print" form is the "End" of the program referenced on the previous "calculate-stratify" form in Exhibit 9A–8.

Exhibit 9A–10 shows a portion of the printed report. Each of the assets listed has been depreciated below its salvage value, and current depreciation is still being calculated. The client's data processing program has no control feature that stops the depreciation calculation properly. Depreciation expense appears to be overstated by $968.

EXHIBIT 9A–9
Report Illustration: Assets Depreciated below Salvage Value

TOUCHE ROSS
STRATA 360

SELECT & PRINT

SEE REVERSE FOR CARD PUNCH

Sequence Number: P S 7 3

REPORT SELECTION CRITERIA (1)

LINE NO. (5–7)	FIELD A (8–10)	OPERATION (11–13)	FIELD B (14–16)	CONSTANT VALUE NUMERIC / ALPHA-NUMERIC (17–24)	DEC. PL. (25)	FIELD C RESULT (26–28)
1 1 0	W06	ADD	W10			T01
1 1 5	T01	G	W05			
1 2 0						
1 2 5						
1 3 0						
1 3 5						
1 4 0						
1 4 5						
1 5 0						
1 5 5						

ALLOWED OPERATIONS

Conditional
- L Less Than
- LE Less Than or Equal to
- E Equal to
- NE Not Equal to
- G Greater Than
- GE Greater Than or Equal to
- RS Random Select
- SC Test Strata Code Field

Mathematical
- ADD Add
- SUB Subtract
- MUL Multiply
- DIV Divide

Other
- ANL Analyze
- MOV Move
- COD Fill Strata Code Field

PRINT SPECIFICATIONS

2 — REPORT NO.: 01 (6–7) — REPORT NAME: ASSETS DEPRC BELOW SALVAGE (8–35)

3 — SORT CONTROL FIELDS FOR RECORDS SELECTED (Major → Minor): W03 (6–8), W01 (9–11), W (12–14)

4 — LINES TO BE PRINTED - (enter Y for Yes)

Details (6)	Major Totals (7)	Intermediate Totals (8)	Minor Totals (9)	Page Totals (10)	Grand Totals (11)
Y	Y	Y			Y

Totals, spacing and breaks are controlled by the corresponding WORK fields specified in Columns 1, 2 and 3 below.

SPACING BETWEEN LINES AND PAGE BREAKS

Details (2) (12)	Major Breaks (3) (13)	Intermediate Breaks (3) (14)	Minor Breaks (3) (15)	Omit Dashed Lines on Totals (Enter Y for Yes) (16)
	3	2		

CONTENTS OF COLUMN (4)

	CONTROL FIELD FOR MAJOR TOTALS/BREAKS			CONTROL FIELD FOR INTERMED. TOTALS/BREAKS			CONTROL FIELD FOR MINOR TOTALS/BREAKS					
	COL. NO.	FIELD	LOW-ORDER POSITION	COL. NO.	FIELD	LOW-ORDER POSITION	COL. NO.	FIELD	LOW-ORDER POSITION	COL. NO.	FIELD	LOW-ORDER POSITION
5	01	W03	002	02	W01	006	03	W12	020	04	W04	040
5	05	W05	048	06	W06	060	07	W07	072	08	W10	084
5	09	W08	096	10	W09	100	11	W14	110	12		
5	13			14			15			16		
5	17			18			19			20		

EXHIBIT 9A–10
Illustration: Report Format and Content

Report No. 1
ABC Company
December 31, 1978

Assets Deprc below Salvage

Class Code	*Asset Number*	*Vendor Ident.*	*Date Acquired*	*Cost*	*Accum. Deprc.*	*Curr. Deprc. Exp.*	*Salvage Value*	*Deprc. Meth.*	*Use Life*	*Deprc. Audit*
1	7678502-1301	10	7.21.68	1000	950	0	100	s1	5	0
1	7678506-1301	2	5.10.69	4500	4500	225	450	s1	10	0
				5500	5450	225	550			0
6	112062394-6	6	2.11.74	3000	2900	63	150	db	5	0
6	639825781-9	2	9.19.55	9500	9000	380	950	s1	25	0
6	938126023-8	7	1.01.58	6000	6300	300	600	s1	20	0
				18500	18200	743	1700			0
				24000	23650	968	2250			0

10

SUBSTANTIVE TESTS WITH STATISTICAL SAMPLING

Substantive tests of transaction details and of account balances center attention on the money amounts under audit. The statistical methods related to such tests are called *sampling for variables*. The term *variables* in this sense refers to measurement of the dollar amounts rather than measurement of the "exception" versus "no-exception" characteristic of control procedures (as discussed in terms of attribute sampling in Chapter 7).

In this chapter the coverage of statistical sampling for variables has three major objectives: (1) to explain how professional judgments may be quantified in a sample-based audit decision, (2) to specify methods for calculating sample size, and (3) to explain how to use statistics in making a decision about the accuracy of a recorded balance or total. Auditors can use statistical models to evaluate evidence, but close attention must be given to the role of professional judgment underlying the statistics. The role of judgment is explained in the chapter.

The Auditor's Problem

Suppose there appears in financial statements the following item classified among the current assets:

	December 31, 1978
Trade accounts receivable	$379,500

Assume also that this total amount is the sum of 8,300 individual customer accounts ranging in amounts from $1 to $6,870.

Management's financial representations include the following:

The 8,300 accounts represent trade customers, and none of the accounts are fictitious.

The total amount is $379,500.

The total amount is due within 12 months.

The auditor's questions include:

Do these 8,300 accounts actually exist and are they from trade customers?

Is $379,500 a materially accurate measurement of the "actual" current accounts receivable total?

The term "actual" is used in this chapter to mean the amount or value that could be determined by an audit of all of the accounts. This kind of problem and the related auditor's questions exist for other accounts such as sales account totals (the sum of many sales invoices), inventory totals (the sum of values for many different inventory items), and any other dollar total that is the sum of many individual dollar amounts. Other *variables* such as weights and lengths can be measured with variables sampling statistics.

The auditor's problem regarding the $379,500 book value of trade accounts receivable is to obtain an estimate of the actual value without auditing *all* the customers' accounts. This unknown actual value (unknown so long as only a *sample* of accounts is audited) may be anything from zero to an amount far greater than $379,500. If internal control is satisfactory, the actual value is likely to be close to $379,500. If the control system is weak, however, the book value may contain many undetected errors and the actual value may be very different.

EXHIBIT 10–1
Range of Possible Actual Values

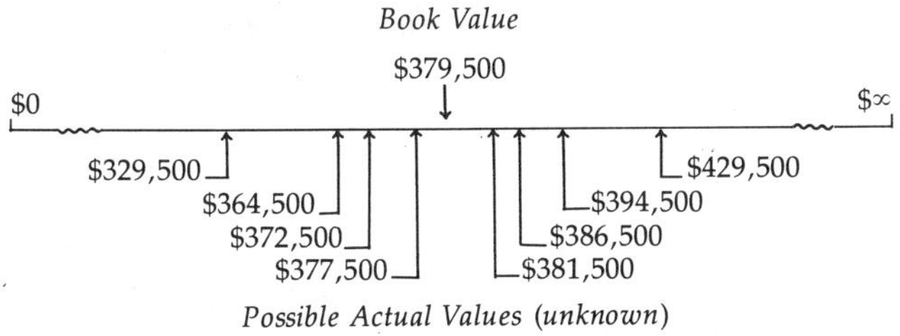

The relationship of actual value to book value is shown in Exhibit 10–1. The auditor's essential *decision problem* is to determine whether the book value of $379,500 is a materially accurate measurement of the actual value. This determination may be made by a direct estimate of the dollar amount (called *mean-per-unit* or MPU measurement) or by an estimate of the error amounts in the balance (called *difference statistic* measurement).

Four Sampling Objectives

The discussion of methods in this chapter mainly relates to what is known as ***representative sampling,*** wherein the population is defined as all constituent items without regard to other characteristics of individual items. The sample selection is intended to produce a set of items that reflects general population characteristics. Three other sampling objectives have been suggested, all of which depend in large degree upon different population definitions.

Corrective sampling has the objective of selecting items that are in error for the purpose of correcting as many errors as possible. The population is judgmentally defined in terms of population segments that have the highest probability of error.

Protective sampling has the objective of selecting items randomly to obtain the greatest coverage of dollar amounts for the purpose of guarding the auditor from missing material errors. The population is judgmentally or mathematically stratified to weigh the sample to high-dollar items.

Preventive sampling has the objective of keeping client personnel uncertain of what items might be sampled and has as its purpose the prevention of any doctoring of areas to be sampled. The population definition depends upon the auditor's judgment of how best to keep other personnel unaware.[1]

Some elementary definitions are given next as a background for considering statistical calculations.

Elementary Definitions

Population (indicated by the letter N). The group of items constituting a dollar balance or total amount under audit is the population. Populations may be judgmentally or mathematically defined by the auditor to suit a particular sampling objective. For example: The 8,300 customer accounts constitute the whole accounts receivable population mentioned earlier. However, an auditor may redefine this population several ways, including the following:

Two subpopulations consisting of:

78 accounts with a total book value of $90,000.

8,222 accounts with a total book value of $289,500.

Three subpopulations consisting of:

All accounts with positive balances.

All accounts with zero balances.

All accounts with negative balances.

[1] Further explanation of the logic and mathematics of these objectives is found in articles by Ijiri and Kaplan, and Hansen and Shaftel cited as sources and additional reading references at the end of this chapter.

379,500 subpopulations each consisting of $1 of the total book value. (This definition is characteristic of dollar-unit sampling, DUS, explained briefly at the end of this chapter.)

These "subpopulations" are *strata* and are obtained by the auditor's *stratification* of the whole population. The subject of stratified sampling is described briefly at the end of this chapter. The point is that auditors can use some judgment in the initial perception of the population and in the definition of the statistical sampling problem.

Item (also known as *sample unit* and *unit of observation*). An item is a single element in the population. Examples include a specific customer's account receivable balance, a specific sales invoice included in a sales account total, a specific inventory line item in an inventory listing, and (in dollar-unit sampling) a single dollar included in a total. A selection of items constitutes a sample from the population under audit.

Sample (indicated by the letter n). A sample is a selection of some of the items from a population. For a random sample, each item in a population or in a stratum must have an equally likely chance of being included in the sample. Random number tables, systematic selection methods, and computer-generated random numbers may be used to identify sample items. In order to perform valid statistical calculations, the sample *must* be random. Calculations based on data from a nonrandom sample indicate lack of knowledge of statistical theory and may be evidence of lack of training and skill as an auditor.

Book Value (indicated by *BV*). The book value is the population dollar amount under audit. It can be the *BV* of the population taken as a whole or of each subpopulation (stratum) defined by the auditor. For the 8,300 customer accounts the *BV* is $379,500.

Book Value of a Sample Item (indicated by x_i). The small letter x is used in this text to symbolize the book value of an individual item. The subscript i identifies the item as the 1st, 2d . . . nth items in the sample.

Book Value of the Sample (indicated by X). The capital letter X is used in this text to symbolize the sum of the book values of the sample items.

Audited Value of a Sample Item (indicated by y_i). The small letter y is used in this text to symbolize the value of the item determined by the auditor after applying audit procedures to gather evidence. For example, suppose the first account receivable in the sample had a book value of $100 ($x_i$) and the auditor found that the customer had not been given proper credit for a payment discount. With this evidence the auditor determines the audited value to be $90 ($y_i$).

These elementary definitions are very important for understanding how to do statistical calculations.

STATISTICAL CALCULATIONS

Auditors deal with the problem of measuring dollar amounts of balances and totals by calculating an average audited item value (MPU measurement) or by calculating an average dollar error in a sample of items (difference statistic measurement.)

Definition. The MPU mean of a sample (indicated by $\bar{Y}$) is an estimator of the audited average of all item values in the population. The "actual" (audited) population average (indicated by the Greek letter μ, *mu*) can be known only after auditing all the items in a population.

Definition. The difference mean of a sample (indicated by $\bar{D}$) is an estimator of the average difference between audited item values and their unaudited book values.[2] Each item difference, d_i, is calculated by subtracting the unaudited item book value from its audited value ($d_i = y_i - x_i$).

A *negative* average difference indicates a book value *overstatement* relative to the audited item values, and a *positive* average difference indicates a book value *understatement.*

Calculation of Means and Point Estimates

Assume the auditor has obtained the following results from a random sample of customer accounts receivable:

Sample Item (i)	*Audited Value (y_i)*	*Book Value (x_i)*	*Difference ($d_i = y_i - x_i$)*
1.	$ 45	$ 50	$-5
2.	26	25	1
3.	100	100	0
4.	37	35	2
5.	17	20	−3
	$225	$230	$−5

MPU sample mean.

$$\bar{Y} = \frac{\sum_{i=1}^{n} y_i}{n} \qquad \text{(Equation 1A)}^{3}$$

$$\bar{Y} = \frac{\$225}{5} = \$45$$

Difference mean.

$$\bar{D} = \frac{\sum_{i=1}^{n} d_i}{n} \qquad \text{(Equation 1B)}$$

$$\bar{D} = \frac{\$-5}{5} = \$-1$$

[2] Means based on differences are *unbiased* estimators of population differences only if a sufficiently large number of nonzero differences are found in the sample. Depending on the size and plus or minus sign of the differences, some 50 to 80 differences should be enough for valid calculations. Examples in this chapter of using only a few differences are for illustrative purposes only.

[3] Similarly, the MPU sample book value mean $= \bar{X} = \frac{\sum_{i=1}^{n} x_i}{n} = \frac{\$230}{5} = \$46.$

The *population* book value mean is indicated in this chapter by *BV/N*. The mean of account book values for the accounts receivable population illustrated in this chapter is $45.72 = $379,500/8300.

Point estimates of total amounts can be obtained by *simple extension;* that is, multiplying the average by the number of items in the population. The MPU point estimate using the audited item values is \$373,500 (= 8,300 × \$45), and the point estimate using the difference is \$−8,300 (= 8,300 × \$−1.00). However, the auditor does not know how reliable these point estimates may be as estimates of population values. The variability of the sample items must be taken into account in order to obtain a measurement of *sampling error*—the erroneous measurement obtained from having a random sample that is actually not representative of the population from which it was drawn.

Calculation of Variability

The dispersion of population values is measured by the statistical *variance* (symbolized by the Greek letter *sigma*, σ^2), usually expressed in terms of its square root—the *standard deviation*. Assume that the term

$$\sum_{i=1}^{N}\left(x_i - \frac{BV}{N}\right)^2$$

given below for the 8,300 accounts receivable mentioned earlier is \$146,820,000.

Standard deviation of population book values.

$$\sigma_x = \sqrt{\frac{\sum_{i=1}^{N}\left(x_i - \frac{BV}{N}\right)^2}{N}} \qquad \text{(Equation 2)}$$

$$\sigma_x = \sqrt{\frac{146,820,000}{8300}} = \sqrt{17,689.253} = \$133$$

Actually, the population standard deviation of *audited values* (σ_y) is important in auditing applications, but this value cannot be known unless all the items are audited. The best the auditor can do is to calculate an estimate of the standard deviation (indicated by the capital letter S) from sample data. To illustrate the calculation, assume the auditor has two separate random samples as follows:

Sample A

i	y_i	x_i	d_i
1	\$ 45	\$ 50	\$−5
2	26	25	1
3	100	100	0
4	37	35	2
5	17	20	−3
	\$225	\$230	\$−5

Sample B

i	y_i	x_i	d_i
1	\$ 70	\$ 75	\$−5
2	41	40	1
3	50	50	0
4	32	30	2
5	32	35	−3
	\$225	\$230	\$−5

MPU measurement.
Standard deviation of sample values.

$$S_y = \sqrt{\frac{\sum_{i=1}^{n} (y_i - \bar{Y})^2}{n-1}} \qquad \text{(Equation 2A)[4]}$$

Sample A

i	y_i	$\bar{Y}$	$(y_i - \bar{Y})^2$
1.	$ 45	$45	$ 0
2.	26	45	361
3.	100	45	3,025
4.	37	45	64
5.	17	45	784
	$225		$4,234

$$S_y = \sqrt{\frac{4234}{4}} = \sqrt{1,058.5} = \$32.53$$

Sample B

i	y_i	$\bar{Y}$	$(y_i - \bar{Y})^2$
1.	$ 70	$45	$ 625
2.	41	45	16
3.	50	45	25
4.	32	45	169
5.	32	45	169
	$225		$1,004

$$S_y = \sqrt{\frac{1,004}{4}} = \sqrt{251} = \$15.84$$

The item values (y_i) are more widely dispersed from the sample mean ($\bar{Y}$) in Sample A than in Sample B. The respective standard deviations reflect this characteristic.[5]

---

[4] This equation and others in the main body of the text omit the *finite population correction factor* $\left(\sqrt{1 - \frac{n}{N}}\right)$ which is useful when the sample constitutes a large proportion of the population (5 percent or more), and each selected sample item is not replaced in the population and available for selection a second time. In the Sample A example, if the five accounts had been chosen from a population of 50 accounts, Equation 2A is properly expressed as:

$$S_y = \sqrt{\frac{\Sigma(y_i - \bar{Y})^2}{n-1}} \times \sqrt{1 - \frac{n}{N}}$$

In the example:

$$S_y = 32.53 \times \sqrt{1 - \frac{5}{50}}$$
$$= 32.53 \times \sqrt{.9}$$
$$= 32.53 \times .9486833$$
$$S_y = 30.86$$

This correction factor contributes to the mathematical accuracy of calculations, but the effect is not greater until $n/N > .05$. (In this case $\sqrt{1 - .05} = .975$, and a 2½-percent difference may be important. When $n/N > .05$ the correction factor is more than 2½ percent.) Refer to Appendix 10–C for the finitely corrected forms of the equations in the text.

[5] For easier computation Equations 2A and 2B can be used as follows:

$$\text{(2A)} \quad S_y = \sqrt{\frac{\sum_{i=1}^{n} (y_i)^2 - n\bar{Y}^2}{n-1}} \qquad \text{(2B)} \quad S_D = \sqrt{\frac{\sum_{i=1}^{n} (d_i)^2 - n\bar{D}^2}{n-1}}$$

Below is the equation and an example of a difference statistic standard deviation calculation using the data from Samples A and B presented earlier.

Difference statistic. Standard deviation of differences.

$$S_D = \sqrt{\frac{\sum_{i=1}^{n} (d_i - \bar{D})^2}{n - 1}} \qquad \text{(Equation 2B)}$$

Sample A

i	y_i	x_i	d_i	$(d_i - \bar{D})^2$
1........	$ 45	$ 50	$−5	$16
2........	26	25	1	4
3........	100	100	0	1
4........	37	35	2	9
5........	17	20	−3	4
	$225	$230	$−5	$34

$$S_D = \sqrt{\frac{34}{4}} = \sqrt{8.5} = \$2.92$$

Sample B: Notice that the differences are identical to Sample A, thus............................ $S_D = \sqrt{\frac{34}{4}} = \sqrt{8.5} = \$2.92$

The difference statistic is potentially valuable because its variance is almost always much smaller than that of the MPU estimator. This relationship contributes to more precise estimates with relatively small samples, provided that a large enough number of dollar errors can be found to overcome problems of statistical bias. Furthermore the measurement of error amounts (the differences) is itself a matter of primary concern in an audit. Notice that the standard deviation of the difference is indeed much smaller in the example above than the standard deviation of the item values themselves. (Compare $2.92 from Equation 2B to $32.53 from Equation 2A for the Sample A data.)

Distribution of Sample Means

Sampling theory contains a *central limit theorem,* which essentially states that repeated samples (of sufficiently large size[6]) will tend to pro-

[6] Accounting populations are often *positively skewed*—containing a few large-dollar items and many small-dollar items. Samples must be large enough to include a representative selection of widely varying amounts so that calculated averages may be *unbiased*. Failure to obtain an unbiased estimate may result in the actual reliability being *less* than the theoretical reliability the auditor wants to obtain.

Cochran states: "There is no safe general rule as to how large n must be for use of the normal approximation in computing confidence limits. For populations in which the principal deviation from normality consists of marked positive skewness, a crude rule I have occasionally found useful is $n > 25\,G_1^2$; where

$$G_1 = \frac{1}{N\sigma^3} \sum_{i=1}^{N} (y_i - \bar{Y})^3 \text{ (a measure of } \textit{skewness}\text{).''}$$

See W. G. Cochran, *Sampling Techniques,* 2d ed. (New York: John Wiley & Sons, Inc., 1963), p. 41.

duce sample means (e.g., $\bar{Y}$ and $\bar{D}$) that cluster around the actual average value of the amount being estimated. Recall that the Greek letter μ was used earlier to indicate the actual but unknown MPU mean of the population. Also, note that μ_D may be used to indicate the actual but unknown average of population errors. Thus:

$\bar{Y}$ is an estimate of μ
$\bar{D}$ is an estimate of μ_D

Repeated sample means tend to take the familiar bell curve shape which is characteristic of the normal distribution of sample means. The standard deviation of the sample means (more often called the *standard error of the mean*) is a measure of the variability of the averages calculated from sample data.

Standard error of the MPU sample mean.

$$S_{\bar{Y}} = \frac{S_Y}{\sqrt{n}} \qquad \text{(Equation 3A)}$$

$$\text{Sample A: } S_{\bar{Y}} = \frac{\$32.53}{\sqrt{5}} = \$14.55$$

$$\text{Sample B: } S_{\bar{Y}} = \frac{\$15.84}{\sqrt{5}} = \$7.08$$

Standard error of the difference statistic average.

$$S_{\bar{D}} = \frac{S_D}{\sqrt{n}} \qquad \text{(Equation 3B)}$$

$$S_{\bar{D}} = \frac{\$2.92}{\sqrt{5}} = \$1.31$$

EXHIBIT 10–2
Normal Distribution of Sample Means

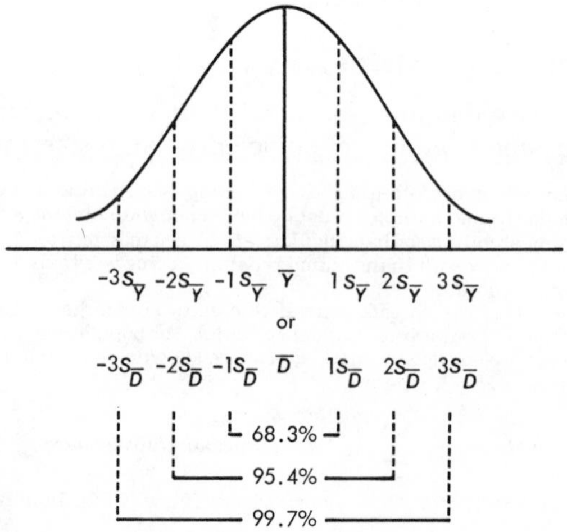

The normal distribution (bell-shaped curve) of sample means enables the auditor to calculate *confidence interval measurements* based on sample data. The curve drawn in Exhibit 10–2 shows the areas under the curve described by intervals of one, two, and three standard errors on either side of the sample mean.

A proper interpretation of 68.3 percent, 95.4 percent and 99.7 percent is that these are the probabilities that intervals based on the sample data include the actual population value (μ or μ_D) when the intervals are centered on the sample mean ($\bar{Y}$ or $\bar{D}$). Auditors may say, for example: "I am 99.7 percent *confident* that the actual population value is within the interval calculated on the basis of three standard errors."

Such calculations are based on an *achieved precision*—a measurement which combines a specified confidence (probability) and the variability found in sample data. *Precision* is defined and calculated as shown in Equations 4A and 4B.

MPU measurement.
Achieved precision.

$$P_Y = Z_\alpha \cdot S_{\bar{Y}} \qquad \text{(Equation 4A)}^7$$

For a 95-percent confidence measurement:
Sample A: $P_Y = 1.96 \cdot \$14.55 = \$28.52$
Sample B: $P_Y = 1.96 \cdot \$\ 7.08 = \$13.88$

Difference statistic.
Achieved precision.

$$P_D = Z_\alpha \cdot S_{\bar{D}} \qquad \text{(Equation 4B)}$$

For a 95-percent confidence measurement:
$P_D = 1.96 \cdot \$1.31 = \$2.57$

Confidence Interval Measurement

The interval measurement itself is obtained by calculating a lower limit (L_1) and an upper limit (L_2). The lower limit is calculated by *subtracting* achieved precision from the sample average ($\bar{Y} - P_Y$ or $\bar{D} - P_D$), and the upper limit is calculated by *adding* achieved precision to the

[7] Z_α represents the number of standard errors associated with the confidence level. Some commonly used ones are:

Confidence	Z_α
80 percent	1.28
90	1.645
95	1.96
99	2.58

These are *two-tailed* coefficients because the interval measurement has both an upper and lower limit. Appendix 10–A contains a table of *two-tailed* coefficients from which the Z_α may be derived. The cell entries in Appendix 10–A represent 1 − Confidence. For example at 1 − .95 = .05, one can find $Z_\alpha = 1.96$ by reading the coefficient at the left and top margins.

sample average ($\bar{Y} + P_Y$ or $\bar{D} + P_D$). Multiplying by the population size (N) and using the book value (with the difference statistic) converts the measurement of an *average* to a measurement of a *total* dollar amount.

MPU Confidence Interval

L_1 (lower limit) $= N(\bar{Y} - P_Y)$

L_2 (upper limit) $= N(\bar{Y} + P_Y)$ (Equation 5A)

Sample A (95 percent confidence):

$L_1 = 8{,}300\ (45 - 28.52) = \$136{,}784$

$L_2 = 8{,}300\ (45 + 28.52) = \$610{,}216$

Sample B (95 percent confidence):

$L_1 = 8{,}300\ (45 - 13.88) = \$258{,}296$

$L_2 = 8{,}300\ (45 + 13.88) = \$488{,}704$

Difference Statistic Confidence Interval

L_1 (lower limit) $= BV + N(\bar{D} - P_D)$

L_2 (upper limit) $= BV + N(\bar{D} + P_D)$ (Equation 5B)

95 percent confidence:

$L_1 = 379{,}500 + 8{,}300(-1 - 2.57) = \$349{,}869$

$L_2 = 379{,}500 + 8{,}300(-1 + 2.57) = \$392{,}531$

Confidence and achieved precision are paired together in the precision calculation. Once sample data are obtained, any number of interval measurements can be calculated, but each one would relate to a specified confidence (which gives the Z_α).

Some examples are shown below.

MPU Measurement (Sample A data)

Confidence	Z_α	P_Y	L_1	L_2
80 percent	1.28	18.62	\$218,954	\$528,046
90	1.645	23.93	174,881	572,119
95	1.96	28.52	136,784	610,216
99	2.58	37.54	61,918	685,082

Difference Statistic Measurement

Confidence	Z_α	P_D	L_1	L_2
80 percent	1.28	1.68	\$357,256	\$385,144
90	1.645	2.15	353,355	389,045
95	1.96	2.57	349,869	392,531
99	2.58	3.38	343,146	399,254

As a general rule, the more precise the measurement (that is, the smaller the distance is between L_1 and L_2) the less confidence an auditor can have that the interval contains the actual value. An auditor can express 95 percent confidence that the actual MPU population value is between \$136,784 and \$610,216 based on Sample A data, but only 80 percent confidence that the actual MPU population value is between \$218,954 and \$528,046.

The MPU confidence intervals based on Sample A data are obviously imprecise (very wide intervals). This happened, in part, because the sample consisted of only five items. Better precision is obtained with larger samples (see Equations 2A and 3A) and with statistics which have lesser variability (e.g., the difference statistic, stratified MPU statistics, and dollar-unit sampling statistics).[8]

DECISION ALTERNATIVES AND RISKS

Statistical models are not substitutes for the exercise of professional judgment. In fact, the mathematical methods are little more than means of making explicit the role and influence of several judgmental factors in a decision about the fair presentation of a balance or total. Five judgmental factors were explained earlier (Chapter 5) in connection with determining the extent of work in substantive audit testing. Below, these five are defined further in the context of statistical methods.

Judgmental Factors	*Statistical Equivalents*
Information about the population	The population size (N) and the population standard deviation (estimated by S_y) are minimal information requirements.
Materiality	The dollar amount (M) of error permitted in a book value without causing misleading financial statements is a judgment required of the auditor.
Internal control evaluation	An acceptable risk of making an erroneous decision must be decided upon by the auditor.
Relative risk	Two risks, named α ("alpha") and β ("beta"), are reviewed below.
Other situation-specific factors	No single statistical model can efficiently account for all conceivable circumstances. Unique factors are not incorporated in general statistical models. Instead, they are handled on a case-by-case judgment standard.

The factors that are easily incorporated in a statistical model can be represented in the form of a four-cell matrix. The matrix brings the statistical model into the context of a decision about a dollar balance.

A Matrix Model of Decision Alternatives

The auditor's approach to the problem of deciding whether a particular dollar amount in financial statements is a materially accurate measure-

[8] Other statistics include ratio and regression estimators which are beyond the scope of this textbook.

ment of the actual value is usually based on an initial hypothesis or statement of the problem. For example, an auditor may say: "I will accept the client's accounts receivable book value of $379,500 as a materially accurate measurement unless the evidence shows that it is not. For this decision I will consider a misstatement of ±$25,000 or more to be material." In effect the auditor has stated a null hypothesis: The actual value is between $354,500 and $404,500 (the $379,500 book value plus and minus $25,000) and a dual alternative hypothesis: The actual value is less than $354,500 or greater than $404,500.

Definition. A material amount (indicated by the capital letter *M*) is a product of the auditor's professional judgment. The amount (±$25,000 in the example given above) is a judgment about the maximum misstatement that could be overlooked or unadjusted, yet the financial statements would still not be considered materially misleading. This concept is very difficult in practice because (1) materiality in an accounting context must be considered—the relationship of error amounts to one or more other financial statement amounts, (2) the materiality limits in other audit areas must be considered (It would do no good to set ±$25,000 in six different audit areas if a total error limit were $100,000), and (3) the special circumstances of the audit (e.g., internal control strengths, susceptibility of the account to irregularities, general risk characteristics of the client's business) have to be weighed and taken into account. The question of "What is materiality" is no more settled in auditing matters than it is in accounting matters. Nevertheless, a judgment of *M* must be made in order to use statistical methods.

The auditor's decision problem, stated simply, is to decide initially whether (1) the book value is a materially accurate measurement of an unknown actual value or (2) the book value represents a material misstatement of the actual value. Exhibit 10–3 shows these decision alternatives and their relationship to correct and erroneous decisions.

The decision matrix shows that prior to any evaluation of evidence four outcomes are possible. Two of them (O_{11} and O_{22}) indicate correct deci-

EXHIBIT 10–3
A Generalized Dollar Amount Decision Matrix

	Unknown Actual Value	
Decision Alternatives	Lies within an acceptable materiality limit ($BV \pm M$)	Lies outside an acceptable materiality limit ($BV \pm M$)
The book value is materially accurate	Correct decision $P(O_{11}) = 1 - \alpha$	Erroneous decision $P(O_{12}) = \beta$ Type II Error
The book value is materially misstated.	Erroneous decision $P(O_{21}) = \alpha$ Type I Error	Correct decision $P(O_{22}) = 1 - \beta$

sions, and two others (O_{12} and O_{21}) indicate erroneous decisions. Substantive procedures such as vouching charges and credits to a customer's account, confirmation of the customer's balance and vouching of payments received on accounts after the cutoff date are ways of obtaining evidence regarding the proper dollar amount for each account receivable selected in an audit sample. These procedures produce audited balances (y_i), which in turn are the basis for statistical calculations. The statistical calculations based on the audit sample provide estimates that assist the auditor in making a decision.

After the auditor evaluates the evidence, he applies a *decision rule* to choose one of the decision alternatives. Once a choice is made, the auditor is subject to only two of the outcomes—a correct decision and an erroneous one. A common decision rule is: Calculate the confidence interval measurement and (1) if the client's book value is within the interval, decide it is materially accurate, or (2) if the client's book value is not within the interval, decide it is materially misstated.

Assume for illustration that the auditor takes a sample of 400 of the 8,300 customer accounts, and the sample standard deviation (S_y) of the MPU measurement is found to be \$20.57. If the actual total value of the 8,300 accounts is \$379,500, the actual MPU population mean is μ = \$45.72 = \$379,500/8,300. Provided that a sample of 400 is large enough, MPU sample means will be normally distributed around the actual mean of \$45.72. (The actual value is not known but is assumed here to be \$379,500 in order to illustrate the decision process.)

For example, using the 80 percent confidence interval measurement: (1) 10 percent of all possible sample means will be less than \$44.40, (2) 80 percent of all possible sample means will be between \$44.40 and \$47.04, and (3) 10 percent of all possible sample means will be greater than \$47.04.[9] These relationships are shown in Exhibit 10–4.

Outcomes O_{11} and O_{21}

If the auditor finds an MPU sample mean between \$44.40 and \$47.04, the 80-percent confidence interval measurement will contain the book value, and the decision rule indicates choice of the alternative: "The book value is materially accurate." If the book value of \$379,500 value is neither overstated nor understated by more than \$25,000, this is a correct decision, and outcome O_{11} has been realized.

For example, if the auditor finds from the sample of 400 accounts a MPU sample mean of \$45.00 and a sample standard deviation of \$20.57, the following calculations would be made:

(1A) MPU mean of audited values = $\bar{Y}$ = \$45.00
(2A) MPU standard deviation = S_y = \$20.57

---

[9] These 80-percent confidence limits are:

(4A) $$P_Y = Z_a \cdot S_{\bar{Y}} = 1.28 \cdot \frac{\$20.57}{\sqrt{400}} = \$1.32$$

(5A) $$L_1 \text{ (MPU average)} = \mu - P_Y = \$45.72 - \$1.32 = \$44.40$$
$$L_2 \text{ (MPU average)} = \mu - P_Y = \$45.72 + \$1.32 = \$47.04$$

EXHIBIT 10–4
Normal Distribution: $n = 400$, $\mu = \$45.72$, $S_y = \$20.57$

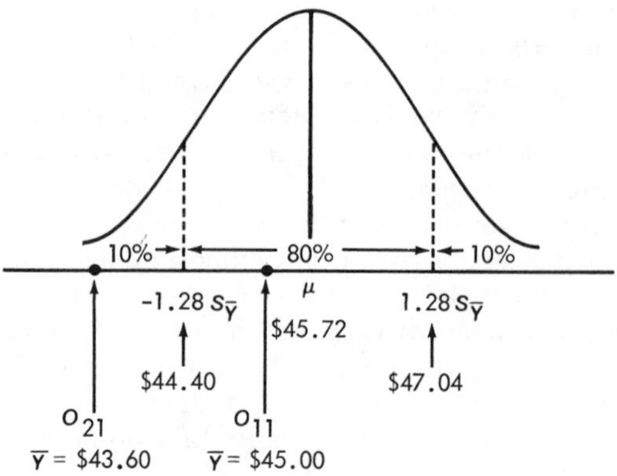

(3A) MPU standard error $= S_{\bar{Y}} = \$20.57/\sqrt{400} = \$1.03$
(4A) MPU achieved precision (80 percent confidence level, $Z_\alpha = 1.28$)

$$P_y = 1.28 \cdot \$1.03 = \$1.32$$

(5A) MPU 80 percent confidence interval

$$L_1 = 8{,}300(\$45 - \$1.32) = \$362{,}544$$
$$L_2 = 8{,}300(\$45 + \$1.32) = \$384{,}456$$

On the other hand, even when the actual value is exactly $379,500, there is a 10-percent chance that the MPU sample mean will be less than $44.40, and a 10-percent chance that it will be greater than $47.04. If the auditor found an MPU sample mean *not* between $44.40 and $47.04, the 80-percent confidence interval measurement would *not* contain the $379,500 book value, and the decision rule would indicate choice of the alternative: "The book value is materially misstated." When this is not the case, the decision is wrong, and outcome O_{21} has been realized.

For example, if the auditor had found from the sample of 400 accounts an MPU sample mean of $43.60 (See Exhibit 10–4) and a sample standard deviation of $20.57, the following calculations would be made:

(1A) MPU mean of audited values $= \bar{Y} = \$43.60$
(2A) MPU standard deviation $= S_y = \$20.57$
(3A) MPU standard error $= S_{\bar{Y}} = \$1.03$
(4A) MPU achieved precision (80 percent confidence level)

$$P_y = 1.28 \cdot \$1.03 = \$1.32$$

(5A) MPU 80 percent confidence interval

$$L_1 = 8{,}300(\$43.60 - \$1.32) = \$350{,}924$$
$$L_2 = 8{,}300(\$43.60 + \$1.32) = \$372{,}836$$

In the above illustrations the probability (α-risk) of the Type I decision error (outcome O_{21}) was 20 percent. There is a 20-percent chance of finding a MPU sample mean less than \$44.40 or greater than \$47.04 when the actual MPU population mean is \$45.72. Thus the expression is: $P(O_{21}) = \alpha = 0.20$. The probability (*reliability*) of the correct decision was $1 - \alpha = 1 - 20\% = 80\%$. Thus the expression is $P(O_{11}) = 1 - \alpha = 0.80$.

In case O_{21}, the auditor made a decision error, deciding that the book value is a material misstatement when in fact it is not. He or she committed the statistical Type I error of rejecting a true hypothesis. Most auditors do not consider the Type I a serious decision error because having decided the balance is materially misstated, efforts will be made to determine why and by how much. The auditor will review the data for evidence of some source of error in an effort to determine a more accurate balance (or the client's personnel will be given duties to determine the amount of error so that an adjustment can be made). The chances are that this subsequent work will reveal that \$379,500 is indeed a materially accurate balance and the initial decision will be reversed. The cost to the auditor is unnecessary work and perhaps the ill will of client personnel.

Thus when exercising professional judgment in specifying α (and $1 - \alpha$, the confidence level), the auditor should think about the additional work that might be involved. The trade-off is that setting a lower α (higher confidence level) causes the sample size to be larger. More explanation of sample size calculation is given later in this chapter.

Outcomes O_{12} and O_{22}

In contrast to the cases discussed above, the book value of \$379,500 may actually be a material misstatement of the actual value. According to the auditor's materiality criterion of ±\$25,000, if the actual value were less than \$354,000 or more than \$404,500 (\$379,500 ± \$25,000), the book value of \$379,500 would be a material misstatement. Assume now for further illustration that the actual value (unknown to the auditor) is exactly \$354,499. Thus the book value is an overstatement of \$25,001. (The example that follows is equally applicable if the actual value were \$404,501, but only one direction of the misstatement is possible at one time.)

This time the auditor may think that the sample is from a distribution around an actual population mean of \$45.72 (= \$379,500/8,300), but in fact it is from a distribution around an actual population mean of \$42.71 μ_{-M} = \$354,499/8,300). Nevertheless the MPU sample mean can turn out to be any one of a number of values as shown before in Exhibit 10–4.

The value of \$354,499 is represented in Exhibit 10–5 by Distribution 1 with a MPU population mean of μ_{-M} = \$42.71 = \$354,499/8,300. (Exhibit 10–5 also shows another material misstatement possibility—the understated book value—represented by Distribution 3 with a MPU population mean of μ_{+M} = \$48.74 = \$404,501/8,300.)

In the preceding section two sample findings were illustrated—one MPU sample mean of \$45.00 and another of \$43.60. *Either of these could*

EXHIBIT 10–5
Distributions of Sample Means from Three Populations (n = 400, μ_{-M} = $42.71, μ_{+M} = $48.74, σ_y = $20.57)

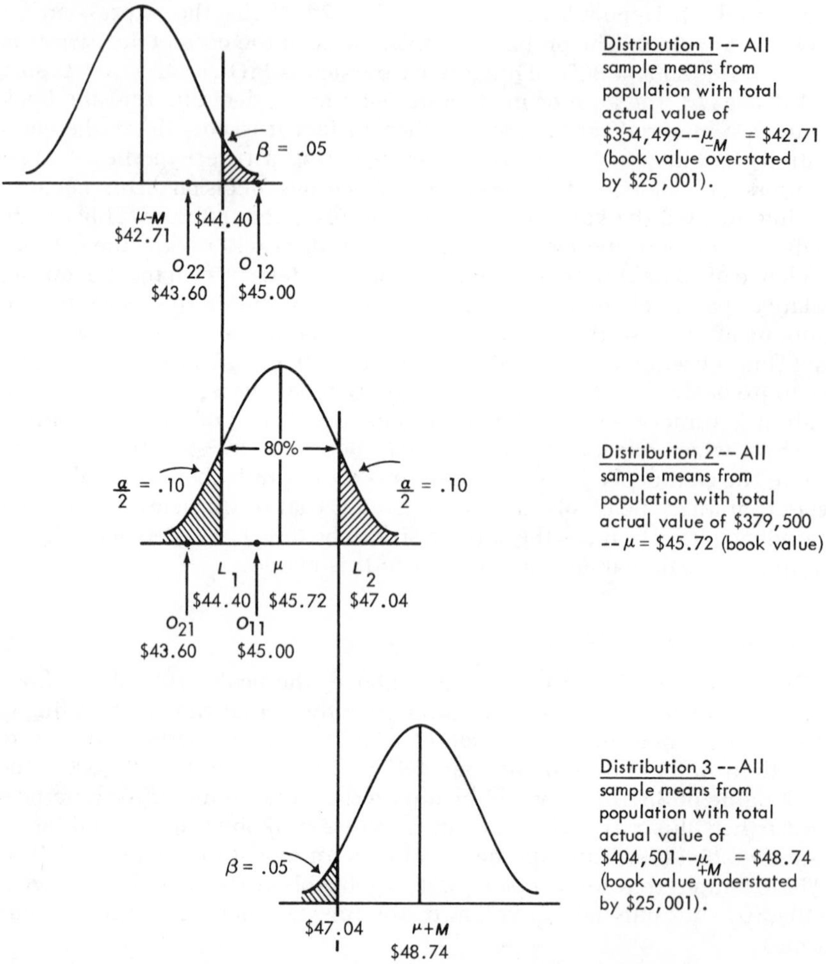

have come from a distribution around an actual MPU population mean of $42.71.

Assuming that the auditor found the MPU sample mean of $45, the decision rule would indicate choice of the alternative: "The book balance is materially accurate." However, when the actual value is $354,499 or less, this is an erroneous decision, and outcome O_{12} will have been realized.

In this accounts receivable illustration, when the MPU population mean is $42.71, there is a 5-percent chance of obtaining a MPU sample mean greater than $44.40—which would lead to the decision that the book value is materially accurate. This 5 percent is the β (beta) risk of a Type II decision error, and the expression is: $P(O_{12}) = \beta = 0.05$.

Had the auditor found a MPU sample mean less than $44.40 (such as the $43.60 illustrated in Exhibit 10–5), the decision rule would indicate the choice: "The book value is materially misstated," and outcome O_{22} would have been realized. This would be a correct decision, and there is a 95-percent chance that a MPU sample mean would be less than $44.40. Hence the expression is: $P(O_{22}) = 1 - \beta = 1 - 0.05 = 0.95$. This is one measure of the reliability.

In outcome O_{22}, the auditor decided correctly that the book value is materially misstated. The next step is to identify the source, type, and amount of errors in order to determine the amount of the adjusting journal entry. Remember, however, that the auditor still does not know that the misstatement is exactly $25,001 and will never know the exact misstatement (unless all the customer accounts are audited). Client's personnel can be assigned the task of analyzing and correcting the balance, and the auditor can review their work.

In outcome O_{12} the auditor made a serious decision error—deciding that the book value is materially accurate when in fact it is a material misstatement of the actual value. This decision error is more serious than the Type I error because the auditor believes the balance is materially accurate and will usually not perform additional procedures to gather more evidence.

A point of emphasis: The risk of making erroneous decisions *always* exists in audits, particularly when evidence is based on samples of data. The risk of audit judgment failure (human error) exists even when all items in a population are audited. Furthermore, the risk of human error *and* sampling error exist when part of the population is audited and a decision (inference) is made about the whole population.

The power of statistical methods lies in the explicit recognition and the attempt to measure and control sampling error.[10] These attempts to control sampling error involve assignment of numerical values to some important professional judgments. The quantification of judgment is discussed below. However, one should be careful to recognize the following discussion as a *framework* or a *model* for thinking about decisions, not as a suggestion that unambiguous numbers can be assigned in place of professional judgments.

Risk Assessment

Auditors act in three ways to minimize the risk of decision errors:

Evaluation of internal accounting control to determine the reliance to be placed on the client's system (review and compliance test procedures).

Performance of other supplementary procedures including analytical review (substantive procedures).

[10] The risk of human error is controlled in general through education, training, and supervision and on a particular engagement through a firm's quality control and review procedures.

Performance of detailed tests of dollar amounts of items (substantive procedures).

Reliance on Internal Control. The first "risk" an auditor faces is the probability that material errors occurred and went through the internal accounting control system undetected. This may happen as a result of weak or ineffective controls or because an influential manager circumvented existing controls. The latter cause is known as "management override" of the control system.

A basic assumption in auditing theory is that the existence of a satisfactory internal control system reduces the probability that material errors in the accounts will occur and go undetected and uncorrected. However, no internal control system is perfect, so errors in the accounts may exist. In short, there is always a probability that material errors may exist, and this probability is higher in systems with poor control and lower in systems with strong control.

The auditor cannot control this probability because it is a function of the data processing system for which management is responsible. All the auditor can do is try to evaluate the system and make a judgment about it in his or her proper study and evaluation of the existing internal control system.

Some information is available from the compliance tests of transaction details performed as a part of the study and evaluation of internal control. The auditor will have obtained CUPLs for several important control attributes. These CUPLs are measures of the proportion of control exceptions that may exist in a system, and they may be taken as indications of the risk that errors (all errors, material and immaterial) went undetected. However, when measuring a CUPL, the auditor takes a risk that the actual exception proportion may be higher.

Thus the auditor must consider: (1) the risk of material errors occurring in the first place and (2) the effectiveness of internal control in detecting and correcting such errors if they do occur. There is little or no practical basis for assessing the first of these risks, so auditing theory treats it conservatively as 100 percent (See *SAS No. 1* Section 320B.36). Consequently, the primary audit judgment is related to the reliability of internal control.

Let this reliability be symbolized by the letter C. An auditor must make a judgment about the reliability of the system and implicitly or explicitly assign a value to the judgment. Some possibilities are shown below:

Evaluation of Internal Control	*C**	*1 − C*
Excellent	90%	10%
Good	70	30
Fair	50	50
Poor	30	70
Unreliable	0	100

* Illustrative only.

The value $1 - C$ is an expression of the risk that material errors will go undetected through the internal accounting control system. As a practical matter of conservatism, auditors do not assign 100 percent reliability to internal control systems.

Risk of Nondiscovery—Supplementary Procedures. Substantive analytical review procedures (e.g., gross margin comparisons, bad debt history analysis) are usually based on overall relationships involving account balance numbers and comparative industry or comparative company statistics. Such procedures may be effective in signaling very large accounting misstatements, but they do not enable the auditor to see many details. Hence, their effectiveness for detecting material errors is not generally considered to be very high. One accounting firm, as a matter of policy, assigns 50 percent or less to the effectiveness of supplementary procedures for detecting material misstatements.

The area of analytical review and supplementary procedures is highly judgmental. With some trepidation one may identify *ESP* (Effectiveness of Supplementary Procedures) and assign a number to it. Thus the value of 1 minus *ESP* represents the risk that supplementary procedures will not enable the auditor to detect material errors.

For further illustration purposes *ESP* is assigned a value of 0 percent, thus $1 - ESP = 1$.

Risk of Nondiscovery—Detail Procedures. The β (beta) risk of making the Type II error is related to the reliability of internal control (C) and the effectiveness of suplementary procedures (ESP) through the concept of *ultimate risk.* Ultimate risk is a combination of three risk elements:

$$\text{Ultimate risk} = \beta\,(1 - C)(1 - ESP),$$

and when $1 - ESP = 1$,

$$\text{Ultimate risk} = \beta\,(1 - C).$$

The auditor wishes to control this ultimate risk of failing to detect material misstatement in financial statements. He or she may simply state: "An ultimate risk of 5 percent is tolerable."

The complement of the ultimate risk is known as *combined reliability* of all the auditing procedures. The ultimate risk and the combined reliability are the quantified equivalents of the concepts of due audit care and a reasonable auditing effort. A high risk (low combined reliability) may indicate a negligent audit. A low risk (high combined reliability) is a mark of an extensive, careful audit. However, an ultimate risk of zero can never be obtained, so some risk must be tolerated.

Putting these concepts together, we get

$$\text{Combined reliability} = 1 - \text{Ultimate risk},$$

and

$$\text{Combined reliability} = 1 - \beta(1 - C)(1 - ESP).$$

Solving this expression, we get

$$\beta = \frac{1 - \text{Combined reliability}}{(1 - C)(1 - ESP)}$$

EXHIBIT 10–6
Internal Control Evaluation and β Quantification

Internal Control Evaluation	*1-C*	*1-ESP*	β	*Combined Reliability*
Excellent	.10	1	.50	.95
Good	.30	1	.17	.95
Fair	.50	1	.10	.95
Poor	.70	1	.07	.95
Unreliable*	1.00	1	.05	.95

* "Unreliable" in this sense means that virtually all evidence depends upon the results of substantive procedures. Situations of abysmal internal controls may exist, and auditors may decide that no amount of testing will produce sufficient competent evidential matter.

Exhibit 10–6 shows the measurement of β for a range of internal control evaluations. Notice that β becomes smaller as internal control is judged to be less reliable. The smaller the value of β, the larger the required sample size (discussed in the next section). Thus, the proper relationship is maintained—the weaker the internal control, the more substantive testing must be done.

These formulations provide a *model* for thinking about audit decisions involving dollar values. It should be apparent that the model depends exclusively on matters of professional judgment. The value of a model is its straightforward recognition of the elements of judgment.

SAMPLE SIZE CALCULATION

A general equation for figuring sample size is shown below. Refer to Appendix 10–C for the same equation stated with the finite correction factor.

$$n = \frac{[S(Z_\alpha + Z_\beta)]^2}{(M/N)^2} \qquad \text{(Equation 6A)}$$

where:

- n is the number of items in the sample.
- S is the estimated standard deviation of the population.
- Z_α is the two-tailed normal deviation coefficient for α.
- Z_β is the one-tailed normal deviation coefficient for β.
- M is the amount judged material.
- N is the population size.

Using this equation on the illustrative data presented in the preceding sections, the auditor obtains a sample size of 400.

$$n = \frac{[(\$20.57)\,(1.28 + 1.645)]^2}{(\$25{,}000/8{,}300)^2} = \text{399 Customer accounts (rounded to 400)}$$

where:

S = \$20.57—the estimated population standard deviation.
Z_α = 1.28—the two-tailed normal deviation coefficient for $\alpha = 0.20$.

Z_β = 1.645—the one-tailed normal deviation coefficient for $\beta = 0.05$.
M = $25,000—the amount judged material.
N = 8,300—the number of customer accounts in the population.

The estimated population standard deviation (S) may be based on a sample of book values. The auditor can calculate S_y (using Equation 2A) based on book values rather than audited values and take the result as a preliminary estimate of S_y in order to calculate a sample size. Later, after the audit work is done, a better estimate of S_y can be obtained.

If the difference statistic is used, S should be an estimate of S_D (Equation 2B). The trouble is that little is known about the differences without performing audit procedures on numerous accounts. One other problem is that 50 to 80 nonzero differences will have to be found in order to obtain unbiased difference measurements. The auditor can make an estimate of the proportion of errors (say 15 percent) and figure the sample size necessary to find a minimum number of errors (in this example, $n = 400$: $15\% \times 400 = 60$). Otherwise some number representing S_D should be used in Equation 6A (in place of S) to calculate a sample size.

The coefficient for Z_α is found in Appendix 10–A. Find the cell entry closest to α and read the coefficient at the left and top margins. For example, $\alpha = .2005$ is the cell entry closest to $\alpha = .20$, read 1.2 at the left margin and .08 at the top margin for $Z_\alpha = 1.28$.

The coefficient for Z_β is found in Appendix 10–B. Find this one-tailed coefficient by finding the entry in the table for $1 - \beta$. For example, for $\beta = 0.05$ (reliability 95 percent), find the number closest to 0.95 ($= 1 - .05$). The value .95 is exactly between 1.64 and 1.65, so it can be read as 1.645. Interpolation on other coefficients is not really necessary.

One more point of emphasis: Sample size calculations as discussed above are usually based on a preliminary estimate of the standard deviation. Subsequent analysis of sample data should be based on the standard deviation of the sample itself.

Some relationships in Equation 6A should be understood. Preliminary sample sizes differ according to the variables decided upon by the auditor. Relationships of sample size to these variables are shown below.

Changes in Variables (taken one at a time)	*Effect on Sample Size*
N: Population size larger	Larger
S_y: Standard deviation larger	Larger
Z_α: α larger ($= Z_\alpha$ smaller)	Smaller
Z_β: β larger ($= Z_\beta$ smaller)	Smaller
M: Material amount larger	Smaller

DECISIONS USING UNSTRATIFIED MPU STATISTICS

When the substantive audit procedures have been completed and the auditor has obtained audited values (y_i) for the sample items, a quantitative test of the material accuracy of the dollar amount can be performed. The steps are shown below with hypothetical results from the sample of 400 accounts illustrated earlier.

Illustration of Positive Decision

A "positive decision" means that the auditor accepts the hypothesis that the book value is materially accurate.

Working with the MPU sample mean of $45.00 illustrated earlier ($n = 400$, $S_y = \$20.57$), the auditor computed an 80-percent confidence interval that contained the book value of $379,500. The decision error possible in this case is the Type II error—accepting a false hypothesis (outcome O_{12}). The associated risk is β (beta). Since the sample size of 400 was based on $\alpha = .20$, $\beta = .05$ and $S = \$20.57$, and S_y is exactly equal to $20.57, the maximum β for this decision is .05.

One further calculation related to β can be performed. The auditor may find some comfort in knowing the maximum probability that the MPU sample mean ($45.00) came from a distribution around an actual mean of $42.71 (actual book value of $354,499 as shown in Distribution 1, Exhibit 10–5).

A formula for this calculation is:

$$Z_\beta = \frac{\bar{Y} - \mu_{-M}}{S_{\bar{Y}}}, \qquad \text{(Equation 7A)[11]}$$

and when $\bar{Y} = \$45.00$

$$Z_\beta = \frac{\$45.00 - \$42.71}{\$1.03} = \frac{\$2.29}{\$1.03} = 2.22$$

The MPU sample mean ($\bar{Y} = \$45.00$) lies a distance of $2.29 from the hypothetical misstated MPU population mean ($\mu_{-M} = \$42.71$), and this represents 2.22 standard errors (= $2.29/$1.03). Using Appendix 10–B, we get $\beta = 0.0132$ for $Z_\beta = 2.22$.

Thus the risk of Type II decision error is 1.32 percent.

Illustration of Negative Decision

A "negative decision" means that the auditor rejects the hypothesis that the book value is materially accurate, accepting instead the alternative—that it misstates the actual value by at least $25,000.

Working with the MPU sample mean of $43.60 illustrated earlier ($n = 400$, $S_y = \$20.57$), the auditor computed an 80-percent confidence

[11] If the sample mean is greater than the book value average, indicating a possible understatement in the book value, equation 7A would be:

$$Z_\beta = \frac{\mu_{+M} - \bar{Y}}{S_{\bar{Y}}}$$

interval that did not contain the book value of \$379,500. The decision error possible in this case is the Type I error—rejecting a true hypothesis (outcome O_{21}). The associated risk is α (alpha). Since the sample size of 400 was based on $\alpha = .20$, $\beta = .05$ and $S = \$20.57$, and S_y is exactly equal to \$20.57, the maximum α for this decision is .20 *if* the actual value is exactly \$379,500.

One further calculation can be made. The auditor can figure the probability that the MPU sample mean came from a distribution around an actual value of \$379,500 ($\mu = \$45.72$). If the MPU sample mean did indeed come from such a distribution, the decision that the book value is overstated by \$25,000 or more is a Type I error. A formula for this calculation is:

$$Z_\alpha = \frac{\mu - \bar{Y}}{S_{\bar{Y}}}, \qquad \text{(Equation 7B)}^{12}$$

and

$$Z_\alpha = \frac{\$45.72 - \$43.60}{\$1.03} = \frac{\$2.12}{\$1.03} = 2.06$$

The MPU sample mean ($\bar{Y} = \$43.60$) lies a distance of \$2.12 from the hypothetical accurate MPU population mean ($\mu = \$45.72$), and this represents 2.06 standard errors (= \$2.12/\$1.03). Using Appendix 10–A, $\alpha = 0.0394$ for $Z_\alpha = 2.06$. Thus the risk is 3.94 percent of deciding that the book value is materially misstated when both the book value and the actual value are equal to \$379,500.

The risk of making this Type I decision error appears to be very small. However, the auditor should also have definite and defensible evidence of the amount and source of the misstatement. Knowledge of the source is needed in order to explain the misstatement to client personnel, and knowledge of the amount is needed to propose an adjusting journal entry. In most cases when the MPU estimate is used, the negative decision leads to more audit work designed to establish a reasonably accurate statement of the balance.

Calculating precise MPU interval estimates using large sample sizes is one way to obtain an estimate of the actual value. Another way is to measure directly the differences between audited values and book values for each item in a sample.

DECISIONS USING DIFFERENCE STATISTICS

The difference measure can be used when: (1) there is a book value for each item, (2) the item book values add up to the control account balance under audit, (3) there are a sufficient number of differences in the sample

---

[12] If the sample mean is greater than the book value average, indicating a possible understatement in the book value, Equation 7B would be:

$$Z_\alpha = \frac{\bar{Y} - \mu}{S_{\bar{Y}}}$$

(50 to 80), and (4) the amounts of the differences are not proportional to their respective book values (e.g., differences are not, for example, 10 percent of the book value in both large and small book values).[13]

The difference statistic is appealing to auditors because it represents a direct measurement of the dollar amount of error. Like the MPU decision model, the critical judgments are the monetary amount considered material and the risk of making a wrong decision.

Auditing standards explain a decision criterion as follows: "The risk that material errors will not be detected in the auditor's examination is measured by the complement of the reliability level used if the auditor compares the upper precision limit of monetary error to the amount he considers material." (*SAS No. 1* Section 320B.30.). The important concept in this standard is the *upper precision limit of monetary error* (indicated by *LME* below).

Notice that the *LME*—a decision-oriented statistical result—is calculated using Z_β, the normal deviation coefficient for β (beta). This differs from the calculation of a difference statistic interval estimate which uses Z_α, the normal deviation coefficient for α (alpha). Refer to Equations 4B and 5B to see Z_α used in the interval estimate.

Definition of LME

1. If the average of the differences is positive, that is,

$$\bar{D} = \frac{\Sigma d_i}{n} > o,$$

where $d_i = y_i - x_i$ (indicating an *understatement* in the book value):

$$LME = N(\bar{D} + Z_\beta S_{\bar{D}}) \qquad \text{(Equation 8A)}$$

2. If the average of the differences is negative, that is,

$$\bar{D} = \frac{\Sigma d_i}{n} < o,$$

where $d_i = y_i - x_i$ (indicating an *overstatement* in the book value):

$$LME = |N(\bar{D} - Z_\beta S_{\bar{D}})| \qquad \text{(Equation 8B)}^{14}$$

By these two definitions, the upper precision limit of monetary error is viewed as the largest value of a difference statistic estimate calculated using the coefficient for Z_β. This value is compared to M, and (1) if the absolute value of the upper precision limit is smaller than M, the amount of error discovered is considered immaterial and the balance is accepted as materially accurate, (2) if the absolute value of the upper precision

[13] The difference measure can be used when differences are proportional to book values, but the ratio statistic is more efficient.

[14] The notation $|N(\bar{D} - Z_\beta S_{\bar{D}})|$ indicates the *absolute* value of the measure, effectively removing the minus sign from the result.

limit is greater than M, the amount of error discovered is considered material and the decision is that the balance is materially misstated.[15]

In the accounts receivable example used throughout this chapter, suppose the auditor obtained the results shown in Exhibit 10–7. For purposes

EXHIBIT 10–7
Illustrative Difference Statistic Data

Sample Item (i)	Audited Value (y_i)	Book Value (x_i)	Difference (d_i)	$(d_i - \bar{D})^2$
1	$ 45	$ 50	$ −5	$ 16
2	26	25	1	4
3	100	100	0	1
4	37	35	2	9
5	17	20	−3	4
.	.	.	.	.
.	.	.	.	.
.	.	.	.	.
225	300	310	−10	81
Sums	$10,125	$10,350	$−225	$86,464
$\bar{Y}$ =	$45			
$\bar{X}$ =		$46		
$\bar{D}$ =			$−1	

of this illustration the book value under audit is the $379,500 recorded amount which will appear in the financial statements. The material amount (M = $25,000) refers to errors in the recorded values and determinations of uncollectible amounts.

The steps in the decision are these:

1. Calculate the average difference (Equation 1B)

$$\bar{D} = \frac{\Sigma d_i}{n} = \frac{\$-225}{225} = \$-1.00$$

2. Calculate the standard deviation (Equation 2B)

$$S_D = \sqrt{\sum_{i=1}^{n} \frac{(d_i - \bar{D})^2}{n-1}} = \sqrt{\frac{86{,}464}{224}}$$
$$= \sqrt{386}$$
$$= \$19.65$$

3. Calculate the standard error (Equation 3B)

$$S_{\bar{D}} = \frac{S_D}{\sqrt{n}} = \frac{\$19.65}{\sqrt{225}} = \$1.31$$

[15] For further explanation of the risk of decision error in this test, see Donald M. Roberts, "A Statistical Interpretation of SAP No. 54," *Journal of Accountancy*, March 1974, pp. 50–53.

4. Calculate *LME* (Equation 8B)

For reliability = 95%, $\beta = 0.05$

$$LME = |N(\bar{D} - Z_\beta S_{\bar{D}})|$$
$$= |8{,}300(-\$1 - (1.645)(\$1.31))| = |-\$26{,}186|$$
$$LME = \$26{,}186$$

5. Apply the decision rule: If $LME < M$, accept the book value as a materially accurate amount. If $LME > M$, decide that the book value is a material misstatement of the actual amount.

In this case the amount of error discovered was a \$225 *overstatement* in the book value—an average of \$1 per customer account audited, or \$8,300 when expressed as a point estimate of the population (= 8,300 × \$1). Statistical measurement gives the information that the amount of error is less than \$26,186 (*overstatement*), with 95 percent reliability. There is a 5-percent risk that the amount of error is greater than \$26,186. The auditor's criterion was to accept a risk of 5 percent that the amount of error might be greater than \$25,000, so the book value fails the decision rule test.

One additional calculation might help. The auditor can ask: "What is the risk that the amount of error exceeds M = \$25,000?" This calculation is shown below.

$$LME = M = |N(\bar{D} - Z_\beta S_{\bar{D}})| = \$25{,}000$$

$$Z_\beta = \frac{M - N|\bar{D}|}{NS_{\bar{D}}} \qquad \text{(Equation 7C)}$$

$$Z_\beta = \frac{\$25{,}000 - 8{,}300\ (\$1)}{8{,}300(\$1.31)} = 1.54$$

$$\beta = 0.0618 \text{ for } Z_\beta = 1.54 \quad \text{(Appendix 10–B)}$$

The risk therefore is 6.18 percent, and the reliability is 93.82 percent. These measures do not meet the auditor's quantitative criteria of 5 percent risk and 95 percent reliability set out at the beginning of the test. Having made this preliminary decision, additional work must be done to determine the source and amount of error so that an adjustment can be made. In contrast to the MPU measurement, however, the auditor has direct measurements of the amount of error.

QUANTITATIVE AND QUALITATIVE ANALYSIS

The explanations up to this point have concerned *quantitative* analysis of audited sample data. Statistical methods provide a means of making such measurements, but auditors' decisions still depend upon professional judgments of acceptable risk of decision error and the monetary amount considered material. In short, an auditor can use statistics, but the statistical measurements and the decision indicated by them must be given an audit interpretation and meaning.

In addition to professional judgments about acceptable risk and material amount, *qualitative* elements of analysis include follow-up of all monetary errors discovered in the sample. The auditor will want to find out whether errors resulted from (1) irregularities—intentional acts to misstate amounts in the accounts or (2) errors—inadvertent mistakes affecting money amounts. Also, the auditor will want to know whether either irregularities or errors involved (*a*) systematic misstatements or random occurrences, (*b*) misapplication of an accounting principle or method, (*c*) certain types of accounts or transactions (e.g., transactions with related parties), or (*d*) cases of management override of controls. For example, the audit of accounts receivable may indicate the systematic error of overstating customers' balances due because discounts allowed are recorded sometime after payment is received. The identification of other kinds of qualitative findings depends on what account is being audited. One other illustration is given below.

> ***Illustration.*** The audit of inventory prices and extensions revealed that unit prices were taken from the purchase orders rather than from the vendors' invoices. In several cases these prices included cash and trade discounts. Statistical analysis showed that the use of these prices caused a material overstatement of the inventory total. Upon request, clients' personnel repriced the inventory by acquisition costs and the auditor reaudited the results.

Knowledge of the source, nature, and amount of monetary errors is very important. Such knowledge is required in order to explain the situation to the client and direct additional work to areas where corrections and adjustments need to be made. The auditor's work is not complete until error analysis and follow-up is done.

SUMMARY OF STATISTICAL METHODOLOGY

To this point in the chapter, the following topics have been covered:

- The auditor's problem.
- Sampling objectives.
- Statistical concepts.
  - Elementary definitions.
  - Calculations of MPU and difference statistics.
  - Risks of decision error.
- Auditing decisions.
  - Quantitative decision rules.
  - Qualitative error analysis.

These topics have been presented in sequence so that the logic of applying a structured methodology to a problem can be clear. Sometimes, however, it is too easy to be overwhelmed by what appears to be a complex approach to problems. This tendency can be avoided by spending a little time on the broad outlines of decision-making methodology. Time, experience, and practice will eventually serve to fill in the technical gaps that may now exist.

EXHIBIT 10–8
Statistical-Based Decisions and a Scientific Method

Statistical-Based Audit Decisions	*Scientific Method*
1. Specify the objectives of the audit test, the nature of the procedures, and define the relevant population of evidential items.	1. Recognize the assertion(s), problems, and preliminary data required to formulate a testable hypothesis statement.
2. Specify the hypothesis to be tested. The general specification is: "The book value is materially accurate"; and the alternative specification is: "The book value is materially misstated."	2. Formulate the hypothesis in such a manner that either acceptance or rejection of it yields a useful auditing decision.
3. Obtain sufficient competent evidential matter.	3. Collect competent evidence that contributes to the decision.
a. Estimate the variability of the population items, set decision criteria for materiality and risk of decision error. Calculate sample size.	*a*. Select applicable evidence-gathering techniques and procedures.
b. Select sample items at random and apply appropriate audit evidence-gathering procedures.	*b*. Perform the techniques and procedures to obtain evidence.
4. Calculate the values of audited data and determine whether the audit findings meet criteria for concluding material accuracy or material misstatement.	4. Evaluate the evidence relative to the decision problem hypothesis and assess its sufficiency for the decision choice.
5. Reach a conclusion as to material accuracy or material misstatement. Document the decision. Based on the decision, decide what to do next in the audit.	5. Make the decision to accept or reject the problem-related hypothesis.

Exhibit 10–8 is presented as a broad summary of the decision-making methodology. The statistical methodology is related to the structured scientific method introduced in Chapter 1.

The last section in the chapter on stratified statistics gives a brief introduction to methods used frequently in practice. Some acquaintance obtained now will make future exposures to course work and technical training much easier.

STRATIFIED STATISTICS

Stratification is a method of achieving sampling efficiency. *Efficiency*, in an audit sampling context, refers to the auditor's performance of enough work (i.e., large enough sample size) to show due audit care and regard for professional standards, yet limit the work (i.e., limit the sample size) to come within reasonable bounds of time and cost on the audit engagement. Concurrently, the auditor has to pay attention to the risks of decision error inherent in sample-based testing.

In the accounts receivable example in this chapter, a hypothetical sample size of 400 was used for illustrative purposes. This number was found using the sample size formula (Equation 6A), incorporating $\alpha = 0.20$, $\beta = 0.05$, $M = 25{,}000$, $N = 8{,}300$ and $S = \$20.57$. Assume instead that $S = \$133$. In this case $n = 5{,}542$ (using the finitely corrected equation in Appendix 10–C), and the "sample" of 5,542 out of 8,300 appears to be extremely large.

The assumption of $S = \$133$ is in fact a realistic relationship. The MPU statistic tends to have a relatively large standard deviation. The sample size equation is very sensitive to the magnitude of the standard deviation, hence MPU statistics appear to require very large samples when unrestricted random sampling is the method used to choose sample items from a single population.

Accounting populations tend to have a few high-dollar items and many small-dollar items. (Populations are "skewed" to the right.) The high-dollar items tend to have a large standard deviation while the small-dollar items tend to have a relatively small standard deviation. As a practical matter, auditors frequently use *stratified* sampling methods in order to control the effect of standard deviation on sample size and to achieve audit objectives with smaller samples.

Stratified Mean-per-Unit Statistics

In stratified sampling the auditor breaks up the whole population into subsets (strata) in order to set aside the high-value items for special attention and achieve sampling efficiency. This stratification has the effect of removing the largest deviations from the population, causing the standard deviation measure of the remaining items to be smaller. Since the calculated sample size is directly related to the magnitude of the standard deviation, the sample sizes for the medium- to low-value strata tend to be smaller in the stratification calculation than they would be in a calculation based on the overall standard deviation.

The efficiency in sampling centers around three features.

A small number of high-value items may be audited completely, and the auditor can thus cover a large dollar volume. The sampling error for a complete audit of this stratum is zero.

The sample sizes in the remaining strata are smaller. The savings through sample size reduction overcome the cost of the complete audit of the high-value stratum.

The estimate of a dollar value can be made more efficiently; that is, more precisely and with fewer total sample items than is possible with an unstratified sample.

In applying methods of stratified sampling, the important audit decisions are: (1) how to identify relevant strata, (2) how to calculate the required sample size, (3) how to apportion the sample to the strata, and (4) how to perform the estimation calculations.

Identifying Relevant Strata

Segments of a population may be identified by professional judgment.[16] The auditor must decide what characteristics of a population are most relevant for the objectives of the audit. For example, the general objective of estimating a total amount calls for stratification of accounts by dollar balances. Dollar value stratification has the effect of differentiating among segments of the population on the basis of relative standard deviation.

For example, suppose that the illustrative accounts receivable population had the following characteristics:[17]

Stratum	*Book Value Interval*	*Number of Accounts*	*Total Dollar Amount*	*Standard Deviation in Stratum*	*Sample Size (Equation 6B)*
0	$512–$6,870	78	$ 90,000	$1,100.00	78
1	$ 64–$ 512	1,000	123,500	$ 224.00	524
2	$ 32–$ 64	1,211	60,000	$ 16.00	45
3	$ 16–$ 32	3,241	81,000	$ 8.00	61
4	$ 1–$ 16	2,770	25,000	7.50	49
Strata 1–4		8,222	$289,500		
Total population		8,300	$379,500	$ 133.00	757

Sample Size Calculation and Allocation

The total sample size for auditing purposes is the sum of the sample sizes computed separately for each stratum. Most auditors would identify a top stratum of high-dollar accounts and audit it completely (Stratum 0 above—78 customer accounts). Equation 6B shown below then would be used to calculate the sample for the remaining 8,222 accounts and allocate it to strata.

[16] Optimal stratification rules are available, but they are beyond the scope of this textbook. See W. G. Cochran, *Sampling Techniques*, 2d ed. (New York: John Wiley & Sons, Inc., 1963).

[17] For reference purposes, these data are adaptations from Population 1 used in *Auditing Research Monograph No. 2*. See citation in the Sources and Additional Reading References at the end of this chapter.

$$n_h = \frac{N_h S_h \sum_{h=1}^{k} N_h S_h}{\left(\frac{M}{Z_\alpha + Z_\beta}\right)^2 + \sum_{h=1}^{k} N_h S_h^2} \qquad \text{(Equation 6B)}$$

where:

$h = 1, 2 \ldots k$	is the number of strata.
n_h	is the sample size for the hth stratum.
N_h	is the number of items in the hth stratum (population size).
S_h	is the estimated standard deviation in the hth stratum.
M	is the total amount considered material.
Z_α and Z_β	are the normal deviation coefficients for specified α and β.
N	is the total population size (sum of N_h, $h = 1 \ldots k$).

One can see that the total sample size using stratified sampling is smaller than the sample size calculated without stratification.[18] Computational details for the above example are set up in Exercise 10.24.

Estimation Calculations with Stratified MPU

The application of stratified sampling produces an interval estimate of the dollar amount in a manner similar to the methods of unstratified estimation explained earlier. However, with stratification the estimate is far more precise because of the reduction of sampling error gained by extensive auditing of the high-dollar items (hence smaller standard error measures).

The midpoint of the interval estimate—the average audited value—is calculated as a weighted average of the strata averages, as shown in Equation 1C below. Computational details are set up in Exercise 10.25.

Stratified MPU mean.

$$\bar{Y}_s = \frac{\sum_{h=0}^{k} (N_h \bar{Y}_h)}{N} \qquad \text{(Equation 1C)}$$

where $\bar{Y}_h$ is the MPU sample mean of the hth stratum.

The sampling error (standard error) is also calculated as a weighted average, as shown in Equation 3C. Computational details are set up in Exercise 10.26.

[18] Equation 6B can be used to calculate n_h for a stratified *difference* statistic by substituting the appropriate standard deviation of the differences for S_h.

Standard error of the stratified MPU mean.

$$S_{\bar{Y}_s} = \left[\frac{\sum_{h=0}^{k} N_h^2 \left(\frac{S_{y_h}}{\sqrt{n_h}} \right)^2}{N^2} \right]^{1/2} \qquad \text{(Equation 3C)}$$

where S_{y_h} is the standard deviation calculated for each stratum using Equation 2A.

The interval estimate is calculated in much the same manner as for unstratified MPU statistics. Equations are shown below and computational details are set up in Exercise 10.27.

Achieved precision using stratified MPU.

$$P_{Y_s} = Z_\alpha \cdot S_{\bar{Y}_s} \qquad \text{(Equation 4C)}$$

Confidence intervals using stratified MPU.

$$\begin{aligned} L_1 &= N(\bar{Y}_s - P_{Y_s}) \\ L_2 &= N(\bar{Y}_s + P_{Y_s}) \end{aligned} \qquad \text{(Equation 5C)}$$

All of the equations above are given in their finitely corrected form in Appendix 10–C.

Dollar-Unit Stratification

Dollar-unit sampling (DUS) is a modified form of attributes sampling that permits the auditor to reach conclusions about dollar amounts. A variation is called *combined attributes-variables* (CAV) sampling. Recall from Chapter 7 the discussion of the point that compliance tests of control procedures based on attribute statistics did not directly incorporate dollar measurements; hence, conclusions were limited to decisions about the proportion of control procedure exceptions found.

DUS is a sampling plan that corresponds dollar amounts to attribute statistics, thus facilitating conclusions about dollar balances and totals. The method has been discussed extensively by Canadian authorities[19] and is the underlying structure for the Deloitte Haskins and Sells sampling plan used by that firm for many years. The method purports to overcome difficulties inherent in other sampling plans, such as:

Unstratified MPU plans call for gigantic sample sizes, and they center attention on audited item values rather than on differences, with which the auditor should be primarily concerned.

Differences statistics suffer problems of bias because a sufficient number of differences may not be found in a sample to permit proper use.

[19] R. Anderson and A. D. Teitlebaum, "Dollar-Unit Sampling," *CA Magazine*, April 1973, pp. 30–39.

Attributes statistics, as conventionally applied, do not associate dollar amounts with statistical measures; hence, they are not useful for decisions about dollar amounts.

First, one must recognize one of the major stumbling blocks of most variables statistics measurements—the statistical standard deviation. When using MPU and difference statistics (unstratified and stratified), the statistical *precision* (P_Y, P_D, and P_Y: see Equations 4A, 4B, and 4C) depends upon the confidence level (Z_α), sample size (n) and the standard deviation (S_y, S_D, S_{y_s}). When using attributes statistics, the statistical *precision* depends on confidence level, sample size, and the number of exceptions found. For example, if one exception was found in a sample of 100, the auditor could have 90 percent reliability that the population exception proportion did not exceed 4 percent. (Refer to Appendix 7–C.3.) Precision in this example is 3 percent—the difference between the sample exception proportion (1 percent) and the CUPL (4 percent).

The trick that enables DUS to correspond dollar amounts to attributes statistics is to define the population as $*BV* individual items, each of which is an item subject to being included in the sample. For example, the 8,300 accounts receivable totaling $379,500 ($*BV*) would be defined as 379,500 dollar units. (Imagine the accounts being represented by 379,500 dollar bills spread out on a table.[20])

Now imagine drawing a sample of 100 individual $1 items (disregarding for the moment which customers' accounts turn up in the sample). Suppose that no exceptions are found. Attributes statistics enables the auditor to measure a computed upper precision limit of 3 percent with 90 percent reliability. (Refer to Appendix 7–C.3.) Furthermore, because the dollar units constituted the population definition, the auditor can also measure an upper limit of dollar error in the amount of $11,385 (= 3% × $379,500) with 90 percent reliability. The only assumption necessary for this calculation is that a customer's account balance (and each dollar in it) cannot be overstated by more than the book value of the account.

Selecting a Dollar-Unit Sample. Continuing with the accounts receivable example of 8,300 accounts totaling $379,500, assume that the auditor wants to select 100 dollar units for audit. Basically the selection process is to obtain a random starting point and select every 3,795th *dollar* as a sample item. (This is a type of *systematic sampling*.) This method assures that the largest customer's account ($6,870) will be included in the sample, and in fact all larger *customer accounts* have a greater likelihood of selection than smaller ones because the former contain more dollar units. (For example, a $2,000 customer account is ten times more likely to contain a dollar chosen in the sample than another customer's $200 account.) This selection is still random, however, because the sample *item* is the dollar, not the customer. The effect is a very high degree of stratification of the population.

---

[20] Anderson and Teitlebaum, "Dollar-Unit Sampling," pp. 30–39.

Pricing the Errors Discovered in a Sample. Assume that upon audit of the 100 dollar units, one such dollar was in a \$1,000 account whose value should be \$750—a 25-percent overstatement. Now the sample consists of 99 dollar units without error and 1 dollar unit with a 25-percent error (a "tainted" dollar). The most conservative expression of the results is the following:[21]

(1) Dollars Sampled	(2) Errors Found	(3) Tainting Percentage	(4) Worst-Case Allocation of Total Upper Error Limit	(5) Net Upper Error Limit (3) × (4)
99	0	100%	3.00%	3.00%
1	1	25	1.00	.25
100			4.00%	3.25%

Thus the auditor's conclusion is that the accounts receivable may be overstated by as much as \$12,333.75 (= 3.25% × \$379,500), with 90 percent reliability.

Sample Size Determination in DUS. The basic formula for the calculation of DUS sample size is:[22]

DUS sample size.

$$n = \frac{BV \times RF}{M} \qquad \text{(Equation 6C)}$$

where:

BV is the total book value.
RF is a DUS "risk factor" related to the probability (β) of a Type II decision error. Risk factors are:

β	*RF*
20%	1.61
15	1.90
10	2.30
5	3.00
2.5	3.69
1	4.61

M is the dollar amount considered material.

[21] Example adapted from Anderson and Teitlebaum, "Dollar-Unit Sampling," pp. 30–39. Using Appendix 7–C introduces some inaccuracy because the computed upper precision limits have been rounded off. More accurate results can be obtained using binomial tables, Poisson approximations of the binomial, or tables packaged for use with DUS.

[22] Adapted from R. J. Anderson, *The External Audit 1* (Toronto: Pitman Publishing, 1977), p. 624.

In the accounts receivable example, with $\beta = 0.10$ the DUS sample size would be \$35 as shown below.

$$n = \frac{BV \times RF}{M} = \frac{379{,}500 \times 2.30}{25{,}000} = 35$$

This calculation of sample size, however, holds some dangers. While the calculation controls β ("beta"), a very high risk of a Type I error exists (α, "alpha"). For example, if 6.5 percent of the dollars in the accounts receivable are 100 percent fictitious (a total overstatement of \$24,667.50 = 6.5% × \$379,500, almost equal to the \$25,000 material amount), the probability of finding at least one such dollar in the sample is 0.90.[23] Thus, with a sample of 35 dollar units from a materially accurate balance, there is a 90-percent chance that the decision will be that the balance is not materially accurate. (Discovering one 100-percent error would cause the computed upper error limit to be about \$42,000 which is greater than M = \$25,000.)

DUS samplers usually take some precautions to control both α and β simultaneously. The effect is to select samples larger than those given by Equation 6C.

SUMMARY

Statistical methods are not substitutes for the auditor's professional judgment. The explanations in this chapter should make it clear that statistical decisions depend upon the auditor's identification and quantification of what dollar amount is considered material, of the effectiveness of internal control, and of the acceptable risks of decision error. Statistics is beneficial, however, because it forces the auditor to think about decision criteria before performing procedures and because it enables him to measure risks and amounts of dollar error.

Having conducted this thoughtful planning process and having gathered evidence from a random sample of items chosen for audit, an auditor can do one or all of the following: (1) test a hypothesis about the balance under audit, (2) calculate an interval measurement, and (3) calculate a risk of decision error. Each of these operations was explained in this chapter first in the general form of an equation and then with a numerical example.

This chapter contains the rudimentary elements of statistical applications that serve as a basis for more advanced practical applications. Almost all field applications employ some form of stratification of a population, and many applications are performed with computerized routines.

---

[23] Recall from Chapter 7 the discovery sampling formulation: $CR\% = 1 - (1 - AUPL)^n = 1 - (1 - .065)^{35} = 0.90$ = the probability of including at least one occurrence of a 100-percent error in a sample of 35 when the proportion of such occurrences is 6.5 percent.

SOURCES AND ADDITIONAL READING REFERENCES

Introduction and Application

Aly, H. F., and Duboff, J. I. "Statistical versus Judgment Sampling: An Empirical Study of Auditing the Accounts Receivable of a Small Retail Store," *Accounting Review,* January 1971, pp. 119–28.

Anderson, Rodney J. "Audit Uses of Statistical Sampling," *Internal Auditor,* May/June 1973, pp. 31–41.

Anderson, Rodney J. *The External Audit 1.* Toronto: Pitman Publishing, 1977. Especially chap. 13, "Statistical Sampling" (pp. 330–77) and chap. 22, "Supplement on Statistical Sampling Theory" (DUS, pp. 610–27).

Anderson, R. J., and Teitlebaum, A. D. "Dollar-Unit Sampling," *CA Magazine,* April 1973, pp. 30–39.

Arkin, Herbert. *Handbook of Sampling for Auditing and Accounting,* 2d. ed. New York: McGraw-Hill Book Co., 1974.

Barrett, M. J., and Ricketts, D. E. "The Statistical Auditor," *The Internal Auditor,* February 1977, pp. 32–37.

Bedingfield, James P. "The Current State of Statistical Sampling and Auditing," *Journal of Accountancy,* December 1975, pp. 48–55.

Deakin, Edward B., and Granof, Michael H. "Regression Analysis as a Means of Determining Audit Sample Size," *Accounting Review,* October 1974, pp. 764–71.

Elliot, R. K., and Rogers, J. R. "Relating Statistical Sampling to Audit Objectives," *Journal of Accountancy,* July 1972, pp. 46–55.

Loebbecke, J. K., and Neter, J. "Statistical Sampling in Confirming Receivables," *Journal of Accountancy,* June 1973, pp. 44–50.

Newman, Maurice S. "Regression Estimates for Accounting Purposes," *Selected Papers,* Haskins & Sells, 1972, pp. 172–94.

Roberts, Donald M. "Statistical Interpretation of SAP No. 54," *Journal of Accountancy,* March 1974, pp. 47–53.

Tummins, M., and Watson, H. J. "Enriching Audit Data," *Internal Auditor,* September/October 1972, pp. 63–73.

Research Papers and Advanced Sources

Barkman, Arnold. "Within-Item Variation: A Stochastic Approach to Audit Uncertainty," *Accounting Review,* April 1977, 450–64.

Cochran, Wm. G. *Sampling Techniques,* 2d ed. New York: John Wiley & Sons, Inc., 1963.

Felix, W. L., Jr., and Grimlund, R. A. "A Sampling Model for Audit Tests of Composite Accounts," *Journal of Accounting Research,* Spring 1977, pp. 23–41.

Hansen, D. R., and Shaftel, T. L. "Sampling for Integrated Objectives in Auditing," *Accounting Review,* January 1977, pp. 109–23.

Ijiri, Y., and Kaplan, R. S. "A Model for Integrating Sampling Objectives in Auditing," *Journal of Accounting Research,* Spring 1971, pp. 73–87.

Kaplan, Robert S. "A Stochastic Model for Auditing," *Journal of Accounting Research,* Spring 1973, pp. 38–46.

Kaplan, Robert S. "Statistical Sampling in Auditing with Auxiliary Information Estimators," *Journal of Accounting Research,* Autumn 1973, pp. 238–58.

Kaplan, Robert S. "Sample Size Computations for Dollar-Unit Sampling," *Journal of Accounting Research,* Supplement 1975, pp. 126–33.

Kinney, Wm. R., Jr. "A Decision Theory Approach to the Sampling Problem in Auditing," *Journal of Accounting Research.* Spring 1975, pp. 117–32.

Kinney, Wm. R., Jr. "Decision Theory Aspects of Internal Control System Design/Compliance and Substantive Tests," *Journal of Accounting Research,* Supplement 1975, pp. 14–37.

Loebbecke, J. K., and Neter, J. "Considerations in Choosing Statistical Sampling Procedures in Auditing," *Journal of Accounting Research,* Supplement 1975, pp. 38–68.

Neter, J., and Loebbecke, J. K. *Behavior of Major Statistical Estimators in Sampling Accounting Populations.* Auditing Research Monograph No. 2 (New York: AICPA, 1975).

Roberts, Donald M. *Statistical Auditing.* New York: American Institute of Certified Public Accountants, 1978.

Smith, K. A. "The Relationship of Internal Control Evaluation and Audit Sample Size," *Accounting Review,* April 1972, pp. 260–69.

Teitlebaum, A. D., and Robinson, C. F. "The Real Risks in Audit Sampling," *Journal of Accounting Research,* Supplement 1975, pp. 70–97.

REVIEW QUESTIONS

10.1. Define sample "item" in the context of an unrestricted random sample of (*a*) accounts receivable and (*b*) inventory.

10.2. Explain what is meant by (*a*) representative, (*b*) corrective, (*c*) protective, and (*d*) preventive sampling.

10.3. Define judgmental sampling. What is its most obvious drawback?

10.4. What is the *materiality criterion* (M) in reference to the audit of a book value?

10.5. Explain what is meant by (*a*) risk and (*b*) reliability in a statistical-auditing context.

10.6. Explain the four possible combinations of decision outcomes in terms of alpha and beta risks in the context of statistical-based audit decisions.

10.7. Explain the two hypothetical decision alternatives in the context of an audit of a book value.

10.8. Identify the relationship to sample size of each of the following: alpha, beta, population size, standard deviation, and material error (M).

10.9. How may *difference estimation* be used by the auditor?

10.10. What is the purpose of employing stratified random sampling for estimation of variables? What important audit decisions are associated with stratified sampling?

EXERCISES AND PROBLEMS

10.11. In sampling for variables (dollar amounts, weights, and the like), what must be known or calculated about the population, and what factors must be decided upon by the auditor in order to determine sample size? What must be calculated and observed from the audited sample findings in order to make a statistical estimate and a statistical-based decision?

10.12. Using the information given below, calculate the MPU confidence interval estimates of the dollar values (*a*) without finite correction, (*b*) with finite correction. Arrange your solution in the following format:

Case ________	*Without Finite Correction*	*With Finite Correction*
Equation		
1A Mean.		
2A Std. Dev.		
3A Std. Error.		
Z_α Coefficient.		
4A Achieved precision.		
5A L_1.		
5A L_2.		

Case	(*a*)	(*b*)	(*c*)
Standard deviation	$25	$25	$25
Material amount	50,000	50,000	50,000
Confidence level	95%	95%	90%
Sample size	225	144	144
Total sample value	$21,825	$15,120	$21,600
Population size	10,000	10,000	10,000
Population total value	$1 million	$1.06 million	$1.5 million

Figures: $\sqrt{1 - \frac{225}{10000}} = .988686 \qquad \sqrt{1 - \frac{144}{10000}} = .992774$

10.13. Chapter 10 illustrates MPU standard deviation calculations based on two sets of sample data. Sample A values are more widely dispersed and the standard deviation is larger than in Sample B. Refer to the illustrations of Equation 2A, 3A, 4A, and 5A calculations in the chapter.

The chapter also contains an illustration of 80 percent, 90 percent, 95 percent, and 99 percent confidence intervals based on Sample A data. The point of interest for the requirements below is to illustrate the relationship of *confidence interval width* to (*a*) confidence level and (*b*) variability.

Required:

a. Prepare a schedule showing *confidence interval width* for Sample A data (see Chapter 10) for confidence levels of 80 percent, 90 percent, 95 percent, and 99 percent.

b. Calculate the 80 percent, 90 percent, 95 percent, and 99 percent confidence intervals for Sample B data and compare these to Sample A.

c. Explain why Sample B intervals are always narrower than Sample A.

10.14. Chapter 10 contains an illustration of outcomes O_{12} and O_{22} in which the following statements are made:

Given a sample of 400 customer accounts from a population of 8,300 with total book value of \$379,500, the mean of the actual values obtained can range from less than \$42.71 to more than \$48.74. When the sample standard deviation is \$20.57:

1. An 80-percent confidence interval based on a MPU sample mean less than \$44.40 will *not* contain \$379,500 (the book value).
2. An 80-percent confidence interval based on any MPU sample mean between \$44.40 and \$47.04 will contain \$379,500 (the book value).
3. An 80-percent confidence interval based on a sample mean greater than \$47.04 will not contain \$379,500 (the book value).

Required:

a. Show calculations demonstrating the relationships stated in 1, 2, and 3 above. (Hint: Use assumed MPU means of \$44.39, \$44.41, \$47.03 and \$47.05.)

b. Assuming that the actual value is \$379,500, which of 1, 2, or 3 represents a decision error? Is it a Type I or Type II error?

c. Assuming that the actual value is \$404,501, which of 1, 2, or 3 represents a decision error? Is it a Type I or Type II error?

d. What *decision rule* did you use in responding to parts *b* and *c* above?

10.15. You desire to evaluate the reasonableness of the book value of the inventory of your client, Draper, Inc. You satisfied yourself earlier as to inventory quantities. During the examination of the pricing and extension of the inventory, the following data were gathered using appropriate unrestricted random sampling with replacement procedures.

Total items in the inventory (N)	12,700
Total items in the sample (n)	400
Total audited value of times in the sample	\$ 38,400
$\sum_{i=1}^{400} (y_i - \bar{Y})^2$	\$312,816
Formula for estimated population standard deviation	$S_y = \sqrt{\dfrac{\sum_{i=1}^{n} (y_i - \bar{Y})^2}{n-1}}$
Formula for estimated standard error of the mean	$S_{\bar{Y}} = \dfrac{S_y}{\sqrt{n}}$
Confidence level coefficient of the standard error of the mean at a 95-percent confidence level	$Z_\alpha = 1.96$

Required:

a. Based on the sample results, what is the point estimate of the total value of the inventory? Show computations in good form.

b. What statistical conclusion can be reached regarding the estimated total inventory value calculated in *a* above at the confidence level of 95 percent? Present computations in good form.

c. What is the probability that your sample result ($\bar{Y}$, above) came from a distribution around a total inventory value of $1,184,148 (with its own actual MPU population mean value of $93.24).

d. Independent of your answers to *a*, *b*, and *c*, assume that the book value of Draper's inventory is $1,700,000, and based on the sample results, the estimated total value (point estimate) of the inventory is $1,690,000. The auditor desires a confidence (reliability) level of 95 percent. Discuss the audit and statistical considerations the auditor must evaluate before deciding whether the sampling results support acceptance of the book value as a fair presentation of Draper's inventory. Assume achieved precision of $35,000 at 95 percent confidence, and an original material amount judgment of M = $45,000. (AICPA adapted)

10.16. During the course of an audit engagement, a CPA attempts to obtain satisfaction that there are no material misstatements in the accounts receivable of a client. Statistical sampling is a tool that the auditor often uses to obtain representative evidence to achieve the desired satisfaction. On a particular engagement an auditor determined that a material misstatement in a population of accounts would be $35,000. To obtain satisfaction, the auditor had to be 95 percent confident that the population of accounts was not in error by $35,000. The auditor decided to use unrestricted random sampling with replacement and took a preliminary random sample of 100 items (n) from a population of 1,000 items (N). The sample produced the following data:

MPU mean of sample items ($\bar{Y}$)	$4,000
Standard deviation of sample items (S_y)	$ 200

Required:

a. Define the statistical terms "reliability" and "precision" as applied to auditing.

b. If all necessary audit work is performed on the preliminary sample items and no errors are detected,
   (1) What can the auditor say about the total amount of accounts receivable at the 95 percent reliability level?
   (2) At what confidence level can the auditor say that the population is not in error by more or less than $35,000? Hint: Calculate the 95 percent confidence interval estimate.
   (3) Assume that the sample was a proper DUS sample of 100 dollars. Also assume that the book amount was $4,039,200. What could the auditor say (measure) about the book value?

c. Assume that the preliminary sample of 100 accounts was sufficient,
   (1) Compute the auditor's point estimate of the population total.
   (2) Indicate how the auditor should relate this estimate to the client's recorded amount. (AICPA adapted)

d. Assume the auditor has decided to accept β (beta) of .05.
   (1) Show calculations indicating whether the sample of 100 accounts does or does not appear to be "sufficient" (*i*) with finite correction, and (*ii*) without finite correction.
   (2) Assume that the book value is $4,039,200, and the auditor has the data given in the problem for a sample of 100 accounts. What value of β (beta) is indicated by the data? Ignore finite correction for calculations.

10.17. Fred's Fertilizer Company is a medium-sized manufacturer of farm and garden fertilizer compounds. Sixty different combinations of fertilizers are mixed by the company, and all of them contain a nitrogen-based powder. The production information system did not provide data on physical quantities used, and the auditor wants to estimate the quantity in order to corroborate evidence of production costs. The data file of materials issue slips contains 4,000 blue slips (prenumbered, starting the year with number 23067) that are used to authorize issue of nitrogen powder.

The auditor wishes to use the statistical method of confidence interval estimation. He has estimated the population standard deviation to be 20 pounds, and he has decided that the maximum error allowable should be 2,000 pounds. He also decides to use a 95 percent confidence level ($\alpha = 0.05$ and $\beta = 0.50$).

Required:

a. Calculate sample size, assuming that finite correction is necessary. (What is "sample" size without finite correction?)

b. Assume that the correct sample size is 2,500, and that the audited average of the issue slips was 250 pounds, and that the standard deviation of the audit sample was actually 18 pounds. What is the auditor's estimate of nitrogen compound material put into production? (Finite correction: $\sqrt{1 - 2{,}500/4{,}000} = .612372$)

10.18. You are planning to confirm accounts receivable of Bainton Farm Products, a wholesale distributor. Company records show that there are 200 customer accounts with a total balance of $300,000. In order to determine how many confirmations to mail, you have decided to use statistical sampling calculations. From a preliminary sample of 50 book values, you have calculated a standard deviation of $300. Other criteria for the sample selection were determined as follows:

Maximum error considered immaterial = $15,000
Alpha (α) = .20
Beta (β) = .05

Required:

a. Calculate sample size (n).

b. Assume that the audit of the sample calculated in *a* above is complete, and the total of the audited values is $125,550. Assume also that the standard deviation of the audited accounts was $300. What decision is indicated by these data?

c. If you decide to accept the hypothesis that the book value is not materially misstated, what is the risk of decision error (β)?

10.19. Your client's physical inventory has a total book value of $1,000,000 and is made up of 10,000 kinds of items of approximately the same value (i.e., there are no identifiable dollar-value strata). You conclude that you can accept the inventory valuation if you can be 95 percent confident that the actual inventory figure is within ±$50,000 of the stated amount of $1,000,000. Based on other audit evidence, you decide to accept a risk of 0.15 of falsely concluding that the book value is a fair presentation.

Required:

a. Your preliminary sample shows a standard deviation of $25. What size sample ($n$) should you choose for examination and evaluation?

b. Assume that the correct sample size is 225 and that the audit of these inventory items gave the the following results. (Ignore the finite correction factor in subsequent calculations.)

	Valuation by		
Item	*(1) Client*	*(2) Auditor*	*Auditor's Value Squared*
1	$ 25.00	$ 25.00	$ 625.00
2	100.50	100.80	10,160.64
3	160.20	165.00	27,225.00
—	—	—	—
—	—	—	—
—	—	—	—
n = 225	85.00	84.00	7,056.00
Totals	$21,728.00	$22,050.00	$2,289,924.00

Hint: Use the formula for S_y shown in footnote 5 in the text.

(1) Calculate the standard deviation of the sample. Is the sample size sufficiently large?

(2) If the sample size is sufficient, what is your conclusion with regard to the hypothesis that the book value is equal to the actual value? If sample size is insufficient, compute the required sample size, and describe the additional actions which the auditor should take.

c. Alter the audit findings of the sample as follows, and rework requirement *b*.

(1) Valuation by client for 225 sample items = $21,375.

(2) Valuation by auditor for 225 sample items = $21,375.

(3) Auditor's value squared, sum = $2,170,625.

10.20. Albert Watson, CPA, had begun the audit of the accounts receivable of the Bunion Boot Manufacturing Company. The company's records were in poor condition because several clerks had handled the bookkeeping during the year, and as soon as one was sufficiently trained, he would resign and another would have to be hired. The controller did not know the extent of error in the accounts but suspected that it was high, and Watson's preliminary tests of transactions showed that errors might run as high as 20 percent. He planned to perform supplemental auditing procedures that at least might have a 50–50 chance of detecting a material error in the accounts receivable control account balance.

Watson decided to use statistical sampling methods to decide whether the accounts receivable were fairly presented in the financial statements. He decided to let α = .05 and to accept a maximum error of $2,250.

The controller gave him a list of 300 customer accounts with balances ranging from zero to several hundred dollars and totaling $54,000. A preliminary random sample of 50 of these accounts gave Watson the basis for figuring a standard deviation estimate of $50.

Required:

a. What measure of β should Watson use for determining the sample to audit?

b. What would be his sample size? What basic substantive procedures would you recommend for the audit of these customer accounts?

c. Can Watson be assured that he has provided for the audit of all the accounts that should be included in the accounts receivable control total?

d. Assume that the audited total of the accounts selected in part *b* was $32,116.50 and that the standard deviation of this sample was $60. What should Watson conclude about the material accuracy of the accounts receivable?

10.21. In planning the audit of inventory valuation, Lois Rose decided to measure the differences (errors) between the audited values she determined and the perpetual inventory record values. The 2,000 perpetual record item values had been summed, and they were equal to the inventory control account balance of $190,000. She selected an unrestricted random sample of 320 perpetual records and vouched the unit prices to the most recent vendor invoices for the items. (The client is on a Fifo inventory basis.) She had decided in advance that any control account misstatement of more than $6,500 would be considered material.

After multiplying the unit prices she obtained from the invoices times the quantity on hand, she found 80 differences when the audited values and the perpetual inventory values were compared. An abstract of her working papers is shown below.

Required:

a. Explain the calculation of the standard deviation (S_D) of the differences with reference to Equation 2B. Check to see if S_D = $19.58 (without finite correction).

b. Calculate the 95-percent confidence interval estimate based on the differences (1) without finite correction and (2) with finite correction. Show the lower (L_1) and upper (L_2) limits and all preceding calculations in good form.

(Figures: $\sqrt{320} = 17.89$, $\sqrt{1 - 320/2000} = .9165$, $\sqrt{319} = 17.86$

EXHIBIT 10.21–1

C-10

X Company
Inventory Valuation Test
December 31, 1978

Prepared by LR
Date January 20

Inventory Item	(1) Audited Value	(2) Book Value	(3) Difference	$(3-6)^2$
R 43	v 812.50	✓ 740.50	72	4970.25
A 42	v 14.00	✓ 14.10	− .10	2.56
B 16	v 83.11	✓ 104.22	− 21.11	511.21
Z 06	v 75.00	✓ 60.00	15.00	182.25
Y 98	v 200.00	✓ 200.00	0	2.25
L 73	v 319.20	✓ 269.20	50	2352.25
Total 320 records	32000	31520	* 480	122297.07

(4) Average (4) 100

(5) Average (5) 98.50

(6) Average (6) * 1.50

v Vouched unit price to recent vendors' invoices and re-calculated inventory item value.

✓ Per perpetual inventory records

Note: Computer run of 2000 inventory records totaled $190,000, equal to control account balance per working trial balance.

* The control account book value appears to be understated.

© WILSON JONES COMPANY G7206 GREEN 7206 BUFF MADE IN U.S.A.

10.22. Auditor Lois Rose wanted to have 95 percent reliability that the amount of error in the inventory balance under audit did not exceed \$6,500.

Required:

Using the data given in Exercise 10.21 above:

a. Calculate the upper precision limit of monetary error (*LME*) both (1) without finite correction and (2) with finite correction. ($S_{\bar{D}} = \$19.58/\sqrt{320} = \$1.09$ in Exercise 10.21*a.*)

b. Should Ms. Rose conclude, on the basis of the quantitative evidence, that the \$190,000 book value of the inventory is not understated by more than \$6,500?

10.23. During the audit of Kingsbury Department Store, you have decided to use stratification sampling techniques to design your selection of accounts receivable for confirmation. You have prepared the following schedule:

Strata (h)	*Number of Items N_h*	*Book Value Total*	*Standard Deviation S_h*
Accounts over \$499	30	\$24,000	\$200
Accounts \$200 to \$499	70	21,000	70
Accounts under \$200	800	32,000	15

You have also decided the following:

$$\alpha = .05$$
$$\beta = .50$$
$$M = \$3,600$$

Required:

Calculate the sample size (number of accounts) for confirmation from each stratum.

10.24. The objective of this exercise is to demonstrate the calculation of stratified sample sizes shown in the example in Chapter 10, using Equation 6B. ($Z_\alpha = 1.28$, $Z_\beta = 1.645$, $M = \$25,000$).

Stratum	*Book Value Interval*	N_h	S_h	N_hS_h	$N_hS_h^2$	n_h
0	\$512–\$6,870	78	\$1,100	85,000	94,380,000	
1	64– 512	1,000	224	224,000	50,176,000	
2	32– 64	1,211	16	19,376	310,016	
3	16– 32	3,241	8	25,928	207,424	
4	1– 16	2,770	7.50	20,775	155,812.5	
Strata 1–4		8,222		290,079	50,849,252.5	
Total population		8,300	\$ 133			

Figures: $(\$25,000/(1.28 + 1.645))^2 = \$73,051,355$

10.25. The objective of this exercise (a continuation of 10.24) is to demonstrate the calculation of the stratified MPU mean using Equation 1C shown in Chapter 10. In order to do this calculation, some hypothetical audit results are assumed, as shown below:

Stratum	n_h	Audited Values	MPU Mean $\bar{Y}_h$	N_h	$N_h\bar{Y}_h$
0	78	$ 88,452		78	
1	524	64,452		1,000	
2	45	2,205		1,211	
3	61	1,464		3,241	
4	49	441		2,770	
	757	$157,014		8,300	

Required:

a. Compute the MPU sample mean for each stratum.
b. Compute the stratified MPU sample mean for the combined strata.
c. Compute the point estimate of the population actual value.

10.26. The objective of this exercise (a continuation of 10.24 and 10.25) is to demonstrate the calculation of the standard error of the stratified MPU sample mean using the finitely corrected form (below) of Equation 3C shown in Chapter 10. The finite correction factor is needed because of the very large samples from strata 0 and 1. (Notice that the standard error associated with stratum 0 is zero, because $\sqrt{1-(78/78)} = 0$.)

$$S_{\bar{Y}_s}\text{, with finite correction (See Appendix 10–C)} = \left[\frac{\sum_{h=0}^{k} N_h^2 \left(\frac{S_h}{\sqrt{n_h}} \cdot \sqrt{1-\frac{n_h}{N_h}}\right)^2}{N^2}\right]^{1/2}$$

Assume the following hypothetical data:

Stratum	N_h	N_h^2	n_h	$\sqrt{n_h}$	$\sqrt{1-\frac{n_h}{N_h}}$	S_h	$N_h^2\left(\frac{S_h}{\sqrt{n_h}}\sqrt{1-\frac{n_h}{N_h}}\right)^2$
0......	78	6,084	78	8.83	0	$1,100	0
1......	1,000	1,000,000	524	22.89	.6899	224	
2......	1,211	1,466,521	45	6.71	.9812	16	8,027,832.3
3......	3,241	10,504,081	61	7.81	.9905	8	10,812,968
4......	2,770	7,672,900	49	7.00	.9911	7.50	8,652,088.1
	8,300		757				73,073,142.4

Required:

a. Compute the amount omitted in the data above.
b. Compute the standard error of the stratified MPU sample mean ($S_{\bar{Y}_s}$).

10.27. The objective of this exercise (a continuation of 10.24, 10.25, and 10.26) is to demonstrate the calculation of the 80-percent confidence interval estimate, based on stratified MPU statistics, using Equations 4C and 5C shown in Chapter 10.

1. For calculation of the 80-percent interval estimate, given the following:

$$\overline{Y}_s = \$45.00$$
$$S_{\bar{Y}_s} = \$\ 1.03 \text{ (with finite correction)}$$
$$Z_\alpha = 1.28$$

Required:

a. Compute the achieved precision (P_{Y_s}).

b. Compute the lower (L_1) and upper (L_2) confidence interval limits at 80 percent confidence.

2. The total book value of the 8,300 customer accounts is \$379,500 (BV/N = \$45.72), and if the actual amount were \$354,499 = \$379,500 − \$25,001, (μ_{-M} = \$354,499/8,300 = \$42.71), the book value would be considered a material misstatement of the actual amount. What is the probability that a stratified MPU sample mean of \$45 or more could have come from a distribution around an actual average of \$42.71?

10.28. Gordon Jacoby plans to apply dollar-unit sampling in the audit of 200,000 customers' electric utility account balances. The total book value of these accounts is \$12 million as of July 31. His planned procedure is to select the sample accounts and vouch payments received in August.

The utility company has established a separate Allowance for Uncollectible Accounts amount of \$600,000 (5 percent of the total). Gordon will be satisfied with this amount if "errors" in the account collections do not differ from \$600,000 by more than ±\$50,000 (=M).

An "error" in a sample account is defined as an account that is not paid (in whole or in part) by the end of August.

From prior experience with this client Gordon expects that the estimate of uncollectible accounts is reasonable. However, he wants to have a 95-percent reliable conclusion based on this audit test (RF = 3).

Required:

a. Compute the DUS sample size.

b. Explain how Gordon can proceed to select the sample.

c. Assume that he selects and audits 700 accounts, and 25 of the accounts, each containing \$1 in the sample, were not paid in August. (None of the accounts had partial payments.) What dollar estimate of uncollectible accounts can Gordon calculate?

10.29. **The "Overfill" Inventory Issue Case**

Ajax Minerals, Inc., mines and ships bulk sulfur in the southeastern United States. The comparison of the physical inventory quantity with the book inventory has consistently revealed an inventory "shortage" of bulk sulfur. This "shortage" occurs at each physical inventory date even though appropriate inventory controls are exercised and material usage requisitions are utilized. However, management policy directs the inventory clerks to fill material requisitions in an expedient manner, and it has been suggested that the clerks have allowed a tendency to overfill to become an accepted practice. In prior years management expressed little concern about the shortage and attributed its occurrence to the overfill tendency, stating that the extra care in weighing was not justified.

At the start of the current year, the company embarked upon a cost reduction program and inventory shortages were reexamined to determine possible causes. The internal audit staff, with the consent of management, began an examination of the problem in an attempt to determine whether the total sulfur shortage could be accounted for by the overfill tendency.

During the year under review, the accounting and inventory records indicated the following transactions for the sulfur inventory:

	Pounds
Beginning inventory	40,000
Receiving reports from mines	752,000
Available for use	792,000
Total material requisitions	722,000
Ending book inventory	70,000
Actual physical inventory on hand	49,700
Inventory "shortage"	20,300

As a means of measuring the amount of overfill in the current period, the internal audit staff selected 100 material requisitions at random during the period and weighed the material supplied for each requisition. A total of 3,000 requisitions for sulfur were prepared during the year and the sample of 100 was from this population. The regular filling routine was not interrupted, and the storeroom clerk was unaware that these verifications were made. The weighing process was somewhat time-consuming, but the weights were accurately determined. See Table 1.

TABLE 1
Summary of Random Sample of Material Requisitions

Sample Selection Number, i	*Requisition Number*	*Recorded Weight* x_i	*Correct Weight* y_i	*Differences* d_i
1	2,471	440	445	5
2	87	170	174	4
—	—	—	—	—
—	—	—	—	—
—	—	—	—	—
99	343	217	217	0
100	400	97	96	−1
Totals		23,400	24,000	600

Other information:

The sum of the squared correct weights was 5,888,304.

The sum of the squared differences between recorded weights and correct weights was 17,856.

Hint: Use the standard deviation equations from footnote 5 in Chapter 10.

Required:

a. What is the sample standard deviation for the (1) MPU statistic and (2) difference statistic? (Ignore finite correction.)

b. What risk of decision error would the internal auditor accept if he decided that the 722,000 pounds of recorded weights was accurate using (1) the MPU statistic and (2) the difference statistic?

c. What accounts for the great difference in the risk of error between the two measures as found in *b* above?

APPENDIX 10–A

Areas in Two Tails of the Normal Curve at Selected Values of Z_α from the Arithmetic Mean

This table shows the black areas:

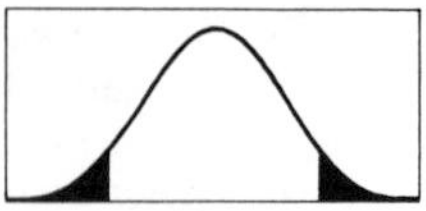

Z_α	.00	.01	.02	.03	.04	.05	.06	.07	.08	.09
0.0	1.0000	.9920	.9840	.9761	.9681	.9601	.9522	.9442	.9362	.9283
0.1	.9203	.9124	.9045	.8966	.8887	.8808	.8729	.8650	.8572	.8493
0.2	.8415	.8337	.8259	.8181	.8103	.8026	.7949	.7872	.7795	.7718
0.3	.7642	.7566	.7490	.7414	.7339	.7263	.7188	.7114	.7039	.6965
0.4	.6892	.6818	.6745	.6672	.6599	.6527	.6455	.6384	.0312	.6241
0.5	.6171	.6101	6031	.5961	.5892	.5823	.5755	.5687	.5619	.5552
0.6	.5485	.5419	.5353	.5287	.5222	.5157	.5093	.5029	.4965	.4902
0.7	.4839	.4777	.4715	.4654	.4593	.4533	.4473	.4413	.4354	.4295
0.8	.4237	.4179	.4122	.4065	.4009	.3953	.3898	.3843	.3789	.3735
0.9	.3681	.3628	.3576	.3524	.3472	.3421	.3371	.3320	.3271	.3222
1.0	.3173	.3125	.3077	.3030	.2983	.2937	.2801	.2846	.2801	.2757
1.1	.2713	.2670	.2627	.2585	.2543	.2501	.2460	.2420	.2380	.2340
1.2	.2301	.2263	.2225	.2187	.2150	.2113	.2077	.2041	.2005	.1971
1.3	.1936	.1902	.1868	.1835	.1802	.1770	.1738	.1707	.1676	.1645
1.4	.1615	.1585	.1556	.1527	.1499	.1471	.1443	.1416	.1389	.1362
1.5	.1336	.1310	.1285	.1260	.1236	.1211	.1188	.1164	.1141	.1118
1.6	.1096	.1074	.1052	.1031	.1010	.0989	.0969	.0949	.0930	.0910
1.7	.0891	.0873	.0854	.0836	.0819	.0801	.0784	.0767	.0751	.0735
1.8	.0719	.0703	.0688	.0672	.0658	.0643	.0629	.0615	.0601	.0588
1.9	.0574	.0561	.0549	.0536	.0524	.0512	.0500	.0488	.0477	.0466
2.0	.0455	.0444	.0434	.0424	.0414	.0404	.0394	.0385	.0375	.0366
2.1	.0357	.0349	.0340	.0332	.0324	.0316	.0308	.0300	.0293	.0285
2.2	.0278	.0271	.0264	.0257	.0251	.0238	.0288	.0232	.0226	.0220
2.3	.0214	.0209	.0203	.0198	.0193	.0188	.0183	.0178	.0173	.0168
2.4	.0164	.0160	.0155	.0151	.0147	.0143	.0139	.0135	.0131	.0128
2.5	.0124	.0121	.0117	.0114	.0111	.0108	.0105	.0102	.00988	.00960
2.6	.00932	.00905	.00879	.00854	.00829	.00805	.00781	.00759	.00736	.00715
2.7	.00693	.00673	.00653	.00633	.00614	.00596	.00578	.00561	.00544	.00527
2.8	.00511	.00495	.00480	.00465	.00451	.00437	.00424	.00410	.00398	.00385
2.9	.00373	.00361	.00350	.00339	.00328	.00318	.00308	.00298	.00288	.00279

Z_α	.0	.1	.2	.3	.4	.5	.6	.7	.8	.9
3	.00270	.00194	.00137	$.0^3967$	$.0^3674$	$.0^3465$	$.0^3318$	$.0^3216$	$.0^3145$	$.0^4962$
4	$.0^4413$	$.0^4413$	$.0^4267$	$.4^4171$	$.0^4108$	$.0^5680$	$.0^5422$	$.0^5260$	$.0^6159$	$.0^6958$
5	$.0^6573$	$.0^4340$	$.0^6199$	$.0^6116$	$.0^7666$	$.0^7380$	$.0^7214$	$.0^7120$	$.0^8663$	$.0^8364$
6	$.0^8197$	$.0^8106$	$.0^9565$	$.0^9298$	$.0^9155$	$.0^{10}803$	$.0^{10}411$	$.0^{10}208$	$.0^{10}105$	$.0^{11}520$

From *Tables of Areas in Two Tails and in One Tail of the Normal Curve*, by Frederick E. Croxton. Copyright, 1949, by Prentice-Hall, Inc.

APPENDIX 10–B

Cumulative Standardized Normal Distribution

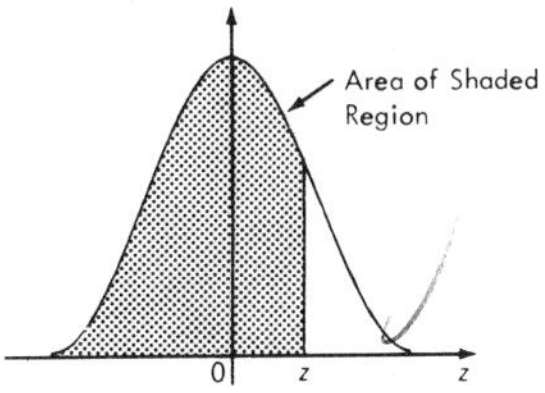

z	.00	.01	.02	.03	.04	.05	.06	.07	.08	.09
.0	.5000	.5040	.5080	.5120	.5160	.5199	.5239	.5279	.5319	.5359
.1	.5398	.5438	.5478	.5517	.5557	.5596	.5636	.5675	.5714	.5753
.2	.5793	.5832	.5871	.5910	.5948	.5987	.6026	.6064	.6103	.6141
.3	.6179	.6217	.6255	.6293	.6331	.6368	.6406	.6443	.6480	.6517
.4	.6554	.6591	.6628	.6664	.6700	.6736	.6772	.6808	.6844	.6879
.5	.6915	.6950	.6985	.7019	.7054	.7088	.7123	.7157	.7190	.7224
.6	.7257	.7291	.7324	.7357	.7389	.7422	.7454	.7486	.7517	.7549
.7	.7580	.7611	.7642	.7673	.7704	.7734	.7764	.7794	.7823	.7852
.8	.7881	.7910	.7939	.7967	.7995	.8023	.8051	.8078	.8106	.8133
.9	.8159	.8186	.8212	.8238	.8264	.8289	.8315	.8340	.8365	.8389
1.0	.8413	.8438	.8461	.8485	.8508	.8531	.8554	.8577	.8599	.8621
1.1	.8643	.8665	.8686	.8708	.8729	.8749	.8770	.8790	.8810	.8830
1.2	.8849	.8869	.8888	.8907	.8925	.8944	.8962	.8980	.8997	.9015
1.3	.9032	.9049	.9066	.9082	.9099	.9115	.9131	.9147	.9162	.9177
1.4	.9192	.9207	.9222	.9236	.9251	.9265	.9279	.9292	.9306	.9319
1.5	.9332	.9345	.9357	.9370	.9382	.9394	.9406	.9418	.9429	.9441
1.6	.9452	.9463	.9474	.9484	.9495	.9505	.9515	.9525	.9535	.9545
1.7	.9554	.9564	.9573	.9582	.9591	.9599	.9608	.9616	.9625	.9633
1.8	.9641	.9649	.9656	.9664	.9671	.9678	.9686	.9693	.9699	.9706
1.9	.9713	.9719	.9726	.9732	.9738	.9744	.9750	.9756	.9761	.9767
2.0	.9772	.9778	.9783	.9788	.9793	.9798	.9803	.9808	.9812	.9817
2.1	.9821	.9826	.9830	.9834	.9838	.9842	.9846	.9850	.9854	.9857
2.2	.9861	.9864	.9868	.9871	.9875	.9878	.9881	.9884	.9887	.9890
2.3	.9893	.9896	.9898	.9901	.9904	.9906	.9909	.9911	.9913	.9916
2.4	.9918	.9920	.9922	.9925	.9927	.9929	.9931	.9932	.9934	.9936
2.5	.9938	.9940	.9941	.9943	.9945	.9946	.9948	.9949	.9951	.9952
2.6	.9953	.9955	.9956	.9957	.9959	.9960	.9961	.9962	.9963	.9964
2.7	.9965	.9966	.9967	.9968	.9969	.9970	.9971	.9972	.9973	.9974
2.8	.9974	.9975	.9976	.9977	.9977	.9978	.9979	.9979	.9980	.9981
2.9	.9981	.9982	.9982	.9983	.9984	.9984	.9985	.9985	.9986	.9986
3.0	.9987	.9987	.9987	.9988	.9988	.9989	.9989	.9989	.9990	.9990
3.1	.9990	.9991	.9991	.9991	.9992	.9992	.9992	.9992	.9993	.9993
3.2	.9993	.9993	.9994	.9994	.9994	.9994	.9994	.9995	.9995	.9995
3.3	.9995	.9995	.9995	.9996	.9996	.9996	.9996	.9996	.9996	.9997
3.4	.9997	.9997	.9997	.9997	.9997	.9997	.9997	.9997	.9997	.9998

The entries from 3.49 to 3.61 all equal .9998. The entries from 3.62 to 3.89 all equal 9999. All entries from 3.90 and up equal 1.0000.

From *Introduction to the Theory of Statistics* by Alexander M. Mood. Copyright 1950, McGraw-Hill Book Co. Used with permission of McGraw-Hill Book Co.

APPENDIX 10–C

Text Equations with Finite Correction

MPU Statistic	*Difference Statistic*	*Stratified Sampling*
(2) Standard deviation (2A) $S_y = \sqrt{\frac{\Sigma(y_i - \bar{Y})^2}{n-1}} \cdot \sqrt{1 - \frac{n}{N}}$	(2B) $S_D = \sqrt{\frac{\Sigma(d_i - \bar{D})^2}{n-1}} \cdot \sqrt{1 - \frac{n}{N}}$	
(3) Standard error—when S_y and S_D are calculated *without* finite correction. (3A) $S_{\bar{Y}} = \frac{S_y}{\sqrt{n}} \cdot \sqrt{1 - \frac{n}{N}}$	(3B) $S_{\bar{D}} = \frac{S_D}{\sqrt{n}} \cdot \sqrt{1 - \frac{n}{N}}$	(3C) $S_{\bar{Y}_s} = \left[\frac{\sum_{h=0}^{k} N_h^2 \left(\frac{S_h}{\sqrt{n_h}} \cdot \sqrt{1 - \frac{n_h}{N_h}} \right)^2}{N^2} \right]^{1/2}$
(4) Achieved precision—when $S_{\bar{Y}}$ and $S_{\bar{D}}$ are calculated *without* finite correction. (4A) $P_Y = Z_\alpha \cdot S_{\bar{Y}} \cdot \sqrt{1 - \frac{n}{N}}$	(4B) $P_D = Z_\alpha \cdot S_{\bar{D}} \cdot \sqrt{1 - \frac{n}{N}}$	When $S_{\bar{Y}_s}$ is already corrected. (4C) $P_{Y_S} = Z_\alpha \cdot S_{\bar{Y}_s}$
(5) Confidence intervals—when P_y and P_D are calculated without finite correction. (5A) $L_1 = N(\bar{Y} - P_Y \sqrt{1 - n/N})$ $L_2 = N(\bar{Y} + P_Y \sqrt{1 - n/N})$	(5B) $L_1 = BV + N(\bar{D} - P_D \sqrt{1 - n/N})$ $L_2 = BV + N(\bar{D} + P_D \sqrt{1 - n/N})$	When P_{y_s} is already corrected. (5C) $L_1 = N(\bar{Y}_s - P_{Y_S})$ $L_2 = N(\bar{Y}_s + P_{Y_S})$
(6) Sample size (6A) $n = \frac{N[S_y(Z_\alpha + Z_\beta)]^2}{N\left(\frac{M}{N}\right)^2 + [S_y(Z_\alpha + Z_\beta)]^2}$	(6A) $n = \frac{N[S_D(Z_\alpha + Z_\beta)]^2}{N\left(\frac{M}{N}\right)^2 + [S_D(Z_\alpha + Z_\beta)]^2}$	(6B) $n_h = \frac{N_h S_h \sum_{h=1}^{k} N_h S_h}{\left(\frac{M}{Z_\alpha + Z_\beta}\right)^2 + \sum_{h=1}^{k} N_h S_h^2}$

(7A) Calculation of $Z_\beta : Z_\beta = (\bar{Y} - \mu_{-M})/(S_{\bar{Y}} \cdot \sqrt{1 - \frac{n}{N}})$, when $S_{\bar{Y}}$ is calculated *without* finite correction.

(7B) Calculation of $Z_\alpha : Z_\alpha = (\mu - \bar{Y})(S_{\bar{Y}} \cdot \sqrt{1 - \frac{n}{N}})$, when $S_{\bar{Y}}$ is calculated *without* finite correction.

(7C) Calculation of Z_β when figuring *LME* measurement, and $S_{\bar{D}}$ is calculated *without* finite correction:

$$Z_\beta = \frac{M - N|\bar{D}|}{N \cdot S_{\bar{D}} \cdot \sqrt{1 - \frac{n}{N}}}$$

(8) Calculation of *LME*—when $S_{\bar{D}}$ is calculated *without* finite correction.

$$\text{(8A)} \quad LME = N\left(\bar{D} + Z_\beta \cdot S_{\bar{D}} \cdot \sqrt{1 - \frac{n}{N}}\right)$$

$$\text{(8B)} \quad LME = \left|N\left(\bar{D} - Z_\beta \cdot S_{\bar{D}} \cdot \sqrt{1 - \frac{n}{N}}\right)\right|$$

PART THREE
Audit Program Applications

11

AUDIT OF REVENUE, RECEIVABLES, CASH RECEIPTS, AND CASH BALANCES

There are four major objectives in this chapter related to the tools and techniques described in previous chapters. The objectives are to explain with relation to revenue, receivables, cash accounts, and cash receipts transactions:

- A business approach to audit objectives concerning existence, valuation cutoff, accounting principles, compliance, and effectiveness.
- Elements of internal accounting control for these accounts and transactions.
- Applications of audit procedures for gathering evidence.
- Types of fraud and misstatement that might occur in these accounts.

The discussion and explanation of each of these four topics are intended to enable students to sharpen their awareness of audit objectives, relevant evidence, relevant audit procedures, and the applications of audit methodology to the specific subset of accounts.

Most programs used in audit field work contain a section of procedures for the audit of revenues, another section for audit of receivables, and another for the testing of cash receipts transactions. In this chapter these three areas are brought together as a related group of accounts and transactions in order to show the close relationship of procedures applied in one area to procedures applied in the others.

A BUSINESS APPROACH TO AUDIT OBJECTIVES

A broad view of operations is very helpful in the planning stage of an audit engagement. Being able to think like a business manager may enable an auditor to gain perspective on each of the primary objectives as they relate to revenue, receivables, cash receipts, and cash balances.

Existence

An understanding of the marketing function is central to understanding features of the existence of cash and receivables balances and the occurrence of revenue-producing transactions. However, the marketing function is even more pervasive in that production plans, inventory management, and research and development programs are also affected by marketing operations.

The first things that an auditor should understand is the company's product and the manner in which it is exchanged. Outright sales create the fewest accounting and auditing problems, but other exchange methods such as leasing, franchising, film distribution, and construction contracting can cause special revenue recognition problems.[1] An auditor should study marketing forecasts, industry trends, market share analyses, and performance monitoring reports for preliminary ideas about real sales volume.

Internal and external influences on selling terms are important. A knowledge of return-merchandise terms and of guarantees and warranties can provide information for later review. In the area of outside economic influences, knowledge of price index movements for specific classes of products can facilitate reconciliation of physical volume and monetary measurement. Awareness of market shifts can lend understanding to a new sales mix. As examples, in 1973–74 the squeeze on gasoline supplies influenced price levels for oil products with consequent effects on the dollar volume of oil company revenues and caused a concurrent shift in the auto industry to a greater sales volume in small cars and reduced volume in large cars.

Marketing realities may have a significant impact also on problems of auditing receivables arising from product exchanges. The number and type of customers are important considerations in planning. It makes a great difference if the company sells to a few large industrial customers (the extreme being a "captive supplier") or to a large number of private individuals who may trade irregularly (as in a department store). Sales to government agencies are significant in that questions of contract continuance may emerge (e.g., contracts with the Department of Defense).

Credit policies of the company and the terms and types of accounts must be understood for an informed audit. The office procedures for sales

---

[1] Technical discussion of special accounting issues can be found in AICPA audit and accounting guides on subjects such as "Accounting for Franchise Fee Revenue," "Accounting for Retail Land Sales," "Banks," "Fire and Casualty Insurance Companies," "Hospitals," "Construction Contractors," and other titles available from the Institute publications division.

order origination, credit approval, billing, shipping, and collection effort form a system of control with which the auditor should become familiar. For example, if these procedures are scattered in many branch locations, an entirely different audit plan would be adopted than had they been centralized in a home office.

The managerial matter of centralization-decentralization is equally important, in an audit planning context, for the cash management function. There is a great difference between cash managed through a single domestic bank account and the situation wherein several accounts are used in widely scattered locations both domestic and foreign. Some companies may have tens or hundreds of accounts, and some accounts may be used only for the deposit of receipts with other accounts used only for various special types of disbursements (e.g., payroll).

A review of historical financial ratios—turnovers related to sales, receivables turnover, and liquidity ratios—can give clues for areas of audit significance. Of particular interest is a preliminary determination of whether the company is in a "tight" cash position. Liquidity problems often magnify risk characteristics in an audit, and in such situations an auditor must be especially careful respecting the existence of cash and receivables assets and sales transactions. Economic troubles can lead to pressures for recording fictitious sales to real or fictitious customers and practices of improper cash cutoff.

Valuation

Cash is the easiest of all assets to value because its counting unit is the same as its measuring unit—the dollar. The principal cash valuation tool is the bank reconciliation. However, valuation problems may arise in connection with expressing foreign balances in U.S. dollars and in situations where cash is restricted in foreign countries. Balances on deposit in domestic institutions under liquidation by the Federal Deposit Insurance Corporation or Federal Savings and Loan Insurance Corporation are more properly considered receivables rather than cash and thus subject to valuation allowances. The facts of foreign holdings and deposits in bankrupt institutions should be learned at an early date.

With respect to sales valuation, the various accounting methods of revenue recognition become of paramount importance. Lease and franchise contract terms should be read with care. When the business is one of construction and the percentage-of-completion method is used, construction sites should be visited for a firsthand view of progress.

Marketing policies for pricing should be understood. Any long-term, fixed price sales commitments should be reviewed in the light of expected product costs over the term of the contract. The policy and experience with returns of goods and allowances should be reviewed in terms of the valuation of net sales.

The valuation of receivables generally relates to collectibility. Factors such as credit policy and collection efforts can have an impact on all types of customer accounts. Analyses of individual account problems or aggregate collection experience can facilitate evaluation of collectibility. Other factors such as conflicts over government contract reimbursement terms and the economic situation in an industry customer group can have an impact on receivables from such customers. Accounts that must be translated from a foreign currency also constitute a valuation problem.

In some cases certain accounts bearing little or no interest may be valued at discounted present value. (See APB *Opinion No. 21.*[2]) The auditor should inquire about customary credit practices and unusual transactions during the year.

Cutoff

Revenue, receivables, and cash receipts transactions are generally subject to significant cutoff problems. With a business overview approach the auditor may wish to compare transaction activity in the last month of the current year to that of the last month of the prior year to detect lack of a proper cutoff. However, some events may be relatively hard to detect—sales of the next period predated by a few days and recorded in the current period or cash receipts *held back* for deposit in the next period, or cash receipts on account recorded as cash sales.

In particular, interbank transfers shown as deposits in transit in one account but omitted from the outstanding checklist in another account will give the auditor problems of both cutoff and proper valuation of cash. This practice of recording the deposit of an interbank transfer before recording the disbursement—thus briefly double-counting the amount as cash—is a form of "kiting," which is an illegitimate way to overstate cash. A careful review of the bank reconciliation and preparation of a schedule of all interbank transfers, showing relevant dates, should reveal attempts at kiting. Exhibit 11–1 shows a working paper schedule of interbank transfers.

Particularly large cutoff errors (in the aggregate) might be detected by a comparison to prior periods. More commonly however, the auditor has to rely on procedures applied in one area to detect cutoff errors in another area. For example, accounts receivable confirmation replies from customers may reveal predated sales, cash payments recorded as cash sales, and cash payments unrecorded until the next period.

Accounting Principles and Disclosure

Accounting principles applicable to all companies require separate disclosure of receivables from directors, officers, subsidiaries, and affiliates. An auditor should as a matter of familiarization, inquire about such transactions with related parties.[3] In the light of industry practices and

[2] "Interest on Receivables and Payables."

[3] As required by auditing standards concerning "Related Party Transactions" (*SAS No. 6*, Section 335) and "Client Representations" (*SAS No. 19*, Section 333).

EXHIBIT 11–1

A-5

ABC Corporation
Schedule of Interbank Transfers
December 31, 1979

Prepared by JR
Date 1-20-80

	Disbursing Bank				Receiving Bank		
Check no.	Bank	Amount	Date per Books	Date per Bank	Bank	Date per Books	Date per Bank
1085	1st National	30000 ✓	12-31-79 x	1-5-80 y	2nd Nat'l.	12-31-79 ⌄	1-3-80 y/x
6114	2nd National	5000 ✓	12-30-79 x	1-4-80 y	1st Nat'l.	12-30-79 ⌄	1-3-80 y/x

✓ Traced to cash disbursements journal.
x Checks properly listed as outstanding on bank reconciliations (A-1, A-3)
y Vouched checks cleared bank in cut-off bank statements.
⌄ Traced to cash receipts journal.
y/x Vouched deposits cleared bank in cut-off bank statement.

Note: We scanned the cash disbursements and cash receipts journals for checks to and deposits from banks. Found none other than the two listed above.

the company's liquidity position, inquiry should also be made of whether any receivables have been sold or assigned or pledged as collateral.

The SEC has rules for disclosures relating to liquidity. Among these rules is the requirement that any cash balance held as a compensating balance pursuant to a formal agreement should be segregated on the balance sheet. Compensating balances not embodied in formal agreements should be disclosed in a footnote. A review of cash management constraints can reveal such formal and informal arrangements.

Companies have to report sales and profits by segments in accordance with FASB *Statement No. 14*. As part of a business approach, the comments given above on awareness of events that influence sales mix (under the discussion of *existence*) are equally applicable to the accounting principles objective. Likewise, several preceding comments on lease, franchise, and construction revenue issues are also relevant to the requirement that all significant accounting policies be disclosed. (See APB *Opinion No.* 22.[4])

Compliance

Respecting cash balances and receivables, the compliance objective is usually associated with private agreements with creditors. Such agreements may take the form of compensating balance requirements or specific assignment of accounts receivable. The auditor should learn about such provisions in debt agreements and look for compliance. Failure to comply may have an impact on the terms or interest rate of the related debt. General restrictive agreements that would apply to such aggregates as total current assets and working capital should be kept in mind when auditing accounts that are included therein.

Regarding receivables and related credit policies and terms, most companies must observe the Truth in Lending Act. A review of disclosures made to debtors can provide evidence of compliance with this law.

In the area of sales more public laws and requirements exist. Sellers must observe the Robinson-Patman Act (dealing with fair pricing), the antitrust acts (relevant to market activities), and various laws governing the use of alcohol and drugs in production. Breweries and distilleries are particularly constrained by law and regulation, but in this environment many reports are made by government auditors and internal auditors, upon which an independent auditor may rely to some extent. The collection and payment of sales and excise taxes on sales is another area where compliance is particularly relevant.

Effectiveness

Internal auditors and management services-minded independent auditors find a fruitful field with revenue, receivables, and cash receipts practices. Below are a few of the areas that are generally amenable to profitable improvement.

---

[4] "Disclosure of Accounting Policies."

Marketing research—mainly in the areas of surveys and product testing—is always subject to a dynamic cost-benefit analysis, which may indicate practices of either overtesting or not enough preliminary testing. The interrelationships of sales plans with production, capital investment, and inventory management can be reviewed for coordination and completeness. For example, gearing a sales force to an effort in excess of production capacity does little good.

Credit management can be reviewed for the soundness of policy and for the effectiveness of collection efforts. This is one area where independent auditors have as much interest as internal auditors because the operation of the credit function has a direct influence on the valuation of accounts receivable.

Cash management is another area that can receive close attention from internal auditors. An effective management will have prepared careful budgets and forecasts and will not allow excess cash to build up in noninterest bearing accounts. Deposits will be made promptly (also of great interest to independent auditors in terms of cash control), and a fine-tuned system may even ride the "float" of the time it takes disbursement checks to clear the bank.

INTERNAL CONTROL

Characteristics of the internal accounting control system are analyzed using techniques of the review and compliance testing phases of a proper study and evaluation of internal accounting control. This study is the means by which independent auditors take their planning overview to the operational phases of the audit examination. Most organizations provide fairly elaborate internal accounting controls over data processing for sales, receivables, and cash receipts transactions.

Review Phase

The essence of an internal control plan lies in three coordinated features:

A plan of organization with proper segregation of functions and restricted access to assets and records,

A system of general or specific authorization for the processing of transaction data, and

A system of error-checking routines for prevention and detection of errors that may occur.

The flowchart exhibits in this chapter show model organizational systems for control of sales, cash receipts, and accounts receivable. Each flowchart shows the segregation of functions considered characteristic of satisfactory internal control. Exhibits 11–4, 11–6, and 11–9 contain internal control questionnaire items that are typical of these systems. Taken together, the flowcharts and the questionnaire items describe desirable control features for each of the three areas.

EXHIBIT 11–2
Sales Invoice Origination

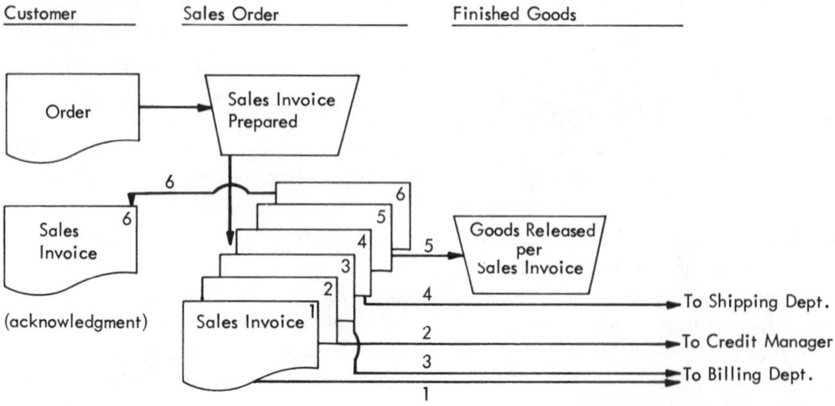

Sales Procedures. Exhibit 11–2 depicts part of a sales procedure system. The external stimulus for a sales transaction is shown as originating with the customer. Thus a customer's purchase order document may exist as a basic file document evidencing the existence of an actual order. Thereafter, the internal data processing system takes over. The flowchart description of such a sales document processing system begins with the operations shown in Exhibit 11–2.

Sales invoice blanks should be controlled in a sales order section of the sales department and issued only on receipt of a stimulus such as a customer's written or telephoned purchase order. Prenumbered sales invoice forms should be used so that someone can check the numbering sequence for missing invoices. If a credit sale is involved, approval of credit should be obtained from a separate credit department prior to final preparation of the sales invoice.

Copies of the approved invoice then are distributed as authority for other departments to act:

Copies 1 and 3 go to the billing department as authority for billing (after matching with the shipping copy),

Copy 2 goes to the credit manager for credit approval (before the other copies are released),

Copy 4 (packing list copy) goes to the shipping department as authority to pack and ship,

Copy 5 goes to an inventory location as authority to release goods to the shipping department, and

Copy 6 is returned to the customer as an acknowledgement of the order.

According to the flowchart, as each action is carried out, copies of the invoice document are transmitted in parallel so that accounting awareness of activities follows the activities themselves. Notice also that segregation of functional responsibilities is maintained among (1) authority to initiate a transaction, (2) physical custody of assets, and (3) responsibility for account recordkeeping.

The sales invoice documents of authorization continue along their way through the shipping, billing, and accounts receivable bookkeeping departments shown in Exhibit 11–3.

Eventually, copies 1, 4, and 6 of the invoice are sent to the customer, and copies 2, 3, and 5 are filed in the credit, billing, and accounts receiv-

EXHIBIT 11–3
Accounting for Sales Invoices

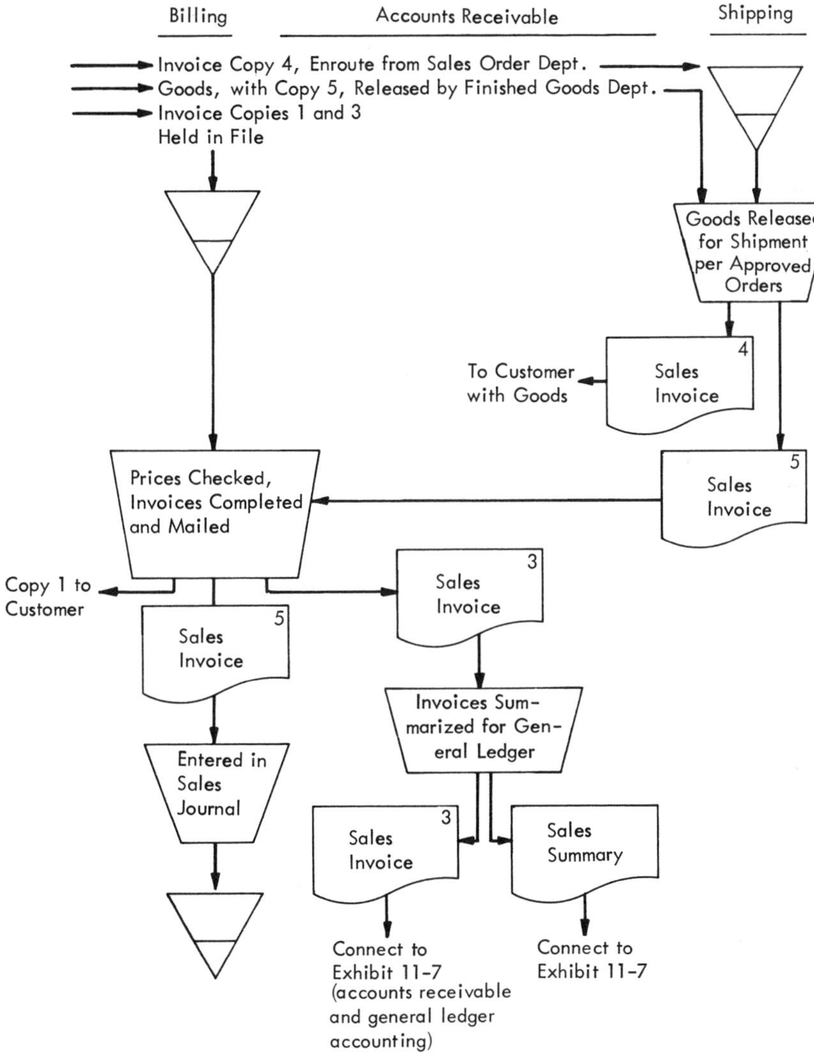

able departments as documentary evidence of the entire process that produced accounting records of a sale and an associated account receivable. Preparation of this flow of documents, duties, operations, and files should give the auditor a thorough understanding of the internal accounting control system. In particular the flowchart should enable the auditor to identify and locate important *files* of accounting records. Knowledge of these files becomes very important for designing detail test of transaction procedures.

EXHIBIT 11–4

INTERNAL CONTROL QUESTIONNAIRE
SALES SYSTEM

1. Are sales invoice blanks prenumbered? Controlled in the sales order department?
2. Are all credit sales approved by the credit department prior to shipment? Explain deviations.
3. Is the credit department independent of the sales department?
4. Are sales prices and terms based on approved standards? Are deviations from standard approved by a responsible officer?
5. Are prenumbered bills of lading or other shipping documents prepared or completed in the shipping department?
6. Are shipping quantities checked against invoice quantities in the billing department? Explain alternate procedures, if any.
7. Are numerical sequences of invoices and shipping documents checked in the billing department?
8. Are sales invoices checked for error in the billing department as to prices, credit terms, extensions and footings, freight allowances, and checked with customers' orders? Explain exceptions.
9. Is there an overall check on arithmetical accuracy of period sales data by a statistical or product line analysis?
10. Are periodic sales data (e.g., weekly total) reported directly to general ledger accounting independent of accounts receivable accounting?
11. Are there adequate safeguards to detect omission or double-counting of sales data? (See items 7 and 9 above.)
12. Are returned sales credits and other credits supported by documentation as to receipt, condition, quantity, and approved by a responsible officer?
13. Are sales of the following types controlled by the same procedures described above? (If not, explain.) Sales to employees, C.O.D. sales, disposals of property, cash sales, scrap sales.
14. Are detail records (product line data, and the like) maintained on an EDP system? If so, complete relevant portions of the EDP internal control questionnaire.

Cash Receipts Procedures. Exhibit 11–5 depicts a cash receipts processing system. It describes procedures for handling checks received in the mail.

When the mail is opened, the system is put in operation. Initial control over cash must be established, and this point is likely to be the most

EXHIBIT 11–5
Initial Cash Receipts Control

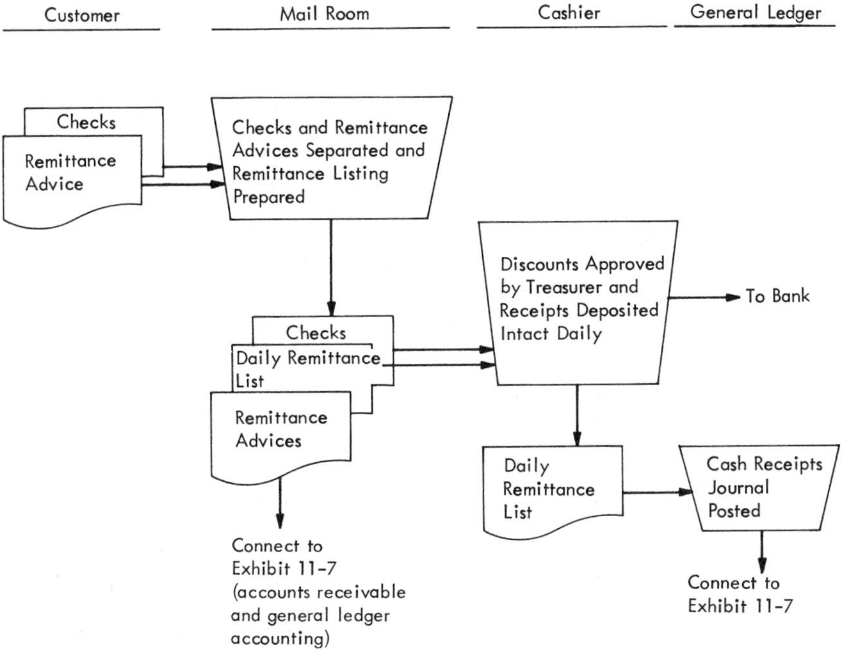

sensitive to control deficiencies. If control is not established through (1) a sales slip and cash register record, or (2) a daily remittance list and remittance advice document, subsequent data processing control features may not be able to detect omission of data in a timely manner.

Throughout the data processing the custody of cash and the recordkeeping functions should be kept separate. Receipts are deposited daily and intact. (No money is removed from petty cash or cash on hand.) Basic documentary evidence of mail cash receipts thus exists in files in the form of remittance lists, bank deposit slips, remittance advice copies, the accounts receivable subsidiary records, and the accounts receivable and cash control accounts. Periodic reconciliation of the accounts receivable subsidiary ledger with the control account should detect errors of posting and errors of a remittance omitted from the daily list and bank deposit.

Not shown in the flowchart, but important for satisfactory control, is the reconciliation of the bank statement. The reconciliation should be done by someone not otherwise responsible for handling cash or cash records. In some companies the internal auditors do the reconciliations. Internal auditors are also involved in control functions respecting access to cash registers and review of deposit slips and other cash records.

A wide variety of cash receipts transactions in addition to those associated with normal sales may occur. Receipts may arise from dividends

EXHIBIT 11–6

INTERNAL CONTROL QUESTIONNAIRE
CASH SYSTEM (RECEIPTS)

A. *General*

1. Are receipts deposited daily, intact, and without delay?
2. Does the cashier control cash from the time it is received in his or her department until deposit?
3. Does someone other than cashier or accounts receivable bookkeeper take the deposits to the bank?
4. Is a duplicate deposit slip retained by the internal auditor or someone other than the employee making up the deposit?
5. Are the duties of the cashier entirely separate from recordkeeping for notes and accounts receivable? From general ledger recordkeeping?
6. Can the cashier obtain access to receivables records or monthly statements?
7. Are all other cash funds (e.g., petty cash) and securities handled by someone other than the cashier? Explain.
8. Does any employee having custody of client cash funds also have custody of nonclient funds (e.g., credit union, benefit funds)?
9. Do branch offices collect cash? Are withdrawals from branch office accounts controlled by a central office?
10. Are rents, dividends, interest, and similar receipts accounted for by accrual or other means in such a way that their nonreceipt would be noticed?
11. Is a bank reconciliation performed monthly by someone who does not have cash custody or recordkeeping responsibility?

B. *Mail and Currency Receipts*

1. Is mail opened by someone other than cashier or accounts receivable recordkeeper? Are daily remittance lists and remittance advices prepared by this person?
2. Is the daily remittance list checked to the daily deposit by someone other than the cashier? Explain when this is done.
3. Are the daily remittance list and deposit slip compared to the cash receipts book and accounts receivable credits entries regularly?
4. Are currency receipts controlled by mechanical devices (e.g., cash registers)? Are machine totals checked by the internal auditor?
5. Are prenumbered sales or receipts books used? Is the numerical sequence checked by the accounting department?
6. Are detail transaction records maintained on an EDP system? If so, complete relevant portions of the EDP internal control questionnaire.

and interest on investments, proceeds from sale of assets or scrap materials, proceeds from loans or other financing transactions, and similar sources. With regard to these receipts, the basic control characteristics of segregation of responsibilities, system of authorization, and system of error-checking routines should exist.

Accounts Receivable Procedures. The accounts receivable recordkeeping is an end point for aspects of both sales and cash receipts transactions, resulting in the maintenance of subsidiary accounts receivable records. Notice that no actual cash (checks, currency, or coin) appears in custody in the operations shown in Exhibit 11–7.

EXHIBIT 11–7
Accounts Receivable and General Ledger Accounting

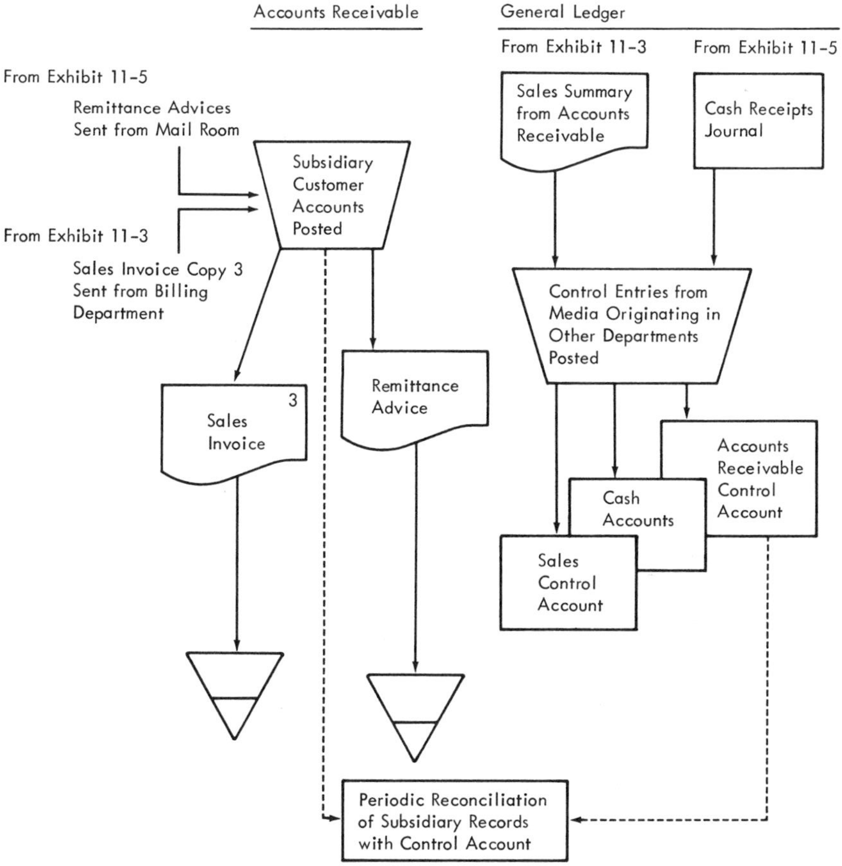

The segment of the flowchart in Exhibit 11–7 also describes maintenance of accounts receivable, cash, and sales general ledger control accounts.

Noncash credits to accounts receivable (e.g., sales returns and allowances, settlement of disputed bills) are shown in Exhibit 11–8. These accounting controls are of particular interest to an auditor. The credit manager's authorization of noncash credits should be in conformity with company policy.

EXHIBIT 11–8
Credit Memo Procedure

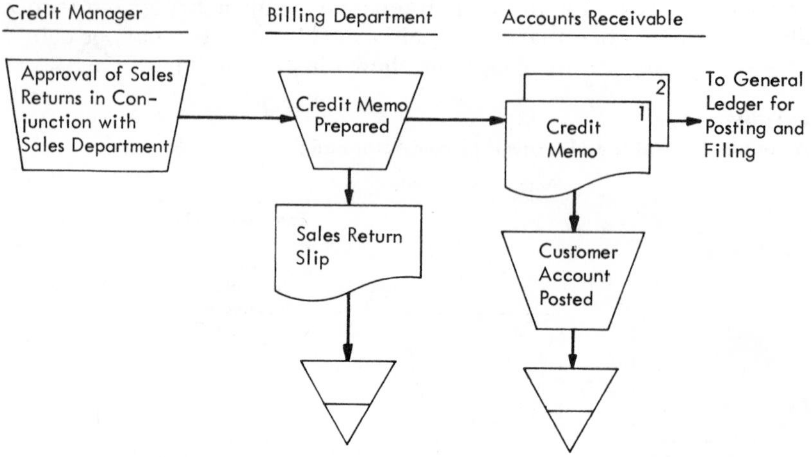

Five accounts receivable control procedures other than the normal processing of charges and credits are important.

1. *Sales returns.* Authority to approve credit for a return should rest with the credit manager, and evidence of the physical return should exist (e.g., sales return receiving slip). The credit manager does not handle cash or keep records relative to the credit memo documents.
2. *Collection effort.* The accounts receivable department analyzes accounts (e.g., aged trial balance) and transmits this information to the credit manager for follow-up.
3. *Account write-offs.* The collection effort coordinates with write-off authority that requires final approval of the treasurer.
4. *Monthly statements.* The mailing of monthly statements is an important regular activity that enhances the control process. The mailing is handled only by the accounts receivable department and should include all accounts each month.
5. *Internal auditors.* The internal auditors may serve as control points in a second-level control over accounts written off and may occasionally conduct a review of credit memos and aged accounts receivable schedules. The internal auditors may also conduct periodic surprise confirmation of accounts as an audit procedure. The auditors may also be especially alert to transactions involving officers, directors, and related affiliates and subsidiaries.

Receivables that arise from sources other than sales (e.g., advances to officers, insurance claims, returned goods claims, deposits, and prepayments) should also be authorized in connection with the activity that causes them. These other activities could involve the cash disbursement

EXHIBIT 11–9

INTERNAL CONTROL QUESTIONNAIRE
ACCOUNTS AND NOTES RECEIVABLE

1. Are customers' subsidiary records maintained by someone who has no access to cash? Is the cashier denied access to these records?
2. Are customers' records balanced monthly with the general ledger control account?
3. Are customers' statements mailed monthly? Is the mailing controlled by the accounts receivable department? Are differences noted by customers routed to someone outside the accounts receivable department?
4. Are delinquent accounts listed periodically for review by someone other than the credit manager (e.g., internal auditor)?
5. Are written-off accounts kept in a memo ledger or credit report file for periodic access?
6. Are credit memo documents prenumbered and controlled?
7. Are noncash credits, discounts allowed after discount rate, and return credits subject to approval by a responsible officer?
8. Are returned goods checked against receiving reports?
9. Is management of the credit department functionally separated from the sales department?
10. Are direct confirmations of accounts and notes obtained periodically by the internal auditor? By other officers?
11. Are notes authorized by a responsible official? Are large loans or advances to related persons approved by the directors?
12. Are notes receivable under the custody of someone other than the cashier or accounts receivable recordkeeper?
13. Is custody of negotiable collateral in the hands of someone not responsible for handling cash or keeping records?
14. Are detail records of accounts and notes transactions and balances maintained on an EDP system? If so, complete relevant portions of the EDP internal control questionnaire.

system, the purchasing-receiving system, or another method of authorization.

Compliance Tests of Transaction Details

In most organizations revenue, receivables, and cash receipts transactions are numerous. Compliance testing of the details of transactions to determine the effectiveness of internal accounting control involves sampling techniques for choosing transactions for audit and for evaluation of the evidence.

Exhibit 11–10 contains a selection of compliance test audit procedures. These steps are designed to enable the auditor to obtain objective evidence about the effectiveness of controls and about the reliability of ac-

EXHIBIT 11–10
Audit Program—Selected Compliance Testing Procedures

A. *Sales*
  1. Trace a sample of shipping documents to related sales invoices.
  2. Scan sales invoices for missing numbers in sequence.
  3. Select a sample of recorded sales invoices:
     a. Perform recalculations to verify arithmetic accuracy.
     b. Vouch to supporting shipping documents. Note dates and quantities.
     c. Vouch prices to approved price lists.
     d. Vouch credit approval.
     e. Trace posting to general ledger and proper customer account.
  4. Observe customer order handling and invoice preparation work.

B. *Cash Receipts*
  1. Select a sample of recorded cash receipts:
     a. Vouch to duplicate deposit slip and remittance list.
     b. Trace to bank statement.
     c. Trace posting to general ledger accounts (e.g., accounts receivable control account, cash accounts).
     d. Trace posting to subsidiary accounts (e.g., customers' accounts receivable).
  2. Select a sample of remittance lists (or daily cash reports):
     a. Trace to cash receipts journal.
     b. Trace journal postings to general ledger.
     c. Trace to bank statement.
  3. Observe the work habits of cashiers, clerks, and their use of cash registers.

C. *Accounts Receivable*
  1. Trace sales invoices to accounts receivable posting (procedure A–3–e above).
  2. Trace cash receipts to accounts receivable posting (procedure B–1–d above).
  3. Select a sample of credit memos:
     a. Review for proper approval.
     b. Trace to posting in customers' accounts.
  4. Select a sample of customers' accounts:
     a. Vouch debits to supporting sales invoices.
     b. Vouch credits to supporting cash receipts documents and approved credit memos.
  5. Observe mailing of monthly customer statements.

counting records (e.g., sales totals, cash amounts, accounts receivable balances). These records contain the basic numbers that appear in the financial statements under audit.

The sales transaction compliance tests include procedures to determine whether shipments were invoiced (A–1); any invoices were lost (A–2); invoices are arithmetically accurate (A–3–a), supported by shipping documents (A–3–b), figured with approved prices (A–3–c), on approved credit (A–3–d), and posted properly to subsidiary and control accounts (A–3–e).

The cash receipts compliance tests are designed to provide evidence as to whether recorded cash receipts are supported by documentary evidence and properly posted to accounts (B–1), and as to whether cash received was recorded and accounted for properly (B–2).

The accounts receivable compliance tests are designed to provide evidence of proper posting of charges and credits to customers' accounts (C–1, C–2, and C–3) and as to whether charges and credits recorded in customers' accounts are properly supported by underlying documents (C–4).

Taken together, these procedures test the important accounts in two directions. One direction is to determine whether transactions that occurred were recorded, and the other direction is to determine whether recorded transactions actually occurred. An example of the first direction is the sample of shipping documents (from the file of all shipping documents) tested to see whether invoices were prepared and recorded. An example of the second direction is the sample of sales invoices (from the file representing all recorded sales) tested to see whether supporting shipping documents exist to verify the fact of an actual shipment. In many instances compliance tests of the attributes of control consist of the two-direction nature of tests which corresponds the contents of one file with the contents of another. The example is illustrated below. (The A–1 and A–3–b codes correspond to the compliance test procedures in Exhibit 11–10.)

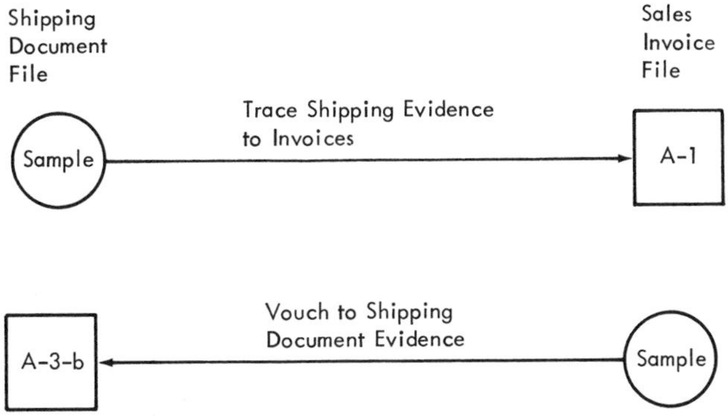

All of the compliance test procedures can be characterized as steps taken to verify the content and character of sample documents from a file and/or correspondence of the sample document with documents in another file. Auditors can expand the simple illustration given above to all the files in a system and develop a chart showing the locations of information in files, the samples from the files, and the procedures applied to the sample transactions.

The evidence obtained in the review phase and in the compliance testing phase should be combined in general and specific conclusions about the reliance that can be vested in the existing internal accounting control system. These judgments will affect the nature, timing, and extent of subsequent auditing procedures, which are discussed in the next section. Descriptions of major deficiencies, weaknesses, and inefficiencies in the system may be incorporated in a report to the client.

SUBSTANTIVE TESTS OF BALANCES

In this section the discussion of audit procedures for auditing balances is organized around each of the eight principal audit procedures. The applicability of each procedure for audit of sales, receivables, and cash is described, and the discussion is expanded to include applicability of procedures to related accounts such as interest, rents, nontrade receivables, and irregular cash receipts.

The construction of an audit program containing these procedures should begin with the auditor's explicit recognition of the assertions in the sales, accounts receivable, and cash balances and in the disclosures related to these balances. The assertions point directly to hypothesis questions that can be tested by gathering sufficient, competent evidential matter. A few of the explicit and implicit assertions typical of this account group are:

Assertions

- Cash is a current asset.
- No cash is restricted to a noncurrent use.
- The amount of cash is neither materially more nor less than the amount shown on the balance sheet.
- Accounts and notes receivable are bona fide claims owed the company.
- Accounts and notes receivable are collectible in the normal course of business.
- None of the accounts or notes receivable are fictitious.
- No accounts or notes receivable have been omitted from the balance sheet.
- Sales transactions occurred in the period under audit.
- Sales transactions recorded in the year under audit did not occur in the period before or the period after.
- Pledged accounts and notes and compensating balances are all disclosed.
- Receivables from directors, officers, and affiliates are all separately disclosed.

The assertions above are not a complete list of all matters of audit interest, but they are illustrative of the types of problems that should be recognized. The next task is to consider the evidence that might support or refute these assertions, and then the auditor can select the most efficient procedures for gathering that evidence.

Recalculation

The first set of auditor recalculations is the reconciliation of subsidiary accounts to general ledger control accounts, and hence to the financial statements and other reports. Footing of sales subsidiary accounts (e.g., product line classifications), the receivables subsidiary file and the aged trial balance of receivables, and the list of bank accounts and cash funds assures the auditor that the set of items represented as supporting detail records do in fact add to the control account totals. In many cases these recalculations may be performed using the computer or by methods of statistical estimation.

If the allowance for uncollectible receivables involves the application of historical collection ratios related to age of accounts, or involves other systematic calculations of discount allowances or unearned income (e.g., installment receivables), then these client calculations can be verified. However, the recalculations should follow the audit of the basic data because a calculation based on unaudited data still produces an unaudited-data result. The arithmetic in a client-prepared bank reconciliation should be recalculated before other audit procedures related to the reconciliation are performed.

Certain other miscellaneous receivable amounts are subject to the recalculation procedure:

Accrued interest receivable. The recalculation is based on the audited interest rate, face amount, and relevant dates of interest-bearing receivables. (See Exhibit 11–11.)

Accrued rent receivable. The recalculation is based on results of audit procedures applied to related property and rental contracts.

Various claims. The bases and calculations of claims for refund on insurance, damaged goods, taxes, and deposits or prepayments can be audited and the receivables amounts recalculated.

Prepaid expenses occupy a classification in current assets near receivables, and these items (similar to accrued amounts receivable) are generally matters of calculation, subject to audit of the bases for the items: for example, prepaid interest, insurance, rent, taxes, salaries, commissions, and the like. Recalculation, following audit of the base data, can complete the audit of items such as these.

Recalculations may serve as a major auditing procedure for revenue based on lease terms, construction contracts, and interest-bearing receivables. For some companies (e.g., banks, savings associations, major lessors) the "sales" item is functionally related to other basic asset data, and the revenue amount can be readily audited by recalculation.

Physical Observation

True physical observation is quite limited for sales, receivables, and cash in the bank because these things are largely intangible. However, the formal documents for notes receivable can be inspected for apparent

EXHIBIT 11–11

A B C Company
B-10 Notes Receivable, Interest Income, Accrued Interest
December 31, 1979

Prepared by J R
Date 1-3-80

Name/Terms	Date of Note	Date Due	Amount 12-31-78	Amount 12-31-79	Interest Income	Accrued Interest
Zephyr Able 10%, interest due 7-1-79	7-1-78	7-1-79	10,000 ν	—	500 ν ₮	-
Y. A. Baker 11%, interest due 1-1-80	1-1-79	1-1-80	— c	5,000 I	550 ₮	550 ₮
Xenon Charlton 10%, interest due 10-1-79 and 4-1-80	4-1-79	4-1-80	c	15,000 I	1,125 ν ₮	375 ₮
			10,000 T	20,000 T	2,175 T	925 T

T Agrees with general ledger.
ν Vouched cash receipts to bank deposit slip.
₮ Recalculated interest income and accrued interest according to terms of notes.
I Inspected notes kept in Treasurer's safe.
c Confirmed amount and terms of notes with debtors. Confirmation replies in Working Papers B-11, B-12.

authenticity, and the auditor can observe the physical safeguards (e.g., safe-deposit box) for control of the notes. Amounts recorded as sales and related trade receivables are evidenced by correspondence and other basic documentation, but inspection of these documents is viewed by auditors as a vouching procedure.

Cash funds on hand may be observed and counted. Petty cash and undeposited cash receipts are typical cash funds on hand. The count should be made in the presence of the fund custodian or another client officer, and that person's signature on a statement that all monies were returned intact should be obtained in order to protect the auditor from later accusations of impropriety. At the same time that one fund is being counted, all other negotiable assets should be under auditor control so that money or securities may not be shifted from one location to another to conceal a shortage. Such control may involve simultaneous count by several auditors of various funds or control by locking up other funds while one is counted.

The documentation of a physical count should contain record of vouchers, checks, bills, and other amounts that have not been entered in the accounts. If these amounts are material, an adjusting entry may be required to record them in the period under audit. The auditor should scan the volume of activity in a fund and the authorization signatures on vouchers for any signs that the fund may have been used improperly.

Some physical observation of production and shipping facilities may give the auditor a perception of physical capacity and potential maximum sales capacity in physical unit terms. These observations may later be useful in performing analyses of interrelationships relevant to the audit of sales dollar totals.

Confirmation

This procedure of obtaining formal statements from outside independent parties is extensively applied in the audit of cash and receivables accounts, and it may be useful for some types of recorded sales.[5]

If sales were made to one or a few major customers, the account activity as well as the balance might be confirmed. In this way the auditor would learn whether the seller's records corresponded with the buyer's records. Confirmation of the terms of leases or construction contracts can yield the basis for recalculation of revenue amounts. Likewise, confirmation of interest rates on loans and mortgages can provide audited data for the recalculation of interest income (the major revenue item in financial institutions).

The standard bank confirmation request form is shown in Exhibit 11–12. This confirmation asks that the bank report its record of account balances for all deposits of the client. (Notice that several other questions on the confirmation request provide information for the audit of direct and contingent liabilities.) The confirmed bank balance should be indicated on the bank reconciliation working paper (shown in Exhibit 5–6.) Confir-

[5] See "Evidential Matter for Receivables" (*SAS No. 1*, Sections 331.01–331.08).

EXHIBIT 11–12

STANDARD BANK CONFIRMATION INQUIRY
Approved 1966 by
AMERICAN INSTITUTE OF CERTIFIED PUBLIC ACCOUNTANTS
and
BANK ADMINISTRATION INSTITUTE (FORMERLY NABAC)

ORIGINAL
To be mailed to accountant

December 30 19 79

Dear Sirs:

Your completion of the following report will be sincerely appreciated. IF THE ANSWER TO ANY ITEM IS "NONE," PLEASE SO STATE. Kindly mail it in the enclosed stamped, addressed envelope *direct* to the accountant named below.

Report from

Yours truly, ABC Company
(ACCOUNT NAME PER BANK RECORDS)

By [illegible]
Authorized Signature

(Bank) Big City National Bank
Main at Michigan Avenue
Chicago, Illinois

Bank customer should check here if confirmation of bank balances only (item 1) is desired. ☐

NOTE—If the space provided is inadequate, please enter totals hereon and attach a statement giving full details as called for by the columnar headings below.

Accountant Anderson, Olds and Watershed
Certified Public Accountants
615 Big City Bank Tower
Chicago, Illinois

Dear Sirs:

1. At the close of business on December 31 19 79 our records showed the following balance(s) to the **credit** of the above named customer. In the event that we could readily ascertain whether there were any balances to the credit of the customer not designated in this request, the appropriate information is given below.

AMOUNT	ACCOUNT NAME	ACCOUNT NUMBER	Subject to Withdrawal by Check?	Interest Bearing? Give Rate
$ 325,325	ABC Company	146-2013	Yes	No

2. The customer was directly liable to us in respect of loans, acceptances, etc., at the close of business on that date in the total amount of $ 100,000, as follows:

AMOUNT	DATE OF LOAN OR DISCOUNT	DUE DATE	INTEREST		DESCRIPTION OF LIABILITY, COLLATERAL, SECURITY INTERESTS, LIENS, ENDORSERS, ETC.
			Rate	Paid to	
$ 100,000	6-30-79	6-30-80	11 %	none	Unsecured

3. The customer was contingently liable as endorser of notes discounted and/or as guarantor at the close of business on that date in the total amount of $ none, as below:

AMOUNT	NAME OF MAKER	DATE OF NOTE	DUE DATE	REMARKS
$				

4. Other direct or contingent liabilities, open letters of credit, and relative collateral, were

none

5. Security agreements under the Uniform Commercial Code or any other agreements providing for restrictions, not noted above, were as follows (if officially recorded, indicate date and office in which filed):

none

Yours truly, (Bank) Big City National Bank

Date January 5, 1980 19

By [illegible], Cashier
Authorized Signature

Additional copies of this form are available from the American Institute of CPAs, 666 Fifth Avenue, New York, N.Y. 10019 mation should be obtained from all banks with which the client did business during the period even if the checking accounts have been closed because the company may have notes payable, contingent liabilities, or other relationships with such banks.

There is also a standard two-page confirmation letter (available from the AICPA) designed to elicit information about compensating balance agreements and other restricting banking relationships. The need for this confirmation is the SEC's requirements for disclosure of compensating balances.

Confirmation of accounts and notes receivable is considered a primary means of obtaining evidence of existence and, to a limited extent, valuation. The accounts and notes to be confirmed may be selected at random or in accordance with a stratification plan consistent with the auditor's objectives. The area of receivables is one in which applications of statistical methods may be very useful. Computer assistance may be utilized to select the accounts and even to print the confirmations. (See the confirmation form in Exhibit 5–3.)

The important points about receivables confirmations are these:

The confirmation letter should be printed on the client's letterhead, or a facsimile, and signed by a client officer.

The auditor should be very careful to be assured that the source of the customer's address is reliable and not subject to alteration by the client in such a way as to misdirect the confirmation letter.

The request should seek information that the debtor can supply, like the amount of a balance or the amounts of specified invoices or notes.

The confirmations should be controlled by the auditor, not given to client personnel for mailing. *Direct* communication is required by auditing standards.

The responses should be returned directly to the auditor, not to the client.

The auditor should endeavor to obtain replies from all positive confirmations by sending second and third requests to nonrespondents. If there is no response or if the response specifies an exception to the client's records, the auditor should carry out vouching procedures to audit the account. When sampling is based on statistical methods, it is important that all accounts in the sample be audited. It is improper to substitute an easy-to-audit customer account not in the sample for one that does not respond to a confirmation request.

The *negative* form of a confirmation asks the other party to the transaction to respond *only if he or she has an exception* to the client's records. Negative confirmations are often used when there are numerous small accounts, such as thousands of electric utility customers. When this form is used, it is the *nonreturn* that is taken as evidence of account correctness.

Confirmation of receivables may be performed at a date other than the year-end. When confirmation is done at an interim date, the audit firm is able to spread work throughout the year and avoid the pressures of overtime that typically occur around December 31. Also, the audit can be completed sooner after the year-end date if confirmation has been done earlier. If the results of confirmation at an interim date are satisfactory, then scanning and limited vouching and analysis can serve to audit the intervening period to the year-end date, provided that reliance on the internal accounting control system is warranted.

The auditor must be careful when confirming advances and notes with officers, directors, affiliated companies, and subsidiaries. These parties are not independent of client management, thus the confirmation is not like one obtained from an independent outside party. To obtain persuasive evidence the auditor may wish to combine the confirmation procedure with other evidence from vouching and inquiry procedures.

Verbal Inquiry

Verbal inquiries directed to officers and employees provide direct evidence only of matters not otherwise evidenced in the accounts or subsidiary records. However, inquiries can lead to a better understanding of the business and to clues for subsequent application of evidence-gathering procedures.

Inquiries about markets and sales activity and of specific economic conditions may contribute to the audit of sales and revenue balances. Information about transportation problems or strikes at customers' plants may explain sales fluctuations or trends. Particularly important for the disclosure of accounting policies is information about the methods of revenue recognition in leasing, franchise, and construction activities. Altogether, responses to verbal inquiries about sales and revenue transactions typically contribute general understanding but little hard evidence. Corroboration with evidence from accounting records is necessary and is usually obtainable.

Inquiries about receivables usually concern questions of classification (e.g., current or long term, from officers) and collectibility. Oftentimes the auditor will have to discuss individual customer accounts with the credit manager or talk about the applicability of historical collection experience to the current receivables balances. Questions about sale, assignment, or pledging of receivables as collateral may also give information for footnote disclosures.

Cash-related inquiries center on any formal or informal restrictions on availability. By this procedure an auditor could learn of compensating balance agreements, loan agreement requirements, or restriction of funds in foreign banks.

Vouching of Documents

Recall that in the vouching procedure documentary evidence is sought for items selected from the records. In the previous discussion of internal control compliance tests, the vouching procedure was used extensively to test attributes of transactions. Vouching is also used in performing substantive tests of details to obtain evidence about monetary balances.

Revenue balances might be audited by selecting a sufficient sample of recorded transactions and vouching them to source documents for authenticity. This task has the objective of auditing the balance and not that of testing internal controls. In statistical model terms, a decision model for a dollar balance would be appropriate and not an application of statistical estimation of error attributes. This vouching would involve examination of the sales invoice (lease contract or other statement of charges), shipping documents, correspondence, and the customer's payment record. The auditor should be especially alert to evidence of transactions with related persons or affiliated companies (particularly with regard for proper exchange prices), and for transactions with subsidiary companies subject to elimination in consolidated statements.

Notice, however, that the vouching procedure accomplishes only an audit of recorded revenue transactions. Such extensive vouching is not common. Usually auditors combine a limited amount of vouching with other analyses of interrelationships to audit revenue balances.

Vouching of documentation underlying receivables balances is generally deferred until after confirmation. Then the procedure (conducted much like the sales vouching application) is directed toward audit of accounts for which confirmations were mailed but no replies received. Vouching may also be carried out to gather evidence about account discrepancies and disputes indicated on confirmation responses.

When confirmation is performed at an interim date, vouching of large items arising between the confirmation date and year-end date may be done to provide safeguard assurance of authenticity. Another application for vouching of receivables lies in the checking of an aged trial balance for proper classification of amounts by age categories. After the year-end, collections on receivables existing at the year-end may be vouched to cash receipts documents for evidence of the existence, valuation, and current asset classification of the receivables balances.

Vouching with respect to cash balances is centered on the examination of the bank reconciliation. (See the reconciliation working paper in Exhibit 5–6.) This vouching essentially amounts to determining whether outstanding checks were really outstanding and that deposits in transit were really mailed before the reconciliation date. The auditor's information source is a *cutoff bank statement.*

The cutoff bank statement is sent by the bank directly to the auditor, and it is usually for a 15- or 20-day period following the reconciliation date. The vouching is a matter of comparing checks that cleared in the cutoff period with the outstanding checklist for evidence that all checks that were written prior to the reconciliation date were on the outstanding checklist. The deposits shown as in transit should be recorded by the bank in the first business days of the cutoff period. If recorded later, there is indication that the deposit may have been made up from receipts of the period after the reconciliation date. For large outstanding checks not clearing in the cutoff period, vouching may be extended to other documentation supporting the disbursement.

These procedures provide evidence of existence, valuation, and proper cutoff of the cash balances.

Retracing

The retracing procedure involves taking samples of transaction data from basic document files and tracing them to the accounts (the opposite direction from the vouching procedure). It is employed extensively in the internal accounting control examination procedures of compliance testing. With regard to sales, receivables, and cash balances, retracing is most often employed to audit for proper cutoff—accounting for transactions in the period in which they actually occurred. The relative risk that sales, receivables, and cash receipts might more likely be overstated than understated reduces the need to rely on retracing as a procedure of searching for unrecorded transactions.

Sales and revenue cutoff is audited by selecting sales invoices, shipping documents, and contracts created in a period (usually ten days to two weeks) before and after the fiscal year-end. The transactions are traced to the sales and receivables accounts to prove that they were recorded in the proper period. Generally this selection of transactions involves a small data population defined for the special cutoff test purpose, and statistical methods are not applied unless the volume of transactions is fairly large.

Scanning

Scanning is a rapid review of records for any unusual transactions. Sales accounts may be scanned for any unusually large individual sales that might deserve additional vouching. The monthly summaries of sales may be reviewed for unusual fluctuations which might signal accounting errors. (One publicly held company reported in an annual report that in December of that year they discovered that sales for the month of November of the *prior year* had been recorded *twice*, resulting in a sales overstatement of $5 million and net income overstatement of $3 million, amounting to $1.60 per share—all material amounts.)

Bank statements for reportedly inactive accounts should be scanned to determine whether they were in fact inactive. Cash receipts records and receivables from officers and directors should be scanned for any apparent payment and reborrowing maneuvers designed to avoid reporting such advances in the financial statements.

Trade accounts and notes receivable should be scanned individually and in total for the period between an interim confirmation date and the fiscal year-end for indications of unusual transactions. This procedure may give the auditor reason to vouch the transaction documentation or make additional inquiries about collectibility.

Analysis of Interrelationships

Several analyses of interrelationships may be used as overall tests to audit sales, receivables, and cash receipts. Relationships such as receivables turnover, gross margin ratio, and sales/asset ratios can be compared to industry statistics and prior years' statistics of the company for evidence of overall reasonableness. Sales and revenue relationships of prior years' audited data to current year data by product line or other classifica-

EXHIBIT 11–13
Audit Program—Selected Substantive Test Procedures

A. *Revenue*
 1. Select a sample of recorded sales invoices and vouch to underlying shipping documents.
 2. Select a sample of shipping documents and trace to sales invoices.
 3. Obtain production records of physical quantities sold and calculate an estimate of sales dollars based on average sales prices.
 4. Recalculate interest income based on average loans outstanding and average interest rates in effect for the year.
 5. Compare revenue dollars and physical quantities with prior year data and industry economic statistics.
 6. Select a sample of sales invoices prepared a few days before and after the balance sheet date and vouch to supporting documents for evidence of proper cutoff.

B. *Cash*
 1. Prepare, or obtain from client, reconciliations of all bank accounts.
 2. Request cutoff bank statements from bank.
 3. Obtain confirmation from banks (standard bank confirmation).
 4. Vouch outstanding checks and deposits in transit to checks and deposits cleared in the cutoff statement.
 5. Prepare a schedule of interbank transfers.
 6. Obtain written representations from the client concerning compensating balance agreements.
 7. Count petty cash funds.

C. *Accounts and Notes Receivable*
 1. Inspect or obtain confirmation of notes receivable.
 2. Recalculate interest income and accrued interest receivable related to notes.
 3. Prepare, or obtain from client, an aged trial balance of customers' accounts receivable. Reconcile total to the accounts receivable control account.
 4. Recalculate the allowance for uncollectible accounts, and discuss past due accounts with the credit manager.
 5. Select a sample of customers' accounts for confirmation.
 6. Obtain written representations from the client concerning pledging of accounts receivable as collateral and as to amounts due from officers and directors.

tion is useful for highlighting changes for further investigation. However, the auditor must be careful when observing data that indicate little or no change from the prior year when changing economic conditions indicate that changes *should* have occurred.

Sales budgets and forecasts can be used for comparison to actual data for indications of unanticipated events. Comparisons of month-to-month sales data with prior year data may highlight any gross accounting errors (such as double-counting a month's sales).

Physical data that is functionally related to sales and production volume may be studied to corroborate sales totals. Shipping tonnage, electricity usage, oil consumption, and other inputs to production will indicate levels of production and shipping activity. In industries having controlled prices, physical sale data may be readily converted into sales dollars as a means of auditing sales. (Of course, the physical data would have to be audited first.)

Account interrelationships can also become a part of the analysis. Sales returns and allowances and sales commissions should vary directly with sales; bad debt expense should vary directly with the amount of sales on credit and accounts receivable balances; freight expenses should vary directly with physical sales volume. As a means of monitoring earlier audit decisions, receivables write-offs should be compared to prior years' allowances for uncollectible accounts.

In general the various analyses of interrelationships are most useful for auditing sales and revenue account balances. Auditors generally rely on evidence produced from many different tests and analyses rather than on vouching sales and revenue transactions in detail. Confirmation and extensive vouching are relied upon much more heavily for the audit of cash and receivables balances, hence additional evidence from analyses of interrelationships is not as important for these accounts.

TYPES OF MAJOR FRAUD AND MISSTATEMENT

Revenue, receivables, and cash receipts transactions provide many of the classic examples of fraud and embezzlement. Sales and other revenue transactions may be deliberately overstated to puff up a poor operating record. Thorough auditing of receivables, alertness for fictitious debtors, and careful reconciliation of cash receipts activity can detect most attempts to overstate sales. Understatement of sales to evade income taxes is harder to detect, but when such understatement is attempted, the receivable and cash collection and the related cost of goods sold records must also be suppressed to hide the omission. About the only way to detect a complete omission of sales and related transactions is through some reconciliation of physical activity with recorded dollar amounts. Incomplete omissions might be detected by careful analyses of account interrelationships (e.g., the gross margin relationship).

Cash is relatively easy to steal, although poor internal accounting controls must exist to make such theft probable. A person who has access both to cash and accounts receivable records may take a cash receipt and then cover it the next day with a payment received for another customer's account. Of course, the second customer does not have credit, so this "lapping" operation must be continued with subsequent receipts. Surprise confirmation or an enforced vacation policy may prevent such activity, but a proper separation of duties is more effective in the long run. If such a person has authority to issue credit memoranda for accounts, it may be possible to hide a theft, but then a high level of noncash credits to receivables should alert a careful auditor to further investigation of credit memoranda.

A cashier who makes out and delivers the bank deposit and also prepares bank reconciliations may abstract cash and hide this fact by falsifying the reconciliation. Inflated "deposits in transit" may be covered by receipts of later days, by underfooting the outstanding checklist, or by omitting outstanding checks from the reconciliation. Regular audit procedures applied to a bank reconciliation should detect these frauds.

An accounts receivable bookkeeper who has access to cash might record a sale in an amount less than the invoice. When payment is received, the "excess" can be stolen. Audit vouching of sales-receivables entries to invoice documents and detail comparison of deposit slip items to accounts receivable credits would detect these embezzlements. Most times, however, finding such an item could amount to trying to find a needle in a haystack, but the independent auditor still needs to be aware of possibilities for embezzlement that might be material with relation to financial statements. Internal auditors, however, may be given an assignment to carry out such a detail investigation for the express purpose of finding isolated instances of embezzlement.

Popular business literature of the 1970s has contained a flood of reports and articles about "computer fraud." The most blatant of these events have involved massive misstatement of sales and revenue totals, receivables, or like kinds of asset balances, and sometimes of cash receipts and cash balances. This text leaves technical issues of computer-assisted fraud for more advanced study, but two observations are in order here. First, when the fraud causes financial results to outrun industry performance and when fictitious customers and fictitious transactions are recorded, the auditor should be able to employ confirmation and vouching procedures sufficiently to find some evidence of massive fraud, even if unable to assess completely its scope and magnitude. Second, if management has aided and abetted the fraud by forging documents, by giving false responses to an auditor's inquiries, and by intercepting confirmation requests, then it is possible that even a careful auditor could be completely fooled while conducting what was thought to be a careful audit.

REVIEW QUESTIONS

11.1. What problems of *valuation* might the auditor encounter with respect to cash? Receivables?

11.2. What accounting principles and disclosures with respect to accounts receivable are of interest to the auditor?

11.3. What features of a sales internal control system would be expected to prevent the omission or double-counting of sales data?

11.4. What feature(s) of a cash receipts internal control system would be expected to prevent (*a*) an employee's absconding with company funds and replacing the funds during audit engagements with cash from the employee pension fund, and (*b*) the cash receipts journal and recorded cash sales from reflecting more than the amount shown on the daily deposit slip?

11.5. What features of a receivables internal control system would be expected to prevent an employee's abstracting cash through the creation of fictitious credit memos?

11.6. What actions might the *internal* auditor take to preserve the integrity of an accounts receivable system?

11.7. What are the *goals* of dual-direction sampling in regard to audit of accounts receivable?

11.8. Distinguish between "positive" and "negative" confirmations. Under what conditions would you expect each type of confirmation to be appropriate?

11.9. What are the important features of the receivables confirmation process?

11.10. From a timing standpoint, when is *vouching* performed on the documentation underlying receivables balances? Explain.

11.11. What is a *cutoff bank statement*? How is it used by the auditor?

11.12. List the information a CPA should solicit in a standard bank confirmation inquiry sent to an audit client's bank.

11.13. How does the auditor test for sales *cutoff*?

11.14. What is "lapping?" What procedures does the auditor employ for its detection?

EXERCISES AND PROBLEMS

11.15. You are the in-charge accountant examining the financial statements of the Gutzler Company for the year ended December 31. During late October you, with the help of Gutzler's controller, completed an internal control questionnaire and prepared the appropriate memoranda describing Gutzler's accounting procedures. Your comments relative to cash receipts are as follows.

All cash receipts are sent directly to the accounts receivable clerk with no processing by the mail department. The accounts receivable clerk keeps the cash receipts journal; prepares the bank deposit slip in duplicate; posts from the deposit slip to the subsidiary accounts receivable ledger; and mails the deposit to the bank.

The controller receives the validated deposit slips directly (unopened) from the bank. She also receives the monthly bank statement directly (unopened) from the bank and promptly reconciles it.

At the end of each month, the accounts receivable clerk notifies the general ledger clerk by journal voucher of the monthly totals of the cash receipts journal for posting to the general ledger.

Each month, with regard to the general ledger cash account, the general ledger clerk makes an entry to record the total debits to Cash from the cash receipts journal. In addition, the general ledger clerk on occasion makes debit entries in the general ledger Cash account from sources other than the cash receipts journal; for example, funds borrowed from the bank.

Certain standard auditing procedures which are listed below have already been performed by you in the audit of cash receipts.

Total and cross-total all columns in the cash receipts journal.

Trace postings from the cash receipts journal to the general ledger.

Examine remittance advices and related correspondence to support entries in the cash receipts journal.

Required:

Considering Gutzler's internal control over cash receipts and standard auditing procedures already performed, list all other auditing procedures and reasons therefore which should be performed to obtain sufficient audit evidence regarding cash receipts. Do not discuss the procedures for cash disbursements and cash balances. Also do not discuss the extent to which any of the procedures are to be performed. Assume adequate controls exist to assure that all sales transactions are recorded. Organize your answer sheet as follows:

Other Audit Procedures	*Reason for Other Audit Procedures*

(AICPA adapted)

11.16. Each of the following situations indicates a weakness in the system of internal control which can be discovered during audit of sales, receivables, and cash receipts transactions. Explain how the auditor will most likely uncover these weaknesses:

a. Identify the population from which you will sample, if appropriate.
b. Describe the specific procedures which can lead to discovery of the weaknesses.

(1) Customers who have not paid debts in the past continue to make charge sales. (Assume that approval for each sale has been given by the credit department.)
(2) Customers who have returned merchandise are frequently overbilled.
(3) Documents supporting receipts from cash sales are frequently destroyed after posting.
(4) Cash receipts are recorded daily but not deposited daily intact.

11.17. Charting, Inc., a new audit client of yours, processes its sales and cash receipts documents in the following manner:

1. *Payment on account.* The mail is opened each morning by a mail clerk in the sales department. The mail clerk prepares a remittance advice

(showing customer and amount paid) if one is not received. The checks and remittance advices are then forwarded to the sales department supervisor who reviews each check and forwards the checks and remittance advices to the accounting department supervisor.

The accounting department supervisor, who also functions as credit manager in approving new credit and all credit limits, reviews all checks for payments on past-due accounts and then forwards the checks and remittance advices to the accounts receivable clerk who arranges the advices in alphabetical order. The remittance advices are posted directly to the accounts receivable ledger cards. The checks are endorsed by stamp and totaled. The total is posted to the cash receipts journal. The remittance advices are filed chronologically.

After receiving the cash from the previous day's cash sales, the accounts receivable clerk prepares the daily deposit slip in triplicate. The third copy of the deposit slip is filed by date, and the second copy and the original accompany the bank deposit.

2. *Sales*. Salesclerks prepare sales invoices in triplicate. The original and second copy are presented to the cashier. The third copy is retained by the salesclerk in the sales book. When the sale is for cash, the customer pays the salesclerk who presents the money to the cashier with the invoice copies.

A credit sale is approved by the cashier from an approved credit list after the salesclerk prepares the three-part invoice. After receiving the cash or approving the invoice, the cashier validates the original copy of the sales invoice and gives it to the customer. At the end of each day the cashier recaps the sales and cash received and forwards the cash and the second copy of all sales invoices to the accounts receivable clerk.

The accounts receivable clerk balances the cash received with cash sales invoices and prepares a daily sales summary. The credit sales invoices are posted to the accounts receivable ledger and then all invoices are sent to the inventory control clerk in the sales department for posting to the inventory control cards. After posting, the inventory control clerk files all invoices numerically. The accounts receivable clerk posts the daily sales summary to the cash receipts journal and sales journal and files the sales summaries by date.

The cash from cash sales is combined with the cash received on account to comprise the daily bank deposit.

3. *Bank deposits.* The bank validates the deposit slip and returns the second copy to the accounting department where it is filed by date by the accounts receivable clerk.

Monthly bank statements are reconciled promptly by the accounting department supervisor and filed by date.

Required:

Construct a flowchart for the sales and cash receipts system of Charting, Inc. (Hint: The column headings, left to right, are Sales Department Clerks, Cashier, Sales Department Supervisor, Accounting Department Supervisor, and Accounts Receivable Clerk.) (AICPA adapted)

11.18. You have been engaged by Central Savings and Loan Association to audit its financial statements for the year ended December 31. The CPA who audited last year's financial statements rendered an unqualified opinion.

In addition to servicing its own mortgage loans, the association acts as a mortgage-servicing agency for three life insurance companies. In this latter activity, the association maintains mortgage records and serves as the collection and escrow agent for the mortgagees (the insurance companies) who pay a fee to the association for these services.

Cash collections (all by mail) on the serviced mortgages are batched daily and entered in an EDP system through an input terminal located in the association's main office. The operator keys the proper mortgage number and enters the receipt information on the terminal keyboard. (This information is obtained from a remittance advice enclosed with the payment.) By this operation, magnetic master files are updated, the transaction data is stored on a random-access disk, and once each month a hard-copy transcript of the account is printed out as a report to the mortgagee. Cash disbursements from the escrow accounts are keypunched on cards, merged monthly with the magnetic master file, also stored on disk, and printed out on the monthly hard-copy report. All disk-stored records are erased after the monthly report is printed. The remittance advices and disbursement authorization documents are filed by mortgage account number.

Required:

You would expect the association to have certain internal controls in effect in the EDP system with input controls, processing controls, and output controls. What controls should be in effect which are unique to the EDP system described above. Controls may be classified as to—

a. Those controls pertaining to input of information.
b. All other types of computer controls. (AICPA adapted)

11.19. Listed below is a selection of items from the Internal Control Questionnaires shown in the chapter. For each one:

a. Identify the control characteristic to which it applies (e.g., segregation of duties—authorization of transactions, access to assets and recordkeeping duties; sound error-checking practice; and so on).
b. Specify one compliance test procedure an auditor could use to determine whether the control was operating effectively.
c. Using your business experience, your logic, and/or your imagination give an example of an error or irregularity that could occur if the control was absent or ineffective.
d. Specify a substantive testing procedure an auditor could use to uncover errors or irregularities, if any, resulting from absence of the control.

(1) Are sales invoice blanks prenumbered? Controlled in the sales order department?
(2) Are sales invoices checked for error in the billing department as to prices, credit terms, extensions and footings, freight allowances, and checked with customers' orders?
(3) Is a bank reconciliation performed monthly by someone who does not have cash custody or recordkeeping responsibility?
(4) Is mail opened by someone other than the cashier or accounts receivable recordkeeper? Are daily remittance advices and/or remittance lists prepared by this person?

(5) Are customers' records balanced monthly with the general ledger control account?

(6) Are noncash credits (to accounts receivable)—discounts, returns—subject to approval by a responsible officer?

11.20. *a.* An independent auditor wishes to test Houston Corporation's sales cutoff at June 30. Describe the steps that the auditor should include in this test.

b. The auditor obtains a July 10 bank statement directly from the bank. Explain how this cutoff bank statement will be used—

(1) In the auditor's review of the June 30 bank reconciliation.

(2) To obtain other audit information. (AICPA adapted)

11.21. The following information was obtained in an audit of the Cash account of Tuck Company as of December 31. Assume that the CPA is satisfied as to the validity of the cash book, the bank statements, and the returned checks, except as noted.

1. The bookkeeper's bank reconciliation at November 30:

Balance per bank statement		$ 19,400
Add deposit in transit		1,100
Total		$ 20,500
Less outstanding checks:		
#2540	$140	
1501	750	
1503	480	
1504	800	
1505	30	2,300
Balance per books		$ 18,200

2. A summary of the bank statement for December:

Balance brought forward	$ 19,400
Deposits	148,700
	$168,100
Charges	132,500
Balance, December 31	$ 35,600

3. A summary of the cash book for December before adjustments:

Balance brought forward	$ 18,200
Receipts	149,690
	$167,890
Disbursements	124,885
Balance, December 31,	$ 43,005

4. Included with the canceled checks returned with the December bank statement were the following:

Number	*Date of Check*	*Amount of Check*	*Explanation*
1501	November 28	$ 75	This check was in payment of an invoice for $750 and was recorded in the cash book as $750.
1503	November 28	580	This check was in payment of an invoice for $580 and was recorded in the cash book as $580.
1523	December 5	150	Examination of this check revealed that it was unsigned. A discussion with the client disclosed that it had been mailed inadvertently before it was signed. The check was endorsed and deposited by the payee and processed by the bank even though it was a legal nullity. The check was recorded in the cash disbursements.
1528	December 12	800	This check replaced No. 1504 that was returned by the payee because it was mutilated. Check No. 1504 was not canceled on the books.
—	December 19	200	This was a counter check drawn at the bank by the president of the company as a cash advance for travel expense. The president overlooked informing the bookkeeper about the check.
—	December 20	300	The drawer of this check was the Tucker Company.
1535	December 20	350	This check had been labeled NSF and returned to the payee because the bank had erroneously believed that the check was drawn by the Luck Company. Subsequently the payee was advised to redeposit the check.
1575	January 5	10,000	This check was given to the payee on December 30 as a postdated check with the understanding that it would not be deposited until January 5. The check was not recorded on the books in December.

5. The Tuck Company discounted its own 60-day note for $9,000 with the bank on December 1. The discount rate was 6 percent. The bookkeeper recorded the proceeds as a cash receipt at the face value of the note.
6. The bookkeeper records customers' dishonored checks as a reduction of cash receipts. When the dishonored checks are redeposited, they are recorded as a regular cash receipt. Two NSF checks for $180 and $220 were returned by the bank during December. The $180 check was redeposited, but the $220 check was still on hand at December 31.

   Cancellations of Tuck Company checks are recorded by a reduction of cash disbursements.
7. December bank charges were $20. In addition a $10 service charge was made in December for the collection of a foreign draft in November. These charges were not recorded on the books.
8. Check No. 2540 listed in the November outstanding checks was drawn three years ago. Since the payee cannot be located, the president of Tuck Company agreed to the CPA's suggestion that the check be written back into the accounts by a journal entry.
9. Outstanding checks at December 31 totaled $4,000 excluding checks No. 2540 and No. 1504.
10. The cutoff bank statement disclosed that the bank had recorded a deposit of $2,400 on January 2. The bookkeeper had recorded this deposit on the books on December 31 and mailed the deposit to the bank.

Required:

Prepare a four-column reconciliation (sometimes called a "proof of cash") of the cash receipts and cash disbursements recorded on the bank statement and on the company's books for the month of December. The reconciliation should agree with the cash figure that will appear in the company's financial statements. (AICPA adapted)

11.22. XYZ operates sales divisions in several cities throughout the country. In addition to other activities the sales divisions are charged with the collection of local receivables; each division maintains a bank account in which all collections are deposited intact. Twice a week these collections are transferred to the home office by check; no other checks are drawn on this bank account. Except for cash receipts and cash disbursements books, no accounting books are kept at the sales offices, but all cash records are retained by them in their files.

As part of your year-end audit you wish to include an audit of cash transfers between the sales divisions and the main office. It is intended that your representative will visit all locations.

Required:

a. What are the purposes of the audit of cash transfers?

b. Assuming that your representative has a full knowledge of audit procedures for regular cash collection to which he will attend at each location, design *only such additional specific* audit steps as the representative will be required to perform to audit the cash transfers from each division to the home office. (AICPA)

11.23. Your client is the Quaker Valley Shopping Center, Inc., a shopping center with 30 store tenants. All leases with the store tenants provide for a fixed rent plus a percentage of sales, net of sales taxes, in excess of a fixed dollar amount computed on an annual basis. Each lease also provides that the landlord may engage a CPA to audit all records of the tenant for assurance that sales are being properly reported to the landlord.

You have been requested by your client to audit the records of the Bali Pearl Restaurant to determine that the sales totaling $390,000 for the year ended December 31 have been properly reported to the landlord. The restaurant and the shopping center entered into a five-year lease on January 1. The Bali Pearl Restaurant offers only table service. No liquor is served. During meal times there are four or five waitresses in attendance who prepare handwritten prenumbered restaurant checks for the customers. Payment is made at a cash register, manned by the proprietor, as the customer leaves. All sales are for cash. The proprietor also is the bookkeeper. Complete files are kept of restaurant checks and cash register tapes. A daily sales book and general ledger are also maintained.

Required:

List the auditing procedures that you would employ to audit the total annual sales of the Bali Pearl Restaurant. (Disregard vending machine sales and counter sales of chewing gum, candy, and the like.) (AICPA adapted)

11.24. Andrew Miller, CPA, is seeking evidence of overall reasonableness in connection with audit of sales and receivables of Van Industries. The following data have been taken from Van's accounting records on December 31 of each year of the following years:

	1978	*1979*
Total sales	$1,000,000	$1,600,000
Credit sales	720,000	1,400,000
Total assets	600,000	800,000
Cost of goods sold	600,000	800,000
Accounts receivable	72,000	350,000
Allowance for uncollectible accounts	12,000	21,000
Sales commissions	20,000	32,000
Average accounts receivable	72,000	280,000
Net income	120,000	320,000
Accounts written off	13,000	112,000

Required:

a. (1) Compute the following ratios for 1978 and 1979.

(*a*) Asset turnover.

(*b*) Return on total sales.

(*c*) Return on total assets.

(*d*) Gross margin percentage.

(*e*) Receivables turnover.

(*f*) Average days to collect receivables.

(2) Compute the amount of cash collected on account in 1979.

b. What indications does the auditor have that the client's policy has changed in regard to granting credit?

c. Is the auditor likely to question the reasonableness of amounts of sales and costs shown for 1979. Explain.

d. List five explanations for the disproportionate increase in cost of goods sold relative to sales, assuming the amounts for 1978 and 1979 are fairly presented.

e. What asset valuation problem might the auditor suspect? Explain.

11.25. The Patrick Company had poor internal control over its cash transactions. Facts about its cash position at November 30 were the following.

The cash books showed a balance of $18,901.62, which included undeposited receipts. A credit of $100 on the bank statement did not appear on the books of the company. The balance according to the bank statement was $15,550.

When the auditor received the cutoff bank statement on December 10, the following canceled checks were enclosed: No. 62 for $116.25, No. 183 for $150.00, No. 284 for $253,25, No. 8621 for $190.71, No. 8623 for $206.80, and No. 8632 for $145.28. The only deposit was in the amount of $3,794.41 on December 7.

The cashier handles all incoming cash and makes the bank deposits personally. He also reconciles the monthly bank statement. His November 30 reconciliation is shown below.

Balance, per books, November 30		$18,901.62
Add: Outstanding checks:		
8621	$190.71	
8623	206.80	
8632	145.28	442.79
		$19,344.41
Less: Undeposited receipts		3,794.41
Balance per bank, November 30		$15,550.00
Deduct: Unrecorded credit		100.00
True cash, November 30		$15,450.00

Required:

a. You suspect that the cashier has stolen some money. Prepare a schedule showing your estimate of the loss.

b. How did the cashier attempt to conceal the thefts?

c. Based only on the information above, name two specific features of internal control which were apparently missing.

d. If the cashier's October 31 reconciliation is known to be in order and you start your audit on December 5, what specific auditing procedures could you perform to discover the theft? (AICPA adapted)

11.26. Archer, CPA, is auditing the financial statements of his new client Flinight Manufacturing Company as of December 31. Flinight makes home kitchen cleaning utensils and markets the products through direct sales to a large network of wholesale distributors located throughout the United States. Some distributors are very successful, purchase a large volume of the products and tend to have large accounts receivable balances with Flinight. A large number of distributors (about 300) are apparently not able just now to penetrate local markets; hence, their purchases and accounts receivable balances tend to be quite small.

There are only 53 of the large accounts, totaling $530,000, and the 300 or so smaller accounts total $250,000. However, accounts receivable constitutes 60 percent of the company's current assets and about 20 percent of total assets. Flinight's stockholders' equity is $500,000, and the company's income for the year (unaudited) was $300,000 before taxes.

Archer's assistant points out that fairly small misstatements of the accounts receivable total could be material with relation to other accounting measurements. For example, a 7-percent overstatement of receivables would also be a 4.2-percent current asset overstatement and would cause Flinight to show a small working capital deficit. Also, this 7 percent overstatement would be 18 percent of the net income. Such an overstatement might result from having too small an allowance for doubtful accounts. In fact, the company treasurer has mentioned that some of the larger wholesalers have not been ordering as much lately, and some of them have not paid as quickly as they did six months ago, even missing the 3-percent cash discount. A few have complained about broken boxes received in shipment.

Archer and his assistant have already obtained evidence that the accounts receivable are properly classified as trade receivables, and no sales are made on terms extending beyond 12 months. They are considering the audit procedures to apply in connection with sending confirmations and evaluating the collectibility of the trade receivables.

Required:

a. Identify and describe the two forms of accounts receivable confirmation requests and indicate what factors should be considered in determining when to use each.

b. Assume the auditors receive satisfactory responses to the confirmation requests. Describe how they could evaluate collectibility of the trade accounts receivable.

11.27. The ABC Appliance Company, a manufacturer of minor electrical appliances, deals exclusively with 20 distributors situated at focal points throughout the country. At December 31, the balance sheet date, receivables from these distributors aggregated $875,000. Total current assets were $1,300,000.

With respect to receivables, the auditor followed the procedures outlined below in the course of the annual examination of financial statements:

1. Reviewed the system of internal accounting control. It was found to be exceptionally good.
2. Tied detail with control account at year-end.
3. Aged accounts. None were overdue.
4. Examined detail sales and collection transactions for the months of February, July, and November.
5. Received positive confirmations of year-end balances.

Required:

You are to criticize the completeness or incompleteness of the above program, giving reasons for your recommendations concerning the addition or omission of any procedures. (AICPA)

11.28. You are in charge of your second yearly examination of the financial statements of Hillsboro Equipment Corporation, a distributor of construction equipment. Hillsboro's equipment sales are either outright cash sales or a combination of a substantial cash payment and one or two 60- or 90-day nonrenewable interest-bearing notes for the balance. Title to the equipment passes to the customer when the initial cash payment is made. The notes, some of which are secured by the customer, are dated when the cash payment is made (the day the equipment is delivered). If the customer prefers to purchase the equipment under an installment payment plan, Hillsboro arranges for the customer to obtain such financing from a local bank.

You begin your field work to examine the December 31 financial statements on January 5, knowing that you must leave temporarily for another engagement on January 7 after outlining the audit program for your assistant. Before leaving, you inquire about the assistant's progress in the examination of notes receivable. Among other things, the assistant shows you a working paper listing the makers' names, the due dates, the interest rates, and amounts of 17 outstanding notes receivable totaling $100,000. The working paper contains the following notations:

1. Reviewed system of internal accounting control and found it to be satisfactory.
2. Total of $100,000 agrees with general ledger control account.
3. Traced listing of notes to sales journal.

You are informed by the assistant that positive confirmation will be requested of the amounts of all outstanding notes receivable and that no other audit work has been performed in the examination of notes receivable and interest arising from equipment sales. There were no outstanding accounts receivable for equipment sales at the end of the year.

Required:

a. List the additional audit procedures that the assistant should apply in the audit of the account for notes receivable arising from equipment sales (Hillsboro has no other notes). No subsidiary ledger is maintained.

b. You ask your assistant to examine all notes receivable on hand before you leave. The assistant returns in 30 minutes from the office safe where the notes are kept and reports that notes on hand total only $75,000.

List the possible explanations that you would expect from the client for the $25,000 difference. (Eliminate fraud or misappropriation from your consideration.) Indicate beside each explanation the audit procedures you would apply to determine if each explanation is correct. (AICPA adapted)

11.29. Several accounts receivable confirmations have been returned with the notation that "verification of vendors' statements is no longer possible because our data processing system does not accumulate each vendor's invoices." What alternative auditing procedures could be used to audit these accounts receivable? (AICPA adapted)

12

AUDIT OF INVENTORIES, COST OF SALES, AND CASH DISBURSEMENTS

This chapter has four major objectives related to the tools and techniques described in earlier chapters. The objectives are to explain with relation to inventories, cost of sales, and cash disbursement transactions:

A business approach to audit objectives concerning existence, valuation, cutoff, accounting principles, compliance, and effectiveness.

Elements of internal control for these accounts and transactions.

Applications of audit procedures for gathering evidence.

Types of fraud and misstatement that might occur in these accounts.

The discussion and explanation of each of these four topics are intended to enable students to sharpen their awareness of audit objectives, relevant evidence, relevant audit procedures, and the application of audit methodology to the specific subset of accounts.

Most programs used in audit field work contain separate sections for procedures related to inventories and for procedures related to cost of sales. The cash disbursement audit procedures are generally combined with procedures for auditing cash receipts transactions and cash balances. In this text, however, cash disbursement audit procedures are grouped with inventory, purchasing, and cost of sales procedures in order to show the flow of a transaction from purchase to account payable and inventory and thence to payment of the liability.

A BUSINESS APPROACH TO AUDIT OBJECTIVES

The broad managerial overview that aids the auditor throughout an engagement is equally useful with regard to inventories, cost of sales, and cash disbursements transactions. The perspective provided by a business approach lends understanding of unique engagement circumstances to each of the auditor's primary objectives.

Existence

The areas of purchasing, inventories, and cost of sales are quite closely related to the marketing function. As before in consideration of sales and receivables, the auditor should become familiar with the client's product. It is important to know whether the product is produced or purchased complete, whether it is perishable, whether it is produced by job order or in a continuous process, whether it is produced on contract only or for shelf inventory or—in nonmanufacturing businesses—whether there is any physical product at all. The size and frequency of sales orders may also be considered in this familiarization with the product.

Marketing plans coordinated with production and purchasing plans should also reveal the composition of input markets. Inputs purchased from only a few suppliers present different auditing problems than when suppliers are numerous and purchases scattered. Knowledge of major types of purchases can facilitate the auditor's subsequent concentration of procedures on the most important elements of cost. The existence of a computer-based purchasing-inventory system that automatically produces standard purchase orders will have an impact on subsequent auditing procedures.

The overview of the product and its input and output markets should also enable the auditor to discern the major cost elements in inventories and cost of sales. Some products are materials cost-intensive, others may be labor cost-intensive, and others may be quite low cost (with attendant heavy expenditures on promotion and advertising). Knowledge of the mix of product line sales and their related gross margins as well as knowledge of the cost element mix can contribute to the auditor's understanding of inventories and cost of sales.

The auditor should also become familiar with the receiving and shipping operations. Receiving practices are important relative to initial control over inventories (both as to quantity and quality), and observations of shipping and selling operations can tell the auditor about inventory on consignment or stored in public warehouses off the client's premises. A tour of inventory storage areas can help in later planning for the observation of a physical inventory count.

With regard to the cash disbursement function, the auditor will want to learn about organization structure—whether the function is centralized at a headquarters level or decentralized in several locations. The extent to which the purchasing function coordinates with the disbursement function is also important. Some companies centralize authority for creation of liabilities through a "purchasing-control" department, while others allow the authority to acquire supplies and services to be dispersed among operating managers. For example, the authority to contract for advertising and promotion may rest with the sales manager without approval from a purchasing department.

The system of accounting for disbursements is also of interest to the auditor. A system that provides for monthly payment of vendors' accounts requires different auditing attention than one that generates schedules of individual invoices by due dates (as in a voucher system). An EDP system that integrates check-writing capabilities with liability records poses still different auditing problems.

Valuation

Inventory valuation is of major interest here. Cost of goods sold valuation represents an allocation of the total costs of goods available for sale, and cash disbursements valuation is derived from the measurement of liabilities arising through regular purchases or other acquisition methods.

In general, the auditor is interested in the major types and dollar volumes of purchases—information that may flow from a familiarization with the product and the manufacturing process. In this connection, information about purchasing department procedures for obtaining prices will be useful. The practice of buying regularly from a small number of suppliers has different implications in comparison to practices of soliciting bids or searching continuously among numerous suppliers for the lowest price.

General and specific economic conditions such as price changes, labor conditions (both in the client's and in suppliers' plants), and market price changes should be related to the circumstances of the engagement. An increase in inventory investment could be the result of higher prices; low inventory turnover could be the result of stockpiling as a hedge against anticipated strikes in suppliers' plants. On the other hand, both of these conditions could also result from having obsolete, worn, or worthless items in the inventory. Attention to market prices and relative product costs will be essential to later determinations of lower-of-cost-or-market inventory values. Special attention to the prices paid to affiliated companies or persons for inventory items is necessary in order to value inventory properly. Knowledge of a new labor contract will certainly affect the audit of labor cost inputs.

Cost of goods sold is an allocation of the total costs of goods available for sale. The valuation problems are partially solved simultaneously with inventory valuation issues discussed above. However, the method of allocation thereafter becomes quite important. In this regard the auditor needs to become familiar with the production technology, its management, and with recent technological changes. Continued use by a company of an obsolete technology may result in incurrence of costs that cannot be recovered through sale of the product. Management of technology and of daily operations should produce analyses of input costs—materials, labor, and overhead—that would show any unusual fluctuations which might require greater audit attention. Changes in technology and the purchase of new equipment should be discussed so that the auditor can look for changes in cost assignments (e.g., more overhead and less direct labor) and for recording of asset disposals, if any. Changes in technology also may alert the auditor to look for reevaluation of standard costs, if such a system is used to allocate costs to the cost of goods sold classification.

Sales levels, gross margins, seasonal fluctuations, and the general efficiency of management in avoiding crises—rush orders, backlog snarls, and so forth—can all be factored into a general understanding of the flow of product from the purchase of inputs to sale. Inefficiencies and lack of planning may mean that excess costs may have been assigned to one or both of inventories and cost of goods sold.

Cutoff

Inventory, cost of sales, and cash disbursement transactions often present significant cutoff problems. Particular problems arise with the reconciliation of a physical inventory count with perpetual inventory records. The auditor must determine whether:

- Goods on hand were counted and included in the inventory compilation,
- Goods consigned-out or stored in outside warehouses (goods owned but not on hand) were included in the inventory compilation,
- Goods in transit (goods actually purchased and recorded but not yet received) were added to the inventory count and included in the inventory compilation,
- Goods on hand but already sold (but not yet delivered) were not counted and were excluded from the inventory compilation, and
- Goods consigned-in (goods on hand but not owned) were excluded from the inventory compilation.

An inventory compilation working paper is shown in Exhibit 12–1.

In connection with inventory and purchase cutoff the auditor should learn about purchasing department and accounts payable department records. The purchasing department's file of open purchase orders (orders placed but goods not yet received) may contain evidence of inventory goods in transit—thus there may exist unrecorded assets (inventory) and unrecorded accounts payable. The accounts payable department may have a file of unmatched receiving reports (reports of goods received awaiting arrival of a vendor's invoice)—indicating the presence of goods that will be included in the physical inventory for which the related accounts payable has not yet been recorded. These files are sources of information about proper accounting cutoff.

Audit of the cost of sales cutoff can be associated with audit work on the sales transaction cutoff. Some overall tests such as inventory turnover and gross margin comparison can yield clues, and comparison of cutoff period sales data with related cost of sales data can provide the association

EXHIBIT 12–1

ABC Company
Inventory Compilation
December 31, 1979

Prepared by JR
Date 1-20-80

Item	Prepared by Client: Quantity	Cost	Amount	Audit Data: Quantity	Cost	Amount
#A601	8928 y	$4.00 ✓	35712			35712 ≠
#F60	13920 y	$3.40	47328	13920	$3.33 X	46353 ≠
#L612	17760 y	$2.40 ✓	42624			42624 ≠
#S801	4560 y	$18.00 ✓	82080			82080 ≠
Inventory per client			207744			
Inventory consigned-out, item #5801			f/≠	1264 (1)	$18	22752 ≠
Inventory per audit						229521 T/B

y Agrees with physical observation and count by DW of audit staff.
✓ FIFO cost vouched to vendor's recent invoices, no exceptions.
X Client failed to exclude cash discount taken on last purchase
≠ Calculated by audit staff
f Footed client's inventory schedule.
T Traced to General Ledger. Book-physical difference was adjusted to the inventory over/short Expense account.
T/B Tied to audit trial balance.
(1) Shipping department records show 1264 units of #5801 shipped to customer December 24 marked "on consignment." Inquiry in billing department revealed this shipping document being held -- no invoice was prepared and no sale was recorded. The normal cost of goods sold entry was made.

Recommended Adjusting Journal Entry

Account	Debit	Credit
Inventory	22752	
Inventory over/short	975	
Inventory		975
Cost of Goods Sold		22752

© WILSON JONES COMPANY G7206 GREEN 7206 BUFF MADE IN U.S.A.

of transaction details. The "cutoff period" begins a few days prior to the client's year-end date and ends a few days after. This is the time when transactions may be recorded in the wrong accounting period.

Cash disbursements cutoff may be facilitated if a schedule of vouchers by due dates is prepared as a part of the cash management function. Generally, however, cash disbursement cutoff is tested in detail with work done on the year-end bank reconciliation. (Refer to Chapter 11.)

Cutoff work on inventories and cash disbursements may be related to other audit work on liabilities (covered in Chapter 15). Unrecorded inventory items (e.g., goods in transit) and cash payments made early in the next year oftentimes pertain to liabilities that should have been recorded in the year under audit, and the search for such events is a part of the liability audit procedure known as the "search for unrecorded liabilities." (See Chapter 15.)

Accounting Principles and Disclosure

Accounting principles of disclosure require that the basis for stating inventories be disclosed as well as any modifications by application of lower-of-cost-or-market valuation. The auditor will want to inquire about the inventory pricing assumption (e.g., Lifo, Fifo). Performance reports and cost analyses should be reviewed. If management uses a method such as Nifo (next-in, first-out) or variable costing for planning purposes, neither of which is in conformity with generally accepted accounting principles, some special attention should be exercised to determine whether such methods are used in the accounts.

The relationships with other companies (affiliates and subsidiaries) should be discussed, and the auditor should learn about typical intercompany transactions. These will have to be considered in consolidated statements or in footnote disclosures.

Marketing, purchasing, and production plans should be reviewed and discussed to determine whether any significant purchase commitments exist. If so, further audit work must be done to determine whether there are any losses to be recognized currently. As a matter of general familiarity, the auditor will want to review the cost accounting system and assess its adequacy for appropriate allocation of overhead and proper assignment of other costs. Surface indications of a haphazard system may spell out significant problems for later audit attention.

Compliance

For most companies compliance with regard to inventories and cost of sales refers to compliance with private contract terms. The auditor will want to learn of any long-term fixed-price sales contracts. It may be necessary to recognize losses if production costs have risen. Many construction and delivery contracts call for monetary penalties for failure to meet deadlines. Such provisions are important, and the auditor may have to review progress on contracts to determine whether any penalties may be anticipated.

Warranty and guarantee terms and quality control management have compliance implications for contracts, and provisions for liability may be appropriate. Poor quality control can have an impact through warranty liabilities and excessive waste and rework cost. In cases where the auditor cannot personally make an evaluation of quality controls, it may be necessary to retain the services of an engineering consultant to assess product quality properly. These considerations have a direct bearing on valuation of inventories as well as on the compliance objective.

In the area of public laws there now exist many product safety statutes and regulations. Through familiarity with the product and discussions with management, the auditor should be apprised of the applicable laws and regulations, both state and federal. An awareness of current events in the news may also serve to alert the auditor to possible product quality issues. As examples, an inventory of drug products that has not been licensed by the Federal Drug Administration may be of doubtful value; stocks of goods banned by government action (e.g., cyclamates, saccharin) may be worthless. An auditor cannot afford either to ignore or overemphasize the potential impact of government regulation on the legality and value of products held in inventory.

Effectiveness

A great many possibilities exist for fruitful consulting activities in management areas concerned with inventories and cost of goods sold. Internal auditors frequently work in these areas, and independent accountants may be able to make useful suggestions for control system improvements. Many cost-saving operational changes stem from information obtained during an audit as well as from extensive special studies.

The independent auditor, as a result of financial audit work, is in the best position to assess the adequacy of the cost accounting system. From a management viewpoint the goal of the system is to produce relevant and timely cost analyses and cost center performance reports for evaluation and control purposes. The auditor will become familiar with the system enough to determine whether these goals are satisfied.

Otherwise, applications of inventory planning and control such as economic order quantity modeling can be usefully employed to assess the efficiency of inventory management. The inventory manager who does not have estimates of inventory carrying and order costs and stock-out costs will not be well prepared to control inventory in an economical fashion. The consultant should look for symptoms of poor control in frequent stock-outs or excessively high inventories.

Effective inventory management is closely related to effective market forecasts, effective production scheduling, and effective purchasing operations. Chronic late deliveries, production bottlenecks, frequent expediting of rush orders, high levels of rework costs, and low inventory turnover all may be indicators of poor planning and coordination. Detailed studies are necessary for prescriptions of corrective action, but observance of such conditions can alert the independent auditor to potential areas for further study in a management advisory services capacity.

Some other areas for effectiveness studies include the operations of the purchasing department, where optimal price selection with considerations of lead time and quality can be a standard. Analyses of make-or-buy alternatives and engineering studies of product improvements may be analyzed or instituted. Shipping and distribution operations can be reviewed for efficiency. Productivity studies may be performed for purposes of production planning and for use in labor contract negotiations.

In the area of cash management, an independent auditor can readily determine if available discounts are being taken. The interest cost implicit in lost discounts can be compared to the company's cost of borrowing funds in order to make timely payments. The auditor can also review the cash disbursement operations for coordination with the overall cash management plan and for coordination with market forecasts, production requirements, and cash budgets.

INTERNAL CONTROL

The characteristics of internal accounting control over purchases, inventory, and cash disbursements may be analyzed initially with the questionnaire and flowchart techniques. Following this review phase of evaluation, tests of transactions may be performed in order to examine objectively the actual effectiveness of controls. Most organizations provide fairly elaborate accounting controls over purchases, inventories, and cash disbursements transactions.

Review Phase

In the first phase of a proper study and evaluation of internal control, the auditor is looking for three coordinated control features:

- A plan of organization with proper segregation of functions and restricted access to assets and records,
- A system of general or specific authorization for the processing of transaction data.
- A system of error-checking routines for prevention and detection of errors that may occur.

With regard to inventories, one special type of error-checking routine is a periodic or cyclical physical count of inventory.

The flowchart exhibits in this chapter show model organizational systems for control of purchase, inventory, and cash disbursement transactions. Each flowchart shows the segregation of functions considered characteristic of satisfactory internal accounting control. Exhibits 12–4, 12–6 and 12–8 contain internal control questionnaire items that are typical of these systems.

EXHIBIT 12–2
Purchase Order Preparation

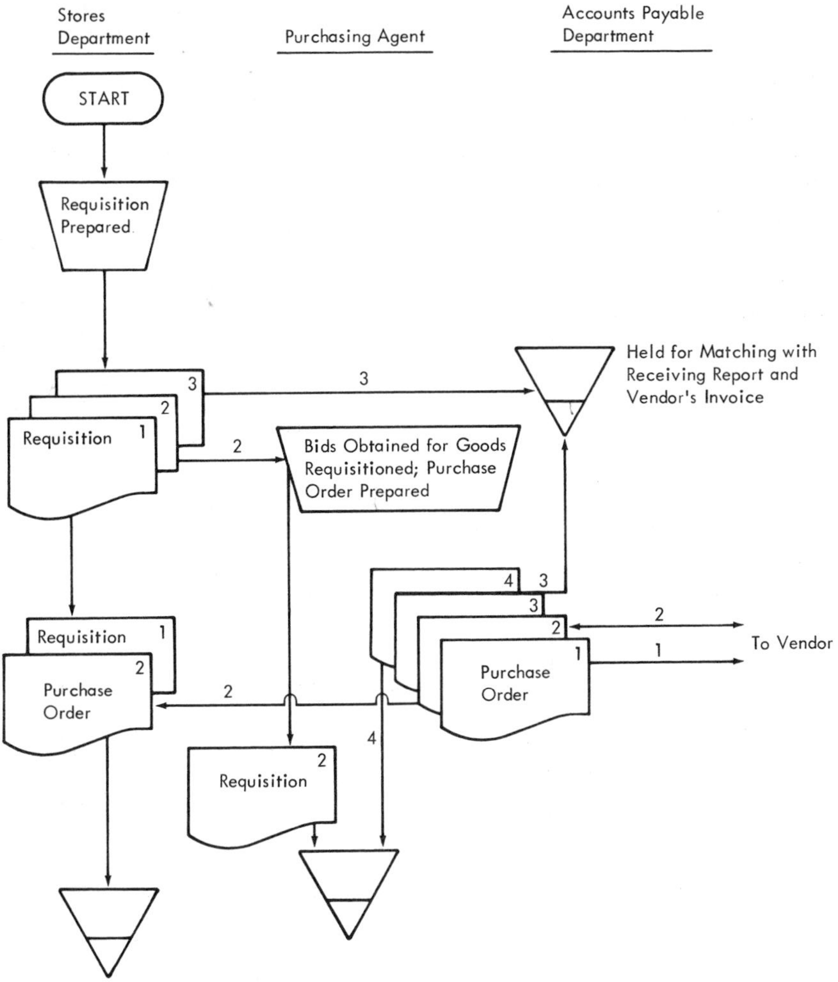

Purchasing Procedures. Exhibit 12–2 shows part of a purchasing procedure system. The internally generated stimulus of a purchase is shown as a requisition originating in the stores (inventory) location. The requisition itself may be originated by a production supervisor, by a sales backorder signal, or by an EDP system that automatically produces a requisition when an inventory item falls to a programmed reorder point quantity.

The requisition serves as an authorization for purchase order preparation, which may be done automatically in an EDP system. In addition to the two copies sent to the vendor (of which Copy 2 is returned as acknowledgement of the order), purchase order copies are used as follows: (*a*) a vendor's copy (Copy 1) which is sent to the supplier; (*b*) an inventory copy (Copy 2) to be matched with the receiving report; (*c*) an accounts payable copy (Copy 3) to be held and matched with the receiving report and vendor's invoice; and (*d*) a purchasing department copy (Copy 4) that is filed with the requisition.

As shown in Exhibit 12–3, while an order is in process there are pending files of goods ordered, but not yet received, in the stores and accounts payable departments. After the goods are received, these open order files are emptied by matching the purchase orders with the receiving report copies.

EXHIBIT 12–3
Receiving, Invoice Processing

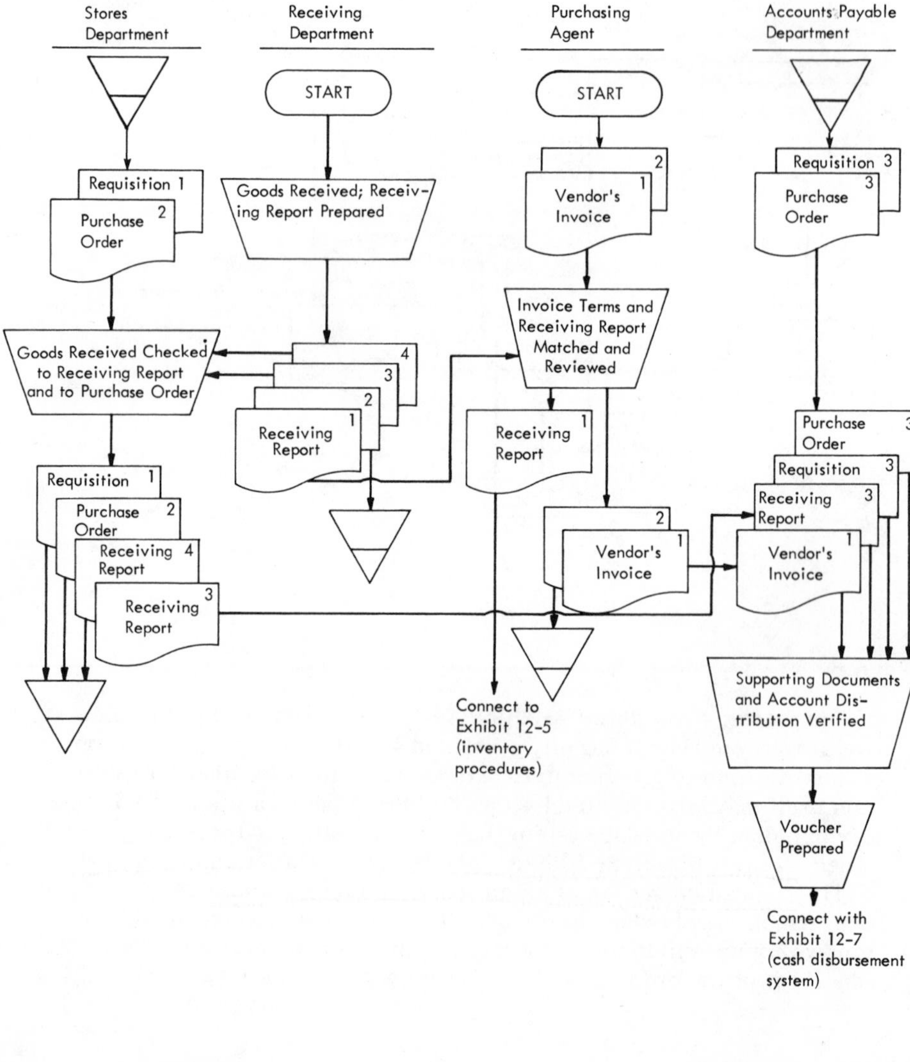

EXHIBIT 12–4

INTERNAL CONTROL QUESTIONNAIRE
PURCHASING AND RECEIVING SYSTEM

1. Is the accounts payable ledger or open voucher register balanced periodically with the general ledger control account?
2. Are vendors' monthly statements checked against accounts payable or unpaid vouchers?
3. Is there a purchasing department independent of the accounting department, receiving department, and shipping department?
4. Are all purchases made only on the basis of approved purchase requisitions?
5. Are all purchases, whether for inventory or expense, routed through the purchasing department?
6. Are the purchase order forms prenumbered and controlled?
7. Are competitive bids received and reviewed for certain items?
8. Are purchase prices approved by a responsible purchasing officer?
9. Are quantity and quality of goods received determined at time of receipt by receiving personnel independent of the purchasing department?
10. Are receiving report forms prenumbered and controlled?
11. Are receiving report copies transmitted to inventory custodians? To purchasing? To accounting department?
12. Is the accounts payable department notified of goods returned to vendors?
13. Are returned goods cleared through shipping department procedures?
14. Are unmatched invoices reviewed frequently for inquiry on receiving?
15. Are unmatched receiving reports reviewed frequently and investigated for proper recording?
16. Are vendors' invoices registered immediately upon receipt?
17. Are vendors' invoices first checked by the purchasing department against purchase orders and receiving reports?
18. Is there an adequate system for recording partial deliveries on a purchase order?
19. Are invoices approved for payment by a responsible officer?
20. Are invoices checked for quantities prices and terms in the accounts payable department against purchase orders and receiving reports?
21. Is there an accounting manual and employee approval for determining distribution of invoice charges to general ledger accounts?
22. Is the distribution of charges double-checked periodically?
23. Are purchases made for employees cleared through the regular purchasing procedures?
24. Are purchases from affiliates and subsidiaries cleared through the regular purchasing procedures? Are these purchases classified separately in general ledger accounts?
25. Are all purchases (material, services, expenses) routed through the accounts payable record and not directly through cash disbursements?
26. If original entry is through the cash disbursements journal, is voucher documentation prepared and filed?
27. Are purchasing and receiving procedures automated in an EDP system? If so, complete relevant portions of the EDP internal control questionnaire.

Exhibit 12–3 shows what happens when the goods and the vendors' invoices are received. The vendor's invoice is received by the purchasing department, where it is reviewed for terms, prices, and quantities and compared to the receiving report. Then the invoice is transmitted to the accounts payable department where it may be held pending transmittal of Copy 3 of the receiving report (if that copy has been delayed in processing). Thus at any one time the accounts payable department may be holding invoices not matched with receiving reports, receiving reports not yet matched with invoices, and purchase orders not matched with either receiving reports or invoices.

At year-end these various pending files contain relevant information for the audit of proper cutoff. Unmatched purchase orders and invoices unmatched with receiving reports may represent inventory in transit, depending on freight and title terms. In both cases liabilities may be unrecorded. Receiving reports unmatched with invoices could also represent unrecorded liabilities. When all documents are matched, a voucher is prepared, the liability and inventory are formally recorded, and the voucher enters the cash disbursement procedural system (Exhibit 12-7). Copy 1 of the receiving report is used to update inventory records as shown in Exhibit 12–5.

EXHIBIT 12–5
Inventory Procedures Flowchart

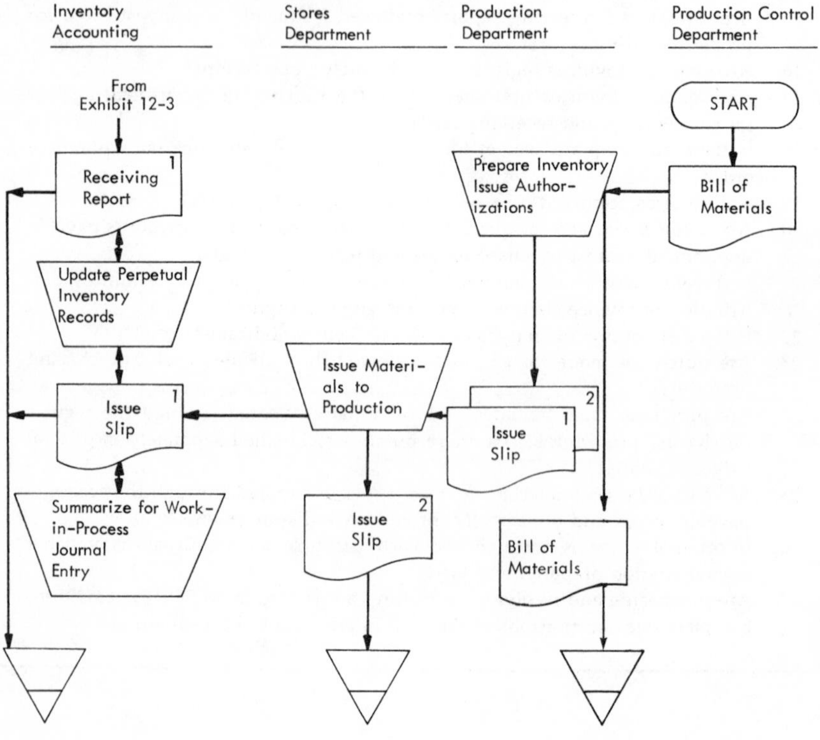

Notice that throughout the purchasing system custody of goods (receiving and stores departments), authority to initiate a transaction (purchasing department), and bookkeeping (accounts payable and inventory records departments) are kept separate. If records are maintained on an EDP system, the transaction data would be transformed into machine-readable media when received by the accounts payable department (requisition, purchase order, receiving report, and invoice). The pending files then would exist on magnetic tapes or disks.

Inventory Procedures and Cost of Goods Sold. Exhibit 12–5 shows an abbreviated set of documents and procedures for updating perpetual inventory records. The additions to inventory flow from the purchasing pro-

EXHIBIT 12–6

INTERNAL CONTROL QUESTIONNAIRE
INVENTORY SYSTEM

1. Are perpetual inventory records kept up to date for raw materials? Supplies? Work in process? Finished goods?
2. Are such perpetual records subsidiary to general ledger control accounts?
3. Do the perpetual records show quantities only? Quantities and prices?
4. Are perpetual records maintained by someone other than the inventory custodian?
5. Are inventory records maintained on an EDP system? If so, complete relevant portions of the EDP internal control questionnaire.
6. Are designated inventory custodians held responsible for physical control over various categories of inventory?
7. Do inventory custodians notify the accounting department of all additions to and issues from inventory?
8. Are issues made only on authority of bills of material and sales invoices?
9. Is there effective control over inventory out on consignment? In outside warehouses? In public warehouses?
10. Is merchandise or materials on consignment-in (i.e., not the property of the client) physically segregated and under effective accounting control?
11. Is there a periodic review for overstocked, slow-moving, or obsolete inventory? Have any adjustments been made during the year?
12. Is a physical inventory count taken during the year? Only at year-end?
13. Are such physical counts made by personnel independent of the inventory custodians?
14. Are priced inventory count sheets double-checked as to cost prices? Market prices? Arithmetic accuracy?
15. If standard costs have been used for inventory pricing, have they been reviewed for current applicability?
16. Are the perpetual records and general ledger accounts adjusted to agree with the physical count and valuation?
17. Are such adjustments reviewed and approved by a responsible officer?
18. Has the client planned for a physical count to be observed by independent auditors?
19. Have such plans been reviewed for completeness and coverage of all inventory items?

cedures flowchart in Exhibit 12–3. Inventory issues to production are originated in a production control department or engineering department with a specification (bill) of materials to be used in manufacture. This bill of materials, or issue slips prepared from it, serve as the stores custodian's authorization to release inventory. The issue slips are then forwarded to inventory accounting where the perpetual records are updated for the issues, and a summary is prepared and priced for a general ledger entry.

Authorizations to release finished goods to the shipping department are effected by sales invoices as described in Chapter 11. Finished goods inventory records would be updated for such issues, and summaries would be prepared for a cost of goods sold journal entry.

Notice in Exhibit 12–5 that the functions of receipt and issue authorization, physical custody, and recordkeeping are performed in different

EXHIBIT 12–7
Cash Disbursements System

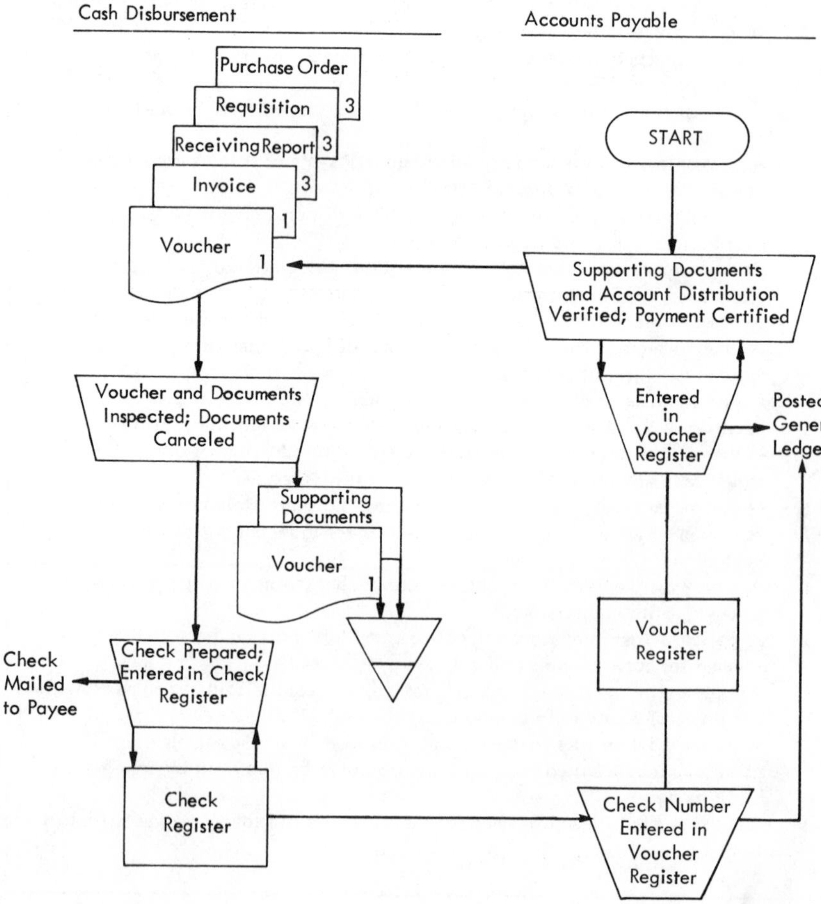

departments. Relevant internal control questionnaire items that further highlight good inventory control practices are presented in Exhibit 12–6.

Cash Disbursement Procedures. The cash disbursement system shown in Exhibit 12–7 presumes that all purchases of inventory items and materials and services expenses (e.g., rent, utilities, advertising) are routed through the purchasing department prior to the preparation of a voucher. In many businesses, however, authority to purchase may be vested in several officers (e.g., advertising manager, maintenance personnel), and supporting documents for receipt or use of goods and services may come to the accounts payable department from sources other than the purchasing department to be matched with an invoice. Decentralized control over purchase authority and invoice transmission may create difficulties in keeping up-to-date records of liabilities.

As shown in Exhibit 12–7, all the supporting documentation is gathered in a voucher that is recorded by the accounts payable depart-

EXHIBIT 12–8

INTERNAL CONTROL QUESTIONNAIRE
CASH DISBURSEMENT SYSTEM

1. Are all disbursements, excepting petty cash, made by check?
2. Are check signing and other cash disbursement procedures automated on EDP equipment? If so, complete relevant portions of the EDP internal control questionnaire.
3. Are all check forms prenumbered and under control?
4. Are voided checks mutilated and retained for inspection?
5. Do checks require two signatures? Is there dual control over machine signature plates?
6. Is the signing and/or countersigning of blank checks prohibited?
7. Are check signers persons who have no access to accounting records, cash receipts, or bank reconciliations?
8. Are check signers prohibited from drawing checks to "cash"?
9. Are bank accounts reconciled by personnel independent of cash custody or recordkeeping personnel?
10. Is the numerical sequence of checks reviewed in the reconciliation process?
11. Are vouchers and other supporting documents reviewed by the check signer? Is the presignature review effective?
12. Are checks mailed directly by the signer and not returned to the accounts payable department for mailing?
13. Are the voucher and supporting documents stamped or impressed "paid" to prevent duplicate payment before being returned to accounts payable for filing?
14. Are payroll checks drawn on a separate payroll bank account? Dividend checks on a separate bank account?
15. Are special disbursement accounts such as for payroll and dividends kept on an imprest basis?
16. Are interbank transfers under effective accounting control to prevent or detect kiting?

ment in a vouchers payable register. When payment is made, a record of payment is entered in the register. Periodically, the open items should be balanced to the liability control account in the general ledger. The voucher is used to record various charges to inventory and expense accounts, with a summary entry transmitted to general ledger accounting.

The voucher original is sent to the cash disbursement section prior to the due date for preparation of a check. The officer responsible for signing checks should review the documentation, approve the voucher, sign the check, then stamp the voucher "paid" so that it cannot be paid a second time in error. The check register is summarized periodically for entries to cash and payables in the general ledger. The authorizing documentation for a cash disbursement originates entirely outside the cash disbursement function. Later, when the bank statement is received, it should be reconciled independently by other personnel not involved in the cash disbursements procedures.

Many companies have automated their ordinary cash disbursements procedures with EDP equipment. Generally the automation involves transferring the voucher data onto magnetic tapes or disks. Daily, the file is searched for vouchers due and checks are printed and signed by machine. In such an EDP system the human approval procedures take place prior to the time data is transformed to machine-readable media. The check-signing control is achieved by special controls over blank check forms, controls over the disbursement computer program, and control over the check signature plate. Other programmed controls such as valid code and limit test checks may also be used as safeguards.

Compliance Tests of Transaction Details

In most manufacturing businesses purchases, inventory, cost of sales, and cash disbursement transactions are numerous. Compliance testing of the details of transactions to determine the effectiveness of internal accounting control involves sampling techniques for choosing transactions for audit and for evaluation of the evidence.

Exhibit 12–9 contains a selection of compliance test audit procedures. These steps are designed to enable the auditor to obtain objective evidence about the effectiveness of controls and about the reliability of accounting records (e.g., purchases totals, inventory accounts, cost of sales, and expense account balances). These records contain the basic numbers that appear in the financial statements under audit.

The inventory-related compliance tests consist of procedures to test the maintenance of the perpetual inventory records. The procedures include tests to determine whether goods received were added to the perpetual records (A–1) and to determine whether goods issued were subtracted from the perpetual records (A–2 and A–3). Another test of the perpetual records is to determine whether additions and issues recorded therein were actual additions (A–4–a) and actual issues (A–4–b). Accept-

EXHIBIT 12–9
Audit Program—Selected Compliance Testing Procedures

A. *Inventory Purchases and Issues*
   1. Select a sample of receiving reports from a numerical sequence file:
      a. Scan for missing receiving reports (missing numbers) vouch to related purchase order.
      b. Trace to inventory record posting of additions.
   2. Select a sample of materials issue slips (or production reports or bills of materials).
      a. Vouch to supporting authorization (signature, production report or bill of materials properly approved).
      b. Trace to inventory record posting of issues.
   3. Select a sample of shipping documents (finished goods) and trace to inventory record posting of issues.
   4. Select a sample of inventory item perpetual records:
      a. Vouch additions to receiving reports.
      b. Vouch issues to issue slips, production reports or bills of material.
   5. Observe work habits of purchasing and receiving department personnel.

B. *Cost of Sales*
   1. With the sample of issues obtained in A–2 above:
      a. Review the accounting summary of quantities and prices for mathematical accuracy.
      b. Trace posting of amounts to general ledger.
   2. Obtain a sample of cost of goods sold entries in the general ledger and vouch to supporting summaries of materials and finished goods issues.
   3. Review (recalculate) the appropriateness of standard costs, if used to price inventory issues. Review the disposition of variances from standard costs.

C. *Cash Disbursements and Other Expenses*
   1. Select a sample of cash disbursement vouchers (or cash disbursement check numbers):
      a. Scan for missing documents (missing numbers).
      b. Vouch supporting documentation for evidence of accurate mathematics, correct classification, proper approval and cancellation of documents.
      c. Trace disbursement debits to general and subsidiary ledger accounts.
   2. Select a sample of recorded expenses from various accounts and vouch them to (*a*) canceled checks, and (*b*) supporting documentation.

able results from these tests may enable the auditor to place reliance on the client's perpetual inventory records. Notice that the tests run in two directions from basic transaction files (A–1, A–2, and A–3) to the perpetual records and from the perpetual records (A–4) to the basic transaction files. A diagram of this two-way test design is shown below. (The codes in the boxes refer to the procedures in Exhibit 12–9.)

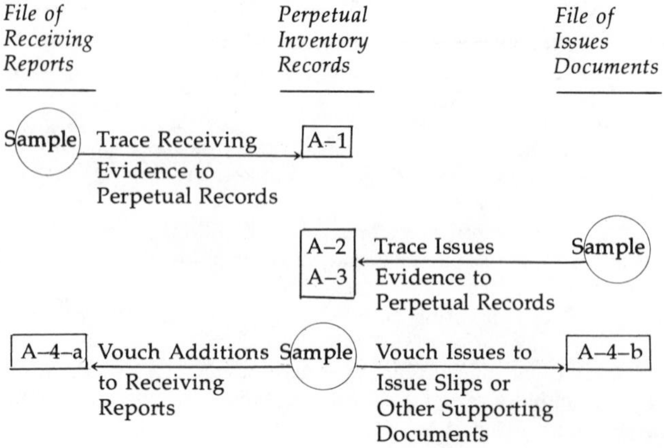

The cost of sales compliance tests are designed to complete the retracing procedure started with the sample of issue slips (or other issue documentation). This time, however, the procedure B–1 involves determining whether the issue documents were properly summarized, priced, and posted to the accounts. The other direction of the test (B–2) is to vouch recorded cost of sales entries to supporting documentation.

The cash disbursement compliance tests are designed to help the auditor determine whether cash disbursements were properly authorized and processed (C–1) and whether recorded cash disbursement debit entries are properly supported by the underlying documentation (C–2).

When purchasing, inventory, cost of sales, and cash disbursement transaction data processing are automated with EDP equipment, the audit problems are multiplied. In general, the several tracing procedures enable the auditor to test the accuracy of data conversion from visible hard-copy documents to machine-readable input media. From that point forward, most control checks are programmed, and some actual decisions such as reorder point and order quantity may be under program control. Thus subsequent testing procedures may utilize computer-control testing methods (e.g., test data, parallel simulation) and review of error messages and reports produced by the client's computer system.

The evidence obtained in the review phase and in the compliance testing phase should be combined in general and specific conclusions about the reliance that can be vested in the existing internal accounting control system. These judgments will affect the nature, timing, and extent of subsequent auditing procedures which are discussed in the next section. Descriptions of major deficiencies, weaknesses, and inefficiencies in the system may be incorporated in a report to the client.

SUBSTANTIVE TESTS OF BALANCES

The eight basic audit procedures are discussed next. Emphasis is placed on applications to inventory, cost of sales, and related accounts.

No further attention is given to cash balances since the related auditing procedures were discussed in Chapter 11. Selected procedures are summarized in Exhibit 12–10.

The construction of an audit program containing these procedures should begin with the auditor's explicit recognition of the assertions in the inventory accounts (including the aggregations of purchases and issues), the cost of sales accounts, and the cash disbursements transactions. The assertions point directly to the hypothesis questions that can be tested by gathering sufficient, competent evidential matter. A few of the assertions typical of this account group are:

- Inventory is a current asset.
- Inventory pledged as collateral is disclosed.
- Inventory is owned by the company.
- Obsolete and unsalable goods have been written off or written down.
- The inventory value does not exceed the applicable measure of market value.
- All purchases are for inventory use or for approved business expenditures.
- All inventory issues are for production.
- Cash disbursements are for properly approved purchase liabilities.
- All cash disbursements are recorded.

The assertions above are not a complete list of all matters of audit interest, but they are illustrative of the types of problems that should be recognized. The next task is to consider the evidence that might support or refute these assertions, and then the auditor can select the most efficient procedures for gathering that evidence.

Physical Observation

It is important to realize that an independent auditor is responsible for *observing* the client's count of inventory and *not* responsible for personally *making* the complete count. Hence the audit procedures involve reviewing the client's plans, observing of the count operations, and making some test counts for tracing to the inventory compilation. The first task for the auditor is to learn about the client's inventory-taking instructions (whether oral or written) and review them for the following characteristics:

Names of client personnel responsible for the count.

Dates and times of inventory taking.

Names of client personnel who will participate in the inventory taking.

Instructions for recording accurate descriptions of inventory items, for count and double-count, and for measuring or translating physical quantities (e.g., counting by measures of gallons, barrels, feet, dozens).

Instructions for making notes of obsolete or worn items.

Instructions for the use of tags, punched cards, count sheets, or other media devices, and for their collection and control.

Plans for shutting down plant operations or for taking inventory after store closing hours, and plans for having goods in proper places (e.g., on store shelves instead of on the floor, or raw materials in a warehouse rather than in transit to a job.)

Plans for counting or controlling movement of goods in receiving and shipping areas if those operations are not shut down during the count.

Instructions for compiling the count media (e.g., tags, punch cards) into final inventory listings or summaries.

Instructions for pricing the inventory items.

Instructions for review and approval of the inventory count; notations of obsolescence or other matters by supervisory personnel.

These characteristics are indicative of a well-planned counting operation. As the plan is carried out, the independent auditor should be present to observe. Many physical inventories are counted at hours that do not conflict with normal business operations.

When the client's records include reasonably well-controlled perpetual inventory records, the auditor's test counting can proceed very much like a test of transactions. A sample of inventory items can be chosen from the perpetual records for test count to ascertain that recorded inventory was counted. In the inventory locations the auditor can count a selection of items, record these, and later trace them to the perpetual records and inventory summary count sheets to ascertain whether all inventory in place was recorded (in perpetual records) or counted (included in the count compilation). This dual-direction sampling for test counting serves the purpose of testing the perpetual records and the count compilation for erroneous counts and for omissions.

As the counting operations proceed, the auditor can continuously evaluate the frequency of actual count errors by recounting the items counted by client personnel. By this evidence the auditor can determine whether the count is satisfactorily accurate. If perpetual records are not maintained and inventory is recorded only on a periodic basis, then the auditor will have to concentrate attention on the physical goods and sufficient test counts in the field.

The foregoing procedures are applicable to the audit of physical quantities when the auditor is present to observe the count and when the count is made on the year-end date. However, the following situations may occur frequently.

A. *Auditor present, physical inventory taken at a date prior or subsequent to year-end date.* The auditor can follow the procedures outlined above for observation of the physical count. However, with a time period intervening between the count date and the year-end, additional auditing of purchase, inventory addition, and issue transactions during that period must be performed. The inventory on the count date can be reconciled to the year-end inventory by appropriate addition or subtraction of the intervening receiving and issue transactions.

B. *Auditor present, physical inventory taken on a cycle basis or on a statistical plan, but never a complete count on a single date.* In this kind of situation the auditor may be present for some counting operations, but only as a matter of "extended procedures" and unusual circumstances would the auditor be present every month (or more frequently) to observe all counts. Businesses that count inventory in this manner generally purport to have accurate perpetual records and carry out the counting as a means of testing the records and maintaining their accuracy. The auditor should arrange to be present during one or two counting operations in order to evaluate the counting plans and their execution. The procedural characteristics enumerated above would be utilized, test counts would be made, and the auditor would be responsible for a conclusion concerning the reasonable accuracy of perpetual quantity records.

C. *Auditor not present, physical inventory taken by the client.* This sort of situation might arise when the auditor is appointed late or when attempting to audit beginning inventories that had not previously been audited. The auditor should review the client's plan for the count as before. Some test counts should be made and traced to current records to the extent needed for a conclusion about the reliability of perpetual records. If the actual count was recent, intervening transaction activity may be reconciled to the year-end inventory. However, the reconciliation over a year's transactions (to unobserved beginning inventories) may be quite difficult. The auditor may employ procedures utilizing interrelationships such as sales activity, physical volume, price indices, and gross profit margins for decisions about reasonableness. Nevertheless, much care must be exercised in "backing into" the audit of a previous inventory.[1]

The auditor should determine where and in what dollar amounts inventories are located off the client's premises, in the custody of consignees, or in public warehouses. If amounts are material and if control is not exceptionally strong, the auditor may wish to visit these locations and conduct on-site test counts. However, if amounts are not material, and/or if related evidence is adequate (e.g., periodic reports, cash receipts, receivables records, shipping records), and if controls are strong, then direct confirmation with the custodian may be considered sufficient competent evidence of the existence of quantities.[2]

Physical observation may also be employed in connection with controlling the cutoff when the auditor is present on the year-end date. In the shipping and receiving locations the numbers of the last receiving report and the last shipping documents may be recorded. A list of items about to be shipped or received, but to be included or excluded from inventory,

---

[1] See "Evidential Matter for . . . Inventory" (*SAS No. 1,* Sections 331.01–.02 and 331.09–.16).

[2] See "Public Warehouses—Controls and Auditing Procedures for Goods Held" (*SAS No. 1,* Section 901).

can be made. These data may later be traced to the inventory compilation, accounts receivable, and payable records, and to sales records as a part of the cutoff audit procedures.

Vouching of Documents

The physical observation procedures are principally designed to audit physical quantities and to facilitate notice of obsolete or worn inventory. Other procedures for inventory valuation mainly involve the audit of unit cost prices used to price, extend, and total the inventory cost. Essentially the procedural application involves sampling inventory items grouped under a unit price. (The quantity × cost extension may be defined as a sample item.) Since the quantity has been audited by observation, there remains the audit of the unit price by vouching the price to a vendor's invoice. The auditor must consider the inventory cost flow assumption in this procedure (e.g., Fifo, Lifo, average) in order to identify the appropriate vendor's price.

When inventory items are manufactured goods, the vouching will be to cost accounting records, standard costs, and thence to vendor's invoices, payroll cost records, and overhead allocation calculations. To the extent that previous tests of transactions have shown the cost accounting system to be reliable, these vouching applications may be limited. However, the auditor should at this point be careful to vouch actual costs sufficiently to reach a conclusion about the reasonableness of standard costs.

Additional attention in vouching operations should be paid to current replacement costs of inventory. If replacement cost prices have fallen below prices used to value the inventory, lower-of-cost-or-market valuation calculations will have to be undertaken. The auditor will then need to obtain selling price data, and data on selling costs, costs to complete work in process, and normal profit margin in order to calculate the cost-or-market ceiling and floor limits.

Inventories of a retail store add complications when the inventory is valued by a retail method estimation. In such cases vouching would be extended to audit the retail price and the cost price and to audit markups and markdowns involved in the retail method calculations.

Vouching should be applied especially to inventory costs associated with purchases from affiliates or subsidiaries. The prices assigned to such goods may be out of line with market prices.[3] Any intercompany profit in inventories would have to be known and eliminated in consolidation.

With regard to cost of goods sold, vouching is a very useful procedure for obtaining specific and detailed evidence. The procedure may in some cases be perceived as a detailed audit of individual cost of goods sold transactions, much like the audit of the value of inventory items. When costs are associated with each sale transaction, the population of recorded data may be defined as the *sales* transactions. With a sample of sales, the related cost of goods sold may be located and then vouched to supporting

[3] See "Related Party Transactions" (*SAS No. 6*, Section 335).

evidence in vendors' invoices or cost accounting records. The other direction of the test would involve a sample of cost of goods sold entries, vouching to supporting documents, then vouching to recorded sales to determine whether all associated costs and revenues were recorded in the same period.

In other situations cost of sales may not be identified specifically with individual sales transactions. In such cases overall tests of reasonableness and recalculations may serve for sufficient audit evidence. Consider the usual calculation of cost of goods sold:

Beginning inventory	$ 300,000
Purchases (net cost)	4,380,000
	$4,680,000
Ending inventory	650,000
Cost of goods sold	$4,030,000

If observation, vouching, recalculation, and other procedures are sufficient to audit beginning and ending inventories and purchases (net of discounts, freight, returns, and the like), the cost of goods sold is also audited in the overall. To the extent that significant items for separate disclosure exist (e.g., significant shrinkage, theft, or casualty losses), then these would have to be identified by other procedures and broken out from the cost of goods sold category. Other procedures for assessing interrelationships relevant to cost of goods sold are covered in sections below.

Recalculation

Recalculations with respect to inventories and cost of sales are performed mostly in connection with price and cost vouching and in testing the clerical accuracy of inventory compilations. The inventory quantity × cost extensions of a sample of items should be recalculated to test accuracy, and the entire inventory compilation should be footed. Various quantity transformations (e.g., units to dozens, gallons to barrels) that match the pricing unit should be tested. Multiplying a per-gross price by quantity measured in dozens can create a significant error. Recalculation is involved in testing the accuracy of job and process cost accumulations relevant for cost-price vouching.

Tests of appropriate pricing by Fifo, Lifo, and so forth, amount to recalculation procedures. The objective here is to determine whether an appropriate cost flow assumption has been applied appropriately. Similarly, recalculations of percentage-of-completion data such as cost accumulations and percent completion serve to test for clerical accuracy and valuation measurement.

The retail method of inventory estimation is a more complex sort of calculation involving cost and retail relationships, markups and markdowns, and cost ratios. The retail method calculation should be carefully analyzed for any errors of logic or of mathematical inaccuracy.

Allocations of cost of goods available to cost of goods sold may be based on calculated amounts (e.g., standard costs). A careful recalculation of such allocations serves to detect clerical errors.

Confirmation

Direct correspondence with outside parties finds limited use with regard to inventories and practically no use with regard to cost of sales. Confirmation of inventory held by consignees or public warehouses may be appropriate under conditions of strong internal control as mentioned earlier. Confirmations may also be used to ascertain the terms of agreements to pledge inventory as security for liabilities and to ascertain or clarify special terms of orders or contracts.

In connection with accounts payable confirmation, if a particular vendor or vendors are large suppliers, the purchasing activity as well as the year-end account balance may be confirmed. In this way a significant portion of the purchases total may be audited by confirmation rather than by extensive vouching of documents.

Verbal Inquiry

Initial inquiries are very useful in the planning of an audit. Information gained in this way would include the locations of inventory, dates for the physical count, inventory held off premises by consignees and public warehouses, the cost flow assumption used to price cost of goods sold and inventories, and the pledging of inventory as collateral. All of this information leads the auditor to other applicable evidence-gathering procedures.

More in the nature of direct evidence, however, would be discussions with knowledgeable client personnel about the status and value of slow-moving inventory, apparently worn, damaged, or obsolete inventory, and the existence of large inventory stockpiles. Sometimes the only evidence of value may be in management's familiarity with the goods and materials in question. Inquiries may also be directed to learning about any significant purchase commitments.

Questions and discussions may lead to explanation of cost overruns on construction projects or manufacturing jobs. Such responses may help explain fluctuations or changes otherwise evident in cost records or inventory prices. Of course, the auditor must be discerning enough to distinguish a factual explanation from an inadequate one. The explanation that "cost of sales increased this year as a result of increased sales and inflation" is one that can be audited. The auditor should be able to ascertain whether inflation did in fact touch the client's inputs (e.g., materials costs, labor rates), and the auditor should be able to ascertain whether sales in fact increased instead of simply being inflated by false entries.

Retracing

In addition to extensive use in the compliance testing phase, retracing may be employed to audit for proper cutoff of purchasing, receiving, and shipping of inventory, and for proper recording of cost of goods sold allocations. The receiving reports and shipping documents for movements just prior to year-end may be traced forward to inventory records and accounts payable of the current year. Likewise, data for shipping and receiving for a short period following the year-end can be retraced to recording in the next accounting period. These procedures will generally serve to audit inventory cutoff, and they may result in the discovery of some unrecorded liabilities.

Cost of goods sold entries should be retraced from related sales transaction data. The correlation of sales cutoff and cost of goods sold cutoff is highly important for a proper matching of costs and revenues. Because the relative risk is that cost of sales entries would be omitted for recorded sales, the relevant data population for the cutoff test is the sales recorded near the year-end date. Statistical methods may be used if the data population is large.

Scanning

When sampling is utilized for test counts, vouching and retracing of inventory quantities and prices, and for cost of sales audit, it is always a good idea to review for large or unusual items that were not included in the sample. By scanning the inventory compilation and accounting records of purchases, cost of sales, and cash disbursements, the large and/or unusual items might be noticed and picked out for additional auditing. The auditor should be specially careful to notice unusual patterns of heavy purchases near year-end or hectic receiving and shipping activity or particularly heavy cash disbursements recorded near the end of the last month. Occurrences of this sort may be a tip-off to efforts to improve the financial statements artificially.

Perpetual inventory records may be scanned to detect slow-moving inventory items. The open purchase order file may be scanned for evidence of any significant purchase commitments. Standard costs not previously audited can be scanned in comparison to standard costs used in the prior year. In this case evidence of no changes in a time of rising prices may indicate that some unit standard costs have not been properly updated for price changes.

Analysis of Interrelationships

The basic historical data interrelationships relevant to inventory and cost of sales accounts are inventory turnover, inventory shrinkage, percentage markups and markdowns, and gross margin percentages. These interrelationships are particularly important for businesses that do not identify specific cost of sales to individual sales transactions (as in retail stores). These turnovers and rates should be analyzed per interperiod trend data for the client and in relation to industrywide statistics. Significant variations from trend or from the industry should be investigated further to provide a satisfactory explanation.

For manufacturing operations the relative ratios of material, labor, and overhead in inventory and in cost of goods sold can be computed and analyzed. Variations may be indicative of amounts misclassified in the accounts. For example, repairs and maintenance expense items improperly classified as materials purchases in the current year would probably change the relative ratios of the inputs enough for questions to be raised and thus cause additional vouching of materials costs.

Expenses that are functionally related to inventory levels and production activity may be correlated with inventory balances and costs of sales. Insurance and certain property tax expenses relate to the value of inventories, and these policies and assessments may be correlated with the account data. Royalty and license payments for use of production techniques may be indicative of production volume. There may even be a special control system set up to gather such data as a basis for figuring royalty payments due. Warehouse receipts may be associated with some types of goods held in public warehouses, and these would bear the seal of

EXHIBIT 12–10
Audit Program—Selected Substantive Test Procedures

A. *Inventories*
1. Review the client's instructions for physical count of the inventory. If the count is based on a statistical sample, review the plan for statistical validity.
2. Test-count a sample of inventory items. Trace test counts to final inventory compilation.
3. Vouch unit prices to vendors' invoices.
4. Recalculate extensions and footings of the final inventory compilation.
5. Test applicability of lower-of-cost-or-market valuation on selected inventory categories.
6. Inquire about inventory out on consignment, if any, and about inventory on hand which is consigned-in from vendors.
7. Confirm inventories held in public warehouses.
8. Inquire about obsolete or damaged goods subject to write-down or write-off. Scan perpetual records for indications of slow-moving inventory.
9. Obtain written representations from the client concerning any pledge of inventory as collateral.

B. *Cost of Sales*
1. Select a sample of recorded cost of sales entries and vouch to supporting documentation.
2. Select a sample of basic transaction documents (e.g., sales invoices, production reports) and determine whether the related cost of goods sold was figured and recorded properly.
3. Determine whether the accounting costing method used by the client (e.g., Fifo, Lifo, standard cost) was applied properly.
4. Compute the gross margin rate and compare to prior years.
5. Compute ratio of cost elements (e.g., labor, materials) to total cost of goods sold and compare to prior years.

the warehouseman. Some selling commission costs may be correlated with consignment sales, and these amounts may be associated with cost of goods sold through consignment arrangements.

If the audit engagement includes subsidiary companies, the auditor can match intercompany purchases of the buyer with intercompany sales of the seller. If other auditors are involved, this same information may be obtained by communication with the other auditors (with management consent respecting information that might be considered confidential).

Budgets, forecasts, performance reports, and variance analysis reports that are a part of the internal management information system should be studied and matched or reconciled to the account data. These reports are generally designed for control purposes to highlight unexpected results and problem areas. Results that differ from expectations and production cost problems are also of interest to the auditor. A review of these reports may supply many explanations or lead to further auditing procedures.

In general, several of the analytical relationships may be combined to provide sufficient evidence concerning fair presentation of cost of goods sold. As a practical matter cost of goods sold is generally audited through a combination of limited vouching and extensive interrelationships analysis. Inventory balances, in contrast, are usually audited with heavy reliance on observation, vouching, and recalculation, with much less emphasis on analytical interrelationships.

TYPES OF MAJOR FRAUD AND MISSTATEMENT

Purchasing operations, inventory custody, and cash disbursement responsibility are all activities susceptible to fraud and error that can achieve material proportions. Each of these areas is interrelated.

Purchasing embezzlement schemes range from the simple to the complex, and oftentimes the former is next to impossible to detect with ordinary auditing procedures. A purchasing agent may take a kickback from a supplier. There is virtually no way to uncover this activity. However, if the kickback is sizable, the supplier's price may be raised out of line with market prices (from other suppliers) to cover the kickback. Audit vouching of prices would draw attention only to the one supplier's price, but a general awareness of the otherwise available market price might trigger a lower-of-cost-or-market valuation calculation for goods in inventory. If the purchasing agent buys goods or services for personal use (e.g., furnishings, home improvements), the agent would have to cover with an authorizing requisition and with some notification of receipt (e.g., receiving report or use report). These maneuvers would involve either access to blank forms or collusion with other employees.

Some persons authorized to purchase may have an easier time without being constrained by a bureaucratic system of requisitions, receipts, and other-person authorizations. Promotion managers, sales representatives, internal news magazine editors, and similar persons have cropped up in the news from time to time for having charged personal trips and amenities for their homes and friends as business expenses. Signs of extravagant habits for a person in a less-well-paid position might be a clue for further investigation. However, an auditor must be very careful about undertaking an expensive investigation when vague suspicions are the auditor's only grounds.

Inventory losses may result from simple theft. Physical safeguards are the best protection against nonemployees. However, an employee who can remove inventory and create an inventory issue authorization (or keep inventory records directly) can cover his or her tracks. Fraudulent overstatement of inventories in order to bolster financial position must be perpetrated by deceiving the auditors. History has recorded the practices of nailing empty cartons to shelves (push at them, they do not move, *ergo* they must be full), by stacking boxes or bales around an empty center (climb to the top and look), and by inserting a full chamber under a measuring hole atop a liquid storage tank, with inventory material in the chamber and water in the remainder of the tank (rattle a rod through the measuring hole to hit the sides of the chamber). These and other deceptions are relatively easy when dishonest persons can predict the auditor's sample selection and degree of suspicion and carefulness.

Production losses may be created by a dishonest inspector who labels good production as defective or as scrap and then is able to remove it. High incidence of such action should become evident in accounting for production quality and inefficiency. Lack of a system for controlling scrap sales and rework operations can make such theft easier, but a sound system of accounting controls, management reports, and follow-up action can prevent or detect the dishonest inspector's activity.

Cash disbursements operations can harbor several opportunities for embezzlement. Generally the process is one of siphoning company funds to a fictitious person or company or to accomplices outside. Fictitious invoices for nonexistent goods or services must reach the check-signing stage with approvals and documents in order. This may involve forged requisitions, purchase orders, and receiving reports, or fraudulent approvals by an authorizing manager. A check so issued may be recorded as an expense item and the funds intercepted by the dishonest manager. Alternatively an accounts payable clerk may simply raise the amount due on an invoice and later recover a share from an accomplice recipient.

Any checks made payable to a bank, to "cash," or to bearer should be investigated and vouched to supporting documents. Checks payable to a bank in repayment of a loan could be intercepted if not mailed directly to the bank, and the interceptor might be able to hide the nonpayment by suppressing due notices, by renewing the note, or by covering with a later embezzlement. Thorough confirmation with all bank creditors would likely uncover this kind of abstraction. Having checks drawn to cash, stolen, not recorded (so as not to falsify any other account balance), and then underfooting the cash receipts journal is another complex embezzlement. However, this one leaves many tracks—a missing check in the check number sequence, the canceled check in the bank statement, and the erroneous cash journal addition. A proof of cash that reconciles receipts and disbursements activity per the bank statement to receipts and disbursements recorded in the accounts would easily detect this maneuver.

REVIEW QUESTIONS

12.1. Explain the auditor's interest in general and specific economic conditions with regard to the objective of determining whether inventories are properly valued.

12.2. What are the primary functions which should be segregated in a purchasing system?

12.3. Identify the users and uses of the receiving report.

12.4. How can the situation in which the *same* supporting documents are used for a duplicate payment be prevented?

12.5. In the auditor's review of a client's inventory-taking instructions, what characteristics is the auditor looking for?

12.6. Explain dual-direction sampling in the context of inventory test counts.

12.7. What procedures are employed to audit inventory when the physical inventory is taken on a cycle basis or on a statistical plan, but never a complete count on a single date?

12.8. What procedures are employed to audit inventory in the custody of consignors or public warehouses?

12.9. What procedures might the auditor employ to test whether cost of goods sold entries are properly recorded and whether associated costs and revenues were recorded in the same period? Explain.

12.10. What procedure might the auditor use to test the propriety of a client's application of the retail method of inventory estimation? Explain.

12.11. What evidence regarding inventories and cost of sales can the auditor typically obtain from *verbal inquiry*?

12.12. In performing an audit, what are the relevant account interrelationships with respect to a retailer's inventory? A manufacturer's inventory?

12.13. What techniques are relied upon most heavily in an audit of cost of goods sold? Inventory balances?

12.14. Describe the major types of fraud and material misstatement with regard to *cash disbursements* of which the auditor should be aware. What procedures are generally relied upon to detect such embezzlement?

EXERCISES AND PROBLEMS

12.15. As the auditor of Adams Manufacturing, Inc., you are concerned about the following responses to verbal inquiries regarding the company's non-EDP system of internal control over cash disbursements, inventory, and cost of sales:

1. Periodically, adjusting entries must be made to correct erroneous postings from vouchers to ledger accounts.
2. Issues of material are not always posted to inventory records.

3. Purchase orders are often made without an authorized requisition.
4. Cash disbursements may not be recorded until the canceled check is received.

Required:

List the steps you would take, including sampling, to obtain objective evidence of the extent of these weaknesses.

12.16. On January 11 at the beginning of your annual audit of the Grover Manufacturing Company's financial statements for the year just ended December 31, the company president confides in you that an employee is living on a scale in excess of that which his salary would support.

The employee has been a buyer in the purchasing department for six years and has charge of purchasing all general materials and supplies. He is authorized to sign purchase orders for amounts up to $200. Purchase orders in excess of $200 require the countersignature of the general purchasing agent.

The president understands that the usual examination of financial statements is not designed to disclose immaterial fraud or conflicts of interest, although their discovery may result. The president authorizes you, however, to expand your regular audit procedures and to apply additional audit procedures to determine whether there is any evidence that the buyer has been misappropriating company funds or has been engaged in activities that were in a conflict of interests.

Required:

a. List the audit procedures that you would apply to the company records and documents in an attempt to—
   (1) Discover evidence within the purchasing department of defalcations being committed by the buyer. Give the purpose of each audit procedure.
   (2) Provide leads as to possible collusion between the buyer and suppliers. Give the purpose of each audit procedure.

b. Assume that your investigation disclosed that some suppliers have been charging the Grover Manufacturing Company in excess of their usual prices and apparently have been making "kickbacks" to the buyer. The excess charges are material in amount.

   What effect, if any, would the defalcation have upon (1) the financial statements that were prepared before the defalcation was uncovered, and (2) your auditor's report? Discuss. (AICPA adapted)

12.17. Listed below is a selection of items from the Internal Control Questionnaires shown in the chapter. For each one:

a. Identify the control characteristic to which it applies (e.g., segregation of duties—authorization of transactions, access to assets and recordkeeping duties; sound error-checking practice; and the like).

b. Specify one compliance test procedure an auditor could use to determine whether the control was operating effectively.

c. Using your business experience, your logic, and/or your imagination, give an example of an error or irregularity that could occur if the control was absent or ineffective.

d. Specify a substantive testing procedure an auditor could use to uncover errors or irregularities, if any, resulting from absence of the control.

(1) Are all purchases made only on the basis of approved purchase requisitions?
(2) Are unmatched invoices (vendors' invoices not yet recorded, awaiting match-up with a receiving report) reviewed frequently for inquiry on receiving?
(3) Are perpetual inventory records kept by someone other than the inventory custodian?
(4) Is there a periodic review for overstocked, slow-moving, or obsolete inventory?
(5) Are all check forms prenumbered and under control?
(6) Are checks mailed directly by the signer and not returned to the accounts payable department for mailing?

12.18. As part of the annual audit of Costello Wholesale Shoes, Inc., you have been assigned to audit the inventory balance. Costello has ten warehouses located throughout the United States to shorten delivery time and provide better service to independent retail outlets. Costello performs its physical inventory using statistical sampling techniques, each year counting a random sample of items in each of three warehouses. The selection of specific warehouses to be included in the physical inventory is a joint decision of the marketing vice president (who makes an annual walk-through of each warehouse to determine if appearance and housekeeping standards are met) and the controller (who evaluates the warehouses in terms of discrepancies reported during the past year). They select for inventory the three warehouses they feel have the most item balances in error. Following is a schedule showing which warehouses have been included in the physical inventory in each of the past three years:

	Warehouse									
Warehouse Year	*1*	*2*	*3*	*4*	*5*	*6*	*7*	*8*	*9*	*10*
Two years ago				X			X	X		
Last year		X		X	X					
Current year			X				X		X	

Based on the results of the inventory for the current year, Costello's controller has concluded that, with 98 percent confidence, the actual balance of the inventory is between $915,000 and $935,000. The book value of the inventory ($927,000) is deemed by the controller to be without material error.

Required:

Assume you have (1) performed test counts of the sampled items, (2) recomputed the controller's calculations, and (3) completed the audit of documentation supporting the sample items.

a. Should you accept the client's conclusions as to the value of the inventory? Explain.

b. Refer to Chapter 10. Which of the four sampling objectives best explains Costello's sampling plan? Explain.

12.19. Your client took a complete physical inventory under your observation as of December 15 and adjusted the inventory control account (perpetual inventory method) to agree with the physical inventory. You have decided to accept the balance of the control account as of December 31, after reflecting transactions recorded therein from December 16 to December 31, in connection with your examination of financial statements for the year ended December 31.

Your examination of the sales cutoff as of December 15 and December 31 disclosed the following items not previously considered. What adjusting journal entries, if any, would you make for each of these items? Explain why each adjustment is necessary.

		Date		
Cost	*Sales Price*	*Shipped*	*Billed*	*Credited to Inventory Control*
$284	$369	12/14	12/16	12/16
391	502	12/10	12/19	12/10
189	213	1/2	12/31	12/31

12.20. In an annual audit for the year ended December 31, you find the following transactions near the closing date:

1. Merchandise costing $1,822 was received on January 3, and the related purchase invoice recorded January 5. The invoice showed the shipment was made on December 29, *F.O.B. destination.*
2. Merchandise costing $625 was received on December 28, and the invoice was not recorded. You located it in the hands of the purchasing agent; it was marked *on consignment.*
3. A packing case containing product costing $816 was standing in the shipping room when the physical inventory was taken. It was not included in the inventory because it was marked *Hold for shipping instructions.* Your investigation revealed that the customer's order was dated December 18, but that the case was shipped and the customer billed on January 10. The product was a stock item of your client.
4. Merchandise received on January 6 costing $720 was entered in the purchase register on January 7. The invoice showed equipment was made F.O.B. supplier's warehouse on December 31. Since it was not on hand at December 31, it was not included in inventory.
5. A special machine, fabricated to order for a customer, was finished and in the shipping room on December 31. The customer was billed on that date and the machine excluded from inventory, although it was shipped on January 4.

Required:

Assume that each of the amounts is material:

a. State whether the merchandise should be included in the client's inventory.

b. Give your reason for your decision on each item in *a* above. (AICPA adapted)

12.21. On January 10, you were engaged to make an examination of the financial statements of Kahl Equipment Corporation for the previous year ended December 31. Kahl has sold trucks and truck parts and accessories for many years but has never had an audit. Kahl maintains good perpetual records for all inventories and takes a complete physical inventory each December 31.

The Parts Inventory account includes the $2,500 cost of obsolete parts. Kahl's executives acknowledge these parts have been worthless for several years, but they have continued to carry the cost as an asset. The amount of $2,500 is material in relation to net income and year-end inventories but not material in relation to total assets or capital at December 31.

Required:

a. List the procedures you would add to your inventory audit program for new trucks because you did not observe the physical inventory taken by the corporation as of December 31 of the year under audit.

b. Should the $2,500 of obsolete parts be carried in inventory as an asset? Discuss. (AICPA adapted)

12.22. Late in December your CPA firm accepted an audit engagement at Fine Jewelers, Inc., a corporation which deals largely in diamonds. The corporation has retail jewelry stores in several eastern cities and a diamond wholesale store in New York City. The wholesale store also sets the diamonds in rings and in other quality jewelry.

The retail stores place orders for diamond jewelry with the wholesale store in New York City. A buyer employed by the wholesale store purchases diamonds in the New York diamond market, and the wholesale store then fills orders from the retail stores and from independent customers and maintains a substantial inventory of diamonds. The corporation values its inventory by the specific identification cost method.

Required:

Assume that at the inventory date you are satisfied that Fine Jewelers, Inc., has no items left by customers for repair or sale on consignment and that no inventory owned by the corporation is in the possession of outsiders.

a. Discuss the problems the auditor should anticipate in planning for the observation of the physical inventory on this engagement because of the—

(1) Different locations of the inventories.

(2) Nature of the inventory.

b. (1) Explain how your audit program for this inventory would be different from that used for most other inventories.

(2) Prepare an audit program for the verification of the corporation's diamond and diamond jewelry inventories, identifying any steps which you would apply only to the retail stores or to the wholesale store. (AICPA adapted)

12.23. Ace Corporation does not conduct a complete annual physical count of purchased parts and supplies in its principal warehouse but uses statistical sampling instead to estimate the year-end inventory. Ace maintains a perpetual inventory record of parts and supplies and believes that statistical sampling is highly effective in determining inventory values and is sufficiently reliable to make a physical count of each item of inventory unnecessary.

Required:

a. Identify the audit procedures that should be used by the independent auditor that change or are in addition to normal required audit procedures when a client utilizes statistical sampling to determine inventory value and does not conduct a 100-percent annual physical count of inventory items.

b. List at least ten normal audit procedures that should be performed to verify physical quantities whenever a client conducts a periodic physical count of all or part of its inventory. (AICPA)

12.24. Your audit client, Household Appliances, Inc., operates a retail store in the center of town. Because of lack of storage space Household keeps inventory that is not on display in a public warehouse outside of town. The warehouseman receives inventory from suppliers and, on request from your client by a shipping advice or telephone call, delivers merchandise to customers or to the retail outlet.

The accounts are maintained at the retail store by a bookkeeper. Each month the warehouseman sends to the bookkeeper a quantity report indicating opening balance, receipts, deliveries, and ending balance. The bookkeeper compares book quantities on hand at month-end with the warehouseman's report and adjusts the books to agree with the report. No physical counts of the merchandise at the warehouse were made by your client during the year.

You are now preparing for your examination of the current year's financial statements in this recurring engagement. Last year you rendered an unqualified opinion.

Required:

a. Prepare an audit program for the observation of the physical inventory of Household Appliances, Inc. (1) at the retail outlet, and (2) at the warehouse.

b. As part of your examination would you verify inventory quantities at the warehouse by means of—

(1) A warehouse confirmation? Why?

(2) Test counts of inventory at the warehouse? Why?

c. Since the bookkeeper adjusts books to quantities shown on the warehouseman's report each month, what significance would you attach to the year-end adjustments if they were substantial? Discuss. (AICPA)

12.25. The Litho Press Company is engaged in the manufacture of large-sized presses under specific contracts and in accordance with customers' specifications. Customers are required to advance 25 percent of the contract price. The company records sales on a shipment basis and accumulates costs by job orders. The normal profit margin over the past few years has been approximately 5 percent of sales, after providing for selling and administrative expenses of about 10 percent of sales. Inventory is valued at the lower-of-cost-or-market.

Among the jobs you are reviewing in the course of your annual examination of the company's December 31 financial statements is Job No. 2357, calling for delivery of a three-color press at a firm contract price of $50,000. Costs accumulated for the job at the year-end aggregated $30,250. The company's engineers estimated that the job was approximately 55 percent complete at that time. Your audit procedures have been as follows:

1. Examined all contracts, noting pertinent provisions.
2. Observed physical inventory of jobs in process and reconciled details to job order accounts.
3. Tested input of labor, material, and overhead charges into the various jobs to determine that such charges were authentic and had been posted correctly. The month of September was selected for test.
4. Confirmed customers' advances at year-end.
5. Balanced work-in-process job ledger with control account.

Required:

With respect to Job No. 2357:

a. State the additional audit procedures, if any, you would employ and explain the purpose of the procedures.

b. Indicate the manner and the amount at which you would include Job No. 2357 in the balance sheet.

c. Comment on the method of choosing cost transactions for the month of September for test. (AICPA adapted)

12.26. *Part A:* During the audit of Mason Co., Inc., for the calendar year 1979, you notice that the company produces aluminum cans at the rate of about 40 million units annually. Also, on the plant tour you notice a large stockpile of raw aluminum in storage. Your inventory observation and pricing procedures showed this stockpile to be the raw materials inventory of 400 tons valued at $240,000 (Lifo cost). Inquiry with the production chief yielded the information that 400 tons was about a four-month supply of raw materials.

Required:

What additional information about the purchase of inventory might you expect to find, and how would you proceed in gathering more information?

Part B: Suppose that you learn that Mason had executed a firm long-term purchase contract with All-Purpose Aluminum Company to purchase raw materials on the following schedule:

Delivery Date	*Quantity*	*Total Price*
Jan. 30, 1980	500 tons	$300,000
June 30, 1980	700 tons	420,000
Dec. 30, 1980	1,000 tons	500,000

Because of recent economic conditions, principally a decline in the demand for raw aluminum and a consequent oversupply, the price stood at 20 cents per pound as of January 15, 1980. Commodities experts predict that this low price will prevail for 12–15 months or until there is a general economic recovery.

Required:

a. Describe the procedures you would employ to gather evidence about this contract (including its initial discovery).

b. In *Part B* above, what facts are cited which an auditor would have to discover for himself?

c. What effect does this contract have on the financial statements?

13

AUDIT OF INVESTMENTS, INTANGIBLES, AND RELATED INCOME AND EXPENSE

The four objectives of this chapter are to explain with relation to investments, intangibles, and related income and expense:

- A business approach to objectives concerning existence, valuation, cutoff, accounting principles, compliance, and effectiveness.
- Elements of internal control for these accounts and transactions.
- Applications of audit procedures for gathering evidence.
- Types of fraud and misstatement that might occur in these accounts.

The discussion and explanation of each of these four topics are intended to enable students to sharpen their awareness of audit objectives, relevant evidence, relevant audit procedures, and the application of audit methodology to the specific subset of accounts.

Most programs used in audit field work contain separate sections for procedures related to investments and for procedures related to intangible assets. This chapter, however, accords with reality in that most audit programs combine the procedures for auditing related revenue with those for the audit of the basic revenue-producing assets. Procedures for auditing expenses related to amortization of intangibles are also typically combined with the program for auditing the intangible assets.

A BUSINESS APPROACH TO AUDIT OBJECTIVES

A broad-based business overview has special relevance to the auditor when considering investments and intangibles because the scope and volume of activities that create these assets vary widely from company to company. In manufacturing businesses investment transactions may be few in number and large in amount while research and development activities may be an extensive effort organized in a separate department. In financial institutions such as banks, savings associations, insurance companies, and mutual funds, the investment activities are ongoing, everyday occurrences involving a large number of transactions; and research activity may be confined to investment advisory research. In the low-activity few-transaction situation the internal control system may be very unstructured, while in the other situation internal control may be as formalized as the sales-receivables system of an industrial or commercial business.

In *Statement of Financial Accounting Standards No.* 2 ("Accounting for Research and Development Costs"), the Financial Accounting Standards Board gave the following definitions of research and development:

> *Research* is planned search or critical investigation aimed at discovery of new knowledge with the hope that such knowledge will be useful in developing a new product or service . . . or a new process or technique, or in bringing about a significant improvement to an existing product or process.
>
> *Development* is the translation of research findings or other knowledge into a plan or design for a new product or process or for a significant improvement to an existing product or process whether intended for sale or use. . . .

Statement No. 2 (hereinafter FASB *No.* 2) also gives several examples of activities that are included in research and development and several examples of activities that are excluded. The definitions and examples are important to auditors because specific disclosure of these costs is required in financial statements.[1]

Existence

At the outset an auditor should be familiar with the client's business. If the client is a financial institution, investments will surely constitute a major proportion of the assets, and income related thereto will constitute the major revenue source. Further familiarity with the entity's investment philosophy—emphasis on growth, or income, or security—will yield insights to the nature of the investment securities.

Industrial companies whose main business is in manufacture or distribution of products and services may engage in investment transactions of a greater variety. Some investments may be in highly liquid securities such as treasury notes or regularly traded common stocks and bonds. These investments may simply be income-producing reservoirs for temporary excess cash. An understanding of the cash management system and its constraints can contribute to recognition of a necessity for temporary investments. Long-term investments may be made for special purposes—to set aside a fund for future expansion or construction purposes or to achieve control over another company through ownership of a

[1] FASB *No.* 2 supercedes APB *Opinion No. 17* ("Intangible Assets") insofar as accounting for research and development costs is concerned.

large block of stock. Long-range plans for the marketing and production functions can lend credence to such investment assets.

The auditor should learn of the client's organizational structure for carrying out investment plans. The existence of an executive finance committee, criteria for directors' approval of investments, and a system for making written investment proposals can all produce evidence in minutes of meetings and other documents. These sources should be reviewed early in the engagement in order to learn of the scope and magnitude of investment transactions. The sale, abandonment, or other disposal of investments should also be channeled through the same system of review and approval.

In a manner similar to the system for approving fixed asset additions and other investments, a framework for proposing acquisitions of intangible assets may also be found. An auditor would be able to learn of an organized research and development department or of an internal task force responsible for merger and acquisition explorations. The activities of departmental and functional groups such as these are of interest in connection with understanding the terms of proposed and completed mergers, and with distinguishing research and development performed on contract for others from research and development performed for the benefit of the client company itself.

Inquiries about the status of investment properties can lead to knowledge of associated income and expenses. Property other than dividend-paying or interest-bearing securities may be held for investment. If such property is being rented in the interim, the auditor can expect to see rental revenue in the accounts. Likewise knowledge of patent or copyright licenses leads the auditor to look for royalty revenue. A controlling interest held in another company means that the investee's financial statements will be important for accounting for income on the equity method.

Valuation

With regard to investments accounted for by the cost or equity methods, most valuation problems are associated with the relation of the accounting value to the market value. Usually this relation is accomplished simply by looking up market quotations in published sources. Investments carried as current assets may be written down to market values lower than cost (FASB *No. 12*, "Accounting for Certain Marketable Securities"). Investments carried as long-term assets may be written down if a value decline is material and apparently permanent. The criterion of "permanent decline" may be hard to test with factual evidence. It may be necessary to analyze values by means other than consulting published market prices.

The auditor should determine whether investments of the client in fact have a market with a reliable quoted price. Some securities may not trade regularly, may be held closely by a small number of shareholders, or may be restricted in some manner (such as "investment letter" stock which cannot be sold without proper SEC registration). Other property such as land, buildings, yachts, or other personal property may not have a readily determinable market value, and they may not be amenable to value analysis in terms of revenue-producing potential.

Some investments may have originated in nonmonetary transactions (APB *Opinion No. 29*)[2] or in transactions which call for imputation of an implicit interest element (APB *Opinion No. 21*)[3]. When notes or other securities have been acquired in this manner, the auditor will want to learn of the circumstances, particularly of the market value of property given in exchange and the market interest rate for such transactions.

The valuation of intangible assets is always a troublesome audit area. The auditor should be familiar with any legal challenges to patents, copyrights, trademarks, and trade names. A lawsuit judgment that invalidates a patent or similar exclusive right may mean that the asset has become worthless. Even without legal action, a patent may lose value if a closely compatible product is marketed in competition. The auditor should thus be aware of competing products in the market. Ultimately some conclusions about the economic life span of an intangible asset will be important for assessing the value of the asset and of the amortization expense flowing from it.

Goodwill is perhaps the most problem-plagued intangible asset in terms of valuation and amortization subsequent to acquisition. Purchased goodwill must be amortized, but the determination of a reasonable lifespan is difficult. Perhaps the most that can be said is that the auditor must constantly be aware of the status, disposition, and use of assets that were a part of the package purchase that gave effect to goodwill. If acquired trade names, market channels, major assets (e.g., store chains), or other significant elements of the package have been sold off or changed, then the capitalized goodwill may be gone as well.

Cutoff

Most investment transactions do not present any unusual cutoff problems. However, auditors should be careful to perceive the status of mergers and acquisition transactions near year-end, and they should carefully evaluate the status of commitments to make major investments. These items are more likely to be matters for footnote disclosure, but in some circumstances they may have an effect on the accounts or on retroactive restatement of prior period financial statements.

A proper cutoff of investment transactions in a financial institution is not unlike that of the purchases cutoff in a manufacturing company. In some entities, such as mutual funds, there may in fact be a flurry of trading near the year-end to "dress up" the portfolio. The auditor's best approach to cutoff, however, is generally through an audit of the transactions, and knowledge of the year-end volume will help him or her plan these procedures.

---

[2] "Accounting for Nonmonetary Transactions."

[3] "Interest on Receivables and Payables."

Transactions respecting intangibles and related income and expense and investment income may also be examined on a test basis for proper cutoff. These procedures may involve the auditor with rent and royalty contracts, published records of dividend payments, and financial statements of affiliated companies. With these procedures there will likely be some auditing overlap with accrued income receivable and accrued expenses on rental property, and possibly with prepaid expenses relating to investments.

Accounting Principles and Disclosure

The current or long-term classification of an investment in securities depends upon two criteria: (1) management's expressed intention that the investment be considered current (or long term), and (2) the marketability of the securities. Management's intentions may be constrained by a contractual agreement to set aside funds for long-term purposes (e.g., bond sinking funds, proceeds of stock offerings earmarked for construction), so the auditor will need to read debt agreements and securities offering prospectuses. If a security has no market, it is difficult to classify it as current, so the auditor should learn of the market, if any. These points may be ones appropriate for footnote disclosures.

Aside from questions of valuation and classification, the most important accounting issues involve compliance with accounting principles dealing with business combinations (APB *Opinion No. 16*), intangible assets (APB *Opinion No. 17*), the equity method of accounting for investments in common stock (APB *Opinion No. 18*), and accounting for research and development costs (FASB *No.* 2).

Business combination agreements must be studied carefully to determine the appropriateness of purchase or pooling accounting and the appropriate recognition of goodwill, if any. The requirements of APB *No. 16* are quite complex in this respect, and the auditor's problem of finding competent evidence of value allocations to a package of assets may involve use of appraisals and other estimates of market values.

Intangible assets may be recognized when purchased in an exchange transaction. However, an intangible asset (e.g., a patent, a computer program) that is purchased only for use in a research and development project and which has no alternative future use is a research and development cost. All research and development costs must be charged to expense when incurred.[4] But if such an intangible has future use in other R&D projects or other alternative uses, only an amortized portion of its cost is a research and development cost. Research and development costs charged to expense during a period must be disclosed separately as a line item in the income statement or in a footnote. Thus the auditor's problem is to obtain sufficient competent evidence to enable the auditor to distinguish R&D costs from non-R&D costs and to distinguish R&D performed

[4] Research and development done under contract for others is not charged to expense but is matched with contract revenue. The R&D expensed under FASB *No.* 2 is R&D that a company conducts for itself.

under contract for others from R&D performed by and for the client company itself.

According to APB *Opinion No. 18*, the equity method of accounting for an investment in common stock must be used if the investor has a "significant controlling influence" over the investee company. Twenty percent or more ownership is the presumptive guideline for defining "significant controlling influence." However, the auditor must become aware of all the facts, not just whether the investor owns more or less than 20 percent of the voting stock. A significant controlling influence may exist with a 15-percent interest in some cases, or a 30-percent interest may not give an investor significant control. (For example, if another investor held 65 percent and was adverse to the client's interest, the client's 30 percent might be powerless.) For these investments and for joint venture investments the auditor may need to obtain financial statements of the investee or of the joint venture. Information about intercompany sales and purchases will have to be gathered to give effect to proper eliminations when the equity method is used.

Compliance

Investments are relatively free of the constraints of legal rules and regulations. An investor, however, must be careful to honor promises made in acquiring securities in a private placement (i.e., without SEC registration). Auditors should be alert to such "letter stock" transactions. Several types of financial institutions such as insurance companies and mutual funds are subject to state and federal regulation of the types of securities they may hold and/or the extent of the holdings. For example, mutual funds are generally prohibited from investing any more than 5 percent of net assets in a single issue of securities. Auditors should be aware of the regulations applicable to financial institutions.

Several of the intangible assets are creatures of law (patents, copyrights, trademarks). Consequently an auditor should review their standing, generally by correspondence with an attorney. Challenges to the patent rights, new competing patents, and the client's own lawsuits for infringement claims all contain relevant audit information. An invalidated patent usually loses all value as an intangible asset, and such an invalidation means that royalties from licensing will no longer exist, and past royalties collected may be subject to dispute.

When in touch with matters of patents and other rights, the auditor could also inquire about the client's status respecting infringement on others' patents. This is a highly technical area, however, and any information in this regard will most likely arise from knowledge of lawsuits against the client.

Effectiveness

The audit of prepaid insurance is one that has drawn independent auditors into an area of effectiveness study concerning the adequacy of insurance coverage. The amount and cost of various types of insurance (e.g., casualty, fidelity bonds, workmen's compensation, business interruption, product liability, directors' indemnity) may be analyzed and reported to management. At present there are no explicit accounting principles that require disclosure of inadequate insurance in financial statements, but the reporting standard that requires adequate disclosure of material financial information may be relevant in extreme cases. Internal auditors would also look upon this sort of analysis as a relevant management services assignment.

Internal research and development projects should be subject to continuous monitoring of costs and benefits. Failure to follow up on such projects is as much a sign of managerial ineffectiveness as failure to monitor and control other more tangible operations and investments. If management and the internal auditors do not exercise such control, the independent auditor may have problems identifying research and development costs for separate disclosure.

Management should also monitor the effectiveness of its program of securities investments. Periodic reports of cost, market value, income returns, holding period, and other factors are relevant for most investment decisions. If such reports are available, the independent auditor may use them to correlate data on cost, sales proceeds, gains and losses, and income with those data shown in the accounts.

INTERNAL CONTROL

The characteristics of internal accounting control over investments, intangibles, and related income and expense may be analyzed initially by using questionnaire and flowchart tools. Subsequent compliance tests may then be performed to examine objectively the actual effectiveness of controls. The breadth and depth of questionnaires and the use of flowcharting, however, depends upon the volume and importance of these transactions in the client's business. The review and compliance testing of a low-volume investment activity in a manufacturing company can be abbreviated. The auditor may decide to audit the balances extensively in lieu of spending a significant amount of audit time on internal accounting control.

Conversely, in the audit of a financial institution that engages in frequent investment and disposal transactions, an auditor would want to analyze internal accounting control closely because some degree of reliance will be placed on it. Extensive research and development activities likewise call for significant audit time to be spent on internal accounting control procedures.

In the discussion that follows, both of the areas of investments and intangibles are treated as though they consisted of high-volume transaction activity. Any adjustments of the amount of audit work done would depend upon the particular characteristics of a company's actual activity in these areas.

Review Phase

The auditor first wants to learn about management's control system in three particular aspects. Each of the three is explained below in such a way as to describe the relationship of control over investments, intangibles, and related income and expense to other control subsystems. Usually there is overlapping control that coordinates investment approval procedures, purchasing procedures, cash receipts procedures, and cash disbursement procedures.

1. *A plan of organization and authorization* that provides for the initiation, review, and approval of investment proposals. The system would resemble the one presented in Chapter 14 depicting procedures for control of fixed asset acquisitions and disposals. The system would also have characteristics of a purchasing control system as shown in Chapter 12.
2. *A system of recordkeeping and physical custody procedures* for accounting for transactions, monitoring results, and ensuring physical control of negotiable securities. The system would contain elements of control over cash receipts and cash disbursements, as shown in Chapter 11, since receipts and disbursements are integral elements of acquisition, disposal, and income and expense transactions.
3. *A system of error-checking routines* for prevention or detection of accounting errors and for reporting on the results of investment and research and development activity. This aspect could include periodic counts or confirmation of securities by internal auditors as well as the common checking routines used in the receipts and disbursements control areas.

The flowchart in Exhibit 13–1 is a composite of procedures relating both to investment transactions (e.g., securities, mergers, joint ventures) and to intangibles transactions (e.g., research and development, acquisitions of companies). The organizational system shows separation of review and approval responsibilities from recordkeeping responsibilities. Not shown in the exhibit are the characteristics of asset custody responsibility. The aspects of custody and other details are discussed below. Exhibit 13–2 and 13–3 contain relevant internal control questionnaire items.

Investment Transaction Procedures

Investments may take a wide variety of characteristics from the newsworthy event of a multimillion dollar tender offer to the day-to-day trading in stocks and bonds; from the simplicity of accounting for securities traded frequently on organized exchanges to the complexities of accounting for a unique investment in a high-technology joint operating venture. Whatever their nature and frequency, however, procedures should be utilized to propose, review, and approve investments; and a management-oriented reporting system should be used to monitor and control such investment activities. Authorizations for transactions may

EXHIBIT 13–1
General Flowchart: Investments and Intangibles Transaction Procedures

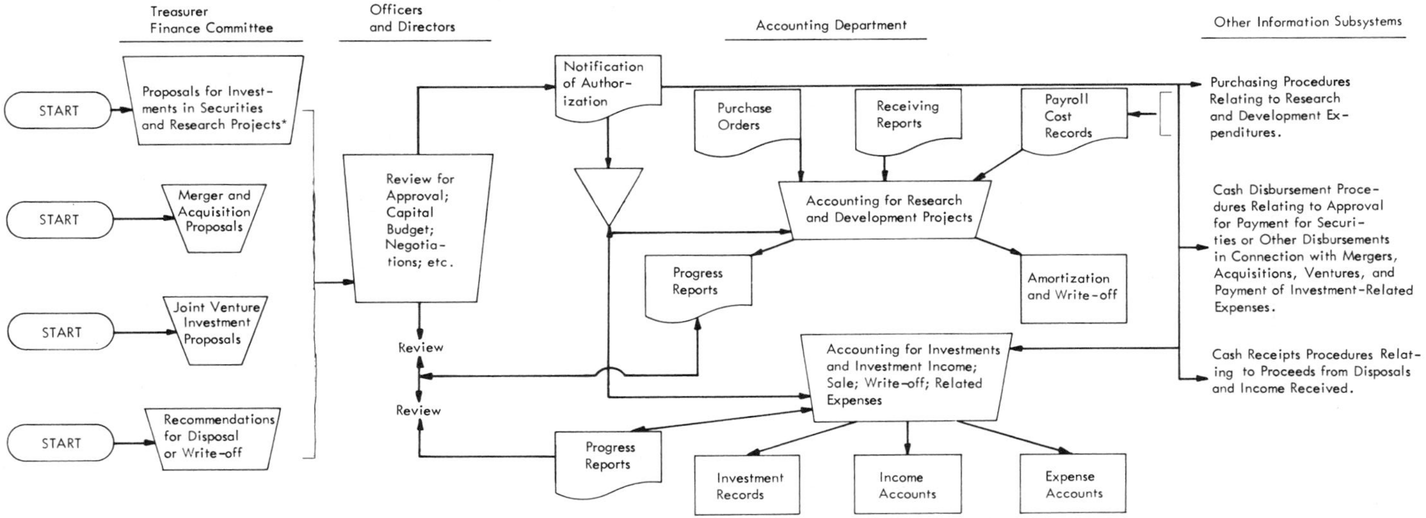

* Research project proposals may originate with scientific, technical, or operating department personnel. Technical and economic data may be transmitted to officers and directors for review and approval.

EXHIBIT 13–2

INTERNAL CONTROL QUESTIONNAIRE
SECURITY INVESTMENTS AND RELATED INCOME

1. Are investment acquisitions and disposals authorized by the board of directors? Executive finance committee? A responsible officer?
2. Is the accounting department informed of income and expense expectations in order to control receipts and disbursements?
3. Have any investments been written off? Are these followed up and controlled for possible remaining value?
4. Do detail investment records contain data on dates, costs, amortization, and certificate numbers?
5. Are all securities in the name of the client? Explain securities held by brokers, trustees, or in name of "bearer."
6. Do the internal auditors or other officers periodically inspect and count securities and compare to the accounting detail records? When was the last such inspection?
7. Are securities held as collateral recorded in memo accounts and safeguarded like those owned by the client?
8. Are securities kept in a vault or safe-deposit box in the name of the client?
9. Does access to the storage place require the presence or signatures of two responsible officers?
10. Are independent trustees or brokers knowledgeable of persons authorized to sell or transfer securities held by them?
11. Are securities records maintained on an EDP system? If so, complete relevant portions of the EDP internal control questionnaire.

be specific as in the case of infrequent or unusual investments such as mergers, joint ventures, or other sizable commitments. Oftentimes, individual officers will be assigned responsibility for monitoring and control. Authorizations may also be general, as in the case of a treasurer's frequent short-term cash management investments or as in the case of a financial institution's buy-sell authority granted to a portfolio manager.

Written record of the authorizations, both general and specific, should be transmitted to the accounting department. Such documents serve the same function as the purchase order and receiving report copies utilized by the accounting department in a purchasing system. They are the source authority that may be consulted in connection with initial accounting for an investment acquisition or disposal. Such authorization documents should contain sufficient detail to inform the accounting department about expected income and expense flows.

Custody of negotiable securities should be controlled. Oftentimes custody is physical, effected by the use of vaults, safe-deposit boxes, or safes. Access to securities should be limited to responsible officers (not persons who keep accounting records), and a dual responsibility whereby removal of securities requires joint actions of two persons is recommended. Such dual control can be attained by using safe-deposit boxes (a record of entry

EXHIBIT 13–3

INTERNAL CONTROL QUESTIONNAIRE
INTANGIBLE ASSETS AND RELATED EXPENSE

1. Are proposals for research, development, leases, acquisitions of franchises, and so forth, approved and authorized by the board of directors? Executive committee? A responsible officer?
2. Is the accounting department informed of authorized projects, budgets, and expenditure expectations?
3. Are detailed project records maintained for research and development? Detailed memorandum records of leases, franchises, and so forth?
4. Have any intangibles been written off or written down? When was the last assessment of intangible values made?
5. Are susceptible transactions (e.g., insurance, rent, taxes, relocation operations) reviewed periodically for appropriate calculation of prepaid expenses and deferred charges? Are such assets under a program for systematic amortization?
6. When actual expenditures exceed amounts authorized, is approval obtained from the directors, executive committee, or a responsible officer?
7. Is there a logical policy in effect for review of transactions for determination of capitalizable values and expense amounts?
8. Is the approval of a responsible officer required for write-off or write-down of intangible assets?
9. Are all patents, copyrights, and trademarks issued in the name of the client? In the names of individuals?

is kept by vault officials), or by using double locks, keys, or combinations for access to storage places. Alternatively, securities may be held by an independent trustee or by a brokerage firm.

Intangibles Transactions Procedures

Intangible assets can take a variety of forms ranging from ordinary calculations of prepaid expenses to complicated evaluations of the cost of patents and goodwill. Prepaid expenses, deferred charges, and similar calculated amounts that are functionally related to other accounting data do not actually arise from a system of control separate from the basic data. For example, prepaid insurance is created through the payment of an insurance premium, and the basic control is exercised through the purchase-cash disbursement system; purchased goodwill is created through an acquisition transaction, and the basic control is through the proposal-review-disbursement system. Accounting propriety and error-checking routines consist of the accountant's analysis of the basic transactions.

Research and development transactions should be controlled at least to the extent that they are properly classified as R&D in an expense account. FASB *No.* 2 requires that R&D performed internally shall be expensed, thus R&D projects do not generate intangible assets. However, the requirement for separate disclosure makes identification of the costs important. Control in this regard would consist of the system for making R&D project proposals and the system for obtaining authorization to spend funds. Notification of authorization to the accounting department, purchasing department, and other responsible personnel would provide the necessary transaction-initiation control. Other controls over accounting accuracy should include definitions in an accounting manual of costs that are included in R&D costs, and of costs that are excluded from the R&D classification.

Investment and intangibles proposals may include plans for lease financing or other long-term payment methods for the acquisition of franchises, distributorships, patents, or other important commercial licenses. Oftentimes these types of transactions are viewed as ordinary and necessary business expenses, but they may in fact create capitalizable asset values. Lease transactions may be construed as purchases of fixed assets. Rights under a lease may be capitalized as leasehold assets under certain circumstances. Long-lasting rights under franchise, distributorship, or other licensing agreements may in fact be intangible assets. The auditor thus should review all proposals introduced in the system for evidence of transactions that could possibly give rise to intangibles of these types.

Compliance Tests of Transaction Details

The extent of tests of transaction details will vary depending on their volume and the materiality of amounts involved in the client's business. The audit program procedures described in Exhibit 13–4 are all stated in terms of compliance tests designed to produce evidence of internal accounting control system reliability. However, in some cases enough of the transactions may be audited to accomplish part of the direct audit of an account balance with these procedures. For example, the vouching procedures related to investments in securities may be 100-percent complete (or nearly so), so that the balance of recorded investment cost will have been partially audited. (Some other procedures relating to physical inspection and confirmation have not yet been performed.)

Transactions in prepaid expenses, R&D, deferred charges, and unusual investments are not usually complicated by problems of EDP processing (except as to original data entry and classification). Analysis, adjustment, reevaluation, and other such judgments cannot be performed by the computer, so the most important accounting problems cannot be imbedded in an EDP system. However, some nonmanufacturing companies (e.g., insurance companies, mutual funds, brokerage houses) may have extensive EDP applications for accounting for investments and investment income. Compliance tests may be used in such audits to test input accuracy, and test data methods, parallel simulation, or other computer-oriented testing methods may be utilized to reach conclusions about system effectiveness.

Evidence obtained through the review and compliance test phases techniques will produce a basis for conclusions about internal accounting

EXHIBIT 13–4
Audit Program—Selected Compliance Testing Procedures

A. *Investments and Related Income*
   1. Review the minutes of board of director's meetings for approval of major investment transactions.
   2. Vouch major investment transactions to approval in director's minutes.
   3. Vouch recorded investments to broker's advice, contract, canceled check, and other supporting documentation.
   4. Review physical security over stock and bond certificates held as investments.
   5. Select a sample of recorded interest or dividend income entries and vouch to bank deposit slip or accrual calculations.

B. *Intangibles and Related Expenses*
   1. Review the minutes of board of director's meetings for approval of major acquisitions of intangibles (e.g., mergers, patents, leases).
   2. Vouch major intangibles transactions to approval in director's minutes.
   3. Vouch recorded intangibles transactions to invoices, contracts, and canceled checks.
   4. Review internal reports of the status and maintenance of intangible assets.
   5. Vouch recorded R&D expense transactions to supporting documentation for evidence of proper classification.
   6. Vouch recorded lease payments to lease contracts and canceled checks.

control reliability, and in some cases, about the fair presentation of balances themselves. For each unique audit engagement the auditor should decide the balance of time *and* effort allocated to the proper study and evaluation of internal accounting control and to the direct audit of balances.

SUBSTANTIVE TESTS OF BALANCES

The eight basic auditing procedures, as applied to the audit of investments, intangibles, and related income and expense, are explained below in detail. The construction of an audit program utilizing these procedures (see Exhibit 13–5) should begin with the auditor's explicit recognition of the assertions contained in investment, intangible asset, and related accounts. The assertions point directly to hypothesis questions that can be tested by gathering sufficient, competent evidential matter. Some of the assertions typical of this account group are:

- Investment securities are on hand or are properly held by a trustee.
- Investment cost does not exceed market value.
- Investments pledged as collateral are properly disclosed.
- Controlling investments are accounted for by the equity method.
- Purchased goodwill is properly recorded.

- Capitalized intangibles costs relate to intangibles acquired in an exchange transaction.
- Amortization is properly calculated.
- Investment income has been received and recorded.
- Research and development costs are properly classified.

The assertions above are not a complete list of all matters of audit interest, but they are illustrative of the types of problems that should be recognized. The next task is to consider the evidence that might support or refute these assertions, and then the auditor can select the most efficient procedures for gathering that evidence.

Verbal Inquiry

Auditors need to know *where* investment securities are held. If the investment securities are in the client's custody, a physical inspection and count can be performed. If the investment securities are held by a trustee or broker, they can be confirmed. The fact that securities are not held by the client may mean that they are pledged as collateral. Further inquiries on this subject should be made and the information combined with other audit procedures related to liabilities and contract obligations.

Inquiries should also deal with the nature of investments and the reasons for holding them. Management's expressed intention that a marketable security investment be considered a long-term investment may be the only available evidence for classifying it as long-term and not as a current asset. Control relations with near-20 percent owned affiliates should be probed with regard to applications of the equity method of accounting for such investments. The status of real estate and personal property held as investments (not in the fixed, productive-property classification) should be reviewed particularly with regard to any rental or lease operations.

Merger and acquisition transactions should be reviewed in terms of the appraisals, judgments, and allocations used to assign portions of the purchase price to tangible assets, intangible assets, liabilities, and goodwill. In the final analysis nothing really substitutes for the audit of transaction documentation, but the verbal inquiries may help the auditor fully understand the circumstances of a merger.

Questions about lawsuits challenging patents, copyrights, or trade names may produce early knowledge of problem areas for further investigation. Likewise discussions and questions about research and development successes and failures may alert the auditor to problems of valuation of assets and related expenses. Responses to questions about licensing of patents can be used later in the audit of related royalty revenue accounts.

Physical Observation

Physical inspection and observation is a procedure having only limited applications in the investment and intangible assets group. Most of these assets have no physical form to observe, but some of them may be evidenced by formal documents that can be inspected and counted by the auditor.

A controlled count of securities is a necessary procedural application. Generally the count consists of the auditor gaining access to the securities in the presence of a responsible client officer. The count is controlled first by simultaneously counting or sealing off other negotiable funds (e.g., securities held as collateral), and second by the auditor conducting the count personally. The count working papers should contain the name of the issuer and description of the security, the number of shares, certificate numbers, maturity value, interest and preferred dividend rates, and the date of issue. When the count is completed, the auditor should obtain a written statement from the client's representative that the securities were returned intact to their safekeeping place.

Investment property may be observed and inspected in a manner similar to the inspection of fixed assets. The principal goal is simply to determine actual existence and condition of the property. Official documents of patents, copyrights, and trademark rights can be inspected to see that they are in fact in the name of the client.

Confirmation

The practice of obtaining independent written confirmation from outside parties is also fairly limited in the area of investments, intangibles, and related income and expense. Securities held by trustees or brokers should be confirmed, and the confirmation request should seek the same descriptive information as obtained in a physical count by the auditor.

Company counsel can be queried as to the knowledge of any lawsuits or defects relating to patents, copyrights, trademarks, or trade names. This confirmation can be sought by a specific request in the attorney's letter.

Cash surrender values of life insurance policies may be confirmed by confirming the in-force status of the policy with the insurance company. (Inspection of the policy itself will produce information of cash surrender values, but possession of the policy document does not guarantee that the policy has not lapsed or that premiums have not been "paid" with policy loans.) For participating life insurance policies the auditor may wish to confirm the amount of accumulated dividends if they have not been used to reduce current cash premiums. In connection with the audit of liabilities the life insurance confirmation may produce evidence of an unrecorded policy loan.

Royalty income from patent licenses received from a single licensee may be confirmed. However, such income amounts are usually audited by vouching the licensee's reports and related cash payment.

Vouching of Documents

The physical inspection of securities is actually a vouching procedure. However, the distinction in this case is unimportant. Other vouching procedures are considerably more significant in the investments-intangibles-related income and expense group.

Investment cost should be vouched to brokers' advices, monthly statements, or other documentary evidence of cost. At this same time it is usually convenient also to vouch the cost of securities sold and retrace the amounts to gain and loss accounts, and to vouch the brokers' statements of sales price and proceeds. The auditor should determine what method of cost-out assignment was used (i.e., Fifo, specific certificate, or average cost) and whether it is consistent with prior years' transactions. The cost of real and personal property can likewise be vouched to invoices or other documents of purchase, and title documents (e.g., on land, buildings) may be inspected.

Prepaid expenses and deferred charges are almost always audited by vouching and recalculation. For prepaid and deferred amounts of insurance, rent, taxes, and so forth the basic documents of policies, contracts, tax notices, and similar associated formal documents are vouched. The auditor looks for terms, dates, periods covered, and amounts as bases for recalculating prepaid and deferred asset amounts.

Vouching may be extensive in the area of research and development efforts. The principal evidential problem is to ascertain whether costs classified as assets or as R&D expense indeed belong in that classification. Amounts recorded are selected, generally on a sample basis, and the purchase orders, receiving reports, payroll records, authorization notices, and management reports are compared to them. Some R&D costs may closely resemble non-R&D costs (e.g., supplies, payroll costs), so the auditor must be very careful in the vouching to perceive costs that appear to relate to other operations.

Income and expense amounts such as rent, interest, dividends, royalties, lease and rent expense, and write-offs can be audited by vouching. In fact if the test of transactions vouching procedure was extensive, these balances may be largely audited already. However, other procedures discussed below can be applied efficiently to the audit of income and expense accounts.

Recalculation and Analysis of Interrelationships

Basic calculations such as footings and crossfooting of investment schedules with reconciliation to ledger accounts should be made by the auditor to check for inadvertent error. Other basic recalculations important for the investment asset-investment income audit involve the auditor with related data from other sources. By consulting quoted market values of securities, the auditor can calculate values and determine whether investments should be written down. If quoted market values are not available, financial statements related to investments must be obtained and analyzed for evidence of basic value. If such financial statements are unaudited, evidence indicated by them is considered extremely weak.

Income amounts can be calculated and audited by consulting published dividend records for quotations of dividends actually declared and paid during a period. Since the auditor knows the holding period of securities, he or she can calculate what dividend income should have been and compare this amount to the account. Any difference could indicate a cutoff error, misclassification, defalcation, or failure to record a dividend receivable. In a similar manner, application of interest rates to bond investments produces a calculated-audited interest income figure (making allowance also for amortization of premium or discount, if applicable).

When investments are accounted for by the equity method, the auditor will have to obtain financial statements of the investee company. These should be audited statements. (Inability to obtain audited statements may indicate that the investor does not really have a control influence.) These statements would be used as the basis for recalculating the amount of the investor's share of income to recognize in the accounts. In addition, these statements may be used to audit the disclosure of investees' assets, liabilities, and income presented in footnotes to the investor's financial statements (a disclosure recommended when investments accounted for by the equity method are material).[5]

Recalculations can be combined with limited vouching procedures to audit rental income and expense, royalty income and expense, and gains and losses on sales of investments. Generally the application involves multiplying rent and royalty rates by time periods and production units. Amounts of accrued income receivable can be recalculated in a similar manner. Gain and loss on investment disposal involves the recalculation of asset cost by the appropriate cost method (e.g., Fifo).

Amortization of goodwill and other intangibles should be recalculated. Like depreciation, amortization expense owes its existence to a calculation, and recalculation based on audited costs and rates is sufficient audit evidence. Likewise recalculation of the amortization of prepaid expenses and deferred charges accomplishes the audit of expense portions; and when combined with audit of the basic expense account, such recalculations accomplish the audit of the remaining unamortized prepaid expense balances.

Retracing and Scanning

In connection with the audit of account balances, the retracing procedure is used primarily for auditing the proper cutoff of transactions that are included in, or which should be excluded from, the balance. In the investments and intangibles area the most sensitive cutoff errors would involve income or expense recognition. For example, the auditor should be careful to audit sales of investments around the year-end. Sales at gains right before year-end and sales at losses right after year-end are indications of a need for more evidence. (In fact the subsequent sale at a loss is convincing evidence for investment write-down at the balance sheet date.) A scanning of journal and account entries made just before and just after the year-end date can reveal such sales of investments.

[5] See "Evidential Matter for Long-Term Investments" (*SAS No. 1*, Section 332).

Vouchers and other invoices recorded in the last two or three weeks and invoices received after year-end should be examined and retraced to the records. There may be a tendency for R&D expense items to be postponed to the next period or to be classified incorrectly at year-end. There is a great deal of latitude in these expenses for income manipulation.

The auditor should scan and review prepaid expenses, accrued revenue, and accrued expenses with relation to his or her knowledge of the underlying intangibles, such as insurance, taxes, leases, royalties, and so forth. It is quite easy for an accrual to be missed.

EXHIBIT 13–5
Audit Program—Selected Substantive Test Procedures

A. *Investments and Related Income*

1. Prepare, or have client prepare, a schedule of all investments. Reconcile with investment accounts per general ledger.
2. Vouch recorded investments to broker's advices, contracts, canceled checks, and other supporting documentation.
3. Inspect or confirm with a trustee or broker the name, number, identification, interest rate, and face amount (if applicable) of securities held as investments.
4. Recalculate interest income and/or look up dividend income in a dividend reporting service (e.g., Moody's Dividend Record).
5. Vouch recorded sales to bank deposit slip and recalculate gain or loss on disposition.
6. Obtain market values of investments and determine whether any write-down or write-off is necessary. Scan transactions soon after the client's year-end to see if any investments were sold at a loss.
7. Inspect title documents, if any, of property held for investment.
8. Review rental agreements on property and trace indicated amounts to income accounts. Vouch a sample of recorded rent income entries to bank deposit slips.
9. Obtain written representations from the client concerning any pledging of investment assets as collateral.
10. Obtain audited financial statements of joint ventures, investee companies (equity method of accounting), subsidiary companies, and other independent entities in which an investment interest is held.

B. *Intangibles and Related Expenses*

1. Review merger documents for proper calculation of purchased goodwill.
2. Inquire of management about legal status of patents, leases, copyrights and other intangibles.
3. Review documentation of new patents, copyrights, leaseholds and franchise agreements.
4. Vouch recorded costs of intangibles to supporting documentation and canceled check(s), if any.
5. Select a sample of recorded R&D expenses. Vouch to supporting documents for evidence of proper classification.
6. Recalculate amortization of goodwill, patents, and other intangibles, if any.

EXHIBIT 13–5 (*continued*)

C. *Other Assets and Income*
1. Confirm cash surrender value of life insurance with insurance company.
2. Recalculate amounts of prepaid insurance. Vouch premium amounts to policies and canceled checks.
3. Prepare, or have client prepare, a schedule of all prepaid expenses. Vouch recorded amounts to supporting documents and canceled checks. Recalculate prepaid amounts.
4. Review royalty agreements. Reconcile terms of agreements with reports from license holder and trace to the related income accounts. Compare amounts to prior years. Vouch recorded income amounts to bank deposit slip.
5. Prepare, or have client prepare, a schedule of accrued income receivable. Reconcile with general ledger account(s). Recalculate amounts. Vouch to supporting documentation.

TYPES OF MAJOR FRAUD AND MISSTATEMENT

Major losses or manipulations in the area of investments and intangibles can be classified in three categories: (1) theft or diversion of funds—securities, sales proceeds, income receipts; (2) manipulation of accounting values through purchase or lease transactions at inflated prices or by fallacious judgment in valuation of intangibles; and (3) business espionage—the unauthorized use or transmittal of secret processes or methods. The first two of these categories are within the auditor's sphere of interest. However, the third area—business espionage—is generally outside the scope of an independent auditor's concern, although he or she should be alert to obvious indications. Internal auditors may be much more involved in matters of business security and investigations along this line.

Theft, diversion, or unauthorized use of investment securities can occur in several ways. If safekeeping controls are weak, securities may simply be stolen, becoming then a police problem rather than an auditing problem. Somewhat more frequent, however, are diversions such as use of securities as collateral during the year, having them returned for a count, then given back to the creditor without disclosure to the auditor. If safekeeping methods require entry signatures (as at a safe-deposit vault), then the auditor may be able to detect the in-and-out movement. The best chance of discovery is that the creditor will confirm the collateral arrangement. In a similar manner securities might be removed by an officer and sold, then repurchased before the auditor's count. The auditor's record of the certificate numbers should reveal this change since the returned certificates (and their numbers) will not be the same as the ones removed.

Cash receipts from interest, royalties on patent licenses, dividends, and sales proceeds might be stolen. The accounting records might or might not be manipulated to cover the theft. In general this kind of defalcation is in the area of cash receipts control, but since these receipts are usually irregular and infrequent, the cash control system may not be as effective as it is for regular receipts on account. If the income accounts are not manipulated to hide stolen receipts, auditors should find less income in the account than the amount indicated by their audit calculations based on other records such as license agreements or published dividend records. If sales of securities are not recorded, the auditor should be able to notice that securities are missing when he or she tries to inspect or confirm them. If the income accounts have been manipulated to hide stolen receipts, vouching of cash receipts should detect the theft, or vouching may reveal some offsetting debit buried in some other account.

Cash received as a return premium on an insurance policy cancellation may be stolen. The auditor's review of policies and recalculation of prepaid insurance may not catch this irregularity unless the policy in-force status is confirmed. Generally, however, such amounts are not material to the financial statements as a whole, and such policy confirmation is considered an "extended procedure."

Accounting values may be manipulated in a number of ways involving purchases at inflated prices, leases with affiliates, acquisitions of patents for stock given to inventor/promoters, sales to affiliates, and fallacious decisions about amortization. Business history has recorded several cases of nonarm's-length transactions with promoters, officers, directors, and controlled companies (even "dummy" companies) designed to drain the company's resources and/or to fool the auditor. In one case a company sold assets to a dummy purchaser set up by a director in order to bolster sagging income with a gain. The auditor did not know that the purchaser was a shell. All the documents of sale looked in order, and cash sales proceeds had been deposited. The auditor was not informed of a secret agreement by the seller to repurchase the assets at a later time. This situation illustrates a very devious manipulation. All transactions with persons closely associated with the company should be audited carefully with reference to market values, particularly when a nonmonetary transaction is involved (e.g., stock exchanged for patent rights). Sales and leaseback and straight lease transactions with insiders should likewise be audited carefully.

Business espionage is an area that tends to be highly technological and oftentimes outside the scope of an auditor's expertise. Often involved is the divulgence of some trade or technological secret that would aid the competition. The toy industry is particularly sensitive to the problem of keeping new toy product development a secret.

Espionage tends to exist in the eye of the beholder, and if it is really a serious matter, litigation will probably begin. At this point the auditor is most likely to learn of the event and disclosure of the litigation will be appropriate. However, the independent auditor is most interested in timely disclosure of events that could result in material adverse effects on financial position and results of operations. The auditor's duty is to insist on disclosure of information about such events as it becomes known and not to speculate on the future effect of present leaky security. Security problems, as matters of internal control, may be brought to the attention of the client.

REVIEW QUESTIONS

13.1. What sources of evidence would the auditor use to become knowledgeable of a client's investment criteria and related approval and authorization system?

13.2. In an adequate system of internal accounting control, how is the custody of negotiable securities controlled?

13.3. What features in the internal accounting control system are of interest to an auditor whose client conducts an extensive product research and development program?

13.4. What procedures do auditors employ in the audit of investment securities to obtain the names of the issuers, the number of shares held, certificate numbers, maturity value, and interest and dividend rates?

13.5. If the dividends accrued on life insurance policies are not used to reduce premiums, how can the auditor obtain evidence of the amount of accumulated dividends?

13.6. What procedures does the auditor employ to obtain evidence of the cost of investments and of investment gains and losses?

13.7. How does the auditor gather evidence of the propriety of amounts of rent currently expensed and deferred?

13.8. Why is the auditor interested in substantial investment losses occurring early in the period following year-end?

EXERCISES AND PROBLEMS

13.9. Listed below is a selection of items from the internal control questionnaires shown in the chapter. For each one:

a. Identify the control characteristic to which it applies (e.g., segregation of duties—authorization of transactions, access to assets and recordkeeping duties; sound error-checking practices and so on).
b. Specify one compliance test procedure an auditor could use to determine whether the control was operating effectively.
c. Using your business experience, your logic, and/or your imagination, give an example of an error or irregularity that could occur if the control was absent or ineffective.
d. Specify a substantive testing procedure an auditor could use to uncover errors or irregularities, if any, resulting from absence of the control.

(1) Is the accounting department informed of income and expense expectations (relating to investments) in order to control receipts and disbursements?
(2) Does access to the storage place (securities investments) require the presence or signatures of two responsible officers?
(3) Are detailed project records maintained for research and development?

(4) Is the approval of a responsible officer required for write-off or write-down of intangible assets?

13.10. The Hertle Engineering Company depends upon innovation and new product development to maintain its position in the market for drilling tool equipment. The company conducts an extensive research and development program for this purpose, and it consistently charges research and development costs to current operations in accordance with *Statement on Financial Accounting Standards No. 2.*

The company began a project called "Project Able" in January 1978 with the goal of patenting a revolutionary drilling bit design. Work continued until October 1979 when the company applied for a patent. Costs were charged to the research and development expense account in both years, except for the cost of computer program which engineers plan to use in "Project Baker," scheduled to start in December. The computer program was purchased from Computeering, Inc., in January 1979 for $45,000.

Required:

a. Give an audit program for the audit of research and development costs on "Project Able." Assume that you are auditing the company for the first time at December 31, 1979.

b. What evidence would you require for the audit of the computer program which has been capitalized as an intangible asset? As of December 31, 1979, this account has a balance of $40,000 (cost less $5,000 amortized as a part of "Project Able").

13.11. Sorenson Manufacturing Corporation was incorporated on January 3, 1978. The corporation's financial statements for its first year's operations were not examined by a CPA. You have been engaged to examine the financial statements for the year ended December 31, 1979, and your examination is substantially completed.

A partial trial balance of the company's accounts is given below:

SORENSON MANUFACTURING CORPORATION
Trial Balance
At December 31, 1979

	Trial Balance	
	Debit	*Credit*
Cash	$11,000	
Accounts receivable	42,500	
Allowance for doubtful accounts		$ 500
Inventories	38,500	
Machinery	75,000	
Equipment	29,000	
Accumulated depreciation		10,000
Patents	85,000	
Leasehold improvements	26,000	
Prepaid expenses	10,500	
Organization expenses	29,000	
Goodwill	24,000	
Licensing agreement No. 1	50,000	
Licensing agreement No. 2	49,000	

The following information relates to accounts which may yet require adjustment:

1. Patents for Sorenson's manufacturing process were purchased January 2, 1979, at a cost of $68,000. An additional $17,000 was spent in December 1979 to improve machinery covered by the patents and charged to the Patents account. The patents had a remaining legal term of 17 years.
2. On January 3, 1978, Sorenson purchased two licensing agreements which were then believed to have unlimited useful lives. The balance in the Licensing Agreement No. 1 account includes its purchase price of $48,000 and $2,000 in acquisition expenses. Licensing Agreement No. 2 was also purchased on January 3, 1978 for $50,000, but it has been reduced by a credit of $1,000 for the advance collection of 1980 revenue from the agreement.

   In December 1978 an explosion caused a permanent 60-percent reduction in the expected revenue-producing value of Licensing Agreement No. 1, and in January 1980 a flood caused additional damage which rendered the agreement worthless.

   A study of Licensing Agreement No. 2 made by Sorenson in January 1979 revealed that its estimated remaining life expectancy was only ten years as of January 1, 1979.
3. The balance in the Goodwill account includes $24,000 paid December 30, 1978, for an advertising program which it is estimated will assist in increasing Sorenson's sales over a period of four years following the disbursement.
4. The Leasehold Improvement account includes (*a*) the $15,000 cost of improvements with a total estimated useful life of 12 years which Sorenson, as tenant, made to leased premises in January 1978; (*b*) movable assembly line equipment costing $8,500 which was installed in the leased premises in December 1979; and (*c*) real estate taxes of $2,500 paid by Sorenson in which under the terms of the lease should have been paid by the landlord. Sorenson paid its rent in full during 1979. A ten-year nonrenewable lease was signed January 3, 1978, for the leased building which Sorenson used in manufacturing operations.
5. The balance in the Organization Expenses account includes preoperating cost incurred during the organizational period.

Required:

Prepare adjusting entries as necessary. (AICPA adapted)

13.12. As a result of highly profitable operations over a number of years, Eastern Manufacturing Corporation accumulated a substantial investment portfolio. In the examination of the financial statements for the year ended December 31, the following information came to the attention of the corporation's CPA:

1. The manufacturing operations of the corporation resulted in an operating loss for the year.
2. The corporation has placed the securities making up the investment portfolio with a financial institution which will serve as custodian of the securities. Formerly the securities were kept in the corporation's safe-deposit box in the local bank.

Required:

a. List the objectives of the CPA's examination of the Investment account.

b. Under what conditions would the CPA accept a confirmation of the securities on hand from the custodian in lieu of personally inspecting and counting the securities? (AICPA adapted)

13.13. You are in charge of the audit of the financial statements of the Demot Corporation for the year ended December 31. The corporation has had the policy of investing its surplus funds in marketable securities. Its stock and bond certificates are kept in a safe-deposit box in a local bank. Only the president or the treasurer of the corporation has access to the box.

You were unable to obtain access to the safe-deposit box on December 31 because neither the president nor the treasurer was available. Arrangements were made for your assistant to accompany the treasurer to the bank on January 11 to examine the securities. Your assistant has never examined securities that were being kept in a safe-deposit box and requires instructions. Your assistant should be able to inspect all securities on hand in an hour.

Required:

a. List the instructions that you would give to your assistant regarding the examination of the stock and bond certificates kept in the safe-deposit box. Include in your instructions the details of the securities to be examined and the reasons for examining these details.

b. After returning from the bank your assistant reported that the treasurer had entered the box on January 4 to remove an old photograph of the corporation's original building. The photograph was loaned to the local chamber of commerce for display purposes. List the additional audit procedures that are required because of the treasurer's action. (AICPA adapted)

13.14. You are engaged in the audit of the financial statements of the Sandy Core Company for the year ended December 31. Sandy Core Company sells lumber and building supplies at wholesale and retail; it has total assets of $1,000,000 and a stockholders' equity of $500,000.

The company's records show an investment of $100,000 for 100 shares of common stock of one of its customers, the Home Building Corporation. You learn that Home Building Corporation is closely held and that its capital stock, consisting of 1,000 shares of issued and outstanding common stock, has no published or quoted market value.

Examination of your client's cash disbursements record reveals an entry of a check for $100,000 drawn on January 23, 1966, to Mr. Felix Wolfe, who is said to be the former holder of the 100 shares of stock. Mr. Wolfe is president of the Sandy Core Company. Sandy Core Company has no other investments.

Required:

a. List the auditing procedures you would employ in connection with the $100,000 investment of your client in the capital stock of the Home Building Corporation.

b. Discuss the presentation of the investment on the balance sheet, including its valuation. (AICPA adapted)

13.15. During your audit of the 1979 financial statements of Longwood, Inc., you find a new account titled "Miscellaneous Assets." Your examination reveals that in 1979 Longwood, Inc., began investing surplus cash in marketable securities, and the corporation's bookkeeper entered all transactions she believed related to investments in this account. Information summarized from the Miscellaneous Assets account appears below:

LONGWOOD, INC.
Information Summarized from
the Miscellaneous Assets Account
For the Year Ended December 31, 1979

Date 1979		*Folio*	*Debit*	*Credit*
	Compudata Common Stock			
Mar. 31	Purchased 500 shares @ 48	CD	$24,000	
July 31	Received cash dividend of $2 per share	CR		$ 1,000
July 31	Sold 100 shares @ 60	CR		6,000
Nov. 15	Pledged 100 shares as security for $4,000 bank loan payable the following February 15	CR		4,000
Nov. 30	Received 150 shares by donation from stockholder whose cost in 1970 was $10 per share	JE	1,500	
	Standard Atomic Common Stock			
Mar. 31	Purchased 900 shares @ 26	CD	23,400	
June 30	Received dividend ($.25 per share in cash and 1 share Standard Atomic preferred for each 5 shares common owned)	CR		225
	Standard Atomic Preferred Stock			
June 30	Received 180 shares as stock dividend on Standard Atomic common	MEMO		
July 31	Sold 80 shares @ 17	CR		1,360
	Interstate Airlines Bonds (due November 30, 1987, with interest at 6 percent payable May 31 and November 30)			
June 30	Purchased 25 $1,000 bonds @ 102	CD	25,625	
Nov. 30	Received interest due	CR		750
Nov. 30	Accumulated amortization	JE		25
Nov. 30	Sold 25 bonds @ 101	CR		25,250
	Other			
July 31	Sold 40 shares of Longwood, Inc., treasury stock @ 82 (purchased in 1975 at $80 per share—carried at cost)	CR		3,280
Dec. 29	Paid 1980 rental charge on safe-deposit box used for investments	CD	35	
	Totals		$74,560	$41,890

All security purchases include brokers' fees, and sales are net of brokers' fees and transfer taxes when applicable. The fair market values (net of brokers' fees and transfer taxes) for each security as of the 1979 date of each transaction were:

Security	*3/31*	*6/30*	*7/31*	*11/15*	*11/30*
Compudata common	48		60	61¼	62
Standard Atomic common	26	30			
Standard Atomic preferred		16⅔	17		
Interstate Airlines bonds		102			101
Longwood, Inc., common			82		

Required:

a. In columns across the top of a worksheet, write the sources of evidence usually consulted in the audit of investments. In rows down the left margin, write each of the account transactions. Indicate by placing an X in the appropriate column the source (s) of evidence most relevant to audit of the transaction.

b. Prepare adjusting journal entries, if any. (AICPA adapted)

13.16. You were engaged to examine the financial statements of Ronlyn Corporation for the year ended June 30.

On May 1, the corporation borrowed $500,000 from Second National Bank to finance plant expansion. However, due to unexpected difficulties in acquiring the building site, the plant expansion had not begun at June 30. To make use of the borrowed funds, management decided to invest in stocks and bonds; and on May 16, the $500,000 was invested in securities.

Required:

In your audit of investments, how would you—

a. Verify the dividend or interest income recorded?

b. Determine market value?

c. Establish the authority for security purchases? (AICPA adapted)

13.17. **Case: Intercompany and Interpersonal Investment Relations**

You have been engaged to audit the financial statements of Hardy Hardware Distributors, Inc., as of December 31. In your review of the corporate nonfinancial records you have found that Hardy Hardware owns 15 percent of the outstanding voting common stock of Hardy Products Corporation. Upon further investigation you learn that Hardy Products Corporation manufactures a line of hardware goods, 90 percent of which is sold to Hardy Hardware.

Mr. James L. Hardy, president of Hardy Hardware, has supplied you with objective evidence that he personally owns 30 percent of the Hardy Products voting stock, and the remaining 55 percent is owned by Mr. John L. Hardy, his brother and president of Hardy Products. James L. Hardy also owns 20 percent of the voting common stock of Hardy Hardware Distributors, another 20 percent is held by an estate of which James and John are beneficiaries, and the remaining 60 percent is publicly held. The stock is listed on the American Stock Exchange.

Hardy Hardware has consistently reported operating profits greater than the industry average. Hardy Products Corporation, however, has a net return on sales of only 1 percent. The Hardy Products investment has always been reported at cost, and no dividends have ever been paid by the company. During the course of your conversations with the Hardy brothers you learn that you were appointed as auditor because they had had a heated disagreement with the former auditor over the issues of accounting for the Hardy Products investment and the prices at which goods had been sold to Hardy Hardware.

For Discussion:

a. Identify the issues in this situation as they relate to (1) conflicts of interest and (2) controlling influences among individuals and corporations.

b. Should the investment in Hardy Products Corporation be accounted for on the equity method?

c. What evidence should the auditor seek with regard to the prices paid by Hardy Hardware for products purchased from Hardy Products Corporation?

d. What information would you consider necessary for adequate disclosure in the financial statements of Hardy Hardware Distributors?

14

AUDIT OF FIXED ASSETS (WITH EDP APPLICATIONS)

The four objectives of this chapter are to explain with relation to fixed assets and related accounts:

A business approach to objectives concerning existence, valuation, cutoff, accounting principles, compliance, and effectiveness.

Elements of internal accounting control for these accounts and transactions.

Applications of audit procedures with generalized EDP software for gathering evidence.

Types of fraud and misstatement that might occur in these accounts.

The discussion and explanation of these topics and the emphasis on using the computer are intended to enable students to sharpen their awareness of audit objectives, relevant evidence, relevant audit procedures, and the ways a computer can be used to perform them.

An audit of fixed assets involves not only the property, plant, and equipment accounts, but also the accounts for depreciation expense, accumulated depreciation, repairs and maintenance expense, property tax expense, insurance expense, and rental expense. This chapter is coordinated with the EDP illustrations that were given in Chapter 9. An additional objective is to suggest applications of generalized audit software in the context of all other relevant non-EDP auditing procedures.

A BUSINESS APPROACH TO AUDIT OBJECTIVES

The nature and utilization of fixed assets varies widely among companies. A broad business approach provides the auditor a familiarity with the type of assets, related maintenance schedules, and associated expenses that are characteristic of the assets of a particular client. Equally important is the nature of the data processing system for asset records. In this chapter, a computer-oriented data processing system is presumed to exist.

Existence

The auditor must recognize that assets in productive use might not be formally recorded in asset accounts. Leased assets might be recorded only as rental expense. Some recorded assets may not be "fixed" in the meaning of "in productive use"; for example, assets held for future disposal, excess capacity, and unrecorded dispositions. Amounts recorded as assets may, in fact, be repair and maintenance expenses, and amounts expensed may be properly capitalized as fixed assets.

During a preliminary plant tour and in the course of conversational inquiries, the auditor should observe the quantity and size of assets, their location and apparent physical condition, and the activity surrounding them. The auditor should also inquire of executives about the ownership or leasing of property.

Further preliminary evidence of existence may be gained by a review of internal management reports. Typical reports include capital expenditure proposals, capital budgets, construction cost or acquisition cost post-analyses, maintenance and repair reports, reports of sales or retirements, and insurance and property tax analyses. A general awareness of social-political-economic forces may also indicate that certain assets may have been acquired or disposed. For example, newspaper reports of consumer groups' complaints about product quality or safety could have caused management to change production methods and equipment. Ecological controversies could have prompted installation of pollution control equipment. In the case of multinational companies, reports of political unrest in foreign countries may predict problems with future expropriation of assets.

Valuation

The valuation of fixed assets may be affected by events other than the normal calculation of annual depreciation. Market conditions and new technologies may create excess capacity. Thus a company may hold assets for disposal, and these should be reported at estimated realizable values. Some assets, such as land, may have substantially appreciated in value and disclosure of market value may be appropriate. An analysis of recent asset disposals can contribute an historical-based insight on the adequacy of depreciation methods and useful lives adopted for asset depreciation calculations.

Cutoff

Problems of proper cutoff are usually not difficult in the audit of fixed assets and related accounts. The failure to record an asset acquisition in the current year (with recording occurring in the subsequent year) usually amounts to an equal understatement of assets and liabilities, although the effect when the liability is a current liability might be significant. Depreciation expense will be understated, but when the cutoff error involves only one or two weeks, the effect is not likely to be material.

More sensitive cutoff issues surround such events as commitments to purchase assets or enter into acquisitions, or agreements to pledge assets as collateral. Initial awareness of these possibilities may arise from general familiarity with operations. The relevant cutoff date for such events, which may not be recorded in the accounts, is the date marking the end of field work (i.e., the date of the auditor's report respecting all important post-balance sheet date events). Other procedures related to objectives of existence and valuation generally produce sufficient evidence related to important cutoff questions.

Accounting Principles and Disclosure

Matters of accounting principles and disclosure can become quite complex. Accounting for leased property, sale and leasebacks, commitments, borrowing agreements and restrictions, pledges of collateral, methods of depreciation, classification of fixed assets, rental property, assets held for disposal, excess capacity, and other matters are all relevant for disclosure in financial statements and footnotes. The business approach described for the existence, valuation, and cutoff objectives can provide preliminary familiarity with a specific situation, and further evidence can provide the information required for proper accounting treatment and adequate disclosures.

The accounting principle that productive assets should be valued at acquisition cost (including all costs of installation and preparation for use) is important, but it is only one of the family of accounting and disclosure issues related to fixed assets. For example, some assets acquired in nonmonetary exchanges may be accounted for at fair market value since any other "cost" amount might be irrelevant in the circumstances. Some leases of property should be capitalized as if they were purchases. Accounting principles contain criteria related to nonmonetary exchanges[1] and proper circumstances for lease capitalization.[2] The auditor's task is to examine transactions and lease contracts to determine if the facts of the situation fit the accounting principle criteria for fair value accounting or lease capitalization.

Compliance

Compliance with borrowing agreements and with rules and regulations of taxing authorities are of interest to both internal auditors and independent auditors. Such agreements may specify certain types of inspection and maintenance, certain insurance coverage, promptness in making tax

[1] APB *Opinion No. 29*, "Accounting for Nonmonetary Transactions."

[2] FASB *Statement of Financial Accounting Standards No. 13*, "Accounting for Leases."

payments, and restrictions as to movement or disposal. Internal auditors are concerned with the policies and procedures for observing agreements, with records of past observance, and with procedures for assuring future observance.

Independent auditors are equally concerned with the record of observance and also with whatever penalties or sanctions might be imposed as a result of nonobservance. Particular importance may be attached to determining whether title to property has been clouded by failure to pay taxes or to comply with other laws. Knowledge of newsworthy events and of court proceedings may give indications of instances of serious noncompliance with laws or other restrictions.

Effectiveness

Effectiveness is an evaluation objective that is more characteristic of the internal auditor's work than that of the independent auditor. An internal auditor would perform procedures designed to yield evidence about the quality of capital expenditure proposals and budgets, the regularity of maintenance and repair operations, and the post-investment follow-up of performance in comparison to budgets and plans. Internal auditors may perform analyses of presently leased property to determine the economies of outright purchase or vice versa. Other analyses may be made of insurance coverage and rates, valuation for property tax purposes, and controls over disposal of equipment. These tasks are of direct service to management, and while they might be interesting and useful to the independent auditor, they are generally tangential to the main objective of rendering an opinion.

INTERNAL CONTROL

By performing procedures of the review and compliance testing phases of a proper study and evaluation of internal accounting control, the auditor should begin to bring into clearer focus some of the information gained from a business approach. Internal accounting controls over fixed asset and related account transactions are usually not elaborate because most companies do not have a large enough volume of such transactions to merit the cost of a specialized control network. (Exceptions to this generality would include large capital-intensive companies and businesses that rent or lease tangible property such as automobiles, trucks, and trailers.)

Review Phase

Functional responsibilities that should be delegated to separate departments or management levels are:

Planning and approval of capital expenditures;

Data processing of documents evidencing delivery or construction, and payment;

Physical custody and operating responsibility for use of assets; and
Authority to idle, sell, or otherwise take assets out of production.

A flowchart of the system of authorization, custody, and recordkeeping may be constructed in order to explain control over fixed asset transactions. Exhibit 14–1 contains a very general representation of such a control system. The flowchart may be analyzed in conjunction with the internal control questionnaire items (Exhibit 14–2) to give a complete picture of important control features.

EXHIBIT 14–1
General Flowchart: Fixed Asset Transactions

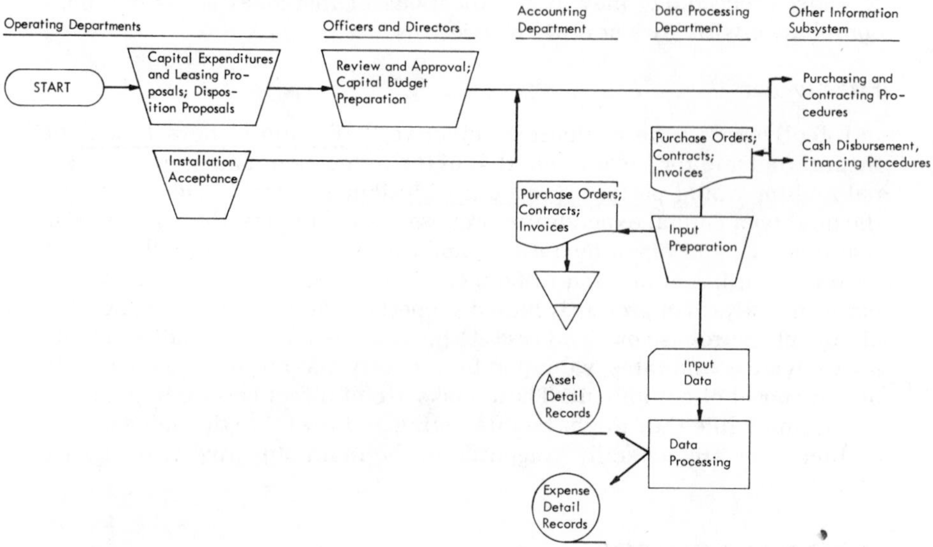

At each point in the flowchart where an explanation of some action is given, the auditor may expect to find documentary evidence. For example:

Operating personnel may prepare analytical proposals.

The directors' minutes and capital budget should contain approvals of expenditures.

Some documentation of installation, acceptance, and readiness should have been prepared.

Orders and approvals for disposal should be in evidence.

The related subsystems for purchasing, cash disbursements, and cash receipts should generate appropriate documentation related to those features of a transaction.

EXHIBIT 14–2

INTERNAL CONTROL QUESTIONNAIRE
FIXED ASSETS AND RELATED ACCOUNTS

1. Are detailed property records maintained for the various units of fixed assets? When were subsidiary records last balanced with general ledger control accounts? (If records are part of an EDP system, complete relevant portions of the EDP Internal Control Questionnaire.)
2. Are capital expenditure and leasing proposals prepared for review and approval by the board of directors or by responsible officers? Describe procedures.
3. When actual expenditures exceed authorized amounts, is the excess approved as in question 2? Describe policy.
4. When was the last physical inspection and inventory? Was it complete?
5. When was the last analysis of insurance coverage? Did it include an appraisal of asset values?
6. When was the last analysis of property tax renditions done?
7. Is there an accounting policy for distinguishing capital additions from repairs and maintenance expenses? Explain, including dollar amount limits.
8. Are memorandum records of leased assets maintained?
9. Is approval of a designated officer or director required for disposal, dismantling, or idling a productive asset? For terminating a lease or rental?
10. Are procedures devised to assure that recording of new assets causes inquiry about accounting for disposal of replaced assets? Describe procedures.
11. Are procedures devised to assure notification to accounting department of asset disposals when there is no replacement? Describe procedures.
12. Is there a uniform policy for assigning depreciation rates, useful lives and salvage values? Describe policy.
13. Describe procedures and analyses performed by internal auditors in the past year.

Notice that the flowchart in Exhibit 14–1 presumes that the transaction and property records are captured on EDP media. Thus some means of reading these records and using the computer are going to be required.

The review of internal accounting control should include a review of computer-based general and applications controls. A selection of questionnaire items for an EDP review is shown in Exhibit 14–3. These items serve the purpose of providing information to the auditor about general controls and application controls. A good design of general controls gives the auditor some comfort that computer operations are well planned and organized. A good set of application controls gives some comfort that material errors may be prevented or detected promptly. The applications controls should be tested for compliance. An auditor can review instructions, sample key-verified cards, observe the use of batch totals, and review error logs for evidential matter concerning the effective operation of computer controls.

EXHIBIT 14–3
Selected Questionnaire Items—EDP General and Application Controls

General Controls

1. Are computer operators or programmers excluded from participating in the input or output control functions?
2. Are programmers excluded from operating equipment?
3. Is there an EDP librarian who is independent of computer operations, systems and programming, and users?
4. Are EDP personnel restricted from initiating, authorizing, or independently processing entries or adjustments to general ledgers or subsidiary ledgers?
5. Is access to the computer room restricted to authorized personnel?
6. Are systems, programs, and data files stored in a fireproof area?
7. Can current files, particularly master files, be reconstructed from files stored in an off-site location?

Application Controls

1. Is conversion of data to machine-readable form done on the basis of up-to-date written instructions?
2. Are important data fields key-verified?
3. Are batch control totals used to reconcile computer-processed data to input control data?
4. Is the EDP department responsible for correcting errors in data arising in EDP operations?
5. Are edit tests used in EDP processing—missing data tests, limit and range tests, check digits, valid codes, proper sequence?
6. Does the computer print an error log?
7. Is computer output reviewed for reasonableness, accuracy, and legibility before distribution to users?

Compliance Tests of Transaction Details

Compliance tests of transaction details are relevant in the case of fixed assets only when the transactions are numerous. When there are only a few major transactions, an audit of all of them will constitute a complete audit of recorded amounts, and testing by sampling will not be necessary. In either event, the auditor's procedures should include an examination of evidential matter in the files. A selection of manual-system-oriented compliance test procedures is given in Exhibit 14–4.

Compliance tests of computer application controls may include the following:

Obtain and read instructions for conversion of data to machine-readable form.

Select a sample of punched cards and inspect them for evidence of key-verification.

Obtain and review check-off sheets showing the proper use of batch control totals.

EXHIBIT 14–4
Audit Program—Selected Compliance Test Procedures

A. *Fixed Assets*
1. Read directors' and other committee minutes and capital budgets for evidence of review and approval of asset acquisitions and disposals.
2. Review the procedures for proposal, approval, analysis, and accounting for leased property.
3. Retrace approved acquisitions and disposals to fixed asset detail records, and:
   a. Determine whether classification is appropriate and whether any capitalized additions should have been expensed as repairs or maintenance.
   b. Vouch asset costs to invoices, contracts, or other supporting documentation.
4. Select a sample* of detail fixed asset records:
   a. Determine whether the records contain mathematical errors.
   b. Vouch additions or disposals to documents indicating proper approval by company officers.
   c. Vouch asset cost to invoices, contracts, or other supporting documents.
5. Select a sample of physical assets in use and trace to detail fixed asset records.

B. *Depreciation*
1. Review the policies and procedures for assigning useful lives and salvage values to assets and for selecting depreciation methods.
2. Select a sample* of asset records:
   a. Determine whether lives, salvage, and methods were assigned in accordance with policy.
   b. Recalculate depreciation expense.
   c. Retrace entries for depreciation expense to general ledger account(s).
3. Select a sample* of asset records and recalculate accumulated depreciation.

C. *Repairs and Maintenance Expense*
1. Prepare, or have client prepare, an analysis of major items of repairs and maintenance and a summary of minor items.
2. For all major items and a sample* of minor items:
   a. Review the charges for approval and correspondence with company policy on capitalization.
   b. Vouch costs to work orders, invoices, contracts, or other supporting documentation.
   c. Determine whether any items expensed should have been capitalized.

* Generalized audit software can be used to select audit samples (random selection or according to the auditor's judgmental criteria) and to perform recalculation of amounts.

Obtain and review error logs and error correction reports.

Prepare and run test data to determine whether programmed edit tests are working properly.

Observe EDP personnel review of output and trace distribution to list(s) of authorized recipients.

Several of the procedures shown in Exhibit 14–4 may be used to audit components of the balance of the fixed asset accounts as well as in the test of transactions for internal control evaluation purposes. The difference is that in the audit of the balance emphasis is placed on condition, existence, and value (cost). In the test of transactions emphasis is placed on errors in connection with such things as lack of approval, mathematical errors, policy errors (e.g., an amount incorrectly expensed rather than capitalized), errors in assigning useful lives, depreciation rates, and salvage values, and the like.

SUBSTANTIVE TESTS OF BALANCES

The construction of an audit program utilizing substantive test procedures should begin with the auditor's explicit recognition of the assertions contained in fixed asset and related expense account records. The assertions can be tested by gathering sufficient, competent evidential matter. Some of the explicit and implicit assertions in fixed assets accounts are:

- All recorded fixed assets are in productive use.
  All asset disposals have been recorded.
  All asset additions have been recorded.
- Repair and maintenance expenses have not been capitalized.
- Asset additions have not been improperly charged to repair and maintenance expense.
- All costs of freight and installation on additions have been capitalized.
- Leases have been capitalized in conformity with FASB *No. 13.*
- Depreciation has been calculated accurately.
- Taxes have been paid or accrued on all taxable asset property.
- Casualty insurance is carried.
- Assets pledged as collateral have not been improperly removed.

The assertions above are not a complete list of all matters of audit interest, but they are illustrative of the types of problems that should be recognized. The next task is to consider the evidence that might support or refute these assertions, and then the auditor can select the most efficient procedures for gathering that evidence. A selection of substantive test procedures is given in Exhibit 14–5.

Recalculation

Mathematical checks are made throughout the internal control examination procedures as a guard against inadvertent error in the accounts. The subsidiary records should be reconciled with the asset control accounts. Expense accounts should be footed. Allocations of insurance premiums and tax assessments and related accruals should be recalculated.

The major set of recalculations involves depreciation provisions and estimates related to disposals and write-offs. Accounting depreciation exists only as a calculated amount, so the audit of it is a recalculation. However, the auditor must first determine by vouching and analysis procedures that the bases for the calculation are accurate (i.e., cost, prior depreciation, useful life and rate, and salvage value). If book and tax methods of depreciation are different, then both will have to be recalculated and the difference considered in connection with amounts of deferred income taxes.

The computer may be used to perform many recalculation procedures. Consider the depreciation calculations. They can be audited 100 percent with the computer in less time than with a manual statistical sampling test. What is required first is that the auditor be satisfied that all the bases for the calculation are accurate. These can be tested by vouching a random sample of records selected by the random selection function of a generalized audit software system. The depreciation formulas may be programmed by the auditor on a specification sheet such as the Calculate-Stratify form shown in the Appendix to Chapter 9. Then running a work file of the client's records on the program will yield audited numbers that are, in effect, a parallel simulation of the recorded depreciation calculations. Discrepancies may be investigated manually on an item-by-item basis.

Physical Observation

Like goods held for sale, tangible assets can be observed and counted (i.e., "inventoried"), although an extensive inventory procedure for fixed assets is generally considered an "extended procedure" to be used only when the internal control system exhibits deficiencies. The procedures A–2 and A–5 shown in Exhibit 14–5 describe the physical observation procedure. In A–5 the assets are inspected and traced to the detail records to ascertain that existing assets are recorded. (For leased assets the tracing may be to lease documents and rental expense records.) In A–2 the recorded assets are inspected in order to determine that they actually exist.

In both procedures, the auditor can make observations on the quantity, quality, condition, and apparent extent of utilization. Assets not in production may have to be classified separately from fixed assets. Obsolete assets may be subject to write-down or write-off.

The computer may be used in two ways in these procedures. Data on the inspected assets (procedure A–5) may be converted to machine-readable form and merged with a work file of detail records in such a way as to identify any absence of recording. As an alternative, a report option selection may call for a printed report of the records purporting to represent the selected assets. (The programmed selection criterion might be an asset identification number.) The selection of detailed asset records (procedure A–2) may be obtained by utilizing the random selection function of a generalized audit software system.

Notice that in these two computer applications the computer is not actually gathering any evidence but is merely assisting the auditor in reading files and selecting items for subsequent manual procedures.

Confirmation

Direct correspondence with independent parties to a fixed asset-related transaction is generally considered an "extended procedure" because most documentary evidence is of the external-internal or formal documents quality. Invoices, contracts, lease agreements, insurance policies, tax notices, canceled checks, and inspection of assets can provide persuasive evidence for audit purposes, and this evidence may be relatively easy to obtain. However, confirmation may be utilized in these situations:

To confirm the terms and status of important leases.
To confirm the in-force status of an insurance policy.
To confirm that title is clear and taxes are paid.

Confirmations may reveal that tangible property has been pledged as collateral for liabilities. Letters addressed to lessors, insurance companies, government officials, and creditors may be used if the auditor feels the need for evidential information of higher persuasive quality than the evidence available in the client's records.

Verbal Inquiry

Questioning of client officers may lead to performance of other procedures. In some cases responses may constitute the only available evidence particularly when the issues concern future commitments, tentative plans to sell assets or to remove them from production, or other actions that are in the planning stage or in early stages of negotiation.

Complete working paper documentation should be kept of inquiries relating to replacement or other dispositions of assets, the pledging of assets as collateral, the accounting treatment of fully depreciated assets, the in-production status of assets, the maintenance of insurance policies in force, the timely payment of any special tax assessments or the fact of any reappraisal of properties for tax purposes, and the maintenance and repair program. Many of these items may not be evidenced anywhere in ordinary accounting records.

Another class of inquiries is directed toward obtaining preliminary information about accounting policies and other matters for disclosure. Responses in this case are usually amenable to corroboration in the records for such things as depreciation methods, the basis of accounting for assets transferred in nonmonetary transactions, methods of accounting for leases, and changes in accounting policies respecting capitalization and depreciation methods. Extensive inquiries about leases may be required because several necessary disclosures relate to future amounts cited in lease agreements but not yet recorded in the rental expense account. These include such items as minimum rental commitments for future years, revenue from existing subleases for future years, and the present value of noncapitalized lease commitments. Other related items include the existence and terms of renewal or purchase options, escalation clauses, guarantees, restrictions on paying dividends, and restrictions on incurring additional debt or further leasing. All leases should be reviewed by the auditor to determine whether the requirements of accounting principles for capitalization have been met by the facts stated in the lease contract documents.

Vouching of Documents

The examination (vouching) of documents generally produces a large portion of the evidence related to fixed asset accounts. Remember that the vouching procedure has been defined as the process of selecting an item in the account records and searching "backward" to find supporting source documents.

In connection with fixed assets the auditor may select fixed asset records and high dollar-value repair and maintenance items for vouching. The random sampling, mathematical limit functions and report selection functions of a generalized audit software system may be employed. Recorded tax and insurance expense items may likewise be selected. However, the purpose for selection of these items is not to test proper internal control and data processing but to audit for evidence of existence, valuation, accounting principles, and cutoff.

Selected asset records may be vouched to invoices, contracts, canceled checks, and other supporting documentation. One important point is to notice any capitalized item that should have been expensed. The vouching of repair and maintenance items to invoices, work orders, and cost records may reveal items expensed that should have been capitalized.

Retracing

The retracing procedure involves finding selected source records and tracing them through the data processing system to entries in the accounts. In connection with the audit of fixed asset accounts the major retracing begins with the directors' authorizations for expenditures and the identification in the capital budget of planned expenditures. This retracing may be carried out during the internal control evaluation or when auditing the asset additions to ascertain whether all authorized additions were indeed acquired. (The findings, however, might be of more interest to an internal auditor than to an independent auditor who does not report on the correspondence of plans to actual events.)

If repair and maintenance work order documents are maintained in a separate file, they may be sampled and traced to the expense account. Misclassifications might then be detected.

EXHIBIT 14–5
Audit Program—Selected Substantive Test Procedures

A. *Fixed Assets*
1. Foot and summarize detail fixed asset subsidiary records and reconcile to general ledger control account(s).*
2. Select a sample* of detail fixed asset records:
   a. Perform a physical observation (inspection) of the assets recorded.
   b. Inspect title documents, if any.
3. Prepare, or have client prepare, a schedule of fixed asset additions and disposals* for the period:
   a. Vouch to documents indicating proper approval,
   b. Vouch costs to invoices, contracts, or other supporting documents,
   c. Determine whether all costs of shipment, installation, testing, and so on have been properly capitalized.
   d. Vouch proceeds (on dispositions) to cash receipts or other asset records.
   e. Recalculate gain or loss on disposition.
   f. Trace amounts to detail fixed asset records and general ledger control account(s).
4. Prepare an analysis of fixed assets subject to investment tax credit for correlation with tax liability audit work.*
5. Observe a physical inventory-taking of the fixed assets, and compare with detail fixed assets records.
6. Obtain written representations from management regarding:
   a. Pledging of assets as security for loans.
   b. Leasing of assets.

B. *Depreciation*
1. Analyze depreciation expense for overall reasonableness with reference to costs of assets and average depreciation rates.
2. Prepare, or have client prepare, a schedule of accumulated depreciation showing beginning balance, current depreciation, disposals, and ending balance. Trace to depreciation expense and asset disposition analyses. Retrace amounts to general ledger account(s).
3. Recalculate depreciation expense for each asset, obtain a total and trace to general ledger account(s).*

C. *Other Accounts*
1. Analyze insurance for adequacy of coverage.
2. Analyze property taxes in detail to determine whether taxes due on assets have been paid or accrued.
3. Recalculate prepaid and/or accrued insurance and tax expenses.
4. Select a sample of rental expense entries.* Vouch to rent/lease contracts to determine whether any leases qualify for capitalization.

* Generalized audit software can be used to (1) foot the detail records maintained on EDP media, (2) select samples, (3) print a report of asset additions and disposals, (4) analyze available investment tax credits, (5) recalculate depreciation expense in detail, and (6) select other samples of expense entries for vouching.

EXHIBIT 14–6

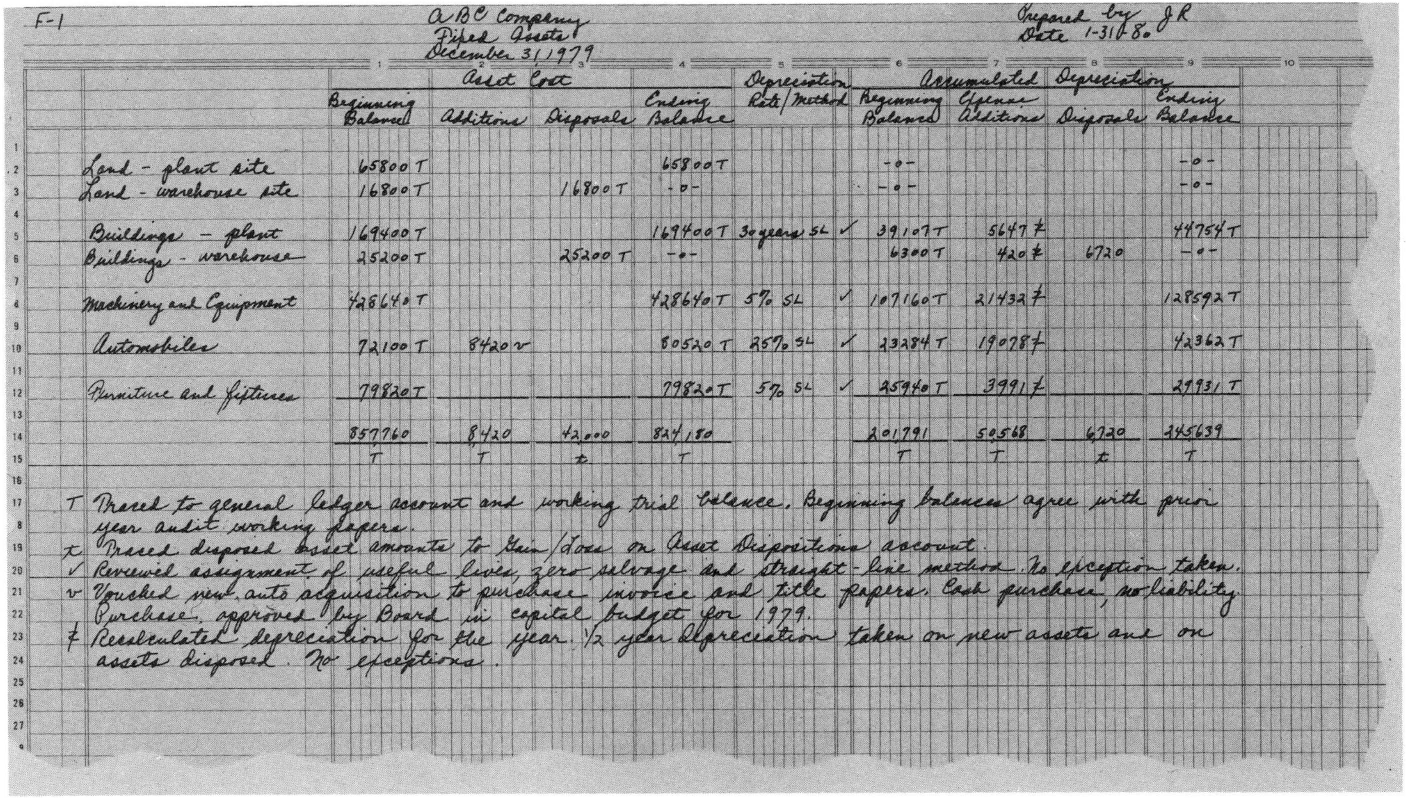

F-1

ABC Company
Fixed Assets
December 31, 1979

Prepared by JR
Date 1-31-80

	Asset Cost: Beginning Balance	Asset Cost: Additions	Asset Cost: Disposals	Asset Cost: Ending Balance	Depreciation Rate/Method		Accumulated Depreciation: Beginning Balance	Accumulated Depreciation: Expense Additions	Accumulated Depreciation: Disposals	Accumulated Depreciation: Ending Balance
Land - plant site	65800 T			65800 T			-0-			-0-
Land - warehouse site	16800 T		16800 T	-0-			-0-			-0-
Buildings - plant	169400 T			169400 T	30 years SL	✓	39107 T	5647 ŧ		44754 T
Buildings - warehouse	25200 T		25200 T	-0-			6300 T	420 ŧ	6720	-0-
Machinery and Equipment	428640 T			428640 T	5% SL	✓	107160 T	21432 ŧ		128592 T
Automobiles	72100 T	8420 v		80520 T	25% SL	✓	23284 T	19078 ŧ		42362 T
Furniture and fixtures	79820 T			79820 T	5% SL	✓	25940 T	3991 ŧ		29931 T
	857760	8420	42,000	824,180			201791	50568	6720	245639
	T	T	t	T			T	T	t	T

T Traced to general ledger account and working trial balance. Beginning balances agree with prior year audit working papers.
t Traced disposed asset amounts to Gain/Loss on Asset Dispositions account.
✓ Reviewed assignment of useful lives, zero salvage and straight-line method. No exception taken.
v Vouched new auto acquisition to purchase invoice and title papers. Cash purchase, no liability. Purchase approved by Board in capital budget for 1979.
ŧ Recalculated depreciation for the year. ½ year depreciation taken on new assets and on assets disposed. No exceptions.

Scanning

Scanning accounts can tip the auditor to such things as unusually large repair items, insurance expenses, tax expenses, or credit entries in these accounts. Anything unusual deserves the auditor's closer attention. The unusually large single items may turn out to be an accounting error, or it may be a clue to items that should be cross-referenced to other accounts. An example is a large insurance premium classified as expense which might be (1) a multiple-year premium, part of which should be deferred; or (2) new insurance on an expensive new asset, which should show up in the asset account.

Scanning may be performed very easily by the computer. Quantified limit criteria and nonnegativity criteria may be programmed. A report of items for further vouching may then be printed.

Analysis of Interrelationships

The primary account relationships are those between asset accounts and expense accounts. Each major asset item should have associated tax and insurance expenses, and conversely each such expense item should be related to an asset or group of assets. The selection of asset and expense records for vouching provides the auditor opportunity to take each item and find its related item in the other accounts. With this procedure the auditor might find assets that are not insured or with taxes unpaid, or the auditor might find insurance and taxes paid on assets that do not exist or have been recorded improperly. Some unrecorded sales or abandonments may thus be discovered. Relating the level of expense and the detail records for repair and maintenance to recorded assets may also reveal assets that have been abandoned or sold.

A sample working paper showing the results of an audit of fixed assets is illustrated in Exhibit 14–6.

TYPES OF MAJOR FRAUD AND MISSTATEMENT

Simple theft of assets and the abstraction of the proceeds of sales of assets relate to matters of internal control and existence. Adequate procedures to inspect and observe assets should reveal material thefts and the failure to record sales of assets properly.

More difficult to detect are practices of purchasing personnel accepting kickbacks from contractors, suppliers, and lessors in consideration of business directed their way. Such practices are undesirable, but since they may not enter the client's accounting records, they are hard to detect. The point for the auditor to watch for is asset costs that are in excess of market prices because of sellers' need to recover the kickback. Such assets may be overvalued in the accounts.

Even more subtle variants are the purchase or lease of assets, or purchase of insurance from companies controlled by insiders (officers, directors, purchasing agents), or from the insider individually. Such transactions may involve prices that are not the same as market determined prices, and disclosure should be made in footnotes to financial statements. At worst, such events as the sham sale of an asset to create a gain in order to bolster income or the siphoning of cash through overcharges can cause material misstatements in financial statements and reports. (The inherent accounting assumption is that transaction data reflect market prices determined in "arm's-length" bargaining transactions.) Internal auditors would be very interested in these types of fraud because they are contrary to managerial policies and criteria of efficiency and effectiveness.

GENERALIZED SOFTWARE AND FIXED ASSET APPLICATION

This chapter was organized to serve two purposes—to cover the techniques and procedures for auditing fixed asset and related accounts, and to suggest some applications of generalized audit software. In this chapter two things should be clear:

Generalized software applications may constitute a relatively small, although important, portion of all audit work on a group of accounts, and

Generalized software can *assist* in the performance of audit procedures (e.g., sample selection), but it can *perform* only a limited amount of auditing (e.g., depreciation recalculations).

The computer makes no decisions that are not carefully defined and programmed by the auditor. In fact, the examples of computer applications show the computer to be a useful audit assistant dependent on the auditor's professional judgments.

REVIEW QUESTIONS

14.1. What accounts are typically grouped in an audit of fixed assets?

14.2. In determining the *existence* of fixed assets, how might the auditor obtain preliminary evidence?

14.3. Explain why a fixed asset account may not properly reflect fixed assets "in productive use."

14.4. In fixed asset management, which functional responsibilities should be delegated to separate departments or management levels?

14.5. What is the difference in emphasis of the audit of the fixed asset balance and the audit of transactions relating to fixed assets?

14.6. Explain the major recalculations performed in an audit of fixed assets.

14.7. When might auditors utilize *confirmation* in their audit of fixed assets? When might they conduct an extensive inventory of fixed assets?

14.8. Why is verbal inquiry important in an audit of fixed assets? What verbal evidence should be documented?

14.9. What unusual transactions would the auditor be looking for in the scanning of fixed asset transactions?

14.10. Identify some major types of fraud and material misstatement related to fixed asset accounts.

EXERCISES AND PROBLEMS

14.11. Listed below is a selection of items from the internal control questionnaires shown in the chapter. For each one:

a. Identify the control characteristic to which it applies (e.g., segregation of duties—authorization of transactions, access to assets and recordkeeping duties; sound error-checking practices, and the like).

b. Specify one compliance test procedure an auditor could use to determine whether the control was operating effectively.

c. Using your business experience, your logic, and/or your imagination, give an example of an error or irregularity that could occur if the control was absent or ineffective.

d. Specify a substantive testing procedure an auditor could use to uncover errors or irregularities, if any, resulting from absence of the control.

(1) When actual expenditures on fixed assets exceed authorized amounts, is the excess approved by the board of directors or by responsible officers?

(2) Is there a policy for distinguishing capital additions from repairs and maintenance expenses?

(3) Is there a uniform policy for assigning depreciation rates, useful lives, and salvage values?

(4) Are important data fields prepared for EDP input key-verified?

(5) Are batch control totals used to reconcile computer-processed data to input control data?

14.12. While auditing an urban bus company in a city of 500,000 population, you encounter the following situation:

1. You have seen an authorization for the purchase of five engines to replace the engines in five buses.
2. The cost of the old engines was removed from property and that of the new engines properly capitalized. The work was done in the company garage.
3. You find no credits for salvage nor for the sale of any scrap metal at any time during the year. You have been in the garage and did not see the old engines.
4. The accountant is also treasurer and office manager. She is an authorized check signer and has access to all cash receipts. Upon inquiry she says she does not recall the sale of the old engines nor of any scrap metal.

Required:

Assuming that the engines were sold as scrap, outline all steps which this fact would cause you to take in connection with your audit. Give consideration to steps beyond those related directly to this one item. (AICPA adapted)

14.13. You have been engaged to make an audit of the financial records of a new client, the ABC Manufacturing Corporation, for its fiscal year ended December 31. Among the fixed assets group are accounts "Land and Buildings," with a balance of $1,007,000, and "Reserve for Depreciation, Land and Buildings," with a balance of $301,000.

The president informs you that "The land and factory were donated by Grand City to the ABC Manufacturing Corporation three years ago. This property had been purchased by Grand City a few months earlier for $1,000,000. ABC Manufacturing Corporation will get title to the donated property seven years from now, provided the average weekly payroll numbers a minimum of 200 each calendar year. The corporation intends to meet these provisions."

List the procedures you would follow in auditing these accounts. (AICPA adapted)

14.14. In connection with a recurring examination of the financial statements of the Louis Manufacturing Company for the year ended December 31, you have been assigned the audit of the Manufacturing Equipment, Manufacturing Equipment—Accumulated Depreciation, and Repairs to Manufacturing Equipment accounts. Your review of Louis's policies and procedures has disclosed the following pertinent information:

1. The Manufacturing Equipment account includes the net invoice price plus related freight and installation costs for all of the equipment in Louis's manufacturing plant.
2. The Manufacturing Equipment and Accumulated Depreciation accounts are supported by a subsidiary ledger which shows the cost and accumulated depreciation for each piece of equipment.
3. An annual budget for capital expenditures of $1,000 or more is prepared by the budget committee and approved by the board of directors. Capital expenditures over $1,000 which are not included in this budget must be approved by the board of directors and variations of 20 percent or more must be explained to the board. Approval by the supervisor of production is required for capital expenditures under $1,000.
4. Company employees handle installation, removal, repair, and rebuilding of the machinery. Work orders are prepared for these activities and are subject to the same budgetary control as other expenditures. Work orders are not required for external expenditures.

Required:

a. Cite the major objectives of your audit of the Manufacturing Equipment, Manufacturing Equipment—Accumulated Depreciation, and Repairs of Manufacturing Equipment accounts. Do not include in this listing the auditing procedures designed to accomplish these objectives.

b. Prepare the portion of your audit program applicable to the review of current-year additions to the Manufacturing Equipment account. (AICPA adapted)

14.15. Hardware Manufacturing Company, a closely held corporation, has operated since 1959 but has not had its financial statements audited. The company now plans to issue additional capital stock expected to be sold to outsiders and wishes to engage you to examine its current transactions and render an opinion on the financial statements for the year ended December 31.

The company had expanded from one plant to three plants and has frequently acquired, modified, and disposed of all types of equipment. Fixed assets have a net book value of 70 percent of total assets and consist of land and buildings, diversified machinery and equipment, and furniture and fixtures. Some property was acquired by donation from stockholders. Depreciation was recorded by several methods using various estimated lives.

Required:

a. May you confine your examination solely to current-year transactions as requested by this prospective client whose financial statements have not previously been examined? Why?

b. Prepare an audit program for the January 1 opening balances of the Land, Building and Equipment, and Accumulated Depreciation accounts at Hardware Manufacturing Company. You need not include tests of current transactions in your program. (AICPA adapted)

14.16. *Part A:* During the course of your audit of Presto Gadgets, Inc., you found the following transaction recorded in the general journal:

Investment in Electro Enterprises common stock	65,000	
Accumulated depreciation—Gear machine, model Y ..	25,000	
Gear machine, model Y		90,000

Explanation: To record exchange of fixed assets for 10,000 shares of Electro common stock.

In a conversation with the treasurer, you are told that the gear machine, model Y, was a fixed asset and that depreciation was recorded to the date of the exchange. The treasurer said that this exchange was a "better deal" than selling the machine outright in the used equipment market where it would probably have brought about $70,000, because Electro's common shares were worth $7.25 each.

Required:

a. What corroborating evidence should you seek by (1) other inquiries, (2) vouching, (3) recalculation, (4) observation, (5) confirmation, and (6) analysis of interrelationships. Explain the purpose of each item of evidence so gathered.

b. Assume that $7.25 per share is a verifiable price for the Electro common stock. Is the Presto journal entry correct? What adjustment, if any, should be made?

Part B: Assume that instead of exchanging its asset for Electro common stock, Presto received from Electro a similar asset (gear machine, model X) and $20,000 in cash in exchange for the gear machine, model Y. The exchange was recorded in Presto's accounts as follows:

Gear machine, model X	45,000	
Cash	20,000	
Accumulated depreciation—Gear machine model Y...	25,000	
Gear machine, model Y		90,000

The treasurer has told you that this was a "good deal" because the model X machine would cost $60,000 in the used equipment market.

Required:

a. What evidence should you obtain about the model X machine?

b. Assume that the $60,000 is a verified market value for the model X machine. Is the Presto journal entry correct? What adjustment, if any, should be made?

14.17. Rivers, CPA, is the auditor for a manufacturing company with a balance sheet that includes the caption "Property, Plant and Equipment." Rivers has been asked by the company's management if audit adjustments or reclassifications are required for the following material items that have been included or excluded from "Property, Plant and Equipment."

1. A tract of land was acquired during the year. The land is the future site of the client's new headquarters which will be constructed in the following year. Commissions were paid to the real estate agent used to acquire the land, and expenditures were made to relocate the previous owner's equipment. These commissions and expenditures were expensed and are excluded from Property, Plant and Equipment.
2. Clearing costs were incurred to make the land ready for construction. These costs were included in Property, Plant and Equipment.
3. During the land clearing process, timber and gravel were recovered and sold. The proceeds from the sale were recorded as other income and are excluded from Property, Plant and Equipment.
4. A group of machines was purchased under a royalty agreement which provides royalty payments based on units of production from the machines. The cost of the machines, freight costs, unloading charges, and royalty payments were capitalized and are included in Property, Plant and Equipment.

Required:

a. Describe the general characteristics of assets, such as land, buildings, improvements, machinery, equipment, fixtures, and so on that should normally be classified as Property, Plant and Equipment, and identify audit objectives in connection with the examination of "Property, Plant and Equipment." *Do not discuss specific audit procedures.*

b. Indicate whether each of the above items numbered 1 to 4 requires one or more audit adjustments or reclassifications, and explain why such adjustments or reclassifications are required or not required. (AICPA adapted)

Organize your answer as follows:

Item Number	*Is Audit Adjustment or Reclassification Required?* Yes or No	*Reasons Why Audit Adjustment or Reclassification Is Required or Not Required*

15

AUDIT OF LIABILITIES, OWNERS' EQUITY, CONTINGENCIES, AND RELATED EXPENSES

The subject matter of this chapter is broad—covering the liability and equity side of the balance sheet with some consideration of major expenses related thereto. The four objectives of the chapter are to provide explanations of the following with relation to liabilities, owners' equity, contingencies, and related expenses:

A business approach to audit objectives concerning existence, valuation, cutoff, accounting principles, compliance, and effectiveness.

Elements of internal accounting control for these accounts and events.

Applications of audit procedures for gathering evidence.

Types of fraud and misstatement that might occur in these accounts and in contingency conditions.

The discussion and explanation of each of these four topics are intended to enable students to sharpen their awareness of audit objectives, relevant evidence, relevant audit procedures, and applications of general audit methodology.

When shifting attention from the asset side of the balance sheet to the liability side, the auditor finds that several aspects of liability, equity, and related expense accounts have already been encountered. The systematic double-entry method of accounting causes these connections. For example, accounts payable were encountered in connection with auditing purchases, notes payable in connection with confirming bank balances, warranty and guarantee liabilities in connection with the inventory-production quality control audit procedures, long-term debt in connection with assets pledged as collateral, and debt restriction disclosures in connection with working capital accounts.

Most programs used in audit field work contain separate sections of procedures applicable to accounts and notes payable, to long-term debt, and to capital stock and other equity accounts. Most often, however, related expenses, dividends, and important items for disclosure are audited along with the related balance sheet accounts.

The account grouping of liabilities, equities, contingencies, and related expenses is very broad. In addition to the usual accounts and dollar balances, there are more supplementary disclosure topics that may not be actually recorded in accounts than there are in other audit areas. The discussion and explanation that follows does not seek to cover every minor account in detail. Major liability, equity, and related expense accounts are emphasized.

A BUSINESS APPROACH TO AUDIT OBJECTIVES

A broad-based business overview is especially useful in the area of liabilities and equities. These accounts and the events associated with them create a wide variety of supplementary footnote disclosures. Such disclosures frequently involve data that are not reduced to summary numbers and entered in accounts in debit-credit form. Examples include disclosures of stock options granted to employees, details of debt agreements and restrictions, and information about lines of credit. Contracts, documents, correspondence and purchase commitments, pension plans, bond indentures, and so forth may be dispersed among various offices and officers instead of being centralized in accounting files. Hence an overview can contribute to the auditor's ability to perceive problem areas and to ask the right questions.

Existence

The business organizational form will dictate many of the auditor's procedures. While most equity transactions are similar in nature, the accounting for them differs as among corporations, partnerships, trade associations, mutual insurance companies, and other types of companies. The type of organization will lead the auditor to the appropriate corporate charter, partnership agreement, or other chartering document for details of the organization and its basic financial structure.

The auditor should learn about the concentration of ownership or managerial control (or lack thereof) in partners, certain stockholders, officers, directors, or trustees. The goals of persons in control of the organization are relevant background information for the auditor. Differing events and accounting problems may be present depending on whether high-level goals include cash flow criteria, stock price attention, maximization of short-run profit or long-run profit, or other objectives that signify success in the eyes of the persons in control.

The auditor should be familiar with the officers and directors, including their principal occupations and employer and any transactions they, or organizations controlled by them, may have had with the client company.

Oftentimes directors are bank officers, underwriters, or officers in related supplier or customer companies. These other companies may interact with the audit client in connection with loans, stock offerings, or as sellers or buyers of goods and services in the ordinary course of business. Transactions with such persons and/or their associated organizations are generally sensitive matters that may require careful disclosure and careful consideration in the performance of subsequent evidence-gathering procedures.

A knowledge of the client's capital structure must be obtained. A brief review of financial statements will usually suffice to tell the auditor of long-term debt, preferred stock, convertible securities, classes of common stock, warrants, options, and other equity classifications. The corporate charter, amendments to the charter, minutes of directors' and stockholders' meetings, loan indentures, and other similar official records may be read to substantiate details of the capital structure.

Questions should be asked about executive and employee compensation and retirement plans. Bonus and stock option plans for executives are matters for disclosure, and they can present complex evidential and accounting problems. Written explanations of the plans should be obtained for review. Likewise, information about pension plan arrangements should be obtained. A description of the plan, of any changes during the year (as to coverage, benefits, or actuarial assumptions), and of the arrangements for management of the plan (by the client or by a trustee) should be obtained for the working papers. The auditor may need an actuarial consultant for special-purpose audit procedures later in the audit engagement.

The nature of the industry, the company, the product(s), and the marketing practices are all of interest in terms of a broad overview. Different industries have different peculiarities of which the auditor should be aware in a general way. For example, textile companies typically engage in factoring accounts receivable; heavy equipment industries often finance asset purchases with equipment trust bonds.

The product characteristics and marketing practices can also create accounts and events of interest. Products sold with warranty or service guarantees create related liabilities. Construction contracting can create unbilled revenue amounts. Installment selling usually creates deferred profit amounts.

For reasons similar to those discussed in Chapters 11 and 13, the auditor should review and understand the cash management system and the company's cash position during the year and at the end of the year. The existence of a "tight" cash position could be indicated by slowness in paying regular trade accounts, heavy short-term borrowings, and reduction or elimination of dividends. Cash management reports should be reviewed for any of these events, and an eye should be kept open to the possibilities of preferred dividends in arrears and debt obligation defaults. In extreme cases the solvency of the business and the auditor's going-concern assumption may be in doubt.

A wide variety of other inquiries and reviews may be conducted. Many corporate offices and officers are likely to have knowledge of financing arrangements and plans that are not matters of accounting record. Included among these are the treasurer's familiarity with lines of credit and their terms, the purchasing agent's familiarity with commitments, the accounting and legal department personnel's familiarity with tax returns and the status of IRS examinations, and legal counsel's familiarity with pending litigation.

Valuation and Cutoff

The valuation of monetary liabilities is not difficult. The audit problem is one of determining whether all the direct monetary liabilities are known, recorded, and properly valued in the financial statements.

The consideration of relative audit risk implies that assets are more likely to be overstated than understated, and liabilities are more likely to be understated (or even omitted) than overstated. For assets it is generally sufficient to audit carefully the recorded amounts, but for liabilities such an approach would not enable the auditor to find any *unrecorded* liabilities. Thus a general set of procedures known as the *search for unrecorded liabilities* is important, and the objective served by such procedures is a mixture of existence, valuation, and cutoff.

The search for unrecorded liabilities may take a variety of procedural forms ranging from standard bank confirmations sent to banks where business has supposedly been terminated, to tests of cutoff for purchase transactions, and including the attorney's written representation letter. These procedures and others have been explained in previous chapters or are explained later in this chapter. At this stage, however, the point is that they can be packaged into a program for the search for unrecorded liabilities. In a broader view, the auditor should be alert to situations that may harbor unrecorded liabilities. Examples of such situations would include the prevalence of poor control over recordkeeping for purchasing-receiving transactions, the existence of discount liability on discounted notes or accounts receivable sold with recourse, and the event of changes in quality control standards or warranty terms.

Some liabilities and deferred credits are not monetary and are subject to valuation uncertainties. Product warranty and guarantee liability is, strictly speaking, a liability contingent on product defects, but accountants ordinarily consider the liability one that is regular, recurring, and subject to estimation. The auditor is concerned with the basis for the estimate, hence interested in the product performance history, quality control criteria, and future costs of replacement parts or services.

Some other credit-balance amounts may simply be mathematical calculations based upon some underlying basic event. Examples are deferred installment sale profit and deferred income taxes. Knowledge of selling practices and of differences in accounting and tax basis records will lead the auditor to further detailed procedures for auditing the deferrals.

Pension plan liabilities are based on actuarial assumptions, and these calculations of liability may best be reviewed by an actuarial consultant. Relevant accounting principle criteria are contained in APB *Opinion No. 8*.[1]

Various contingencies and commitments may present difficult auditing problems that range from events of known amounts but uncertain future contingencies (e.g., discounted notes or accommodation endorsements), to events of known occurrence but uncertain amount (e.g., litigation involving unsettled monetary damages). Adequate disclosure of amounts and the contingent events and their probabilities is the auditor's goal, and all information that sheds light on these factors is useful.[2]

Valuation in owner equity accounts may be affected by noncash capital contributions. In such cases the fair value of assets received or of securities given must be ascertained. Similar valuation problems arise out of the granting of compensatory stock options and the issuance of stock warrants attached to debt instruments. In all these cases, market values of the securities must be determined and accounted for properly. The criteria in APB *Opinion No. 14*,[3] *No. 25*,[4] and *No. 29*[5] are all relevant to the auditing decisions.

Accounting Principles and Disclosure

Accounting principles and disclosure issues fall mainly into two categories: (1) measurement and classification and (2) detailed and specific disclosures. When information concerning existence, valuation, and cutoff has been gathered, most of the raw material for proper measurement and classification is also available.

The most complex matter of classification arises when a business is in poor financial condition, bordering on collapse, bankruptcy, or reorganization. When such events are probable, traditional accounting theory tied to the going-concern concepts breaks down. One result is effectively to void the concept of historical cost measurement for assets. Another effect is that the current versus long-term classification of liabilities becomes clouded, and the seniority features of debt and the preferences in liquidation of preferred stock become more critical. Under some conditions all liabilities may become due immediately, and debt that was once considered long-term may suddenly be current. Dividends on preferred stock may be in arrears. In such cases auditors may still give a report, but they must be careful about stating the invalidity of the going-concern concept and about making full disclosure of knowable contingencies.

Detailed and specific disclosures are required in a number of areas related to liabilities and owner equity. Many of these requirements are contained in a variety of APB *Opinions*, and many others are contained in

[1] "Accounting for the Cost of Pension Plans."

[2] FASB *No. 5*, "Accounting for Contingencies."

[3] "Accounting for Convertible Debt and Debt Issued with Stock Purchase Warrants."

[4] "Accounting for Stock Issued to Employees."

[5] "Accounting for Nonmonetary Transactions."

accounting series releases and in other SEC rules and regulations. The SEC entered the disclosure arena actively in the early 1970s and has in many instances required disclosure of information that had not been required by preexisting accounting principles. Both the SEC and APB-FASB sources must be familiar ground to the auditor in order that he or she may be aware of the required and recommended disclosure details.

Since this textbook is primarily concerned with professional auditing and secondarily concerned with accounting issues, the details of accounting disclosure principles are not discussed as they would be in an accounting textbook. Below, however, is a condensed list of items for supplementary disclosure with references to accounting principles sources. References to SEC requirements are not given, but the subject of reporting to the SEC is recommended as suitable for additional study with a text specifically devoted to the subject.

Leases and lease commitments (FASB *No. 13*).

Deferred income taxes (APB *Opinions No. 11, No. 23,* and FASB *No. 9*).

Pension plans (APB *Opinion No. 8*).

Contingencies and executory contracts (ARB chapter 50 and FASB *No. 5*).

Contracts—construction, fixed fee, defense (ARB *No. 43,* Chapters 11–A, 11–B, and 11–C; ARB *No. 45*).

Stockholders' equity—capital structure, preferred stock, changes, restrictions, options (APB *Opinions No. 6, No. 10, No. 12, No. 15, No. 25,* ARB *No. 43,* Chapter 13–B, ARB *No. 46*).

Early extinguishment of debt (APB *Opinion No. 26,* and FASB *No. 4*).

Nonmonetary transactions (APB *Opinion No. 29*).

Proposed business combinations (APB *Opinion No. 16*).

Accounting changes (APB *Opinion No. 20*).

Translation of foreign currencies (FASB *No. 8*).

Accounting by debtors and creditors for troubled debt restructurings (FASB *No. 15*).

Compliance

Matters of compliance related to liabilities and owner equity fall into two categories: (1) private contractual agreements and (2) public laws, rules, and regulations. In this latter category compliance with various taxation statutes are relevant, including those related to sales and excise taxes, payroll taxes, and income taxes. Sales and excise tax liabilities (and the related expense amounts) can be material and important. For example, the excise taxes collected on gasoline and tires runs into the hundreds of million dollars for large oil companies and tire manufacturing companies. In local retail outlets similar collections and remittances for general sales taxes and various excise taxes are dictated by local, state, and federal law. An employer has similar responsibilities to withhold and remit social security and income taxes from employees' pay.

Income tax compliance is important for every company. An auditor is responsible for ascertaining the accurate measurement of the tax liability, and in this respect the auditor should determine that all taxable income is included and that all deductions are lawful. In this audit area, the auditor may see opportunities for tax savings and can bring these to the attention of the client. However, such advice should be reviewed with persons on the tax staff if the auditor does not have considerable tax expertise.

The auditor should be familiar with state laws governing legal capital requirements, dividends, and constraints on treasury stock transactions. Such laws vary among states. Also relevant in the compliance context is the client's observance of the corporate charter and its own bylaws. These documents generally contain statements of the type of business the corporation is licensed for, the classes and number of shares of authorized stock, and provision for notice of stockholder meetings and certain transactions of which the stockholders must approve (e.g., election of directors, appointment of auditors).

In the area of securities regulation the federal securities acts must be observed in connection with offering and trading securities in interstate commerce. Also, most states have securities registration laws governing intrastate offerings. Auditors are usually involved closely in the preparation of documents filed with the SEC and state regulatory agencies. Many CPA firms have auditors who are trained as specialists in these laws, and these persons are responsible for technical compliance with many complex provisions of the law.

In the area of private contractual agreements, debt indentures and trust agreements should be studied by the auditor. These documents generally contain restricting specifications involving pledge of assets, dividend payment restrictions, working capital requirements, and other items that define the responsibilities of the debtor. If all or part of an agreement is being violated, the debt may be accelerated, the interest rate may increase, or some other adverse event may be forthcoming. The auditor should include among his or her audit procedures directions to compare financial data with the terms of restricting covenants.[6]

Likewise the terms of securities should be examined for an understanding of stock preferences, dividend requirements, conversion rights, and the terms of warrants and options. When auditing a partnership, the partnership agreement contract should be reviewed for provisions as to salaries, profit sharing, and other terms and conditions. In some large partnerships where some partners are limited, silent, or not involved in management, strict observance of the partnership agreement is very important.

Pension and option plans and union contracts are among other contractual agreements that warrant close attention. Benefits, rights, job classifications, wage rates, and obligations to withhold union dues should be reviewed and correlated with related liabilities and unfunded past service pension costs. Data from these documents are also relevant for the

[6] Oftentimes an audit engagement will provide for a special report, addressed to the creditor(s), on compliance with restrictive covenants.

audit understanding of related pension, compensation, and payroll costs and expenses.

Effectiveness

There are many avenues for analyses in the area of capital management, ranging from lease-or-buy decisions for fixed assets to tax planning. Cash management is one area of financial analysis that can have an impact on several categories of debt and equity capital. Cash budgeting can reveal seasonal needs for short-term borrowing, and coordinated capital budgets can show needs for long-term financing through debt or stock issues. Even when a comprehensive system of cash and capital management is not in use, special-purpose studies may be performed to support important decisions. Internal auditors may frequently find themselves with assignments to evaluate the economics of various financing alternatives.

On an ongoing basis management should provide a system for monitoring compliance with existing debt indenture agreements. Similarly, such liabilities (and associated expenses) of warranties and guarantees and pension plans should be analyzed periodically for comparison to forecast expectations. If an independent auditor finds that management reporting and awareness in these areas are deficient or nonexistent, special attention will be warranted in more detailed subsequent auditing procedures.

Tax planning is an important area in financial management. When extensive needs are perceived, the auditor may properly recommend that the client seek to employ an expert or engage a tax consultant for services that go beyond the scope of the auditor's duties.

Many management advisory services engagements can also stem from the auditor's familiarity with a client's capital structure, the goals of management, and the system for effecting those goals. When opportunities for consulting benefits involve complex problems that go beyond the auditor's principal task of attesting to financial statements, the auditor may suggest that the client seek help from management advisory service consultants.

INTERNAL CONTROL

In the account grouping of liabilities and owner equity, internal accounting control systems and procedures may be classified three ways, depending upon the volume and nature of transactions:

1. *Accounts payable and notes payable.* Internal control systems and procedures are generally fairly elaborate with document authorization, recordkeeping, and custody responsibilities designed to handle numerous transactions.

2. *Derivative liabilities, for example, sales and excise taxes, income taxes, payroll taxes.* These transactions generally are controlled within the system that controls the basic transactions from which the liabilities are derived. For example, the sales transaction control system, the tax

planning function, and the payroll system essentially control the related liabilities for sales and excise taxes, income taxes, and payroll taxes.

3. *Long-term debt and capital stock.* Transactions in these accounts are generally few in number and large in amount and may be handled on a special event basis rather than as a part of an elaborate system of procedures. Oftentimes stockholder records are under the control of independent registrars, transfer agents, and dividend disbursing agents.

As a practical matter questionnaires are generally relied upon heavily to analyze internal control over most liability and equity transactions. However, for more elaborate control systems flowchart descriptions may be quite useful.

Review Phase

Even in cases where the system of internal control procedures is not elaborate, the independent auditor is still interested in the existence of satisfactory control that provides for:

A plan of organization that assigns high-level responsibility for review and approval of major financing transactions,

A system of accounting data processing that is independent of the review and approval level, and

A system of accounting review to check for errors in data processing.

In the area of accounts and notes payable these features may be bureaucratized to a large extent. For infrequent debt and equity transactions the system may not be especially well defined.

Accounts and Notes Payable Procedures. Exhibit 15–1 contains features discussed in Chapter 12 relating to purchases, accounts payable, and cash disbursements. Parts of Exhibit 15–1 are a combination of elements of the purchasing system and the cash disbursement system. Notice that the essential characteristic of the system is the separation of authorization and approval to initiate a transaction from the responsibility for recordkeeping.

The authorization documents may be multicopy and may pass through several departments as in the case for materials purchases. On the other hand the authorizations may be less formal and nonstandardized as may be the case with loans or purchases of some services (e.g., consultants' studies). Whatever specific forms, documents, or procedures are used, the independent auditor would consider a system well controlled if for every transaction that created a liability there was an initial general or specific written authorization on file. To the extent that authorizing documents are missing, additional audit work will have to be performed.

Recordkeeping control procedures should exist to double-check the coding and classification of costs and expenses represented by account and note payable obligations. Cash disbursement procedures should be controlled in such a way as to ensure proper payment of all liabilities and duplicate payment of none. (Refer to the discussion of cash disbursement procedures in Chapter 12.)

EXHIBIT 15–1
General Flowchart: Accounts and Notes Payable Procedures

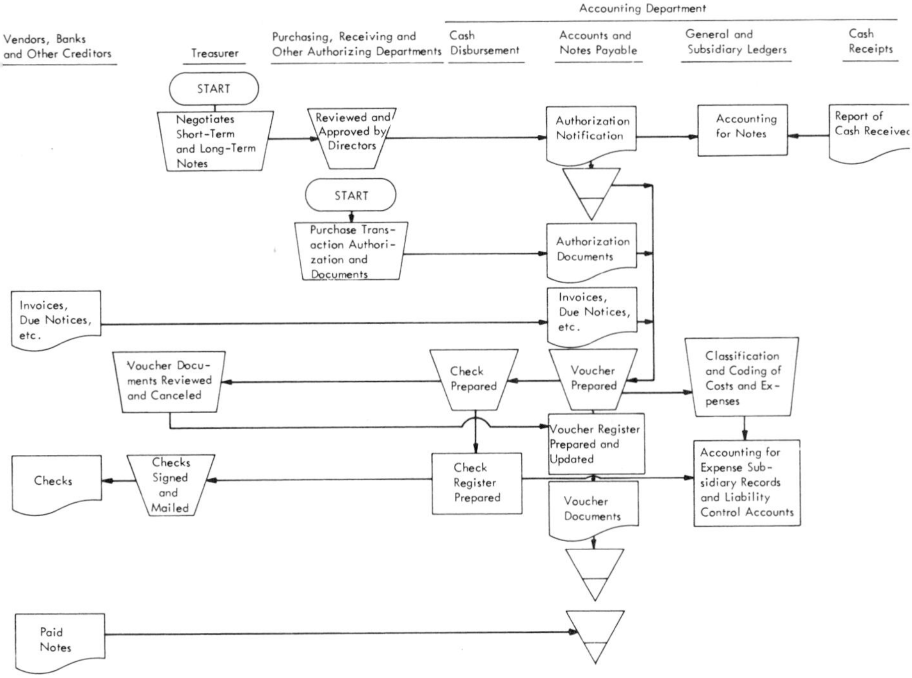

Relevant internal control questionnaire items are contained in Exhibit 15–2. Notice that several of these questions are duplicates of ones presented in Chapter 12 for the purchasing and receiving system and the cash disbursement system.

Long-Term Debt and Capital Stock Transactions. Major financing transactions generally receive formal review and exhaustive analysis by officers, directors, and analysts in the organization. Such reviews are usually described in formal proposals, board minutes, and finally in prospectuses and correspondence accompanying the offer and sale of securities. Some transactions in these categories may require stockholders' approval, and in some cases they may require amendment of the corporate charter (e.g., authorization of new classes of stock or of increase in number of authorized shares). Stock dividends, stock splits, option plans, and treasury stock transactions fall into this category of major financing transactions subject to high-level review and regulation.

The circumstances and constraints surrounding major financing transactions generally are sufficient for control. The documentation is usually voluminous, though nonstandardized, and ample exposure to review and approval is common. Accounting for such transactions—large in amount but few in number—usually does not involve extensive double-

EXHIBIT 15–2

INTERNAL CONTROL QUESTIONNAIRE
ACCOUNTS AND NOTES PAYABLE

1. Are direct borrowings on notes payable authorized by the directors? The treasurer?
2. Are two or more authorized signatures required on notes?
3. Are notes payable records kept by someone who cannot sign notes or checks?
4. Are paid notes canceled, stamped "paid," and filed?
5. Is the voucher register or subsidiary of open accounts payable and notes payable periodically reconciled with the general ledger control account(s)?
6. Are vendors' statements and bank due notices compared with records of unpaid liabilities?
7. Are any adjustments made as a result of this comparison? Are adjustments approved by a responsible officer?

(From the Purchasing and Receiving System Questionnaire)

1. Is the accounts payable ledger or open voucher register balanced periodically with the general ledger control account?
2. Are vendors' monthly statements checked against accounts payable or unpaid vouchers?
5. Are all purchases, whether for inventory or expense, routed through the purchasing department?
12. Is the accounts payable department notified of goods returned to vendors?
16. Are vendors' invoices registered immediately upon receipt?
17. Are vendors' invoices first checked by the purchasing department against purchase orders and receiving reports?
19. Are invoices approved for payment by a responsible officer?
21. Is there an accounting manual and employee approval for determining distribution of invoice charges to general ledger accounts?
22. Is the distribution of charges double-checked periodically?

(From the Cash Disbursement System Questionnaire)

1. Are all disbursements, excepting petty cash, made by check?
4. Are voided checks mutilated and retained for inspection?
5. Do checks require two signatures? Is there dual control over machine signature plates?
7. Are check signers persons who have no access to accounting records, cash receipts, or bank reconciliations?
11. Are vouchers and other supporting documents reviewed by the check signer? Is the presignature review effective?
12. Are checks mailed directly by the signer and not returned to the accounts payable department for mailing?
13. Are the voucher and supporting documents stamped or impressed "paid" to prevent duplicate payment before being returned to accounts payable for filing?

checking and review for errors in the same systematic sense that would be appropriate for large-volume transaction events. An auditor (independent auditor or internal auditor) can recheck completely for accounting error in a very short time.

Relevant internal control points are set forth in the internal control questionnaire items in Exhibit 15–3. Notice that the questionnaire directs the auditor to additional control features when independent trustees, registrars, transfer agents, and payment agents are not employed.

EXHIBIT 15–3

INTERNAL CONTROL QUESTIONNAIRE
LONG-TERM DEBT AND CAPITAL STOCK

1. Are approvals for sale of securities recorded in the minutes and transmitted to the accounting department?
2. Are an independent trustee and an independent interest-paying agent employed?
3. Are retired notes and bonds and redeemed interest coupons mutilated or imprinted "paid" and filed or destroyed? Are destruction certificates obtained?
4. Are an independent registrar, transfer agent, and dividend-paying agent employed?
5. If not, are stockholder subsidiary records and stock transfer records maintained under satisfactory control?
   a. Are unissued certificates and stubs for issued certificates in custody of a responsible officer?
   b. Are surrendered certificates canceled and new ones issued?
   c. Are stock transfer tax stamps in the custody and control of a responsible officer?
6. If dividends are paid directly by the company:
   a. Is a special dividend disbursement bank account used?
   b. Are the dividend checks made out to stockholders of record on the record date?
   c. Are amounts of dividend checks reconciled to the directors' dividend declaration?
   d. Are unclaimed dividend checks redeposited and accounted for as liabilities?

Compliance Tests of Transaction Details

Tests of transaction details are more extensive in the accounts and notes payable transactions than in other accounts in the liabilities and owner equity grouping. Some aspects of these objective tests have already been encountered in connection with tests of purchase and cash disbursement transactions (See Chapter 12). In Exhibit 15–4 portions of earlier tests are abstracted from Chapter 12 and set in the context of a test of liability transactions. To the extent that sufficient tests have already been performed during the audit, these tests will not have to be repeated.

EXHIBIT 15–4
Audit Program—Selected Compliance Test Procedures

A. *Notes Payable*
   1. Read director's and finance committee minutes for authorization of financing transactions (e.g., short-term notes payable, bond offerings).
   2. Select a sample of paid notes:
      a. Recalculate interest expense for the period under audit.
      b. Retrace interest expense to general ledger account.
      c. Vouch payment to canceled checks.
   3. Select a sample of notes payable:
      a. Vouch to authorization by director's or finance committee.
      b. Vouch cash receipt to bank statement.

B. *Accounts Payable*
   1. Select a sample of open accounts payable and vouch to supporting documents of purchase (e.g., vendor's invoices).
   2. Retrace debits arising from accounts payable transactions for proper classification.
   3. Select a sample of accounts payable entries recorded after the balance sheet date and vouch to supporting documents for evidence of proper cutoff—evidence that a liability should have been recorded as of the balance sheet date.

Each of the procedures in Exhibit 15–4 describes one or more attributes relevant for the design of statistical-based tests. In the event that note transactions are few in number, however, they may be audited 100 percent. If such is the case then the test of transaction procedures will have been adapted to accomplish a large part of the audit of the notes payable and interest expense balances.

If data processing of accounts payable transactions is automated with EDP equipment, the tests accomplish an audit of input data accuracy. Other procedures utilizing test data or parallel simulation may be employed to audit computer-controlled accounting for costs, expenses, assets, and payables. Generalized audit software programs may be used to select samples for the vouching tests.

Minor and/or Infrequent Transactions. Several accounts in the category of liabilities and equities are not generally characterized by elaborate transaction control systems. Sales and excise taxes, payroll taxes and other payroll withholdings, income taxes payable, and accrued expenses are amounts derived from other basic transactions. The year-end liability balances in these accounts stem from the basic transactions, and control is generally effected through the other systems of control. Some examples are:

Sales and excise tax amounts are controlled by the sales system. Correlation with sales along with vouching cash payments and tax reports are sufficient to test the transactions and usually accomplish the audit of the balance as well.

Payroll taxes and other withholdings are controlled by the payroll system. Correlation with payroll along with vouching payroll tax reports and cash payments are sufficient to test the transactions and audit the year-end balances.

Income taxes payable are a function of the income measurement, the tax estimate, and tax payments. Vouching the payments along with the tax return audit procedures are sufficient to test transactions and audit the balances.

Accrued expenses are tested and audited along with the interest, rent, taxes, or other basic events that created the accrual.

Transactions in long-term debt, capital stock, warrants, options, paid-in capital, and retained earnings are usually not tested as a matter of an internal control evaluation. These transactions are generally audited completely by reference to authorizations, by tracing them to events reflected in the accounts and related disclosures, and by vouching to cash receipts and cash disbursements and other formal documentation for verification of the transaction amounts. Because of the limited number and the great importance of these transactions, they are usually subjected to detailed substantive audit procedures.

Summary and Conclusion. The evaluation of internal accounting control over liabilities, owner equity, and related expenses involves the auditor in two different control environments. Regarding the accounts and notes payable system, the compliance tests may be quite extensive; yet in areas like long-term debt and owner equity, the auditor may perform a direct audit of the balance. Depending on the nature of the accounts and the transactions—their frequency, volume, and amount—the proper study and evaluation of internal accounting control may be a complementary mixture of the review and the compliance test phase procedures, or it may end with the questionnaire stage of the review phase.

Near the end of the audit, when the procedures described thus far in this chapter are usually performed, the distinction between procedural applications for compliance tests of transaction details and procedures applied to the substantive tests of balances begins to blur. One appears, as a practical matter, to be the same as the other.

SUBSTANTIVE TESTS OF BALANCES

The construction of an audit program of substantive test procedures should begin with the auditor's recognition of the explicit and implicit assertions contained in accounts and disclosures relating to liabilities, owners' equity, and contingencies. The assertions point directly to questions that can be tested by gathering sufficient, competent evidential matter. A few of the assertions typical to this group of accounts and disclosures are:

- All material liabilities are recorded.
- Liabilities are properly classified as to their contingent or direct nature.
- Liabilities are properly classified as to their current or long-term status.
- Terms, conditions, and restrictions relating to debt are adequately disclosed.
- Capital stock terms and features are adequately disclosed.
- Options, warrants, and other stock issue plans are properly accounted for and disclosed.
- All important contingencies are either provided for in the accounts or disclosed in footnotes.

The assertions above are not a complete list of all matters of audit interest, but they are illustrative of the types of problems that should be recognized. The next task is to consider the evidence that might support or refute these assertions. A selection of substantive test procedures is shown in Exhibit 15–5.

Vouching of Documents

Vouching may be utilized extensively to audit the recorded balances of liabilities, owners' equity, and related expense accounts. In a manner similar to the test of transactions vouching procedures, selected trade creditor balances, note balances, payroll taxes withheld, income taxes payable, and similar liability, balances may be vouched to documentation of the transaction or series of transactions that created the balance. Notice that the procedure differs somewhat from the test of transactions in that a balance (e.g., account payable to a supplier) is selected instead of one purchase from a supplier. Thus balances may be audited by (1) vouching an accounts payable balance to recent invoices and recent payments, (2) vouching a note or bond payable balance to cash receipts and the loan agreement, (3) vouching payroll tax liabilities to payroll records and tax returns, (4) vouching income tax payable to the income tax return. Additional vouching whereby the auditor compares year-end liability amounts to cash payments made in the subsequent period serves the dual purpose of producing evidence of the year-end balance and possible evidence of unrecorded liabilities (if subsequent payment includes an amount not properly recorded at the balance sheet date).

Liabilities for and disclosures about pension and profit-sharing plans should be vouched to the plan or contract as to terms, conditions, and amounts. In most cases the audit will also involve important recalculations of amounts, sometimes performed by a consulting actuary in the case of complex pension plans.

In connection with the capital accounts there may be changes in the number of authorized shares, issues of warrants, grants of stock options, dividends, treasury stock transactions, appropriations or restrictions of retained earnings, or other events of major significance. In many cases

EXHIBIT 15–5
Audit Program—Selected Substantive Test Procedures

A. *Notes Payable*
   1. Prepare, or have client prepare, a schedule of notes payable showing beginning balances, new notes, repayment and ending balances. Trace to general ledger accounts.
   2. Confirm notes payable—amount, interest rate, due date, collateral, other terms—with creditors.
   3. Review standard bank confirmation for evidence of unrecorded notes.
   4. Obtain written representations from management concerning notes payable, collateral agreements, and restrictive covenants.

B. *Accounts Payable*
   1. Confirm payable amounts with creditors, especially those with small or zero balances.
   2. Retrace payments on account made after the balance sheet date to accounts payable as of the balance sheet date.
   3. Reconcile vendors' monthly statement with recorded accounts payable.

C. *Other Accounts and Disclosures*
   1. Prepare, or have client prepare, a schedule of all accrued and estimated liabilities (e.g., accrued interest, wages, taxes).
   2. Recalculate accrued amounts.
   3. Based on average interest rates and amount of debt outstanding, recalculate interest expense for the period under audit.
   4. Confirm outstanding common and preferred stock with stock registrar agent.
   5. Vouch payroll taxes payable to tax returns.
   6. Vouch stock option and profit-sharing plan disclosures to contracts and plan documents.
   7. Vouch treasury stock transactions to cash receipts and cash disbursement records and to director's authorization. Inspect treasury stock certificates.

the auditor will vouch the transaction to directors' minutes, stockholders' approvals, stock option and warrant plan documents, or other authorization for the transaction. When cash receipts or cash disbursements are involved, the appropriate cash receipt and canceled check documents may be examined. New issues of debt or capital stock may be vouched to securities registration documents as well as to cash receipts records and loan agreements.

Many major expense account balances are audited by vouching. A common audit program procedure is: "Analyze the Professional Fees Expense account and vouch all entries over $200." An account analysis in this sense consists of a listing of all the expense entries over $200 with a full description of the date, payee, and amount. A lump-sum item for "all entries under $200" is inserted to make the analysis reconcile with the account balance. Each entry over $200 is vouched to supporting invoices, contracts, correspondence, or other documents in order to determine whether the expense is recorded in the right account at the proper amount.

The analysis of professional fees gives the auditor the names of attorneys, other accountants, or consultants who have been engaged by the client. Some of these persons, for example the attorneys, may be questioned about contingent events related to the client's financial statements.

Retracing and Scanning

These two procedures may be used extensively in the search for unrecorded liabilities. The essence of the search is that the auditor examines the basic file records (e.g., purchases, receiving reports, payments, vouchers) and retraces the data processing to determine whether transactions were recorded in the proper period. The transactions included in the search are ones recorded during the two- or three-week periods both immediately before and immediately after the balance sheet date. Many innocent errors of unrecorded liabilities result from simple cutoff errors, and their detection is not difficult.

The auditor obtains the invoices recorded in the post-year-end period, many of which may have been received for the first time (say, on January 10 for a December 31 year-end). By a combination of retracing from the invoices to the records and vouching from the records to the invoices, cutoff errors (including unrecorded liability errors) can be found. The auditor documents these items in the working papers and records his or her decision as to whether they are material enough to require an adjustment of the accounts. A working paper showing a search based on subsequent cash disbursements is illustrated in Exhibit 15–6.

Another particularly relevant application of retracing procedures involves the examination of IRS audit reports and correspondence and the audit reports of state and local tax authorities. Errors and deficiencies revealed and assessed in such reports should be retraced to the accounts to ascertain that they are properly accounted for. Tax audits typically lag, and the period of the last completed audit may be disclosed in footnotes to the financial statements. Oftentimes this review of tax agents' reports reveals some deductions or assessments in dispute. Information on such matters is important for disclosure of contingent liabilities if probable assessments have not already been recorded.

Basic files, vouchers, invoices, receiving reports, cash disbursements, cash receipts, and other such records may be scanned for unusual amounts. Sometimes when the transaction volume is large in the cutoff period, the items chosen for audit are selected by scanning for amounts larger than a relevant limit (for example, every transaction over $300). An alternative selection method would be random selection, augmented by scanning the items not selected for any unusual characteristics.

Analysis of Interrelationships

In the liability and equity accounts two different overall interrelationships can be analyzed to support conclusions about transaction activity

EXHIBIT 15–6

G-2

A B C Company
Search for Unrecorded Liabilities
December 31, 1979

Prepared by JC
Date 1-31-80

Check no.	Payee	Date	Amount	
1101	Smalltown Utility Co.	1-5-80	733 00	x December 1979 utility bill
1102	Mortons Vendomat	1-6-80	1032 00	x Christmas party costs
1103	Vendorama	1-6-80	7628 00	✓ Inventory received 12-26-79
~				
1189	Adams Apple	1-31-80	321 00	y Supplies received 1-10-80

✓ Traced to accounts payable balance as of 12-31-79. Properly recorded.
x Account payable was not recorded in 1979.
y Payment on liability arising after 12-31-79

Recommended adjustment

Utility Expense	733	
Miscellaneous Expense	1032	
Accounts Payable		1765

© WILSON JONES COMPANY G7206 GREEN 7206 BUFF MADE IN U.S.A.

and account balances. The general level of activity as evidenced by physical production volume, purchasing activity, inventory stockpiling, and cost of goods sold amounts should correspond with credits to trade accounts payable. When production, purchases, and sales are increasing, accounts payable activity and period-end balances will likely be greater also. These relationships, coupled with the cash position and payment activity, are essential clues to the reasonableness of trade accounts payable totals.

Also in the area of overall relationships, certain liabilities are functions of other basic transactions. Sales taxes are functionally related to sales dollar totals, payroll taxes to payroll totals, excise taxes to sales dollars or volume, income taxes to income.

Interest expense is generally related item-by-item to interest-bearing liabilities. At the same time that the liabilities are audited (including those that have been paid during the year), the related interest expense amounts can be recalculated based on the amount of debt, the interest rate, and the time period. By comparing the results to the interest expense account, auditors may be able to detect (1) greater expense than their calculations show, indicating some interest paid on debt unknown to them, possibly an unrecorded liability; (2) lesser expense than their calculations show, indicating misclassification, failure to accrue interest, or an interest payment default; or (3) interest expense equal to their calculations. The first two possibilities raise questions for further study and the third shows a correct correlation between debt and debt-related expense.

An example of a working paper showing recalculation of interest expense and other notes payable procedures is in Exhibit 15–7.

Retained earnings is definitely interrelated with income and dividends. In fact, retained earnings balances are little more than the accumulated results of such transactions. The retained earnings balance is essentially audited by relating charges and credits to income and dividend amounts, which themselves may be audited by retracing, vouching, and recalculation. (If there are other entries in retained earnings such as prior period adjustments or error correction entries, the audit would also involve vouching of the transaction documentation.)

Recalculation

Many liability balances owe both existence and valuation to a calculation. All the accrued expense liabilities (e.g., accrued interest payable, rent payable, salaries and wages payable) fall into this category as well as sales and excise taxes payable, income tax payable, warranty and guarantee liabilities, unamoritized bond discount or premium, deferred installment income and other liability and deferred credit balances. Most changes in partners' capital accounts are essentially calculated allocations of partnership net income.

The audit of such balances may depend in large part on the auditor's recalculations, supported by appropriate vouching to basic transactions or contract agreements. As suggested in previous discussion, accrued ex-

EXHIBIT 15–7

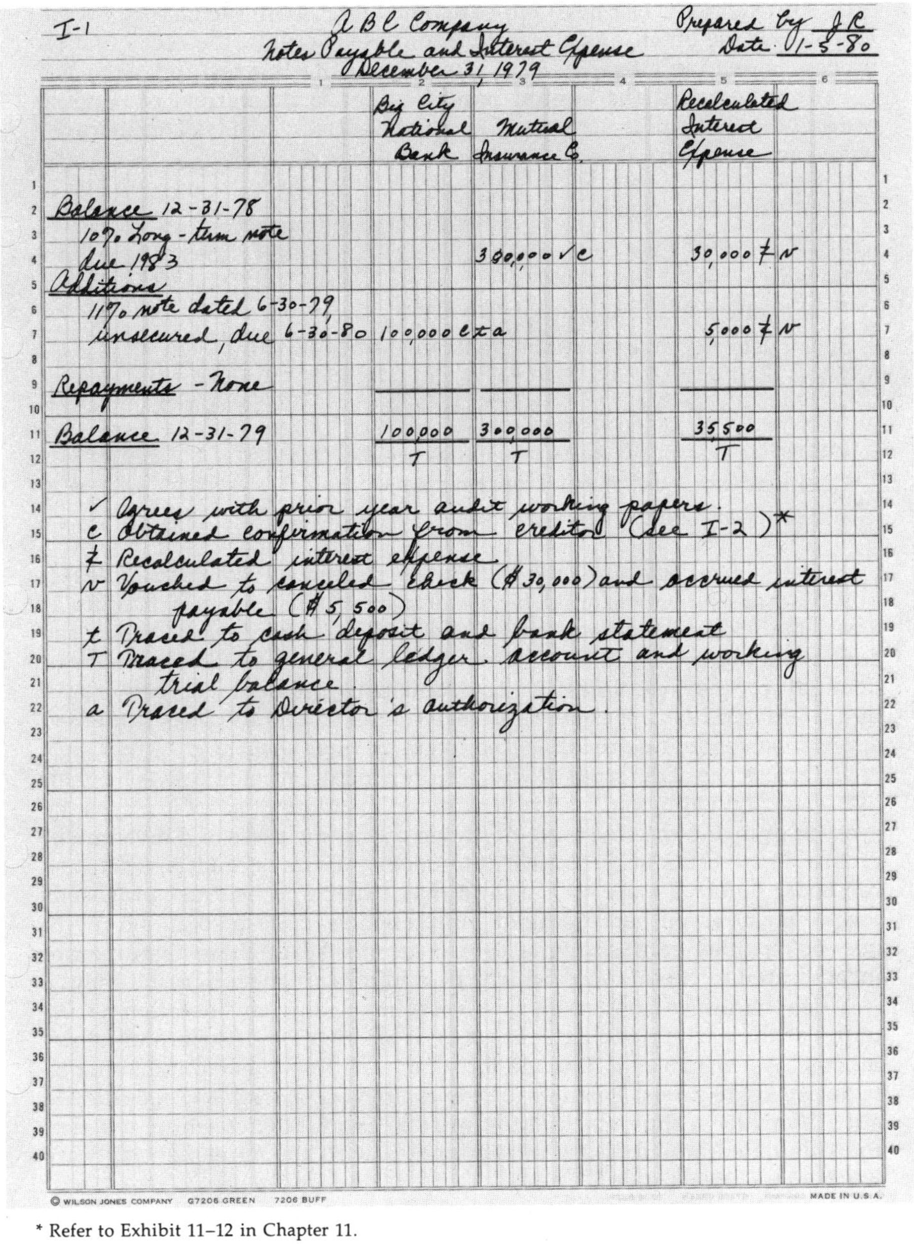

I-1

ABC Company
Notes Payable and Interest Expense
December 31, 1979

Prepared by JR
Date 1-5-80

	Big City National Bank	Mutual Insurance Co.	Recalculated Interest Expense
Balance 12-31-78			
10% Long-term note			
due 1983		300,000 ✓ c	30,000 ⱡ v
Additions			
11% note dated 6-30-79,			
unsecured, due 6-30-80	100,000 c t a		5,000 ⱡ v
Repayments - None			
Balance 12-31-79	100,000 T	300,000 T	35,500 T

✓ Agrees with prior year audit working papers.
c Obtained confirmation from creditor (See I-2)*
ⱡ Recalculated interest expense
v Vouched to canceled check ($30,000) and accrued interest payable ($5,500)
t Traced to cash deposit and bank statement
T Traced to general ledger account and working trial balance.
a Traced to Director's authorization.

© WILSON JONES COMPANY G7206 GREEN 7206 BUFF MADE IN U.S.A.

* Refer to Exhibit 11–12 in Chapter 11.

penses are recalculated with reference to interest rates, wage rates, tax rates, time periods, last payment date, and other definitive factors. To the extent that the client has already made these accruals, the recalculation process is relatively simple. In all cases, particularly when the client has not made accruals, the auditor must be alert to the variety of possible accruals so that one is not overlooked and omitted entirely. The short list below contains typical accrual items.

Salaries, wages, and bonuses.
Sales commissions.
Royalties.
Real estate and personal property taxes.
Social security and unemployment insurance taxes.
Insurance.
Rents.
Interest.
Compensation cost of stock option plans.
Warranty and guarantee expenses.

Lease obligations and the liabilities related to capitalized lease-purchase agreements should be recalculated. When such a liability is based on the discounted present value of future contractual payments, the auditor should use the mathematics of present value calculations in his or her audit procedures. Similarly, in connection with debt discount or premium amortization, present value or straight-line amortization method applications should be recalculated to check their accuracy.

Several types of deferred credits also depend upon calculations for their existence and valuation. Deferred profit on installment sales involves the gross margin and the sale amount; deferred income taxes and investment credits involve tax-book timing differences, tax rates, and amortization methods; deferred contract revenue may depend on contract provisions for prepayment, on percentage-of-completion revenue recognition methods, or on other terms unique to a contract. All of these features are incorporated in calculations which the auditor can check for accuracy.

When auditing partnerships, a very important consideration is the terms of the partnership agreement for allocation and distribution of net income. A contract may provide for salaries, interest on capital, and distribution share ratios. Partners are generally very sensitive to accuracy in such allocations; thus, the auditor must be careful to determine whether the calculated amounts are in accordance with the agreement and are mathematically correct.

Corporate earnings presentation are complicated by earnings per share calculations. Accounting Principles Board *Opinion No. 15*[7] gives criteria for a number of calculations including weighted average of shares outstanding, common stock equivalent shares, use of the "treasury stock"

[7] "Earnings per Share."

method, shares assumed under full dilution, and net income to common stockholders. Additional calculations may be included in pro forma disclosures when capital structure changes occur after the year-end.

Physical Observation

Opportunities to use the physical observation technique in connection with liabilities and owners' equity accounts are limited. With regard to liabilities the auditor may wish to inspect assets pledged as collateral in order to ascertain whether they are kept in the location and/or condition required by the collateral agreement. This inspection may involve looking at fixed assets or inventory pledged, observing their condition and safekeeping; or it may involve inspection of securities pledged but in the custody of the client. Bonds, notes, other formal debt instruments, and shares of common or preferred stock that have been redeemed, retired, converted, or acquired as treasury bonds or stock may be inspected in much the same manner as security investment assets are inspected.

Confirmation and Verbal Inquiry

Capital stock may be subject to confirmation when independent registrars and transfer agents are employed. Such agents are responsible for knowing the number of shares authorized and issued and for keeping lists of stockholders' names. The basic information about capital stock such as numbers of shares, classes of stock, preferred dividend rates, conversion terms, dividend payments, shares held in the company name, expiration dates and terms of warrants, and stock dividends and splits can be confirmed with the independent agents. Many of these information items can be corroborated by the auditor's own inspection and reading of stock certificates, charter authorizations, directors' minutes, and offering prospectuses. When there are no independent agents, however, most audit evidence is gathered by vouching stock record documents (e.g., certificate book, stubs). When circumstances call for extended procedures, information on outstanding stock may be confirmed directly with the holders.

Independent written confirmations are usually obtained for notes and bonds payable. In the case of notes payable to banks the standard bank confirmation may be used. The amount and terms of bonds payable, mortgages payable, and other formal debt instruments can be confirmed by letter to the holder or trustee. The confirmation request should include questions not only of amount, interest rate, and due date but also questions about collateral, restrictive covenants, and other items of agreement entered into between lender and borrower. Confirmation requests should be sent to lenders with whom the company has done business in the recent past, even if no liability balance is shown at the confirmation date. Such extra confirmation coverage is a part of the search for unrecorded liabilities.

Confirmations may also be used to audit trade accounts payable. However, there is a great difference between accounts payable confirmation and accounts receivable confirmation. When confirming receivables, the auditor is primarily interested in evidence of the existence of a real claim on a real debtor. The relative risk is that recorded receivables may be overstated. In contrast, the relative risk respecting payables is that they may be omitted or otherwise understated. A confirmation sample of accounts payable with balances greater than zero can only reveal omission of invoices (which could result from cutoff errors), but such a sample would not provide any means of detecting accounts that were entirely omitted.

The accounts payable confirmation sample should include all suppliers with whom the client has done business recently (or at least the major ones), regardless of the size of the balance at the confirmation date. With this selection, the confirmation procedure becomes a part of the search for unrecorded liabilities. Similarly, payable amounts that are old, past due, in dispute, or have other unusual characteristics should be confirmed.

Confirmation and inquiry procedures may be used to obtain responses on a class of items that can be loosely termed "off-balance sheet information." Within this category are such things as terms of loan agreements, leases, endorsements, guarantees, and insurance policies (whether issued by a client insurance company or owned by the client). Among these items is the difficult-to-define set of *contingencies* and *commitments* that oftentimes pose evidence-gathering problems to the auditor. Frequently encountered types of contingencies and commitments are listed below:

Type of Contingency or Commitment	*Typical Procedures and Sources of Evidence*
1. Endorsements on discounted notes.	1. Standard bank confirmation.
2. Debt guarantees (e.g., obligations of subsidiaries).	2. Inquiry of client management, confirmation by direct debtor.
3. Repurchase or remarketing agreements.	3. Vouching of contracts, confirmation by customer, inquiry of client management.
4. Commitments to purchase at fixed prices.	4. Vouching of open purchase orders, inquiry of purchasing personnel, confirmation by supplier.
5. Commitments to sell at fixed prices.	5. Vouching of sales contracts, inquiry of sales personnel, confirmation by customer.
6. Loan commitments (as in a savings and loan association).	6. Vouching of open commitment file, inquiry of loan officers.
7. Lease commitments.	7. Vouching of lease agreement, confirmation with lessor or lessee.
8. Legal judgments, litigation, pending litigation, claims, assessments.	8. Confirmation with client counsel (i.e., attorney's representation letter).

All of the items listed above may become subjects for footnote disclosures. Some of them may be amenable to estimation and valuation and thus may be recorded in the accounts and shown in the financial statements themselves (e.g., obligations for endorsements on defaulted debts of others, losses on fixed-price purchase commitments, probable tax deficiency settlements).

One of the most important confirmations is the response known as the attorney's representation letter. The letter is described in *Statement on Auditing Standards No. 1*, Section 560.12(d), as follows: "Inquire of client's legal counsel concerning litigation, claims and assessments."

Prior to 1976 some difficulties had arisen over lawyers' willingness to respond to auditors' requests for information about contingencies, litigation, claims, and assessments. Lawyers themselves were facing legal liability for failure to respond properly. At about the same time the FASB issued *Statement of Financial Accounting Standards No. 5*, "Accounting for Contingencies," which defined pending litigation, claims, assessments, and the "probable," "reasonably possible" and "remote" likelihoods that future events (e.g., court judgment) would confirm a loss from an existing contingency. FASB *No. 5* sets forth standards for accrual and disclosure of litigation, claims, and assessments in financial statements.

Statement on Auditing Standards No. 12 (Section 337) entitled "Inquiry of a Client's Lawyer concerning Litigation, Claims and Assessments," issued in 1976, is the auditors' counterpart of FASB *No. 5*. This SAS requires auditors to make certain inquiries designed to elicit the information upon which accounting in conformity with FASB *No. 5* can be determined.

The attorney's letter serves as a major means for the auditor to learn of material contingencies. Even so, a devious or forgetful management or a careless attorney may fail to tell the auditor of some important factor or development. The auditor somehow has to be alert and sensitive to all possible contingencies so that he or she can ask the right questions at the right time. Such questions should be directed not only to attorneys but also to management because an auditor has the right to expect to be informed by management about all material contingent liabilities. Audit procedures useful in this regard include:[8]

Inquire and discuss with management the policies and procedures for identifying, evaluating, and accounting for litigation, claims, and assessments.

Obtain from management a description and evaluation of litigation, claims, and assessments. . . .

Examine documents in the client's possession concerning litigation, claims, and assessments, including correspondence and invoices from lawyers.

Obtain assurance from management that it has disclosed all unasserted claims that the lawyer has advised them are probable of assertion. . . .

Read minutes of meetings of stockholders, directors, and appropriate committees. . . .

---

[8] *SAS No. 12* (Sections 337.04–.07).

Read contracts, loan agreements, leases and correspondence from taxing or other governmental agencies. . . .

Obtain information concerning guarantees from bank confirmation forms.

Auditors have a natural conservative tendency to look out for adverse contingencies. However, potentially favorable events should also be investigated and disclosed (e.g., the contingency of litigation for damages wherein the client is the plaintiff). In an effort to assist management in observing the law and to provide adequate disclosure of information in financial statements, the auditor should be alert to all types of contingencies.

TYPES OF MAJOR FRAUD AND MISSTATEMENT

The kinds of fraud and misstatement connected with liability and owners' equity accounts differ significantly from those associated with asset and revenue accounts. Few employees are tempted to steal a liability, although fictitious liabilities may be created in the records as a means of misdirecting cash payments into the hands of an employee. The auditor should be alert for such fictions in the same sense that he or she is alert to the possibility of having fictitious accounts receivable.

Although there are opportunities for employee fraud on the company, the area of liabilities and owners' equity also opens up possibilities for company fraud on outsiders. This class of fraud is most often accomplished through material misrepresentations or omissions in financial statements and related disclosures.

In addition to various means of misappropriating cash by manipulation of liability records, officers and employees might use stock or bond instruments improperly. Unissued stock or bonds and treasury stock or bonds might be used as collateral for personal loans. Even though the company may not be damaged or suffer loss by this action (unless the employee defaults and the securities are seized), the practice is unauthorized and contrary to company interests. Similarly, employees might gain access to stockholder lists and unissued or treasury bond coupons and cause improper payments of dividends and interest on securities that are not outstanding. Proper custodial control of securities (either by physical means such as limited-access vaults or by control of an independent disbursing agent) would prevent most such occurrences. An auditing procedure of reconciling authorized dividend and interest payments (calculated using declared dividend rates, coupon interest rates, and known quantities of outstanding securities) to actual payments would detect unauthorized payments. If the company does not perform this checking procedure, the auditor may include it among his or her own overall recalculation procedures.

Many liability, equity, and "off-balance sheet" transactions are above the reach of normal internal control systems, which can operate effectively over ordinary large-volume transactions (e.g., purchases, sales) processed by clerks and machines. The size, impact, and infrequency of many liability and equity transactions, however, cause them to be handled by high corporate officers, and these persons have power to override normal procedural control systems. Thus the auditor is generally justified in auditing liability, equity, and high-level-managed transactions and agreements extensively since control depends in large part on the abilities of management.

Income tax evasion and fraud result from actions taken by managers and experts. Evasion and fraud may be accomplished by simple omission of income, by taking unlawful deductions (e.g., contributions to political campaigns, depreciation on nonexistent assets, or depreciation in excess of cost), or by contriving sham transactions for the sole purpose of avoiding taxation. An auditor should be able to detect errors of the first two categories if the actual income and expense data has been sufficiently audited in the financial statements. The last category—contrived sham transactions—are hard to detect, because a dishonest management generally disguises them skillfully.

Financial statements may be materially misstated by reason of omission or understatement of liabilities and by failure to disclose technical defaults on loan agreement restrictions. The several means of auditing to discover unrecorded liabilities through a "search for unrecorded liabilities" may be used to attempt to discover such omissions and understatements. If auditors discover that loan agreement terms have been violated, they should bring the information to the client's attention, and they should insist upon proper disclosure in footnotes to the financial statements. In both situations (liability understatement and loan default disclosure) management's actions, reactions, and willingness to adjust the financial figures and make adverse disclosures will be important inputs to an auditor's subjective evaluation of managerial integrity. An accumulation of inputs relevant to managerial integrity can have an important bearing on the auditor's perception of relative risk for the audit engagement taken as a whole.

A company, individual managers, and the auditors can run afoul of securities regulations if they are not careful. The general framework of regulation by the SEC was reviewed briefly in Chapter 4. Auditors must be cognizant of the general provisions of the securities laws to the extent that they can identify situations that constitute obvious fraud and to the extent that they can identify transactions that *might* be subject to the law. Having once recognized or raised questions about a securities transaction, the auditor should under no circumstances proceed to act as his or her own attorney. The facts should be submitted to competent legal counsel for an opinion. Even though the auditor is not expected to be a legal expert, he or she does have the duty to recognize obvious instances of impropriety and pursue an investigation with the aid of legal experts.

Similarly the auditor should assist the client in observing SEC rules and regulations on matters of timely disclosure. In general, the timely disclosure rules are phrased in terms of management's duties, and they do not *require* the auditor to do any specific procedures or make any specific disclosures. Their purpose and spirit are to require management to disseminate to the public any material information, whether favorable or unfavorable, so that the market can incorporate it in investment decisions. Various rule provisions require announcements and disclosures very soon after information becomes known. Oftentimes relevant situations arise during the year when the independent auditors are not present, so of course they cannot be held responsible or liable. In other situations, however, the auditor may learn of information inadvertently or the auditor's advice may be sought by the client. In such cases the accountant should act in the public interest as an auditor, consistent with the requirements of law and regulation.

Pressures are presently on the auditor to discover more information about "off-balance sheet" contingencies and commitments and to discover the facts of management involvement with other parties to transactions. As explained earlier in this chapter, the auditor's knowledge of contingencies and commitments that are not evidenced in accounting records depends almost entirely on what management and its attorneys will reveal. Management's control of buyers and sellers and the existence of side guarantees in purchase and sale transactions may be concealed from the auditor with relative ease. The current pressures on the auditor to discover more information is a part of the public pressure on the auditor to take more responsibility for fraud detection.

REVIEW QUESTIONS

15.1. What matters of *compliance* is the auditor interested in with respect to owner's equity?

15.2. What are the essential internal control features relative to capital stock when an independent registrar and transfer agent are *not* used?

15.3. Generally, how much emphasis is placed upon adequate internal control in the audit of long-term debt, capital stock, warrants, options, paid-in capital, and retained earnings? Explain.

15.4. In a partnership, what procedures are relied upon most heavily to audit salaries of partners, interest on capital balances, and other income allocations?

15.5. What things should an auditor know are important about capital stock for an effective audit?

15.6. How is a confirmation used in auditing notes and bonds payable?

15.7. In regard to contingencies and commitments, why would an auditor vouch open purchase orders?

15.8. How might the auditor's opinion be affected by the following reply to a confirmation request by client's counsel regarding a pending lawsuit against a client? Explain. "Several agreements and contracts to which the company is a party are not covered by this response since we have not advised or been consulted in their regard."

15.9. What ethics problem does the auditor face in connection with his or her knowledge of facts considered to be inside information but which are not disclosed by management?

EXERCISES AND PROBLEMS

15.10. Listed below is a selection of items from the internal control questionnaires shown in the chapter. For each one:

a. Identify the control characteristic to which it applies (e.g., segregation of duties—authorization of transactions, access to assets and recordkeeping duties; sound error-checking practice; and so on).
b. Specify one compliance test procedure an auditor could use to determine whether the control was operating effectively.
c. Using your business experience, your logic, and/or your imagination, give an example of an error or irregularity that could occur if the control was absent or ineffective.
d. Specify a substantive testing procedure an auditor could use to uncover errors or irregularities, if any, resulting from absence of the control.

(1) Is direct borrowing on notes payable authorized by the directors? The treasurer?
(2) Are notes payable records kept by someone who cannot sign notes or checks?
(3) Are vendors' statements and bank due notices compared with records of unpaid liabilities?
(4) Are retired notes and bonds and redeemed interest coupons mutilated or imprinted "paid" and filed or destroyed? Are destruction certificates obtained?
(5) Are amounts of dividend checks reconciled to the director's dividend declaration?

15.11. *a.* (1) Define *loss contingency*.
(2) Give three methods of reflecting loss contingencies in the financial statements.

b. In an examination of the Marco Corporation as of December 31, 1979, you have learned that the following situations exist. No entries in respect thereto have been made in the accounting records. What *entries* would you recommend and what *disclosures,* if any, would you make of these situations in the financial statements for December 31, 1979?

(1) The Marco Corporation has guaranteed the payment of interest on the ten-year, first-mortgage bonds of the Newart Company, an affiliate. Outstanding bonds of the Newart Company amount to $150,000 with interest payable at 9 percent per annum, due June 1 and December 1 of each year. The bonds were issued by the Newart Company on December 1, 1977, and all interest payments have been met by that company with the exception of the payment due December 1, 1979. The Marco Corporation states that it will pay the defaulted interest to the bondholders on January 15.

(2) During the year 1979 the Marco Corporation was named as a defendant in a suit for damages by the Dalton Company for breach of contract. An adverse decision to the Marco Corporation was rendered, and the Dalton Company was awarded $40,000 damages. At the time of the audit, the case was under appeal to a higher court.

(3) On December 23, 1979, the Marco Corporation declared a common stock dividend of 1,000 shares, par $100,000, of its common stock, payable February 2, 1980, to the common stockholders of record December 30, 1979.

c. What procedures might an auditor use to discover the situations described in part (*b*) above. (AICPA adapted)

15.12. You were in the final stages of your examination of the financial statements of Ozine Corporation for the year ended December 31, 1979, when you were consulted by the corporation's president who believes there is no point to your examining the 1980 voucher register and testing data in support of 1980 entries. He stated that (1) bills pertaining to 1979 which were received too late to be included in the December voucher register were recorded as of the year-end by the corporation by journal entry, (2) the internal auditor made tests after the year-end, and (3) he would furnish you with a letter certifying that there were no unrecorded liabilities.

Required:

a. Should a CPA's test for unrecorded liabilities be affected by the fact that the client made a journal entry to record 1979 bills which were received late? Explain.

b. Should a CPA's test for unrecorded liabilities be affected by the fact that a letter is obtained in which a responsible management official certifies that to the best of his knowledge all liabilities have been recorded? Explain.

c. Should a CPA's test for unrecorded liabilities be eliminated or reduced because of the internal audit test? Explain.

d. What sources in addition to the 1980 voucher register should the CPA consider to locate possible unrecorded liabilities? (AICPA adapted)

15.13. Prepare an audit program which would bring to light various types of contingent liabilities and commitments. (The program should be in general terms for each area covered and should describe briefly the type of contingent item which might be found under each step. Ignore the fact that several of the steps in the program might normally be included in programs for other parts of your examination.) In order to consider a wide variety of contingencies, organize the program around the following persons and documents:

a. Bank confirmation.
b. Client counsel.
c. Board minutes.
d. Purchasing agent.
e. Personnel director.
f. President. (AICPA adapted)

15.14. The Hymine Manufacturing Company, Inc., which has been doing business for ten years, has engaged you to examine its financial statements.

The company has never before engaged the services of a CPA. Its federal income tax returns have been prepared by the company's chief accountant.

Required:

a. In an initial engagement the CPA usually applies the auditing procedure of reviewing the client's federal income tax returns for prior years. What are the general purposes or objectives of this auditing procedure? (In this part do not list specific items of information available from this source.)

b. An objective of the review of prior years' income tax returns is to obtain specific items of information pertaining to the client's accounting and income tax practices. List these specific items and explain each item's relevance to the CPA's examination. (For example, prior years' income tax returns would be reviewed for any net operating loss carryover which would be applied to any income tax liability for the year under examination.) (AICPA)

15.15. You have been assigned to the audit of Southampton Shipping Company. The company has adopted a funded pension plan in the past year which allows management to add annually a discretionary amount to a pension fund, recognizing concurrently a liability equal to the amount in the fund.

Required:

a. One of your objectives as an auditor is to determine that all liabilities are reflected in the financial statement in the proper amounts. In view of this objective, why might you dispute Southampton's pension plan?

b. Assume the amounts associated with the pension plan are material to the company's financial position. If the plan is accounted for as proposed by management, what effect would this have on the audit opinion?

c. What procedures might you use to audit the pension fund liability account?

15.16. You were engaged to examine the financial statements of Ronlyn Corporation for the year ended June 30.

On May 1, the corporation borrowed $500,000 from Second National Bank to finance plant expansion. The long-term note agreement provided for the annual payment of principal and interest over five years. The existing plant was pledged as security for the loan.

Due to unexpected difficulties in acquiring the building site, the plant expansion had not begun at June 30. To make use of the borrowed funds, management decided to invest in stocks and bonds, and on May 16, the $500,000 was invested in securities.

Required:

a. What are the audit objectives in the examination of long-term debt?

b. Prepare an audit program for the examination of the long-term note agreement between Ronlyn and Second National Bank. (AICPA adapted)

15.17. The following covenants are extracted from the indenture of a bond issue. The indenture provides that failure to comply with its terms in any respect automatically advances the due date of the loan to the date of noncompliance (the regular date is 20 years hence). Give any audit steps or reporting requirements you believe should be taken or recognized in connection with each one of the following:

1. "The debtor company shall endeavor to maintain a working capital ratio of 2 to 1 at all times, and in any fiscal year following a failure to maintain said ratio, the company shall restrict compensation of officers to a total of $100,000. Officers for this purpose shall include chairman of the board of directors, president, all vice presidents, secretary, and treasurer."
2. "The debtor company shall keep all property which is security for this debt insured against loss by fire to the extent of 100 percent of its actual value. Policies of insurance comprising this protection shall be filed with the trustee."
3. "The debtor company shall pay all taxes legally assessed against property which is security for this debt within the time provided by law for payment without penalty and shall deposit receipted tax bills or equally acceptable evidence of payment of same with the trustee."
4. "A sinking fund shall be deposited with the trustee by semiannual payments of $300,000, from which the trustee shall, in his discretion, purchase bonds of this issue." (AICPA)

15.18. Clark and his partner Kent, both CPAs, are planning their audit program for the audit of accounts payable on the Marlboro Corporation annual audit. This Saturday afternoon they have reviewed the thick file of last year's working papers, and both of them remember all too well the six days they spent on accounts payable.

Last year Clark had suggested that they mail confirmation to 100 of Marlboro's suppliers. The company regularly purchases from about 1,000 suppliers, and these account payable balances fluctuate widely, depending on the volume of purchases and the terms Marlboro's purchasing agent is able to negotiate. Clark's sample of 100 was designed to include accounts with large balances. In fact the 100 accounts confirmed last year covered 80 percent of the total accounts payable.

Both Clark and Kent spent many hours tracking down minor differences reported in confirmation responses. Nonresponding accounts were investigated by comparing Marlboro's balance with monthly statements received from suppliers.

Required:

a. Identify the accounts payable audit objectives that the auditors must consider in determining the audit procedures to be followed.

b. Identify situations when the auditors should use accounts payable confirmations, and discuss whether they are required to use them.

c. Discuss why the use of large dollar balances as the basis for selecting accounts payable for confirmation might not be the most efficient approach, and indicate what more efficient sample selection procedures could be followed when choosing accounts payable for confirmation.

15.19. During the audit of Zinco Enterprises, you found the following transaction:

Retained earnings	10,000	
Common stock		10,000

To record the issuance of 1,000 shares of no-par common stock pursuant to executive stock option plan.

Required:

a. What evidence would the auditor require to determine whether the above-mentioned stock option plan is compensatory or noncompensatory? What sources of evidence would the auditor most likely use?

b. Assume you have determined that the plan is compensatory. Your examination has also revealed that the plan is for newly hired personnel in a management development program and is compensation for future services. What adjusting entry would you propose?

15.20. You are a CPA engaged in an examination of the financial statements of Pate Corporation for the year ended December 31. The financial statements and records of Pate Corporation have not been audited by a CPA in prior years.

The stockholders' equity section of Pate Corporation's balance sheet at December 31, follows:

Stockholders' equity:

Capital stock—10,000 shares of $10 par value authorized; 5,000 shares issued and outstanding....................................	$ 50,000
Capital contributed in excess of par value of capital stock	32,580
Retained earnings	47,320
Total stockholders' equity	$129,900

Pate Corporation was founded in 1970. The corporation has ten stockholders and serves as its own registrar and transfer agent. There are no capital stock subscription contracts in effect.

Required:

a. Prepare the detailed audit program for the examination of the three accounts comprising the stockholder's equity section of Pate Corporation's balance sheet. (Do not include in the audit program the audit of the results of the current year's operations.)

b. After every other figure on the balance sheet has been audited by the CPA, it might appear that the retained earnings figure is a balancing figure and requires no further audit work. Why does the CPA audit retained earnings as he does the other figures on the balance sheet? Discuss. (AICPA adapted)

15.21. A and B form a corporation and transfer to it oil leases owned by them equally for which they had paid $30 in capitalized fees. They had also paid $1,280 for delay lease rentals which they had charged to expense in the year paid by them as individuals. The transferor stockholders had no other costs or expenses applicable to these leases. At the time of the transfer there were favorable geological and geophysical reports on the property, but there had been no production in the area. The board of directors of the new corporation issued $300,000 par value common stock for the leases, one half the stock going to A and one half to B. A and B donated concurrently one half of their respective shares to the corporate treasury to be sold at par for working capital.

Required:

a. Discuss the proper balance sheet presentation of the leases and of the capital and donated stock.

b. What audit procedures would you apply to the leases?

c. Must this stock issue be reported or registered with the SEC? Explain. (AICPA adapted)

16

AUDIT OF PAYROLL, OTHER REVENUE AND EXPENSE, AND COMPLETION OF FIELD WORK

This chapter is divided into two major sections. The first one covers the audit of payroll and the audit of other revenues and expenses which have not been covered in previous chapters. In this section the objectives are to explain with relation to payroll and other revenue and expense:

- A business approach to audit objectives concerning existence, valuation, cutoff, accounting principles, compliance, and effectiveness.
- Elements of internal accounting control relevant to these accounts.
- Applications of audit procedures for gathering evidence.
- Types of fraud and misstatement that might occur.

The second section covers the process of completing the field work and gathering up the loose ends of the audit. In this section the principal points covered are:

- Obtaining written management representations.
- Audit procedures for "subsequent events."
- Review of the work by audit managers and partners.
- Quality control and review of practice in general.

I. AUDIT OF PAYROLL AND OTHER REVENUE AND EXPENSE

Decisions about payroll and other compensation costs are usually important because the labor input is usually large. The payroll grouping of accounts includes not only wages and salaries but also vacation pay, pension benefits, deferred compensation contracts, compensatory stock option plans, employee benefits (e.g., health insurance), payroll taxes, and related accrued liabilities for these costs. Audit procedures explained in this chapter pertain mostly to techniques for testing transactions and auditing balances of wage and salary accounts.

The payroll and compensation cost accounting system may be simple or it may be complex. Cost and expense accounts may be few in number (e.g., executive salaries, sales commissions, and sales salaries in a retailing business) or they may be represented by a wide variety of account classifications dispersed throughout a cost accounting system (e.g., direct labor, indirect labor, asset construction wages, general overhead, and idle time costs in a manufacturing operation).

A BUSINESS APPROACH TO AUDIT OBJECTIVES

An overview of the personnel management system in a client company can contribute a significant understanding of payroll and compensation cost. Such an overview can assist in planning the compliance tests of transactions, and in most cases it can contribute significantly to planning the procedures for auditing balances (especially when the management control system is functioning effectively).

Existence

There is no question that payroll and other compensation costs will exist in a business. The real questions concern the amount, efficiency, and control over utilization of human resources. The auditor should first determine whether the business is labor-intensive or capital-intensive. The absolute magnitude and the percent relationship of payroll costs to total revenue and total expense will tell the auditor the degree of importance he or she should attach to the audit of such costs.

The general design of the data processing system is also important. Some companies may account for payroll costs in a simple manner to satisfy legal requirements—classifying output in a few accounts for direct labor, indirect labor, sales salaries and executive salaries. The legal requirements include payroll accounting for tax reporting and withholding purposes and inventory-production cost accounting for income tax purposes.

In contrast, other companies may use a complex managerial accounting and reporting system. Of course, such a system must be designed to satisfy basic legal recordkeeping requirements, but the system of reporting, analyzing, and controlling costs may be far more elaborate than the simple legalistic-system output. A managerial-oriented system may segment direct and indirect labor into several budgetary categories and may segment costs by responsibility centers or by cost centers. Thus aggregate sums of related costs (e.g., direct labor) may not appear in a single account but instead may be subclassified in a wide variety of accounts.

If the system is a simple legalistic one, the opportunities for close managerial control are minimized, and the auditor will probably have to conduct extensive compliance and substantive tests. A more complex managerial-oriented system, on the other hand, provides for closer managerial review and control of errors and out-of-line costs. Auditors may thus rely on managerial control to some extent, provided that they can find evidence that the review-control system is actually used effectively by managers.

In connection with understanding the client's business, the auditor can incorporate his or her earlier acquired knowledge of the marketing and production functions. Payroll costs and accounting for standard, repetitive marketing and production operations tend to be more systemized and uncomplicated than when marketing and production is oriented to special orders, special promotions, and nonrepetitive operations. A good understanding of the business also contributes insights to relative staff levels in production, marketing, maintenance, administration, and research and development functions. The nature of seasonal fluctuations and the mode of payment (e.g., hourly, monthly, bonus, commission) can also be discerned through knowledge of marketing and production organization features.

Valuation

For the most part payroll cost valuation problems are not difficult. However, some compensation costs and benefit programs (e.g., stock options, bonuses, pension plans) typically involve complex measurement methods and issues.

The auditor should determine how the client sets pay rates. For executives such determinations may be a matter of record in the directors' minutes, or they may be recorded in reports of periodic salary review committees. In the case of office and production workers, the personnel department generally includes a wage and salary administration function. Pay scales for unionized workers may be formalized in a union contract. In general, the more formal the system the better because objective evidence of basic rates is then available in documentary sources.

Valuation becomes less objective when nonproductive costs such as idle time and cost overruns have occurred. An effective managerial accounting system may have already identified such costs, and the audit of them may amount to a fairly straightforward analysis of management's explanations and calculations. However, when the reporting system does not identify such costs, the auditor must be alert for excessive labor costs in inventory or in self-constructed assets.

Another type of valuation problem may arise in audits of medium-to-small businesses. The Internal Revenue Code requires that compensation be "reasonable" in order to qualify as a business deduction, otherwise a portion of an unreasonably large salary may be considered a "dividend" paid by a corporation. When this happens, the corporation's income tax liability may be increased materially. The auditor should be alert to unreasonably large salaries, especially when paid to officers who are controlling stockholders.

Pension and stock option cost measurement principles are specified in APB *Opinion No. 8*[1] and APB *Opinion No. 25*[2]. The audit of these costs and other costs computed as bonuses, incentive pay, and deferred compensation require that the auditor obtain copies of the plans and contracts in order to understand the valuation problems.

Accounting Principles and Disclosure and Cutoff

Accounting measurement principles and proper cutoff are usually satisfied by providing appropriate accruals of cost at the fiscal year-end date. Familiarity with the types of compensation and benefits can provide the auditor with a checklist of costs for which accruals may be required. The audit of proper period cutoff may be facilitated by the existence of a management reporting system (e.g., budgetary, responsibility centered) that would highlight large variances in the period before year-end. Lacking such a system, a review of the payroll system payments, an analysis of sales commission accruals (and interrelationship with sales activity), and vouching of payroll tax returns would generally serve to satisfy the auditor that no material cutoff errors or measurement errors had occurred.

In addition to accounting measurement and cutoff issues, however, other areas of disclosure are important. The status of union negotiations, retroactive settlements, or new agreements as to wages constitute material information. Actions taken against the company by the Equal Employment Opportunity Commission (EEOC) and by the U.S. Labor Department (regarding industrial safety laws) may constitute contingencies respecting penalties or retroactive pay settlements.

Oftentimes managements write analytical explanations of the financial effect on results of operations of strikes, work stoppages, new union contracts, and other labor-related events for inclusion in the annual report. Such information is usually carried in management's explanations of financial operations and not in the financial statement footnotes. The auditor's responsibility regarding such financial data presented elsewhere in an annual report is to determine that the information does not contradict or distort related disclosures in the audited financial statements and footnotes. It is a common practice for auditors to review printer's proof of an annual report in order to ascertain that financial data in the president's letter and other narrative sections of the annual report correspond with the audited financial statement data.

Compliance

Personnel and payroll administration are subject to a wide variety of laws and regulations. The major ones are: federal, state, and local income tax withholding regulations, social security withholding and contribution regulations, federal and state unemployment insurance laws, workmen's

---

[1] "Accounting for the Cost of Pension Plans."

[2] "Accounting for Stock Issued to Employees."

compensation insurance laws, minimum wage laws, equal employment opportunity laws, industrial safety laws, the federal welfare and pension plans disclosure act, and the pension reform act of 1974 (ERISA—Employee Retirement Income Security Act). With almost every session of the U.S. Congress, some form of social legislation impacting on workingmen—their wages, working conditions, pensions, benefits, and so forth—is proposed.

Auditors need to be thoroughly familiar with the laws that produce regular and direct business expenses (e.g., social security, unemployment insurance, withholding regulations, workmen's compensation insurance). The effect of other social legislation concerning employment opportunities and industrial safety, however, are difficult to evaluate in an audit situation, and the auditor's duties in such cases are like those associated with other kinds of contingencies.

Compliance with plans, contracts, and union agreements respecting compensation should be reviewed by the auditor. These private agreements contain rights and obligations that create liabilities for the company. Failure to comply with one or more provisions of such agreements may mean the client has not recorded compensation cost and a related liability. For example, failure to award stock options, failure to program payment of a cost-of-living wage escalator, or failure to pay employees the rate required by their job classifications are all errors in compensation cost measurement that result from noncompliance.

Effectiveness

The independent auditor should be very interested in finding evidence of the effectiveness of a managerial-oriented labor cost reporting system. Budgetary comparisons, variance analyses, responsibility center reports, and cost center reports that are *used* by managers to initiate and direct corrective action are supporting evidence of existence, valuation, cutoff, and measurement accuracy. The auditor's task is to find signals in the reports (e.g., large efficiency variances) that should stimulate managerial action; then by inquiry and review of subsequent reports determine whether corrective action was actually taken. Such evidence of an effective system can mean that the auditor can rely on the system and thus limit subsequent detail audit work on payroll and compensation cost elements.

Internal auditors and management consultants are equally interested in determining whether a reporting system is effective, but their goals relate more to profitability and potential improvements and changes to increase profits. They may incorporate into the analysis job performance statistics, work measurements, and productivity standards as a means of making more complete evaluations of the efficiency of human resource utilization.

In Chapter 5, under the heading of Programs for Internal Audits, an example of the direction of a review of the payroll function was given. Recall that among the internal auditor's concerns were the payroll department's staffing and work flow characteristics, an analysis of overtime work scheduling, an evaluation of labor turnover, and an analysis of night maintenance personnel scheduling. Effectiveness studies involve audits of personnel planning; studies of cause, effect, and trend relationships; and evaluations of personnel development programs. The effectiveness objective also includes evaluations of employee recordkeeping procedures, labor relations and negotiation functions, and wage and salary administration operations.

INTERNAL CONTROL

Questionnaire and flowchart tools may be used to review the overall system for controlling payroll costs. Compliance tests of transaction details are an integral element of the internal accounting control examination, because by such means the basic input accuracy for managerial reports can be assessed. The input accuracy for these reports largely governs the effectiveness of the reports for managers' and auditors' purposes. Thus while the managerial reports may serve several audit purposes, decisions to rely on such reports must *follow* an assessment of their basic transaction input accuracy. If the auditor finds that accuracy or reliability is lacking in one or more specific reporting areas, then he or she may have identified another audit area that requires closer audit attention. (For example, inaccuracy of reporting and controlling labor costs charged to assets under construction would mean that the asset costs could bear more detailed audit work.)

Review Phase

A payroll data processing control system should exhibit separation of five functional responsibilities. These responsibilities overlap with the cash disbursements and accounts payable internal control systems.

1. Personnel or Labor Relations Department. Persons independent of the other functions should have transaction initiation authority to add new employees to the payroll, to delete terminated employees, to obtain authorizations for deductions (e.g., insurance, savings bonds, withholding tax exemptions), and to transmit authority for rate changes to the payroll department.

2. Timekeeping and Cost Accounting. Data on which pay is based (e.g., hours, piece-rate volume, incentives) should be accumulated independent of other functions. Cost data thus accumulated can be entered into the cost accounting system.

3. Supervision. All pay base data should be approved by an employee's immediate supervisor.

4. Payroll Accounting. Using rate and deduction information supplied by the personnel function and base data supplied by the timekeeping-supervision functions, independent persons should prepare individual paychecks, employee wage and salary records, and summary accounting journal entries.

5. *Payroll Distribution.* Actual custody of paychecks and cash should be controlled in distribution to employees so that the checks or cash do not return to persons involved in any of the other four functions.

These functional responsibilities relate primarily to nonsalaried employees of a manufacturing business. For salaried employees the system is simplified by not having to collect timekeeping data. In nonmanufacturing businesses the cost accounting operations may be very simple or even nonexistent. The relative importance of each of these five areas should be determined for each engagement in light of the nature and organization of the client's operations.

EXHIBIT 16–1
Employment and Timekeeping

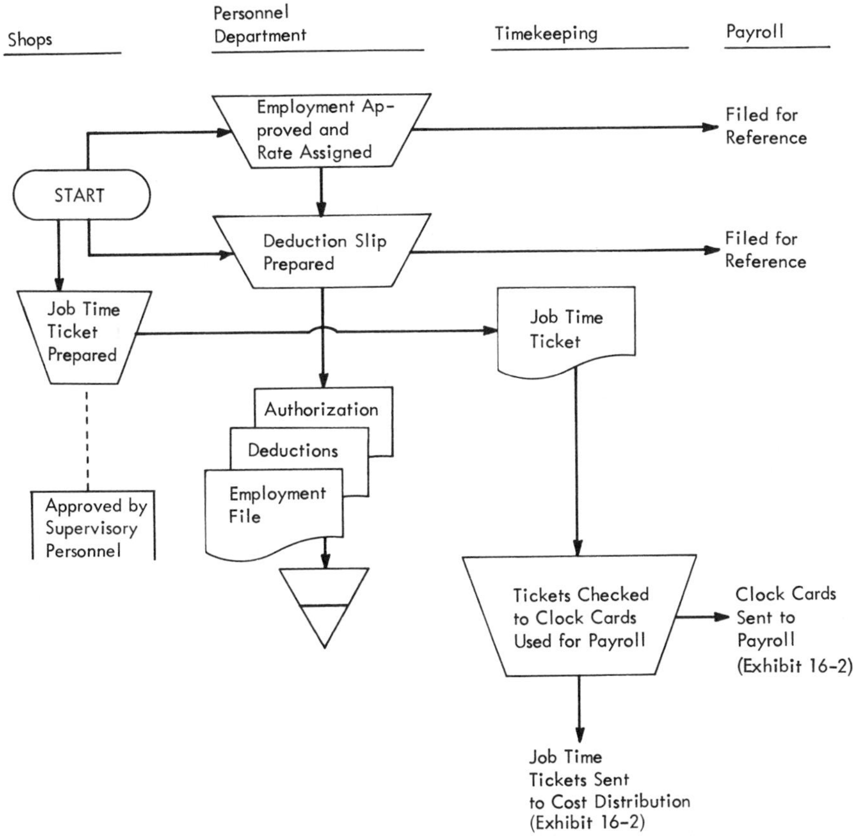

The flowchart in Exhibit 16–1 shows segregation of functional responsibilities related to employment authorization (personnel department), timekeeping and supervisor's approval. The remaining payroll responsibilities center in the preparation and distribution of checks. Exhibit 16–2 shows a proper segregation of duties and flow of transaction docu-

EXHIBIT 16–2
Check Preparation and Cost Accounting

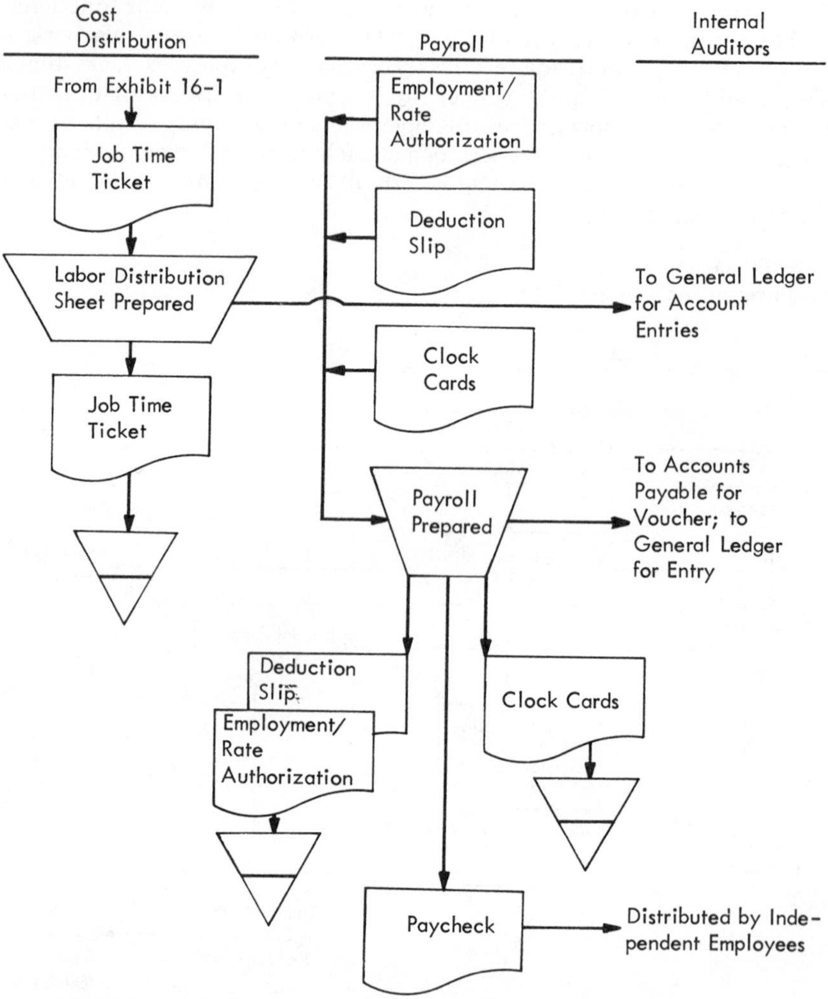

ments. Internal control questionnaire items relating to a payroll system are in Exhibit 16–3.

These procedures produce documentary files that can be sampled in the compliance tests of transaction details. The most important files are: (1) personnel department personnel files, (2) rate and deduction authorizations filed in Payroll, (3) job time tickets filed in Cost Distribution and the labor distribution worksheet filed in General Ledger, and (4) clock cards filed in Payroll and the payroll listing filed in Accounts Payable. Each of these files coordinate with one or more of the others, and they can

EXHIBIT 16–3

INTERNAL CONTROL QUESTIONNAIRE
PAYROLL SYSTEM

1. Are names of employees hired or terminated reported in writing to the payroll department by the personnel department?
2. Is the payroll compared to personnel files periodically? How often? By internal auditors?
3. Are all wage rates determined by contract, agreement, or policy and approved by a responsible personnel officer?
4. Are authorizations for deductions signed by the employees on file?
5. Are all employees paid by check?
6. Are payroll check blanks prenumbered? Is a special payroll bank account used?
7. Are payroll checks signed by persons who do not prepare the payroll or the checks, nor have custody of the other cash funds, nor keep accounting records?
8. Are checks distributed by someone other than the employee's immediate supervisor?
9. Is the payroll bank account reconciled by someone who does not prepare payrolls, sign checks, or distribute paychecks?
10. If payments are made in cash: Is an independent agent such as an armored car service used? Is currency placed in envelopes by employees who do not prepare payrolls? Are receipts obtained from employees?
11. Are unclaimed wages deposited in a special bank account or otherwise controlled by a responsible officer.
12. Is there a timekeeping department (function) independent of the payroll department?
13. Are timekeeping and cost accounting records (e.g., hours, dollars) reconciled with payroll department calculations of wages and salaries?
14. Are timecards or piece work reports prepared by the employee approved by his or her supervisor? Is a time clock or other electromechanical system in use?
15. Are payroll department personnel rotated in their duties? Required to take vacations? Bonded?
16. Is the payroll sheet itself signed and approved prior to payment by the employee preparing it? By a responsible officer?
17. Are payrolls audited periodically by internal auditors?
18. Do internal auditors conduct occasional surprise distributions of paychecks or cash?
19. Is the payroll preparation, check preparation, or check signature performed with EDP equipment? If so, complete the relevant portions of the EDP Internal Control Questionnaire.

be cross-tested as suggested in the discussion accompanying Exhibit 16–4.

By reference to the internal control questionnaire and flowchart, several kinds of error-checking procedures may be noted, including:

Periodic comparison of the payroll to the personnel department files (to check for terminated employees not deleted).

EXHIBIT 16–4
Audit Program—Selected Compliance Test Procedures

A. *Personnel Files and Compensation Documents*
   1. Select a sample of personnel files and review them for complete information on employment date, job classification, wage rate, authorized deductions. If files are on magnetic tape, use generalized audit software to select the sample.
   2. Retrace pay rate and deduction information to payroll department files used in payroll preparation. This tracing may be to a machine-readable master file on tape or disk.
   3. Review director's minutes for authorization of officers' salaries.
   4. Obtain copies and review pension plans, stock options, profit sharing, and bonus plans.

B. *Payrolls*
   1. Select a sample of payroll sheet entries:
      a. Vouch pay rate and deductions to personnel files or other authorizations.
      b. Vouch hours worked to clock cards. Note supervisor's approval.
      c. Recalculate gross pay, deductions, net pay.
      d. Foot (recalculate addition) of a selection of periodic payrolls.
      e. Vouch to canceled payroll check. Examine employees' endorsement.
      Note: Sample selection and the recalculations may be done with generalized audit software.
   2. Select a sample of clock cards, note supervisor's approval, and retrace to periodic payroll sheets.
   3. Vouch a sample of periodic payroll totals to payroll bank account transfer vouchers, and vouch payroll bank account deposit slip for cash transfer.
   4. Retrace a sample of employees' payroll entries to cumulative payroll records maintained for tax reporting purposes. Reconcile total of employees' payroll records with payrolls paid for the year.
      Note: The reconciliation may be started using generalized audit software.
   5. Review computer-printed error messages for evidence of the use of check digits, valid codes, limit tests and other input, processing and output editing controls. Retrace correction or resolution of errors.
   6. Retrace payroll information to management reports and to general ledger account postings.
   7. Obtain control of a periodic payroll and conduct a surprise distribution of paychecks.

C. *Cost Distribution Reports*
   1. Select a sample of cost accounting analyses of payroll:
      a. Reconcile periodic (e.g., weekly) totals with payroll payments for the same periods.
      b. Vouch to time records (e.g., job time tickets).
   2. Retrace cost accounting labor cost distributions to management reports and postings in general ledger and subsidiary account(s).
   3. Select a sample of labor cost items in (*a*) ledger accounts and/or (*b*) management reports. Vouch to supporting cost accounting analyses.
      Note: Sample selections from accounts management reports and cost accounting analyses may involve using generalized audit software to read computerized data base files.

Periodic rechecking of wage rate authorizations.
Payroll bank account reconciliation.
Rotation of employee duties.
Reconciliation of payroll data with cost accounting data.

Compliance Test of Transaction Details

Payroll systems are frequently automated with EDP equipment. However, in both manual and EDP systems, compliance tests of transaction details are highly important because the evidence produced bears heavily on the reliability of internal management reports and analyses. In turn, reliance on these reports and analyses, along with other analytical relationships, constitutes a major portion of the audit of payroll, compensation costs, and cost accounting balances.

Typical compliance test procedures are listed in Exhibit 16–4. Along with the procedures are indications of some ways in which typical manual-oriented tests may be coordinated with tests in an EDP environment.

These compliance tests are designed to produce evidence of the following:

- Adequacy of personnel files, especially the authorizations of pay rate and deductions used in calculating pay. The compliance tests run in two directions (codes below refer to procedures in Exhibit 16–4).

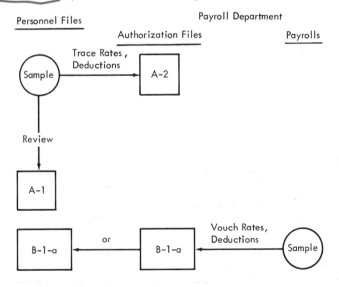

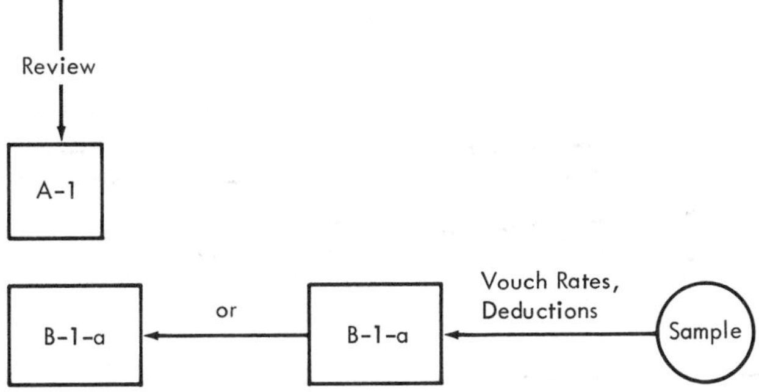

- Accuracy of the periodic payrolls recorded in accounts and in employees' cumulative wage records. The compliance tests tend to center on the periodic payrolls. The diagram below shows that the sample of employees' paycheck entries and totals from payrolls are both vouched to supporting documents and retraced to other records and reports.

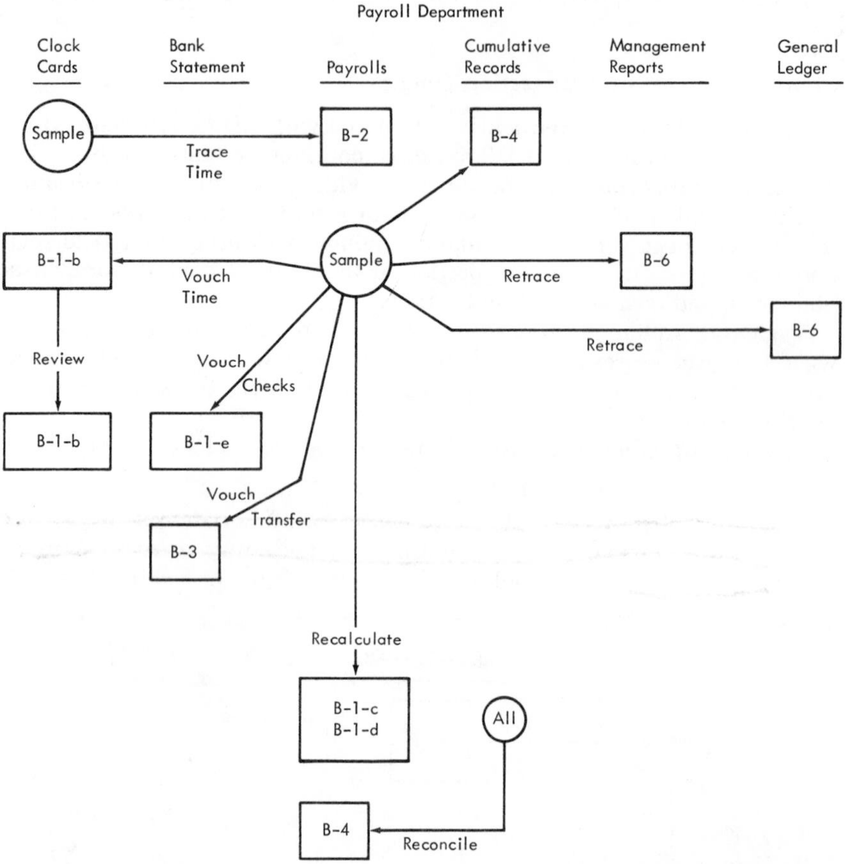

- Accuracy of cost accounting distributions and management reports. The cost accounting for labor costs must be reasonably accurate because good management reports contribute to cost control. The auditor who wishes to rely on the cost accounting system must determine whether it contains and transmits accurate information. Procedure B–6 is part of this test. Other tests are shown in the diagram on page 553.

In connection with these tests for overstatement, auditors may perform a *surprise observation* of a payroll distribution. Such an observation involves taking control of paychecks and accompanying a client representative as the distribution takes place. The auditor is careful to see that each employee is identified and that only one check is given to each individual. Unclaimed checks are controlled, and in this manner the auditor hopes to detect any fictitious persons on the payroll.

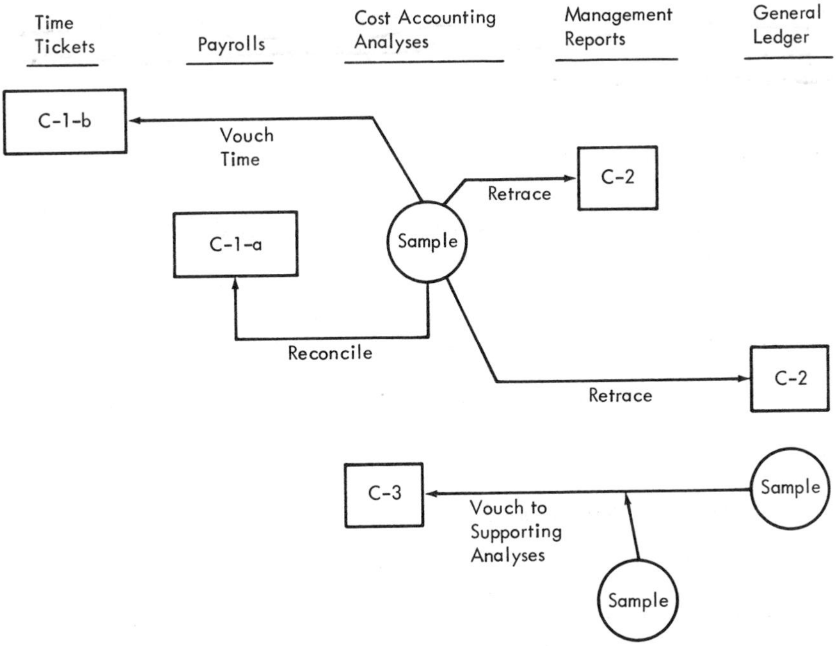

Computerized payroll and cost accounting systems are encountered frequently. Their complexity, however, may range from an application of simply writing payroll checks to an integrated system that prepares management reports and cost analyses based on payroll and cost distribution inputs. Methods of test data utilization are frequently employed to test controls in such systems, and parallel simulation may be applied efficiently to test an integrated system.

SUBSTANTIVE TESTS OF BALANCES

Payroll balances tend to be scattered among the following accounts: Administrative Salaries, Sales Salaries, Labor Cost in Inventory, Labor Cost in Cost of Goods Sold, Labor Cost in Constructed Assets, and a variety of other account classifications. In addition, compensation costs may be characterized by pension plan costs, employee fringe benefits, sales commissions, profit-sharing plans, deferred compensation contracts, and stock option compensation to name a few.

Audit problems respecting balances of a large segment of payroll costs (i.e., manufacturing labor) are compounded by the fact that the balances have little or no independent existence outside the accumulation of numerous payroll transactions. An account receivable is also a net accumulation of transactions, but there exists a customer to confirm the balance. No one can confirm the total of labor cost in inventory. It cannot be physically observed. Inquiries about it are not particularly convincing. Consequently, the principal procedures for auditing payroll and compensation costs are recalculation and analysis of interrelationships, verbal inquiry, vouching of documents, and reliance on internal control and internally generated reports.

Verbal Inquiry and Vouching

Inquiries are initially useful for learning about compensation that takes the form of commissions, fringe benefits, pensions, profit-sharing plans, bonus plans, deferred compensation contracts, and stock options. As a result of the inquiries the auditor knows to vouch the documents that set out the terms of such arrangements and can then audit related cost and expense balances by vouching account entries to the supporting contracts, documents, and plans. This segment of the audit may also involve retracing of compensation authorizations to accounts and recalculations of amounts.

Recalculation and Analysis of Interrelationships

The types of compensation costs mentioned above tend to exist in the form of infrequent, formally defined transactions that can be audited by specific identification. A large portion of costs, however, may fall in the category of aggregations of voluminous transactions. These aggregations are generally audited by means of recalculations and analyses in overall (analytical) tests.

Administrative salaries may be audited by adding up the salaries authorized by the directors and comparing the amount to the account balance. In a like manner sales commissions based on sales dollars or units may be recalculated by applying the contract rate to the base (sales dollars or physical volume as determined by the audit of sales).

Interrelationships become particularly important with respect to labor costs in inventories, cost of sales, and constructed assets. Among the relevant relationships are:

Gross margin.

Percentage of labor to total inventory cost.

Trends in these ratios.

Trends in gross payroll dollar amounts.

Variances from budget or standard.

Per unit labor costs.

Idle-time costs.

Research and development classifications of payroll cost compared to R&D activity.

Many of these ratios and relationships should be evidenced in internal management reports, and to the extent that the reports themselves have been found reliable, they may be used by the auditor for decision purposes. In some cases the auditor may have to calculate ratios and relationships, looking for any unusual occurrences or changes that would indicate a need for further evidence.

AUDIT OF REVENUE

As the field work nears an end, the auditor needs to consider other revenue accounts that have not been audited previously in connection with account groupings. As a brief review, the following types of revenue and related topics will have already been audited either in whole or in part at this stage of the engagement.

Revenue and Related Topics	*Related Account Groups*	*Chapter(s) in This Text*
Sales and sales returns	Revenue and receivables	11
Lease revenue	Fixed assets, revenue and receivables	11, 14
Franchise revenue	Receivables, intangibles	11, 13
Construction revenue	Revenue and receivables	11
Dividends and interest	Receivables, investments	11, 13
Gain, loss on asset disposals	Fixed assets, revenue and receivables, investments	11, 13, 14
Rental revenue	Revenue and receivables, investments	11, 13
Royalty and license revenue	Revenue and receivables, investments	11, 13
Long-term sales commitments	Revenue and receivables	11
Product line reporting	Revenue and receivables	11
Accounting policy disclosure	Revenue and receivables	11
Earnings per share	Equities	15

To the extent that these revenue items have been audited completely, the audit working papers should show cross-reference indexing to the revenue account in the trial balance. The accounts that have not been audited completely will be evident. The auditor should ascertain by reference to the trial balance (or other source if the trial balance does not contain sufficient detail) that he or she has a list of all the revenue and gain or loss accounts and amounts.

Additional audit procedures along the lines explained in earlier chapters may be applied to provide finishing touches to the evidence-gathering process. Other procedural reviews may be carried out as analyses of interrelationships and specific account analyses.

Analysis of Interrelationships

The revenue accounts and amounts should be compared to prior year data and to multiple year trends to ascertain whether any unusual fluctuations (or lack thereof) are present. Comparisons should also be made to budgets, monthly internal reports, and to forecasts, to ascertain whether there have been events that required explanation or analysis by management. These explanations themselves may then be subjected to audit. For example, a sales dollar increase may be explained as a consequence of a price increase—which can be corroborated by reference to transaction tests of price lists performed during the compliance testing of sales transaction control.

The auditor should also ascertain whether account classifications, aggregations, and summarizations are consistent with those of the prior year. This information will have a bearing on the consistency portion of the auditor's opinion.

Analysis of Miscellaneous Revenue—Vouching

All "miscellaneous" or "other" revenue accounts and all "clearing" accounts with credit balances should be analyzed. *Account analysis* in this context refers to the identification of each important item and amount in the account, following by vouching and inquiry to determine whether amounts should be classified elsewhere. All clearing accounts should be eliminated, and the amounts classified as revenue, deferred revenue, liabilities, deposits, or contra-assets as the case may be.

Miscellaneous and other accounts can harbor many accounting errors. Proceeds from sale of assets, insurance premium refunds, insurance proceeds, and other receipts may simply be credited to the account. Oftentimes the finding of such items as these reveal unrecorded asset disposals, expiration of insurance recorded as prepaid, or other asset losses covered by insurance. Exercise 16.19 at the end of this chapter shows an account analysis of a prepaid expense account.

Revenue Recognition and Unusual Transactions

Significant audit evidence and reporting problems can arise with transactions that are designed by management to manufacture earnings. Oftentimes such transactions are complicated through a structure of subsidiaries, affiliates, and related parties. Generally the amounts of revenue are large. The transactions themselves may not be concealed, but certain guarantees may have been made by management and not revealed to the auditor. The timing of the transactions may be carefully arranged to provide the most favorable income result.

These unusual types of transactions take a wide variety of characteristics that it is difficult to classify them for useful generalization. Controveries have arisen in the past over revenue recognized on the construction percentage-of-completion method, over sales of assets at inflated prices to management-controlled dummy corporations, over sales of real estate to independent parties with whom the seller later associates for development of the property (making guarantees as to indemnification for losses), and over disclosure of revenues by source. These revenue issues are a combination of evidential problems, auditor responsibility for detecting errors and irregularities, and reporting-disclosure standards. Three illustrations of such problems are given below.

Illustration. National Fried Chicken, Inc., a large fast-food franchiser, began negotiations to purchase State Hot Dog Company, a smaller convenience food chain, in August. At August 1, 1979, State's net worth was $7 million, and National proposed to pay $8 million cash for all the outstanding stock. On June 1, 1980, the merger was consumated, and National paid $8 million even though State's net worth had dropped to $6 million. Consistent with prior years State lost $1 million in the ten months ended June 1; and as in the past, the company showed a net profit of $1.5 million for June and July. At June 1, 1980, the fair value of State's net assets was $6 million, and National accounted for the acquisition as a purchase, recording $2 million goodwill. National proposed to show in consolidated financial statements the $1.5 million of post-acquisition income, and $50,000 amortization of goodwill.

Audit Resolution. The auditors discovered that the purchase price was basically set at 16 times expected earnings and that management had carefully chosen the consummation date in order to maximize goodwill (and reportable net income after amortization in fiscal 1980). The auditors required that $1 million of "goodwill" be treated as prepaid expenses which expired in the year ended July 31, 1980, so that bottom-line income would be $500,000.

Illustration. In August the company sold three real estate properties to BMC for $5,399,000 and recognized profit of $550,000. The letter agreement that covered the sale committed the company to use its best efforts to obtain permanent financing and to pay underwriting costs for BMC, and it provided BMC with an absolute guarantee against loss from ownership and a commitment by the company to complete construction of the properties.

SEC Resolution (ARS 153; February 25, 1974). The terms of this agreement made the recognition of profit improper because the company had not shifted the risk of loss to BMC.

Illustration. In December 1979, White Company sold one half of a tract of undeveloped land to Black Company in an arm's-length transaction. The portion sold had a book value of $1.5 million, and Black Company paid $2.5 million in cash. Black Company planned to build and sell apartment houses on the acquired land. In January 1980, White and Black announced a new joint venture to develop the entire tract. The two companies formed a partnership, each contributing its one half of the total tract of land. They agreed to share equally in future capital requirements and profits or losses.

Audit Resolution. The $1 million profit from the sale was not recognized as income in White's 1979 financial statements, but instead was classified as a deferred credit. White's investment in the joint venture was valued at $1.5 million. White's continued involvement in development of the property and the uncertainty of future costs and losses were cited as reasons.

AUDIT OF EXPENSES

Although many major expense items will have been audited in connection with other account groupings, numerous minor expenses may still remain unaudited. As a brief review the following major expenses and related topics have been audited in whole or in part at this late stage of the engagement.

Expenses and Related Topics	*Related Account Groups*	*Chapter(s) in This Text*
Purchases, cost of goods sold	Inventories and cost of goods sold	12
Inventory valuation losses	Inventories and cost of goods sold	12
Warranty and guarantee expense	Inventories and cost of goods sold, liabilities and equity	12, 15
Royalty and license expense	Inventories and cost of goods sold	12
Marketing and product R&D	Investments and intangibles	13
Investment value losses	Investments and intangibles	13
Rental property expenses	Investments and intangibles	13
Amortization of intangibles	Investments and intangibles	13
Bad debt expense	Revenue and receivables	11
Depreciation expense	Fixed assets	14
Property taxes, insurance	Fixed assets, liabilities and equity	14, 15
Lease and rental expense	Fixed assets	14
Repairs and maintenance	Fixed assets	14
Income tax expense	Liabilities and equity	15
Legal and professional fees	Liabilities and equity	15
Interest expense	Liabilities and equity	15
Pension and retirement benefits	Liabilities and equity, payroll	15, 16
Payroll and compensation costs	Payroll	16
Sales commissions	Payroll	16
Administrative compensation	Payroll	16
Contingencies	Liabilities and equity	15

Like the revenue accounts mentioned in the previous section, if audit work is complete as to expense accounts, the working papers should show cross-reference indexing from the evidential papers to the trial balance. Some of the expenses may not have been audited completely (e.g., property tax expense), and some finishing-touch vouching of supporting documents may be required.

Analysis of Interrelationships

Several minor expenses such as office supplies, telephone, utilities, and similar accounts are not audited until late in the engagement. Generally the dollar amounts in these accounts are not material (taken singly) and the relative risk is small that they might be misstated in such a way as to create misleading financial statements. Auditors usually audit these kinds of accounts by "comparison." With this method, a list of the expenses is made with comparative balances from one or more prior periods, and the dollar amounts are reviewed for unusual changes (or lack of unusual changes if reasons therefor are known).

Such a comparison may be enough to satisfy the auditor as to a decision that the amounts are fairly presented. On the other hand, questions might be raised and additional evidence might be sought. In the latter case the auditor may vouch some expenses to supporting documents (i.e., invoices and canceled checks). In many cases expense entries in the accounts will have been audited during the test of cash disbursement and accounts payable transactions, and the evidence thus produced in other phases of the audit should not be overlooked.

Comparisons to budgets, internal reports, and forecasts may also be made. Variations from budget may have been subject already to management explanation, or the auditor may need to explain variations.

Analysis of Expense Accounts—Vouching

All "miscellaneous" or "other" expense accounts and "clearing" accounts with debit balances should be analyzed by listing each important item on a working paper and vouching it to supporting documents. Miscellaneous and other expenses may include abandonments of property, items not deductible for tax purposes, or payments that should be classified in other expense accounts. Clearing accounts should likewise be analyzed, and items therein classified according to their nature or source so that all clearing account balances are removed and accounted for properly. (See Exercise 16.19 at the end of this chapter for an example of such an analysis.)

Advertising expense, travel and entertainment expense, and contributions are accounts that are typically analyzed in detail. These accounts are particularly sensitive to income tax consequences. Travel, entertainment, and contributions must be documented carefully in order to stand the IRS auditor's examination. Questionable items may have an impact on the income tax expense and liability.

Along with advertising, these expenses sometimes harbor abuses of company policy respecting expense allowances, and minor embezzlements or cheating sometimes can be detected by a careful auditor. For the most part a detailed audit of expense-account payments may be of greater interest to the efficiency-minded internal auditor than to the independent auditor. As far as the independent auditor is concerned, even if employees did overstate their reimbursable expenses, the actual paid-out amount is still fairly presented as a financial fact. If there is evidence of expense-account cheating, the independent auditor may present the data to management.

TYPES OF MAJOR FRAUD AND MISSTATEMENT

Payroll-related frauds can be ingenious, and they are usually carried out in an environment of internal control weaknesses. The most obvious type of payroll fraud is the "padded" payroll—fictitious persons on the payroll. Theoretically, a corrupt personnel department employee could authorize entry of a ghost on the rolls. However, the employee would also have to provide for receiving the paycheck and annual W–2 tax form and make sure that no one ever wondered where "Joe" worked and why "Joe" was never seen. Complications are added if "Joe" has to submit periodic time reports (a supervisor would have to approve them) or if he has to participate in a periodic salary review program.

Employees in collusion with supervisors might pad their time or production reports and share the overpayments. Lack of managerial review of productivity statistics, including a reconciliation of production shown in pay records with actual production output, would permit such overpayments to go unnoticed. Similarly, approval of overtime not worked or failure to notify the payroll department of a terminated employee could work the same way.

The auditor's best hope to detect such frauds would be through the tests of transactions described earlier in this chapter. Chances are that a minor fraud might escape attention by not being included in a random test sample and by being minor enough to not show up in gross overall test statistics. However, if a payroll fraud is massive and pervasive, one or more examples are likely to emerge in transaction test samples. The auditor's duty is to recognize them when they turn up in a sample.

Payroll department employees might themselves write paychecks for fictitious persons or for employees they know have terminated. If a weak control system permits such employees access to checks after they have been signed, the checks could then be taken. If payroll department employees have access to unclaimed paychecks, the same abstraction could be accomplished. The payroll might then have to be added short to reconcile with comparison totals (e.g., cost accounting labor accumulations or approved salary lists). In these cases the auditor's surprise observation of a payroll distribution and his recalculation of the arithmetic of the periodic payroll could detect the frauds.

"Computer fraud" might be more ingenious, but essentially the same manipulations would have to be carried out and similar weaknesses would have to exist. The central control feature in a computerized payroll system is the master file of active employees. This file generally contains name, identifying number, pay rate, information for deductions, and cumulative payroll records. When a current payroll is run, the active employee master file is consulted for information necessary to compute net pay. Improper entries on the master file and absence of processing controls (e.g., provision for an error message when a name is entered and no master record is on file) would make it possible to pay a fictitious person. Of course, the problem of delivering the check would still exist, and non-EDP controls would also have to be deficient. The auditor's work can begin with tests of master file data (e.g., vouching to personnel files) and proceed to tests of application controls to see if a ghost could be paid by the computer.

Major financial statement misstatement may occur through errors in the auditor's own judgment, prompted by managerial pressure to approve a particular accounting treatment or a particular unique transaction. Such misstatements generally arise over revenue recognition and timing judgments which were discussed in this chapter under the heading of *Audit of Revenue.* They may also arise from erroneous judgments to defer costs that ultimately turn out to have no value. If such events are to be called frauds, they are usually frauds on the auditor, perpetrated by managers. Whatever they are called, the result in the view of a disappointed investor is a materially misleading financial statement. Such events can lead to lawsuits for damages, creating problems of legal liability.

II. COMPLETION OF FIELD WORK

Return for a moment to Chapter 1 and review the definition of auditing according to the American Accounting Association's Committee on Basic Auditing Concepts.

> Auditing is a systematic process of objectively obtaining and evaluating evidence regarding assertions about economic actions and events to ascertain the degree of correspondence between those assertions and established criteria and communicating the results to interested users.

Throughout the intervening chapters emphasis has been placed on the systematic decision-oriented processes for gathering and evaluating evidence. The process begins with recognition of the economic things and events that are presented for audit, and it continues with an audit program organization of objectives and procedures designed to produce sufficient, competent evidential matter upon which to base a series of decisions.

A SEQUENCE OF AUDIT EVENTS

One finds it easy to visualize the auditor performing some audit work at an interim period sometime before a balance sheet date, and then completing the work *on* the magic balance sheet date. True, much audit work is done months before the balance sheet date, with the auditor working for a time, leaving the client's offices, and then returning for the year-end work. Actually, the auditor may not even do any audit work on the balance sheet date itself, but he or she *always* is engaged in evidence-gathering *after* that date—sometimes as much as six months afterwards.

Interim and Final Audit Work in Independent Auditing

In the interim audit work the auditor is generally involved deeply in a preliminary study and evaluation of internal accounting control—completing the questionnaire, constructing flowcharts, writing narratives, and planning the compliance tests. Some compliance tests are usually performed at interim, and tentative judgments about internal accounting control reliability are made early. Also, the auditor can apply audit procedures for substantive testing of balances as of an interim date, and in this way a significant amount of recalculating, vouching, observation, and confirmation can be performed early.

When the auditor returns around the year-end and receives final unaudited financial statements that have been prepared by management, he can start where he left off at interim and complete the work on internal accounting control evaluation and audit of balances. As a capstone to the programmed procedures the auditor always obtains written management representations.

Client Representations

Management makes many responses to inquiries during the course of an audit. Many of these responses are very important, sometimes constituting the basic evidence upon which an auditor makes decisions. To the extent that additional evidence is obtainable through other procedures, the auditor should corroborate client representations.

In addition, *Statement on Auditing Standards, No. 19* (Section 333), "Client Representations," issued in 1977, requires that the auditor obtain *written* client representations on matters of audit importance. These written representations, however, are not substitutes for corroborating evidence obtainable through applying other auditing procedures. The written representations take the form of a letter on the client's letterhead, addressed to the auditor, signed by a responsible officer (normally the chief executive officer and/or chief financial officer), and dated as of the date of the auditor's report. Thus, the letter covers events and representations running beyond the balance sheet date up to the end of all important field work.

SAS No. 19 (Section 333) contains a list of 20 matters and discussions of several other points that may be included in a written client representation letter. The SAS also contains a sample letter. Matters that may be in such a letter include the following:

Management's acknowledgement of primary responsibility for fair presentation of financial statements in conformity with generally accepted accounting principles.

Completeness of the minutes of stockholders', directors' and important committee meetings.

Information concerning related party transactions.

Information concerning events occurring subsequent to the balance sheet date.

Management plans and intentions that influence accounting treatments (e.g., excluding a short-term obligation from current liabilities because of intent to refinance with a long-term obligation).

The written client representations are evidence of the extent of management's cooperation with the auditor. If information is withheld or erroneous information is given by management, the letter serves as a record. Should a lawsuit or other controversy arise, management may be called to account for misinformation given in written client representations.

Prior to writing the representation letter, however, the auditor will have performed procedures during a time after the balance sheet date on (1) balances and events that existed *at* the balance sheet date, and (2) events that occurred *after* the balance sheet date.

EVENTS SUBSEQUENT TO THE BALANCE SHEET DATE

Two types of events that occur subsequent to the balance sheet date but before the end of field work (thus before issuance of the audit opinion) attract the auditor's attention. The first type involves adjustment of the accounts *as of the balance sheet date*. *Statements on Auditing Standards No. 1* (Section 560.03) gives the following explanation:

> The first type consists of those events that provide additional evidence with respect to conditions that existed at the date of the balance sheet and affect the estimates inherent in the process of preparing financial statements. All information that becomes available prior to the issuance of the financial statements should be used by management in its evaluation of the conditions on which the estimates were based. The financial statements should be adjusted for any changes in estimates resulting from the use of such evidence.

The auditor normally performs some procedures directed to subsequent events as a matter of ordinary due audit care. For example:

Using a cutoff bank statement to—

- Examine checks paid after year-end that are, or should have been, listed on the bank reconciliation.
- Examine bank posting of deposits in transit listed on the bank reconciliation.

Vouching collections on accounts receivable in the month following year-end for evidence of existence and collectibility of the year-end balance.

Retracing cash disbursements of the month after year-end to accounts payable for evidence of any liabilities unrecorded at year-end.

Vouching of write-downs of fixed assets after year-end for evidence that such valuation problems existed at the year-end date.

Vouching of sales of investment securities, write-downs, or write-offs in the months after the audit date for evidence of valuation at the year-end date.

Vouching and retracing sales transactions in the month after year-end for evidence of proper sales and cost of sales cutoff.

SAS No. 1 (Section 560.04) gives further explanation and examples as follows:

> Identifying events that require adjustment of the financial statements under the criteria stated above calls for the exercise of judgment and knowledge of the facts and circumstances. For example, a loss on an uncollectible trade

account receivable as a result of a customer's deteriorating financial condition leading to bankruptcy subsequent to the balance sheet date would be indicative of conditions existing at the balance sheet date, thereby calling for adjustment of the financial statements before their issuance. On the other hand, a similar loss resulting from a customer's major casualty such as a fire or flood subsequent to the balance sheet date would not be indicative of conditions existing at the balance sheet date and adjustment of the financial statements would not be appropriate. The settlement of litigation for an amount different from the liability recorded in the accounts would require adjustment of the financial statements if the events, such as personal injury or patent infringement, that gave rise to the litigation had taken place prior to the balance sheet date.

The second type of subsequent event involves occurrences that had both their cause and manifestation arising *after* the balance sheet date. Recall that the auditor's responsibility for adequate disclosure runs to the date marking the end of the field work.[3] Consequently even for those events that occurred after the balance sheet date and are not of the first type requiring financial statement adjustment, the auditor must consider their impact on the financial statements and footnotes taken as a whole, and he may insist that disclosure be made.

SAS No. 1 (Sections 560.05–.06) offers a concise explanation of the second type of subsequent event as follows:

> The second type consists of those events that provide evidence with respect to conditions that did not exist at the date of the balance sheet being reported on but arose subsequent to that date. These events should not result in adjustment of the financial statements.* Some of these events, however, may be of such a nature that disclosure of them is required to keep the financial statements from being misleading. Occasionally such an event may be so significant that disclosure can best be made by supplementing the historical financial statements with pro forma financial data giving effect to the event as if it had occurred on the date of the balance sheet. It may be desirable to present pro forma statements, usually a balance sheet only, in columnar form on the face of the historical statements.
>
> Examples of events of the second type that require disclosure in the financial statements (but should not result in adjustment) are:
>
> *a.* Sale of a bond or capital stock issue.
> *b.* Purchase of a business.
> *c.* Settlement of litigation when the event giving rise to the claim took place subsequent to the balance sheet date.
> *d.* Loss of plant or inventories as a result of fire or flood.
> *e.* Losses on receivables resulting from conditions (such as a customer's major casualty) arising subsequent to the balance sheet date.
>
> * This paragraph is not intended to preclude giving effect in the balance sheet, with appropriate disclosure, to stock dividends or stock splits or reverse splits consummated after the balance sheet date but before issuance of the financial statements.

The aspect of retroactive recognition of the effect of stock dividends and splits is an exception that may be explained briefly with an example.

[3] In connection with a registration statement filed under the Securities Act of 1933, responsibility runs to the effective date of the registration statement.

The problem is one of timing and one of informative communication to financial statement users. When the financial statements reach the users, the stock dividend or split may have been effected, and to report financial data as if it had not occurred might be considered misleading.

Illustration. The company approved a 2-for-1 stock split to be effective February 1. The fiscal year-end was December 31, and the financial statements as of December 31 showed 50 million shares authorized, 10 million shares issued and outstanding, and earnings per share of $3.

Audit Resolution. Footnote disclosure was made of the split and of the relevant dates. The equity section of the balance sheet showed 50 million shares authorized, 20 million shares issued and outstanding, and earnings per share of $1.50 was shown along with the income statement. Earnings per share of prior years were adjusted accordingly. The footnote disclosed comparative earnings per share on the predividend shares. The audit report was dated February 25.

Dual Dating in the Audit Report

Sometimes it happens that *after* completion of field work (but before issuance of the report), a significant event comes to the auditor's attention. Imagine that in the illustration given above that field work had been completed on January 20, and that the audit report was to be so dated; then the auditor learned of the 2-for-1 stock dividend while in the process of writing the report and opinion.

Dual dating refers to the dating of the opinion as of the end of field work along with a later date attached to disclosure of the significant subsequent event. Thus in the illustration, the opinion would be dated "January 20, except as to Footnote X which is dated February 1." The audit resolution described above would be the same as before.

The purpose of dual dating is twofold: (1) to provide a means of inserting important information in the financial statements even when learned after field work is complete, while at the same time (2) to inform users that the auditor takes full responsibility for subsequent events only up to the end of field work (i.e., January 20) and for the specifically identified later event but does not take responsibility for other events which may have occurred between January 20 and February 1. (Audit standards associated with reporting events that become known *after the report is issued* are covered in Chapter 18.)

Audit Program for the Subsequent Period

Some audit procedures performed in the period subsequent to the balance sheet date may be part of the audit program for determining cutoff and proper valuation of balances as of the balance sheet date. However, the procedures specifically designed for gathering evidence about the two types of subsequent events is different and apart from the rest of the audit program. The procedures shown in Exhibit 16–5 should be performed at or near the completion of field work (or near the effective date in the case of an SEC registration engagement).

EXHIBIT 16–5

AUDITING PROCEDURES FOR SUBSEQUENT EVENTS

a. Read the latest available interim financial statements; compare them with the financial statements being reported upon; and make any other comparisons considered appropriate in the circumstances. In order to make these procedures as meaningful as possible for the purpose expressed above, the auditor should inquire of officers and other executives having responsibility for financial and accounting matters as to whether the interim statements have been prepared on the same basis as that used for the statements under examination.

b. Inquire of and discuss with officers and other executives having responsibility for financial and accounting matters (limited where appropriate to major locations) as to:

(i) Whether any substantial contingent liabilities or commitments existed at the date of the balance sheet being reported on or at the date of inquiry.

(ii) Whether there was any significant change in the capital stock, long-term debt, or working capital to the date of inquiry.

(iii) The current status of items, in the financial statements being reported on, that were accounted for on the basis of tentative, preliminary, or inconclusive data.

(iv) Whether any unusual adjustments have been made during the period from the balance sheet date to the date of inquiry.

c. Read the available minutes of meetings of stockholders, directors, and appropriate committees; as to meetings for which minutes are not available, inquire about matters dealt with at such meetings.

d. Inquire of client's legal counsel concerning litigation, claims, and assessments. (See *SAS No. 12*, Section 337, covered in Chapter 15 of this textbook.)

e. Obtain a letter of representations, dated as of the date of the auditor's report, from appropriate officials, generally the chief executive officer and chief financial officer, as to whether any events occurred subsequent to the date of the financial statements being reported on by the independent auditor that in the officer's opinion would require adjustment or disclosure in these statements. The auditor may elect to have the client include representations as to significant matters disclosed to the auditor in his performance of the procedures in subparagraphs (*a*) to (*d*) above and (*f*) below.

f. Make such additional inquiries or perform such procedures as he considers necessary and appropriate to dispose of questions that arise in carrying out the foregoing procedures, inquiries, and discussions.

Source: *Statement on Auditing Standards No. 1* (Section 560.12), "Subsequent Events."

The auditing procedures for subsequent events constitute a large part of the "S–1 review," which is the audit for subsequent events contemplated by the Securities Act of 1933 respecting the auditor's responsibility running to the effective date of a registration statement. In addition to the procedures listed above the auditor should read the entire prospectus and other pertinent portions of the registration statement, and make inquires and obtain written representations (as in part *e* in Exhibit 16–5) up to the effective date. (Refer to *SAS No.1*, Section 710, "Filings under Federal Securities Statutes.")

However, recall that in the *Escott* v. *BarChris* lawsuit (Appendix 4–B), the S–1 review was found to be deficient. The audit program for the review was in accordance with generally accepted auditing standards, but the court found that its execution was faulty. Notwithstanding the fact that the several procedures are set out by the AICPA in an authoritative pronouncement, an auditor must be careful to see that the execution of them will stand the test of a reasonable critical review. In addition the auditor must be careful to apply procedures that are not in the list if circumstances indicate matters that should be investigated further. Reliance on the *form* of the list in *SAS No. 1 may not* serve as a complete defense in some future controversy.

QUALITY CONTROL REVIEW PROGRAM

Quality control of the audit work on each engagement is achieved by exercising supervision at all levels. The partner in charge of the engagement reviews the work of the manager; the manager reviews the work done by the in-charge accountant and the assistant accountants; the in-charge accountant reviews the work done by the assistants. At each stage of review, more work may be indicated to clear up unresolved exceptions, incomplete procedures and, in general, to put the working papers in good form.

In addition, many audit firms practice "cold review." A partner not in charge of the audit engagement reviews the draft report and the working papers before the job is closed. The objective is to obtain another expert review by someone who is not closely involved with the everyday work on the engagement. Such a person may notice deficiencies that have escaped the attention of persons directly involved in the audit details.

Quality control concerns on a professionwide basis first entered the auditing standards literature in 1974 with the issuance of *Statement on Auditing Standards No. 4* (Section 160) entitled, "Quality Control Considerations for a Firm of Independent Auditors." This SAS addressed the problem of identifying policies and procedures that may affect the quality of work on audit engagements. The elements of quality control which should be considered by firms are the following:

Independence of personnel.

Assigning qualified personnel to engagements.

Consultation with experts.

Supervision of work at all organizational levels.

Hiring of personnel.

Professional development and continuing education.

Advancement of personnel in the firm.

Acceptance and continuance of clients.

Inspection—"internal audit" of the effectiveness of the other quality control considerations.

As a result of congressional criticism of the accounting profession prompted by some dramatic fraud and bankruptcy cases, the AICPA has acted to strengthen the profession's commitment to quality control. A new senior committee—the Quality Control Standards Committee—was formed early in 1978. This committee has begun to consider various topics for official pronouncements on quality control.

When the Quality Control Standards Committee was created, some professionwide quality control programs already existed. Materials available to guide firms in setting policies and procedures for the elements identified in *SAS No. 4* included a program approved by the AICPA in 1976 and two guidance documents issued by the Special Committee on Proposed Standards for Quality Control Policies and Procedures (as revised, 1978).

Voluntary Quality Control Review Program for CPA Firms (AICPA, 1976). This pamphlet describes a voluntary program whereby CPA firms can request review by the AICPA staff and a selected panel of experts.

Quality Control Policies and Procedures for Participating CPA Firms (AICPA, 1978). This booklet gives examples of specific policies and procedures for firms to use as a guide for preparing their own quality control documents.

Performing and Reporting on Quality Control Compliance Reviews (AICPA, 1978). This document provides guidance for firms intending to participate in the voluntary review program. The guide discusses the objectives of a compliance review and the nature and extent of procedures that would be performed by a review team conducting and reporting on a compliance review.

A quality control review is very similar to an audit. Of course, in an audit a business's financial statements are the representations taken under examination. In a quality control review, an auditing firm's *quality control document* contains the "representations" about the policies and procedures which will be reviewed. These documents, which range from 30 to over 100 pages in length (depending on the size of the firm), contain a wealth of information about a firm's professional activities. Students—prospective employees of the firms—should obtain and read the document. Policies include specific firm procedures concerning ownership of stock in clients, pay, rotation of duties, promotion, continuing education, and other matters of special interest to new employees.

Quality control review is an integral element of the membership rules for the SEC practice firms and the private companies practice firms sections of the AICPA's division for firms. In addition, the SEC practice firms section will have a public oversight board composed of prominent persons not otherwise connected with the accounting profession. (The firm of Arthur Andersen & Co. has had such an oversight board for several years.

This board has issued public reports on its review of the firm.) The objective of such a board is to provide a detached but expert view of the operations of the profession.

An apparently acceptable method of obtaining *peer review* is for one auditing firm to hire another auditing firm to conduct a review. As of early 1978 almost all of the "Big Eight" firms and a number of smaller firms had retained one another to conduct quality control reviews. Some of the firms have published reports resulting from completed reviews.

TO THE REPORTING OBLIGATION

No matter where the study of auditing is begun, all roads lead to one end product—the auditor's report. The next four chapters deal with the attestation rendered by independent auditors and with reports of internal auditors and governmental auditors. All the decisions based on sufficient competent evidential matter finally become a part of the reporting decision. It is here that accounting, auditing, and one's professional sense of fairness in communication join in the art of report construction. The auditor's reporting obligation is the obligation to serve the public interest.

REVIEW QUESTIONS

16.1. What grouping of accounts is associated with "payroll"?

16.2. In a payroll system, what duties should be separated?

16.3. Why might an auditor conduct a surprise observation of a payroll distribution? What should be observed?

16.4. Generally, what procedures are used in the audit of miscellaneous revenue accounts?

16.5. How are minor expenses such as telephone and utilities expenses usually audited?

16.6. Why are advertising expense, travel and entertainment expense, and charitable contributions given special attention during an audit?

16.7. What is the purpose of a client representation letter? What representations would you expect management to make in a client representation letter with respect to receivables? Inventories? Minutes of meetings?

16.8. What are the two types of "subsequent events"? In what way(s) are they different?

16.9. What treatment is given stock dividends and splits which occur after the balance sheet date, but before the audit report is issued? Explain.

16.10. What is the purpose of "dual dating"?

16.11. Of what use is an inquiry of management during the subsequent period?

16.12. Generally, what additional actions should the auditor take in the period between the audit report date and the effective date of a registration statement?

16.13. Describe a "cold review." What is its purpose?

16.14. What is the objective of the AICPA Quality Control Standards Committee?

EXERCISES AND PROBLEMS

16.15. Listed below is a selection of items from the internal control questionnaires shown in the chapter. For each one:

a. Identify the control characteristic to which it applies (e.g., segregation of duties—authorization of transactions, access to assets and recordkeeping duties; sound error-checking practices and the like).
b. Specify one compliance test procedure an auditor could use to determine whether the control was operating effectively.
c. Using your business experience, your logic, and/or your imagination, give an example of an error or irregularity that could occur if the control was absent or ineffective.
d. Specify a substantive testing procedure an auditor could use to uncover errors or irregularities, if any, resulting from absence of the control.

(1) Are names of employees hired or terminated reported in writing to the payroll department by the personnel department?
(2) Are payroll checks signed by persons who do not prepare the payroll or checks, nor have custody of other cash funds, nor keep accounting records?
(3) Is there a timekeeping department (function) independent of the payroll department?
(4) Are timekeeping and cost accounting records (e.g., hours, dollars) reconciled with payroll department calculations of wages and salaries?

16.16. You are engaged in auditing the financial statements of Henry Brown, a large independent contractor. All employees are paid in cash because Mr. Brown believes this arrangement reduces clerical expenses and is preferred by his employees.

During the audit you find in the petty cash fund approximately $200 of which $185 is stated to be unclaimed wages. Further investigation reveals that Mr. Brown has installed the procedure of putting any unclaimed wages in the petty cash fund so that the cash can be used for disbursements. When the claimant to the wages appears, he is paid from the petty cash fund. Mr. Brown contends that this procedure reduces the number of checks drawn to replenish the petty cash fund and centers the responsibility for all cash on hand in one person inasmuch as the petty cash custodian distributes the pay envelopes.

Required:

a. Does Mr. Brown's system provide proper internal control of unclaimed wages? Explain fully.
b. Because Mr. Brown insists on paying salaries in cash, what procedures would you recommend to provide better internal control over unclaimed wages? (AICPA)

16.17. You are the senior in charge of the annual audit of ABC Manufacturing Corporation for the year ending December 31. You are informed by the partner supervising the engagement that the estimated time required for the audit for you and one assistant is two weeks for "preliminary work" in November and three weeks for "final work" after the books are closed for the year.

You find that the client's internal control over hourly payrolls is not perfect in that the size of the organization does not permit complete diversification of duties, yet there are no outstanding weaknesses. The 300 hourly employees are paid biweekly by check. Wage rates are set forth in a union contract, a copy of which is furnished to you.

Required:

a. Prepare an audit program for the examination of hourly payrolls to be performed during "preliminary work."

b. State what, if any, additional auditing procedures would be required in connection with hourly payrolls during the "final work" on the audit. (AICPA adapted)

16.18. The Generous Loan Company has 100 branch loan offices. Each office has a manager and four or five subordinates who are employed by the manager. Branch managers prepare the weekly payroll, including their own salaries, and pay employees from cash on hand. Employees sign the payroll sheet signifying receipt of their salary. Hours worked by hourly personnel are inserted in the payroll sheet from timecards prepared by the employees and approved by the manager.

The weekly payroll sheets are sent to the home office along with other accounting statements and reports. The home office compiles employee earnings records and prepares all federal and state salary reports from the weekly payroll sheets.

Salaries are established by home office job-evaluation schedules. Salary adjustments, promotions, and transfers of full-time employees are approved by a home office salary committee based upon the recommendations of branch managers and area supervisors. Branch managers advise the salary committee of new full-time employees and terminations. Part-time and temporary employees are hired without referral to the salary committee.

Required:

a. Based upon your review of the payroll system, how might funds for payroll be diverted?

b. Prepare a payroll audit program to be used in the home office to audit the branch office payrolls of the Generous Loan Company. (AICPA adapted)

16.19. You are examining the financial statements of the ABY Company, a retail enterprise, for the year ended December 31, 1979. The client's accounting department presented you with an analysis of the Prepaid Expenses account balance of $31,400 at December 31, 1979, as shown below.

ABY COMPANY
Analysis of Prepaid Expenses Account
December 31, 1979

Description	*Balance December 31, 1979*
Unexpired insurance:	
Fire	$ 750
Liability	4,900
Utility deposits	2,000
Loan to officer	500
Purchase of postage meter machine, one half of invoice price	400
Bond discount	3,000
Advertising of store opening	9,600
Amount due for overpayment on purchase of furniture and fixtures	675
Unsaleable inventory—entered June 30, 1979	8,300
Contributions from employees to employee welfare fund	(275)
Book value of obsolete machinery held for resale	550
Funds delivered to Skyhigh Stores with purchase offer	1,000
Total	$31,400

Additional information includes the following:

1. Insurance policy data:

Type	*Period Covered*	*Premium*
Fire	12/31/78 to 12/31/80	$1,000
Liability	6/30/79 to 6/30/80	9,500

2. The postage meter machine was delivered in November, and the balance due was paid in January. Unused postage of $700 in the machine at December 31, 1979, was recorded as expense at time of purchase.
3. Bond discount represents the unamortized portion applicable to bonds maturing in 1980.
4. The $9,600 paid and recorded for advertising was for the cost of an advertisement to be run in a monthly magazine for six months, beginning in December 1979. You examined an invoice received from the advertising agency and extracted the following description:

   "Advertising services rendered for store opened in November 1979 . . . $6,900"

5. ABY has contracted to purchase Skyhigh Stores and has been required to accompany its offer with a check for $1,000 to be held in escrow as an indication of good faith. An examination of canceled checks revealed the check had not been returned from the bank through January 1980.

Required:

a. What is the correct balance of prepaid expenses?

b. For each item in the account analysis, give—

(1) The evidence that should be gathered.

(2) The adjusting entry, if any. (AICPA adapted)

16.20. XYZ Corporation has several hundred employee travel advances outstanding at all times. Subsidiary ledger cards for individual employees are controlled by a general ledger account. Certain advances are specifically designated "permanent"; all others are intended to be cleared at the end of each field trip. All cash transactions for advances, reimbursements, or returns, and all expenses reported are posted to the subsidiary ledger cards.

Required:

Assuming no restrictions have been placed on the scope of your audit, prepare an audit program for the examination of the outstanding travel advances and the general ledger control account. (AICPA)

16.21. You are examining the records of a moderate-sized manufacturing corporation in connection with the preparation of a balance sheet and operating statement to be submitted with your opinion. There is some internal control but the office and bookkeeping staff comprises only three persons. You decide to audit a sample of transactions in detail. The sales are $1 million per year.

Submit a detailed, explicit audit program setting forth the steps you believe are necessary in connection with the following expense accounts. (The total of one year's charges in each account is set forth opposite each caption):

a.	Advertising	$60,000
b.	Rent	8,000
c.	Salesperson's commissions	39,000
d.	Insurance	4,000

16.22. In connection with a general audit of a manufacturing company, it is necessary to make an examination of *miscellaneous cash receipts*, as distinguished from *general receipts*.

State specifically the procedures auditors should follow to satisfy themselves that all cash from the following sources has been received that should have been received:

1. Interest and dividends on securities owned, and interest on notes receivable.
2. Amounts received for equipment sold or exchanged.
3. Proceeds from bank loans.
4. Refunds of advances for travel expenses.
5. Refunds of insurance premiums.
6. Rentals from property owned.
7. Royalties received.
8. Sales of scrap.
9. Sales of capital stock and bond issues.
10. Sales of securities owned. (AICPA)

16.23. You are in the process of "winding up" the field work on XYZ Stove Corporation, a company engaged in the manufacture and sale of kerosene space heating stoves. To date there has been every indication that the financial statements of the client present fairly the position of the company at December 31 and the results of its operations for the year then ended. The company had total assets at December 31 of $4 million and a net profit for the year (after deducting federal and state income tax provisions) of $285,000. The principal records of the company are a general ledger, cash receipts record, voucher register, sales register, check register, and general journal. Financial statements are prepared monthly. Your field work will be completed on February 20, and you plan to deliver the report to the client by March 12.

Required:

a. Prepare a brief statement as to the purpose and period to be covered in a review of subsequent events.

b. Outline the post-audit review program which you would follow to determine what transactions involving material amounts, if any, have occurred since the balance sheet date. (AICPA adapted)

16.24. The following events occurred in different cases, but in each instance the event happened after the close of the fiscal year under audit, but before all representatives of the auditor had left the office of the client. State in each case what notice, if any, you would take in your report on the fiscal year; the closing date in each instance is December 31.

1. Merchandise handled by the company had been traded in the open markets in which it procures its supplies at $1.40 on December 31. This price had prevailed for two weeks, following an official market report that predicted vastly enlarged supplies; however, no purchases were made at $1.40. The price throughout the preceding year had been about $2 which is the level experienced over several years. On January 18 the price returned to $2, following public disclosure of an error in the official calculations of the prior December, correction of which destroyed the expectations of excessive supplies. Inventory at December 31 was on a cost-or-market basis.
2. On February 1, the board of directors adopted a resolution accepting the offer of an investment banker to guarantee the marketing of $100 million of preferred stock.
3. On January 22, one of the three major plants of the client burned with a loss of $50 million which was covered to the extent of $40 million by insurance.
4. The client in this case is an investment company of the open-end type. In January a wholly new management came into control. By February 20, the new management had sold 90 percent of the investments carried at December 31 and had purchased others of a substantially more speculative character.
5. This company has a wholly owned but not consolidated subsidiary producing oil in a foreign country. A serious rebellion began in that country on January 18 and continued beyond the completion of your audit work. The press in this country has carried extensive coverage of the progress of the fighting. (AICPA adapted)

16.25. In connection with your examination of the financial statements of Olars Manufacturing Corporation for the year ended December 31, your post-balance sheet date review disclosed the following items:

1. *January 3:* The state government approved a plan for the construction of an express highway. The plan will result in the appropriation of a portion of the land area owned by Olars Manufacturing Corporation. Construction will begin late next year. No estimate of the condemnation award is available.
2. *January 4:* The funds for a $25,000 loan to the corporation made by Mr. Olars on July 15 were obtained by him by a loan on his personal life insurance policy. The loan was recorded in the account Loan from Officers. Mr. Olars's source of the funds was not disclosed in the company records. The corporation pays the premiums on the life insurance policy, and Mrs. Olars, wife of the president, is the owner and beneficiary of the policy.
3. *January 7:* The mineral content of a shipment of ore en route on December 31 was determined to be 72 percent. The shipment was recorded at year-end at an estimated content of 50 percent by a debit to Raw Material Inventory and a credit to Accounts Payable in the amount of $20,600. The final liability to the vendor is based on the actual mineral content of the shipment.
4. *January 15:* Culminating a series of personal disagreements between Mr. Olars, the president, and his brother-in-law, the treasurer, the latter resigned, effective immediately, under an agreement whereby the corporation would purchase his 10 percent stock ownership at book value as of December 31. Payment is to be made in two equal amounts in cash on April 1 and October 1. In December the treasurer had obtained a divorce from his wife who was Mr. Olars's sister.
5. *January 31:* As a result of reduced sales, production was curtailed in mid-January and some workers were laid off. On February 5 all the remaining workers went on strike. To date the strike is unsettled.
6. *February 10:* A contract was signed whereby Mammoth Enterprises purchased from Olars Manufacturing Corporation all of the latter's fixed assets (including rights to receive the proceeds of any property condemnation), inventories, and the right to conduct business under the name "Olars Manufacturing Division." The effective date of the transfer will be March 1. The sale price was $500,000 subject to adjustment following the taking of a physical inventory. Important factors contributing to the decision to enter into the contract were the policy of the board of directors of Mammoth Industries to diversity the firm's activities and the report of a survey conducted by an independent market appraisal firm which revealed a declining market for Olars products.

Required:

Assume that the above items came to your attention prior to completion of your audit work on February 15, and that you will render a short-form report. For *each* of the above items:

a. Give the audit procedures, if any, that would have brought the item to your attention. Indicate other sources of information that may have revealed the item.

b. Discuss the disclosure that you would recommend for the item, listing all details that you would suggest should be disclosed. Indicate those items or details, if any, that should not be disclosed. Give your reasons for recommending or not recommending disclosure of the items or details. (AICPA adapted)

16.26. In connection with your audit, you request that the management furnish you with a letter or letters containing certain representations. For example, such representations might include the following: (1) the client has satisfactory title to all assets; (2) no contingent or unrecorded liabilities exist except as disclosed in the letter; (3) no shares of the company's stock are reserved for options, warrants, or other rights; and (4) the company is not obligated to repurchase any of its outstanding shares under any circumstances.

Required:

a. Explain why you believe a letter of representation should be furnished to you.

b. In what way, if any, do client representations affect your audit procedures and responsibilities? (AICPA adapted)

16.27. The major written understandings between a CPA and client, in connection with an examination of financial statements, are the engagement (arrangements) letter and the client's representation letter.

Required:

a. (1) What are the objectives of the engagement (arrangements) letter?
(2) Who should prepare and sign the engagement letter?
(3) When should the engagement letter be sent?
(4) Why should the engagement letter be renewed periodically?

b. (1) What are the objectives of the client's representation letter?
(2) Who should prepare and sign the client's representation letter?
(3) When should the client's representation letter be obtained?
(4) Why should the client's representation letter be prepared for each examination?

c. A CPA's responsibilities for providing accounting services sometimes involve the association with unaudited financial statements. Discuss the need in this circumstance for:
(1) An engagement letter.
(2) Client's representation letter. (AICPA)

16.28. You have been assigned to perform a cold review of a correspondent CPA firm's audit of Oxford Millwork Company for the calendar year ending December 31. In the audited financial statements of Oxford Millwork Company, you find the following representations:

Common stock, $10 par value, 100,000 shares outstanding, 400,000 shares authorized (Note 1)	$1,000,000

Note 1: *Subsequent event* (dated January 20). The board of directors approved a 3-for-1 stock split effective January 20. At the effective date, the par value of outstanding common stock is $3,000,000.

You have reviewed the correspondent CPA firm's audit report and found the opinion dated "January 15, 19xx, except as to Note 1 which is dated January 20, 19xx."

Required:

a. What is the purpose of a cold review?

b. What is the purpose of dual-dating?

c. What recommendations would you make to the CPA firm concerning presentation of the subsequent event?

16.29. **Case: Recognizing Income of a Purchased Subsidiary**

The following brief dialogue occurred in a controversy wherein a plaintiff claimed that management back-dated the effective date of an acquisition in order to pump up earnings improperly. The independent auditors, Eastford and Redwood, are involved because they signed an unqualified opinion on the consolidated financial statements in question.

Plaintiff's Attorney: Plaintiff alleges that COSIF Company's purchase of 100 percent of the stock of Prosper, Inc., was effective on April 28, almost four months after the beginning of COSIF's fiscal year on January 1. COSIF included in consolidated income the results of Prosper's operations for the full 12 months ended December 31. This was improper accounting which failed to reflect the substance of the transaction.

Eastford and Redwood knew, or should have known, that the effective date was April 28. The evidence shown today proves that the first written agreement concerning the acquisition was a memorandum agreement dated March 5 which set forth the general terms of the transaction. The final written agreement was signed and dated on April 28. Their unqualified opinion was improperly rendered.

Eastford and Redwood. The issue is whether January 1 or some later date should have been used as the acquisition date for accounting purposes. We stipulate that the first written memorandum was dated May 5 and the final agreement April 28. However, we have also introduced into evidence written representations from the president of COSIF and COSIF's outside counsel that an oral agreement substantially equivalent to the May 5 memorandum agreement was reached on or about January 1. COSIF's outside counsel is one of the most highly regarded law firms on the east coast.

These representations were meaningful to us because we were not engaged as COSIF's auditors until November 14 and were not present when the actual negotiations took place.

Plaintiff alleges that applicable accounting principles were misapplied (APB *Opinion No. 16*, paragraph 93, Section 1091.93) because no written agreement existed *on* January 1.

We insist that elements of the April 28 agreement, which made the acquisition effective *as of* January 1, show that the *substance* of the transaction supports our conclusion that January 1 was the proper accounting date. We cite the following:

COSIF and Prosper clearly intended an effective date of January 1.

The fixed portion of the purchase price depended upon a minimum amount of Prosper's income through December 31 of the year preceding. (At May 5 the audit of Prosper's prior fiscal year had not yet been completed.)

The contingent portion of the purchase price depended upon an agreed minimum amount of Prosper's income for the year beginning January 1 and two years thereafter.

Warranties made by Prosper as to assets and liabilities were *as of* December 31 (just prior to the January 1 effective date).

Interest on COSIF's notes issued as a part of the payment package ran from January 1.

The full amount of Prosper's earnings from January 1 inured to the benefit of COSIF.

Question:

What is the proper accounting date for COSIF's investment in Prosper?

PART FOUR

Reporting Obligations

17

REPORTS BY INDEPENDENT AUDITORS

Reports rendered by independent auditors as attestations to financial statements may take a variety of forms and variations. Auditors have definite reporting *obligations* under generally accepted auditing standards.

Independent auditors accept and discharge their social obligations to public users of financial statements through the medium of the attestation report. The decisions required in formulating a report have characteristics of ethical decisions, wherein the auditor must objectively evaluate the impact of the report on users' decisions; and the decisions have characteristics of technical decisions, wherein the auditor must be cognizant of generally accepted accounting principles and recognized professional standards.

AN ETHICAL-TECHNICAL ENVIRONMENT

One of the first rules of ethics relevant in the reporting context is Rule 301: "A member shall not disclose any confidential information obtained in the course of a professional engagement except with the consent of the client." However, Rule 301 also states: "This rule shall not be construed (*a*) to relieve a member of his obligation under Rules 202 and 203. . . ." The latter two rules require an auditor to comply with generally accepted auditing standards and to report on compliance with generally accepted accounting principles. Both the auditing standards of reporting and the accounting principles require adequate disclosure of financial information that is materially important for users' economic decisions.

Thus the confidential information rule is inoperative respecting information that is necessary for adequate financial communication to report users. In a social context the user's needs are superior to the issuers' (i.e., management) desires to consider information confidential. However, the distinction between materially important information and unimportant information is often difficult to make in practice. In questionable situations auditors find themselves involved in a process of ethical reflective choice, particularly in the role of projecting thoughts about information forward to the users' decision models and the potential uses of information.

With regard to technical aspects of the decision about what type of report to issue an auditor must consider several quantitative and qualitative elements.

Magnitude. The quantitative size of an amount in question is one feature of its importance. Size—materiality—may be analyzed in terms of absolute amount or in relation to other financial statement amounts.

Uncertainty of Outcome. An event whose occurence is probable is more important than one whose occurrence is merely possible or remote.

Likelihood of Error. A financial statement item in a high-risk area (e.g., receivables on land sales contracts) deserves more attention than one in a low-risk or routine area.

Expertise of the Auditor. Whether the auditor can reach a decision or needs to call upon the skills of another expert has an impact on the reporting decision. For example, valuations of diamond inventories or mineral reserves are usually beyond the expertise of the auditor. Also, the auditor's ability to predict the future is usually no better than some other person's ability (e.g., predicting the outcome of litigation in progress).

Pervasive Impact on Financial Statements. Financial statements items may impact on only a few accounts or on many. Errors in inventory valuation, for example, affect cost of goods sold, gross margin, net income, income tax expense, inventory balances, and tax liabilities. Items with such pervasive effects are handled differently from items that have limited or isolated effects.

Nature of the Item. The qualitative description of the item itself may override all other considerations of importance. For example, clear evidence of an illegal act makes the event important in and of itself, without regard to money amounts or other considerations.

Subordination of Time-Cost Constraints

Throughout this text there has been an underlying presumption that an audit must be completed in a timely manner and at a cost acceptable to management and sufficient for the auditor. However applicable these time and cost constraints may be in the performance of field work, they are ultimately subordinate when writing the report. Consistent with a scientific decision-making approach and consistent with the third AICPA field work standard (requiring sufficient competent evidential matter as a basis for an opinion), the quality and quantity of evidential matter is ultimately evaluated independently of the time and cost taken to obtain it.

If the evidence is insufficient at the time the report is written, an unqualified opinion cannot be rendered. This is true even if for some reasons of time or cost it would have been impossible or very costly to obtain sufficient competent evidence to support an unqualified opinion. The attestation report decisions are governed by what is known through evidence without any "discount" for the ease or difficulty experienced in gathering the evidence.

Consequently, the auditor cannot resort to the device known as *negative assurance* when writing an attestation opinion on financial statements purporting to show financial position and results of operations. A negative assurance is a statement to the effect that "Nothing came to our attention which would indicate that these statements are not fairly presented." The negative assurance of this type does not adequately indicate whether appropriate attention was given by the auditor in such a way that he or she had opportunity to know whether statements were or were not fairly presented.[1]

Basic Content of the Short-Form Report

The unqualified short-form report was introduced in Chapter 1 of this text. The technical explanation of the contents of the report is not repeated here but should be reviewed at this time.

Scope Paragraph. The current report (adopted in 1971) consists of two segments. The *scope paragraph* is the auditor's report of the character of his or her own work in the audit examination. This portion of the report is vitally important for disclosure of the quality and extent of the audit itself. The auditor must render a fair presentation of his own work as well as an opinion on the fair presentation of financial statements.

Over the years the scope paragraph has been modified. Audit reports prior to 1941 described procedures, explanations, sources of information, and review of accounting methods (internal control) in explicit terms. In 1941 the SEC required reports filed with the commission to state whether the audit was made in accordance with generally accepted auditing standards. Consequently reports issued after 1941 described the audit "in accordance with generally accepted auditing standards" and omitted more detailed descriptions of procedures. All of the meaning of the general and field work standards is implicit in the scope paragraph, including: (1) the auditors were trained and proficient, (2) the auditors were independent, (3) due professional care was exercised, (4) the work was planned and supervised, (5) internal control was properly studied and evaluated, and (6) sufficient competent evidential matter was obtained.

To the extent that one or more of these general and field work standards is *not* actually satisfied during an audit, the scope paragraph must be *qualified*. A qualification in this paragraph means the addition of wording

---

[1] *Statement on Auditing Standards No. 1* (Section 518.01). However, negative assurances are permitted in letters to underwriters and in certain financial statements that do not purport to present financial position and results of operations (Sections 518.02, 518.03), in certain kinds of special reports (*SAS No. 14*, Sections 621.15–.19 "Special Reports") and in certain reports on a limited review of interim financial information (*SAS No. 10*, Section 720.22).

that explains exactly what standard was not satisfied and why it was not satisified. Such qualifications may be caused by lack of independence, lack of sufficient competent evidence, or by restrictions on procedures imposed by the client.

Opinion Paragraph. The other basic segment of the report is the *opinion paragraph.* Users of audited financial statements are generally most interested in the opinion. The opinion paragraph is the public manifestation of the auditor's private decision-making process.

The reporting standards listed below are incorporated in the opinion paragraph.

1. The report shall state whether the financial statements are presented in accordance with generally accepted accounting principles.
2. The report shall state whether such principles have been consistently observed in the current period in relation to the preceding period.
3. Informative disclosures in the financial statements are to be regarded as reasonably adequate unless otherwise stated in the report.
4. The report shall either contain an expression of opinion regarding the financial statements, taken as a whole, or an assertion to the effect that an opinion cannot be expressed. When an overall opinion cannot be expressed, the reasons should be stated. In all cases wherein an auditor's name is associated with financial statements, the report should contain a clear-cut indication of the character of the auditor's examination, if any, and the degree of responsibility he is taking.

When reading the reporting standards, one should understand the term "financial statements" to include not only the traditional balance sheet, income statement, and statement of changes in financial position but also all the footnote disclosures and additional information (e.g., earnings per share calculations) that are integral elements of a complete financial presentation. In this regard, the third reporting standard, with its reference to *informative disclosures*, is open-ended. It is through this opening that auditors may exercise a wide latitude of professional judgment in deciding what information must be disclosed. It is also the opening that disgruntled investors often use as a basis for lawsuits.

The objective of the fourth reporting standard is to enable shareholders, credit grantors, and others who use financial statements to determine the extent to which financial statements reported on by CPAs may be relied upon.[2] This standard requires that when an auditor's name is associated with financial statements the auditor should (1) express an opinion on the financial statements taken as a whole or (2) assert that an opinion cannot be expressed. These two alternatives essentially define the degree of responsibility taken by the auditor.

A disclaimer of opinion is an assertion that an opinion cannot be expressed. When a disclaimer of opinion is given, the auditor takes no re-

[2] D. R. Carmichael, *The Auditor's Reporting Obligation: The Meaning and Implementation of the Fourth Standard of Reporting*, Auditing Research Monograph No. 1 (New York: AICPA, 1972), p. 1.

sponsibility whatsoever for the fair presentation of the financial statements. This assertion is a "no opinion." The auditor does not know whether the statements are fairly presented or materially misleading. A disclaimer is always given on unaudited financial statements because by the definition of "unaudited" the auditor does not have sufficient competent evidential matter upon which to base an opinion. The disclaimer can also be given when the going-concern assumption is in doubt.

Both the unqualified opinion and the adverse opinion are opinions regarding the financial statements taken as a whole. The unqualified opinion states that financial statements *are* fairly presented, and the adverse opinion states that they *are not*. As a practical matter, even though the adverse opinion is an "overall opinion," reasons are always given to explain why the opinion is adverse. One should be aware that an auditor needs at least as much evidence to support an adverse opinion as for an unqualified opinion. Both opinions assert that the auditor *knows*, and knowing requires a sufficient competent evidential basis. With both types of opinion the auditor takes full responsibility.

However, the degree of responsibility taken may be less than "full responsibility" when some kinds of *qualified opinions* are rendered. Qualified opinions are opinions on financial statements "taken as a whole" but with an exception taken to one or more specific discrepancies or uncertainties. Auditing standards also provide for the use of "subject to" qualification language when uncertainties exist in the client's business. Examples of uncertainties include questions about the realizable value of equipment held for sale and the future outcome of significant lawsuits. Evidence is not obtainable in the case of future outcomes, so auditors can flag the uncertainty by writing that the opinion is "subject to" the outcome of the specific matter. The theory is that using the "subject to" language takes the flagged item out of the auditor's responsibility.

Some opinion qualifications, however, are matters of auditor knowledge and auditor responsibility. A qualification based on a departure from generally accepted accounting principles or on an inconsistency in the application of accounting principles becomes a qualification because the auditor has full knowledge of it. Flagging matters such as these as the reasons for a qualified opinion means that the auditor takes responsibility for the accuracy of his or her statement about the item in question.

The reporting obligations are subject to fairly complex conditions and criteria for appropriate use. The remainder of this chapter examines them in more detail.

REPORTS AND THE MATERIALITY DIMENSION

Immaterial or unimportant information can usually be ignored—treated as if it did not exist—when an auditor makes decisions about the audit report. However, when information passes a materiality threshold, the audit report decision is affected. In connection with reporting decisions there is also a theory of "lesser" and "greater" materiality. *Lesser materiality* merely means that the item in question is important and

EXHIBIT 17–1
The Effect of Materiality on Audit Reports

Circumstances for Departure from Standard Audit Report	*Required Type of Report*	
Limitation on scope (509.10–.13)	*Qualified* "except for" Opinion paragraph refers to possible effects on financial statements	*Disclaimer* Separate paragraph discloses limitation—no reference to procedures performed
Opinion based partially on report of another auditor (509.14, 543)	*Unqualified* Scope paragraph discloses reliance and opinion paragraph refers to report of other auditors. (See Chapter 18 for details.)	
Departure from GAAP (509.15–.17)	*Qualified* "except for" Separate paragraph discloses substantive reasons and principal effects	*Adverse* Separate paragraph discloses substantive reasons and principal effects
Departure from an official pronouncement (509.18–.19)	*Qualified** "except for" Separate paragraph discloses substantive reasons and principal effects	*Adverse** Separate paragraph discloses substantive reasons and principal effects
Lack of consistency (509.20, 546)	See Exhibit 17–6	
Auditor is not independent (571)	*Disclaimer* Scope paragraph states explicitly that the auditor is not independent	
Uncertainty (509.21–.25)	*Qualified* "subject to" Separate paragraph discloses substantive reasons	*Disclaimer* Separate paragraph discloses substantive reasons
Emphasis of a matter (509.27)	*Unqualified* Separate paragraph discusses the matter	
Materiality dimension	←—— *Lesser* ***Materiality (risk)***	***Greater*** ——→

* Where the departure is *necessary* to make the financials not misleading, an unqualified opinion is issued with an explanation of the circumstances.

Source: Adapted from D. Causey, "Newly Emerging Standards of Auditor Responsibility," *Accounting Review*, January 1976, p. 25.

needs to be disclosed and/or dealt with in a qualified opinion. The information cannot simply be ignored.

Greater materiality means that the item in question is very important and has an extreme impact on the reporting decision. Both lesser and greater materiality involve considerations of magnitude, uncertainty, likelihood of error, auditor expertise, pervasive impact, and nature of the item.

Statement on Auditing Standards No. 2 (Section 509), "Reports on Audited Financial Statements," refers to eight circumstances that can result in departures from the standard unqualified audit report. These circumstances are shown in Exhibit 17–1 in relation to a materiality dimension. Each report that is qualified when the item is of "lesser materiality" becomes a disclaimer or an adverse report when the item is of "greater materiality."

REPORTS AND THE EVIDENCE DIMENSION

The subject of decisions about the content of an audit report may also be organized along an evidence dimension. The discussion below adopts the evidence dimension because it pervades all choices of report form and content and because it is directly related to the technical-procedural elements of an audit. The remaining coverage in this chapter is limited to "financial statements taken as a whole which purport to present financial position and results of operations."

FULLY SUFFICIENT COMPETENT EVIDENCE

Auditors are in the most comfortable position when they have all the evidence needed to make a report decision. The short form of the opinion can be used without modification if the unqualified opinion is decided upon. Likewise, the auditor must have sufficient competent evidence in order to decide to use the adverse form of the opinion.

Unqualified Opinion

Auditing standards explain the unqualified opinion as follows:

> An unqualified opinion states that the financial statements present fairly financial position, results of operations, and changes in financial position in conformity with generally accepted accounting principles (which include adequate disclosure) consistently applied. . . . This conclusion may be expressed only when the auditor has formed such an opinion on the basis of an examination made in accordance with generally accepted auditing standards.[3]

This explanation ties the quality of "present fairly" closely to conformity with generally accepted accounting principles, but the parenthetical phrase—"(which include adequate disclosure)"—opens the possibility that matters on which official accounting pronouncements are silent might be

---

[3] *Statement on Auditing Standards No.* 2 (Section 509.28).

necessary for a fair presentation. In fact, Ethics Rule 203 provides for the possibility that *adherence* to pronouncements of accounting standards *might* create misleading financial statements.

Rule 203. A member shall not express an opinion that financial statements are presented in conformity with generally accepted accounting principles if such statements contain any departure from an accounting principle promulgated by the body designated by Council to establish such principles which has a material effect on the statements taken as a whole, *unless* the member can demonstrate that due to unusual circumstances the financial statements would otherwise have been misleading. In such cases his report must describe the departure, the approximate effects thereof, if practicable, and the reasons why compliance with the principle would result in a misleading statement. [Emphasis added.]

Auditing standards place some emphasis on Rule 203 by providing that when such unusual circumstances exist, the auditor's report should explain them in a middle paragraph(s). In such cases the opinion paragraph can be unqualified with respect to conformity with generally accepted accounting principles.[4] Public opinion and court cases have tended to assert dominance of the idea of "present fairly" over "conformity with generally accepted accounting principles." Ethics Rule 203 and the auditing standards tend to confirm this dominance.

A typical unqualified opinion is shown in Exhibit 17–2. The report covers comparative financial statements of two years. The report in Ex-

EXHIBIT 17–2
Unqualified Opinion

To the Shareholders and Directors of the United States Shoe Corporation:

We have examined the consolidated balance sheets of THE UNITED STATES SHOE CORPORATION (an Ohio corporation) and subsidiaries as of July 31, 1977 and 1976, and the related consolidated statements of earnings and retained earnings and changes in financial position for the years then ended. Our examination was made in accordance with generally accepted auditing standards and, accordingly, included such tests of the accounting records and such other auditing procedures as we considered necessary in the circumstances.

In our opinion, the accompanying consolidated financial statements referred to above present fairly the financial position of the United States Shoe Corporation and subsidiaries as of July 31, 1977 and 1976, and the results of their operations and changes in their financial position for the years then ended in conformity with generally accepted accounting principles applied during the periods.

ARTHUR ANDERSEN & CO.
September 27, 1977

[4] *SAS No.* 2 (Section 509.19). This provision has the effect of allowing financial statements to contain a departure from an official pronouncement, allowing the auditor to explain why the departure was necessary in order that financial statements *not* be misleading, and then allowing the departure to be "in conformity with generally accepted accounting principles" as would be indicated by the unqualified opinion paragraph.

hibit 17–3 is an example of an unqualified opinion that conforms with Ethics Rule 203, noting a departure from generally accepted accounting principles. Generally, however, departures from accounting principles cause the auditor to render an adverse or qualified opinion.

EXHIBIT 17–3
Opinion Conforming to Ethics Rule 203

Board of Directors
Health Industries, Inc.
Columbia, Maryland

We have examined the consolidated balance sheet of Health Industries, Inc., and subsidiaries as of December 31, 1975 and 1974, and the related statements of operations and deficit and changes in financial position for the years then ended. Our examination was made in accordance with generally accepted auditing standards and, accordingly, included such tests of the accounting records and such other auditing procedures as we considered necessary in the circumstances.

As explained in Note B, the company has changed its method of recording revenues from recognition at the time of sale to recognition over the membership term and has applied this change retroactively in the accompanying financial statements. Accounting Principles Board (APB) *Opinion Number 20*, "Accounting Changes," provides that such a change be made by including, as an element of net earnings during the year of change, the cumulative effect of the change on prior years. Had APB *Opinion Number 20* been followed literally, the cumulative effect of the accounting change would have been included as a charge in the 1975 statements of operations. Because of the magnitude and pervasiveness of this change, we believe a literal application of APB *Opinion Number 20* would result in a misleading presentation, and that this change should therefore be made on a retroactive basis.

In our opinion, the aforementioned consolidated financial statements present fairly the financial position of Health Industries, Inc., and subsidiaries at December 31, 1975 and 1974, and the results of their operations and the changes in their financial position for the years then ended, in conformity with generally accepted accounting principles applied on a consistent basis after restatement for the change described in the preceding paragraph and the changes described in Note C to the financial statements, with all of which we concur.

TOUCHE ROSS & CO.
Certified Public Accountants

NOTE B—CHANGE IN ACCOUNTING FOR REVENUES AND COSTS

In prior years, revenue from sale of memberships, less a deferred portion, was taken into income at the time of sale. The deferred portion was taken into income on a straight-line basis over the membership term and was equivalent to the estimated future cost of providing facilities and services. These costs consisted of a prorata share of estimated future operating expenses.

In December 1974, the company's independent accountants, Touche Ross & Co., informed the company that they had taken a position as a firm, which they suggested should be effective for fiscal years ended after December 31, 1974, to recognize membership fee revenue and associated costs over the period of membership.

EXHIBIT 17–3 (*continued*)

The company has concluded that even though the change has not been required by an authoritative accounting body, there is sufficient authoritative support within similar industries, and it will accept the change suggested by its auditors.

Accounting Principles Board (APB) *Opinion Number 20*, "Accounting Changes," provides that such a change be made by including, as an element of net earnings during the year of change, the cumulative effect of the change on prior years. Had APB *Opinion Number 20* been followed literally, the cumulative effect of the accounting change would have been included as a charge, net of tax benefits, in the 1975 statement of operations and would have resulted in reporting a net loss of $14,143,147 and $8,555,662 ($1.55 and $.94 per share) for 1975 and 1974, respectively. Because of the magnitude and pervasiveness of this change, the company believes a literal application of APB *Opinion Number 20* would result in a misleading presentation and that this change should, therefore, be made on a retroactive basis.

As the result of retroactive treatment of the change in the method of accounting for membership revenues, the financial statements for prior years have been restated. The effect of the change was to decrease net earnings by $138,306 and decrease the net loss by $6,438,389 ($.02 and $.71 per share) in 1975 and 1974, respectively. The increase in deferred revenue at January 1, 1974, net of related tax benefits, resulted in an adjustment to opening retained earnings of $21,131,266.

In determining contract lives for years prior to 1975, permanent memberships and other long-lived contracts were assigned a term of 36 months, since in the opinion of management, this term reasonably approximates the effective membership term and is consistent with present operating practices that limit the term of a membership to 30 months. Costs directly related to the sale of memberships were calculated using current operating experience and adjusted for known changes and practices not experienced in prior years in arriving at the amount of costs to be deferred for prior years.

NOTE C—ACCOUNTING FOR DISCOUNT EXPENSE AND REPORTING OF FINANCE SUBSIDIARIES:

Accounting for Discount Expense

In accordance with the recommendations issued by the accounting standards division of the American Institute of Certified Public Accountants, the company, during 1975, changed its method of recording discounts on sales of receivables with recourse. The discount expense had previously been charged to expense at the time of sale and is currently being deferred and charged to expense over the term of the receivables using the effective yield (sum-of-the-digits) method. The amount of such deferred discount, net of amortization, was $710,000 at December 31, 1975.

Reporting of Finance Subsidiaries

Two finance subsidiaries, previously accounted for by the equity method of accounting, are now fully consolidated since substantially all of their revenue is derived from the company. The effects of this change are to include all finance revenues and expenses as well as all assets and liabilities of Newport Acceptance Corporation and Universal Guardian Acceptance Corporation in the consolidated statements for 1975 and 1974. This change has no effect on the net earnings or loss.

Adverse Opinion

An adverse opinion is exactly the opposite of the unqualified opinion. In this type of opinion the auditor says that the financial statements *do not* fairly present financial position, results of operations, and changes in financial position in conformity with generally accepted accounting principles. The scope paragraph should not be qualified, because in order to decide to use the adverse opinion, the auditor must possess all evidence necessary to reach the decision. When this opinion is given, the auditor must disclose *all* the substantive reasons in the report in explanatory paragraphs.

As a practical matter, however, an auditor generally requires *more* evidence to support an adverse opinion than to support an unqualified opinion.[5] Perhaps this phenomenon can be attributed to auditors' reluctance to be bearers of bad news. In addition, client relations considerations typically are intermingled in the decision process. However, auditing standards are quite clear on the point that, if an auditor has a basis for an adverse opinion, he cannot extricate himself from an uncomfortable position by giving a disclaimer of opinion.[6]

An example of an adverse opinion is given in Exhibit 17–4.

In making decisions on whether to use the adverse opinion, the materiality dimension is important. If there is a departure from accounting principles and sufficient evidence shows the effect to be immaterial, an unqualified opinion may be rendered (as if the departure had not existed). If the effect of the departure is material (but not extremely material) and isolated to a single event, a qualified opinion may be given. (An example of such a qualification is shown in Exhibit 17–5.)

Adverse opinions may arise from situations other than events of departure from officially promulgated accounting principles. In *Auditing Research Monograph No. 1* the adverse opinion is described as the auditor's means of expressing strong disapproval of the financial representations of management, especially in the significant situation wherein the intent of management appears to be to mislead readers of the financial statements.[7] In some other situations evidence may clearly indicate that the going-concern assumption is not valid and that the company faces bankruptcy or liquidation; hence financial statements prepared on the cost basis of accounting are not appropriate. In such cases, when evidence is fully persuasive, an adverse opinion may be given.

Consistency Qualifications in the Opinion

The second standard of reporting (the "consistency standard") requires that the report shall state whether accounting principles have been consistently observed in the current period in relation to the preceding period.

---

[5] Carmichael, *The Auditor's Reporting Obligation*, pp. 123, 126.

[6] *Statement on Auditing Standards No. 2*, (Section 509.45).

[7] Carmichael, *The Auditor's Reporting Obligation*, p. 126.

EXHIBIT 17–4
Adverse Opinion

To the Board of Directors and Shareholders of the
Manhattan Life Insurance Company:

We have examined the balance sheet (statutory basis) of the Manhattan Life Insurance Company as of December 31, 1975, and the related statements (statutory basis) of income, surplus, and changes in financial position for the year then ended. Our examination was made in accordance with generally accepted auditing standards and, accordingly, included such tests of the accounting records and such other auditing procedures as we considered necessary in the circumstances. We previously examined and reported upon the financial statements for 1974.

The company presents its financial statements in conformity with accounting practices prescribed or permitted by the Insurance Department of the State of New York. The effects on the accompanying financial statements of the variances between such practices and generally accepted accounting principles are described in Note 10.

It is our opinion that, because of the materiality of the effects of the differences between generally accepted accounting principles and the accounting practices referred to in the preceding paragraph, the aforementioned financial statements do not present fairly the financial position of the Manhattan Life Insurance Company at December 31, 1975 and 1974, or the results of its operations or changes in its financial position for the years then ended, in conformity with generally accepted accounting principles. It is our opinion, however, that the supplementary data included in Note 10 present fairly surplus at December 31, 1975 and 1974, and net income for the years then ended, in conformity with generally accepted accounting principles applied on a consistent basis. Also in our opinion, the accompanying statutory financial statements present fairly the financial position of the Manhattan Life Insurance Company at December 31, 1975 and 1974, and results of its operations and changes in its financial position for the years then ended, in conformity with accounting practices prescribed or permitted by the Insurance Department of the State of New York which, except for the change in computing policy reserves as described in Note 12 to the financial statements, have been applied on a consistent basis.

COOPERS & LYBRAND
New York, New York
March 8, 1976

The materiality dimension is explicit in the objective of this reporting standard, as stated below:

> The objective of the consistency standard is (*a*) to give assurance that the comparability of financial statements between periods has not been *materially* affected by changes in accounting principles, which include not only accounting principles and practices but also the methods of applying them, or (*b*) if comparability has been *materially* affected by such changes, to require appropriate reporting by the independent auditor regarding such

EXHIBIT 17–5
Opinions Qualified with an Exception for Departure from Generally Accepted Accounting Principles

A. Exception Based on Generally Accepted Accounting Principles without Reference to an Official Pronouncement

To the Board of Directors, Wisconsin Natural Gas Company:

We have examined the balance sheet of Wisconsin Natural Gas Company as of December 31, 1975 and 1974, and the related statements of income, retained earnings and changes in financial position for the years then ended. Our examinations were made in accordance with generally accepted auditing standards and accordingly included such tests of the accounting records and such other auditing procedures as we considered necessary in the circumstances.

As more fully set forth in Note A of Notes to Financial Statements, the company has unbilled revenues which would increase net income and shareholder's equity if recorded in the accounts.

In our opinion, except that unbilled revenues have not been recorded as described in the preceding paragraph, the financial statements examined by us present fairly the financial position of Wisconsin Natural Gas Company at December 31, 1975 and 1974, the results of its operations and changes in financial position for the years then ended, in conformity with generally accepted accounting principles consistently applied.

PRICE WATERHOUSE & CO.
Milwaukee, Wisconsin

Unbilled Revenues

In accordance with predominant industry practice, the company records revenues from customers at the time billings are rendered. The effect of this practice on results of operations for prior years has not been material. However, because of 1975 rate increases and December weather conditions, net income for 1975 would have been increased by approximately $1,404,000 after income taxes if such revenues, computed on the basis of gas delivered to customers, had been recorded. The corresponding increase in net income for 1974 would have been approximately $569,000.

The accumulation of unbilled revenues of approximately $11.1 million at December 31, 1975, if recorded in the accounts, would increase shareholder's equity by approximately $5,356,000 after income taxes.

B. Exception Based on Generally Accepted Accounting Principles with Reference to an Official Pronouncement (APB *Opinion No. 30*)

The Board of Directors
Post Corporation

We have examined the consolidated balance sheets of Post Corporation and subsidiaries as of December 31, 1976 and 1975, and the related consolidated statements of operations, stockholders' equity, and changes in financial position, and supporting schedules for the years then ended. Except as explained in the following paragraph, our examination was made in accordance with generally accepted audit-

EXHIBIT 17–5 (*continued*)

ing standards and, accordingly, included such tests of the accounting records and such other auditing procedures as we considered necessary in the circumstances.

In connection with the disposition of its investment in All-Star Insurance Corporation during 1975, which is more fully described in Note 2 to the consolidated financial statements, the company did not make a determination of and did not report separately in the consolidated statement of operations the amount of the loss representing the company's equity in All-Star's results of operations in 1975 through the date of disposal and the amount representing the loss on the disposal. *Opinion No. 30* of the Accounting Principles Board requires that, in connection with the disposal of a segment of a business, such amounts be reported separately. The failure to report such amounts separately had no effect on the company's consolidated net loss reported for the year ended December 31, 1975.

In our opinion, except for the effect of the matter discussed in the preceding paragraph, the aforementioned consolidated financial statements present fairly the financial position of Post Corporation and subsidiaries at December 31, 1976 and 1975, and the results of their operations and the changes in their financial position for the years then ended, in conformity with generally accepted accounting principles applied on a consistent basis, and the supporting schedules, in our opinion, present fairly the information set forth therein.

PEAT, MARWICK, MITCHELL & CO.
Milwaukee, Wisconsin
February 23, 1977

(2) LOSS ON ALL-STAR INSURANCE CORPORATION

Under an agreement dated and effective October 30, 1975, the company disposed of its 99.8 percent ownership interest in All-Star Insurance Corporation by transfer of all of the All-Star shares held by it to Stellar Investment Corporation, an unaffiliated company. The transfer was made without receiving any consideration therefore. The loss on All-Star for 1975 represents the write-off of the investment of $4,265,170 at December 31, 1974, based on cost adjusted for equity in net losses of All-Star through that date less income taxes applicable to the loss resulting from the write-off. The company has not made a determination of the portion of the loss applicable to operations of All-Star in 1975 through the date of disposal. Unaudited total revenues of All-Star in 1975 through the date of disposal consisted of net premiums earned of $5,904,436 and investment income of $486,282.

changes. It is implicit in the objective that such principles have been consistently observed *within* each period. (Emphasis added.)[8]

While materiality is a consideration in deciding whether to write a consistency exception, the magnitude of materiality is usually not a reason for modifying the opinion in any other way. In other words, a change in accounting principle or application method may double or triple reported net income, but this is not viewed by practicing auditors as reason enough to

[8] *Statement on Auditing Standards No. 1* (Section 420.02).

give an adverse opinion, only a consistency qualification and full disclosure. An exception to this general observation exists in the case of failure to restate prior year financial statements after a business combination accounted for as a pooling of interests. This failure is also a departure from GAAP. (See *SAS No. 1*, Section 546.12.) An opinion qualified because of a departure from GAAP, possibly an adverse opinion, may be appropriate.

Consistency qualifications arise from knowledge based on sufficient competent evidence. In order to state an explicit qualification, the auditor must definitely know of it and must have evidence of the magnitude (quantitative materiality) of the effect. However, in some cases of first-time audits an engagement may not be extended to prior periods sufficiently to attest to consistency. In such cases a form of "disclaimer of consistency" may be given by omitting the consistency phrase, with adequate disclosure of the reasons for the omission. The consistency phrase may simply be omitted in a report on a business's first year of operations.

Statements on Auditing Standards No. 1 explains circumstances that do and do not require consistency exceptions in the auditor's report (Sections 420 and 546). The circumstances requiring exceptions are condensed and described in Exhibit 17–6. These circumstances parallel very closely the accounting prescribed in *APB Opinion No. 20* ("Accounting Changes").

However, FASB *Interpretation No. 20* (an interpretation of APB *No. 20*) provides that "an enterprise making a change in accounting principle to conform with the recommendations of an AICPA *Statement of Position* (an accounting guide issued by the AICPA Accounting Standards Executive Committee) shall report the change as specified in the statement. If an AICPA *Statement of Position* does not specify the manner of reporting a change in accounting principle to conform with its recommendations, an enterprise making a change in accounting principle to conform with the recommendations of the statement shall report the change as specified by *APB No. 20*." Notwithstanding specified methods of accounting for changes, whether in an FASB *Statement of Accounting Standards* or in an AICPA *Statement of Position*, the auditor's governing standard is: "Changes in accounting principle having a material effect on the financial statements require recognition in the independent auditor's opinion as to consistency." (*SAS No. 1*, Section 420.05.)

In 1978 the Commission on Auditors' Responsibilities recommended that the consistency reporting requirement be dropped from the auditor's short-form report. The commission's reasoning was that the consistency language effectively made the auditor an *originator* of financial statement information. The commission prefers to see auditors strictly in the role of attestors to financial information prepared by management. Since generally accepted accounting principles (e.g., APB *Opinion No. 20*, FASB *Interpretation No. 20*) prescribe the manner of accounting for changes, the commission sees no need for auditors to write a consistency phrase in the opinion.

Without a consistency phrase in the reporting scheme, auditors would

EXHIBIT 17–6
Reporting on Inconsistency

Nature of Possible Inconsistency Requiring Departure from Standard Report	*Required Type of Report*		*Middle Paragraph Required*	*Restatement of Prior Years' Financials When Presented for Comparison*
	Material Inconsistency	*Greatly Material Inconsistency*		
1. Change from GAAP to GAAP reported by restating prior financials (546.02).	*Modified Opinion Paragraph* State consistent after giving retroactive effect to change.		No	Yes
2. Change from GAAP to GAAP reported by means other than restating prior financials (546.03). Including change in principle inseparable from change in estimate (420.11).	*Modified Opinion Paragraph* State "except for the change . . . have been applied on a consistent basis."		No	No
3. Change from GAAP to GAAP without reasonable justification (546.06).	*Qualified* "except for" relates to both GAAP and consistency.	*Adverse*	Yes	Yes
4. Change to principle not conforming to GAAP (546.05).	*Qualified* "except for."	*Adverse* No reference to consistency since not in conformance with GAAP.	Yes	No
5. Scope limitation in first audit situation due to client restriction or inadequate prior year records preclude opinion on consistency (546.15).	*Qualified* Scope paragraph states: "except as indicated in the following paragraph."		Yes	No
6. Prior financials kept on cash basis and restatement impracticable (546.16).	*Modified Opinion Paragraph* Make no mention of consistency while middle paragraph explains prior financials.		Yes	No
7. Change from principle not conforming to GAAP (420.10).	*Modified Opinion Paragraph* State consistent after giving retroactive effect to change.		No	Yes

Source: D. Causey, "Newly Emerging Standards of Auditor Responsibility: A Reply," *Accounting Review*, January 1977, p. 260.

write a qualified opinion taking exception to an accounting change if the enterprise did not conform to generally accepted accounting principles in accounting for and disclosing the change. However, as of late 1978, the Auditing Standards Board had not acted on this recommendation.

When evaluating a change in accounting principle, the auditor must be satisfied that management's justification for the change is reasonable. APB *Opinion No. 20*, "Accounting Changes," states: "The presumption that an entity should not change an accounting principle may be overcome only if the enterprise justifies the use of an alternative acceptable accounting principle on the basis that it is preferable." A change solely "to increase profits" may be preferable from management's viewpoint, but such a reason is not reasonable justification for most auditors. When a change is made, the auditor must state his concurrence or disagreement using language like "with which we concur," or language of an opinion qualification in cases of disagreement.[9] In reports on subsequent years' financial statements appropriate reference to the change should be made in the audit report as long as the year of change is included in the years reported on.

An example of the opinion qualified as to consistency is shown in Exhibit 17–7.

EXHIBIT 17–7
Consistency Qualification

A. Accounting Change Not Related to Official Pronouncements

To the Stockholders and Board of Directors of
New Jersey Natural Gas Company:

We have examined the balance sheet of New Jersey Natural Gas Company as of September 30, 1977 and 1976, and the related statements of operations and retained earnings and changes in financial position for the years then ended. Our examinations were made in accordance with generally accepted auditing standards and, accordingly, included such tests of the accounting records and such other auditing procedures as we considered necessary in the circumstances.

In our opinion, the accompanying financial statements present fairly the financial position of the company at September 30, 1977 and 1976, and the results of its operations and changes in its financial position for the years then ended, in conformity with generally accepted accounting principles consistently applied subsequent to the changes (with which we concur) made as of October 1, 1975, in the methods of accounting for unbilled revenues and purchased fuel costs, as described in Note 2 to the financial statements.

HASKINS & SELLS
Newark, New Jersey
November 15, 1977

2. ACCOUNTING CHANGES

Effective October 1, 1975, the company changed its method of accounting to (*a*) accrue the amount of unbilled revenues for estimated services provided from the

[9] SEC *Accounting Series Release No. 177* requires independent accountants to submit a letter stating whether a change is to a preferable principle—one that provides a better measure of business operations. This requirement relates to the filing of quarterly financial statements on Form 10–Q.

EXHIBIT 17–7 (*continued*)

monthly cycle meter reading dates to month end and to (*b*) charge operations for emergency fuel costs in the period in which these costs are recovered under the purchase gas adjustment clause in the company's tariffs. These changes were made to match more closely costs and revenues. Deferred taxes have been provided to the extent that these amounts will not be included as income for federal income tax purposes.

These changes increased net income and earnings per share by $545,000 and $.22, respectively, for the year ended September 30, 1976, and were recorded in the fourth quarter.

B. Accounting Changes Related to Official Pronouncements (*FASB 8 and 13*)

To the Stockholders and Board of Directors of
Air Products and Chemicals, Inc.:

We have examined the consolidated balance sheets of Air Products and Chemicals, Inc. (a Delaware corporation), and subsidiaries as of 30 September 1977 and 30 September 1976 and the related statements of consolidated income, changes in shareholders' equity, and changes in consolidated financial position for the years then ended. Our examination was made in accordance with generally accepted auditing standards and, accordingly, included such tests of the accounting records and such other auditing procedures as we considered necessary in the circumstances.

In our opinion, the above-mentioned financial statements present fairly the financial position of Air Products and Chemicals, Inc., and subsidiaries as of 30 September 1977 and 30 September 1976, and the results of their operations and the changes in their financial position for the years then ended in conformity with generally accepted accounting principles consistently applied during the periods, after giving retroactive effect to the changes (with which we concur) in the method of accounting for the translation of foreign currency transactions and foreign currency financial statements and the method of accounting for capital leases both as described in Note 1 to the financial statements.

ARTHUR ANDERSEN & CO.
Philadelphia, Pennsylvania
4 November 1977

1. ACCOUNTING CHANGES

In September 1977 the company elected early adoption of the retroactive provisions of *Statement on Financial Accounting Standards No. 13* pertaining to the capitalization of capital leases. The effect on fiscal year 1977 net income and earnings per share was to decrease earnings by $1,011,000 or $.04 per share.

Effective 1 October 1976, the company changed its accounting policies for translation of foreign currencies to comply with *Statement on Financial Accounting Standards No. 8*.

These two accounting standards require retroactive application, and accordingly, prior year financial statements have been restated. The effect of the changes on fiscal year 1976 net income and earnings per share was to decrease earnings by $1,180,000 or $.04 per share.

Summary: Reporting with Fully Sufficient Competent Evidence

Fully sufficient competent evidential matter is required for several reporting alternatives. This basis in evidence is clearly required for the unqualified opinion and for the adverse opinion because they are factual and definite statements made by the auditor. Equally factual and definite are the auditor's statements concerning departures from generally accepted accounting principles and consistency (or lack thereof) in the application of accounting principles. In all these types of opinions and their variations, auditors must possess the knowledge that supports the message in the opinion paragraphs.

REPORTING UNDER PERVASIVE EVIDENTIAL DEFICIENCIES

At the other end of the evidence continuum lies the situation wherein the auditor has been unable to obtain sufficient competent evidence upon which to base an opinion on financial statements taken as a whole. Such situations involve uncertainties about continuation of the entity (i.e., the going-concern assumption) and engagements in which a complete audit is not performed. Disclaimers of an opinion—a statement that *no opinion* is given—result from pervasive evidential deficiencies.

General Disclaimer of Opinion

When lack of evidence is a consequence of a client's imposed restriction on the scope of audit field work or when important audit evidence could not be obtained for other reasons, the scope paragraph of the report should be modified to explain the circumstances. Such a scope qualification should be used only when the restriction on procedures or the inability to perform procedures has resulted in lack of sufficient competent evidential matter, further resulting in a qualified opinion or a disclaimer of opinion. If the audit scope has been restricted in some specific respect (for example, a client's refusal to let the auditor confirm receivables), but sufficient competent evidence is gathered by other procedures, the auditor need not modify the standard scope paragraph. The general guide is that scope paragraph qualification is necessary only when there will be an associated opinion qualification or disclaimer.

Whenever an opinion is disclaimed, the auditor should give all substantive reasons for the expression of no opinion. An example of a disclaimer based on going-concern uncertainties is presented in Exhibit 17–8.

Under conditions of massive uncertainty, if auditors could definitely determine that the business was failing, financial statements conforming to going-concern-based accounting principles would definitely *not* be a fair presentation of financial position and results of operations. In this case the adverse opinion would be attached to financial statements that were in conformity with generally accepted accounting principles for going-concern companies.

EXHIBIT 17–8
Disclaimer of Opinion

To the Board of Directors
Pacific Coast Properties, Inc.
Santa Monica, California

We have examined the consolidated balance sheets of Pacific Coast Properties, Inc., and subsidiaries as of December 31, 1976 and 1975, and the related consolidated statements of operations and shareholders' equity, and changes in financial position for the years then ended. Our examinations were made in accordance with generally accepted auditing standards and, accordingly, included such tests of the accounting records and such other auditing procedures as we considered necessary in the circumstances.

As more fully described in Notes 1 and 2, Pacific Coast Properties, Inc., has been experiencing severe liquidity problems since 1974. The company's ability to continue as a going concern is contingent upon successfully marketing its inventory, continued financing from lenders, and obtaining infusions of equity capital. Inventory has been valued at amounts which the company expects to realize, assuming a prompt but orderly disposition. However, because of the company's liquidity problems and difficulties in marketing its inventory, the company's ability to recover its inventory carrying value is uncertain.

The matters and conditions set forth above are of a complex nature and their resolution is dependent on many factors not susceptible of conclusive evaluation. We, therefore, are unable to make a determination regarding the resolution of these matters.

The consolidated financial statements at December 31, 1976 and 1975, and for the years then ended have been prepared on the basis of the continuation of the company as a going concern. However, the company has incurred substantial losses and continuation of the company as a going concern is dependent upon its ability to attain profitable future operations, recover the carrying value of its inventory, and obtain adequate financing.

Because of material uncertainties relating to the continuance of operations discussed in the preceding paragraphs, we are unable to and do not express an opinion on the consolidated financial statements of Pacific Coast Properties, Inc., and subsidiaries at December 31, 1976 and 1975, or for the years then ended.

KENNETH LEVENTHAL & COMPANY
March 24, 1977

NOTE 1—STATEMENT OF SIGNIFICANT ACCOUNTING POLICIES

Real Estate

All properties included in inventory of real estate are stated at cost, which is not in excess of net realizable value. Net realizable value is defined as the value which the company could reasonably expect to receive upon sale of its inventory, assuming a prompt but orderly disposition, after giving consideration to its current liquidity problem (see Notes 2, 4 and 12), reduced by costs of disposal and carrying costs (including interest and property taxes) until the projected date of sale. The

EXHIBIT 17–8 *(continued)*

company recognizes losses on projects in its inventory in the accounting period in which they become apparent.

The company follows a policy of capitalizing interest until completion of construction, or in the case of land held for sale, until the property is sold. Loan fees, property taxes, leasing costs, and other costs directly related to the inventory of real estate are also capitalized as a cost of the project. Income or loss from the rental operations of completed properties developed by the company for sale in the ordinary course of business are charged or credited against the carrying value of such properties. There were no such operations in 1976. Obligations incurred by the company pursuant to rental performance guarantees are reflected in the computation of the cost of real estate sold. There were no guarantees outstanding during 1976.

Accounting for Sales of Real Estate

Revenues and costs from the disposition of inventory are recognized in conformity with criteria and rules promulgated in an industry accounting guide applicable to real estate transactions issued by the American Institute of Certified Public Accountants.

NOTE 2—OPERATIONS

Commencing in 1974 and through 1976, the company experienced severe liquidity problems. These problems have continued into 1977 and caused the company during 1974 to suspend its historical business activities of acquiring and developing for sale commercial, industrial, and residential real estate properties. Since the middle of 1974, the company has been attempting to dispose of its inventory in an effort to generate cash to meet current expenses and repay outstanding debt. The company has not commenced any new development work since April 1974. During 1975, through renegotiation, the company terminated all of its remaining guarantee/leaseback arrangements in an effort to reduce its cash outflow.

The company continues its attempts to improve its liquidity position and to acquire additional capital. The survival of the company as a going concern is dependent upon the success of its acquiring such capital and improving its liquidity. Acquisition of capital might be accomplished as a result of successful marketing of inventory and/or the infusion of equity capital.

If the company's efforts as to the marketing of its inventory and obtaining additional capital are unsuccessful, the company will be forced to seek a solution by means of judicial proceeding which could ultimately result in the liquidation of the company.

Disclaimers on Unaudited Financial Statements

Oftentimes clients will want a CPA to become associated with the preparation or delivery of financial statements without engaging the CPA for a complete audit. Sometimes such work may involve the CPA only in writing up the financial statements in proper form from the client's books and records. Such financial statements are *unaudited* if the CPA has not applied any auditing procedures or has not applied procedures which produced sufficient evidence upon which to base an opinion on the statements taken as a whole.

Clients generally desire the association of the CPA's name in order to lend some credibility to the statements—which is the essence of the attest function. But CPAs cannot afford to lend credibility in this manner and accept exposure to liability without performing an audit in accordance with generally accepted auditing standards.

Consequently, in all cases where a CPA is associated with unaudited financial statements, he or she must submit disclaimer like the one shown in Exhibit 17–9. In addition, the guides listed below should be followed:

1. If the statements are prepared for the client's internal use only, a sentence to that effect should be inserted in the disclaimer.
2. If the CPA should learn that the statements are not in conformity with generally accepted accounting principles (including adequate disclosures), the departures should be explained in the disclaimer.
3. If prior years' unaudited statements are presented, the disclaimer should cover them as well as the current year statements.
4. Each page of the statements should be clearly labeled as unaudited.

EXHIBIT 17–9
Disclaimer for Unaudited Financial Statements

MacGregor Leisure Corporation
Houston, Texas

The accompanying consolidated balance sheet of MacGregor Leisure Corporation and subsidiaries, as of August 31, 1976 and 1975, and the related consolidated statements of net loss, retained earnings (deficit), changes in financial position, and the supplemental material for the years then ended were not audited by us and accordingly we do not express an opinion on them.

SEIDMAN & SEIDMAN
December 31, 1976

Disclaimer When CPA Is Not Independent

Independence is the foundation of the attest function. *When independence is lacking an audit in accordance with generally accepted auditing standards is impossible to perform*. These strong assertions reveal that an audit is not just the applications of tools, techniques, and procedures of auditing, but also the independence in mental attitude of the auditor. Nowhere in auditing standards is this idea set forth more clearly than in the following excerpt:

> When a certified public accountant who is not independent is associated with financial statements . . . , any procedures he might perform would not be

in accordance with generally accepted auditing standards, and accordingly he would be precluded from expressing an opinion on such statements.[10]

In keeping with this standard, evidence gathered by an auditor who is not independent is not considered sufficient competent evidence. The pervasive deficiency lies in the lack of independence. In such cases the disclaimer shown in Exhibit 17–10 is appropriate. In addition, these guides should be followed:

1. The report should not mention any reasons for not being independent because readers might erroneously interpret them as unimportant.
2. The report should make no mention whatsoever of any audit procedures applied because readers might erroneously conclude that they were sufficient.
3. If the CPA should learn that the statements are not in conformity with generally accepted accounting principles (including adequate disclosures), the departures should be explained in the disclaimer.
4. Each page of the financial statements should be clearly labeled as unaudited.

EXHIBIT 17–10
Disclaimer When a CPA Is Not Independent

The Board of Directors
The Austin Symphony Orchestra Society, Inc.

We are not independent with respect to the Austin Symphony Orchestra Society, Inc., and the accompanying balance sheet as of June 30, 1977, and the related statements of revenues and expenditures and changes in fund balances for the year then ended were not audited by us; accordingly, we do not express an opinion on them.

Peat, Marwick, Mitchell & Co.

November 8, 1977

Summary: Pervasive Evidential Deficiencies

Where there is a general lack of evidence, for whatever reason, the auditor should issue a disclaimer of opinion. A general lack of evidence can result from inability to perform some important procedures or as a consequence of the existence of a massive uncertainty about the validity of the going-concern assumption. Statements that are unaudited and statements with respect to which the CPA is not independent should carry a clear expression of "no opinion."

Sometimes, however, it is difficult to distinguish a *pervasive* evidential deficiency from an *isolated* evidential deficiency, or a *massive* uncertainty

[10] *Statement on Auditing Standards No. 1* (Section 517.01).

from an *ordinary* uncertainty. In the next section opinion qualifications based on these finer distinctions are discussed.

ISOLATED EVIDENTIAL DEFICIENCIES AND UNCERTAINTIES

Difficult decision problems arise when the auditor finds himself in the position of having too little evidence to support a clear-cut unqualified or adverse opinion and too much evidence to justify an outright disclaimer. Most often such problems result from a lack of evidence about some specific event, amount, or account. The lack of evidence many times is attributable to restrictions on the scope of the audit, to the fact that important procedures were impracticable, or to the circumstances of an uncertainty about which evidence is simply not available at the time the report decision has to be made.

Once the evidential or circumstantial uncertainty is identified, the auditor has to attempt to assess the potential importance and materiality of the amount involved. Materiality in this context is multidimensional, referring not only to the absolute or relative dollar amount of an item but also to (1) its nature, (2) its probability, and (3) its time horizon. As a broad general rule of thumb such problems are resolved with mild qualification language (sometimes even with an unqualified opinion) when (1) the potential monetary impact is small, (2) the item itself is not especially dramatic, (3) the probability of serious adversity is small, and (4) the time of likely occurrence is distant. When each of these four facets have the opposite characteristics, a report decision would lean toward a disclaimer (or even an adverse opinion where the going-concern assumption is persuasively in doubt). The report decision is more complex when the four facets are not all at one extreme.

Scope Paragraph Qualifications

The auditor's report of his own work should describe any evidential deficiency that resulted from failure to perform auditing procedures necessary in the circumstances of the engagement. Evidential deficiencies may arise in a variety of situations. Common ones involve inability to confirm receivables, inability to observe the physical count of inventories, and inability to obtain evidence about investments accounted for on the equity method (e.g., information on the value of such investments and in the transactions between investor and investee that should be eliminated under the equity method).[11] For example: The client may refuse to permit confirmation of important receivables; the auditor might be engaged after the physical count of inventory has been conducted; the auditor may be unable to obtain audited financial statements of investees and detailed information about investor-investee transactions.

If these types of evidential deficiencies can be overcome by obtaining

[11] See *Statement on Auditing Standards No. 1* (Section 542).

sufficient, competent evidence through alternative procedures, no scope qualification is required and an unqualified opinion may be given. For example, receivables may be audited through the alternative procedure of vouching payments received after the balance sheet date. However, observation of inventories must be performed (even if at a date subsequent to the balance sheet date), and reliable information on investor-investee transactions must be obtained in order to audit the intercompany eliminations.

When evidential deficiencies persist, auditors usually add language to the scope paragraph calling attention to an exception. For example: "Our examination was made in accordance with generally accepted auditing standards . . . , except as stated in the following paragraph." The middle paragraph then explains the circumstances and the nature of the evidential deficiency. If the auditor was unable to observe beginning inventory because he was not engaged until later but was able to observe the ending inventory, the paragraph would say so. In this case the opinion could be a disclaimer on the results of operations and changes in financial position (because beginning inventory enters into income determination) and an unqualified opinion on financial position (because the ending inventory was audited).

Reporting When Uncertainties Exist

A different type of evidential deficiency arises when uncertainties exist. An auditing "uncertainty" is essentially the same thing as an accounting "contingency" which is defined in *FASB Statement No. 5* as follows:

> A contingency is defined as an existing condition, situation, or set of circumstances involving uncertainty as to possible gain ("gain contingency") or loss ("loss contingency") to an enterprise that will ultimately be resolved when one or more future events occur or fail to occur. Resolution of the uncertainty may *confirm* the acquisition of an asset or the reduction of a liability or the loss or impairment of an asset or the incurrence of a liability. . . . (Emphasis added.)

FASB No. 5 sets forth accounting and disclosure standards for handling contingencies. One of the most common contingencies involves the uncertain outcome of litigation pending against the client. Auditing uncertainties include such things as the value of fixed assets that are presently held for sale (e.g., a whole plant or warehouse facility) and the status of assets involved in foreign expropriations.

Auditors may perform procedures in accordance with generally accepted auditing standards, yet the uncertainty and lack of evidence may persist. The problem is that it is impossible to obtain audit "evidence" about the future. The concept of audit evidence includes information knowable at the time a reporting decision is made and does not include predictions about the future resolution of uncertainties.

Consequently, auditors usually do not qualify the scope paragraph when contingencies and uncertainties exist. The audit usually has been performed in accordance with generally accepted auditing standards, and the auditor has done all the things possible in the circumstances. Auditors cannot predict the future much better than anyone else. Of course auditors have extrapolated the future in ordinary accounting ways (e.g., estimating collectibility of trade receivables based on collection history and assessing useful lives of fixed assets based on the client's pattern of use), and thus have reduced the "information risk" to users of the financial statements. *Information risk* refers to the probability that erroneous accounting measurements of the ordinary type are published in financial statements.

However, the auditor can do nothing to reduce the "business risk" faced by the client company. *Business risk* refers to such environmental forces as the ups and downs of demand in markets, fluctuation of prices, exposures in foreign economies, and the unusual uncertainties that may arise from litigation and from holding major assets for sale.

In 1978 the Commission on Auditors' Responsibilities concluded that auditors have an obligation to mitigate information risk. This obligation is fulfilled in the auditor's report by using "except for" language in connection with scope limitations and clients' nonconformity with accounting principles. The disclaimer of opinion is another way to put users on guard against information risk.

The commission also concluded that assessment of business risk was the responsibility of the users of financial statements. The client's accountants are responsible for full disclosure and proper accounting for contingencies (using *FASB No. 5* standards), and the auditor's responsibility is to determine whether the client's accounting and disclosure is in conformity with generally accepted accounting principles. If so, according to the commission, an unqualified opinion should be given.

This commission recommendation would effectively eliminate the opinion known as the "subject to opinion," which has been used by auditors for many years. The "subject to opinion" directs attention to material uncertainties/contingencies and is considered a useful "red flag" for financial statement users. The Auditing Standards Board is studying the entire form and content of auditors' reports on financial statements, but as of late 1978 no wholesale changes had been enacted in authoritative pronouncements.

"Subject to" Language

Significant uncertainties about future events may exist with regard to such things as tax deficiency assessments, contract disputes, recoverability of asset costs, lawsuits, and other important contingencies. The matter should be explained clearly and completely in a paragraph(s) following the scope paragraph, and the opinion may contain a statement that the overall opinion on financial statements taken as a whole is "subject to" the ultimate future outcome. Two examples of such situations and qualifications are given in Exhibit 17–11.

EXHIBIT 17–11
Reporting When Uncertainties Exist

A. Isolated Uncertainty Subject of Opinion Paragraph Modification

The Board of Directors
Tony Lama Company, Inc.:

We have examined the consolidated balance sheets of Tony Lama Company, Inc., and subsidiary as of July 31, 1977 and 1976, and the related consolidated statements of earnings and retained earnings and changes in financial position for the years then ended. Our examination was made in accordance with generally accepted auditing standards and, accordingly, included such tests of the accounting records and such other auditing procedures as we considered necessary in the circumstances.

As discussed in Note 10 to the consolidated financial statements, the company is contingently liable in connection with certain customs penalties; the amount of such liability is not presently determinable.

In our opinion, subject to the effect on the consolidated financial statements of the ultimate resolution of the matter discussed in the preceding paragraph, the aforementioned consolidated financial statements present fairly the financial position of Tony Lama Company, Inc., and subsidiary at July 31, 1977 and 1976, and the results of their operations and the changes in their financial position for the years then ended, in conformity with generally accepted accounting principles applied on a consistent basis.

PEAT, MARWICK, MITCHELL & CO.
September 30, 1977

(10) Contingency

During the year ended July 31, 1976, the U.S. Customs Service instituted an investigation of the duty declarations made by the company in connection with the importation of footwear parts from Mexico during the period from October 1969 to May 1976. Upon completion of its internal investigation of the customs matter in accordance with guidelines suggested by the Customs Service, the company, on November 1, 1976, filed with the service a schedule of applicable costs which reflected unpaid duties aggregating approximately $365,000 and provision was made for this amount in the 1976 consolidated financial statements.

During fiscal 1977 the Customs Service completed its investigation of the company's duty declarations, and the company was assessed an additional $145,000 for duties lost. This additional deficiency was charged to operations during fiscal 1977, and the aggregate amount of duties lost as determined by the Customs Service was paid by the company during the year.

In August 1977 the company pleaded guilty to criminal charges in connection with the duty declarations and subsequently paid a fine of $15,000. In addition, the Customs Service assessed the company a civil penalty of approximately $36 million, which represents the forfeiture value of the goods imported during the period in question. The company is preparing its petition for mitigation of the penalty, and normally such penalties are mitigated to a multiple (generally from one to eight) of the alleged loss of revenue (510,000). The company has made provision in its 1977 consolidated financial statements for $510,000, the minimum penalty it expects to incur in connection with the customs matter; however, the penalty ultimately as-

EXHIBIT 17–11 (*continued*)

sessed may be substantially in excess of this amount. The total ultimate liability to the company which may result from the customs matter is not presently determinable. Customs penalties normally may be repaid with interest over a period of five years from the date of final adjudication. Such penalties are not deductible for federal income tax purposes.

B. Isolated Uncertainties Combined to Yield Going-Concern Doubt and a Disclaimer of Opinion

Board of Directors
Aeronca, Inc.
Torrance, California

We have examined the consolidated balance sheet of Aeronca, Inc., and subsidiaries as of December 31, 1975 and 1974, and the related statements of operations, stockholders' equity, and changes in financial position for the years then ended. Our examination was made in accordance with generally accepted auditing standards and, accordingly, included such tests of the accounting records and such other auditing procedures as we considered necessary in the circumstances.

As discussed in Note 2, the company is currently involved in negotiations for the determination of the final contract price for a significant long-term contract. The effect upon the consolidated financial statements is dependent on such negotiations. As set forth in Note 3, work in process under the L–1011 program includes substantial costs, the recovery of which requires additional sales authorizations of approximately 100 shipsets. As indicated in Note 10, the company may be assessed for additional property taxes.

The accompanying financial statements have been prepared on a going-concern basis. Satisfactory negotiation of the credit arrangements referred to in Note 5 had not been consummated as of March 1, 1976, and such arrangements are necessary to the continuation of the company as a going concern.

Because of the significance of the matters referred to in the previous paragraphs we are unable to and do not express an opinion on the accompanying consolidated financial statements for the year ended December 31, 1975.

TOUCHE ROSS & CO.
March 1, 1976

Reporting Obligations—A Summary

In the final analysis the auditor's reporting decision rests upon how much is known about the financial statements—the evidence dimension. The standard unqualified short-form report is the basic starting point for a reporting decision, but several circumstances may exist that require departure from the standard language. The circumstances covered in this chapter include:

Departure from GAAP—an accounting deficiency.

Departure from an official pronouncement—an accounting deficiency (modified by Ethics Rule 203).

Lack of consistency—an accounting deficiency.

Limitation on scope—an evidential deficiency.

Uncertainty—related to future events.

Unaudited financial statements—pervasive absence of audit evidence.

Auditor is not independent—related to auditing standards.

Emphasis of a matter—separate paragraphs used to highlight and explain.

One other modification of the standard short-form report language is used when one auditor relies on the work and reports of other independent auditors. This topic and others related to reporting are covered in Chapter 18.

SOURCES AND ADDITIONAL READING REFERENCES

Anderson, H. M., and Giese, J. W. "The Auditor's Belief and His Opinion—The Need for Consistency," *The CPA Journal*, January 1973, pp. 49–54.

Bernstein, L. A. "The Concept of Materiality," *Accounting Review*, January 1967, pp. 86–95.

Boatsman, J. R., and Robertson, J. C. "Policy-Capturing on Some Selected Materiality Judgments," *Accounting Review*, April 1974.

Carmichael, D. R. "Auditor's Reports—A Search for Criteria," *Journal of Accountancy*, September 1972, pp. 67–74.

______. *The Auditor's Reporting Obligation: The Meaning and Implementation of the Fourth Standard of Reporting, Auditing Research Monograph No. 1*, New York: AICPA, 1972.

Commission on Auditors' Responsibilities. "Reporting on Significant Uncertainties," sec. 3 in *Report, Conclusions, and Recommendations* (New York: CAR, 1978), pp. 23–30.

Cooper, K., and Keim, G. D. "Unsettled Issues in Corporate Disclosure," *The CPA Journal*, March 1977, pp. 27–30.

Cumming, John. "Modification in Unaudited Reports," *The CPA Journal*, December 1976, pp. 17–22.

Dominiak, G. F., and Louderback, III, J. G. " 'Present Fairly' and Generally Accepted Accounting Principles," *The CPA Journal*, January 1972, pp. 45–49.

Hill, Henry. "Reporting on Uncertainties by Independent Auditors," *Journal of Accountancy*, January 1973, pp. 55–60.

Isbell, David B., and Carmichael, D. R. "Disclaimers and Liability—The Rhode Island Trust Case," *Journal of Accountancy*, April 1973, pp. 37–42.

Mautz, R. K., and Sharaf, H. A. *The Philosophy of Auditing*, especially chap. 7, "Fair Presentation," American Accounting Assn., 1961.

Newton, Lauren K. "The Risk Factor in Materiality Decisions," *Accounting Review*, January 1977, pp. 97–108.

Olson, Wallace E. "A Look at the Responsibility Gap," *Journal of Accountancy*, January 1975, pp. 52–57.

______. "The Search for Fairness in Financial Reporting," *Journal of Accountancy*. May 1976, pp. 82–86.

Rosenfield, Paul, and Lorensen, L. "Auditor's Responsibilities and the Audit Report," *Journal of Accountancy*, September 1974, pp. 73–83.

Unaudited Financial Statements Task Force. *Guide for Engagements of CPAs to Prepare Unaudited Financial Statements* (AICPA, 1975).

REVIEW QUESTIONS

17.1. What is the relationship of the time-cost constraint to the type of report issued by an independent auditor?

17.2. What is a "negative assurance"? Why is it generally prohibited? When is a negative assurance permitted?

17.3. In what type of audit report does the auditor take full responsibility? No responsibility?

17.4. Explain how the *evidence dimension* affects the auditor's report when the client refuses to allow the auditor to confirm an extremely material amount of receivables?

17.5. Explain the effect of the *materiality dimension* on an auditor's report when the client uses an accounting method that departs from generally accepted accounting principles.

17.6. When might omission of the standard consistency phrase be appropriate?

17.7. What are unaudited statements? In connection with unaudited statements, what general guides should the auditor follow?

17.8. If an auditor is not independent with respect to a client, what type of opinion must be issued? Why?

17.9. Explain how materiality is multidimensional.

17.10. In what circumstances would an auditor render an "except for" opinion? A disclaimer of opinion?

EXERCISES AND PROBLEMS

17.11. Roscoe, CPA, has completed the examination of the financial statements of Excelsior Corporation as of and for the year ended December 31, 1978. Roscoe also examined and reported on the Excelsior financial statements for the prior year. Roscoe drafted the following report for 1978.

March 15, 1979

We have examined the balance sheet and statements of income and retained earnings of Excelsior Corporation as of December 31, 1978. Our examination was made in accordance with generally accepted accounting standards and, accordingly, included such tests of the accounting records as we considered necessary in the circumstances.

In our opinion the above-mentioned financial statements are accurately prepared and fairly presented in accordance with generally accepted accounting principles in effect at December 31, 1978.

Roscoe, CPA
(Signed)

Other information:

a. Excelsior is presenting comparative financial statements.
b. Excelsior does not wish to present a statement of changes in financial position for either year.
c. During 1978 Excelsior changed its method of accounting for long-term construction contracts and properly reflected the effect of the change in the current year's financial statements and restated the prior year's statements. Roscoe is satisfied with Excelsior's justification for making the change. The change is discussed in footnote number 12.
d. Roscoe was unable to perform normal accounts receivable confirmation procedures, but alternate procedures were used to satisfy Roscoe as to the validity of the receivables.
e. Excelsior Corporation is the defendant in a litigation, the outcome of which is highly uncertain. If the case is settled in favor of the plaintiff, Excelsior will be required to pay a substantial amount of cash which might require the sale of certain fixed assets. The litigation and the possible effects have been properly disclosed in footnote number 11.
f. Excelsior issued debentures on January 31, 1977, in the amount of $10,000,000. The funds obtained from the issuance were used to finance the expansion of plant facilities. The debenture agreement restricts the payment of future cash dividends to earnings after December 31, 1983. Excelsior declined to disclose this essential data in the footnotes to the financial statements.

Required:

Consider all facts given and rewrite the auditor's report in acceptable and complete format incorporating any necessary departures from the standard (short form) report. (AICPA adapted)

17.12. Pauline Burke, CPA, has completed field work for her examination of the Willingham Corporation for the year ended December 31, 1977, and now is in the process of determining whether to modify her report. Presented below are two independent, unrelated situations which have arisen.

Situation I

In September 1977, a lawsuit was filed against Willingham to have the court order it to install pollution-control equipment in one of its older plants. Willingham's legal counsel has informed Burke that it is not possible to forecast the outcome of this litigation; however, Willingham's management has informed Burke that the cost of the pollution-control equipment is not economically feasible and that the plant will be closed if the case is lost. In addition, Burke has been told by management that the plant and its production equipment would have only minimal resale values and that the production that would be lost could not be recovered at other plants.

Situation II

During 1977, Willingham purchased a franchise amounting to 20 percent of its assets for the exclusive right to produce and sell a newly patented product in the northeastern United States. There has been no production in marketable quantities of the product anywhere to date. Neither the franchisor nor any franchisee has conducted any market research with respect to the product.

Required:

In deciding the type-of-report modification, if any, Ms. Burke should take into account such considerations as follows:

Relative magnitude.
Uncertainty of outcome.
Likelihood of error.
Expertise of the auditor.
Pervasive impact on the financial statements.
Inherent importance of the item.

Discuss Burke's type-of-report decision for each situation in terms of the above and other appropriate considerations. Assume each situation is adequately disclosed in the notes to the financial statements. Each situation should be considered independently. In discussing each situation, ignore the other. It is not necessary for you to decide the type of report which should be issued. (AICPA)

17.13. The assets of The Men's Custom Shop at May 31, 1979, are listed below:

Assets	*Amount*
Cash	$ 60,000
Accounts receivable (net)	190,000
Merchandise inventory	460,000
Equipment (net)	105,000
Total	$815,000

During the course of your annual examination of the company's financial statements, the owner advises you that he will not permit confirmation of the accounts receivable because his customers would resent it.

Required:

a. State the conditions, if any, under which you would render an unqualified opinion on the financial statements, and providing the conditions are met,

b. Prepare the short-form report you would render on these financial statements. (AICPA adapted)

17.14. Client Corporation (whose fiscal year will end December 31, 1979) informs you on December 18, 1979, that it has a serious shortage of working capital because of heavy operating losses incurred since October 1, 1979. Application has been made to a bank for a loan, and the bank's loan officer has requested financial statements.

Required:

Indicate the type of opinion you would render under each of the following independent sets of circumstances. Give the reasons for your decision.

a. Client Corporation asks that you save time by auditing the financial statements prepared by Client's chief accountant as of September 30, 1979. The scope of your audit would not be limited by Client in any way.

b. Client Corporation asks that you conduct an audit as of December 15,

1979. The scope of your audit would not be limited by Client in any way.

c. Client Corporation asks that you conduct an audit as of December 31, 1979, and render a report by January 16. To save time and reduce the cost of the audit, it is requested that your examination not include confirmation of accounts receivable or observation of the taking of inventory.

d. Client Corporation asks that you prepare financial statements as of December 15, 1979, from the books and records of the company without audit. The statements are to be submitted on plain paper without your name being associated in any way with them. The reason for your preparing the statements is your familiarity with proper form for financial statements. (AICPA adapted)

17.15. A CPA was engaged by the Alba Nursing Home to prepare, on the CPA's stationery and without audit, financial statements for 1979 and its 1979 income tax return. From the accounting and other records the CPA learned the following information about the Nursing Home:

1. The Alba Nursing Home is a partnership that was formed early in 1979. The nursing home occupies a large old mansion that stands on a sizable piece of ground beside a busy highway. The property was purchased by the partnership from an estate that out-of-state heirs wanted to settle. The heirs were unfamiliar with the local real estate market and sold the property at the bargain price of $10,000 for the house and $5,000 for the land.
2. A few weeks after the purchase the partnership employed a competent independent appraisal firm that appraised the house at $50,000 and the land at $100,000.
3. The property was then written up on the partnership books to its appraisal value, and the partners' capital accounts were credited with the amount of the write-up.
4. Additional funds were invested to convert the mansion to a nursing home, to purchase the necessary equipment and supplies, and to provide working capital.

Required:

a. Assume that the CPA prepared the financial statements of the Alba Nursing Home from the accounting records, placed them on her stationery, and labeled each page "Prepared without Audit." In accordance with the client's preference, the assets were reported only at appraisal values. Under the circumstances presented, what is the CPA's responsibility, if any, to disclose the method of valuation of the assets? Discuss.

b. In this situation, how does the CPA's responsibility for disclosure of the valuation basis of the assets differ, if at all, from the responsibility she would have had if she had made a typical examination of the financial statements?

c. In this situation, would it be proper for the CPA to prepare, and sign as preparer, the 1979 federal income tax return for the partnership if the mansion is shown on the income tax return at its appraisal value? Discuss. (AICPA adapted)

17.16. Nancy Miller, CPA, has completed field work for her examination of the financial statements of Nickles Manufacturers, Inc., for the year ended March 31, 1979, and now is preparing her auditor's report.

She was engaged on April 15, 1979, to examine the financial statements for the year ended March 31, 1979, and was not present to observe the taking of the physical inventory on March 31, 1979. Her alternative procedures included examination of shipping and receiving documents with regard to transactions since the year-end; extensive review of the inventory-count sheets; and discussion of the physical inventory procedures with responsible company personnel. She has also satisfied herself as to inventory valuation and consistency in valuation method. Inventory quantities are determined solely by means of physical count. (Note: Assume that the CPA is properly relying upon the examination of another auditor with respect to the beginning inventory.)

Required:

a. Discuss the appropriate disclosures, if any, in the financial statements and accompanying footnotes.

b. Discuss the effect, if any, on the auditor's short-form report. (AICPA adapted)

17.17. The CPA must comply with the generally accepted auditing standards of reporting when he prepares his opinion on the client's financial statements. One of the reporting standards relates to consistency.

Required:

a. Discuss the statement regarding consistency that the CPA is required to include in his opinion. What is the objective of requiring the CPA to make this statement about consistency?

b. Discuss what mention of consistency, if any, the CPA must make in his opinion relating to his first audit of the financial statements of the following companies:
   (1) A newly organized company ending its first accounting period.
   (2) A company established for a number of years.

c. Discuss whether the changes described in each of the cases below would require recognition in the CPA's opinion as to consistency. (Assume the amounts are material.)
   (1) The company disposed of one of its three subsidiaries that had been included in its consolidated statements for prior years.
   (2) After two years of computing depreciation under the declining-balance method for income tax purposes and under the straight-line method for reporting purposes, the declining-balance method was adopted for reporting purposes.
   (3) The estimated remaining useful life of plant property was reduced because of obsolescence. (AICPA)

17.18. Various types of "accounting changes" can affect the second reporting standard of the generally accepted auditing standards. This standard reads, "The report shall state whether such principles have been consistently observed in the current period in relation to the preceding period."

Assume that the following list describes changes which have a material effect on a client's financial statements for the current year.

1. A change from the completed-contract method to the percentage-of-completion method of accounting for long-term construction-type contracts.

2. A change in the estimated useful life of previously recorded fixed assets based on newly acquired information.
3. Correction of a mathematical error in inventory pricing made in a prior period.
4. A change from prime costing to full absorption costing for inventory valuation.
5. A change from presentation of statements of individual companies to presentation of consolidated statements.
6. A change from deferring and amortizing preproduction costs to recording such costs as an expense when incurred because future benefits of the costs have become doubtful. The new accounting method was adopted in recognition of the change in estimated future benefits.
7. A change to including the employer share of FICA taxes as "retirement benefits" on the income statement from including it with "other taxes."
8. A change from the Fifo method of inventory pricing to the Lifo method of inventory pricing.

Required:

Identify the type of change which is described in each item above, state whether any modification is required in the auditor's report *as it relates to the second standard of reporting,* and state whether the prior year's financial statements should be restated when presented in comparative form with the current year's statements. Organize your answer sheet as shown below.

For example, a change from the Lifo method of inventory pricing to the Fifo method of inventory pricing would appear as shown. (AICPA)

Item No.	*Type of Change*	*Should Auditor's Report be Modified?*	*Should Prior Year's Statements Be Restated?*
Example	An accounting change from one generally accepted accounting principle to another generally accepted accounting principle.	Yes	Yes

17.19. The concept of materiality is important to the CPA in his examination of financial statements and expression of opinion upon these statements.

Required:

Discuss the following:

a. How are materiality (and immateriality) related to the proper presentation of financial statements?

b. What factors and measures should the CPA consider in assessing the materiality of an exception to financial statement presentation?

c. How will the materiality of a CPA's exceptions to financial statements influence the type of opinion he expresses? (The relationship of materiality to *each type* of auditor's opinion should be considered in your answer.) (AICPA adapted)

17.20. You have been assigned to the examination of the Cap Sales Company's fire insurance policies. All audit procedures with regard to the fire insurance register have been completed.

You conclude that the insurance coverage against loss by fire is inadequate and that if loss occurs the company may have insufficient assets to liquidate its debts. After a discussion with you management stated that they were not going to increase the amount of insurance coverage and refused to disclose factual information about insurance in the financial statements.

Required:

a. What mention will you make of this condition and contingency in your short-form report? Why?

b. What effect will this condition and contingency have upon your opinion? Give the reasons for your position.

17.21. The following audit report was written by your partner yesterday. You need to describe the reporting deficiencies, explain the reasons for them, and discuss with him how the report should be corrected. This may be a hard job because he has always felt somewhat threatened because you were the first woman partner in the firm. You have decided to write up a three-column worksheet showing the deficiencies, the reasons, and the correction needed. This was his report:

> I made my examination in accordance with generally accepted auditing standards. However, I am not independent with respect to Mavis Corporation because my wife owns 5 percent of the outstanding common stock of the company. The accompanying balance sheet as of December 31, 1979, and the related statements of income and retained earnings and changes in financial position for the year then ended were not audited by me; accordingly, I do not express an opinion on them.

Required:

Prepare the worksheet described above.

DISCUSSION CASES

17.22. **Information Disclosure—Fallhard Manufacturing Company**

In 1978 Fallhard Manufacturing Company was experiencing financial difficulty. After reporting a small profit in 1976, the loss for 1977 was $3.8 million. Total assets were $89 million, shareholders' equity was $38 million, and outstanding long-term and short-term debt to financial institutions was $31.6 million as of December 31, 1977. The company obtained shareholder approval to sell $10 million of 9 percent cumulative preferred stock to Gofast, Inc., and closed the sale in December, 1978. The proceeds were used to pay off $5 million of the short-term debt and $5 million of the long-term debt.

After purchasing the preferred stock, Gofast, Inc., became a "related party" as defined in *SAS No. 6* (Section 335).

However, in December 1977, prior to the stock transaction Gofast had purchased a manufacturing facility from Fallhard for $3 million, which was Fallhard's book value of the plant. Repayment terms were (1) immediate down payment of $500,000, (2) 50¢ for each unit of product produced at the plant, payable semiannually, and (3) 5/6 of the proceeds from the sale of any equipment or real estate transferred with the plant property. Fallhard took a nonrecourse note for $2.5 million, and at December 31, 1977, this amount was classified as a noncurrent asset.

After Fallhard reported a $1 million loss in 1978, some stockholders began to complain. One spoke up at the annual meeting, held on March 1, 1979, saying: "The comparative financial statements in the annual report for 1977 and 1978 are materially misleading. In particular, they fail to disclose the nature and terms of the related party transaction with Gofast, Inc. We might have grounds for a lawsuit."

For Discussion:

a. Gofast, Inc., was not a related party in 1977 when the plant was purchased. Should the nature and terms of the transaction and the note have been disclosed anyway?

b. As of December 31, 1978, however, Gofast, Inc., had become a related party. Should the auditor qualify the opinion on the 1978 statements because Fallhard did not retroactively apply the related party transaction disclosure rules to the plant sale transaction?

17.23. **Going-Concern Problems—Tenfour Company***

On December 10, 1976, you are trying to complete the audit for the year ended September 30 of Tenfour Company, a manufacturer of CB (citizen's band) radios. Tenfour is a major company in the industry and has enjoyed the boom times of heavy demand for CB radio units. Earlier in 1976 investors snatched up a public stock offering at $25 per share, a price that amounted to 15 times 1975 earnings per share.

Late in the day you are studying, for the tenth time, the following footnote disclosures that have been prepared by Tenfour management. They are very accurate.

NOTE E. GOVERNMENT REGULATION

Because of serious overcrowding of citizen's radio bands the Federal Communications Commission has banned the sale of 23-channel CB radios. Forty channels are now authorized, but the FCC has ruled that manufacturers can accept no orders prior to January 1, 1977. Consumers apparently do not want to buy the old 23-channel units, and the result has been a dramatic turndown in sales as the company approaches the traditionally busy Christmas season.

NOTE F. BANK DEBT

The company's $40 million bank debt, bearing 11 percent interest, is in default as a result of lack of sales and sales revenue. Temporary waivers of default action have been obtained, and the company is renegotiating the terms of the debt.

---

* The 1976 and 1977 dates in this case are used because FCC actions occurred at that time.

NOTE G. QUARTERLY RESULTS (UNAUDITED)

	Fiscal Year 1975		Fiscal Year 1976	
Sales in Millions	*Sales*	*EPS*	*Sales*	*EPS*
Quarter ended:				
December 31	$15	$ .53	$18	$ .60
March 31	10	.36	12	.38
June 30	12	.43	7	(.15)
September 30	10	.35	2	(.58)
	$47	$1.67	$39	$0.25

NOTE H. PENDING LITIGATION

Certain shareholders who purchased stock in the January 1976 public offering have filed suit in federal district court claiming unspecified damages and alleging the company's violation of the Securities Act of 1933. The company's outside legal counsel has not had opportunity to study the complaint, and proceedings are still in the discovery phase. Company management believes this lawsuit has no merit and that its ultimate resolution will have no material effect on the company's financial position.

After re-reading these notes you also review certain other information.

The company has a huge inventory of 23-channel CB units. When consumer demand was heavy, distributors would book multiple orders to ensure a supply. Now that demand has dried up, they are canceling orders and refusing to accept shipments.

Sixteen other manufacturing companies compete in the domestic market. Four of them have already declared bankruptcy and sought protection under Chapter XI of the Bankruptcy Act.

The company has not switched to 40-channel production, counting instead on marketing a $25 converter that will be sold with a 23-channel unit. Right now there is extremely sharp price-cutting among manufacturers on 40-channel sets.

An analysis by a respected investment research organization has predicted a serious shake-out among companies in the industry. The analyst's report guesses that half the companies will fold, but no predictions were made about which ones.

Industry lobbyists in Washington, D.C., are pushing hard for a substantial increase in import duties on cheaper Japanese units. However, the government's inflation fighting and counterpressures in favor of free trade may blunt this effort.

The industry is in a mess, but Tenfour has a recent history of great success. If 1977 demand picks up, if consumers want the 23-channel set + converter package, if cash holds out until the demand develops, and if foreign competition doesn't drive prices down too much, the company might have a decent chance to return to profitability.

The company is anxious to see the audit report. Tenfour's president has already told you that he has to hand-carry a copy to the lending banks, and he thinks that anything less than an unqualified opinion will make the renegotiations very tough.

For Discussion:

a. Is Tenfour Company going or gone?

b. Will a disclaimer of opinion on the grounds of a massive going-concern uncertainty *cause* Tenfour to declare bankruptcy?
c. Would the auditor be in a better professional position if he or she did not have to try to predict the outcome of future events?
d. What kind of opinion would you give on the Tenfour Company financial statements?

17.24. **"Internal Use Only" Statements—Welsch Chocolate Company**

As a partner of Able Auditor's Associates you managed the engagement to prepare unaudited financial statements for the Welsch Chocolate Company, a small ($2 million assets), but growing, company in Medium City (population 750,000). The company was formed two years ago and business has been very good. Demand for Welsch's Confections is high, and a new candy plant was erected last year. The fast pace of the business has created heavy workloads for four members of the Welsch family, who own and manage the business, and the staff of six accountants have their hands full with internal cost accounting and monitoring of construction cost projects. They simply have no time to prepare general-purpose financial reports. However, the accounts and records are well-kept, and data processing is conducted in an atmosphere of good control.

John Welsch, the president, has hired Able Auditor's to prepare unaudited financial statements. He has emphasized that all he wants is the basic financial schedules and not "all that footnote and earnings per share stuff." Mr. Welsch just wants to keep tabs on all aspects of the business's overall profitability.

The engagement did not prove difficult and nothing unusual turned up. You wrote the standard unaudited financial statement disclaimer on a cover page, marked all the financial schedules "unaudited," and included in the disclaimer these sentences:

> These financial statements are incomplete presentations because they do not include all the disclosures required by generally accepted accounting principles. They are for internal use only and should not be distributed to, nor used by, anyone who is not a member of the company's management.

John Welsch thought the disclaimer was a needless bit of trivia, but he thanked you anyway, took 20 copies of the report, paid your bill on the spot, and promised to call on you next year.

Very recently you were involved in the audit of First National Bank, Medium City's largest. While reviewing the loan files on new loans, you were surprised (to say the least) to find a new loan of $1 million to Welsch Chocolate Company. The file also contained two copies of your report, complete with the cover sheet, your disclaimer, and the notice about internal use. A bank officer had penciled on one of the copies "Able is known to be a group of especially competent accountants."

Notwithstanding the compliment, you are disturbed over the fact that John Welsch used your report in connection with the bank loan. You are beginning to think you should do something about it.

For Discussion:

a. To whom does the audit report belong, once it is delivered?
b. Should the owner of the report be free to do with it whatever he or she wishes?
c. What action should you take now? Consider communications with (1) First National Bank, (2) John Welsch.

18

REPORTS BY INDEPENDENT AUDITORS (CONCLUDED)

Several situations may arise in practice which do not fit the system of reporting criteria and options explained in Chapter 17. In this chapter the objective is to explain reporting standards with regard to:

Reporting on comparative financial statements of two or more years presented in a document (*SAS No. 15,* Section 505).

Obligations regarding *other information* in documents containing audited financial statements (*SAS No. 8,* Section 550).

Auditing of *segment information* in conformity with FASB *No. 14* (*SAS No. 21,* Section 435).

Reliance on the work of other independent auditors when giving an opinion on financial statements (*SAS No. 1,* Section 543).

Omission of whole financial statement schedules (*SAS No. 1,* Section 545).

Subsequent discovery of facts after an opinion on financial statements has been issued (*SAS No. 1,* Section 561).

Special reports and engagements (*SAS No. 14,* Section 621).

Long-form reports (*SAS No. 1,* Section 610).

Letters for underwriters (*SAS No. 1,* Section 630).

Personal financial statements.

REPORTING ON COMPARATIVE STATEMENTS

Companies usually present financial schedules (income statement, balance sheet and statement of changes in financial position) for at least one prior year in comparison with the current year. Financial statement footnotes also usually contain numerical data in comparative form, although narrative-descriptive disclosures often relate only to the current year. Auditor's reports relate to "financial statements taken as a whole" (i.e., financial schedules and footnotes taken together), and *Statement on Auditing Standards No. 15* (Section 505) expanded the concept of "financial statements taken as a whole" to include the statements of one or more comparative prior periods as well as the current year statements.

When an auditor has previously issued a report on prior year statements presented in current year comparative form, he should *update* the report previously issued. An *updated report* is one based not only on the prior year audit but also on information that has come to light since then (particularly in the course of the current year audit work). An updated report may be the same (e.g., unqualified, qualified) as previously issued, or it may be different depending on whether current information causes a retroactive change in the auditor's reporting decision.

The language of a report on comparative financial statements cites two (or more) balance sheet dates and two (or more) accounting periods and expresses the opinion on all of the statements. The date of the report is the date on which all important field work was completed on the current year audit.[1]

Complications arise and care must be taken with report language when the two (or more) comparative statements carry differing opinions. Differing opinions cases involve the following:

Qualified opinion on current year's financial statements with prior year unqualified.

Qualified opinion on prior year's financial statements with the current year qualified for the same and an additional reason.

Unqualified opinion on the current year's financial statements with disclaimer of opinion on the prior year's statement of income.

Unqualified opinion on current year's balance sheet with disclaimer of opinion on prior year's unaudited financial statements.

Disclaimer of opinion on current year's unaudited financial statements with opinion on prior year's audited financial statements.

An example of a differing opinion is shown in Exhibit 18–1. The auditor's report on fiscal 1976, when issued in 1976, contained qualifying language related to an uncertainty about the losses which might be incurred on disposition of a subsidiary. In 1977 the uncertainty was resolved, and the updated opinion on 1976 financial statements, when issued in 1977 in comparative form, was changed to an unqualified opinion.

---

[1] An *updated report* differs from the *reissuance* of a previously expressed report. A reissuance is essentially providing more copies of the report or giving permission to use it in another document sometime after its original delivery date. The report *date* is the original date of the end of field work on that year's audit, indicating a cutoff date for the auditor's responsibility to report on subsequent events. (See *SAS No. 1*, Sections 530.06–.08.)

EXHIBIT 18–1
Comparative Statement Opinion Changed from Qualified to Unqualified

Directors and Shareholders
Caesars World, Inc.:

We have examined the consolidated balance sheet of Caesars World, Inc., and subsidiaries as of July 31, 1977 and 1976, and the related consolidated statements of operations, shareholders' equity, and changes in financial position for the years then ended. Our examination was made in accordance with generally accepted auditing standards and, accordingly, included such tests of the accounting records and such other auditing procedures as we considered necessary in the circumstances.

As discussed in Note 17, since September 1975 the Securities and Exchange Commission has been investigating the adequacy of disclosures and other matters in connection with certain transactions. In our report dated October 1, 1976 (except as to certain notes which were as of October 25, 1976), our opinion on the July 31, 1976, financial statements was qualified as being subject to the effects, if any, on such financial statements of the ultimate resolution of this matter. Since that date, the company's board of directors has received a report from special counsel, engaged at the request of the board's audit committee to investigate the questioned transactions entered into by the company. Based on this report, the audit committee has concluded that the description of the transactions contained in Note 17 is accurate and that the outcome of the Securities and Exchange Commission investigation will have no material adverse effect upon the company's financial condition. Also, after considering the report of special counsel, corporate counsel and general counsel have reaffirmed their opinions that the transactions were adequately disclosed and that the company has committed no violations of federal securities laws in connection therewith. In view of the foregoing and inasmuch as no information has come to our attention which would cause us to conclude that the aforementioned matters would have a material adverse effect on the accompanying financial statements, our present unqualified opinion on the July 31, 1976, financial statements as presented herein is different from that expressed in our previous report.

In our opinion, the financial statements referred to above present fairly the consolidated financial position of Caesars World, Inc., and subsidiaries as of July 31, 1977 and 1976, and the consolidated results of their operations and the changes in their financial position for the years then ended, in conformity with generally accepted accounting principles applied on a consistent basis.

ALEXANDER GRANT & COMPANY
Van Nuys, California
October 17, 1977

17. (EXCERPTS) SECURITIES AND EXCHANGE COMMISSION INVESTIGATION

Since September 1975, the Securities and Exchange Commission has been investigating the adequacy of the disclosures and other matters in connection with certain transactions. The company and its counsel believe that these transactions have been adequately disclosed and that the company has committed no violations of federal securities laws in connection therewith. The company also believes the outcome of the Securities and Exchange Commission investigation will not have a

EXHIBIT 18–1 (*continued*)

material adverse effect upon the financial condition of the company. The transactions and other occurrences about which inquiries have been made included the following: (Note: Disclosure details omitted.)

Each of the above transactions involved the same people or their relatives. In addition, since 1972 the chairman of the board of directors of the company (chairman) had been a stockholder with a one-third interest and a participant in a significant Flordia real estate venture with these people. All of the participants guaranteed substantial mortgage debts, but the chairman provided (1972 to March 1977) less than 5 percent of the funds provided by all the participants which were required above the mortgage commitment. In 1975 the chairman made a loan to one of the other participants which was repaid in 1977. In March 1977, the chairman assigned his stock interest to the other participants but remained liable for the quaranteed mortgage debts.

During 1977, the company's board of directors received a report from special counsel, engaged at the request of the board's audit committee to investigate the aforementioned transactions. Based on this report and on their own knowledge of the transaction, the audit committee has concluded that the description of the aforementioned transactions is accurate and that the outcome of the Securities and Exchange Commission investigation will not have a material adverse effect upon the company's financial condition.

OBLIGATIONS REGARDING "OTHER INFORMATION"

Audit clients disseminate financial information in many forms—in press releases, interviews with financial analysts, unaudited quarterly financial statements, and in other parts of documents that contain audited financial statements. Almost all annual reports and filings with regulatory agencies contain sections such as a president's letter and management's analysis of operations, but these sections are separate from the audited financial statements and are not covered by the audit opinion. Nevertheless, auditors have an obligation under generally accepted auditing standards to read the other information and determine whether it is inconsistent with the audited financial statements.

This obligation exists only with regard to (*a*) other information in documents that contain audited financial statements (e.g., annual reports, 10–K reports filed with the SEC)[2] and (*b*) other information in other kinds of documents reviewed at the request of the client. The auditor is not obligated to review press releases, analysts' interviews, or other forms of irregular financial event releases unless requested by the client to do so.

---

[2] *SAS No. 1* (Sections 630 and 710) specify the kinds of "other information" that should be reviewed in connection with letters for underwriters and documents filed under the Securities Act of 1933 (see Sections 630.36–.41 and 710.07). These types of "other information" are defined more narrowly that the "other information" discussed in this portion of the textbook.

An example of "other information" is a president's letter remark that: "Earnings increased from $1 million to $2 million, an increase of 50c per share." This is a statement that can be corroborated by comparison to the audited financial statements. The president's comment would be considered inconsistent if the $1 million was income after a significant extraordinary gain and the $2 million was income before an extraordinary loss, or if the 50c change in EPS was the difference between last year's fully diluted EPS and this year's primary EPS. The president has selected numbers without due regard to their meaningful comparison. Other kinds of "other information," however, might not be so directly related to audited figures. For example, the marketing vice president might write that: "This year's sales represent a 20-percent share of the total market for our product."

EXHIBIT 18–2
Action When Other Information Is Materially Inconsistent (*SAS No. 8,* Section 550.04)

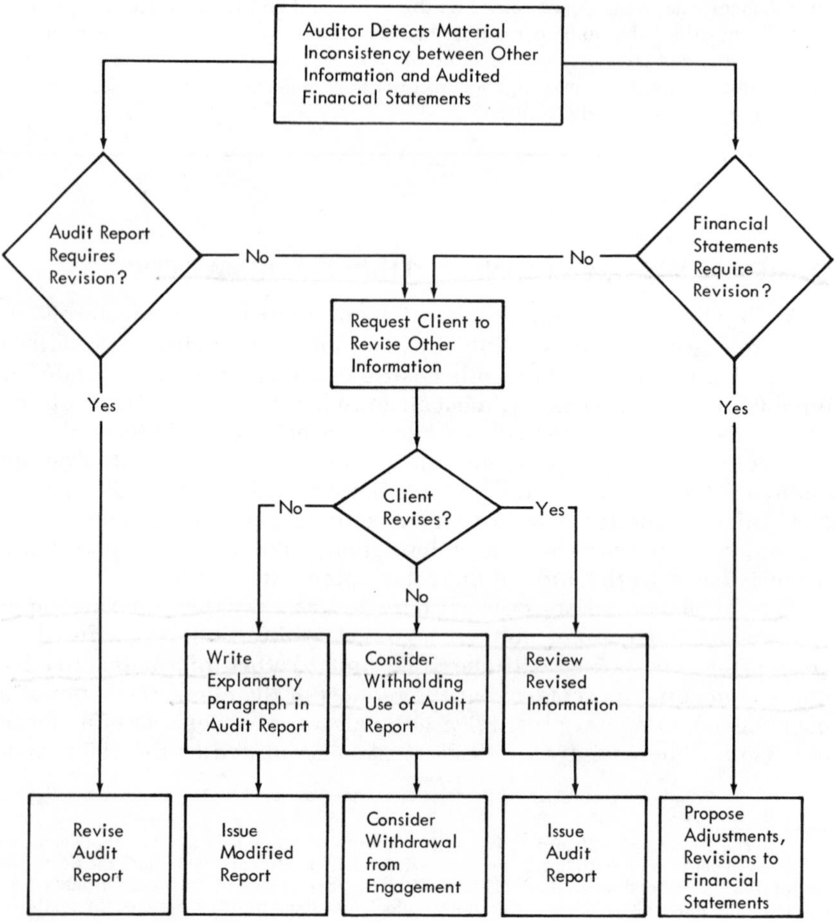

If the auditor decides there is a material inconsistency in other information such as the president's selective use of audited financial statement numbers, a course of action is required. The auditor's actions are diagrammed in Exhibit 18–2.

If the auditor detects what he or she believes might be a material misstatement of fact (not necessarily a direct inconsistency with audited financial statement numbers), the information should be discussed with the client. One example would be the marketing vice president's comment about market share. The auditor must decide whether he or she has the expertise to evaluate the information in question, whether management has experts who developed the information, and whether consultation with some other expert is needed. This last step would be taken only if the auditor has a valid basis for pursuing the matter and it concerns information that is particularly important.

If a misstatement of material fact exists, auditing standards provide the following: (1) Notify the client in writing of the auditor's views, (2) consult with legal counsel about appropriate action to take, (3) take the action indicated by professional judgment in the particular circumstances. These three points are vague, to say the least, mainly because there is no catalog of "other information" that is *not* under the auditor's opinion. Likewise, there is little or no guidance to be offered as to what is a "material misstatement of fact in other information" that is *not* presented in financial statements prepared in conformity with generally accepted accounting principles. This portion of auditing standards provides the auditor some latitute to decide what to do about material misstatement of "other information," providing an analogy to the third AICPA reporting standard (informative disclosures in the financial statements are to be regarded as reasonably adequate unless otherwise stated in the report) regarding information that *is in* audited financial statements.

AUDITED SEGMENT INFORMATION

Segment information has appeared in published financial statements for many years, and auditors' opinions have covered the segment classifications as well as the financial statements taken as a whole. In 1976 the Financial Accounting Standards Board issued *Statement on Financial Accounting Standards No. 14*, "Financial Reporting for Segments of a Business Enterprise," and required the disclosure of segment information in financial statements presented in conformity with generally accepted accounting principles. The information is a disaggregation of elements of a business's financial statements—revenue, operating profit or loss, identifiable assets, depreciation, capital expenditures—on the basis of industries, foreign operations, export sales, and major customers.

Prior to 1977 auditing standards did not include any guidelines about auditing segment information. However, when FASB *No. 14* made such presentations a requirement of generally accepted accounting principles, *Statement on Auditing Standards No. 21* (Section 435), "Segment Information" was issued (December 1977).

According to *SAS No. 21* (Section 435.03) the objective of auditing procedures applied to segment information is to provide the auditor a basis for concluding whether the information is presented in conformity with FASB *No. 14.* The procedures do not necessarily enable the auditor to express an opinion on the segment information taken by itself. The spirit of *SAS No. 21* is to guide the auditor with respect to the segment information when expressing an opinion on the financial statements taken as a whole. Notwithstanding the context of "financial statements taken as a whole," the auditor's objective is to report on the conformity with FASB *No. 14* of the segment information presentation.

A client may represent to the auditor that there are no segments of the business requiring disaggregated presentation in conformity with FASB *No. 14.* In such cases the auditor must be able to use his or her knowledge of the business and the industry to determine whether the client's representation is correct. If so, an unqualified opinion may be rendered. However, if the auditor cannot determine whether segments exist and the client declines to develop further information, the auditor faces a *limitation on the scope of the audit.* In such a case the scope paragraph of the report would be qualified to explain the lack of evidence, and the opinion paragraph would be qualified with the language: "In our opinion, except for the possible omission of segment information, the financial statements present. . . ." (See *SAS No. 21,* Sections 435.15–.16, for other examples of illustrative qualification language.)

When segment information is presented, the following procedures should be applied:

Review, evaluate and *become acquainted with:*

Internal accounting control in operating segments.

Nature, number, and size of industry segments, subsidiaries and divisions, and geographic areas.

Accounting principles used in industry segments and geographic areas.

Inquire of management concerning methods of determining segment information, and *evaluate* the reasonableness of those methods.

Inquire as to the basis of accounting for sales or transfers among segments and areas, and *audit* a sample of such transactions.

Audit the disaggregation of financial statement information into segment information, utilizing *analytical review* (substantive test) comparisons.

Inquire about allocation methods, *evaluate* reasonableness of the methods, and *audit* a sample of the allocations.

Determine whether segment accounting methods and segment information are presented consistently from period to period.

These procedures essentially outline the application of compliance tests and substantive tests to segment information. They appear to call for no less than sufficient competent evidence regarding the disaggregated segment information.

The standard short-form report on the financial statements need not be modified unless there is (1) material error in the segment information, (2) technical misapplication of FASB *No. 14*, (3) omission of segment information, or (4) inconsistency in the presentation of the segment information. The *materiality* in each of these cases is evaluated with reference to the "financial statements taken as a whole." However, the auditor must be careful to consider not only the relative dollar amount of errors, misapplications or omissions, but also the *qualitative* characteristics of the information. For example, a material error (say, 30 percent) in the revenue attributed to a small segment may amount to only 2 percent of total company revenue, but if the segment is represented by management as a key segment for business development and future profitability, the error should be considered material. Other qualitative features would include errors that distort segment trends or errors involved in segments representing politically sensitive foreign countries.

When a material error, misapplication, omission or inconsistency exists, the auditor's report is modified with language indicating either a departure from generally accepted accounting principles (FASB *No. 14*) or a consistency exception that affects the financial statements taken as a whole. Consistency matters related strictly to the segment information (not affecting the aggregated financial statements) are covered in FASB *No. 14*, so any change not accounted for and disclosed in conformity with FASB *No. 14* would cause an opinion qualified as to nonconformity with accounting principles rather than a consistency exception.

In early 1978 the Financial Accounting Standards Board took notice of arguments that small businesses were burdened by unnecessary technical accounting and reporting requirements. This controversy has been known as the "Big GAAP-Little GAAP" question. As a result the FASB *suspended* application of *FASB No. 14* (as well as *APB No. 15* on "Earnings per Share") to nonpublic companies, pending some future resolution of the "Big GAAP-Little GAAP" question. Acting rapidly, the Auditing Standards Executive Committee issued an auditing interpretation of *SAS No. 21* (*Journal of Accountancy*, May 1978) which permitted auditors to issue an unqualified opinion on financial statements of nonpublic companies which omitted the segment information. The interpretation explained that the need for this provision arose from a highly unusual situation and should not be taken as a precedent on future revisions or amendments of FASB statements. The situation was in limbo in 1978 and was awaiting resolution of reporting requirements by the FASB.

USING THE WORK AND REPORTS OF OTHER INDEPENDENT AUDITORS

Often an auditor audits a material portion of a reporting entity's assets, liabilities, revenues and expenses, but at the same time another independent auditor(s) may be engaged to audit subsidiaries, divisions, branches, components, or investments that are included in the reporting entity's financial statements. Generally, the principal auditor is the one whose signature appears on the report of the financial statements of a consolidated or parent entity. The auditor of the reporting entity must first determine if he or she is the "principal auditor" and then must make other decisions regarding use of the work and reports of the other independent auditor(s).

First the principal auditor is obliged to satisfy himself as to the independence and professional responsibility of the other auditor(s). If the principal auditor is satisfied with these qualities, next he must decide whether to make reference in the audit report to the other auditor. The principal auditor may decide to make no reference, and the audit report may follow the form and wording of the standard short-form report.

On the other hand, the principal auditor may decide to refer to the work and reports of other auditors in his or her own audit report. Such a reference is not in itself a scope or an opinion qualification. The decision to refer would be to show divided responsibility for the audit work, and the explanation should show very clearly the extent of the divided responsibility (e.g., disclosing percent or amount of assets, revenues, and expenses covered by other auditors' work). However, the opinion that follows the

EXHIBIT 18–3
Reference to Work and Report of Other Auditors

To the Board of Directors
The Black and Decker Manufacturing Company:

We have examined the consolidated statement of financial condition of the Black and Decker Manufacturing Company and subsidiaries as of September 25, 1977, and September 26, 1976, and the related consolidated statements of earnings, changes in stockholders' equity, and changes in financial position for the years then ended. Our examinations were made in accordance with generally accepted auditing standards and, accordingly, included such tests of the accounting records and such other auditing procedures as we considered necessary in the circumstances. We did not examine the financial statements of certain consolidated subsidiaries located outside the United States which statements reflect total assets and revenues constituting 29 percent and 36 percent in the 1977 and 31 percent and 41 percent in 1976, respectively, of the related consolidated totals. These statements were examined by other independent accountants whose reports thereon have been furnished to us, and our opinion expressed herein, insofar as it relates to the amounts included for these subsidiaries, is based solely on the reports of the other independent accountants.

In our opinion, based upon our examinations and the reports of the other independent accountants, the financial statements referred to above present fairly the consolidated financial position of the Black and Decker Manufacturing Company and subsidiaries at September 25, 1977, and September 26, 1976, and the consolidated results of their operations and changes in their financial position for the years then ended, in conformity with generally accepted accounting principles applied on a consistent basis.

/s/ Ernst & Ernst

EXHIBIT 18–4

Using the Work and Reports of Other Auditors (interpretation of *SAP No. 45,* Section 543 of *SAS No. 1*)

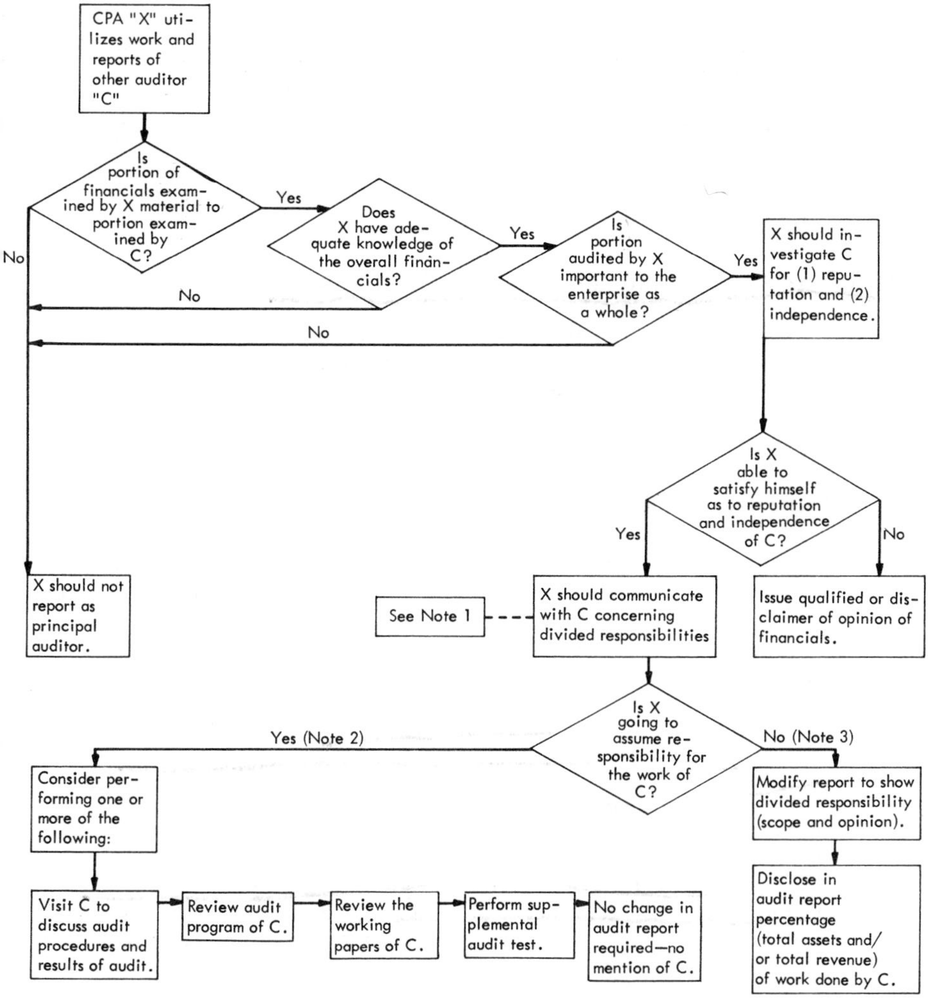

Note 1: X should insure that C understands (1) that the financials examined by him will be included in financials reported on by X, (2) United States GAAP and auditing standards, (3) the relevant reporting requirements of the SEC (if appropriate) and (4) a review will be made of (*a*) matters affecting intercompany eliminations, and, if appropriate, (*b*) uniformity of accounting practices employed in component statements.

Note 2: Ordinarily this alternative is adopted when C (other auditor) is a correspondent firm, an agent of X or the portion of financials examined by C is not material.

Note 3: This alternative is usually adopted when (1) it is impracticable for X to review C's work or apply other procedures to gain satisfaction and (2) financials examined by C are material in relation to overall financials.

Source: *Journal of Accountancy,* March 1974, p. 84. Copyright © 1974 by the American Institute of Certified Public Accountants, Inc.

reference must be consistent with the sufficiency and competency of evidence gathered by all the auditors. If other auditors have rendered opinions qualified in some way, the circumstances must be considered by the principal auditor in writing his or her own opinion.

An example of an opinion with references to work and reports of other auditors is shown in Exhibit 18–3.

Exhibit 18–4 contains a detailed explanation of the several elements of a principal auditor's decision on whether to use, rely upon, and/or refer to the work of other auditors. These decisions involve the materiality of financial operations audited by others and the extent of familiarity with the other auditors' professional qualifications.

OMISSION OF BASIC FINANCIAL STATEMENT(S)

APB *Opinion No. 19* ("Reporting on Changes in Financial Position") requires that a statement of changes in financial position be presented with financial statements of a for-profit entity which purport to show both financial position and results of operations. If such a statement of changes is omitted, the auditor's report would be qualified by reason of a departure from generally accepted accounting principles.

Normally a failure to disclose required information results in the auditor including that information in his or her report. However, auditing standards make an exception in this case to the effect that it is not appropriate for an auditor to prepare and present a whole financial schedule in the audit report.[3] Consequently the recommended report form is as follows. (Notice that there is no mention of the statement of changes in financial position in the scope paragraph.)

> We have examined the balance sheet of X Company as of December 31, 19__, and the related statements of income and retained earnings for the year then ended. Our examination was made in accordance with generally accepted auditing standards and, accordingly, included such tests of the accounting records and such other auditing procedures as we considered necessary in the circumstances.
>
> The company declined to present a statement of changes in financial position for the year ended December 31, 19__. Presentation of such statement summarizing the company's financing and investing activities and other changes in its financial position is required by *Opinion No. 19* of the Accounting Principles Board.
>
> In our opinion, except that the omission of a statement of changes in financial position results in an incomplete presentation as explained in the preceding paragraph, the aforementioned financial statements present fairly the financial position of X Company at December 31, 19__, and the results of its operations for the year then ended in conformity with generally accepted accounting principles applied on a basis consistent with that of the preceding year.

The sequence of decisions involved in reporting on the omission of the statement of changes is shown in Exhibit 18–5.

---

[3] *Statement on Auditing Standards No. 1* (Section 545.05), as amended by *SAS No. 21* (1977).

EXHIBIT 18–5

Reporting on the Statement of Changes in Financial Position (interpretation of *SAP No. 50,* Sections 420.15–.16, 516.08 and 545.04–.05 of *SAS No. 1*)

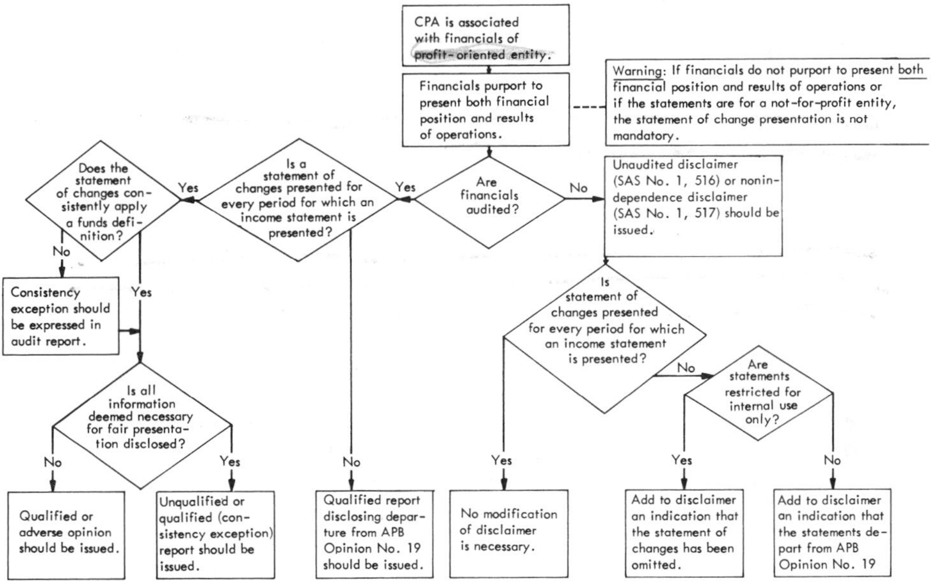

Source: *Journal of Accountancy,* March 1974, p. 86. Copyright © 1974 by the American Institute of Certified Public Accountants, Inc.

In some engagements an auditor may be requested to report on only one aspect of financial affairs; for example, only on financial position and not on results of operations, or only on results of operations and not on financial position. Auditing standards interpret such constraints as limited reporting objectives and not as limitations on the scope of an engagement.[4] However, this kind of situation creates a problem because APB *Opinion No. 19* requires *three* financial schedules (balance sheet, income statement, and statement of changes in financial position) in order to present *two* financial aspects (financial position and results of operations).

Current auditing standards permit auditors to associate the income statement schedule with a report on results of operations and the balance sheet with a report on financial position. The statement of changes in financial position seems to be associated with neither when they are presented separately, but it is a required and integral statement when they are presented together.

Consequently, an opinion only on the fair presentation of financial position may be on the balance sheet alone, and an opinion only on results of operations may be on the income statement alone. In either case it is not

[4] *Statement on Auditing Standards No. 1* (Section 509.13).

considered necessary to supply the missing financial statements in the audit report itself or to modify the audit report in any way other than to omit any mention in the scope and opinion paragraphs of the omitted financial statements. Thus auditors do not insist that each and every financial presentation be complete with all three financial statements.

SUBSEQUENT DISCOVERY OF FACTS EXISTING AT THE DATE OF THE AUDITOR'S REPORT

Several generally accepted auditing standards deal with the subject of "subsequent events." Actually, the standards deal with two things: (1) *events* that actually occur after the balance sheet date and (2) *knowledge* gained after the balance sheet date of events that occurred or conditions that existed on or before the balance sheet date. The subsequent event or subsequently acquired knowledge may arise (1) before the end of audit field work, (2) after the end of field work but before issuance of the report, or (3) after the audit report is issued.

Exhibit 18–6 shows a time continuum of these combinations with a key to the auditing standards sections that deal with them. *SAS No. 1*, Sections 530, 560, and 710 were discussed in Chapter 16 of this textbook in connection with the completion of field work topic.

EXHIBIT 18–6
Subsequent Events and Subsequent Discovery

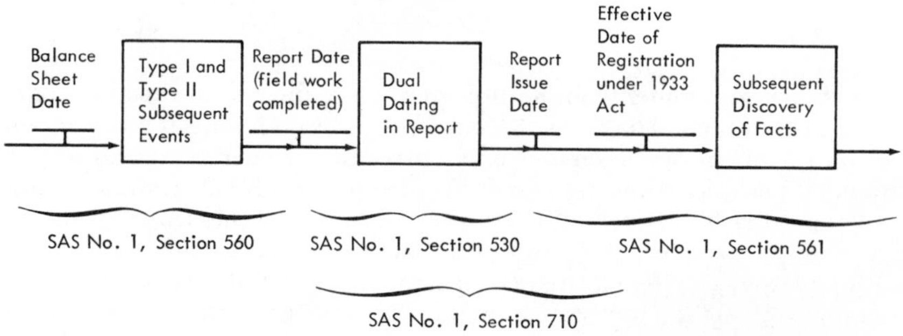

Auditing standards relating to discovery of facts subsequent to report issuance may be traced to the *Yale Express* case (*Fischer* v. *Kletz*, see Appendix 4–B). The situation is one in which the auditor has already issued an audit report and later becomes aware of facts that existed at the report date. Auditors are under no general obligation to continue performance of any auditing procedures past the report date (except when engaged on an SEC registration statement), but when they happen to learn of facts that are apparently important, they have the obligation to determine whether the information is reliable and whether the facts existed at the date of the report.[5]

[5] *Statement on Auditing Standards No. 1* (Section 561.04).

EXHIBIT 18–7
Subsequent Discovery of Facts Existing at the Date of the Auditor's Report (interpretation of *SAP No. 41,* Section 561 of *SAS No. 1*)

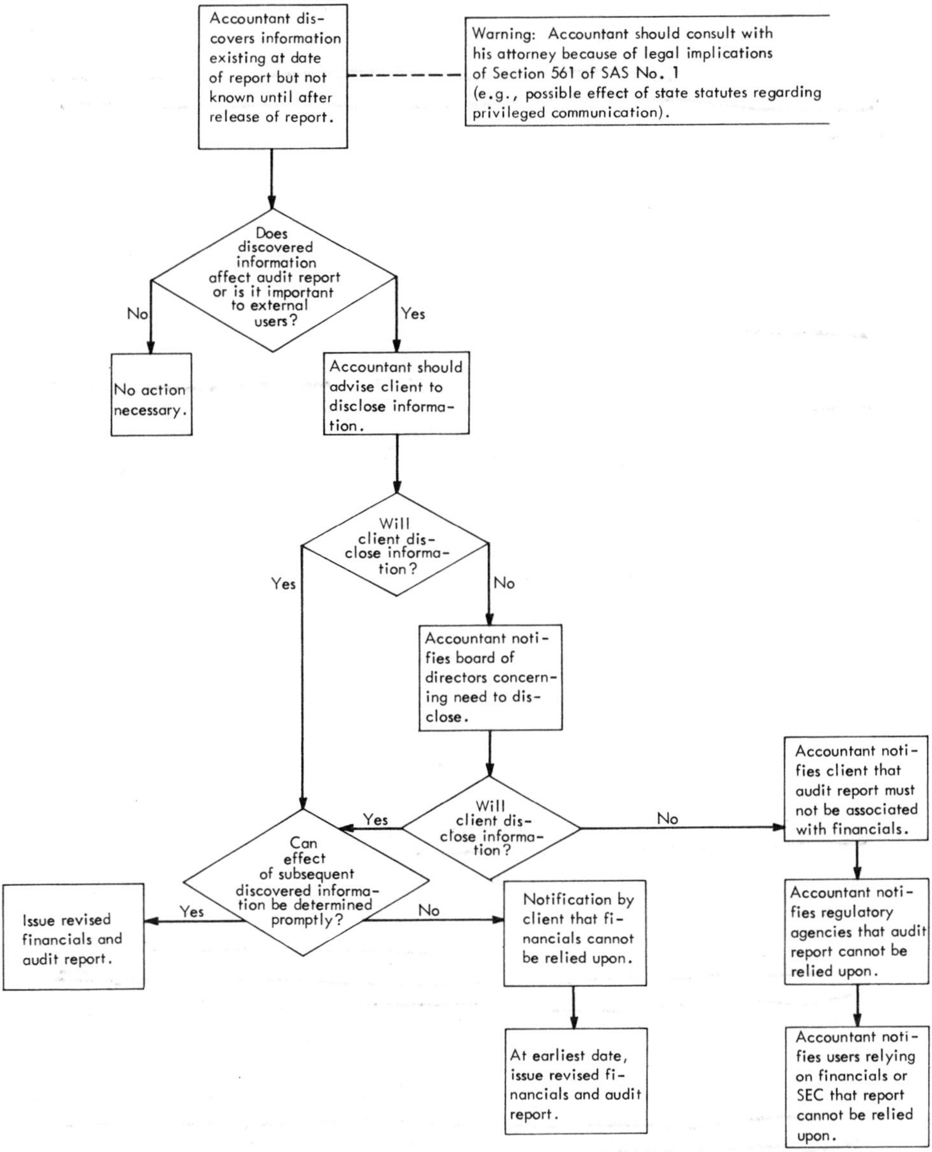

Source: *Journal of Accountancy,* March 1974, p. 82. Copyright © 1974 by the American Institute of Certified Public Accountants, Inc.

When both of these conditions are affirmed and the auditor believes that his or her report would have been different and that there are persons relying on the report, the auditor should take steps to withdraw the first report, issue a new report, and inform persons currently relying on the financial statements. These measures are facilitated by cooperation on the part of the client. However, the auditor's duties to notify the public that an earlier report should not be relied upon are not relieved by client objections.

The sequence of decisions embodied in these standards is explained in Exhibit 18–7. Basically these decisions relate to the importance and impact of the information, the cooperation of the client in taking the necessary action, and the actions to be taken.

SPECIAL REPORTS

Auditors may perform a variety of services, *acting in the capacity of auditor* (*not* as tax advisor or management consultant), that require a report for which the usual wording of the short-form report is inappropriate. Such services involve reports issued in connection with:

Financial statements prepared in accordance with a comprehensive basis of accounting other than generally accepted accounting principles.

Specified elements, accounts, or items of a financial statement.

Compliance with aspects of contractual agreements or regulatory requirements related to audited financial statements.

Financial statements presented in prescribed (governmental or regulatory agency) forms or schedules that require a prescribed form of auditor's report.

Other Comprehensive Bases of Accounting

The first AICPA reporting standard ("The report shall state whether the financial statements are presented in accordance with generally accepted accounting principles") is satisfied in *special report* situations by disclosing in the auditor's report that the statements are not intended to conform with generally accepted accounting principles. An opinion (or disclaimer of opinion) may then be expressed with regard to conformity with the comprehensive basis of accounting used. (*SAS No. 1*, Section 410.02, as amended by *SAS No. 14*).

Comprehensive bases of accounting other than generally accepted accounting principles include prescribed uniform systems of accounts (e.g., by a state insurance commission, Interstate Commerce Commission uniform accounts), tax-basis accounting, cash receipts and disbursements accounting, and other definite sets of criteria having substantial support (e.g., general price-level adjusted statements as described in APB *Opinion No. 3*). Adequate informative disclosures must also be considered when reporting on financial statements presented on a non-GAAP comprehensive basis of accounting.

The special report relating to a comprehensive basis of accounting other than GAAP should include the following elements:

A scope paragraph identifying the financial statements examined and stating whether the examination was made in accordance with generally accepted auditing standards. Identifying terms such as "balance sheet," "statement of financial position," "statement of income," "statement of operations," and "statement of changes in financial position" are generally used to refer to financial statements prepared in conformity with generally accepted accounting principles. Thus other titles such as "statement of assets and liabilities arising from cash transactions," "statement of income—statutory basis," and other titles that describe other bases of accounting should be used in special report situations.

A middle paragraph stating that the financial statements are not intended to be presented in conformity with GAAP, and reference to a footnote disclosure of the basis of accounting and how it differs from GAAP.

A reporting paragraph that expresses an opinion or disclaims an opinion that the financial statements are presented fairly in conformity with the basis of accounting described. An explanation of reasons must be given if the opinion is other than unqualified.

A phrase reporting on consistent application of the basis of accounting described.

An example of a report on cash basis financial statements is given in Exhibit 18–8.

Specified Elements, Accounts, or Items

Auditors may be requested to render special reports on such things as rentals, royalties, profit participations, or a provision for income taxes. In some cases, clients may ask auditors to perform a specified set of procedures and report on the findings.

The first AICPA reporting standard does not apply because the specified element, account, or item does not purport to be a financial statement of financial position or results of operations. The second AICPA reporting standard (consistency) applies only if the element, account, or item is measured according to some provision of generally accepted accounting principles.

Special engagements with limited objectives enable auditors to provide needed services to clients. *SAS No. 14* (Section 621.14) gives examples of reports relating to amount of sales used in computing rental, reports relating to royalties, reports on a profit participation, and a report on the adequacy of a tax provision in financial statements. Exhibit 18–9 contains a hypothetical report on prize payments made by a magazine.

EXHIBIT 18–8
Cash Basis Statement Opinion

To the Directors of the Corner Grocery:

We have examined the Statement of Assets and Liabilities—Cash Basis of the Corner Grocery as of August 31, 1979, and the related Statement of Cash Receipts and Disbursements for the year then ended. Our examination was made in accordance with generally accepted auditing standards and, accordingly, included such tests of the accounting records and such other auditing procedures as we considered necessary in the circumstances.

As described in Footnote 1 the company's policy is to prepare financial statements on the basis of cash receipts and disbursements. Consequently, revenue and related assets are recognized in the financial statements when received rather than when earned, and expenses are recognized when paid rather than when the obligation is incurred. Accordingly, the accompanying financial statements are not intended to present financial position and results of operations in conformity with generally accepted accounting principles.

In our opinion, the financial statements referred to above present fairly the assets and liabilities, arising from cash transactions of the Corner Grocery as of August 31, 1979, and the revenue collected and expenses paid during the year then ended, on the basis of accounting described in Footnote 1, which basis has been applied in a manner consistent with that of the preceding year.

Johnson & Johnson, CPAs
September 21, 1979

EXHIBIT 18–9
Report on a Financial Element

To *American Handy Magazine:*

We have examined the schedule of cash prize payments as defined by *America Handy Magazine* for the period January 1, 1977, through January 31, 1979. Our examination was made in accordance with generally accepted auditing standards and, accordingly, included such tests of the accounting records relating to prize payments and such other auditing procedures as we considered necessary in the circumstances.

In our opinion, the schedule of cash prize payments showing a total amount of $117,655 presents fairly the cash prizes paid by *American Handy Magazine* for the period January 1, 1977, through January 31, 1979, according to the definition of cash prizes set forth in official contest disclosure circulars distributed with entry blanks.

Lamb & Company
Certified Public Accountants
February 4, 1979

Compliance with Contractual Agreements or Regulatory Requirements

Clients may have restrictive covenants in loan agreements. Lenders may require a periodic report on whether the client has complied with such contractual agreements. Following a standard scope paragraph, the auditor may give a *negative assurance* of the following type:

> In connection with our examination, nothing came to our attention that caused us to believe that the company was not in compliance with any of the terms, covenants, provisions, or conditions of sections 32 through 46 of the indenture dated January 1, 1976, with First National Bank. However, it should be understood that our examination was not directed primarily toward obtaining knowledge of such noncompliance.

A similar negative assurance may be given with regard to federal and state regulatory requirements. Examples would include limitation on investments according to section 993(*d*)(2) and (3) of the 1954 Internal Revenue Code, or state insurance department regulations about the nature of insurance company investments.

Regulatory agencies may seek to have auditors sign assertions in prescribed report language that goes beyond acceptable professional reporting responsibilities and involve auditors in areas outside their function and responsibility. In such cases, the auditor should insert additional wording in the prescribed report language or write a completely revised report which reflects adequately his position and responsibility.

LONG-FORM REPORTS

The decision of whether to issue the standard short-form report or a long-form report depends upon the needs of the client, which may be derived from the needs of the report recipient. In addition to the basic financial statements and disclosures (which would be covered by a short-form report), the long-form report may contain one or more of the following:

1. Detail schedules of items in the basic financial statements (e.g., an aged schedule of accounts receivable).
2. Statistical data (e.g., the distribution of sales among large and small customers, government and private customers).
3. Explanatory comments (e.g., descriptions of accounting methods, explanations of credit policies, explanation of transactions with insiders).
4. Explanatory descriptions of the audit scope (e.g., the number of accounts receivable confirmations mailed, returned, those with errors and without errors).

Whatever the specific content of the long-form report, the auditor must observe the reporting standards. Generally the fourth standard is observed by including a standard short-form opinion on the basic financial statements. Along with the additional information, supplementary expressions of opinion may be added. When presenting the additional information, the auditor should be careful to maintain a clear distinction between management's representations (e.g., detail schedules, statistical data, and explanatory comments) and the auditor's own representations (i.e., explanations of the audit scope). The auditor should clearly establish his or her position regarding the additional information. Furthermore, the auditor should be extremely careful that none of the additional information stands in contradiction of the overall opinion on the financial statements taken as a whole.

Long-form reports are often rendered to owners and managers of small businesses that do not have the accounting staff to produce regular analytical reports. Banks and other lenders also often request the long-form report on small businesses for similar reasons—in order to analyze the business and assess the lending risk more fully. In the light of these needs, one must consider whether the basic financial statements with a short-form report are suitable for all general financial decisions as they purport to be. The existence of the standards for long-form reports seems to suggest that all information necessary for a fair presentation—for the purpose of specialized decisions—may not be contained in the basic financial statements.

However, one must realize that the long-form report standards were written in 1957 (*Statement on Auditing Procedure No.* 27), before the proliferation of accounting principles that required many additional disclosures. A comparative content analysis might reveal that the basic financial statements prepared according to current accounting standards contain much of the detail and explanation that characterized the long-form reports of the 1950s. To a certain extent the long-form report has been institutionalized by securities law in the registration statements and annual reports required to be filed with the SEC.

LETTERS FOR UNDERWRITERS

In connection with public offerings of securities auditors become involved with serving the needs of underwriters as well as serving the public need with an opinion on financial statements. *Underwriters* are persons who take securities of an issuer for the purpose of making a public distribution. They have a duty for diligence regarding misleading statements or omissions as defined in Section 11(b) of the Securities Act of 1933. Underwriters have sought the assistance of independent auditors in meeting this diligence requirement, and the assistance comes in the form of *letters for underwriters* (sometimes called "comfort letters").

The letter to an underwriter is not required by the 1933 act, and it is not a report filed with the SEC. The letter, in the opinion of underwriters, is supposed to be evidence of their discharge of the duty to conduct a reasonable investigation of financial matters that are not otherwise covered by the opinion of an expert (e.g., the independent auditor). Thus the independent auditor acts as agent for the underwriter and reports on his or her findings.

Bear in mind that the "reasonable investigation" required of the underwriter is relevant only to unaudited financial data. The audited statements are covered by the expert independent auditor's opinion, and the underwriter is justified in relying upon that expert opinion. Thus the procedures contemplated by the underwriter's diligence duty do not constitute a complete audit, and the letter is not a true audit report. At best, the limited procedures pursuant to an underwriter's letter can produce negative assurances made by the auditor to the underwriter.

In keeping with the context of letters for underwriters, auditing standards prescribe that it is the underwriter's responsibility to specify the investigatory procedures that are considered necessary and sufficient in the circumstances.[6] The auditor may make suggestions in order to assist the underwriters. Nevertheless, the ultimate responsibility rests with the underwriter because it is the underwriter's diligence duty that is being discharged.

In outline, matters covered in a typical letter are:

a. A statement as to the independence of the accountants.

b. An opinion as to whether the audited financial statements and schedules included in the registration statement comply as to form in all material respects with the applicable accounting requirements of the act and the published rules and regulations thereunder.

c. Negative assurances as to whether the unaudited financial statements and schedules included in the registration statement:

  (i) Comply as to form with the applicable accounting requirements of the act and the published rules and regulations thereunder.

  (ii) Are fairly presented in conformity with generally accepted accounting principles on a basis substantially consistent with that of the audited financial statements and schedules included therein.

d. Negative assurances as to whether, during a specified period following the date of the latest financial statements in the registration statement and prospectus, there has been any change in capital stock or long-term debt or any decrease in other specified financial-statement items.

Upon performing procedures for the underwriter, the auditor may learn of matters (e.g., material decreases in a financial balance, or misstatement in the unaudited financial statements) that should be disclosed in the registration statement. If disclosure is appropriate but management decides not to disclose the matter in the registration statement, mention of it should be made in the letter to the underwriter. In this manner the underwriter may be considered to have learned of a material misstatement or omission. The auditor will have to decide what impact such a discovery will have on his own report on the financial statements.

[6] *Statement on Auditing Standards No. 1* (Section 630.07).

EXHIBIT 18–10
Report on Personal Financial Statements

MR. AND MRS. INDIVIDUAL
Statement of Assets and Liabilities
December 31, 1978

	Column A: Cost Basis	*Column B:* Estimated Value Basis
Assets:		
Cash	$ 11,079	$ 11,079
Marketable securities (Note 2)	29,578	42,227
Cash value of life insurance	4,647	4,647
Net assets of ABC Proprietorship (Notes 1 and 3)	47,970	65,280
Interest in net assets of XYZ Corp.		
~~		
appreciation (Note 7)	—	24,230
Total liabilities	$ 40,480	$ 64,710
Excess of assets over liabilities	$149,772	$222,463

The Notes to the Financial Statements are an integral part of this statement.

To Mr. and Mrs. Individual:

We have examined the statement of assets and liabilities of Mr. and Mrs. Individual on the cost basis (Column A) as of December 31, 1978, and the related statement of changes in net assets for the year then ended. Our examination was made in accordance with generally accepted auditing standards and, accordingly, included such tests of the accounting records and such other auditing procedures as we considered necessary in the circumstances.

In our opinion, the accompanying statements on the cost basis (Column A) present fairly the assets and liabilities of Mr. and Mrs. Individual at December 31, 1978, and the changes in their net assets for the year then ended, in conformity with generally accepted accounting principles applied on a basis consistent with that of the preceding period.

We have also determined that the additional information set forth in the accompanying statements on the estimated value basis (Column B) is presented on the bases described in the statements or in the footnotes. However, we do not express an opinion on the amounts shown as estimated values.

Able and Baker, CPAs
January 24, 1979

Source: Adapted from *Audits of Personal Financial Statements* (New York: AICPA, 1968), pp. 18, 21.

PERSONAL FINANCIAL STATEMENTS

Personal financial statements may be prepared for an individual, a husband and wife, or a larger family group, as the circumstances may require.[7] The general guidelines for such statements are as follows:

1. Financial statements should be prepared on a cost basis in conformity with generally accepted accounting principles.
2. Accrual accounting should be used, and cash basis statements are not appropriate.
3. A statement of assets and liabilities restated at estimated values should be included as additional information. (Use two parallel columns, one for cost basis and the other for estimated value basis.)
4. The title of the position statement should be "Statement of Assets and Liabilities."

The auditor's report should refer separately to the cost basis and estimated value basis information, showing clearly the responsibility taken for each. Exhibit 18–10 contains an abbreviated portion of a personal financial statement and the recommended report form. The apparent need for audited personal financial statements arose in the mid-1960s in connection with candidates for political office. However, they may be useful in a wide variety of personal financial transactions.

SOURCES AND ADDITIONAL READING REFERENCES

Burton, John C., ed. *Corporate Financial Reporting: Conflicts and Challenges.* New York: American Institute of Certified Public Accountants, 1969.

Committee on Personal Financial Statements of AICPA. "Audits of Personal Financial Statements." New York: American Institute of Certified Public Accountants, 1968.

Guy, Dan M. "SAP Flowcharts," *Journal of Accountancy,* March 1974, pp. 81–86.

———, and Mann, H. "A Practical Guide for Reporting on Limited Examinations of Financial Statements," *CPA Journal,* July 1973, pp. 555–62.

New York Stock Exchange, Inc. "Recommendations and Comments on Financial Reporting to Shareholders and Related Matters." A White Paper, 1973.

Reiss, Harry F., Jr. "Letters for Underwriters," *CPA Journal,* December 1971, pp. 935–37.

Smith, E. W., and Shellenberger, J. S. "Some Unpublished Audit Reports," *Journal of Accountancy,* November 1970, pp. 45–52.

Sommer, A. A., Jr. "Financial Reporting: Who Is Liable? (1) Legal Liability of Accountants, (2) Reporting Obligations of Financial Executives," *Financial Executive,* March 1974, pp. 18–29.

Wade, Allison. "Launching a Stock Registration—A Joint Accountant-Attorney Effort to Lead the Client through the Maze," *CPA Journal,* April 1972, pp. 279–87, and May 1972, pp. 399–402.

[7] Standards for audits of personal financial statements are explained fully in the AICPA industry audit guide entitled *Audits of Personal Financial Statements* (New York: AICPA, 1968).

REVIEW QUESTIONS

18.1. What criteria define a "principal auditor"?

18.2. What actions are taken by the principal auditor *only* if he or she assumes full responsibility for the work of another auditor?

18.3. Is the reference in an audit report to work performed by another auditor a scope qualification? Explain.

18.4. If subsequent to issuance of a report an auditor discovers information which existed at the report date and materially impacts on the financial statements, what actions should the auditor take if the client (including the board of directors) refuses to make disclosure?

18.5. Assuming the same facts in 18.4 except that the client consents to disclosure, what action should be taken if the effect of the subsequent information is presently indeterminate?

18.6. What type of report is indicated if all financial statements are fairly presented but the statement of changes in financial position is omitted? Explain.

18.7. If a statement of changes is not presented in unaudited statements that are "restricted to internal use," what is the effect on the auditor's opinion? What is the effect if the statements are unrestricted?

18.8. What general conditions indicate that a *special report* format should be used?

18.9. What are the AICPA guidelines for personal financial statements?

18.10. In long-form reports, to what special problems should the auditor be alert?

18.11. What types of additional information not given in the short-form report are typically included in long-form reports?

18.12. What is an underwriter? In letters to underwriters, what representations does the auditor make with respect to audited financial statements? Unaudited financial statements and schedules?

EXERCISES AND PROBLEMS

18.13. Dewey, Cheatem, and Howe, CPAs, have prepared the following financial statement and accompanying report for Flash Babbler, candidate for the U.S. Senate.

FLASH BABBLER
Balance Sheet
December 31, 1978

Assets:	
Cash	$ 22,000
Marketable securities (lower of cost or market)	56,719
Cash value of life insurance	2,111
Interest in Babbler Brothers Brothels, Inc. (cost)	164,150
Real estate (cost)	526,480
Automobile (estimated value)	8,540
Total Assets	$780,000

Liabilities:	
Short-term credit	$ 1,965
Personal loan—Southern Bank	51,000
U.S. government—income taxes	105,000
Real estate mortgage	265,410
Total Liabilities	$423,375
Equity in assets	356,625
Total Liabilities and Equity	$780,000

REPORT OF THE AUDITORS

Mr. Flash Babbler:

We have examined the balance sheet of Mr. Flash Babbler as of December 31, 1978. Our examination was made in accordance with generally accepted auditing standards and, accordingly, included such tests of the accounting records and such other auditing procedures as we considered necessary in the circumstances. However, we did not inspect the securities, and we cannot predict who will prevail in the dispute over title to certain real estate owned by Mr. Babbler, but nothing came to our attention to cause us to believe that Mr. Babbler will not retain the land in question.

All things considered, we believe the statement above is fairly accurate insofar as reflecting the assets, liabilities, and equity of Mr. Babbler.

Dewey, Cheatem, and Howe, CPAs

Required:

a. Criticize the personal financial statements.

b. Criticize the audit report prepared by the CPA firm.

18.14. You have finished field work in connection with the annual audit of Western Associates Corporation for the year ended December 31 and are preparing to render your opinion. Western's management has not prepared a statement of changes in financial position. All audit work performed with respect to the other basic financial statements has been completed to your satisfaction, and you have the *audited* information available to prepare the statement of changes.

Required:

a. Generally, what is the auditor's obligation with respect to information which the client refuses to disclose but which is necessary for adequate disclosure?

b. Should the auditor prepare the statement of changes in financial position? Explain.

c. Prepare the middle paragraph (if applicable) and the opinion paragraph of your audit report for Western Associates Corporation.

d. Assume that all financial statements are *unaudited.* Prepare the audit report if the statement of changes is omitted.

18.15. Albert and Hannibal, CPAs, have been contacted by Kelly Underwriters to prepare an underwriter's letter in connection with a public offering of stock by Norris Needle Corporation. Norris has made several contracts which require cash in the near future, and they are pressing the underwriters and auditors to expedite registration and issue of the securities. To speed up the registration process, Albert and Hannibal sent the underwriters a list of procedures they would perform, unless otherwise notified by either Norris or Kelly. During application of these procedures, Norris notified the CPAs of a long-term secured note payable recently made with Everett Bank, payable in five years. The proceeds from the note increased long-term liabilities by 10 percent. An opinion included in the letter from the CPAs to Kelly Underwriters is shown below:

> In our opinion, the financial statements and schedules, the summary of earnings, and the interim unaudited financial statements (dated March 31) examined by us are presented fairly and comply as to form in all material respects with the applicable accounting requirements of the act and the published rules and regulations thereunder.

Required:

a. What problems do you see with the agreement between the CPAs and the underwriters concerning which audit procedures will be performed?

b. In accord with current auditing practice, what action would the auditor take to disclose the increase in long-term debt, if any?

c. Is the excerpted opinion prepared by Albert and Hannibal satisfactory? Explain.

18.16. On June 1, A. J. Faultless & Co., CPAs, became aware of certain information which had existed at the date of their audit report (February 25) prepared in connection with the audit of Hopkirk Company for the year ended the previous December 31. Faultless determined that the information would probably affect the decisions of external users and advised Hopkirk's chief executive to make proper disclosure. The executive flatly refused to make the disclosure, arguing that the information was immaterial. On June 17, Faultless provided the subsequent information in question to a news reporter, and it was printed in *The Wall Street Journal* along with a statement that the financial statements and accompanying audit report, dated February 25, could not be relied upon.

Required:

Evaluate the actions of Faultless & Co., CPAs, with respect to the subsequent information discovered. What are the possible legal effects of the firm's actions, if any?

18.17. What are the limitations in applying the generally accepted auditing standard of *an opinion as to conformity of financial statements with generally accepted principles of accounting*? Indicate the general effects of its application on the wording of the opinion in the auditor's *special report* on the statements in each of the two following cases.

1. The financial statements of the XYZ Market, a retail grocery operated as an individual proprietorship, are prepared on the basis of cash receipts and disbursements. These statements do not purport to present the financial position and results of operation of the company.
2. The financial statements of the Able Insurance Company are prepared in accordance with the principles and practices of uniform accounting prescribed by the State Insurance Department. These statements purport to present the financial position and results of operation of Able. (AICPA adapted)

18.18. Jiffy Clerical Services is a corporation which furnishes temporary office help to its customers. Billings are rendered monthly based on predetermined hourly rates. You have examined the company's financial statements for several years. Following is an abbreviated statement of assets and liabilities on the cash basis as of December 31.

Assets:	
Cash	$20,000
Advances to employees	1,000
Equipment and autos, less allowance for depreciation	25,000
Total Assets	$46,000
Liabilities:	
Employees's income taxes withheld	$ 8,000
Bank loan payable	10,000
Estimated federal income taxes on cash basis profits	10,000
Total Liabilities	$28,000
Net Assets	$18,000
Represented by:	
Common stock	$ 3,000
Cash profits retained in the business	15,000
	$18,000

Unrecorded receivables were $55,000, and payables were $30,000.

Required:

a. Prepare the opinion you would issue covering the statement of assets and liabilities as of December 31, as summarized above, and the related statement of cash income and expenses for the year ended that date.

b. Briefly discuss *and* justify your modifications of the conventional opinion on accrual basis statements. (AICPA adapted)

18.19. Independent certified public accountants may issue two types of auditor's reports in connection with an examination of financial statements: a so-called short-form of auditor's report in connection with financial statements intended for publication; and a so-called long-form of auditor's report for the purposes of management and other parties.

Required:

a. Outline in *general terms* the kinds of materials which are commonly included in a long-form report other than those commonly included in a short-form report.

b. Does the auditor assume the same degree of responsibility for other data in the long-form report that is assumed for individual items in the customary basic financial statements (balance sheet and statements of income, retained income and capital)? State the reasons for your answer. (AICPA)

18.20. You are newly engaged by the James Company, a New England manufacturer with a sales office and warehouse located in a western state. The James Company audit must be made at the peak of your busy season when you will not have a senior auditor available for travel to the western outlet.

Furthermore, the James Company is reluctant to bear the travel expenses of an out-of-town auditor.

Required:

a. Under what conditions would you, the principal auditor, be willing to accept full responsibility for the work of another auditor?

b. What would be your requirements with respect to the integrity of the other auditor? To whom would you direct inquiries about the other auditor?

c. What reference, if any, would you make to the other auditor in your report if you were:

(1) Assuming full responsibility for the auditor's work?

(2) Not assuming responsibility for the auditor's work? (AICPA)

18.21. Albacore Fish Food Fabricators produces specialty fish food products for two markets. The domestic United States market for pet store products is supplied by the output of the Richmond plant. The foreign market for commercial fish farm products is served from the Norfolk plant. Overseas shipments are put on freighters for shipment to Europe and Africa. Corporate headquarters is in Richmond.

Albacore proposes to make the following segment information disclosure in a footnote:

SEGMENT INFORMATION

Albacore operates in two markets—domestic and foreign. The domestic market is principally pet store products, and the foreign market is principally commercial fish farm products. Information related to these two segments of the business is given below. There were no significant intersegment sales or transfers. Identifiable assets by segment consists of inventories, land, and plant directly identified with each segment. General corporate assets (net) consists of all cash, receivables, investments, headquarters property, and liabilities. Albacore has no major customers as defined in FASB *Statement No. 14.*

Year ended 19XX (000)	*Domestic*	*Foreign*	*Headquarters*	*Combined*
Sales and revenue	$135,000	$117,494	—	$252,494
Operating profit	$ 12,718	$ 10,231	—	$ 22,949
General corporate expense			$ 4,265	(4,265)
Interest expense			3,121	(3,121)
Net income				$ 15,563
Identifiable assets	$113,193	$126,869	$42,931	$282,993
Capital expenditures	16,701	12,932	1,121	30,754

Required:

a. Do you detect any omission of segment information as presented above?

b. Albacore management has made representations that there were no significant intersegment sales and no "major customers" as defined by FASB *No. 14.* What should the auditor do with respect to these representations?

c. Give four specific procedures to be applied in the audit of the segment information.

d. Should the audit opinion be qualified in any way that you can see?

18.22. **Changing the Opinion—Fallhard Manufacturing Company**

Refer to the fact situation concerning purchase of a plant by Gofast, Inc., from Fallhard Manufacturing Company as given in Exercise 17.22.

For Discussion:

The 1978 annual report contained 1977 and 1978 financial statements in comparative form. Assume that Fallhard failed to disclose the nature of the repayment terms of the note and the auditors wanted to qualify the opinion on the 1978 financial statements for this reason. The previously issued audit report on the 1977 financial statements was unqualified, and Gofast, Inc., did not become a related party until after the 1977 report was delivered.

Required:

a. Should the 1978 opinion qualification be extended to cover the 1977 financial statements, effectively applying the related party transaction disclosure rules retroactively?

b. Assume that the auditor decides to qualify the opinion on 1977 financial statements issued in comparative form with the 1978 statements. Write the report.

18.23. **Special Report on Nonfinancial Information**

Aggieland, Inc., is a farm management company. Aggieland sells parcels of land to investors who seek a tax shelter. Tenant farmers work the land in corn, paying all expenses of production. The crop is harvested by independent contractors using mechanized equipment. When the crop is sold, tenants' costs are paid plus a salary based on production and the contractors are paid a fee for the harvesting. Any remaining net cash flow is paid to the investors.

Usually , there is no remaining cash flow for investors. Their expectation of investment return is based mainly on appreciation in value of the land, which is located near a large urban area.

The harvest season is approaching. Aggieland's president wants you to provide an audit report on the reasonable measurement of the harvest in terms of bushels of corn. The report will be sent to the investors. He does not want you to audit Aggieland's Inc., financial statements.

If you accept this engagement, you can review the grain harvest procedures, observe the harvest in process, trace observed harvest truckloads to harvest records, confirm acreage with independent surveyors, review reports from storage elevators, recalculate accuracy of harvest records, and confirm yields per acre with the tenants.

For Discussion:

Does *Statement on Auditing Standards No. 14* (Section 621) provide for issuance of a report like the one requested by Aggieland? If so, what kind of report would be issued?

19

UNAUDITED INFORMATION AND NONOPINION REPORTS

This chapter is divided into two parts:

I. Unaudited information in audited financial statements.
II. Nonopinion reports.

The *unaudited information* topic is a phenomenon new since 1975. As financial accounting evolves and changes, new information tends to enter financial presentations without being subject to a complete audit and without being covered by the audit opinion. In contrast to unaudited *financial statements,* unaudited *information* is like a small island of special information placed in the midst of the audited financial statements.

Nonopinion reports are auditors' reports that do not purport to be directly related to financial statement presentations. These reports include independent auditors' reports on internal control and MAS engagements and the reports rendered by governmental and internal auditors on their work assignments. They are informative reports of the audit work performed, the results and findings, and the recommendations for improvement.

I. UNAUDITED INFORMATION IN AUDITED FINANCIAL STATEMENTS

The U.S. Securities and Exchange Commission has vigorously pursued a policy of mandating disclosure of financial information which is not otherwise required to be disclosed under generally accepted accounting principles. SEC power in this area flows from various rules under *Regulation S-X*—the regulatory rules which specify disclosures that must be made in 10–Q (quarterly) and 10–K (annual) financial statements filed with the commission. The SEC, however, has stopped short of requiring that the audit opinion cover such information. Nevertheless, auditors are *associated with* the information because it appears in a document containing audited financial statements. (Refer to the discussion in Chapter 18 of auditors' responsibilities regarding "Other Information in Documents containing Audited Financial Statements", *SAS No. 8*, Section 550.)

The SEC has enacted rules requiring footnote disclosure in audited financial statements of (1) interim financial information and (2) replacement cost information. Such footnotes may be placed in the financial statements and covered by the auditor's opinion, but the information must then be audited in accordance with generally accepted auditing standards. Predominant practice is to label the footnotes "unaudited" and follow applicable auditing standards, which are explained below.

INTERIM FINANCIAL INFORMATION

Rule 3–16 (*t*) of *Regulation S–X* requires disclosure of selected quarterly financial data in notes to financial statements filed with the SEC by large companies whose shares are actively traded. The data includes quarterly sales, gross profit, income and earnings per share for the two most recent fiscal years, as well as other explanatory information. When this rule was originally proposed, the SEC wanted to have the information audited, but the final form of the rule permits the interim financial information footnote to be labeled "unaudited." The reasons for wanting auditor involvement included past problems with quarterly statements and "surprise" fourth quarter adjustments made by companies. The SEC believed that auditor involvement would improve the quality of quarterly financial information.

Regulation S–X provides the following:

> If the financial statements covered by the accountant's report designate as "unaudited" the note required by Rule 3–16 (*t*) (of *Regulation S–X*), it shall be presumed that appropriate professional standards and procedures with respect to the data in the note have been followed by the independent accountant who is associated with the unaudited footnote by virtue of reporting on the financial statements in which it is included.

The key phrase in this requirement is: "it shall be presumed that *appropriate professional standards and procedures* with respect to the data in the note have been followed by the independent accountant. . . ." Auditing standards are found in *SAS No. 10* (Section 720) entitled "Limited Review of Interim Financial Information" and in *SAS No. 13* (Section 519) entitled "Reports on a Limited Review of Interim Financial Information."

Limited Review Engagement

A *limited review* is considerably different from an audit. According to *SAS No. 10* (Section 720.06) the objective of a limited review of interim financial information is to give the accountant a basis for preparing a report to the board of directors. A limited review, strictly speaking, does not require a complete study and evaluation of internal accounting control each quarter or the gathering of sufficient competent evidential matter on which to base an opinion on interim financial statements taken as a whole. At best, the accountant may be able to recommend improvements in the system for producing interim statements and adjustments for accounting errors that may have been discovered.

Nature of Review Procedures. The nature of limited review procedures consists mainly of inquiry and analytical review (analysis of interrelationships). *SAS No. 10* (Sections 720.10–.11) suggests the following:

Inquire about the accounting system.
 Obtain an understanding of the system.
 Determine whether there have been any significant changes in the system used to produce interim information.
Perform analytical review, comparing current interim information with budgets, comparative prior periods, and financial relationships characteristic of the client's accounts.
Read the minutes of stockholder, board of director, and board committee meetings to identify actions or events that may affect interim financial information.
Inquire about conformity of the information with generally accepted accounting principles.
Obtain letters from other accountants who perform limited reviews of significant segments, subsidiaries, or other investees.
Inquire of officers and executives about:
 Conformity with generally accepted accounting principles.
 Changes in the client's business or accounting practices.
 Matters about which questions have arisen as a result of applying other procedures (listed above).
 Events subsequent to the date of the interim information.

Timing of Review Procedures. Review procedures should be performed at or near the date of the interim information. Starting the engagement prior to the cutoff date will give the auditor a chance to deal with problems and questions without undue deadline pressures.

Extent of Review Procedures. The accountant needs to acquire a sufficient knowledge of the client's business, just as if the engagement were a regular audit. Knowledge of strengths and weaknesses in the internal control system and of problem accounting areas is very useful in judging the extent of review procedures. Basically, the extent of review procedures depends upon the accountant's professional judgment of what problem areas may exist in the system of internal accounting control, the severity of unique accounting principles problems and the errors that have occurred in the past. With knowledge of these areas, the accountant can direct and fine-tune the review procedures in the interest of improving the quality of the interim information.

SAS No. 10 (Sections 720.19–.22) describes a report to the client's board of directors containing the following:

Identification of the interim information reviewed.

Description of the procedures performed, or a reference to procedures described in an engagement letter.

Statement that an audit in accordance with generally accepted auditing standards was *not* performed *and* a disclaimer of opinion. Any departures from accounting principles should also be reported.

Statement that a limited review would not necessarily disclose all matters of significance.

Description of the results of the review (including proposed adjustments, if any, and recommendations about the system of internal accounting control).

Statement that the report is for the board of directors and may be furnished to management, but it should not be otherwise used.

This report is prescribed for the board of directors—an internal report. However, accountants also have responsibilities respecting external reports on interim information.

Reporting on a Limited Review

An accountant may consent to use of his or her name in an external report on interim information, provided that a limited review has been satisfactorily completed. The basic content of the report is (*SAS No. 13*, Section 519.04):

A statement that a limited review was made in accordance with standards for such reviews.

An identification of the interim information reviewed.

A statement that an audit was not made *and* a disclaimer of opinion.

When the client submits interim information in a 10–Q report filed with the SEC, the client may state that a limited review was performed and must also state whether effect was given to adjustments and disclosures, if any, proposed by the accountant. In addition to the three report elements above, the accountant's report must also contain a comment confirming or otherwise commenting on the client's disposition of proposed adjustments and disclosures.

When interim financial information is presented in a footnote to audited financial statements and labeled "unaudited" (see Exhibit 19–1), the regular report on the audited financial statements need not be modified to refer to the limited review. Labeling the footnote "unaudited" is enough. However, the report on the audited financial statements will be

EXHIBIT 19–1
Interim Information in Footnote Labeled "Unaudited"

Howell Industries, Inc.
Note 1—Summary of Quarterly Financial Information (unaudited)

Following is selected quarterly financial data for 1977. In the opinion of management: all adjustments, which include only normal recurring accruals, necessary to present fairly the results of operations for quarterly periods were made.

	Quarter ended			
	10/31/76	*1/31/77*	*4/30/77*	*7/31/77*
	(dollars in thousands except per share data)			
Net sales	$5,427	$6,297	$7,162	$6,896
Cost of products sold	4,685	5,427	5,958	5,262
Net earnings	222	304	422	247
Earnings per share	$ .15	$ .21	$ .30	$ .17

modified with appropriate explanatory language under the following conditions and circumstances:

The footnote indicates that a limited review was performed but does not indicate that the accountant expresses no opinion on the interim information.

The footnote is not properly marked "unaudited."

The scope of a limited review was restricted or the review was not completed (unless the note makes this disclosure).

The interim information is not presented in conformity with generally accepted accounting principles.

REPLACEMENT COST INFORMATION

Rule 3–17 of *Regulation S–X* requires disclosure by certain large capital-intensive companies of "replacement cost information." The goal of the information is to disclose the effects of changing specific prices on the cost of fixed assets, accumulated depreciation, depreciation expense, and cost of goods sold elements of financial statements. The information is supplementary, and it is viewed by proponents as a first step in showing how inflation affects a business.

The replacement cost disclosure rule (announced in SEC *Accounting Series Release No. 190* in 1976) had a stormy birth because there was a great deal of opposition to having to make the measurements and disclose the results. In part, *ASR 190* was an opening salvo on the concept of historical cost accounting. The ongoing "conceptual framework of accounting and reporting" project on the FASB agenda is related to the efforts being made to reexamine the measurement basis used in financial accounting. As time passes, changes in the kind of supplementary information offered to explain changing prices may take place. In the meantime, *ASR 190* and the SEC replacement cost disclosures serve as the only company-issued, nonhistorical published accounting data.

Replacement cost information appears in an "unaudited" footnote in a qualifying registrant's 10–K annual report. It may be included in the published annual report or a reference may simply be made to the availability of the 10–K. In either event the auditor is associated with the information because it appears in a document containing audited financial statements.

Audit standards, as expressed in *SAS No. 18* (Section 730), "Unaudited Replacement Cost Information," prescribes certain limited procedures an auditor should perform. In the same sense that a limited review of interim financial information does not constitute an audit in accordance with generally accepted auditing standards, neither does a review of replacement cost information constitute an audit. The limited procedures include the following:

Inquire of management as to whether the information has been prepared and presented in accordance with Rule 3–17 of *Regulation S–X*.

Inquire of management as to the methods used to calculate replacement cost information.

Inquire of management as to procedures used to compile the data supporting the replacement cost information and the relationship to the data supporting the related audited financial statement information. (For example: Fixed asset useful lives for depreciation calculation purposes should generally be the same.)

Inquire of management as to the bases for supplemental explanatory disclosures accompanying the replacement cost measurements.

Inquire as to changes and reasons therefore in methods of calculating replacement costs.

Since the footnote is labeled "unaudited," the audit report on the financial statements ordinarily need not be modified and need not ordinarily make reference to the replacement cost information footnote. However, in keeping with auditing standards regarding "other information" (*SAS No. 8,* Section 550), the auditor must resolve any apparent inconsistency or material misstatement of fact.

Also, the auditor's report should be *expanded* if (*a*) the limited review reveals that the replacement cost information is not prepared or presented in accordance with *Regulation S–X* requirements, or (*b*) the auditor has been unable to apply the limited procedures related to the information, or (*c*) the footnote reveals that the auditor performed limited procedures but does not state that an opinion is disclaimed. The standard short-form audit report is *expanded* by adding a middle paragraph with explanatory language that sets the record straight—disclosing inability to perform limited review procedures, disclosing nonconformity with *Regulation S–X*, or disclaiming an opinion on the information, as the circumstances may require. *SAS No. 18* (Section 730.08) gives illustrative language for expanding the audit report.

An example of an unaudited replacement cost information disclosure is shown in Exhibit 19–2.

EXHIBIT 19–2
Unaudited Replacement Cost Footnote

American Telephone & Telegraph Co., Form 10–K

Replacement Cost (unaudited)—In response to Securities and Exchange Commission requirements, the following figures compare telephone plant investment as shown on the balance sheet of the American company and its consolidated subsidiaries at December 31, 1976, with the approximate cost to replace its productive capacity at that date. The figures also compare accumulated depreciation at that date with the amount that would have been provided had past depreciation accruals contemplated such replacement costs. Additionally, they compare depreciation expense for the consolidated companies for the year ended December 31, 1976, with depreciation expense computed (using historic depreciation assumptions) on these estimates of replacement cost.

	Thousands of Dollars		
	As Stated	*At Replacement Cost*	*Difference*
Telephone plant investment:			
For which replacement cost has been determined	$90,659,997	$130,404,652	$39,744,655
Included at historic cost	3,507,486	3,507,486	—
Total	$94,167,483	$133,912,138	$39,744,655
Accumulated depreciation	18,245,477	32,634,432	14,388,955
Net telephone plant investment	$75,922,006	$101,277,706	$25,355,700
Depreciation expense	$ 4,483,906	$ 5,979,672	$ 1,495,766

These replacement cost figures are theoretical, based on the assumptions that, as of December 31, 1976, electronic switching systems would replace all electromechanical switching systems; most other telephone plant would be replaced in accordance with present replacement practices; and building space would be reduced because of the use of electronic switching systems. Certain telephone plant categories are included at historic cost: principally land, telephone plant under construction, and telephone plant held for future use.

The difference between historic and estimated replacement cost of net telephone plant investment does not represent additional book value for the American company's stock. The above replacement cost is an approximation of the amount of capital that could have been required were the consolidated companies to have replaced the entire productive capacity of

EXHIBIT 19–2 (*continued*)

such plant on December 31, 1976. Replacement actually will take place over many years and the funds needed will be derived from sources similar to those available during 1976.

Depreciation expense based on an estimate of replacement cost also is a theoretical figure and not deductible in determining income tax expense. The excess of depreciation on replacement cost over that determined on historic cost is a measure of the extent to which current operations have not been making provision for the higher replacement cost of present plant capacity. Such provision, if made, would provide funds which would be used in lieu of funds from other sources for plant construction.

It would be unrealistic to impute a reduced net income by the difference between depreciation based on historic cost and that based on estimates of replacement cost. New plant is likely to provide largely offsetting additional revenue-generating services and operating efficiencies. Additionally, replacement of plant will take place over many years. It is true, however, that the earnings of the consolidated companies must be high enough to provide some equity capital from reinvested earnings and to attract additional debt and equity to provide funds for any replacement cost in excess of depreciation accruals based on the historic cost of the plant.

II. NONOPINION REPORTS

Independent auditors, governmental auditors, internal auditors, and management advisory services consultants all render reports that do not contain opinions on fair presentation of financial position and results of operations. This section provides a review of such nonopinion reports by these four types of auditors. The objective is to connect the general approach and objectives of auditing with the reports of both independent auditors and other types of auditors.

REPORTS ON INTERNAL CONTROL

Independent auditors report publicly on the condition of internal accounting control only in the extreme case where it is so unreliable as to prevent the economic accumulation of sufficient competent evidence. In such cases the opinion on financial statements is disclaimed. However, in some audits an expression of findings about internal control is either requested or required, as in the case of audits of banks, brokerage firms, and holders of government grants.

Auditors' reports on internal control are not *opinions* on internal control. Auditing standards respecting such reports are found in:

SAS No. 1 (Section 640), "Reports on Internal Control."

SAS No. 1 (Section 641), "Reports on Internal Control Based on Criteria Established by Governmental Agencies."

SAS No. 20 (Section 323), "Required Communication of Material Weaknesses in Internal Accounting Control."

Explanations and illustrations of the report form were placed at the end of Chapter 6 of this textbook, in order to be closely related to the internal control theory topic.

As a result of a Commission on Auditors' Responsibilities recommendation in 1978, the Auditing Standards Board has begun a study of the feasibility of public reporting on internal control. Before too long, a new scheme for such reports may develop.

REPORTS OF GOVERNMENTAL AUDITORS

Auditing standards for audit of government organizations, programs, activities, and functions were introduced in Chapters 1 and 2. The GAO views governmental auditing not as restricted to financial reports alone, but as extended to three areas:

1. *Financial and compliance.* The emphasis is on fair presentation of financial statements and on compliance with applicable laws and regulations.
2. *Economy and efficiency.* The emphasis is on economical and efficient resource utilization by management, including studies of management information systems, administrative procedures, and organizational structure.
3. *Program results.* The emphasis is on determining whether objectives set by a legislative or other program authorizing body are being met, including studies of alternative means of achieving desired results at lower cost.

These three areas may be viewed as a hierarchy, the first one most closely resembling current practice in independent auditing and the next two moving toward systems-oriented auditing and management consultation. The latter two areas are consistent with the GAO mission—to serve Congress as consultants.

In 1973 the AICPA Committee on Relations with the General Accounting Office completed its study of the GAO standards and issued a report. The committee's conclusions and recommendations consisted of the following points:

- The GAO standards follow the same general organization as the generally accepted auditing standards of the AICPA, and the standards applicable to financial audits are intended to be identical. However, in GAO's definition, an audit may also be concerned with efficiency and economy of operations, compliance with both financial and nonfinancial laws and regulations, and with program effectiveness. This broader definition of an audit will require that agreement be reached as to criteria for evaluating economy, efficiency, and effectiveness.
- Independent public accountants should be encouraged to participate in audits of the types contemplated by the GAO standards but should be cautioned to define carefully, in an engagement agreement, the scope of each engagement and the method of reporting. The profession should work to further define standards for performing such audits.

- When the scope of an audit goes beyond examination of financial presentations, the auditor should ascertain whether criteria are available (in audit guides or other sources) for use in reviewing compliance with laws and regulations, and in evaluating efficiency and economy of operations and program effectiveness.
- When nonaccounting expertise is needed, the independent auditor should determine in advance its availability and cost. He should further determine how his use of the work of nonaccounting experts will be made known in his report.
- A CPA should recognize that the GAO standards do not contemplate that he will express an opinion as to the economy and efficiency of operations or as to program effectiveness. In reporting on reviews covering these matters, the auditor should limit his opinion to fairness of presentation of financial information in conformity with generally accepted accounting principles, or with other principles prescribed for the entity or program audited, and the consistency of application of such principles. This does not preclude an auditor from disclosing lack of compliance with laws and regulations. Also the auditor may identify areas in which improvements in methods or practices are possible and may make appropriate recommendations. He may also point out areas in which noteworthy accomplishments have occurred or in which further study may be required.
- Audits concerned with economy, efficiency, and program effectiveness will presumably require more time than those covering only financial presentations. Care should be taken to provide for sufficient time to complete the engagement.[1]

Exhibit 19–3 contains an example of findings from a report by governmental auditors. This example is highly condensed from a more lengthy report, but it shows the nature and emphasis of typical governmental audit reports.

The emphasis of this report is on economical and efficient resource utilization by Department of Agriculture managers of the Commodity Distribution Program (a program enacted by Congress). The general audit assignment was to assess how efficiently the program was being operated. One feature of efficiency is highlighted in the excerpts in Exhibit 19–3—the package sizes and used in commodity distributions.

Administrative instructions from the Department of Agriculture directed agents to distribute to institutions (schools, and so on) in the "most economical size packages," whatever that size might be, but presumably the large sizes suggested in the report. The auditors found, however, that small sizes were being used at a considerable cost that could be avoided. Judging strictly on a dollar-cost basis, the programs were found to be inefficient.

Conceivably an independent CPA could have conducted this investigation. While he or she would not be expected to render some kind of overall opinion on "efficiency," there is no doubt that a CPA could have reached the same conclusions and made the same recommendations. In fact, this

[1] Committee on Relations with the GAO, *Auditing Standards Established by the GAO: Their Meaning and Significance for CPAs* (New York: AICPA, 1973), pp. 10–11.

EXHIBIT 19–3

Audit Findings Regarding Efficiency and Economy in Using Resources

Example: Uneconomical Package Sizes Used in a Commodity Distribution Program

In an audit of the Commodity Distribution Program of the Department of Agriculture, GAO reported that savings could be realized if larger package sizes of commodities are used when possible.

Criteria Used to Measure Efficiency and Economy

The Department of Agriculture's instructions to state distribution agencies require that, to the extent practicable, commodities be donated to schools and institutions in the most economical size packages. When commodities are available in packages of more than one size, the instructions require that state agencies requisition the commodities to the maximum extent practicable, in large-size packages—such as 50-pound containers—for schools and institutions.

Conditions Found by Auditors

In seven states covered by the review, distributing agencies were requisitioning foodstuffs for large users in small-size packages instead of large-size packages.

Effect of the Conditions

A substantial part of the additional costs of providing flour, shortening, and nonfat dry milk in small containers to schools and institutions could be saved. GAO estimated that, nationwide, for fiscal year 1970 these additional costs totaled about $1.6 million.

Cause of the Situation

Agriculture regional officials said that, although they encouraged state distributing agencies to requisition commodities in the most economical size package practicable, they had not questioned the propriety of state agencies requesting commodities in small-size packages for schools and institutions and that they had not required the agencies to justify such requests because they believed the agencies were making the proper determinations as to packages sizes.

Auditors' Recommendations

In view of the savings available by acquiring commodities in large-size packages, GAO recommended that Agriculture take appropriate action to have regional offices vigorously enforce the requirement that state agencies requisition commodities—particularly, flour, vegetable shortening, and nonfat dry milk—in the most economical size packages practicable. GAO recommended also that state agencies be required to justify, when necessary, the requisitioning of the commodities in small-size packages for schools and institutions.

Source: "Examples of Findings from Governmental Audits," *Audit Standards Supplement Series No. 4* (U.S. General Accounting Office, 1973), pp. 19–20.

assignment is probably very similar to some tasks undertaken as management advisory services engagements. A CPA could operate both within the expectations of GAO audit standards and within the suggestions expressed by the AICPA Committee on Relations with the GAO.

INTERNAL AUDIT REPORTS

The viewpoint of internal auditors is one of providing services and assistance to management. Among companies that have organized internal audit staffs the following are frequently cited in policy statements as the functions and responsibilities that may be assigned to internal auditors.

1. To review compliance with, and implementation of managements' policies, procedures, and assigned tasks.
2. To safeguard the assets of the company, including assignments to detect frauds and irregularities.
3. To evaluate the systems of internal accounting and managerial control.
4. To recommend improvements and corrective action respecting programs and functions.

These audit areas are almost identical to the GAO conception of auditing. The first and second are equivalent to auditing *financial matters and compliance* (although emphasizing company policy rather than applicable laws and regulations); the third is similar to auditing for *economy and efficiency* (with its emphasis on control systems); and the fourth is similar to auditing *program results* (to the extent of evaluating alternatives that yield recommendations for improvement and correction).

The reporting stage is the internal auditor's opportunity to capture management's undivided attention. But to be truly effective, a report cannot be unduly long, tedious, technical, and laden with minutiae. It must be accurate, concise, clear, and timely. There is no standard form for internal audit reports, and there will likely never be one given the diversity of assignments and the diversity of managers' abilities and interests.

Exhibit 19–4 contains an example of an internal audit report on the study of a personnel department. Notice that the report begins with a summary or overall conclusion that conveys the essential findings and captures the attention of the reader. The personnel department report may be characterized as a broad evaluation of a management function.

MAS ENGAGEMENT REPORTS BY CPAs

In contrast to the well-defined areas of audit and tax practice, independent accountants' practice in management advisory services (MAS) can be described only by cataloging a variety of such services. On a specific engagement basis, independent accountants, acting as management consultants, perform services in areas as diverse as those performed by internal auditors. In fact, much MAS practice is very similar to some internal

EXHIBIT 19–4

Corporate Operations Analysis Department
Summary Letter Report

Personnel Director
ABC Company

Dear Bob,

Our analysis of your Personnel Department is now completed. This report summarizes our findings and recommendations.

Focus

Personnel services 2,200 office and technical employees who are loacted in five different divisions or operating units within the metropolitan area. Approximately one half of these employees are in the XYZ Division.

The department has 36 people and operates on a budget of about $600,000 annually.

Our analysis was confined to the three major personnel functional responsibilities of Placement, Manpower Development/Training, and Compensation Practices.

XYZ Personnel provides service to operating management on an "as requested" basis; when provided, our review revealed this service to be generally adequate.

Overall Assessment

However, XYZ Personnel's role in the management of office and technical personnel is mainly passive. As such, most personnel practices are handled by the operating people, who are not technically trained in personnel administration.

Further, the personnel department is not knowledgeable in the extent, quality, and consistency of personnel administration practices performed by the operating people.

Finally, we believe that Personnel concentrates too much of its efforts and resources on activities that are of low priority in the management of human resources.

The department's whole approach to the acquisition, development, and retention of people does not assure operating management of optimum use of their investment in manpower.

Major Recommendations

1. Analyze and define the role of the residential personnel department.

   The personnel department does not play a major role in the administering of personnel practices upon employees. Personnel does not know either the extent, quality, or consistency (and inconsistency) of these practices among the many managers and departments.

   Many important personnel practices are the complete prerogative of individual operating managers.

   Examples of these practices are:

   a. Manpower requirement forecasting.
   b. Employee performance appraisals.
   c. Career counseling and career development.
   d. Determination of specific individual training needs and training received.
   e. Early identification of "marginal" and "failing" employees. Establishment of corrective action programs.

EXHIBIT 19–4 (*continued*)

f. Analysis of absenteeism levels and control.
g. Information flow to employee's personnel jackets.

Personnel usually does not participate in, or monitor, these activities. We contribute this passive role to two factors:

The lack of a formally defined charter from top management.

A low level of expertise among departmental employees, below the managerial positions, due to an agressive job rotation policy. (Department management considers this necessary to keep employees challenged.)

Several steps are required before Personnel can undertake a more aggressive, employee-oriented service role.

- Develop a formal written charter of operations, approved by top divisional management. Describe areas of personnel administration where the personnel department has sole responsibility. Delineate those areas where Personnel should play an advisory or monitoring role.
- Discontinue the rapid rotation practice. Develop greater vertical growth potential within the personnel department.
- Gradually implement the above charter through assignments of specific action programs to individual department employees.

The major benefit of this effort will be to give assurance that the biggest investment—the investment in people—is always being well managed.

2. Improve the accuracy of the manpower forecast.
3. Implement a disciplined program for job description development and maintenance.
4. Assist and monitor operating management in the employee appraisal function. Utilize appraisal information.
5. Guide and monitor personnel training activities.
6. Compile and utilize statistical information to improve effectiveness and efficiency in personnel activities.
7. Improve the quality and completeness of employee personnel information.
8. Investigate the desirability of an organizational realignment.

We believe that implementation of our recommendations will substantially increase and improve the level of service now being offered by the Personnel function to operating management. Furthermore, the company will have greater assurance that their biggest investment—the investment in people—is being well managed.

The specific details supporting these and other recommendations are contained in the interim recommendation reports which have been furnished you.

____
Manager

____
Lead Analyst

Source: From Lawrence B. Sawyer, *The Practice of Modern Internal Auditing*. Copyright 1973 by The Institute of Internal Auditors, Inc. 249 Maitland Ave., Altamonte Springs, Florida. Reprinted with permission.

audit assignments. The independent consultant may accept engagements to evaluate compliance, economy and efficiency, and program results—all areas that are identified by the GAO auditing standards.

Consequently, MAS engagement reports should exhibit the same characteristics as internal audit reports and GAO reports. The problem must be identified; some explanation of the investigation should be given; and the findings and recommendations should be expressed clearly and concisely.

The MAS report in Exhibit 19–5 is the full text of an actual report. The assignment was a relatively uncomplicated one—evaluation of the system for controlling inventory—and the resultant report is a good example of clarity and direct communication.

EXHIBIT 19–5
MAS Report by a CPA

Mr. C. D. Derfin,
Control Instruments, Inc.

Dear Mr. Derfin:

We have completed our review of the cost accounting system of Control Instruments, Inc., as outlined in our engagement letter to you. The primary objective of our review was to determine if a new system should be designed or if the existing one should be modified. Our conclusion is that the present system for controlling inventory is sound. It is simple, but it should provide for good control of inventory. The problem is one of improper utilization of the existing system.

We believe that control of inventory is vital to company operations. We understand there are numerous shortages of parts which delay the assembly process. However, we do not believe that this problem is primarily due to a systems weakness. We observed that additions to inventory are properly entered on the perpetual records when receiving reports are received by the inventory control clerk. Items are deleted from the records when they are pulled from the warehouse, and an adequate system exists for keeping track of material shortages. We believe that the warehouse operation is the primary source of inventory control problems. Our observations and recommendations in this area are summarized below.

Warehouse Operation

Warehouse personnel are currently taking cycle counts of raw materials to locate differences between perpetual records and actual quantities on hand. We noted that there were many such discrepancies. In an attempt to find a reason for these discrepancies, we unpacked three pulled orders in the warehouse and compared actual items packed with the amounts indicated as being packed on the bills of material. In each case we found discrepancies.

In order to identify the source of these errors, we recommend that the warehousemen be required to initial the bills of material for the orders they pull. They have already been instructed to do this. The production supervisor currently unpacks all pulled orders and counts the contents before the orders go to the production line. We believe he should take the additional step of reporting the exact discrepancies daily to John Roberts. Additional recommendations to improve the

EXHIBIT 19–5 (*continued*)

warehouse operation are summarized below. Some of these recommendations are already being implemented.

1. Continue the cycle count procedure, but take time to resolve differences daily. Report reasons for differences to John Roberts.
2. Temporarily assign a man full-time to maintaining inventory records.
3. Stock inventory in the correct locations, or attach a note to the bin, stating where additional items are located.
4. Adopt a "last bag" system for control of "C" items.
5. When an order for several units on the small line requires more than one box, pack all of one type part in the same box.
6. When pulling an order for several units on the large line, pack as many complete units as possible, and limit the shortages to the remaining units.
7. Require warehousemen to pack orders neatly, particularly general kits.
8. Adopt a daily routine in the warehouse as follows:
   a. Stock the items received,
   b. Fill short orders,
   c. Fill remaining orders,
   d. Special projects.

We noted that physical control of inventory has been substantially improved by constructing a chain link fence around the warehouse area. Since access to the warehouse is now very limited, it will be difficult for unauthorized personnel to remove parts.

General Observations

While most of our time was spent in the warehouse, we also noted some opportunities to improve the general operation of the Control Instruments facility. Our recommendations are summarized below:

1. Revise the cost book to contain an accurate description and the current cost of each item.
2. Revise the Bills of Material to make them accurate and adopt a formal procedure for keeping them current.
3. Redesign the forms used for the Bills of Material. They can be changed to indicate more clearly the number of items packed versus the number of items specified. They could also indicate which items are used in the electrical subassembly process, so these items could be packed together. These forms should be ordered as snap-out multiple part forms.
4. Redesign the "owe sheets" to make them consistent and easy to understand.
5. Assign part numbers to all purchased parts except common nuts and bolts.
6. Assign part numbers to sheet metal parts, and include these parts in the cost book and Bills of Material.
7. Adopt a tag method for keeping track of labor hours spent on individual units, and revise labor time standards as appropriate.

Accounting Procedures

There is some confusion over exactly what accounting procedures have been employed in the past. We recommend that the following procedures be used in the

EXHIBIT 19–5 (*concluded*)

future to account for the costs of materials and labor. We believe most of these procedures are already understood by accounting personnel and are being used.

1. Record raw materials purchases at standard cost and maintain a purchase price variance account. For internal financial statements, the variance can be treated as part of cost of goods sold.
2. Charge labor to cost of goods sold at standard time. Charge the difference between standard and actual to labor efficiency variance, which is part of cost of goods sold.
3. At the end of each month, count the finished goods inventory and estimate work-in-process inventory.

We would be pleased to discuss this letter further at your convenience. We appreciate this opportunity to be of service to you.

Very truly yours,
Alexander Grant & Co., CPAs

The CPA's report, like the internal auditor's report, gets to the main problem quickly, identifying the source of trouble as the warehouse operation. Notice that the consultants found and reported that the trouble was not the result of a basic system weakness. The report makes specific points and recommendations on inventory handling procedures as well as on recordkeeping procedures. This particular engagement required not only ordinary expertise as an accountant but also an ability to perceive some elementary materials-handling problems and offer commonsense solutions to them.

SOURCES AND ADDITIONAL READING REFERENCES

Bromage, M. C. "Wording the Management Audit Report," *Journal of Accountancy*, February 1972, pp. 50–57.

Committee on Relations with the General Accounting Office of AICPA. "Auditing Standards Established by the GAO: Their Meaning and Significance for CPAs." New York: American Institute of Certified Public Accountants, 1973.

Comptroller General of the United States. "Examples of Findings from Governmental Audits," *Audit Standards Supplement Series No. 4*. U.S. General Accounting Office, 1973.

Konrath, Larry. "The CPA's Risk in Evaluating Internal Control," *Journal of Accountancy*, October 1971, pp. 53–56.

Levy, L. E., and Kern, D. P. "SAP No. 49: 'Reports on Internal Control'—Small Step or Giant Leap," *CPA Journal*, December 1972, pp. 1019–23.

Morse, E. H., and Carmichael, D. R. "Letters to the Editor—Critique of Report on Internal Control and Response," *Journal of Accountancy*, May 1972, pp. 30–33.

Sawyer, Lawrence B. *The Practice of Modern Internal Auditing*. Altamonte Springs, Florida: The Institute of Internal Auditors, Inc., 1973.

Securities and Exchange Commission. "Notice of Adoption of Amendments to Form 10–Q and *Regulation S–X* regarding Interim Financial Reporting," *Accounting Series Release No. 177,* September 10, 1975.

Securities and Exchange Commission. "Notice of Adoption of Amendments to *Regulation S–X* Requiring Disclosure of Certain Replacement Cost Data." *Accounting Series Release No. 190,* March 23, 1976.

Swieringa, R. J., and Carmichael, D. R. "A Positional Analysis of Internal Control," *Journal of Accountancy,* February 1971, pp. 34–43.

REVIEW QUESTIONS

19.1. What is the difference between *unaudited financial statements* and *unaudited information* in a document containing audited financial statements?

19.2. Why do you think the SEC wants to see independent auditors involved with reviews of unaudited interim and replacement cost information?

19.3. Give at least six procedures an auditor should perform in a limited review of interim financial information.

19.4. Is a disclaimer of opinion required in an auditor's report on a limited review of interim financial information?

19.5. Explain the connection between auditors' responsibilities for "other information in documents containing audited financial statements" (*SAS No. 8,* Section 550) and responsibilities for unaudited interim financial information and replacement cost information.

19.6. If an independent auditor discovers that the scope of a GAO-type audit engagement goes beyond the examination of financial statements, what problems must the auditor resolve to continue with the engagement?

19.7. In a GAO-type audit engagement, what are the likely attributes of the auditor's report?

19.8. Identify the functions and responsibilities typically assigned to internal auditors.

19.9. What general characteristics do MAS engagement reports share with GAO and internal audit reports?

EXERCISES AND PROBLEMS

19.10. When unaudited financial statements are presented, it is not sufficient to simply mark each page "unaudited." A disclaimer of opinion must be attached.

However, footnotes (in audited financial statements) containing unaudited interim information and replacement cost information are usually labeled "unaudited." When management does not disclose the performance of any limited review, the audit opinion may be unqualified and contain no reference at all to the "unaudited" footnotes.

For Discussion:

This set of reporting guidelines seems to create a double standard regarding unaudited statements and certain types of unaudited information.

Can you give reasons why an explicit disclaimer is not always required whenever any kind of unaudited information appears in association with a CPA's name?

19.11. Ajax Pipefitting Company fabricates pipe joints and flow systems for customers. The joints are electrically welded, and Ajax uses a ZB40 x-ray machine to inspect the strength of the welds. Ajax bought its ZB40 three years ago for $60,000. Most such x-ray machines last ten years, so Ajax has recorded $6,000 depreciation expense for the current year—the third year the machine has been used.

A new ZB40 now costs $75,000. Ajax is planning to purchase a second one because no technologically improved machine is on the market.

When Ajax's accountants prepared the replacement cost information, the ZB40 was reflected as follows:

Machinery and equipment	$75,000
Accumulated depreciation................	22,500
Current year depreciation expense	7,500

Required:

a. Auditing standards specify some review procedures that an auditor should perform with regard to unaudited replacement cost information. With reference to the ZB40 machine, explain the procedures.

b. How do these procedures differ from those specified in auditing standards for a limited review of unaudited interim financial information?

19.12. The report excerpts reproduced below were taken from an audit performed by an association of consultants (one of which is a prominent public accounting firm) under a contract with a state auditor. The audit was a comprehensive study of the state's school construction program, one aspect of which was design review.

Criteria Used to Measure Efficiency and Economy

The design review branch of the department of general services is responsible for making design reviews for all the state's school construction. A minimum of four reviews is made of each school construction project. The department's standard is 15 days for each review.

Conditions Found by Auditor

The audit of the design review process disclosed that each design draft takes an average of 31 days for review as compared with the department's time standard of 15 days.

Effect of the Conditions

The total impact of this delay exceeds $14,000 for each $1 million of school construction.

Also, if lengthy design reviews prevent the architect from meeting his established schedule, the department of education may not be able to satisfy critical facility needs.

Causes of the Situation

The department of general services was not meeting its design review schedule because it lacked the needed data to perform reviews, the review process had unnecessary steps, and there was no follow-up to detect time lags in the review.

Required:

a. Refer to the GAO General Audit Standards (Chapter 2). What is the scope of the above audit? Explain.

b. Based on the above facts, draft a paragraph summarizing your recommendations for improvement suitable for inclusion in a report conforming to GAO audit standards. (Adapted from "Examples of Findings from Governmental Audits," U.S. General Accounting Office, 1973.)

19.13. Environmental Protection Agency auditors audited a three-year grant awarded to a state environmental service agency under the Federal Water Pollution Control Act (FWPCA) and reported that the state agency did not meet its objective. The grant required the development of a comprehensive pollution control and abatement plan for controlling water pollution in the state harbor. Excerpts from the report are reproduced below.

Goal of the Program

Section 3(c) of FWPCA established a program to make grants to a state or states not to exceed 50 percent of the administrative expenses of a planning agency for a period not to exceed three years, if such agency provides for adequate representation of appropriate state, interstate, local, or international interests in the basin, or portion thereof involved, and is capable of developing an effective, comprehensive water quality control and abatement plan for a basin.

The state agency was awarded a grant from January 1970 to January 1973 for developing a comprehensive pollution control and abatement plan to define the program to be used for controlling water pollution in the state harbor.

Condition Found by the Auditor

The review disclosed that the state agency had not accomplished grant objectives. A comprehensive pollution control and abatement plan for the state harbor had not yet been developed, although the three-year grant period had expired.

Effect of Not Meeting the Goal

A total of $196,000 in federal funds has been paid to the state agency for developing a plan; yet none of the major objectives have been accomplished.

Cause Which Contributed to Failure to Meet the Goal

In the auditors' opinion, the state agency's administration of the project was inadequate, and it did not make a concerted effort to complete the project. Although the agency defined five subgoals to achieve the objectives of the grant, none of the goals were completed, nor had substantial progress been made in their completion.

Required:

a. Refer to the GAO General Audit Standards (Chapter 2). What is the scope of the above audit? Explain.

b. Based on the above facts, draft a paragraph summarizing your recommendations for inclusion in a report conforming to GAO audit standards. (Adapted from "Examples of Findings from Governmental Audits," U.S. General Accounting Office, 1973.)

19.14. As an internal auditor for Foghorn Company, a medium-sized manufacturer of special machinery, you have recently completed an internal audit covering (1) procedures for materials requisition, (2) procedures for materials receipt and storage, (3) purchasing department duties, and (4) accounting department duties.

Prepare a report of your audit findings and recommendations which is to be sent to the president, K. L. McDonald. Your report should include identification of system weaknesses and recommended corrective actions, based on your summary of the audit findings shown below. In setting forth the weaknesses and recommendations, organize this part of your report around the four areas identified above.

Purchasing and Subsequent Procedures

After approval by manufacturing department foremen, material purchase requisitions are forwarded to the purchasing department supervisor who distributes such requisitions to the several employees under his control. The latter employees prepare prenumbered purchase orders in triplicate, account for all numbers, and send the original purchase order to the vendor. One copy of the purchase order is sent to the receiving department where it is used as a receiving report. The other copy is filed in the purchasing department.

When the materials are received, they are moved directly to the storeroom and issued to the foremen on informal requests. The receiving department sends a receiving report (with its copy of the purchase order attached) to the purchasing department and sends copies of the receiving report to the storeroom and to the accounting department.

Vendors' invoices for material purchases, received in duplicate in the mail room, are sent to the purchasing department and directed to the employee who placed the related order. The employee then compares the invoice with the copy of the purchase order on file in the purchasing department for price and terms and compares the invoice quantity with the quantity received as reported by the shipping and receiving department on its copy of the purchase order. The purchasing department employee also checks discounts, footings, and extensions and initials the invoice to indicate approval for payment. The invoice is then sent to the voucher section of the accounting department where it is coded for account distribution, assigned a voucher number, entered in the voucher register, and filed according to payment due date.

On payment dates prenumbered checks are requisitioned by the voucher section from the cashier and prepared except for signature. After the checks are prepared, they are returned to the cashier, who puts them through a check signing machine, accounts for the sequence of numbers, and passes them to the cash disbursements bookkeeper for entry in the cash disbursement book. The cash disbursements bookkeeper then returns the checks to the voucher section which then notes payment dates in the voucher register, places the checks in envelopes, and sends them to the mail room. The vouchers are then filed in numerical sequence. At the end of each month one of the voucher clerks prepares an adding machine tape of unpaid items in the voucher register and compares the total thereof with the general ledger balance and investigates any difference disclosed by such comparison.

20

COMMUNICATION WITH USERS—REPORTING HORIZONS

Auditors' reporting obligations are constantly under evaluation. Several recommendations and proposals for evolution and change are under consideration, some of which may be near to adoption, others quite far away. This chapter contains brief reviews of six areas that represent reporting horizons:

Accounting and review services.

Commission on Auditors' Responsibilities' communication recommendations.

Involvement with forecasts.

Involvement with price level-adjusted financial statements.

Involvement with current value financial statements.

Management audit reports.

ACCOUNTING AND REVIEW SERVICES

The topic of "accounting and review services" is an outgrowth of a long-running problem with *unaudited financial statements*. The profession was shocked by the court decision imposing monetary liability on an accountant in 1967 (See Appendix 4–A, *1136 Tenants' Corp.* v. *Max Rothenberg & Co.*) and met the problem by issuing auditing standards in 1967 ("Unaudited Financial Statements," *SAS No. 1*, Section 516), in 1970 ("Reporting When a CPA is Not Independent," *SAS No. 1*, Section 517), and in 1975 publishing the *Guide for Engagements of CPAs to Prepare Unaudited Financial Statements* (AICPA, 1975). The motivation behind these standards was two-fold: (1) Only one level of assurance was believed to be attainable—the assurance provided by performance of an audit in accordance with generally accepted auditing standards (GAAS) and (2) any CPA association short of an audit in accordance with GAAS should carry an explicit disclaimer in order to avoid legal liability problems.

The troublesome feature is that the unaudited statement standards are burdensome. Many small CPA firms conduct practice in "accounting and review services" for small business clients. These engagements include bookkeeping, financial statement preparation, and financial statement review to help small businesses prepare financial communications. Auditing standards that recognize only one level of assurance based on a full audit appeared to deny small clients the full benefit of the CPA's services.

The Moss and Metcalf investigations in 1977–78 highlighted the problem by centering attention on the idea that auditing standards handicapped the business of small CPA firms and their services to small business clients. The argument has become known as the "Big GAAS—Little GAAS" question. "Big GAAS" has been portrayed as the villain in the play under the proposition that existing standards were enacted under the influence of large CPA firms whose practice is centered on big business. Even though this proposition is not true, the fact is that small CPA firms *want* to give, and small businesses *want* to receive, some level of assurance as a result of accountants' work even though an audit in accordance with GAAS is not performed.

Recognizing the tenacity of the issue and the heat of congressional criticism, the AICPA formed a new senior technical committee in 1977—the Accounting and Review Services Committee. The committee has continuing responsibility to develop and issue pronouncements of standards concerning the services and reports a CPA may render in connection with unaudited financial statements of clients. The committee's authority extends only to CPA-client relationships with businesses that are *not* required to file financial statements with a regulatory agency (e.g., SEC). Thus the profession has: (1) the Auditing Standards Board (Auditing Standards Executive Committee until 1978) which promulgates standards that *must* be observed in engagements involving regulatory filings and in cases where the other committee has not enacted standards and (2) the Accounting and Review Services Committee which will issue standards pertinent to nonregulatory unaudited financial statements.

The new committee issued its first exposure draft in January 1978, entitled "Proposed Statement on Standards for Accounting and Review Services: Compilation and Review Services." *Compilation* services and *review* services represent two different kinds of engagements, both of which are less than a full audit.

In a *review services* engagement a CPA performs some procedures to achieve a level of assurance. This level is not the same as that which could be attained by performing an audit in accordance with GAAS. The objective of a review of financial statements, according to the exposure draft is:

> To achieve, through the performance of inquiry and analytical procedures, limited assurance that there are no material modifications that should be made to the statements in order for them to be in conformity with generally accepted accounting principles or, if applicable, with another comprehensive basis of accounting.

A review service does not provide a basis for expression of an opinion on financial statements. Each page of the financial statements should be marked "See Accompanying CPA's Report." The report on a complete review services engagement should include the following:

Statement that a review service was performed in accordance with standards promulgated by the AICPA.

Statement that a review service is substantially less in scope than an audit, and an opinion on financial statements is not expressed.

Statement that all information is the representation of management or owners of the business.

Statement that the CPA is not aware of any material modifications that should be made, or, if aware, a disclosure of departure(s) from generally accepted accounting principles.

A CPA who is not independent may not issue a review services report. However, a compilation report can be issued.

A *compilation service* is one in which the CPA performs few, if any, procedures, and it is substantially less than a review service. The objective of a compilation of financial statements, according to the exposure draft, is:

> To present in the form of financial statements information supplied by an entity without achieving any assurance as to whether there are material modifications that should be made to the statements in order for them to be in conformity with generally accepted accounting principles or, if applicable, with another comprehensive basis of accounting.

In a compilation service a CPA should read the financial statements, looking for obvious clerical or accounting principle errors, but no other procedures need be performed. Each page of the financial statements should be marked "See Accompanying CPA's Report." The report can be issued by a CPA who is not independent, if that fact is disclosed. The report should contain the following:

Statement that a compilation service has been performed.

Statement that all information is the representation of the management or owner(s) of the business.

Statement that a compilation service is limited to presentation of information supplied by management or owners without achievement by the CPA of any assurance as to whether any material modifications should be made to make them conform to generally accepted accounting principles or another comprehensive basis of accounting.

Two other report items may be included when applicable: (1) A statement that management or owners have elected to omit substantially all footnote-style disclosures, and if they were included, they might influence the users' conclusions about the business and (2) a statement that the CPA is not independent if such be the case.

COMMISSION ON AUDITORS' RESPONSIBILITIES

In its 1978 final *Report, Conclusions, and Recommendations* the Commission on Auditors' Responsibilities addressed three different areas. The recommendations shown below are under study by the AICPA. This project is expected to be quite long range.

Forming an Opinion[1]

The commission made the following conclusions and recommendations on areas that relate to current reporting practices. Their thrust is to raise the level of auditors' obligations respecting choice of accounting principles and content of the audit report.

> Numerous attempts have been made to analyze the meaning of the phrase in the auditor's report, "present fairly . . . in conformity with generally accepted accounting principles." A more useful approach is to explore the nature of generally accepted accounting principles and generally accepted auditing standards and to analyze the judgments and decisions they require. One of the most effective ways of describing, clarifying, or considering expansion of the auditor's responsibilities in forming an opinion on financial statements is to focus on the judgments and decisions that must be made about the selection and application of accounting principles. When this is done, the phrase "present fairly" becomes unnecessary, and it should be deleted from the auditor's report.
>
> Management's selection and application of accounting principles require decisions based on judgments as to the appropriateness of the principles to the underlying events or transactions considered both individually and collectively. The auditor is responsible for determining whether management's judgments were appropriate.
>
> The auditor's evaluation requires a decision if two or more alternative principles are generally accepted and criteria for selecting among them are insufficient. The auditor should analyze the underlying facts and circumstances to determine whether one of the alternatives would result in a presentation more closely in accord with the substance of a transaction or event.
>
> The mere absence of authoritative literature specifying how the choice among alternatives should be made is not sufficient grounds for the auditor to accept management's selection. He should not accept management's selection of an accounting principle simply because its use is not forbidden, and he should not accept management's rejection of a principle simply because it is not required.
>
> Accounting principles appropriate to individual circumstances may be

[1] Commission on Auditors' Responsibilities, Section 2, "Forming an Opinion on Financial Presentations" in *Report, Conclusions, and Recommendations* (New York: CAR, 1978), pp. 13–22. Copyright © 1978 by the American Institute of Certified Public Accountants, Inc.

selected and applied properly; yet the resulting financial statements as a whole may be biased or misleading. The auditor should make an evaluation of the cumulative effect of management's judgment in the presentation of financial statements.

Corporate Code of Conduct[2]

The commission ventured into a new field with recommendations about auditor involvement with corporations' statements of policy on corporate conduct. This area is one that has attracted a great deal of public interest. The principle recommendations are these:

> Corporations should be required to adopt statements of policy indicating in detail the conduct that will not be tolerated. The statement of policy should be made available to shareholders and should be distributed to the appropriate level of employees. Corporations should also adopt procedures to provide for effective monitoring of compliance.
>
> Until a requirement for adoption of a statement of policy on improper conduct is implemented by an appropriate body, corporations and their auditors are encouraged voluntarily to begin implementation of the commission's proposals.
>
> When a code of conduct has been adopted by the corporation, the auditor should be willing to provide users with assurance on whether a company is taking effective action to control illegal or questionable conduct. The auditor should review the company's code of conduct and the procedures adopted to monitor compliance with it. The auditor should determine whether there are material weaknesses in the related monitoring procedures and indicate his conclusion on these matters in his report.
>
> If a company has adopted a corporate code of conduct, the report by management in the annual report should include a statement that such a code exists and that procedures have been implemented to monitor compliance. The auditor's report should state that he has reviewed the company's code of conduct and should describe his review of the company's monitoring procedures and his conclusions on those aspects that can be audited.

Changing the Report[3]

One of the most radical of the commission's recommendations was to change substantially the form and content of the auditor's report. The commission saw the current standard short-form report as an "unread symbol" more like a Good Housekeeping Seal than a communication to users of financial statements. The major recommendation among the ones listed below is a dual report: (1) a report from management, plus (2) an auditor's report. The commission's suggested tentative management report is reproduced in Exhibit 20–1 and the suggested auditor's report in Exhibit 20–2. An innovative statement given by Olin Corporation management in that company's 1977 annual report is shown in Exhibit 20–3.

---

[2] Section 5, "Corporate Accountability and the Law," *Report, Conclusions, and Recommendations*, pp. 41–50.

[3] Section 7, "The Auditor's Communication with Users," *Report, Conclusions and Recommendations*, pp. 71–84.

Evidence abounds that communication between the auditor and users of his work—especially through the auditor's standard report—is unsatisfactory. The present report has remained essentially unchanged since 1948 and its shortcomings have often been discussed. Recent research suggests that many users misunderstand the auditor's role and responsibilities, and the present standard report only adds to the confusion. Users are unaware of the limitations of the audit function and are confused about the distinction between the responsibilities of management and those of the auditor.

The present means of communicating the work of the independent auditor to users has not kept pace with developments in auditing and the financial reporting environment. The acceptance and discharge of added responsibilities should be communicated by the auditor to the users of his work. The additional messages, for example, should cover other information in the annual report, association with interim information, internal accounting controls, corporate codes of conduct, and meetings with the audit committee of the company's board of directors.

Generally accepted accounting principles now make reporting on consistency management's, not the auditor's, responsibility. The auditor's proper function is to consider the propriety of management's accounting for changes in accounting principles and the adequacy of management's disclosures concerning consistency in the application of accounting principles, not to report that accounting principles have or have not been consistently applied. The illustration of a revised auditor's report in this section omits reference to consistency.

To facilitate implementation of the recommendation to eliminate the auditor's reference to consistency, another useful change would be for the Financial Accounting Standards Board to amend APB *Opinion No. 20* to require a standard note to the financial statements covering accounting changes. The note should disclose all changes that materially affect interperiod comparability, including both changes in accounting principles and changes in accounting estimates.

The commission recommends that the present method of referring to other auditors be eliminated. Either one of two means would provide users with sufficient information on the responsibilities taken. As is presently acceptable, the auditor can do enough additional work so that he does not need to refer to the other auditor. Alternatively, management could present the reports of the other auditors. If there are many reports from other auditors, management may appropriately list those reports that do not contain qualified or adverse opinions on any of the information reported on.

Reporting requirements should be made consistent by requiring the auditor to report on all unaudited financial information with which he is associated, including that appearing in a document containing audited financial statements.

INVOLVEMENT WITH FORECASTS

Ethics Rule 201 (*e*) prohibits the association of an accountant's name with a forecast of future transactions in a manner which may lead readers to the belief that the accountant vouches for the *achievability* of the forecast. Notice, however, that this prohibition is strictly limited to the matter of *achievability*. Accountants and auditors may be associated by name

EXHIBIT 20–1
Recommended Report by Management

Financial Statements

We prepared the accompanying consolidated balance sheet of XYZ Company as of December 31, 1976, and the related statements of consolidated income and changes in consolidated financial position for the year then ended, including the notes [or, (the named statements) have been prepared on our behalf by our independent auditor from the company's records and other relevant sources.]. The statements have been prepared in conformity with generally accepted accounting principles appropriate in the circumstances and necessarily include some amounts that are based on our best estimates and judgments. The financial information in the remainder of this annual report [or other document] is consistent with that in the financial statements.

Internal Accounting Controls

The company maintains an accounting system and related controls to provide reasonable assurance that assets are safeguarded against loss from unauthorized use or disposition and that financial records are reliable for preparing financial statements and maintaining accountability for assets. There are inherent limitations that should be recognized in considering the potential effectiveness of any system of internal accounting control. The concept of reasonable assurance is based on the recognition that the cost of a system of internal control should not exceed the benefits derived and that the evaluation of those factors requires estimates and judgments by management. The company's system provides such reasonable assurance. We have corrected all material weaknesses of the accounting and control systems identified by our independent auditors, Test Check & Co., Certified Public Accountants [or, We are in the process of correcting all material weaknesses . . .] [or, We have corrected some of the material weaknesses but have not corrected others because. . . .].

Other Matters

The functioning of the accounting system and related controls is under the general oversight of the board of directors [or the audit committee of the board of directors]. The members of the audit committee are associated with the company only through being directors. The accounting system and related controls are reviewed by an extensive program of internal audits and by the company's independent auditors. The audit committee [or the board of directors] meets regularly with the internal auditors and the independent auditors and reviews and approves their fee arrangements, the scope and timing of their audits, and their findings.

We believe that the company's position in regard to litigation, claims, and assessments is appropriately accounted for or disclosed in the financial statements. In this connection we have consulted with our legal counsel concerned with such matters and they concur with the presentation of the position.

The company has prepared and distributed to its employees a statement of its policies prohibiting certain activities deemed illegal, unethical, or against the best interests of the company. (The statement was included in the 197X annual report of the company; copies are available on request.) In consultation with our independent auditors we have developed and instituted additional internal controls and internal audit procedures designed to prevent or detect violations of those policies. We believe that the policies and procedures provide reasonable assurance that our operations are conducted in conformity with the law and with a high standard of business conduct.

EXHIBIT 20–1 (*continued*)

[If applicable, During the past year our independent auditors provided the company with certain nonaudit services. They advised us in the preparation of [or, if applicable, They prepared] the company's income tax return; they assisted in the design and installation of a new inventory control system; and they performed the actuarial computations in connection with the company's pension plan.]

[If applicable, The board of directors of the company in March 1976 engaged Super, Sede & Co., Certified Public Accountants, as our independent auditors to replace Test Check & Co., following disagreements on [accounting principles, disclosures, or the scope of the examination]. Test Check & Co. agrees with that description of disagreements.]

Source: Commission on Auditors' Responsibilities, *Report, Conclusions, and Recommendations* (New York: CAR, 1978), pp. 79–80. Copyright © by the American Institute of Certified Public Accountants, Inc.

with the underlying assumptions and calculations involved in forecasts as long as their reports do not indicate that the forecast results will actually be realized.

There are two important features of forecasts: (1) the underlying economic assumptions and (2) the accounting calculations and compilations that flow therefrom. Accountants should consider both of these features when defining their responsibilities. Taking responsibility for review of the reasonableness of the assumptions involves greater risk and responsibility than taking responsibility only for the resultant calculations.

EXHIBIT 20–2
Recommended Audit Report

Financial Statements

The accompanying consolidated balance sheet of XYZ Company as of December 31, 1976, and the related statements of consolidated income and changes in consolidated financial position for the year then ended, including the notes, are the representations of XYZ Company's management, as explained in the report by management.

In our opinion, those financial statements in all material respects present the financial position of XYZ Company at December 31, 1976, and the results of its operations and changes in financial position for the year then ended in conformity with generally accepted accounting principles appropriate in the circumstances.

We audited the financial statements and the accounting records supporting them in accordance with generally accepted auditing standards. Our audit included a study and evaluation of the company's accounting system and the related controls, tests of details of selected balances and transactions, and an analytical review of the information presented in the statements. We believe our auditing procedures were adequate in the circumstances to support our opinion.

EXHIBIT 20–2 (*continued*)

Other Financial Information

We reviewed the information appearing in the annual report [or other document], in addition to the financial statements, and found nothing inconsistent in such other information with the statements or the knowledge obtained in the course of our audits. [Any other information reviewed, such as replacement cost data, would be identified.]

We reviewed the interim information released during the year. Our reviews were conducted each quarter [or times as explained] and consisted primarily of making appropriate inquiries to obtain knowledge of the internal accounting control system, the process followed in preparing such information and of financial and operating developments during the periods, and determining that the information appeared reasonable in the light of the knowledge we obtained from our inquiries during the current year, from any procedures completed to the interim date in connection with our audit for such year, and from our audits for preceding years. Any adjustments or additional disclosures we recommended have been reflected in the information.

Internal Accounting Controls

Based on our study and evaluation of the accounting system and related controls, we concur with the description of the system and controls in the report by management [or, Based on our study and evaluation of the accounting system and controls over it, we believe the system and controls have the following uncorrected material weaknesses not described in the report by management. . .] [or other disagreements with the description of the system and controls in the report by management] [or a description of uncorrected material weaknesses found if there is no report by management]. Nevertheless, in the performance of most control procedures, errors can result from personal factors, and also control procedures can be circumvented by collusion or overridden. Projection of any evaluation of internal accounting control to future periods is subject to the risk that changes in conditions may cause procedures to become inadequate and the degree of compliance with them to deteriorate.

Other Matters

We reviewed the company's policy statement on employee conduct, described in the report by management, and reviewed and tested the related controls and internal audit procedures. While no controls or procedures can prevent or detect all individual misconduct, we believe the controls and internal audit procedures have been appropriately designed and applied during the year.

We met with the audit committee [or the board of directors] of XYZ Company as often as we thought necessary to inform it of the scope of our audit and to discuss any significant accounting or auditing problems encountered and any other services provided to the company [or indication of failure to meet or insufficient meetings or failure to discuss pertinent problems].

Test Check & Co.
Certified Public Accountants

Source: Commission on Auditors' Responsibilities, *Report, Conclusions, and Recommendations* (New York: CAR, 1978), pp. 77–79. Copyright © 1978 by the American Institute of Certified Public Accountants, Inc.

EXHIBIT 20–3
Illustration of a Management Responsibility Statement

Responsibility for Financial Statements

The management of Olin Corporation is responsible for the integrity of its consolidated financial statements and their preparation in accordance with generally accepted accounting principles. To fulfill this responsibility requires the maintenance of sound accounting systems supported by strong internal controls. The company believes it has sound accounting systems and a high level of internal control which are maintained by the recruitment and training of qualified personnel, appropriate divisions of responsibility, the development and communication of accounting and other procedures, and comprehensive internal audits.

Our independent public accountants are engaged to examine, and to render an opinion on, the fairness of our consolidated financial statements in conformity with generally accepted accounting principles. Their opinion appears on this page. Our independent public accountants evaluate the effectiveness of our internal accounting control systems, review selected transactions and carry out other auditing procedures before expressing their opinion on our financial statements.

The Board of Directors has appointed an Audit Committee composed of outside directors which meets with the independent public accountants, management, and the internal auditors periodically to review the work of each. The public accountants and the company's internal audit department have free access to meet with the Audit Committee without management's presence.

Source: Olin Corporation Annual Report, 1977, p. 35.

Reports on Forecasts in the United Kingdom

In 1969, as a reaction to frequent takeover bid and merger activity in Great Britain, an accounting group introduced standards of practice related to presentation of forecast information. In brief the standards require that where forecasts appear in a circular addressed to shareholders in connection with a takeover bid or merger offer (1) the assumptions upon which the directors have based their profit forecasts must be stated in the document and (2) the accounting bases and calculations for the forecasts must be examined and reported on by the auditors or consultant accountants.[4]

The U.K. standards thus officially limit the accountants' reports to the accounting bases and calculations. An example of the reports appearing in a British offering circular is shown in Exhibit 20–4.

Even though responsibility is limited to accounting bases and calculations and their consistency with underlying assumptions, British accountants report that they are concerned with the reasonableness of the as-

[4] The Institute of Chartered Accountants in England and Wales, "Accountants' Reports on Profit Forecasts," July 1969.

EXHIBIT 20–4
Reports on a British Profit Forecast

Disclosure by Directors

(*a*) Assumptions—The forecast has been arrived at on the assumptions that there will be no significant changes in exchange rates from those ruling at 30 June, 1977, and no changes in legislation nor serious industrial disputes which could have material effect on the forecast.

(*b*) Bases—

(i) The forecast includes the nine months interim results ended 30 June 1977.

(ii) Airco, Inc., has not been asked to make a formal forecast of profits for the year to 30 September, 1977, instead BOC has included within its group forecast the Group's share of the Airco, Inc., published quarterly profit before tax for the nine months ended 30 June, 1977, amounting to £14.7 million, together with BOC's assessment of Airco's likely result for the September quarter 1977.

(*c*) The following are copies of letters from Coopers & Lybrand and Lazard Brothers Co., Limited, concerning the profit forecast—

Report of Auditors

The Directors,
BOC International, Limited

Dear Sirs,

We have reviewed the accounting bases and calculations for the Group profit forecast of BOC International, Limited, for the year ending 30 September, 1977, referred to on page 2 of the Rights Issue document to be dated 8 September, 1977, with the exception of those for the results of Airco, Inc., included therein. The Group forecast, for which the Directors are solely responsible, includes results shown by the unaudited accounts for the nine months ended 30 June, 1977.

Apart from the results of Airco, Inc., which we have not reviewed, in our opinion the Group forecast, so far as the accounting bases and calculations are concerned, has been properly compiled on the basis of the assumptions made by the Directors set out on page 10 of the Rights Issue document to be dated 8 September, 1977, and is presented on a basis consistent with the accounting policies normally adopted by the Group.

Yours truly,
COOPERS & LYBRAND,
Chartered Accountants
September 2, 1977

Report of Underwriters

The Directors,
BOC International, Limited

Dear Sirs,

We write with reference to the Rights Issue document to be dated 8 September, 1977, addressed to the Ordinary shareholders of BOC International, Limited, which includes a profit forecast of the Group (treating Airco, Inc., on the basis explained

EXHIBIT 20–4 (*continued*)

therein) for the year ending 30 September, 1977, referred to on page 2 of the document.

We have discussed with officers of your Company the assumptions which form the basis on which the profit forecast has been made, and we have also considered the letter addressed to yourselves from Coopers & Lybrand, regarding the accounting bases and calculations underlying such forecast.

As a result of the discussions we have had with officers of your Company, and in the light of the letter from Coopers & Lybrand, we have formed the opinion that the forecast of the Group's profit for the year ending 30 September, 1977, for which you are solely responsible, has been prepared with due care and consideration.

Yours faithfully,
Lazard Brothers & Co., Limited
September 2, 1977

sumptions on which a forecast is based. Lacking satisfaction as to reasonableness, British accountants reportedly either withhold the report on the forecast or issue a qualified report (pointing out the unreasonable assumptions(s)).[5]

Forecasts in the United States

Until 1973 the SEC prohibited earnings forecasts in statements filed with the Commission. However, there was public dissatisfaction over the uneven dissemination of forecast information by companies. Thus, the SEC changed its rules to permit (but not require) forecasts in statements and required companies that released forecast information to release it publicly and not to just a few favored analysts. At that time, however, the SEC *prohibited* any association of auditors' names and reports with the forecasts.

The times changed, however, and in 1975 the SEC proposed new rules to the effect that (1) companies that made public disclosure of forecast information would be required to file certain data about the forecasts with the Commission and (2) if a company represented that a third-party review had been performed (e.g., by a CPA firm), the reviewer's report would have to be filed. The proposed rules were not popular, received considerable criticism, and were withdrawn. Late in 1978 the SEC adopted new voluntary guidelines designed to encourage corporate forecasts, and accountants may perform and report on a "review" of the forecast.

A blue-ribbon SEC Advisory Committee on Corporate Disclosure completed its work in 1978 and recommended more attention to disclosure of "soft" information such as forecasts. The atmosphere may be a little more

[5] D. R. Carmichael, "Reporting on Forecasts: A U.K. Perspective," *Journal of Accountancy*, January 1973, pp. 39–40.

EXHIBIT 20–5
Accountant's Report on a Forecast

New Jersey Sports and Exposition Authority
1100 Raymond Boulevard
Newark, New Jersey 07102

Gentlemen:

The projections of annual operating cash flows for the sports complex to be built at the Hackensack Meadowlands site by the New Jersey Sports and Exposition Authority, which you have engaged us to prepare, are in the attached report. The report includes descriptions of the approach, assumptions made, and results. The scope of the projections includes:

Annual operating receipts, expenditures, and net cash flow from the specified 100 nights of harness and 60 days of thoroughbred racing at the racetrack.

Annual operating receipts, expenditures, and net cash flow from the football stadium.

Annual operating expenditures related to the overall operation and administration of the planned complex as it relates to the racetrack and stadium.

It is our understanding that these projections will be used by the Authority together with land and construction cost estimates and other information furnished by separate parties to evaluate the financial feasibility of the complex.

The projections have, of course, been prepared from estimates based on numerous assumptions about current and future events. However, since the time that the assumptions underlying the projections were originally identified and evaluated, a shortage of petroleum products and other forms of energy has apparently occurred. It is not possible to measure the effect of this apparent shortage on the underlying assumptions, and consequently, we are unable to express an opinion as to their reasonableness. Further, because all projections are based on assumptions about circumstances and events that have not yet taken place, these projections are subject to the variations that may arise as future operations actually occur. Accordingly, we cannot express an opinion as to whether the projected results will be attained.

Very truly yours,
Touche Ross & Co.
December 13, 1973

congenial than it was in 1975 because two publications have had time to circulate, and CPAs may have had more time to decide what kind of involvement with forecasts is feasible. The two publications are:

Statement of Position on *Presentation and Disclosure of Financial Forecasts* (AICPA Accounting Standards Executive Committee, August 1975).

Management Advisory Services Executive Committee. *Guidelines for Systems for the Preparation of Financial Forecasts.* Guideline Series No. 3 (AICPA, 1975).

The Commission on Auditors' Responsibilities spoke on the issue of forecasts, making the observation that the process of preparing forecast information is not as standardized as it is for other accounting information. The Commission seems to believe that reviews could be made by auditors when some reasonable degree of standardization is developed on the type of information to be used for input, processing, recording, and documenting forecasts. However, the development of such standards, according to the Commission, is presently in a primitive state.

Even though auditors have not been associated with business forecasts for profit-organized entities, they have not avoided association with documents for securities of governmental and nonprofit organizations. Accountants' reports have appeared in prospectuses offering bonds for such organizations as hospitals and governmental projects. A report on one such forecast is shown in Exhibit 20–5.

INVOLVEMENT WITH NEW ACCOUNTING MEASUREMENTS

The FASB has begun a new series of statements on Financial Accounting Concepts. This series is the product of the project known as the "Conceptual Framework for Financial Accounting and Reporting," which is a massive reexamination of the foundations of accounting. The project is the locus of "inflation accounting" studies in the United States.

The United Kingdom and Australian accountants led the world with studies and reports on inflation accounting, mainly because those two countries experienced rapid rates of price change in 1973–75. The Sandilands and Morpeth committees in the U.K. developed an exposure draft calling for current cost accounting, but the effort lost some steam in 1977 when accountants voted to make such accounting voluntary rather than mandatory. The accountants in Australia adopted a provisional accounting standard calling for a form of current cost accounting.

In the United States the study of alternatives goes on. The principal candidates for supplementary nonhistorical cost financial statements are price level-adjusted financial statements and current value accounting statements.

Price Level-Adjusted Statements

The accounting framework for price level-adjusted financial statements is found in APB *Statement No. 3*, "Financial Statements Restated for General Price Level Changes" (1969), and in an FASB exposure draft released in 1974. The FASB exposure draft entitled "Financial Reporting in Units of General Purchasing Power" was withdrawn when SEC *Accounting Series Release No. 190* was issued, and the whole question was deferred to the outcome of the conceptual framework project.

No explicit standards exist to guide auditors' involvement with price level-adjusted statements except for one bare mention in *SAS No. 14* ("Special Reports," Section 621). Section 621.04 (*d*) defines as one of the "comprehensive bases of accounting other than generally accepted accounting principles" the following:

> A definite set of criteria having substantial support that is applied to all material items appearing in financial statements, such as the price-level basis of accounting described in *Accounting Principles Board Statement No. 3*.

Thus auditors can render a "special report" on price level-adjusted financial statements. The financial statements and audit report in Exhibit 20–6 is an example of auditor's involvement with such statements.

Current Value Statements

Accounting theorists have for a long time favored various measurements in current value accounting, including discounted present value of cash flows, entry values (replacement cost, current cost), and exit values (disposal value, current cash equivalent). Measurement by anything other than historical cost received little notice from the practicing profession until the mid-1970s when five things happened: (1) United States and worldwide inflation accelerated, (2) critics voiced loud discontent with historical cost measurement, (3) British, Australian, Dutch, and other accountants started promoting accounting measurement alternatives, (4) the SEC issued *Accounting Series Release No. 190*, and (5) the FASB Conceptual Framework for Financial Accounting and Reporting moved into the phase of considering measurement bases, including some kinds of current value accounting.

The state of the art in 1978 (and probably for some years to come) is that companies presenting current value information will have to write their own full disclosures of the measurement methods used and their rationale for using them. The *basis of accounting* may differ from one company to another. Nevertheless, auditors may render reports on such information. An example of condensed financial statements and an auditor's report is shown in Exhibit 20–7. The first, fourth, and fifth paragraphs of the auditor's report relate specifically to the special report on the current value financial statements.

MANAGEMENT AUDIT REPORTS

Auditing history is replete with appeals from time to time to "extend the attest function." The ultimate goal is unmistakable. Persons who seek extension want auditors to lend credibility to, and take partial responsibility for, representations made by management that are not already attested.

Perhaps the most radical extension contemplated to date is auditor involvement with reporting on the adequacy of management. Lacking a better term, this proposal for extension has been called "independent audit of management." In essence, the audit of management, in full form, proposes to incorporate all the information and operations of various information sources into an *auditor's evaluative report on the management of an enterprise*. This form of evaluation report is altogether different from conventional attestation reports.

EXHIBIT 20–6

INDIANA TELEPHONE CORPORATION
Consolidated Statements of Income
For the Years Ended December 31, 1976 and 1975

	Column A Historical Cost		*Column B Historical Cost Restated to Current Purchasing Power*	
	1976	*1975*	*1976*	*1975*
Operating Revenues:				
Local service	$ 9,823,102	$ 8,995,077	$10,017,668	$ 9,713,407
Toll service	9,477,156	8,494,729	9,664,870	9,173,103
Miscellaneous	764,252	653,622	779,390	705,819
Total Operating Revenues	$20,064,510	$18,143,428	$20,461,928	$19,592,329
Operating Expenses:				
Depreciation and amortization, Notes 1(c) and 7	$ 3,861,825	$ 3,517,540	$ 5,718,137	$ 5,452,409
Equipment lease expense, Note 9	47,872	—	48,870	—
Maintenance	3,342,797	2,768,997	3,409,008	2,990,125
Total Depreciation, Maintenance and Other	$ 7,252,494	$ 6,286,537	$ 9,176,015	$ 8,442,534
Traffic	1,433,369	1,380,068	1,461,760	1,490,278
Commercial	1,076,834	984,722	1,098,163	1,063,360
General and administrative	2,267,556	2,313,362	2,330,089	2,511,934
State, local and miscellaneous federal taxes	1,444,843	1,343,502	1,473,461	1,450,791
Federal income taxes, Notes 1(d) and 6—				
Currently payable	726,622	721,059	812,786	778,641
Deferred until future years	355,000	821,000	362,032	889,543
Deferred investment tax credit (net)	918,004	594,705	893,716	607,089
Total Operating Expenses	$15,474,722	$14,444,955	$17,608,022	$17,234,170
Operating Income	$ 4,589,788	$ 3,698,473	$ 2,853,906	$ 2,358,159

Nonoperating (income) and Expenses:				
Interest on long-term debt	$ 2,400,209	$ 1,516,284	$ 2,447,750	$ 1,637,372
Other deductions	268,917	231,694	267,844	244,867
Allowance for funds used during construction, Note 1(f)	(196,170)	(213,612)	(200,056)	(230,671)
Other income	(587,735)	(235,631)	(599,377)	(254,448)
Federal income taxes	53,150	(103,064)	(54,203)	(111,294)
Gain from retirement of long-term debt through operation of sinking funds	(16,181)	(28,114)	(16,502)	(30,360)
Price-level gain from retirement of long-term debt, Note 1(a)—				
From operation of sinking funds	—	—	(180,010)	(175,104)
From maturities	—	—	—	(332,630)
Gain from retirement of preferred stock through operation of sinking funds	(11,154)	(11,517)	(11,375)	(12,437)
Price-level gain from retirement of preferred stock, Note 1(a)	—	—	(39,592)	(37,743)
Price-level (gain) loss from monetary items, Note 1(a)	—	—	103,388	(59,491)
Total Nonoperating (income) and Expenses	$ 1,911,036	$ 1,156,040	$ 1,826,273	$ 638,061
Net Income, Note 1(*a*)	$ 2,678,752	$ 2,542,433	$ 1,027,633	$ 1,720,098
Preferred stock dividends	95,640	94,173	97,535	101,694
Earnings Applicable to Common Stock	$ 2,583,112	$ 2,448,260	$ 930,098	$ 1,618,404
Earnings per Common Share, Note 4	$ 5.04	$ 4.78	$ 1.82	$ 3.16

EXHIBIT 20–6 (*concluded*)

Auditors' Report

To the Shareholders of Indiana Telephone Corporation:

We have examined the consolidated statements of assets and capital of INDIANA TELEPHONE CORPORATION (an Indiana corporation) and subsidiary and the corporate statements of assets and capital of INDIANA TELEPHONE CORPORATION as of December 31, 1976 and 1975, and the related consolidated and corporate statements of income, retained earnings, and changes in financial position for the years then ended. Our examination was made in accordance with generally accepted auditing standards and, accordingly, included such tests of the accounting records and such other auditing procedures as we considered necessary in the circumstances.

As discussed more fully in Note 8 to the consolidated and corporate financial statements, a proceeding between Indiana Telephone Corporation and Indiana Bell Telephone Company, Incorporated, relating to settlements between the two companies for jointly used message toll and special services facilities is pending in the Public Service Commission of Indiana. As a result of this proceeding, Indiana Telephone Corporation may be entitled to receive additional settlement revenues retroactive to January 1, 1974. Whether any such additional revenues will be allowed is not now determinable.

In our opinion, subject to the effect of such adjustment, if any, as may be required as a result of the matter referred to above, the accompanying financial statements shown under Column A present fairly the financial positions of Indiana Telephone Corporation and subsidiary and of Indiana Telephone Corporation as of December 31, 1976 and 1975, and the results of their operations and the changes in their financial position for the years then ended, in conformity with generally accepted accounting principles consistently applied during the periods.

In our opinion, however, subject to the effect of such adjustment, if any, as may be required as a result of the matter referred to above, the accompanying financial statements shown under Column B more fairly present the financial positions of Indiana Telephone Corporation and subsidiary and of Indiana Telephone Corporation as of December 31, 1976 and 1975, and the results of their operations and the changes in their financial position for the years then ended, as recognition has been given to changes in the purchasing power of the dollar, on the basis explained in Note 1(a).

Indianapolis, Indiana
February 11, 1977

ARTHUR ANDERSEN & CO.

A number of fundamental questions must be studied when considering independent audits of management by CPAs. They include:

Generally accepted auditing standards and procedures for management audits.

Kinds of financial data and other informational materials to be covered in such audits.

A body of standards for the evaluation of managerial abilities and performance.

Competence of auditors to conduct and report on such audits.

Auditor independence and objectivity in management auditing.

Legal liability of auditors with regard to such audits.[6]

These issues have been studied by a wide variety of persons in an eclectic manner, and very little has been done to formulate a cohesive statement relating to performance of management audits. However, one proposal for an opinion on management performance has been suggested, and it is reproduced in Exhibit 20–8 as a means of summarizing the issues involved in audits of management.

In a more conventional context, auditors may be moving toward deeper involvement with management issues in areas other than "independent audits of management." The GAO statement of three auditing areas points toward audits that resemble evaluations of management performance, or at least evaluations of managerial decisions. In connection with their review of the GAO audit standards, the AICPA Committee on Relations with the GAO concluded on the following note, which is also a fitting conclusion for the final chapter of this text.

> Audits of government activities provide both opportunities and challenges to the public accounting profession. Government agencies, CPAs, and others must deal with the need to develop techniques for measuring economy, efficiency, and effectiveness, including techniques for measuring social considerations such as the success of an educational or environmental improvement program. Responding to this need will undoubtedly require much study and considerable time. The profession should be willing to work with government agencies and others toward developing measurement criteria and audit techniques.
>
> The accounting profession should also consider developing professional study courses on the subject of auditing for efficiency, economy, and effectiveness and should consider whether standards are needed for reliance on nonaccounting experts. In this latter connection, the profession should not neglect to consider the extent to which reporting on efficiency, economy, and effectiveness falls within the area of expertise of CPAs.
>
> The members of this committee agree with the philosophy and objectives advocated by the GAO in its standards and believe that the GAO's broadened definition of auditing is a logical and worthwhile continuation of the evolution and growth of the auditing discipline.

[6] T. G. Secoy, "A CPA's Opinion on Management Performance," *Journal of Accountancy*, July 1971, p. 53. Copyright © 1971 by the American Institute of Certified Public Accountants, Inc.

EXHIBIT 20–7
Current Value Statements and Auditor's Report

THE ROUSE COMPANY AND SUBSIDIARIES
Consolidated Cost Basis and Current Value
Balance Sheet (condensed)
December 31, 1977

	Current Value Basis	*Cost Basis*
Assets		
Operating properties (note A):		
Current value	$461,794,000	
Cost		$366,556,000
Less accumulated depreciation		60,323,000
		$306,233,000
Other property	67,568,000	64,920,000
Other assets	74,454,000	74,454,000
Total	$603,816,000	$445,607,000
Liabilities, Deferred Credits and Shareholders' Equity		
Debt	$390,997,000	$390,997,000
Deferred income taxes (note B)	21,900,000	650,000
Other liabilities and deferred credits	30,314,000	30,314,000
Shareholders' equity:		
Book cost	23,646,000	23,646,000
Revaluation equity	136,959,000	
Total Shareholders' Equity	$160,605,000	$ 23,646,000
Total	$603,816,000	$445,607,000

Consolidated Current Value Basis Statement
of Changes in Revaluation Equity
December 31, 1977

	Year Ended December 31, 1977	Seven Months Ended December 31, 1976 (as restated, note 2)
Revaluation equity at beginning of period, as previously reported	$ 122,249	$ 112,873
Cumulative effect of change in accounting for leases (note 2)	(948)	(1,195)
Present value of income taxes related to revaluation equity (note 1)	(17,800)	(16,400)
Revaluation equity at beginning of period, as restated	$ 103,501	$ 95,278
Changes in revaluation equity during period:		
Increase in value of properties in operation at beginning of period	$ 25,602	$ 6,160
Value of new projects opened during period	10,745	2,926
Increase (decrease) in value of mortgage banking operations notes receivable	(262)	244
Increase in replacement cost of other property, net of related accumulated depreciation	823	293
Increase in present value of income taxes, net of increase in cost basis deferred taxes	(3,450)	(1,400)
Net change in revaluation equity during period	$ 33,458	$ 8,223
Revaluation equity at end of period	$ 136,959	$ 103,501

Note A: Only properties in operation at December 31, 1977, have been appraised. Properties under development but not yet open have been carried at their cost.

Note B: New methodology has been utilized in establishing a provision against current value shareholders' equity—to reflect the estimated present value of potential future income taxes.

EXHIBIT 20–7 (*continued*)

The Board of Directors
The Rouse Company:

We have examined the consolidated cost basis and current value basis balance sheets of the Rouse Company and subsidiaries as of December 31, 1977 and 1976, and the related consolidated cost basis statements of operations, shareholders' equity, changes in financial position, and current value basis statements of changes in revaluation equity for the year ended December 31, 1977, and the seven months ended December 31, 1976. Our examinations were made in accordance with generally accepted auditing standards and, accordingly, included such tests of the accounting records and such other auditing procedures as we considered necessary in the circumstances. We did not examine the consolidated financial statements of Rouse-Wates, Incorporated, and subsidiaries (Rouse-Wates) as of and for the seven months ended December 31, 1976, which were examined by other auditors whose qualified report thereon has been furnished to us, and our opinion expressed herein, insofar as it relates to the amounts included for Rouse-Wates for 1976, is based upon the report of the other auditors except as described below.

As explained in Note 8 to the consolidated financial statements, Rouse-Wates' financial statements for 1977 and 1976 have been prepared on a liquidation basis, and reserves have been provided for estimated losses on the disposal of assets. The opinion of the other auditors on the financial statements of Rouse-Wates for 1976 is "subject to the effect on the financial statements of any adjustments, which in our judgment could be material, arising because of differences between the estimates referred to (above) and the actual amounts ultimately realized or incurred and subject to the Rouse Company making additional advances as needed to enable the company (Rouse-Wates) to meet the obligations to its creditors."

In our report dated February 15, 1977, our opinion on the consolidated financial statements of the Rouse Company and subsidiaries for 1976 was qualified as being subject to the effect thereon of the matters underlying the qualification of the other auditors described above. As explained in Note 8, during 1977 Rouse-Wates disposed of several properties and obtained commitments for the disposition of certain other properties on terms which established the adequacy of the previously recorded reserves for estimated losses and the reserves for estimated losses on the remaining properties are considered adequate as of December 31, 1977. Also as explained in Note 8, additional advances were made to Rouse-Wates by the Rouse Company during 1977 and any additional advances which may be needed will be funded by the Rouse Company. Accordingly, we do not qualify our present opinion on the consolidated financial statements.

As more fully described in Note 1, the current value basis financial statements supplement the financial statements prepared on a cost basis. However, they are not intended to present financial position and changes in shareholders' equity in conformity with generally accepted accounting principles. In our opinion, such current value basis financial statements provide relevant financial information about the company which is not provided by the cost basis financial statements.

In our opinion, based upon our examinations and for 1976 the report of the other auditors as described above, the aforementioned consolidated cost basis financial statements present fairly the financial position of the Rouse Company and subsidiaries at December 31, 1977 and 1976, and the results of their operations and the changes in their financial position for the year ended December 31, 1977, and the seven months ended December 31, 1976, in conformity with generally accepted accounting principles; and the consolidated current value basis financial statements present fairly the information set forth therein at December 31, 1977 and 1976, and for the year ended December 31, 1977, and the seven months ended December 31, 1976, on the basis of accounting described in Note 1. The aforementioned accounting principles and current value basis of accounting have been applied on a consistent basis after restatement for the changes, with which we concur, in the method of accounting for leases as described in Note 2(d) and the method of accounting for income taxes in the current value basis financial statements as described in Note 1.

February 24, 1978

Peat, Marwick, Mitchell & Co.

EXHIBIT 20–8
Proposed Opinion on Management Performance

To the Audit Committee of the Board of Directors and the Stockholders of XYZ Manufacturing Corporation:

We have investigated the management of XYZ Manufacturing Corporation for the year ended December 31, 1970. In carrying out our investigation, we focused on the following areas: the organizational structure of the company; the information system; the system of managerial controls and procedures; and the managerial plans, policies, and goals for the year under investigation. Our investigation did not include managerial forecasts of earnings and cash flows, or the projected results of planned projects, operations, and financial position in future years.

In conducting our investigation and evaluating managerial performance, we used objective research procedures and available standards, both absolute and comparative, which we considered necessary and appropriate in the circumstances.

In our judgment, XYZ Manufacturing Corporation was managed with reasonable efficiency during the year ended December 31, 1970, judged in the light of our findings and the circumstances in which the company operated during that year.

Your attention is called to the report on our examination of the financial statements of the company for the year ended December 31, 1970, on page 10 of this annual report.

A summary of the major findings of our investigation follows. First, the systems of informational, financial, and operational controls and procedures were found to be well established and working on a basis consistent with the organizational structure of the company. There were good relationships among the various levels of management, and the management personnel displayed mutual respect and empathy in their work. There was convincing evidence of a satisfactory degree of motivation at all levels of management.

Second, the plans, policies, and goals of management for the year were evaluated and found to be reasonable and attainable. The organizational structure fostered the attainment of the goals, while the plans and policies were found to be efficiently designed and implemented.

Third, the most important opportunity for improving management was found in the areas of the information system. We found several cases in which information communicated from lower supervisory levels was either incomplete, irrelevant, or so classified and summarized that it did not provide an adequate basis for decision making. As a result, additional costs were incurred to obtain adequate information, decisions were often delayed, and faulty decisions were made. We have provided management with a detailed description of this deficiency, a list of the actions we recommend to overcome it, and have been assured that they will be implemented immediately.

It will be understood that our firm assumes no responsibility for the activities of the management of the company or the results of such activities.

John Doe & Company
Certified Public Accountants
February 21, 1971

Source: T. G. Secoy, "A CPA's Opinion on Management Performance," *Journal of Accountancy*, July 1971, p. 59.

SOURCES AND ADDITIONAL READING REFERENCES

Asebrook, R. J., and Carmichael, D. R. "Reporting on Forecasts: A Survey of Attitudes," *Journal of Accountancy,* August 1973.

Belda, B. J. "Reporting on Forecasts of Future Developments," *Journal of Accountancy,* December 1970, pp. 54–58.

Bissell, G. S. "A Professional Investor Looks at Earnings Forecasts," *Financial Analysts Journal,* May/June 1972, pp. 73–78.

Brown, R. G. "Ethical and Other Problems in Publishing Financial Forecasts," *Financial Analysts Journal,* March/April 1972, pp. 38–45.

Burton, John C. "Management Auditing," *Journal of Accountancy,* May 1968, pp. 41–46.

———. "Fair Presentation: Another View," *The CPA Journal,* June 1975, pp. 13–19.

Carmichael, D. R. "Reporting on Forecasts: A U.K. Perspective," *Journal of Accountancy,* January 1973, pp. 36–47.

———. "The Attest Function—Auditing at the Crossroads," *Journal of Accountancy,* September 1974, pp. 64–72.

Commission on Auditors' Responsibilities, *Report, Conclusions, and Recommendations.* New York: CAR, 1978.

Cummings, Joseph P. "Financial Forecasts and the Certified Public Accountant: A Statement to the SEC." Peat, Marwick, Mitchell & Co., November 1972.

Gregory, Wm. R. "Unaudited, But O.K.?" *Journal of Accountancy,* February 1978, pp. 61–65.

Guy, Dan M. "Auditing Projected Financial Statements," *Management Accounting,* November 1972, pp. 33–38.

———. "A Proposed Statement of Audit Responsibility for Projected Financial Statements," *CPA Journal,* December 1972, pp. 1009–19.

Ijiri, Yuji. "On Budgeting Principles and Budget-Auditing Standards," *Accounting Review,* October 1968, pp. 662–67.

Institute of Chartered Accountants in England and Wales. *Accountant's Reports on Profit Forecasts,* July 1969.

Lahey, J. M. "Toward a More Understandable Auditor's Report," *Journal of Accountancy,* April 1972, pp. 48–53.

Langenderfer, H. Q., and Robertson, J. C. "A Theoretical Structure for Independent Audits of Management," *Accounting Review,* October 1969, pp. 777–87.

Management Advisory Services Executive Committee. *Guidelines for Systems for the Preparation of Financial Forecasts.* Guideline Series No. 3. AICPA, 1975.

———. *Guidelines for Participation in Government Audit Engagements to Evaluate Economy, Efficiency, and Program Results.* Guideline Series No. 6. AICPA, 1977.

Mautz, R. K., and Sharaf, Hussein A. *The Philosophy of Auditing,* American Accounting Association Monograph No. 6. American Accounting Assn., 1961.

New York Stock Exchange, Inc. "Recommendations and Comments on Financial Reporting to Shareholders and Related Matters." A White Paper, 1973.

Norgaard, C. T. "Extending the Boundaries of the Attest Function," *Accounting Review,* July 1972, pp. 433–42.

Revsine, Lawrence. "The Preferability Dilemma," *Journal of Accountancy,* September 1977, pp. 80–89.

Robertson, J. C., and Clarke, R. W. "Verification of Management Representations: A First Step toward Independent Audits of Management," *Accounting Review,* July 1971, pp. 562–71.

Secoy, T. G. "A CPA's Opinion on Management Performance," *Journal of Accountancy,* July 1971, pp. 53–59.

Shank, J. K., and Calfee, J. B., Jr. "Case of the Fuqua Forecast," *Harvard Business Review,* November-December 1973.

Sommer, A. A. "Reporting Obligations of the Financial Executive," *Financial Executive,* March 1974, pp. 25–29.

Unaudited Financial Statements Task Force, *Guide For Engagements of CPAs to Prepare Unaudited Financial Statements.* AICPA, 1975.

Willingham, J. J.; Smith, C. H.; and Taylor, M. E. "Should the CPA's Opinion Be Extended to Include Forecasts?" *Financial Executive,* September 1970, pp. 80–89.

REVIEW QUESTIONS

20.1. Discuss the influences and pressures that led to creation of the Accounting and Review Services Committee.

20.2. In what area(s) of practice are Accounting and Review Service Committee pronouncements applicable?

20.3. What is the difference between a *review services engagement* and a *compilation service engagement*? Compare both of these to an *audit engagement*.

20.4. How would you characterize the Commission on Auditors' Responsibilities' recommendations regarding the topics of (*a*) "forming an opinion," (*b*) "corporate code of conduct," and (*c*) "changing the report?"

20.5. What auditing standards govern the form and content of a report on price level-adjusted financial statements? Current value financial statements?

20.6. What restrictions are placed upon auditors' association with forecasts by Ethics Rule 201(e)?

20.7. In the United Kingdom, to what aspects of a forecast is the audit directed? Explain the U.K. auditor's responsibility for the assumptions upon which a forecast is based.

20.8. What problem areas have been identified with respect to attesting to forecasts?

20.9. What fundamental areas have been suggested to require further study in connection with independent audits of management by CPAs?

EXERCISES AND PROBLEMS

20.10. You have been engaged by the Coffin brothers to compile their financial schedules from books and records maintained by James Coffin. The brothers own and operate three auto parts stores in Central City, and even though their business is growing, they have not wanted to employ a full-time bookkeeper. James specifies that all he wants is a balance sheet, a statement of operations, and a statement of changes in financial position. He does not have time to write up footnote disclosures to accompany the statement.

James directed the physical count of inventory on June 30 and adjusted and closed the books on that date. You find that he is actually a good accountant, having taken some night courses at the community college. The accounts appear to have been maintained in conformity with generally accepted accounting principles. At least, you have noticed no obvious errors.

Required:

You are independent with respect to the Coffin brothers and their Coffin Auto Speed Shop business. Prepare a report on your compilation services engagement.

20.11. One portion of the report on a review services engagement may read as follows:

> Based on my (our) review, I am (we are) not aware of any material modifications that should be made to the accompanying financial statements in order for them to be in conformity with generally accepted accounting principles.

Required:

a. Is this paragraph a "negative assurance" given by the CPA?
b. Why is "negative assurance" generally prohibited in *audit* reports?
c. What justification is there for permitting "negative assurance" in a review services report?

20.12. Hughes-Hyland Freight Company (HH) operates a large overland trucking business. HH has a fleet of 100 trucks based in 10 depots scattered throught 12 western states. Freight customers contract for pick-up and delivery and pay rates regulated by the Interstate Commerce Commission.

Customers who use HH frequently are billed monthly on the basis of shipments delivered. Other customers pay the freight charges at the time of pick-up. HH is obligated to deliver the shipment in good condition to the destination. If goods are damaged in transit (a rare occurrence), HH must refund the freight charges. However, HH is not liable for the damage, and customers usually purchase their own insurance.

Several years ago Arch Conserve, the corporate controller, chose to use the "delivered method" of recognizing freight revenue. However, an alternative method ("picked up") is now used by about two thirds of the companies in the industry. These two methods are described below:

Delivered Method. Upon reaching the destination the truck driver records the time and date on a copy of the shipping papers. This copy is returned to the accounting office and (1) serves as the basis for billing customers who receive monthly statements, or (2) serves as the basis for transferring amounts from the Deposit Revenue account to the Revenue account for customers who paid at the time of pick-up. At the fiscal year-end an entry is made to defer to the next year some operating costs related to shipments in transit. This deferral is never very large because the time between pick-up and delivery seldom exceeds ten days.

Picked-Up Method. Under this method revenue is recognized at the time of pick-up without regard to when the shipment is actually delivered. At the fiscal year-end estimated operating expenses related to shipments in transit (delivered in the next accounting period) are accrued. This method is simpler than the "delivered method" because drivers' reports of delivery time and date do not have to be processed directly through the revenue recognition accounting system.

For Discussion:

a. As an auditor, would you be able to evaluate management's choice of the "delivered method?" Is it an appropriate accounting method that properly reflects the substance of HH's revenue recognition transactions?

b. Assume that a new controller took over and changed to the "picked-up method." As a successor auditor (newly engaged by HH), would you be able to evaluate management's new choice of method? Is it an appropriate accounting method that properly reflects the substance of HH's revenue recognition transactions?

c. Assume that you were the auditor both before and after HH's change of method and that you have to prepare a report stating whether the change was to a "preferable accounting method that provides a better measure of business operations." Would you be able to decide whether the "picked-up method" was or was not preferable in this sense?

d. Independent of your response in (*c*) above, would your decision be harder or easier if GG Truck Lines, another client, used the "delivered method" and did not plan to change?

20.13. Your client, the Neighborhood Paper Company, has a fiscal year-end of December 31. NPC needs to borrow money from a local bank and believes that current value financial statements that reported the appreciated value of its assets would be helpful. A loan is needed for working capital purposes.

NPC owns two paper recycling processors. Old paper is chemically processed, reduced to a wet mass, then pressed out into semifinished thick paper mats. The mats are sold to customers who use them for packing material. Recycling processors are fairly complex pieces of integrated machinery, and they are built on a customized basis by a few specialized engineering firms.

NPC has owned one of the processors for five years. It was appraised last year at $135,000 by a qualified engineering appraiser. The second processor was purchased last month for $125,000—its appraised value—and $10,000 was spent in bringing certain maintenance up to date. Both processors have identical through-put production capacities.

The other major asset is a nine-acre plot of land NPC bought four years ago when management thought the plant would have to be moved. The land was purchased for $195,000 and was appraised by a qualified appraiser at $250,000 only 20 months after the purchase date. The nine acres is located near a rapidly expanding industrial area.

Management has prepared the balance sheet summary shown below:

	Cost	Current Value		Cost	Current Value
Cash	$ 5,000	$ 5,000	Accounts payable	$ 6,000	$ 6,000
Accounts receivable	7,000	7,000	Long-term debts	100,000	100,000
Recycling processors	210,000	270,000	Stockholders' equity	316,000	316,000
Land	195,000	250,000	Reevaluation equity		110,000
	$422,000	$532,000		$422,000	$532,000

Since the recycling processors were appraised/purchased so recently, management does not want to bear the expense of new appraisals this year. No plans have been made to obtain a new appraisal on the land. NPC, however, is a profitable operation. The unaudited income statement for the current year (historical cost basis) shows net income of $46,000.

You have accepted the engagement to review and report on the current value balance sheet in conjunction with your regular annual audit of the historical cost financial statements.

For Discussion:

a. What auditing standards are applicable to the engagement to review and report on the current value balance sheet?

b. What primary auditing procedures should you apply in addition to those necessary for the audit of the historical cost financial statements?

c. Will any additional disclosures in footnotes be necessary?

d. Are there any evidential problems in the NPC situation that might prevent your rendering a report on the current value balance sheet?

20.14. You have been engaged by the Dodd Manufacturing Corporation to attest to the reasonableness of the assumptions underlying their forecast of revenues, costs, and net income for the calendar year 1980. Four of the assumptions which they have made are shown below. For each assumption, state the evidence sources and procedures you would use to determine the reasonableness.

a. The company intends to sell certain real estate and other facilities held by Division B at an aftertax profit of $600,000; the proceeds of this sale will be used to retire outstanding debt, as described below.

b. The company will call and retire all outstanding 9 percent subordinated debentures (callable at 108). The debentures are expected to require the full call premium given present market interest rates of 7 percent on similar debt. A rise in market interest rates to 8 percent would reduce the loss on bond retirement from the projected $200,000 to $190,000.

c. Current labor contracts expire on September 1, 1980, and the new contract is expected to result in a wage increase of 5½ percent. Given the projected levels of production and sales, aftertax operating earnings would be reduced approximately $50,000 for each percentage point wage increase in excess of the expected contract settlement.

d. The sales projection for Division A assumes that the new Portsmouth facility will be fully completed and operating at 40 percent of capacity at February 1, 1980. It is highly improbable that the facility will be operational before January of 1980. Each month's delay would reduce sales of Division A approximately $80,000 and operating earnings by $30,000.

20.15. In Professor Secoy's opinion on management performance (refer to the text), an overall assessment of management is stated as follows:

> In our judgment, XYZ Manufacturing Corporation was managed with reasonable efficiency during the year ended December 31, 1970, judged in light of our findings and the circumstances in which the company operated during that year.

Required:

a. For auditors to render opinions on the overall efficiency or effectiveness of management, it is evident that *categories* must be developed into which a company's management can be classified, for example, "good," "bad," "mediocre." Propose (define) categories which you deem suitable for expressing the overall efficiency or effectiveness of management.

b. Sets of criteria have been proposed by various researchers for assessing the quality of management. For each of the proposals shown below, cite the primary advantage(s) and disadvantage(s).
  (1) The quality of a company's management can be assessed through comparing management's techniques and processes to generally accepted principles of management.
  (2) The quality of a company's management should be determined on the basis of how the company performed in regard to specific financial measures such as
    (*a*) Earnings per share of company compared to industry average.
    (*b*) Rate of return on sales of company compared to industry average.
    (*c*) Rate of return on assets of company compared to industry average.
    (*d*) Sales per employee of company compared to industry average.

20.16. 1. Explain briefly the justification for extending the attest function, where possible, to the nonfinancial statement representations of management.
2. In regard to extending the attest function to nonfinancial statement management representations, what role do you see for studies of the needs of users of financial statements and associated nonfinancial representations?

20.17. You have been engaged to attest to the nonfinancial representations in the corporate annual report of Rotidua Roller Bearings Corporation. However, you believe that management's representations in connection with the marketability of a new product are materially misleading. Management will not alter the representations.

Required:

a. Propose how you might disclose the misleading representations in your audit report.

b. Assume management contends its position regarding the representations is justifiable and wants the opportunity to challenge the auditor's judgment. What support can you find for including management's comments as part of your audit report?

INDEX

E

J–K

L

N

Q

This book has been set in 9 and 8 point Primer, leaded 2 points, Part numbers and titles are in 24 point Palatino. Chapter numbers are in Weiss Series I and chapter titles are in 20 point Palatino. The size of the type page is 27 x 45½ picas.